■ Introduction

My experience has taught me that what students want most from a study guide is help in mastering course material in order to do well on examinations. I have developed this *Study Guide* to respond specifically to that demand. Using this *Study Guide* alone, however, is not enough to guarantee that you will do well in your course. In order to help you overcome the problems and difficulties that most students encounter, I have some general advice on how to study, as well as some specific advice on how best to use this *Study Guide.*

Economics requires a different style of thinking than what you may encounter in other courses. Economists make extensive use of assumptions to break down complex problems into simple, analytically manageable parts. This analytical style, while ultimately not more demanding than the styles of thinking in other disciplines, feels unfamiliar to most students and requires practice. As a result, it is not as easy to do well in economics on the basis of your raw intelligence and high-school knowledge as it is in many other courses. Many students who come to my office are frustrated and puzzled by the fact that they are getting A's and B's in their other courses but only a C or worse in economics. They have not recognized that economics is different and requires practice. In order to avoid a frustrating visit to your instructor after your first test, I suggest you do the following.

◆ ***Don't rely solely on your high-school economics.*** If you took high-school economics, you have seen the material on supply and demand which your instructor will lecture on in the first few weeks. Don't be lulled into feeling that the course will be easy. Your high-school knowledge of economic concepts will be very useful, but it will not be enough to guarantee high scores on exams. Your college or university instructors will demand much more detailed knowledge of concepts and ask you to apply them in new circumstances.

◆ ***Keep up with the course material on a weekly basis.*** Skim the appropriate chapter in the textbook *before* your instructor lectures on it. In this initial reading, don't worry about details or arguments you can't quite follow — just try to get a general understanding of the basic concepts and issues. You may be amazed at how your instructor's ability to teach improves when you come to class prepared. As soon as your instructor has finished covering a chapter, complete the corresponding *Study Guide* chapter. Avoid cramming the day before or even just the week before an exam. Because economics requires practice, cramming is an almost certain recipe for failure.

◆ ***Keep a good set of lecture notes.*** Good lecture notes are vital for focusing your studying. Your instructor will only lecture on a subset of topics from the textbook. The topics your instructor covers in a lecture should usually be given priority when studying. Also give priority to studying the figures and graphs covered in the lecture.

Instructors do differ in their emphasis on lecture notes and the textbook, so ask early on in the course which is *more* important in reviewing for exams — lecture notes or the textbook. If your instructor answers that both are important, then ask the following, typical economic question: which will be more beneficial — spending an extra hour re-reading your lecture notes or an extra hour re-reading the textbook? This question assumes that you have read each textbook chapter twice (once before lecture for a general understanding, and then later for a thorough understanding); that you have prepared a good set of lecture notes; and that you have worked through all of the problems in the appropriate *Study Guide* chapters. By applying this style of analysis to the problem of efficiently allocating your study time, you are already beginning to think like an economist!

◆ ***Use your instructor and/or teaching assistants for help.*** When you have questions or problems with course material, come to the office to ask questions. Remember, you are paying for your education and instructors are there to help you learn. I am often amazed at how few students come to see me during office hours. Don't be shy. The personal contact that comes from one-on-one tutoring is professionally gratifying for instructors as well as (hopefully) beneficial for you.

◆ *Form a study group.* A very useful way to motivate your studying and to learn economics is to discuss the course material and problems with other students. Explaining the answer to a question *out loud* is a very effective way of discovering how well you understand the question. When you answer a question only in your head, you often skip steps in the chain of reasoning without realizing it. When you are forced to explain your reasoning aloud, gaps and mistakes quickly appear, and you (with your fellow group members) can quickly correct your reasoning. The "You're the Teacher" questions in the *Study Guide* and the Review questions at the end of each textbook chapter are extremely good study group material. You might also get together *after* having worked the *Study Guide* problems, but *before* looking at the answers, and help each other solve unsolved problems. You may also find it useful to participate in the on-line, E-mail discussion located on the internet at ParkinSt@AW.COM.

◆ *Work old exams.* One of the most effective ways of studying is to work through exams your instructor has given in previous years. Old exams give you a feel for the style of question your instructor may ask, and give you the opportunity to get used to time pressure if you force yourself to do the exam in the allotted time. Studying from old exams is not cheating, as long as you have obtained a copy of the exam legally. Some institutions keep old exams in the library, others in the department. Students who have previously taken the course are usually a good source as well. Remember, though, that old exams are a useful study aid only if you use them to *understand* the reasoning behind each question. If you simply memorize answers in the hopes that your instructor will repeat the identical question, you are likely to fail. From year to year, instructors routinely change the questions or change the numerical values for similar questions.

◆ *Use Economics in Action.* This is state-of-the-art interactive software for IBM-compatible computers. It is an integrated tutorial, graphing, demonstration, and testing program that covers all the main themes in the textbook using three modes. The tutorial mode places you in an economics-related job situation and leads you through assignments that reveal and explore economic concepts and principles. The free mode allows you to interact with economic models by changing parameters and observing the effects on graphs. The quiz mode gives you graphical or data-related multiple-choice questions. When you select an answer, you are given a detailed explanation (and graphical illustration) of why your answer is right or wrong. All software modes are closely integrated with the textbook.

■ Using Your *Study Guide*

You should only attempt to complete a chapter in the *Study Guide* after you have read the corresponding textbook chapter and listened to your instructor lecture on the material. Each *Study Guide* chapter contains the following sections.

Key Concepts. This first section is a short summary, in point form, of all key definitions, concepts and material from the textbook chapter. Key terms from the textbook appear in bold. This section is designed to focus you quickly and precisely on the core material that you *must* master. It is an excellent study aid for the night before an exam. Think of it as crib notes that will serve as a final check of the key concepts you have studied.

Helpful Hints. When you encounter difficulty in mastering concepts or techniques, you will not be alone. Many students find certain concepts difficult and often make the same kinds of mistakes. I have taught over 12,000 students the principles of economics and I have seen these common mistakes often enough to have learned how to help students avoid them. The hints point out these mistakes and offer tips to avoid them. The hints focus on the most important concepts, equations, and techniques for problem solving. They also review crucial graphs that appear on every instructor's exams. I hope that this section will be very useful, because instructors always ask exam questions designed to test these possible mistakes in your understanding.

Self-Test. This will be one of the most useful sections of the *Study Guide.* The questions are designed to give you practice and to test skills and techniques you must master to do well on exams.

There are plenty of multiple-choice type of questions and other types of questions in the Self-Test, each with a specific pedagogical purpose. Before I describe the four parts of the Self-Test section, here are some general tips that apply to all parts.

STUDY GUIDE

PARKIN
MICROECONOMICS
THIRD EDITION

MARK RUSH
University of Florida

AVI J. COHEN
York University
Contributer

HARVEY B. KING
University of Regina
Contributer

Addison-Wesley Publishing Company
Reading, Massachusetts • Menlo Park, California • New York • Don Mills, Ontario
Harlow, United Kingdom • Amsterdam • Bonn • Sydney • Singapore • Tokyo
Madrid • San Juan • Milan • Paris

Reproduced by Addison-Wesley from camera-ready copy supplied by the author.

Reprinted with corrections May, 1996.

ISBN 0-201-60983-5
2 3 4 5 6 7 8 9 10-CRS-99989796

Use a pencil to write your answers in the *Study Guide* so you have neat, complete pages from which to study. Draw graphs wherever they are applicable. Some questions will ask explicitly for graphs; many others will not but will require a chain of reasoning that involves shifts of curves on a graph. *Always draw the graph.* Don't try to work through the reasoning in your head — you are much more likely to make mistakes that way. Whenever you draw a graph, even in the margins of the *Study Guide,* label the axes. You may think that you can keep the labels in your head, but you will be confronting many different graphs with many different variables on the axes. Avoid confusion and label. As an added incentive, remember that on exams where graphs are required, instructors will deduct points for unlabelled axes.

Do the Self-Test questions as if they were real exam questions, which means do them *without looking at the answers.* This is the single most important tip I can give you about effectively using the *Study Guide* to improve your exam performance. Struggling for the answers to questions that you find difficult is one of the most effective ways to learn. The adage — no pain, no gain — applies well to studying. You will learn the most from right answers you had to struggle for and from your wrong answers and mistakes. Only after you have attempted all the questions should you look at the answers. When you finally do check the answers, be sure to understand where you went wrong and why the right answer is correct.

There are many questions in each chapter, and it will take you somewhere between two and six hours to answer all of them. If you get tired (or bored), don't burn yourself out by trying to work through all of the questions in one sitting. Consider breaking up your Self-Test over two (or more) study sessions.

The four parts of the Self-Test section are:

True/False/Uncertain and Explain. These questions test basic knowledge of concepts and your ability to apply the concepts. Some of the questions challenge your understanding, to see if you can identify mistakes in statements using basic concepts. These questions will identify gaps in your knowledge and are useful to answer out loud in a study group.

When answering, identify each statement as *true, false,* or whether you are *uncertain* because the statement may be true or false depending on circumstances or assumptions. Explain your answer in one sentence in the space underneath each question.

Multiple-Choice. These more difficult questions test your analytical abilities by asking you to apply concepts to new situations, manipulate information and solve numerical and graphical problems.

This is the most frequently used type of exam question, and the Self-Test contains many of them in a scrambled order to reflect a real exam situation.

Read each question and all four choices carefully before you answer. Many of the choices will be plausible and will differ only slightly. You must choose the one *best* answer. A useful strategy in working these questions is first to eliminate any obviously wrong choices and then to focus on the remaining alternatives. Don't get frustrated or think that you are dim if you can't immediately see the correct answer. These questions are designed to make you work to find the correct choice.

Short Answer. Each chapter contains several Short Answer questions. Some are straightforward questions about basic concepts. They can generally be answered in a few sentences or, at most, in one paragraph. Others are problems. The best way to learn to do economics is to do problems. Problems are also the second-most popular type of exam question — practice them as much as possible!

You're the Teacher. Each chapter contains from one to three questions that either cover very broad issues or errors that all too common among students. These questions may be the most valuable you will encounter for use in your study group. Take turns by pretending that you are the teacher and answer the questions for the rest of your group. Who knows, you may like this process so much that you actually do become a professor at a university teaching economics!

Answers. The Self-Test is followed by answers to all questions. Unlike other study guides on the market, I have included complete answers because I believe that reading complete answers will help you master the material ... and that's what this *Study Guide* is all about! But do *not* look at an answer until you have attempted a question. When you do finally look, use the answers to understand where you went wrong and why the right answer is correct.

Part Overview Problem. Every few chapters, at the end of each of the parts of the textbook, you will find a special problem (and answer). These multi-part problems draw on material from the part you have just concluded and are similar to the "Reading Between the Lines" sections in your textbook. There is also a self-test that contains four multiple choice questions drawn from each chapter in the section. The questions are in order, with the first four from the first chapter in the section, the second four from the second chapter, and so forth. If you miss several questions from one chapter, you'll know to spend more time on that chapter when preparing for your exam. These multiple choice questions are written in a different style than those in the chapter because instructors have different ways of writing questions. By encountering different styles, you will be better prepared for *your* test.

If you effectively combine the use of the textbook, the *Study Guide, Economics in Action,* and all other course resources, you will be well prepared for exams. You will also have developed analytical skills and powers of reasoning that will benefit you throughout your life and in whatever career you choose.

Your Future and Economics

After your class is concluded, you may well wonder about economics as a major. The last chapter in this *Study Guide*, written by Robert Whaples, helps examine your future by discussing whether economics is the major for you. I invite you to read this chapter and consider the information in it.

Final Comments

I have tried to make the *Study Guide* as helpful and useful as possible. Undoubtedly I have made some mistakes; mistakes that you may see. If you find any, I, and succeeding generations of students, would be grateful if you could point them out to me. At the end of my class at the University of Florida, when I ask my students for their advice, I point out to them that this advice won't help them at all because they have just completed the class. But, comments they make will influence how future students are taught. Thus, just as they owe a debt of gratitude for the comments and suggestions that I received from students before them, so too will students after them owe them an (unpaid and unpayable) debt. You are in the same situation. If you have questions, suggestions, or simply comments, let me know. My address is to the right, or you can reach me via E-mail at either ParkinEd@AW.COM or else directly at RUSH@DALE.CBA.UFL.EDU. Your input probably won't benefit you directly, but they will benefit following generations. And, if you give me permission, I will note your name and school in following editions so that any younger siblings (or, years down the road, maybe even your children!) will see your name and offer up thanks.

To date, students who have uncovered errors and to whom we all owe a debt of gratitude include:

- Jeanie Callen at the University of Minnesota-Twin Cities.
- Brian Mulligan at the University of Florida
- Patrick Lusby at the University of Florida
- Jonathan Baskind at the University of Florida

I also owe Avi J. Cohen, of York University, and Harvey B. King, of University of Regina. Their superb study guide for the Canadian edition of Michael Parkin's book was the basis for this study guide. This book uses many of their chapter summaries, helpful hints, and questions. Much of what is good about the book is a direct reflection of their work.

Robert Whaples of Wake Forest University not only wrote the last section of the *Study Guide* but checked the entire manuscript for accuracy. The errors he caught were embarrassingly numerous and the suggestions he made invariably useful. Marilyn Freedman at Addison Wesley played a key role coordinating my work; without her cheerfulness, this book would have been much different and much poorer. I owe Cindy Johnson of Publishing Services an immense debt. She is a computer expert, a publishing expert, a technology expert, and an economic expert all in one package; she shaped this book from beginning to end. Jerry Moore was the long-suffering copy editor of this project. It is thanks to Jerry that the English in the following chapters approaches conventional usage; any errors in this preface are mine because he ain't seen this section yet. I need to thank Michael Parkin and Robin Bade. Michael has written such a superior book that it was easy to be enthusiastic about writing the *Study Guide* to accompany it and both Michael and Robin made suggestions that vastly improved the *Study Guide.* I finally want to thank my family: Susan, Tommy, Bobby, and Kathryn, who, respectively: allowed me to be late for dinner so I could work on this book; allowed me to type this book on his computer; kept me company in his brother's room while I worked; and allowed me to skip changing her diapers so that I could type. Thanks a lot!

Mark Rush
Economics Department
University of Florida
Gainesville, Florida 32611
April, 1996.

Table of Contents

1 WHAT IS ECONOMICS?

Key Concepts

■ Economics and Scarcity

Economics is a broad subject, addressing issues such as technological change, the proper role for the government, international trade, and income growth.

The **fundamental economic problem is scarcity.**

- Because the available resources are not enough to satisfy everyone's wants, choices are necessary.
- Economics studies how we use limited resources to try to satisfy unlimited wants.
- The *opportunity cost* of a choice is the value of the best forgone alternative; opportunity cost is different than money cost.

Marginal analysis and the **principle of substitution** play important roles in making choices.

- **Marginal analysis** compares the *additional* cost — the marginal cost — of an action to the *additional* benefit — the marginal benefit — of the action.
- The **principle of substitution** states that, when the opportunity cost of an action rises, people substitute other activities that now have lower relative opportunity costs. In other words, people respond to **incentives**. After a change in incentives, competition creates second round effects throughout the economy.

■ What Economists Do

Economics is divided into **microeconomics**, the study of individual firms, individual consumers, or individual markets, and **macroeconomics**, the study of national and global economies and the factors that shape them.

Economic science strives to uncover how the world works; **economic policy** strives to make society better off.

All sciences distinguish between:

- **Positive statements** — statements about what is. These can be shown to be true or false through observation and measurement.
- **Normative statements** — statements about what ought to be. These are matters of opinion.

Economic science is a collection of positive statements that are consistent with the real world.

An **economic theory** is constructed by building and testing **economic models**, which are simplified descriptions of the world that include only the factors considered most important. When developing models and theories, economists use the idea of ***ceteris paribus***, Latin for "other things being equal" to focus on the effect of one particular factor. In the development of theories and models, two pitfalls are possible:

- **Fallacy of composition** — the assertion that what is true for a part must be true for the whole or what is true for the whole must be true for each of the parts.
- ***Post hoc*** **fallacy** — the assertion that one event caused another because the first occurred before the other.

Economic policy is guided by four policy objectives:

- **Economic efficiency** — when production costs are as low as possible, everyone buys the bundle of goods and services that makes them as well off as possible, and people specialize in occupations that give them the maximum possible economic benefit.
- **Equity** — equity means "fairness." What is equitable is an issue that lacks consensus.
- **Economic growth** — increases in income and output per person.
- **Economic stability** — when swings in the level of economic activity have been prevented.

■ The Economy: An Overview

The economy allocates resources among alternative uses and determines the answers to five questions:

- ♦ What goods and services are produced?
- ♦ How are the goods and services produced?
- ♦ When are the goods and services produced?
- ♦ Where are the goods and services produced?
- ♦ Who consumes the goods and services produced?

An economy is comprised of **decision makers** (households, firms, and governments) and **markets** (such as factor markets and goods markets). In factor markets households supply the factors of production (labor, land, capital, and entrepreneurial ability) and firms demand factors. In goods markets, firms supply goods and households (and governments) demand them.

In all markets, decisions must be coordinated. Price adjustments can be used to coordinate decisions and determine answers to the "what," "how," "when," "where," and "who" questions. Alternatively, decisions can be coordinated using a *command mechanism* whereby some group determines the answers to the questions and then gives instructions about how they are to be answered.

Helpful Hints

1. The definition of economics (how people use limited resources to try to satisfy unlimited wants) leads directly to three important economic concepts — choice, opportunity cost, and competition. Because wants exceed resources, people cannot have everything they want and therefore must make choices among alternatives. In making choices, people forgo other alternatives. The opportunity cost of any choice is the value of the best forgone alternative. Finally, because wants exceed resources, an individual's wants, as well the wants from different individuals, must compete against each other for the scarce resources.
2. The basic assumption made by economists about human behavior is that people try to make themselves as well off as possible. As a result, people respond to changed incentives by changing their decisions. Marginal analysis is the key tool used by economists to determine how people's behavior will change. The idea of marginal analysis is that an individual compares the additional (or "marginal") benefits from taking an action to the additional (or "marginal") costs of the action. If the additional benefits from the action exceed the additional costs, taking the action makes the person better off and so economists assume that the person takes the action. Conversely, if the marginal benefits fall short of the marginal costs, economists assume that the action is not taken. An important aspect of marginal analysis is that only the *additional* benefits and costs and not the *total* benefits and costs of the action are considered. Only the additional benefits and additional costs are relevant because they are the benefits and costs that the person will enjoy and pay only if the action is undertaken. Hence, when deciding on the desirability of an action, marginal analysis is the approach we take.
3. In attempting to understand how and why something works (for example, an airplane or an economy), we can use description or we can use theory. A description is a list of facts about something. But it does not tell us which facts are essential for understanding how an airplane works (the shape of the wings) and which facts are less important (the color of the paint). Scientists use theory to abstract from the complex descriptive facts of the real world and focus only on those elements essential for understanding. These essential elements are fashioned into models — highly simplified representations of the real world. Economic models focus on the essential forces (such as competition) operating in the economy, while abstracting from less important forces (such as whims or advertising). In a real sense, models are like maps, which are useful precisely because they abstract from real world detail. A map that reproduced all the details of the real world (street lights, traffic signs, electric wires) would be useless. A useful map offers a simplified view, which is carefully selected according to the purpose of the map. A useful theory is similar: It gives guidance and insight into how the immensely complicated real world functions and reacts to changes
4. This chapter of the text is designed to give you a broad introduction to economics. Because of its

introductory nature, it covers a lot of ground. The following chapters are more focused. They examine specific topics to help fill in the details that are sketched in this overview chapter. After you complete this course, you will find it enlightening and fun to return to this chapter and read quickly through it. You will be amazed at how much you have learned and at the insights and understanding that your course has given you into how the world functions!

Questions

True/False/Uncertain and Explain

1. Scarcity is a problem only for economies that use prices to coordinate decisions.

2. Because resources are limited, people must learn how to limit their wants.

3. The principle of substitution suggests that, when the opportunity cost of an action increases, people want to take more of that action because it now must be higher quality.

4. The opportunity cost of buying a slice of pizza for $2 rather than a burrito for $2 is the burrito and not the two dollars that was spent on the pizza.

5. When economic activity is coordinated by a command mechanism, the decisions of what, how, and where are the result of price adjustment.

6. In economics, a closed economy is one in which there is very limited economic freedom.

7. The problem of allocating scarce resources is faced by every economy, regardless of whether it uses prices or a command mechanism to coordinate decisions.

8. Economics is not a science because it deals with the study of willful human beings and not inanimate objects in nature.

9. A positive economic statement is one that economists are "positive" is correct.

10. A positive statement is about what is; a normative statement is about what will be.

11. Detailed description alone is the key to understanding what makes things work.

12. An example of the "how" question is: "How does the nation decide who gets the goods and services that are produced?"

13. Macroeconomics studies the causes of inflation.

14. The idea of *ceteris paribus* is used whenever a *post hoc* fallacy is being discussed.

15. When the predictions of a model conflict with the relevant facts, the model must be discarded or modified.

Multiple Choice

1. The fact that human wants cannot be fully satisfied with available resources is called the problem of
   a. opportunity cost.

   b. scarcity.
   c. what to produce.
   d. for whom to produce.

2. From 9 to 10 A.M., Fred can sleep in, go to his economics lecture, or play tennis. Suppose that Fred decides to go to the lecture but thinks that, if he hadn't, he would otherwise have slept in. The opportunity cost of attending the lecture is
   a. sleeping in *and* playing tennis.
   b. playing tennis.

   c. sleeping in.
   d. one hour of time.

3. One student from a thirty-person class can easily walk through a door. Assuming that all thirty students simultaneously can therefore easily walk through the same door is an example of the
   a. opportunity cost fallacy.
   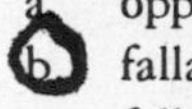
   b. fallacy of composition
   c. fallacy of substitution.
   d. *post hoc* fallacy.

4. The problem of scarcity exists
   a. only in the past but not anymore.
   b. only in very poor economies.
   c. in all economies.
   d. now but will be eliminated with economic growth.

5. When the government chooses to use resources to build a dam, these resources are no longer available to build a highway. This choice illustrates the concept of
   a. a market mechanism.
   b. macroeconomics.
   c. opportunity cost.
   d. a closed economy.

6. A positive statement is
   a. about what ought to be.
   b. about what is.
   c. always true.
   d. one that does not use the *ceteris paribus* clause.

7. The opportunity cost to a customer of getting a $10 haircut is the
   a. customer's best alternative use of the $10.
   b. customer's best alternative use of the time it takes to get a haircut.
   c. customer's best alternative use of both the $10 and the time it takes to get a haircut.
   d. value to the barber of $10 and the time it takes to give a haircut.

8. The question "Should personal computers or mainframe computers be produced?" is an example of the
   a. what question.
   b. how question.
   c. where question.
   d. who question.

9. Suppose that Lea and Brent both must skip work for an hour to take an exam. If Lea's job pays $12 per hour and Brent's pays $9 an hour, the opportunity cost of taking the exam
   a. is higher for Lea.
   b. is higher for Brent.
   c. is the same for Lea and Brent.
   d. cannot be compared for Lea and Brent.

10. The *post hoc* fallacy is the
   a. assertion that what is true for a part of the whole must be true for the whole.
   b. claim that one event caused another because the first event came first.
   c. use of *ceteris paribus* in order to study the impact of one factor.
   d. claim that the timing of two events has nothing to do with which event caused the other.

11. Which of the following is a positive statement?
   a. The government must lower the price of a pizza so that more students can afford to buy it.
   b. The best level of taxation is zero percent because then people get to keep everything they earn.
   c. My economics class should last for two terms because it is my favorite class.
   d. An increase in college tuition will cause fewer students to apply to college.

12. Marginal analysis
   a. states that an individual compares the total benefits and total costs before taking an action to decide if the action is worthwhile.
   b. assumes that a person will not use his or her scarce resources unless there is a very large positive benefit from so doing.
   c. suggests that someone undertakes an action only when the marginal costs of the action are less than the marginal benefits.
   d. applies only in a nation that does not use a command mechanism to allocate resources.

13. The Latin term *ceteris paribus* means
   a. "false unless proven true."
   b. "other things the same."
   c. "after this, then because of this."
   d. "not correct, even though it is logical."

14. What coordinates economic activity in markets?
   a. Firms.
   b. Households.
   c. Planners.
   d. Prices.

15. Which of the following is NOT a factor of production?
    a. The labor hired by a business.
    b. The capital equipment used by a business.
    c. The money a business has in the bank.
    d. The land used by a business.

16. Scarcity can be eliminated through
    a. competition.
    b. market mechanisms.
    c. command mechanisms.
    d. none of the above because scarcity cannot be eliminated.

17. Economic efficiency is attained in part when
    a. people's incomes are equal.
    b. the economy grows as rapidly as possible.
    c. there are no major fluctuations in economic activity.
    d. the costs of producing the goods consumers want are as low as possible.

18. Second round effects are caused by
    a. the fact that the first round effects are never sufficient to solve the "what" question.
    b. the substitutions people make in response to changed incentives.
    c. the impact of scarcity combined with positive analysis.
    d. incomplete first round effects.

19. An economic model includes
    a. only normative statements.
    b. no use of *ceteris paribus*.
    c. all known facts about a situation.
    d. only details considered essential.

20. Which of the following is a positive statement?
    a. Low rents will restrict the supply of housing.
    b. Low rents are good because they make apartments more affordable.
    c. Housing costs too much.
    d. Owners of apartment buildings ought to be free to charge whatever rent they want.

21. In an economy in which markets are used to coordinate economic decisions, what solves the economic questions of "what," "how," "where," "when," and "who"?
    a. Commands, issued by planners, pass through the chain of markets and answer the questions.
    b. Prices in markets answer the economic questions.
    c. Laws instruct individuals about the proper answers.
    d. The principle of scarcity answers the questions by allocating scarce resources to where they are most needed.

22. An example of a "what" question is
    a. "Will buses or subways be produced?"
    b. "Will professional football players or video game programmers be paid more?"
    c. "What hours is the local Taco Bell open?"
    d. "Will rice be grown in Kansas or California?"

23. Opportunity cost does NOT include
    a. external cost.
    b. value of the best alternative forgone.
    c. value of all alternatives forgone.
    d. time cost.

24. Which of the following is a microeconomic topic?
    a. The reasons why Kathy buys less orange juice.
    b. The reasons for a decline in average prices.
    c. The cause of recessions.
    d. The effect of the government budget deficit on inflation.

■ Short Answer Problems

1. "In the future, as our technology advances even further, eventually we will whip scarcity. In the high-tech future, scarcity will be gone." Do you agree or disagree with this claim? Explain your answer and what scarcity is. Also, why does the existence of scarcity require choices?

2. In sciences such as chemistry, controlled experiments play a key role. How does that relate to economists' use of *ceteris paribus*?

3. What are the four objectives of economic policy? Is one of these either distinctly more or distinctly less important than the others? Explain your answer.
4. "Education is basic right. Just as kindergarten through 12th grade education is free, so, too, should a college education be free and guaranteed to every American." This statement can be analyzed by using the economic concepts discussed in this chapter to answer the following questions.
   a. What would be the opportunity cost of providing a free college education for everyone?
   b. Is providing this education free from the perspective of society as a whole?
5. Ashley, Doug, and Mei-Lin are planning to travel from New York to Boston. The trip takes one hour by airplane and five hours by train. The air fare is $100 and train fare is $60. They all have to take time off from work while traveling. Ashley earns $5 per hour in her job, Doug $10 per hour, and Mei-Lin $12 per hour.

   Calculate the opportunity cost of air and train travel for each person. If each wants to travel at the lowest possible cost, how will each of them travel to Boston?
6. Indicate whether each of the following statements is positive or normative. If it is normative, rewrite it so that it becomes positive. If it is positive, rewrite it so that it becomes normative.
   a. The government ought to reduce the size of its budget deficit in order to lower interest rates.
   b. Government imposition of a tax on tobacco products will reduce their consumption.
   c. Health care costs should be lower so that poorer people can afford quality health care.
7. A student-athlete is contemplating whether to return to college for his senior year or enter the NFL draft. If he returns, tuition costs $5,000, room and board $7,000, and books $800. His college has given him a scholarship that will cover his tuition, books, and $6,500 of his room and board. If he enters the NFL draft, he will be a first-round draft choice and receive a contract worth $2 million for his first year. If he is in the NFL, he will incur incidental expenses of $100,000 a year. What is the student's opportunity cost of returning to college for his senior year?

■ You're the Teacher

1. "Economic theories are useless because the models on which they are based are totally unrealistic. They leave out so many descriptive details about the real world, they can't possibly be useful for understanding how the economy works." Defend the fact that economic theories are much simpler than reality.
2. "Does everything have an opportunity cost?" This student is asking a very good question; provide an equally good answer!

Answers

True/False Answers

1. **F** Scarcity exists because people's wants exceed their ability to meet those wants, and this fact of life is true for *any* economy.
2. **F** Wants describe the amount that people would take if everything were free; wants are unlimited but the amount that people actually buy is limited.
3. **F** The principle of substitution points out that when the opportunity cost of an action increases, people undertake less of the action.
4. **T** The opportunity cost is the burrito that was sacrificed in order to buy the pizza.
5. **F** In an economy coordinated by a command mechanism, commands from some central planner provide answers to the economic questions.
6. **F** A closed economy is one that does not trade with any other country.
7. **T** *Every* economy faces scarcity, so every economy must (somehow) allocate its scarce resources among competing opportunities.
8. **F** Economics is a science because it generates predictions about the real world.
9. **F** Positive statements attempt to describe how the world works.
10. **F** A normative statement tells what policies should be followed.
11. **F** Detailed description is not a fruitful source for understanding how things work because too many details cause confusion. A theory that focuses only on key elements is more useful.
12. **F** The "how" question asks, "How are goods and services produced?"
13. **T** Inflation involves the prices of all goods and services and so is one of the major topics studied in macroeconomics.
14. **F** *Ceteris paribus* is used in order to focus on the effect from a change in one factor.
15. **T** A model's predictions must be consistent with the facts to become part of accepted theory.

Multiple Choice Answers

1. **b** Scarcity refers to the observation that human wants are unlimited but that the resources available to satisfy these wants are limited.
2. **c** The opportunity cost of any action is the (single) best alternative forgone by taking the action.
3. **b** In this case, the fallacy of composition is arguing that what is true for a part must necessarily be true for the whole.
4. **c** Scarcity — the fact that wants exceed the resources available to satisfy all the wants — will exist forever in all economies.
5. **c** Because the resources are used to build a dam, the opportunity of using them to build a highway is lost.
6. **b** Positive statements describe how the world is and how it works.
7. **c** The opportunity cost of purchasing a good includes the time spent buying it as well as the other goods that can no longer be purchased.
8. **a** The "what" question asks, "What goods and services will be produced?".
9. **a** The cost in terms of time spent taking the test is the same for Lea and Brent. However, Lea passes up buying $12 worth of things, and Brent loses the ability to buy only $9.
10. **b** The usual *post hoc* fallacy is to claim that one event caused another because the first event occurred before the second.
11. **d** This statement is the only one that tries to describe how the world actually works; all the others are normative statements that describe a policy that should be pursued.
12. **c** This is an example of marginal analysis, a very important concept in economics.
13. **b** *Ceteris paribus* is the economic equivalent of a controlled experiment: Its use allows us to determine the effect of changing only one factor at a time.
14. **d** Prices are used in a market economy to coordinate households' desires about what to buy and firms' plans about what to sell.
15. **c** Factors of production are the actual inputs used to produce goods and services, not money in a bank.

16. **d** Scarcity is the universal condition that human wants always exceed the resources available.
17. **d** In part, economic efficiency requires that the goods being produced are those that consumers want; another part of economic efficiency requires that these goods be produced as inexpensively — as efficiently! — as possible.
18. **b** As people respond to the price changes created by the first-round effect, second-, and then third-, fourth-, etc., round effects occur.
19. **d** By including only essential details, economic models are vastly simpler than reality.
20. **a** This statement is the only one that describes how the world works.
21. **b** We begin exploring the role that prices play in answering these economic questions Chapter 4.
22. **a** The "what" questions asks, "What is produced?" — in this case, busses or subways?
23. **c** Opportunity cost includes only the *best* alternative forgone, not all alternatives forgone.
24. **a** Kathy is an individual consumer, so the reasons why she reduces her purchases of orange juice is a microeconomic topic.

■ Answers to Short Answer Problems

1. This claim is incorrect. Scarcity will always exist. Scarcity occurs because people's wants are unlimited, but the resources available to satisfy these wants are finite. As a result, not all of everyone's wants can be satisfied; the goods and services that are needed to meet all the wants are simply unavailable. For instance, think about the number of people who want to spend all winter skiing on uncrowded slopes. Regardless of the level of technology, there simply are not enough ski slopes available to allow everyone who wants to spend all winter skiing in near isolation to do so. Uncrowded ski slopes are scarce and will remain so forever. Thus technology can never eliminate scarcity.

   At its most basic level, scarcity is a problem of essentially infinite wants and limited resources. Because not all the goods and services wanted can be produced, choices must be made about which wants will be satisfied and which wants will be disappointed.

2. Chemists can check the predictions of a model by conducting controlled experiments and observing the outcomes. For instance, when determining the effect of temperature on a particular reaction, chemists can ensure that, between different experiments, *only* the temperature changes. Everything else is held constant. Economists usually cannot perform such controlled experiments and instead must change one variable at a time in a model and compare the results. This approach involves the use of *ceteris paribus*, wherein only one factor is allowed to change. Additionally, the differences in the model's outcomes can be tested only against variations in data that occur naturally in the economy. This constraint means economists face more difficult and less precise model building and testing than is possible for the controlled experiments of chemists and other scientists.

3. The four objectives of economic policy are economic efficiency, equity, economic growth, and economic stability. The issue of whether one of these is more important than the others is a normative question. Some people may feel that efficiency is vital; others may opt for equity or growth. Thus we cannot unambiguously conclude that one of these objectives is more or less important than the others.

4. a. Even though a college education may be offered without charge ("free"), opportunity costs still exist. The opportunity cost of providing such education is the best alternative use of the resources used to construct the necessary universities and the best alternative use of the resources (including human resources) used in the operation of the schools.

   b. Providing a "free" college education is hardly free from the perspective of society. The resources used in this endeavor would no longer be available for other activities. For instance, the resources used to construct a new college cannot be used to construct a hospital to provide better health care. Additionally, the time and effort spent by the faculty, staff, and students operating and attending colleges has a substantial opportunity cost, namely, that these individuals cannot participate fully in other sectors of the economy. These examples show that providing a "free" college education to everyone is not free to society!

Table 1.1 Short Answer Problem 5

Traveler		Train	Plane
Ashley			
(a)	Fare	$60	$100
(b)	Opportunity cost of travel time at $5/hr	25	5
	Total cost	85	105
Doug			
(a)	Fare	$60	$100
(b)	Opportunity cost of travel time at $10/hr	50	10
	Total cost	110	110
Mei-Lin			
(a)	Fare	$60	$100
(b)	Opportunity cost of travel time at $12/hr	60	12
	Total cost	120	112

5. The main point in this question is that the total opportunity cost of travel includes both the best alternative value of the travel time and the train or air fare. The total opportunity costs of train and air travel for Ashley, Doug, and Mei-Lin are calculated in Table 1.1. Based on the calculations in Table 1.1, Ashley will take the train, Mei-Lin will take the plane, and Doug might take either.
6. a. This statement is normative. A positive statement is: "If the government reduced its budget deficit, interest rates would fall."
   b. This statement is positive. A normative statement is: "The government should tax tobacco products in order to reduce their consumption."
   c. This statement is normative. A positive statement is: "If health care costs were lower, more poor people would receive health care."
7. If the student returns to college, the opportunity cost comprises the alternatives he has sacrificed. Because his scholarship covers tuition and books, they are not part of the opportunity cost; he does not have to pay for them and so does not sacrifice anything. However, because only $6,500 of the $7,000 room and board expenses are paid by the scholarship, the remaining $500 the student pays is part of the opportunity cost of returning to college. The major component of the opportunity cost, though, is the fact that the student must pass up being drafted by the NFL. If the student plays in the NFL, he will receive $2,000,000, less his expenses of $100,000. Thus by playing in the NFL, the student would net $1,900,000. By returning to school, the student loses the opportunity to earn $1,900,000. This, then is part of the opportunity cost of returning to college for his senior year. Hence the student's opportunity cost of returning to school is $1,900,000 plus $500, or $1,900,500.

■ You're the Teacher

1. "Economic theories are like maps, which are useful precisely because they abstract from real world detail. A useful map offers a simplified view, which is carefully selected according to the purpose of the map. No map maker would claim that the world is as simple (or as flat) as the map, and economists do not claim that the real economy is as simple as their theories. What economists do claim is that their theories isolate the effects of real forces operating in the economy, yield predictions that can be tested against real-world data, and that these predictions often are correct.

   "As Milton Friedman (a Nobel Prize winner in Economics) said on this topic: 'A theory or its 'assumptions' cannot possibly be thoroughly 'realistic' in the immediate descriptive sense.... A completely 'realistic' theory of the wheat market would have to include not only the conditions directly underlying the supply and demand for wheat but also the kind of coins or credit instruments used to make exchanges; the personal characteristics of wheat-traders such as the color of each trader's hair and eyes, ... the number of members of his family, their characteristics, ... the kind of soil on which the wheat was grown, ... the weather prevailing during the growing season; ... and so on indefinitely. Any attempt to move very far in achieving this kind of 'realism' is certain to render a theory utterly useless.'"

From Milton Friedman, "The Methodology of Positive Economics," in *Essays in Positive Economics.* (Chicago: University of Chicago Press, 1953), 32.

2. "Virtually everything has an opportunity cost. People sometimes say that viewing a beautiful sunset or using sand from the middle of the Sahara Desert have no opportunity costs. But that isn't strictly true. Viewing the sunset has an opportunity cost in terms of the time spent watching it. The time could have been utilized in some other activity and, whatever the next highest valued opportunity might have been, that is the opportunity cost of watching the sunset. Similarly, making use of sand from the Sahara also must have some opportunity cost, be it the time spent in gathering the sand or the resources spent in gathering it. Thus, from the widest of perspectives, the answer is: Yes, everything does have an opportunity cost."

2 MAKING AND USING GRAPHS

Key Concepts

Graphing Data

Graphs represent quantity as a distance on a line. On a two-dimensional graph:

- the horizontal line is the **x-axis.**
- the vertical line is the **y-axis.**
- the intersection of the two lines is the **origin.**

The three main types of economic graphs are:

- **Scatter diagrams** — show the relationship between two variables, one measured on the x-axis and the other on the y-axis. Such a relationship indicates how the variables are *correlated*, not whether one variable *causes* the other.

  Time-series graphs — demonstrate the relationship between time (measured on the x-axis) and other variable(s) (measured on the y-axis). They reveal the variable's level, direction of change, speed of change, and **trend**, which is its general tendency to rise or fall.
- **Cross-section graphs** — show the values for different groups of one variable at a point in time.

Graphs can be misleading when they stretch or squeeze the measurement scale to exaggerate or understate the magnitude of the variation of the variables.

Graphs Used in Economic Models

The four important relationships between variables are:

- **Positive** — the variables move together in same direction, as illustrated in Figure 2.1. The relationship is upward-sloping, so the slope is a positive number.
- **Negative** — the variables move in opposite directions, as shown in Figure 2.2. The relationship is downward-sloping and so the slope is a negative number.

FIGURE **2.1**
A Positive Relationship

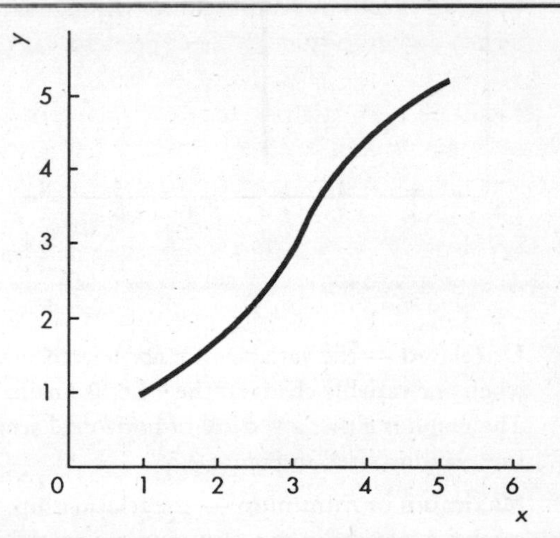

FIGURE **2.2**
A Negative Relationship

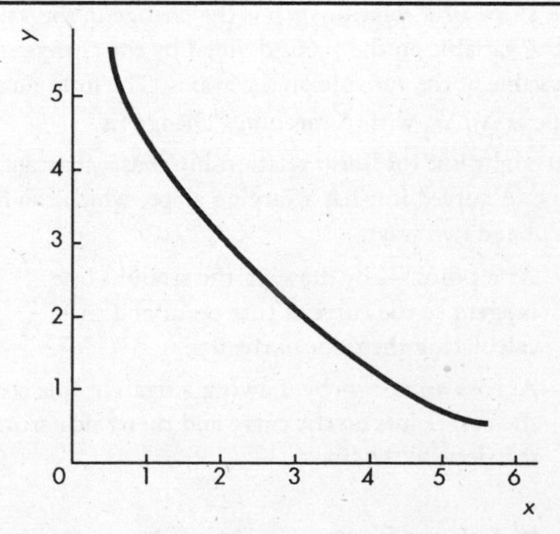

FIGURE **2.3**
No Relationship

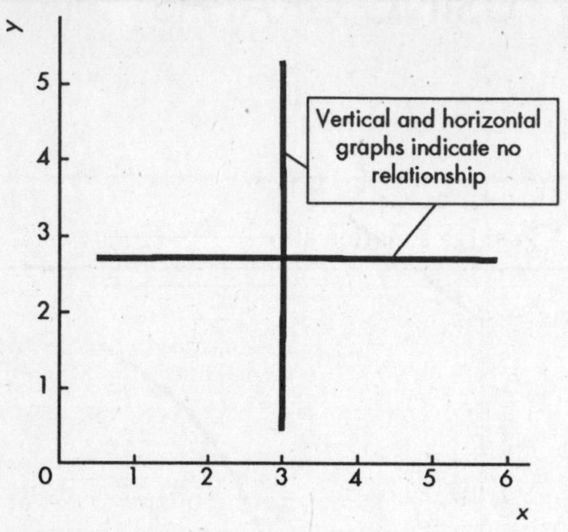

FIGURE **2.4**
A Minimum

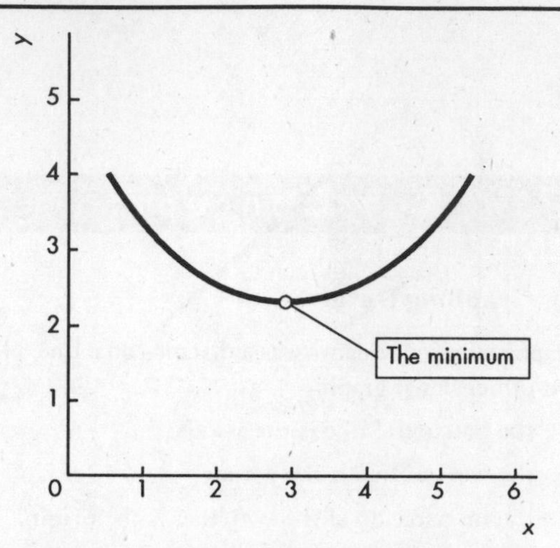

- **Unrelated** — the variables are not related so that, when one variable changes, the other is unaffected. The graph is either a vertical or horizontal straight line, as illustrated in Figure 2.3.
- **Maximum or minimum** — the relationship reaches a maximum or a minimum point, then changes direction. Figure 2.4 shows a minimum.

The Slope of a Relationship

The **slope of a relationship** is the change in the value of the variable on the *y*-axis divided by the change in the value of the variable on the *x*-axis. The formula for slope is $\Delta y/\Delta x$, with Δ meaning "change in."

A straight line (or linear relationship) has a constant slope. A curved line has a varying slope, which can be calculated two ways:

- **At a point** — by drawing the straight line tangent to the curve at that point and then calculating the slope of the line.
- **Across an arc** — by drawing a straight line across the two points on the curve and then calculating the slope of the line.

Relationships Among More Than Two Variables

Relationships between more than two variables can be graphed by holding constant the values of all the variables except two (a *ceteris paribus* assumption) and then graphing the relationship between the two. When one of the variables not illustrated changes, the entire relationship between the two that have been graphed shifts.

Helpful Hints

1. Economists almost always use graphs to present relationships between variables. This fact should not "scare" you nor give you pause. Economists do so because graphs *simplify* the analysis. All the key concepts you need to master are presented in this chapter. Once you understand them, you will realize how graphs make learning economics much easier. Keep in mind that, if at some later point in this course, you become confused by a graphing concept — slope, the meaning of a positive relationship, or whatever — you can return to this chapter and review the relevant material.
2. If your experience with graphical analysis is limited, this chapter is crucial to your ability to readily understand economic analysis. However, if you are experienced in constructing and using graphs, this chapter may be "old hat." Even so, you should skim the chapter and work through the questions in this supplement.

FIGURE **2.5**
Rise Over Run

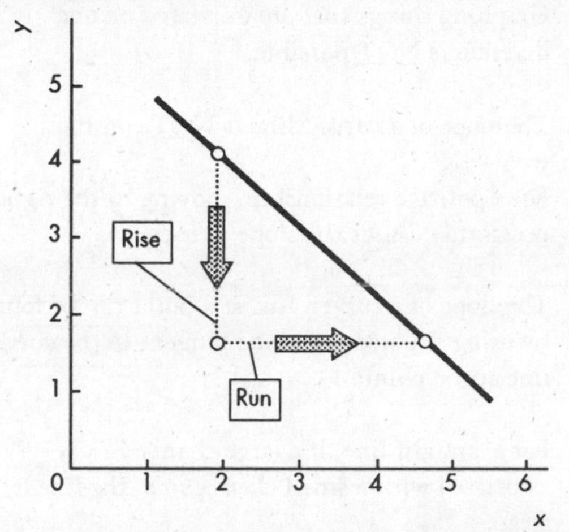

FIGURE **2.6**
Graph of a Straight Line

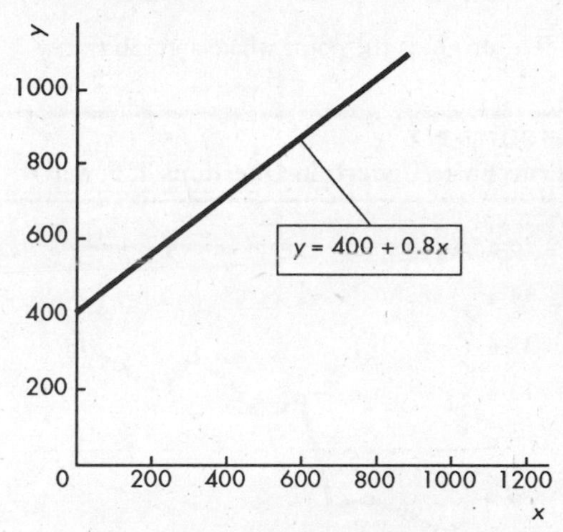

3. Often the slopes of various relationships are important. Usually what is key is the sign of the slope — whether the slope is positive or negative — rather than the actual value of the slope. An easy way to remember the formula for slope is to think of it as the "the rise over the run," a saying used by carpenters and others. The idea is simple. As illustrated in Figure 2.5, the *rise* is the change in the variable measured on the vertical axis, or in terms of symbols, Δy. The *run* is the change in the variable measured on the horizontal axis, or Δx. This "rise over the run" formula also makes it easy to remember whether the slope is positive or negative. If the rise is actually a drop, as shown in Figure 2.5, then the slope is negative: When the variable measured on the horizontal axis increases, the variable measured on the vertical axis decreases. However, if the rise actually is an increase, then the slope is positive. In this case, an increase in the variable measured on the *x*-axis is associated with an increase in the variable measured on the *y*-axis.

4. The general equation of a straight line is sometimes useful to remember. Any straight line on a graph has as its general formula

$$y = a + bx$$

In this formula, the *a* term is the vertical intercept — that is, it gives the value of the variable on the vertical axis where the line crosses this axis. In other words, it is the value of the variable on the vertical axis when the variable on the horizontal axis equals zero. The *b* term is the slope of the line. Thus the sign of *b* indicates immediately whether the relationship between *x* and *y* is positive (when *b* is positive) or negative (when *b* is negative).

With this equation, you can use these two facts to determine instantly the vertical intercept and the slope. For example, if

$$y = 400 + 0.8x$$

the vertical intercept is 400; that is, when *x* equals zero, *y* equals 400. The slope of the line is 0.8. Because the slope is a positive number, the relationship between *x* and *y* is positive. When graphed, as in Figure 2.6, the line slopes up and to the right.

Questions

True/False/Uncertain and Explain

1. If the graph of the relationship between two variables slopes upward and to the right, the relationship between the variables is positive.

2. If the relationship between *y* (measured on the vertical axis) and *x* (measured on the horizontal

axis) is one in which y reaches a maximum, the slope of the relationship must be negative before and positive after the maximum.

3. The origin is the point where a graph starts.

FIGURE **2.7**

True/False/Uncertain Questions 4, 5, and 6

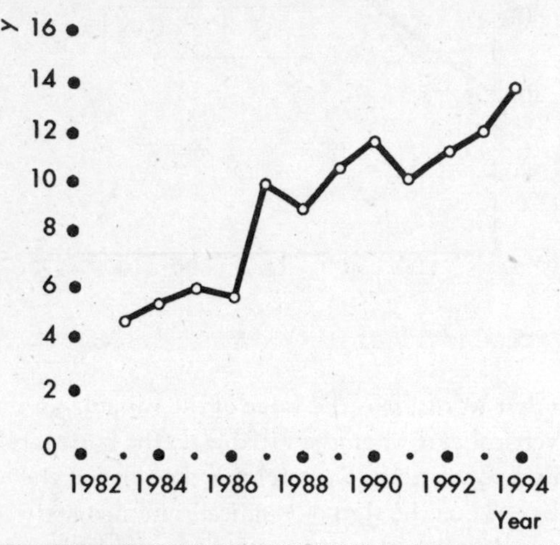

4. In Figure 2.7, the value of y decreased between 1990 and 1991.

5. In Figure 2.7, the value of y increased most rapidly between 1993 and 1994.

6. Figure 2.7 shows a trend with y generally increasing.

7. The slope of a straight line is calculated by dividing the change in the value of the variable measured on the horizontal axis by the change in the value of the variable measured on the vertical axis.

8. A graph showing a positive relationship between stock prices and the nation's output means that an increase in stock prices causes an increase in output.

9. A cross-section graph compares values of a variable for different groups at a single point in time.

10. To the left of a minimum point, the slope is negative; to the right the slope is positive.

11. Graphing things that are unrelated on one diagram is <u>NOT</u> possible.

12. The slope of a curved line is <u>NOT</u> constant.

13. For a positive relationship, moving to the right necessarily causes the slope to increase.

14. The slope of a curved line at a point can be found by using the slope of a line tangent to the curved line at the point.

15. For a straight line, if a large change in y is associated with a small change in x, the line is steep.

■ Multiple Choice

1. Demonstrating how an economic variable changes from one year to the next is best illustrated by a
   a. one-variable graph.
   b. time-series graph.
   c. linear graph.
   d. cross-section graph.

2. If variables x and y move up and down together, they are
   a. positively related.
   b. negative related.
   c. unrelated.
   d. trend related

3. Which type of graph can mislead?
   a. A time series graph.
   b. A cross-section graph.
   c. A scatter diagram.
   d. *Any* type of graph might mislead.

4. The term "direct relationship" means the same as
   a. correlation.
   b. trend.
   c. positive relationship.
   d. negative relationship

FIGURE 2.8
Multiple Choice Question 5

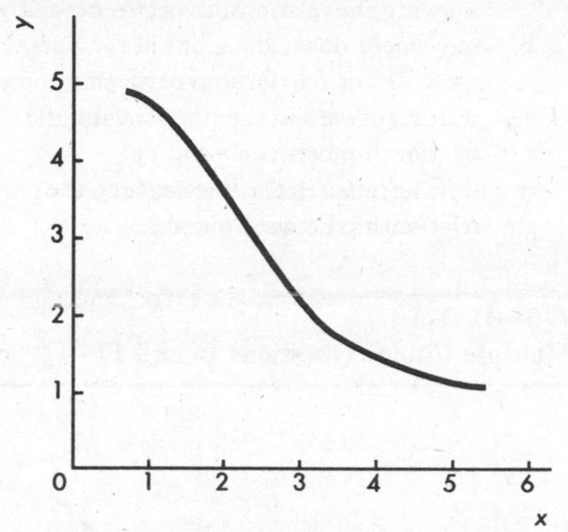

FIGURE 2.9
Multiple Choice Questions 9 and 10

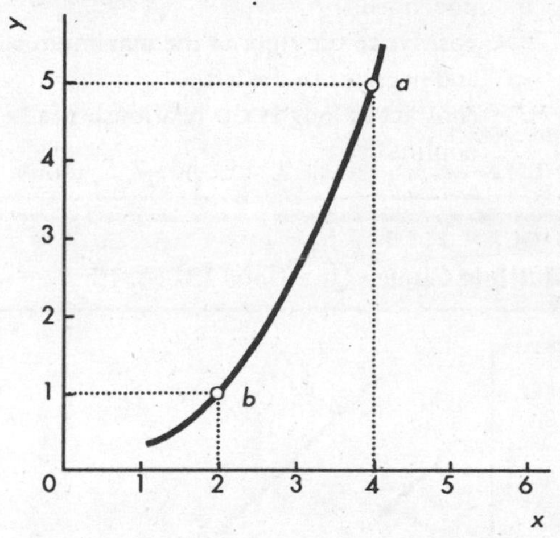

5. Figure 2.8 shows
   a. a positive relationship.
   b. a time-series relationship.
   c. a negative relationship.
   d. no relationship between the variables.

6. A nonlinear relationship
   a. always has a maximum.
   b. always has a constant slope.
   c. always slopes up to the right.
   d. never has a constant slope.

7. The relationship between two variables, *x* and *y*, is a vertical line. Thus, *x* and *y* are
   a. positively correlated.
   b. negatively correlated.
   c. not related.
   d. falsely related.

8. You think that the total amount of goods produced in the United States has generally increased. Thus in a time-series graph illustrating the total amount produced, you expect to find
   a. an upward trend.
   b. no relationship between time and the amount of goods produced.
   c. an inverse relationship between time and the amount of goods produced.
   d. a linear relationship.

9. The relationship between *x* and *y* in Figure 2.9 is
   a. positive with an increasing slope.
   b. positive with a decreasing slope.
   c. negative with an increasing slope.
   d. negative with a decreasing slope.

10. In Figure 2.9, the slope across the arc between points *a* and *b* equals
    a. 5.
    b. 4.
    c. 2.
    d. 1.

11. You hypothesize that more natural gas is sold in the Northeast when winters are colder. Which of the following possibilities would best reveal if this relationship is correct?
    a. A time-series diagram showing the amount of natural gas sold in the Northeast during last 30 years.
    b. A time-series diagram showing the average temperature in the Northeast during the last 30 years.
    c. A scatter-diagram plotting the average temperature in the Northeast against the amount of natural gas sold.
    d. A trend diagram that plots the trend in natural gas sales over the last 30 years against the average temperature in the Northeast 30 years ago and this year.

12. The slope of a negative relationship is
    a. negative.
    b. undefined.
    c. positive to the right of the maximum point and negative to the left.
    d. constant as long as the relationship is nonlinear.

FIGURE **2.10**
Multiple Choice Questions 13, 14, 15

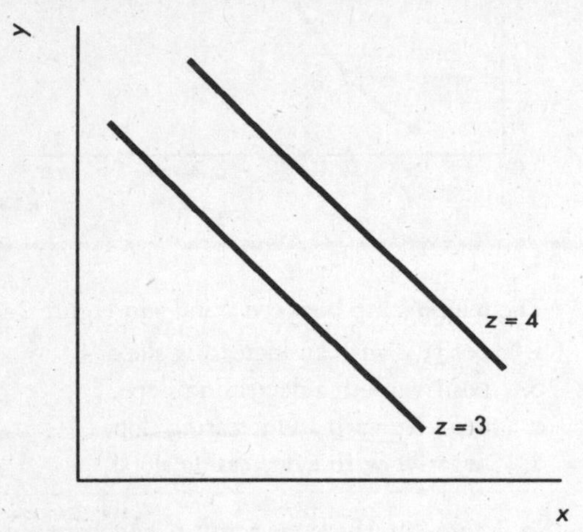

13. In Figure 2.10, x is
    a. positively related to y and negatively related to z.
    b. positively related to both y and z.
    c. negatively related to y and positively related to z.
    d. negatively related to both y and z.

14. In Figure 2.10, *ceteris paribus*, an increase in x is associated with
    a. an increase in y.
    b. a decrease in y.
    c. an increase in z.
    d. a decrease in z.

15. In Figure 2.10, an increase in z causes a
    a. movement up along one of the lines showing the relationship between x and y.
    b. movement down along one of the lines showing the relationship between x and y.
    c. shift rightward in the line showing the relationship between x and y.
    d. shift leftward in the line showing the relationship between x and y.

FIGURE **2.11**
Multiple Choice Questions 16 and 17

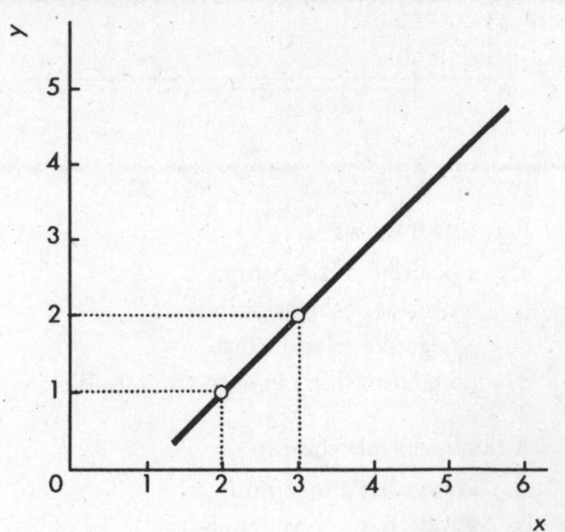

16. In Figure 2.11, between $x = 2$ and $x = 3$, what is the slope of the line?
    a. 1.
    b. –1.
    c. 2.
    d. 3.

17. In Figure 2.11, how does the slope of the line between $x = 4$ and $x = 5$ compare with the slope between $x = 2$ and $x = 3$?
    a. The slope is greater between $x = 4$ and $x = 5$.
    b. The slope is greater between $x = 2$ and $x = 3$.
    c. The slope is the same.
    d. The slope is not comparable.

18. You notice that, when the inflation rate increases, interest rates also tend to increase. This fact indicates that
   a. there may false causality between inflation and interest rates.
   b. higher inflation rates must cause higher interest rates.
   c. a scatter diagram of the inflation rate and the interest rate will show a positive relationship.
   d. a cross-section graph of the inflation rate and the interest rate will show a positive relationship

FIGURE 2.12
Multiple Choice Questions 19 and 20

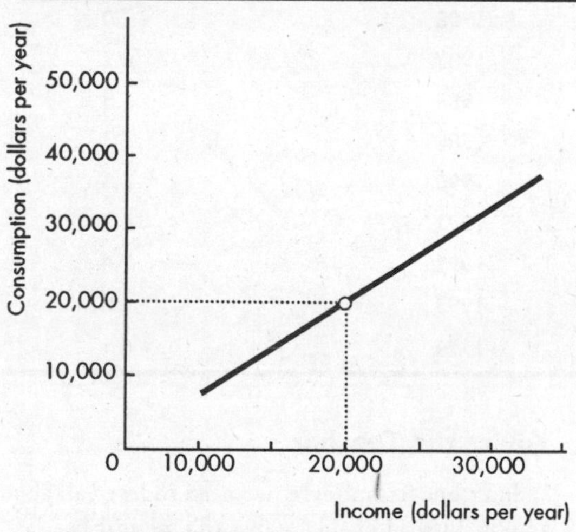

19. In Figure 2.12, when income equals $20,000, what does consumption equal?
   a. $0.
   b. $10,000.
   c. $20,000.
   d. Impossible to tell.

20. The relationship between income and consumption illustrated in Figure 2.12 is
   a. positive and linear.
   b. positive and nonlinear.
   c. negative and linear.
   d. negative and nonlinear.

Short Answer Problems

Table 2.1 Short Answer Problem 1

x	y
1	2
2	4
3	6
4	8
5	6
6	4

1. a. Use the data in Table 2.1 to graph the relationship between x and y.
   b. Over what range of values for x is this relationship positive? Over what range is it negative?
   c. Calculate the slope between $x = 1$ and $x = 2$.
   d. Calculate the slope between $x = 5$ and $x = 6$.
   e. What relationships do your answers to parts c and d have to your answer for part b?

Table 2.2 Short Answer Problem 2

Price (dollars per compact disc	Quantity of compact discs purchased, low income	Quantity of compact discs purchased, high income
$11	5	6
12	4	5
13	3	4
14	1	3
15	0	2

2. a. Bobby says that he buys fewer compact discs when the price of a compact disc is higher. Bobby also says that he will buy more compact discs after he graduates and his income is higher. Is the relationship between the number of compact discs Bobby buys and the price positive or negative? Is the relationship between Bobby's income and the number of compact discs positive or negative?
   b. Table 2.2 shows the number of compact discs Bobby buys in a month at different prices when his income is low and when his income is high. On a diagram with price on the

vertical axis and the quantity purchased on the horizontal axis, plot the relationship between the number of discs purchased and the price when Bobby's income is low.

c. On the same diagram, draw the relationship when Bobby's income is high.

d. Does an increase in Bobby's income cause the relationship between the price of a compact disc and the number purchased to shift rightward or leftward?

FIGURE **2.13**

Short Answer Problem 3

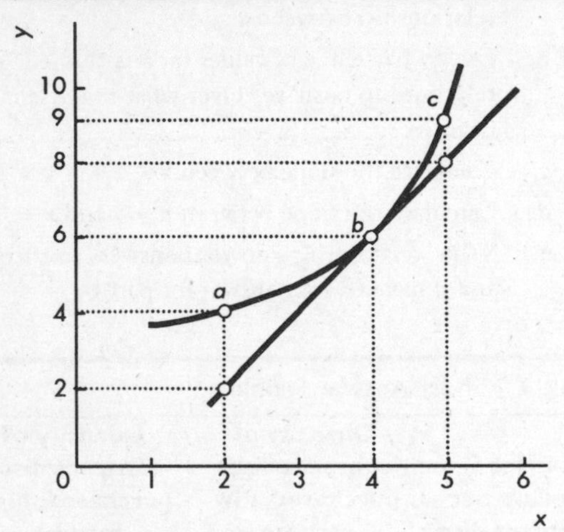

3. a. In Figure 2.13, use the tangent line in the figure to calculate the slope at point *b*.
   b. Compute the slope across the arc between points *b* and *a*.
   c. Calculate the slope across the arc between points *c* and *b*.
4. Can a curve to have a positive but decreasing slope? If so, draw an example.
5. a. The data in Table 2.3 show the unemployment rate in the United States between 1974 and 1994. Draw a time-series graph of these data.
   b. In what year was the unemployment rate the highest?
   c. Has there been a trend in the unemployment rate?

Table 2.3 Short Answer Problem 5

Year	Unemployment rate
1974	5.6%
1975	8.5
1976	7.7
1977	7.1
1978	6.1
1979	5.8
1980	7.1
1981	7.6
1982	9.7
1983	9.6
1984	7.5
1985	7.2
1986	7.0
1987	6.2
1988	5.5
1989	5.3
1990	5.5
1991	6.7
1992	7.4
1993	6.8
1994	6.1

You're the Teacher

1. "I don't understand why we need to learn all about graphs. Instead of this, why can't we just use numbers? If there is any sort of relationship we need to see, we can see it easier using numbers instead of all these complicated graphs!" Explain why graphs are useful when studying economics.
2. "There must be a relationship between the direction a curve is sloping, what its slope is, and whether the curve shows a positive or negative relationship between two variables. But I can't see the tie. Is there one? And what is it?" Help this student by answering the questions posed.
3. "Hey, I thought this was an *economics* class, not a *math* class. Where's the economics? All I've seen so far is math!" Your friend's complaint is related to the previous comment. Now, however, reassure your friend by explaining why the concentration in this chapter is on mathematics rather than economics.

Answers

True/False Answers

1. **T** If the graph slopes upward to the right, then an increase in the variable measured along the horizontal axis is associated with an increase in the variable measured on the vertical axis.
2. **F** As Figure 2.14 illustrates, before the maximum is reached, the relationship must be positive; after the maximum is attained, the relationship must be negative.

FIGURE **2.14**
True/False/Uncertain Question 2

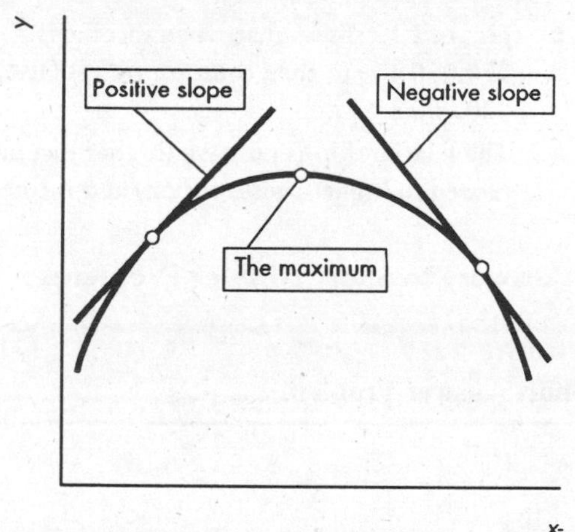

3. **F** The origin is where the horizontal and vertical axis start, *not* where the graph starts.
4. **T** According to the figure, *y* decreased from about 12 to about 10.
5. **F** *y* rose the most between 1986 and 1987.
6. **T** As the figure makes clear, there has been an upward trend in *y*. Note how the time-series graph made answering the last questions easy.
7. **F** Just the reverse is true: Divide the change in the variable on the *vertical* axis by the change in the variable on the *horizontal* axis.
8. **F** The graph shows a correlation between stock prices and increases in output, but that does not necessarily mean that the increase in stock prices causes the increase in output.
9. **T** This is the definition of a cross-section graph.
10. **T** To verify this answer, flip Figure 2.14 upside down. Note that to the left of the minimum the line is falling, so its slope is negative; to the right the line is rising, so its slope is positive.
11. **F** If two unrelated variables are graphed on the same diagram, the "relationship" between the two is either a vertical or a horizontal straight line.
12. **T** Only the slope of a straight line is constant.
13. **F** Figure 2.15 shows a positive relationship whose slope decreases when moving up along it from point *a* to point *b*.

FIGURE **2.15**
True/False/Uncertain Question 13

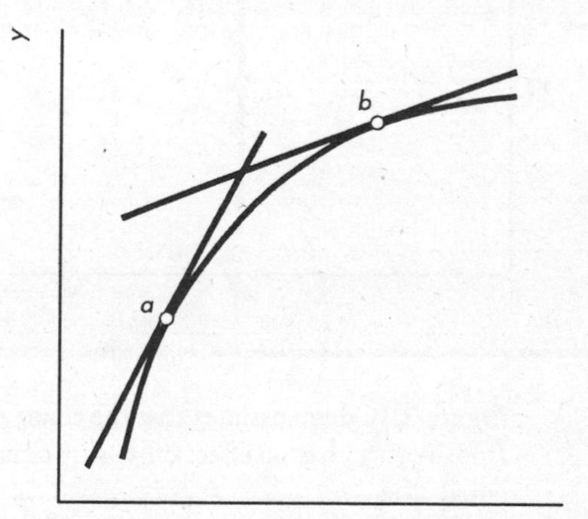

14. **T** This statement is precisely how the slope at a point on a curved line is calculated.
15. **T** The definition of slope is $\Delta y/\Delta x$. Thus, if a large change in *y* (the numerator) is associated with a small change in *x* (the denominator), the slope is relatively large, indicating that the line is relatively steep.

Multiple Choice Answers

1. **b** A time-series graph illustrates how the variable has changed over time.
2. **a** In this case, an increase (or decrease) in *x* is associated with an increase (or decrease) in *y*, so the variables are positively related.

3. **d** Any type of graph can be misleading.
4. **c** The term "positive relationship" means the same as "direct relationship."
5. **c** As x increases, y decreases; thus the relationship between x and y is negative.
6. **d** A straight line — that is, a linear relationship — has a constant slope whereas nonlinear relationships have slopes that vary.

FIGURE **2.16**
Multiple Choice Question 7

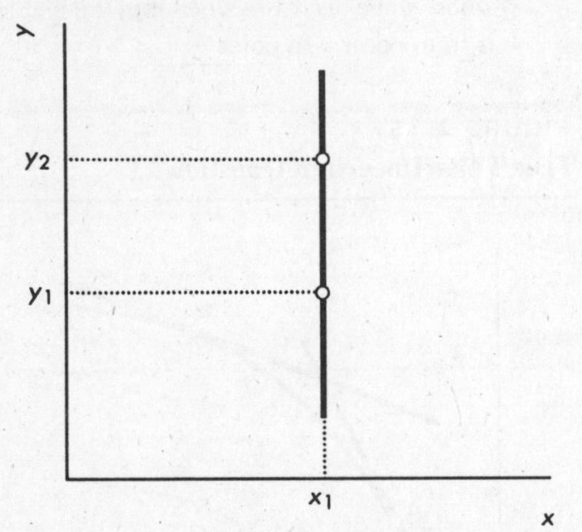

7. **c** Figure 2.16 demonstrates that the change in y from y_1 to y_2 has no effect on x — it remains equal to x_1.
8. **a** The upward trend indicates a general increase in production over time.
9. **a** The slope is positive and, because the line is becoming steeper, the slope is increasing.
10. **c** The slope between the two points equals the change in the vertical distance divided by the change in the horizontal distance, that is $(5-1)/(4-2)$, which gives 2.
11. **c** This scatter diagram will show the correlation between temperature and natural gas sales.
12. **a** A negative relationship has a negative slope; a positive relationship has a positive slope.
13. **c** The curves showing the relationship between x and y demonstrate that x and y are negatively related. For any value of y, an increase in z is associated with a higher value for x, so x and z are positively related.
14. **b** Moving along one of the lines showing the relationship between x and y (say, the line with $z = 3$) shows that, as x increases, y decreases.
15. **c** The higher value of z shifts the entire relationship between x and y rightward.
16. **a** The slope equals the "rise over the run," or $(2-1)/(3-2) = 1$.
17. **c** The figure shows a straight line. The slope of a straight line is constant, so the slope between $x = 4$ and $x = 5$ is the same as the slope between $x = 2$ and $x = 3$.
18. **c** A positive correlation between inflation rates and interest rates is reflected in a scatter diagram as a positive relationship; that is, the dots would tend to cluster along a line that slopes upward to the right.
19. **c** Figure 2.12 shows that when income is $20,000 a year, then consumption is (also) $20,000 a year.
20. **a** The relationship is positive (higher income is related to higher consumption) and is linear.

Answers to Short Answer Problems

FIGURE **2.17**
Short Answer Problem 1

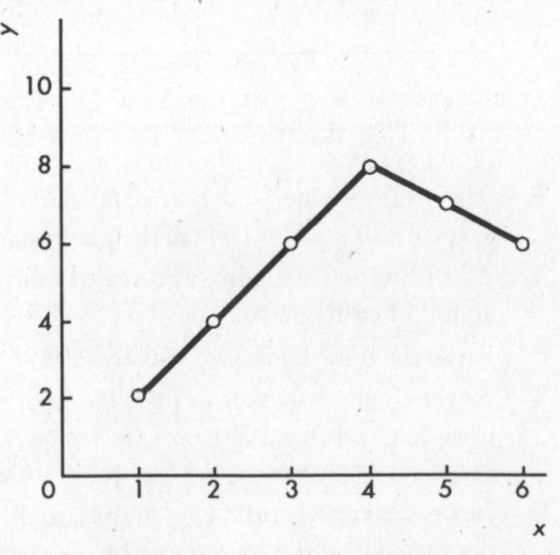

1. a. The relationship between x and y is illustrated in Figure 2.17.

b. The relationship between x and y is positive between $x = 1$ and $x = 4$. Between $x = 4$ and $x = 6$, the relationship is negative.

c. The slope equals $\Delta y/\Delta x$ or, in this case between $x = 1$ and $x = 2$, the slope is $(2 - 4)/(1 - 2) = 2$.

d. Between $x = 5$ and $x = 6$, the slope is equal to $(6 - 4)/(5 - 6) = -2$.

e. Over the range of values where the relationship between x and y is positive — from $x = 1$ to $x = 4$ — the slope is positive. Over the range where the relationship between x and y is negative — from $x = 4$ to $x = 6$ — the slope is negative. Thus positive relationships have positive slopes and negative relationships have negative slopes.

2. a. Because Bobby buys more compact discs when their price is lower, the relationship between the number of compact discs Bobby buys and the price is negative. Similarly, the relationship between Bobby's income and the number of compact discs he buys is positive.

b. Figure 2.18 illustrates the relationship between the price of a compact disc and the number Bobby buys when his income is low.

c. Also illustrated in Figure 2.18 is the relationship between the number of compact discs Bobby buys and their price when Bobby's income is high.

d. An increase in Bobby's income shifts the relationship between the price of a compact disc and the number Bobby buys rightward.

3. a. The slope is $(8 - 2)/(5 - 2) = 2$.

b. The slope is $(6 - 4)/(4 - 2) = 1$.

c. The slope is $(9 - 6)/(5 - 4) = 3$.

4. Yes, a curve can have a positive, decreasing slope. Figure 2.19 illustrates such a relationship. In it, at relatively low values of x the slope is quite steep, indicating a high value for the slope. But, as x increases, the curve becomes flatter, which means that the slope decreases. (To verify this set of results, draw the tangent lines at points a and b and then compare their slopes.) This figure points out that there is a major difference between the value of a relationship at some point and its slope at that point!

FIGURE 2.18
Short Answer Problem 2

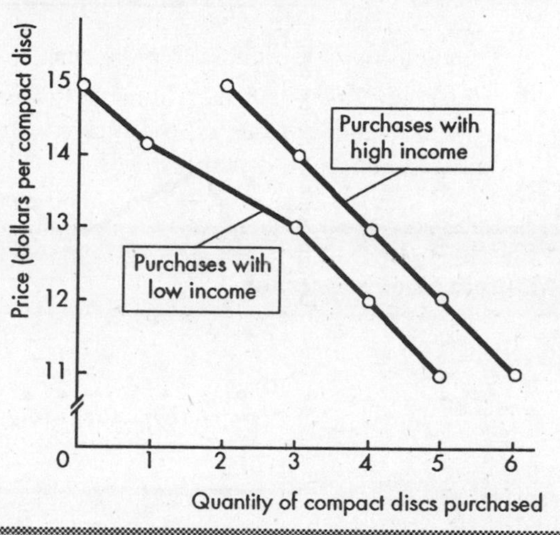

FIGURE 2.19
Short Answer Problem 4

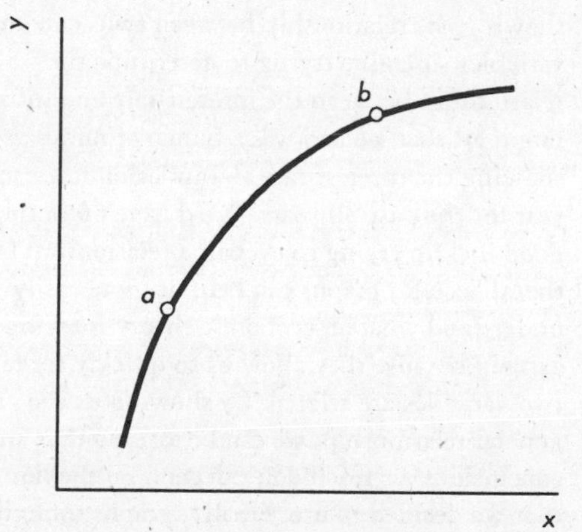

5. a. Figure 2.20 (on the next page) shows the time series of unemployment rates in the United States.

b. The unemployment rate was the highest in 1982, when it equaled 9.7 percent.

c. There does not seem to be much of a trend toward either generally higher or generally lower unemployment rates.

FIGURE 2.20
Short Answer Problem 5

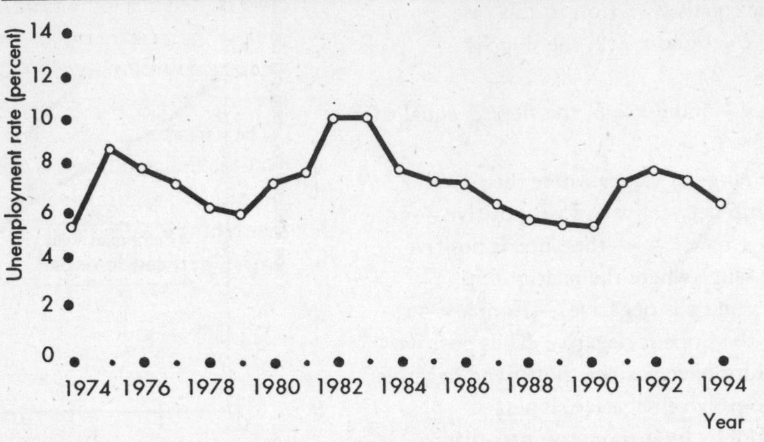

■ You're the Teacher

1. "Graphs make understanding economics and the relationships between economic variables easier in three ways. First, graphs are extremely useful in showing the relationship between two economic variables. Imagine trying to determine the relationship between the interest rate and inflation rate if all that we had was a bunch of numbers showing the interest rate and inflation rate each year for the past 30 years. We'd have 60 numbers; good luck in trying to eyeball a relationship from them! Second, graphs can help us more easily understand what an economic theory is trying to explain because they allow us to quickly see how two variables are related. By showing us the general relationship, we can be assured that any conclusions we reach don't depend on the numbers that we decided to use. Finally, graphs sometimes show us a result we might not have otherwise noticed. If all we had were numbers, we could easily become lost trying to keep track of them. Graphs make our work easier, and for this reason we need to know how to use them!"

"The connection between the direction a line slopes, its slope and whether the relationship is positive or negative is easy — once you see it! Take a look at Figure 2.21. In this figure, the line slopes upward to the right. The slope of this line is positive: An increase in *x* is associated with an increase in *y*. Because increases in *x* are related to increases in *y*, the graph shows a positive relationship between *x* and *y*. Now look at Figure 2.22 (on the next page). Here the line slopes downward to the right. The slope of this line is negative: An increase in *x* is related to a decrease in *y*. Because *x* and *y* are inversely related, the relationship shown in Figure 2.22 is negative. I can summarize these results for you so that you'll

FIGURE 2.21
You're the Teacher Question 2

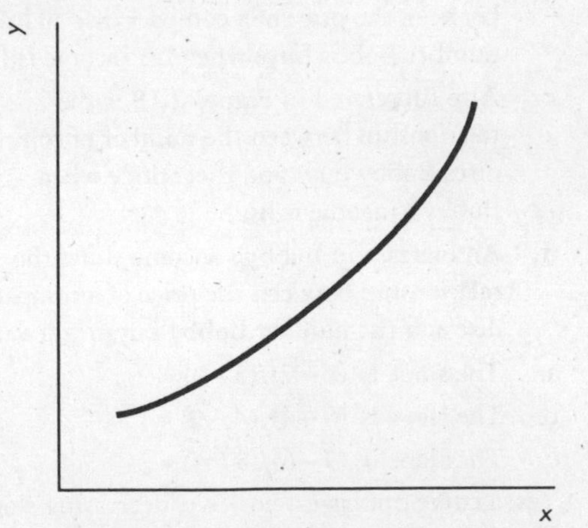

FIGURE 2.22
You're the Teacher Question 2

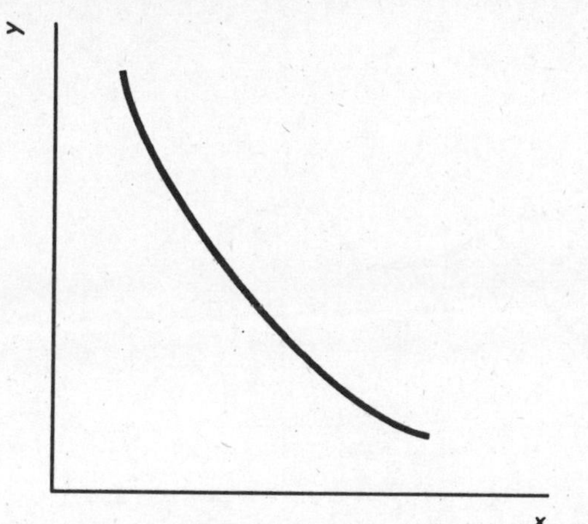

always be able to remember them by putting them all together:

Direction of line		Sign of slope		Type of relationship
Upward to the right	⇔	Positive	⇔	Positive
Downward to the right	⇔	Negative	⇔	Negative

This summary should help you keep everything straight."

3. "This *is* an economics class. But understanding some simple graphing ideas makes economics a lot easier to learn. Learning about graphing for its own sake is not important in this class; what is important is learning about graphing to help with the economics that we'll take up in the next chapter. So, look at this chapter as a resource. Whether you already knew everything in it before you looked at it or even if everything in it was brand new, anytime you get confused by something dealing with a technical point on a graph, you can look back at this chapter for help. So, chill out; we'll get to the economics in the next chapter!"

3 PRODUCTION, GROWTH, AND TRADE

Key Concepts

The Production Possibility Frontier (*PPF*)

Production involves changing factors of production — labor, land, capital, and entrepreneurial ability — into goods and services. Production is limited by the amount of resources available. The **production possibility frontier** (*PPF*):

- is the boundary between unattainable and attainable production possibilities.
- shows maximum combinations of outputs (goods and services) that can be produced with given resources and technology.

FIGURE 3.1
A Linear *PPF*

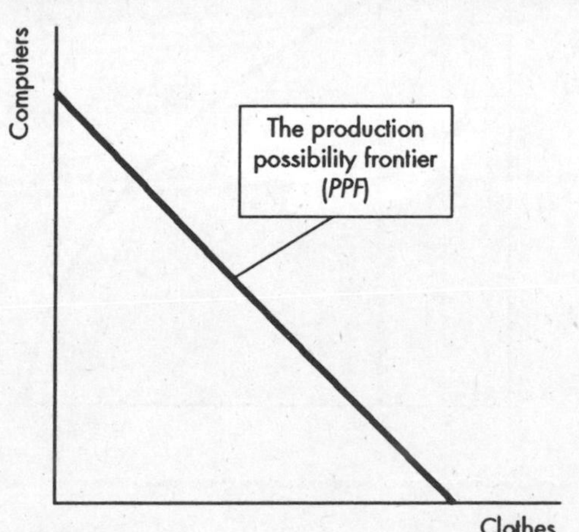

A linear *PPF* for an economy is illustrated in Figure 3.1. This figure shows three characteristics in common to all production possibility frontiers:

- Production points inside the *PPF* are attainable. They are not maximum combinations of outputs, and so are attainable but are inefficient and occur with unemployed or misallocated resources.
- Points on the *PPF* are both attainable and efficient. In moving between two points on the *PPF*, more computers can be obtained only by producing fewer clothes; the ***opportunity cost*** of more computers is the amount of clothes forgone.
- Points outside the *PPF* are unattainable.

Increasing Opportunity Cost

When resources are not equally productive in producing different goods and services, the *PPF* has increasing opportunity costs and bows outward, as illustrated in Figure 3.2.

FIGURE 3.2
A *PPF* with Increasing Opportunity Costs

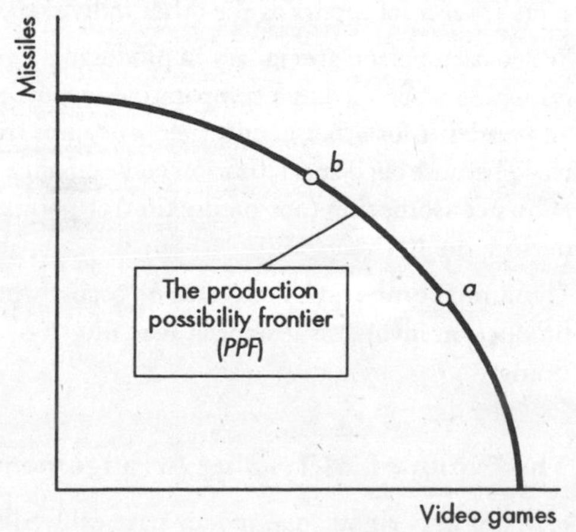

- The opportunity cost of moving from point *a* to *b* and producing more missiles is the amount of video games that are foregone.
- The bowed out shape of the *PPF* illustrates increasing opportunity cost. As more missiles are

produced, the opportunity cost — the video games that must be sacrificed — increases.

■ Economic Growth

Economic growth occurs when the *PPF* shifts out. The faster it shifts, the more rapid is economic growth.

- ♦ *Technological progress* and *capital accumulation* shift the *PPF* outward and are causes of economic growth.
- ♦ The opportunity cost of economic growth (through capital accumulation and technological progress) is today's foregone production and consumption.
- ♦ Nations that devote more resources to capital accumulation grow more rapidly than nations that devote fewer resources to it.

■ Gains from Trade

- ♦ Between two people, an individual has a **comparative advantage** in producing a good if he or she can produce it at lower opportunity cost than the other person.
- ♦ Comparative advantage is different from absolute advantage. **Absolute advantage** occurs when a person can produce more of *both* goods using the same amount of inputs as the other individual.
- ♦ When each person specializes in producing a good for which he or she has a comparative advantage and trades it for other goods, there are gains from trade because such specialization and exchange allows consumption (not production) at points outside the *PPF*.
- ♦ **Dynamic comparative advantage** occurs when production involves substantial **learning-by-doing.**

■ The Evolution of Trading Arrangements

Markets, property rights, and money have evolved to help reap the gains from specialization.

- ♦ Markets pool information into a price, which signals buyers and sellers about the actions they should take.
- ♦ **Property rights** are social arrangements that set the terms of the ownership, use, and disposal of factors of production, goods, and services.
- ♦ Monetary exchange overcomes the **barter** problem of requiring a double coincidence of wants before a trade can be consummated.

Helpful Hints

1. This chapter reviews the crucial concept of opportunity cost — the best alternative forgone — that was introduced in Chapter 1. A helpful formula for opportunity cost, which works well in solving problems— especially problems that involve moving up or down a production possibility frontier (*PPF*)—is:

$$\text{Opportunity cost} = \frac{\text{Give up}}{\text{Get}}$$

The opportunity cost equals the quantity of goods you must give up divided by the quantity of goods you will get. For instance, Courtney can grow corn or produce cloth. Consider the three possibilities on her *PPF* in Figure 3.3.

FIGURE 3.3
A *PPF* Between Corn and Cloth

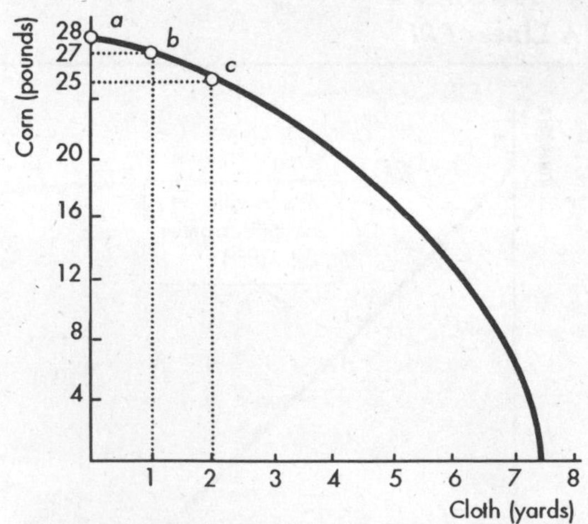

If we move down the *PPF*, first from *a* to *b*, what is the opportunity cost of an additional yard of cloth? Courtney must give up 1 pound of corn (28 – 27) to get 1 yard of cloth (1 – 0). Putting these quantities into the formula, we get the opportunity cost of the first yard of cloth:

$$\frac{\text{1 pound corn}}{\text{1 yard cloth}} = \text{1 pound corn per yard of cloth}$$

Next, if we move from *b* to *c*, the opportunity cost of the second yard of cloth is calculated the same way and is 2 pounds of corn. (The opportunity cost is increasing as more cloth is produced, which accounts for the bowed-out shape of the *PPF*.)

Now, if we move up the *PPF* from *c* to *b*, what is the opportunity cost of an additional pound of corn? Jane must give up 1 yard of cloth (2 – 1) to get 2 pounds of corn (27 – 25). Substituting into the formula yields:

$$\frac{1 \text{ yard cloth}}{2 \text{ pounds corn}} = \frac{1}{2} \text{ yard cloth per pound of corn}$$

Opportunity cost is always measured in the units of the forgone good.

2. Opportunity cost also can be related to the slope of the *PPF*. As we move *down* between any two points on the *PPF*, the opportunity cost of an additional unit of the good on the *horizontal axis* is:

$$|\text{Slope of the } PPF|$$

(The slope of the *PPF* is negative, but economists describe opportunity cost in terms of a positive quantity of forgone goods, so we use the absolute value of the slope to calculate the desired positive number.) The point that the slope equals thc opportunity cost can be verified by looking at the slope between points *a* and *b* in the first hint. The slope between *a* and *b* is:

$$\frac{\text{Change in vertical distance between } a \text{ and } b}{\text{Change in horizontal distance between } a \text{ and } b}$$

Comparing this formula with the calculations used to compute the opportunity cost of moving from point *a* to point *b* shows that they are identical. Thus the slope of the *PPF* equals the opportunity cost of gaining an additional unit of the good measured on the horizontal axis.

Similarly, as we move *up* between any two points on the *PPF*, the opportunity cost of an additional unit of the good on the *vertical axis* is:

$$\left|\frac{1}{\text{Slope of } PPF}\right|$$

These formulas show us the reciprocal relation between the opportunity costs of moving from *b* to *c* and moving from *c* to *b* in the first hint. The opportunity cost of an additional unit of cloth (on the horizontal axis) between *b* and *c* is 2 pounds of corn. The opportunity cost of an additional unit of corn (on the vertical axis) between *c* and *b* is ½ yard of cloth.

3. The *PPF* provides a good example of the role played by simplifying assumptions in economic analysis. Clearly, no society in the world produces only two items. Reality is the extreme complexity of the real world with billions of people and hundreds of millions of goods and services. But, by assuming that there are such "two-good" nations or people, we can gain invaluable insights into real-world affairs.

For instance, once a nation is producing on its production possibilities frontier, the two-good *PPF* reveals that producing more of one good has an opportunity cost in terms of the forgone production of the other good. So, too, is the case in the real world. No matter how many goods an economy produces, once it is on its production possibilities frontier, to increase the production of one good necessarily has an opportunity cost in terms of some other good or goods that must be forgone. Thus it is not free to produce more, say, video games; there is an opportunity cost that must be paid, perhaps in the form of hand calculators that can not be produced.

In addition, the model allows us to explain several phenomena that we observe in the world, such as specialization and exchange. The *PPF* also has some more implications or predictions. For example, the *PPF* shows that countries that devote a larger proportion of their resources to capital accumulation will have more rapidly expanding production possibilities. The model can be tested by comparing this prediction to real-world observations.

Like all economic models and theories, the *PPF* is based on assumptions that vastly simplify the complex reality in which we live. But, like all economic models and theories, the *PPF* is useful because these simplifications allow us to see more clearly the underlying issues and truths.

4. The production possibilities frontier shows the *maximum* combinations of goods that can be produced. Hence anything that changes the maximum causes the frontier to shift. For instance, changes in resources available to a nation or changes in technology, cause the *PPF* to shift. (Increases in resources and technology shift the

PPF rightward; decreases in resources shift the *PPF* leftward.)

To produce less than the maximum is always possible — that is, to produce inside the *PPF* curve. This condition occurs whenever some inefficiency emerges within the economy. For example, excessive unemployment of any resource (labor, capital, or whatever) or an inefficient use of resources cause a nation to produce at a point within the boundary illustrated by the *PPF*. However, "deficient" technology or a reduction in the resources available to the society do not cause it to produce within its *PPF*. Technology and the nation's resource base set the limits to production, that is, determine where the *PPF* boundary is located. So if, for some reason, technology is lost or resources shrink, the *PPF* shifts in, but the nation does not necessarily produce at some point within the new *PPF* curve.

Questions

True/False/Uncertain and Explain

1. Increasing opportunity costs cause the *PPF* to be bowed out.
2. Exchange using barter requires a double coincidence of wants.
3. Daphne has a comparative advantage in producing sweaters if she can produce more than Lisa while using the same number of inputs.
4. There is an opportunity cost to increasing a nation's economic growth rate.
5. Production levels within the *PPF* are not attainable.
6. If two individuals have different opportunity costs of producing goods, both can gain from specialization and trade.
7. Learning-by-doing can lead to dynamic comparative advantage.
8. If the United States has an absolute advantage in growing corn and making computers, it must have a comparative advantage in growing corn.

FIGURE 3.4
True/False/Uncertain Questions 9 and 10

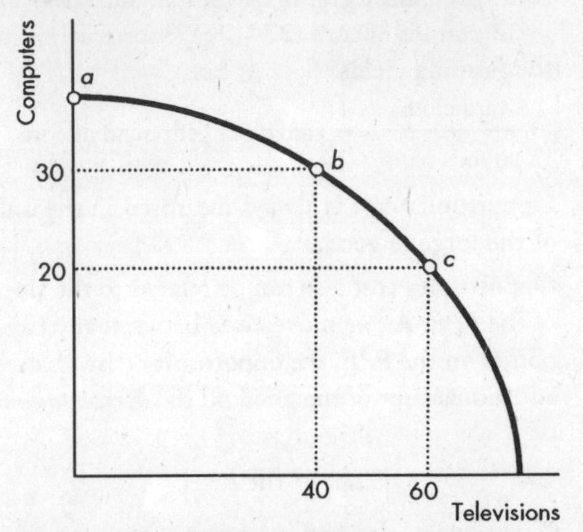

9. In Figure 3.4, point *a* is NOT attainable.
10. In Figure 3.4, the opportunity cost of moving from point *b* to point *c* is 10 computers.
11. Economic growth causes the *PPF* to shift outward.
12. From a point within the *PPF*, rearranging production and producing more of *all* goods is possible.
13. From a point on the *PPF*, rearranging production and producing more of *all* goods is possible.
14. Along a bowed-out *PPF*, as more of a good is produced, the opportunity cost of producing it diminishes.
15. If the natural resources available to a nation decrease, the nation's *PPF* shifts leftward.

Multiple Choice

1. If the United States can increase its production of automobiles without decreasing its production of any other good, the
   a. United States must be producing at a point within its *PPF*.
   b. United States must be producing at a point on its *PPF*.
   c. problem of scarcity has been solved in the United States.
   d. None of the above are correct because increasing the production of one good without decreasing the production of another good is never possible.

2. Economic growth
   a. creates unemployment.
   b. has no opportunity cost.
   c. shifts the *PPF* rightward.
   d. makes it more difficult for a nation to produce on its *PPF*.

3. The bowed-out (convex) shape of a *PPF*
   a. is due to capital accumulation.
   b. reflects the unequal application of technology in production.
   c. illustrates the fact that no opportunity cost is incurred for increasing the production of the good measured on the horizontal axis.
   d. is due to the existence of increasing opportunity cost.

4. An increase in the nation's capital stock will
   a. shift the *PPF* rightward.
   b. cause a movement along the *PPF* upward and to the left.
   c. cause a movement along the *PPF* downward and to the right.
   d. move the nation from producing within the *PPF* to producing at a point closer to the *PPF*.

5. The opportunity cost of economic growth is
   a. capital accumulation.
   b. technological change.
   c. reduced current consumption.
   d. the gain in future consumption.

FIGURE **3.5**
Multiple Choice Questions 6 and 7

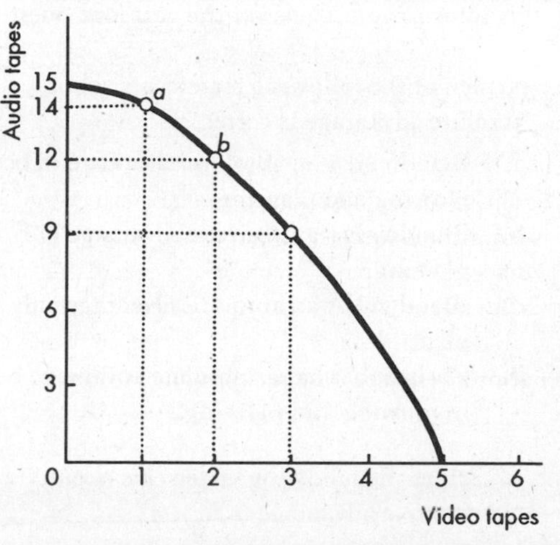

6. In Figure 3.5, at point *a* what is the opportunity cost of producing one more video tape?
   a. 14 audio tapes.
   b. 3 audio tapes.
   c. 2 audio tapes.
   d. There is no opportunity cost.

7. In Figure 3.5, at point *b* what is the opportunity cost of producing one more video tape?
   a. 12 audio tapes.
   b. 3 audio tapes.
   c. 2 audio tapes.
   d. There is no opportunity cost

8. Production points on the *PPF* itself are
   a. efficient but not attainable.
   b. efficient and attainable
   c. inefficient but not attainable.
   d. inefficient and attainable.

9. Which of the following statements about points on the production possibilities frontier is correct?
   a. All points on the *PPF* are efficient.
   b. All points on the *PPF* are efficient except those that are on the vertical and horizontal axes.
   c. Only one point on the *PPF* is efficient.
   d. None of the above statements is correct.

In one day Brandon can either plow 40 acres of land or plant 20 acres. In one day, Christopher can either plow 28 acres of land or plant 7 acres. Use this information to answer the next four questions.

10. Which of the following statements about absolute advantage is correct?
    a. Brandon has an absolute advantage in both plowing and planting.
    b. Brandon has an absolute advantage only in plowing.
    c. Brandon has an absolute advantage only in planting.
    d. Christopher has an absolute advantage both in plowing and planting.

11. Which of the following statements about comparative advantage is correct?
    a. Brandon has a comparative advantage both in plowing and planting.
    b. Brandon has a comparative advantage only in plowing.
    c. Brandon has a comparative advantage only in planting.
    d. Christopher has a comparative advantage both in plowing and planting.

12. Christopher has
    a. an absolute advantage only in planting.
    b. an absolute advantage only in plowing.
    c. a comparative advantage only in planting.
    d. a comparative advantage only in plowing.

13. Brandon and Christopher can
    a. gain from exchange if Brandon specializes in planting and Christopher in plowing.
    b. gain from exchange if Brandon specializes in plowing and Christopher in planting.
    c. exchange, but only Brandon will gain from the exchange.
    d. exchange, but only Christopher will gain from the exchange.

14. Which of the following did <u>NOT</u> evolve to help reap the gains from specialization?
    a. Property rights.
    b. Markets.
    c. Comparative advantage.
    d. Monetary exchange.

15. If all resources are equally productive in all activities,
    a. the problem of scarcity would be solved.
    b. the nation would produce within its *PPF*.
    c. barter would be as efficient as monetary exchange.
    d. the *PPF* would be linear.

16. The *PPF* shifts if
    a. the unemployment rate falls.
    b. people decide they want more of one good and less of another.
    c. the prices of the goods and services produced rise.
    d. the resources available to the nation change.

17. In general, the more resources that are devoted to technological research, the
    a. greater is current consumption.
    b. higher is the unemployment rate.
    c. faster the *PPF* shifts out.
    d. more the *PPF* will bow out.

18. "Double coincidence of wants" refers to
    a. barter transactions.
    b. a problem overcome by the introduction of property rights.
    c. an issue that does not arise with specialization.
    d. the one instance when comparative advantage does not hold.

19. The scarcity of resources means that the *PPF* is
    a. bowed out.
    b. linear.
    c. negatively sloped.
    d. positively sloped

20. Production efficiency means that
    a. scarcity is no longer a problem.
    b. producing more of one good without producing less of some other good is not possible.
    c. as few resources as possible are being used in production.
    d. there is no opportunity cost to the production of a good

Suppose that a nation produces only two goods — yak butter and rutabagas. Three alternative combinations of production that are on its *PPF* are given in Table 3.1. Use this information to answer the next three questions.

Table 3.1 Production Possibilities

Possibility	Pounds of yak butter	Number of rutabagas
a	600	0
b	400	100
c	0	200

21. In moving from combination *a* to *b*, the opportunity cost of producing more rutabagas is
    a. 6 pounds of yak butter per rutabaga.
    b. 4 pounds of yak butter per rutabaga.
    c. 2 pounds of yak butter per rutabaga.
    d. 0 pounds of yak butter per rutabaga.

22. In moving from combination *b* to *a*, the opportunity cost of producing more pounds of yak butter is
    a. 0.10 rutabaga per pound of yak butter.
    b. 0.50 rutabaga per pound of yak butter.
    c. 1.00 rutabaga per pound of yak butter.
    d. 2.00 rutabagas per pound of yak butter.

23. Producing 400 pounds of yak butter and 50 rutabagas is
    a. not possible for this nation.
    b. possible and is an efficient production point.
    c. possible but is an inefficient production point.
    d. an abhorrent thought.

24. You and your friend studied the same amount of time; you received an A in your economics and math classes, but your friend received lower grades. Based on these results, you
    a. definitely have a comparative advantage in economics.
    b. definitely have an absolute advantage in economics.
    c. perhaps have an absolute advantage in economics.
    d. definitely have both an absolute and comparative advantage in economics.

25. Directly exchanging one cow for five pigs is an example of
    a. property rights.
    b. specialization.
    c. barter.
    d. None of the above

26. In order to achieve the maximum gains from trade, people should specialize according to
    a. property rights.
    b. *PPF*.
    c. absolute advantage.
    d. comparative advantage.

27. A nation can *produce* at a point outside its *PPF*
    a. when it trades with other nations.
    b. when it is producing products as efficiently as possible.
    c. when there is no unemployment.
    d. never.

28. A nation can *consume* at a point outside its *PPF*
    a. when it trades with other nations.
    b. when it is producing products as efficiently as possible.
    c. when there is no unemployment.
    d. never.

29. A bowed-out *PPF* means that
    a. people are not specializing according to their comparative advantages.
    b. some resources are not available to the nation.
    c. the economy is not producing as efficiently as possible.
    d. the opportunity cost of producing additional units of a good is increasing.

■ Short Answer Problems

1. What does the negative slope of the *PPF* mean? Why might a *PPF* be bowed out?
2. How does the production possibilities frontier illustrate the idea of scarcity?
3. A nation produces only two goods. One uses a lot of capital and only a little labor; the other uses a lot of labor and only a little capital. Draw a *PPF* for this country, putting the labor-intensive good on the horizontal axis. Suppose that immigration

into the country increases so that the labor force increases. Show the effect of the increase on the *PPF*. Can you state for sure whether the nation produces more or less of the labor-intensive good? Use the *PPFs* you have drawn to support your answer.

4. In Figure 3.6, indicate which points are efficient and which are inefficient. Also show which points are attainable and which are not attainable.

FIGURE 3.6
Short Answer Problem 4

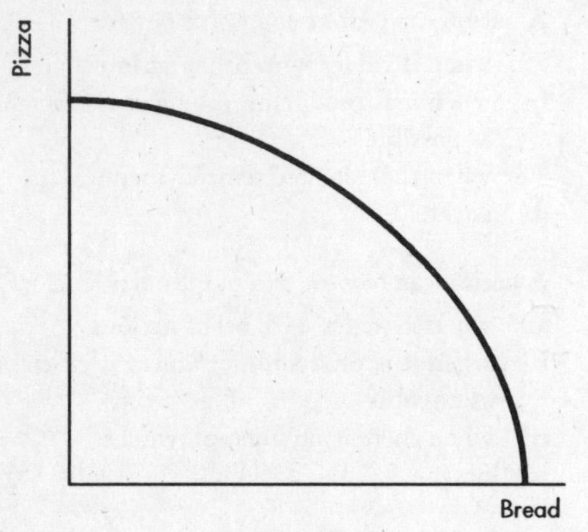

Table 3.2 Sydna's Production Possibilities

Possibility	Dates gathered	Fish caught
a	54	0
b	50	1
c	42	2
d	32	3
e	20	4
f	0	5

5. Sydna is stranded on a desert island and can either fish or harvest dates. Six points on her production possibilities frontier are given in Table 3.2.
   a. In Figure 3.7, plot these possibilities, label the points, and draw the *PPF*.

FIGURE 3.7
Short Answer Problem 5

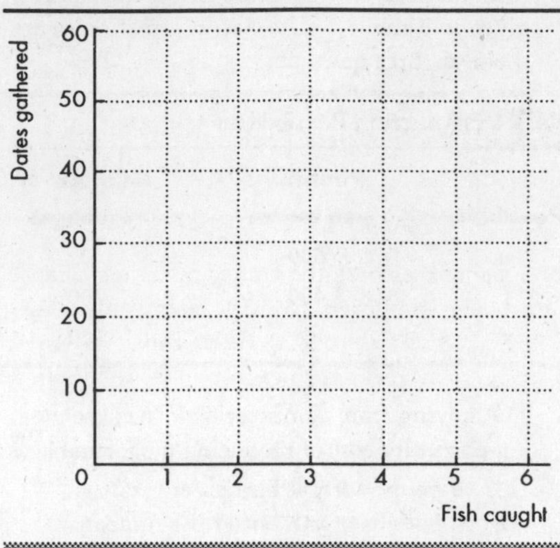

   b. If Sydna moves from possibility *c* to possibility *d*, what is the opportunity cost per fish?
   c. If Sydna moves from possibility *d* to possibility *e*, what is the opportunity cost per fish?
   d. In general terms, what happens to the opportunity cost of a fish as the output of fish increases?
   e. In general terms, what happens to the opportunity cost of dates as the output of dates increases?
   f. Based on the original *PPF* you plotted, is a combination of 40 dates and 1 fish attainable? Is this combination an efficient one? Explain.

6. If the following events occurred (each is a separate event, unaccompanied by any other event), what would happen to the *PPF* in Problem 5?
   a. A new fishing pond is discovered.
   b. The output of dates is increased.
   c. Sydna finds a ladder that enables her to gather slightly more dates.
   d. A second person, with the same set of fish catching and date gathering skills as Sydna, is stranded on the island.

Table 3.3 Production in France and the United States

	Computers produced in an hour by a worker	Bottles of wine produced in an hour by a worker
United States	10	20
France	6	8

7. Suppose that both the United States and France produce computers and wine, using only labor. Each nation has 1000 workers. Table 3.3 shows what a worker in each country can produce in an hour.
   a. On graph paper, draw the *PPF* for the United States. What is the maximum amount of wine that can be produced in the United States? The maximum number of computers?
   b. On graph paper, draw the *PPF* for France. What is the maximum number of bottles of wine that can be produced in France? The maximum number of computers?
   c. Complete Table 3.4

Table 3.4 Short Answer Problem 7 (c)

	Opportunity cost of one computer	Opportunity cost of one bottle of wine
United States	___	___
France	___	___

   d. In what good(s) does the United States have an absolute advantage? France?
   e. In what good(s) does the United States have a comparative advantage? France?
   f. Suppose that the United States shifted one worker from producing computers to producing wine and that France shifted two workers from making wine to manufacturing computers. What happens to the output of computers and wine in the United States and France combined?
8. How do property rights affect people's incentives to innovate?
9. Suppose that you wanted eggs for breakfast but were in an economy that used barter. Your only skill is as a comedian. Describe what you would have to do to get your eggs and relate this to the benefits from monetary exchange.

■ You're the Teacher

1. "The idea of the production possibilities frontier is stupid. I mean, after all, who ever heard of a nation that produces only two goods. Come on; every nation produces millions, probably billions of goods. Why do I have to bother to learn about the production possibilities frontier when it is so unrealistic?" One reason for this student to learn about the production possibilities frontier is because it likely will be featured on exams. But there are other reasons. Explain some of these reasons to help motivate this student.
2. Your friend, who is not in your economics class, says: "I always thought that economic growth was good, and the more rapid the growth the better. At least, this is what I hear politicians saying. Now you tell me that economic growth inevitably has some costs. I don't understand this at all; can you explain it to me again?"

Answers

True/False Answers

1. **T** If resources are not equally productive in all activities, there is increasing opportunity cost and the *PPF* is bowed out.
2. **T** The double coincidence of wants is the major drawback to barter because it makes finding trading partners very difficult.
3. **U** Based on the information in the problem, Daphne definitely has an absolute advantage, but without more information we cannot tell whether she has a comparative advantage.
4. **T** The opportunity cost is the loss of current consumption.
5. **F** These points are attainable but inefficient.
6. **T** A key observation is that *both* individuals gain.
7. **T** Learning-by-doing means that the costs of producing a good fall as more is produced, so the nation (or person) ultimately may acquire a comparative advantage in making the good.
8. **F** Comparative advantage requires *comparing* the opportunity costs of producing corn in the United States with the opportunity costs of producing it elsewhere.
9. **F** *Any* point on the production possibilities frontier is attainable, even points where the *PPF* intersects the axes.
10. **T** The opportunity cost equals the number of computers sacrificed, in this case the drop from 30 computers at point *b* to 20 at point *c*.
11. **T** As the *PPF* shifts rightward, the nation is able to produce more of all goods.
12. **T** Points within the frontier are inefficient, which means that rearranging production and boosting the output of all goods and services is possible. This condition is illustrated in Figure 3.8, where from (the inefficient) point *a*, it is possible to rearrange production and move to points such as *b* or *c* where more of both books and magazines are produced.

FIGURE **3.8**
True/False/Uncertain Question 12

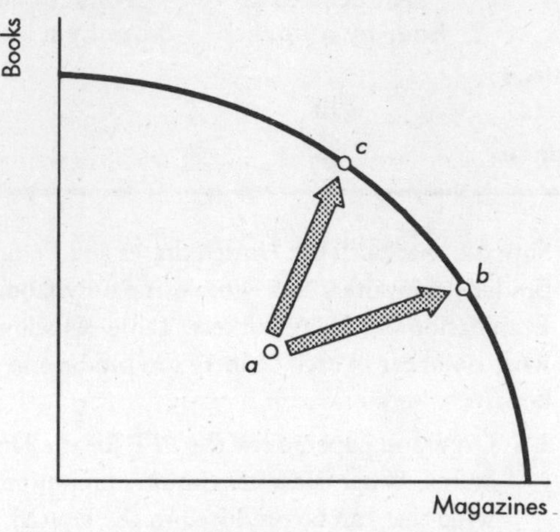

13. **F** Points on the frontier are efficient, so increasing the production of one good necessarily requires producing less of some other good.
14. **F** As more of a good is produced, the opportunity cost of additional units increases.
15. **T** If fewer factors of production are available, less can be produced, so the *PPF* shifts leftward.

Multiple Choice Answers

1. **a** Only from points within the frontier can the production of a good increase without decreasing the production of another good.
2. **c** Economic growth makes attainable previously unattainable production levels.
3. **d** Increasing opportunity costs means that, as more of a good is produced, its opportunity cost increases, which causes the *PPF* to bow out.
4. **a** Increases in the capital stock are one of the engines of economic growth.
5. **c** If a nation devotes more resources to capital accumulation or technological development, which are the main sources of growth, fewer resources can be used to produce goods for current consumption.

6. **c** By producing 1 more video tape, audio tape production falls by 2 (from 14 to 12), so the opportunity cost is 2 audio tapes.
7. **b** In accordance with the law of increasing opportunity costs, as more video tapes are produced, the opportunity cost of an additional video tape gets larger.
8. **b** *Only* points on the frontier are both attainable and efficient.
9. **a** *All* points on the *PPF* are efficient.
10. **a** Brandon can produce more of both goods with the same inputs as Christopher, so Brandon has an absolute advantage.
11. **c** Brandon's opportunity cost of planting 1 acre of land is plowing 2 acres, whereas Christopher's opportunity cost of planting an acre is plowing 4 acres.
12. **d** Christopher's opportunity cost of plowing an acre is planting ¼ of an acre, while Brandon's opportunity cost of plowing an acre is planting ½ an acre.
13. **a** By specializing according to their comparative advantages, both can gain from exchange.
14. **c** Comparative advantage promotes specialization but did not evolve to help reap the gains from it.
15. **d** Only in this case is the *PPF* not bowed out because the opportunity cost of producing additional units of a good is constant rather than increasing.
16. **d** An increase in resources shifts the *PPF* rightward; a decrease shifts it leftward. (A decrease in the unemployment rate moves the nation from a point in the interior of the *PPF* to a point closer to the frontier.)
17. **c** The more resources used for technological research, the more rapid is economic growth.
18. **a** The "double coincidence of wants" refers to the problem with barter wherein exchange can occur only when each trading partner has the good wanted by the other.
19. **c** Once production is on the *PPF*, if more of one good is produced, then because resources are scarce some other good must be foregone, which means that the *PPF* has a negative slope.
20. **b** This answer is the definition of production efficiency.
21. **c** Moving from *a* to *b* gains 100 rutabagas and loses 200 pounds of yak butter, so the opportunity cost is (200 pounds of yak butter)/(100 rutabagas), or 2 pounds of yak butter per rutabaga.
22. **b** 100 rutabagas are sacrificed, so the opportunity cost is (100 rutabagas)/(200 pounds of yak butter) or 0.50 rutabagas per pound of yak butter. Note how the opportunity cost of a rutabaga is the reciprocal of the opportunity cost of a pound of yak butter, as calculated in question 21.
23. **c** When 400 pounds of yak butter are produced, a maximum of 100 rutabagas can be produced; because only 50 rutabagas are produced, the combination is inefficient.
24. **b** You produced more than did your friend, using the same amount of inputs.
25. **c** The exchange of one good directly for another is barter.
26. **d** Specializing according to comparative advantage reduces the opportunity cost of producing goods and services.
27. **d** The *PPF* shows the maximum amounts that can be produced.
28. **a** When a nation specializes according to its comparative advantage and trades with another specialist nation, both can consume at levels beyond their *PPFs*.
29. **d** Increasing opportunity costs accounts for the bowed-out shape of the *PPF*.

■ Answers to Short Answer Problems

1. The negative slope of the *PPF* indicates that increasing the production of one good causes the production of some other good to decline.

   A *PPF* can be bowed out because the existence of nonhomogeneous resources creates an increasing opportunity cost as the production of either good is increased. In other words, because resources are not identical, some are better suited for producing one good than another. So, when resources are switched from producing items for which they are well suited to producing goods for which they are ill suited, the opportunity cost of increasing the output of these goods rises.

2. The very existence of the production possibilities frontier itself indicates that unlimited production of all things (or anything) is impossible. The limits to production are the result of scarcity of resources, so the frontier illustrates the existence of scarcity.

   Additionally, the fact that the frontier has a negative slope shows that increasing the production of one good must be accompanied by producing less of some other good. The fundamental reason that the production of another good must be reduced is scarcity: Not enough resources are available to produce more of one item without reducing the production of some other good.

3. The *PPF* for this nation is illustrated in Figure 3.9. The increase in immigration raises the nation's labor force. As a result, its *PPF* shifts rightward. Note in Figure 3.9 that the shift is not "parallel"; that is, the shift along the horizontal axis is larger than the shift along the vertical axis. The reason for this difference is straightforward: Because the one good is labor intensive, the increase in the labor force means that substantially more of that good can be produced. For the capital-intensive good, however, the increase in the labor force does not have such a large impact. As shown, more of it can be produced, but because it uses primarily capital in its production, the increase is not as large.

   We cannot state for sure whether the nation will produce more (or less) of the labor- intensive good. People's preferences between the two goods play a role in determining what is produced. If people decide that they want more of the labor-intensive good, more will be produced. For instance, the economy may move from producing at point *a* on the old *PPF* to point *b* on the new *PPF*. But if people decide that they want more of the capital-intensive good, the nation might move from point *a* to point *c* and actually end up producing less of the labor-intensive good. Essentially the *PPF* presents a menu of production points available to the nation and people's preferences between the different goods play a key role in determining which production point is chosen.

FIGURE **3.9**
Short Answer Problem 3

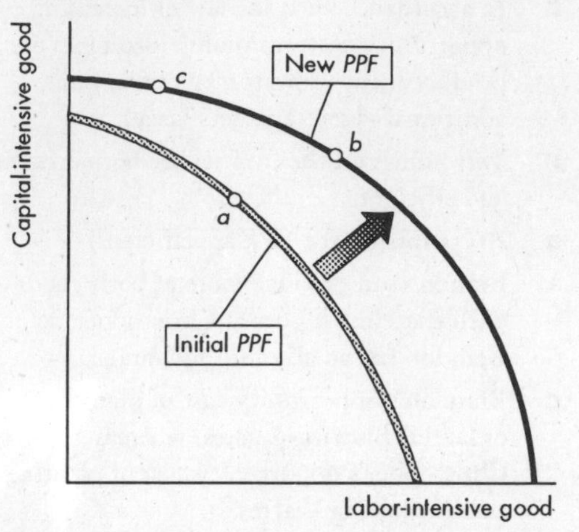

FIGURE **3.10**
Short Answer Problem 4

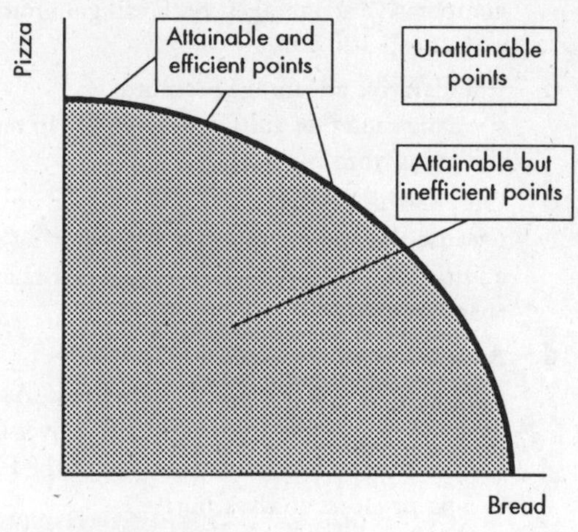

4. Figure 3.10 shows the efficient/inefficient points and attainable/not attainable points. The attainable but inefficient points are shaded; the attainable and efficient points lie on the *PPF* itself; and the unattainable points lie beyond the *PPF*.

FIGURE **3.11**
Short Answer Problem 5

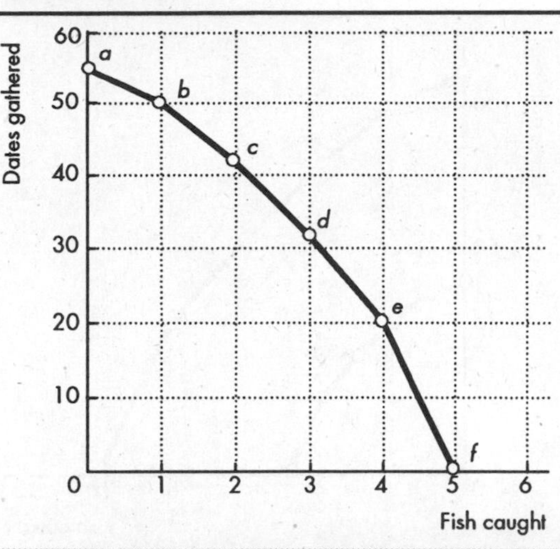

5. a. Figure 3.11 shows the *PPF*.

b. Moving from *c* to *d* means that the number fish caught increases by 1 while the number of dates gathered falls from 42 to 32. Hence catching 1 fish costs 10 dates, so the opportunity cost of the fish is 10 dates. In terms of a formula, the opportunity cost of this fish is:

$$\frac{42 \text{ dates} - 32 \text{ dates}}{3 \text{ fish} - 2 \text{ fish}} = 10 \text{ dates per fish.}$$

c. Moving from *d* to *e* indicates that the opportunity cost of the fish is 12 dates: the number of dates gathered falls from 32 to 20 while the number of fish caught increases by 1.

d. As more fish are caught, the opportunity cost of an additional fish rises. In particular, the first fish has an opportunity cost of only 4 dates; the second, 8 dates; the third, 10 dates; the fourth, 12 dates; and the fifth, 20 dates.

e. As more dates are gathered, the opportunity cost of a date rises. Moving from *f* to *e* shows that the first 20 dates cost only 1 fish so that the opportunity cost of a date here is $1/20$ of a fish. Going from *e* to *d*, however, makes the opportunity cost of a date $1/12$ of a fish. As more dates are gathered, their opportunity cost increases until moving from *b* to *a* the opportunity cost of a date is $1/4$ fish.

As parts (d) and (e) demonstrate, there is increasing opportunity cost moving along the *PPF*. That is, as more fish are caught, their opportunity cost — in terms of forgone dates — increases and as more dates are gathered, their opportunity cost — in terms of foregone fish — also increases.

f. This combination is within the *PPF* and is attainable. It is inefficient because Sydna could produce more of either or both goods. Therefore she is not organizing her activities as efficiently as possible.

FIGURE **3.12**
Short Answer Problem 6 (a)

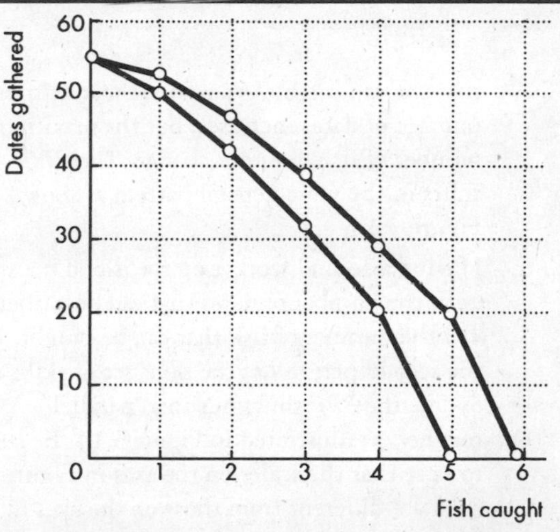

6. a. A new fishing pond increases the number of fish Sydna can catch, but it does not affect the maximum number of dates she can gather. As a result, her *PPF* shifts generally as shown in Figure 3.12.

b. Increasing her output of dates does not affect the *PPF*. Sydna might increase her gathering of dates either by moving from a point within the *PPF* curve to a point on (or closer to) the frontier or by moving along the frontier itself. However, neither of these actions changes the *PPF*.

c. The ladder increases the number of dates that Sydna can gather but has no effect on the fish

FIGURE **3.13**

Short Answer Problem 7 (c)

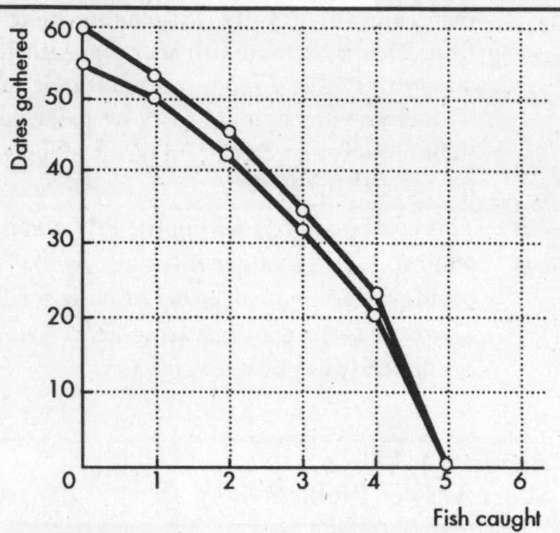

FIGURE **3.14**

Short Answer Problem 7 (d)

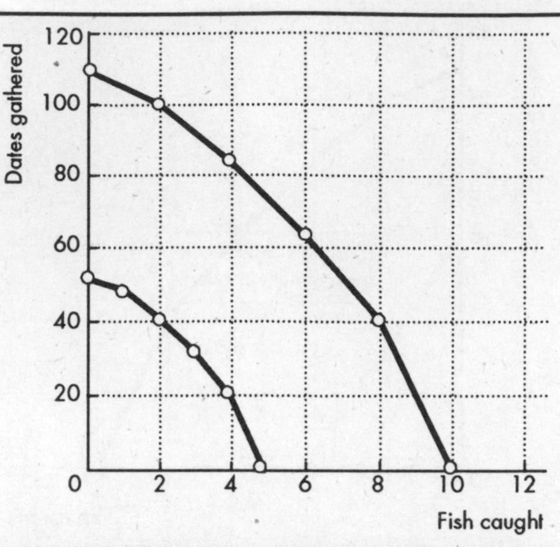

that she can catch. As a result, the maximum number of dates increases, but the maximum number of fish does not change. The *PPF* shifts in the same general pattern as shown in Figure 3.13.

d. Having a second worker on the island boosts both the number of dates that can be gathered *and* the number of fish that can be caught. If the second person has the same set of skills as Sydna, the *PPF* shifts out in a "parallel" manner, as illustrated in Figure 3.14. Be sure to note that the scales on the axes in Figure 3.14 are different from those on the axes in Figures 3.11–3.14.

7. a. Figure 3.15 shows the U.S. *PPF*. The maximum amount of wine that can be produced is 20,000 bottles, when everyone specializes in producing only wine. The maximum number of computers that can be produced is 10,000, attainable when everyone produces only computers.

FIGURE **3.15**

Short Answer Problem 8 (a)

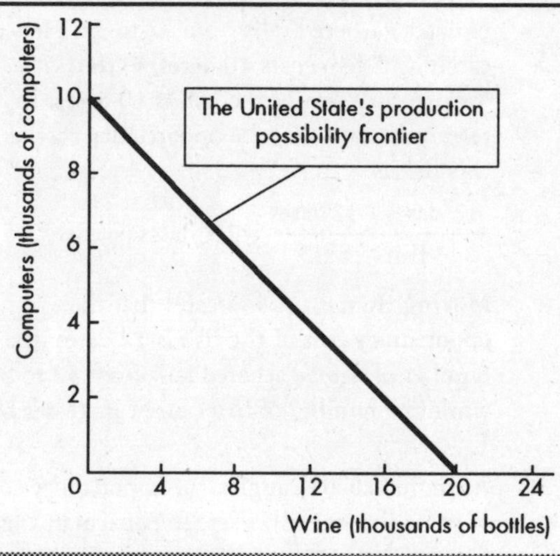

FIGURE **3.16**
Short Answer Problem 8 (b)

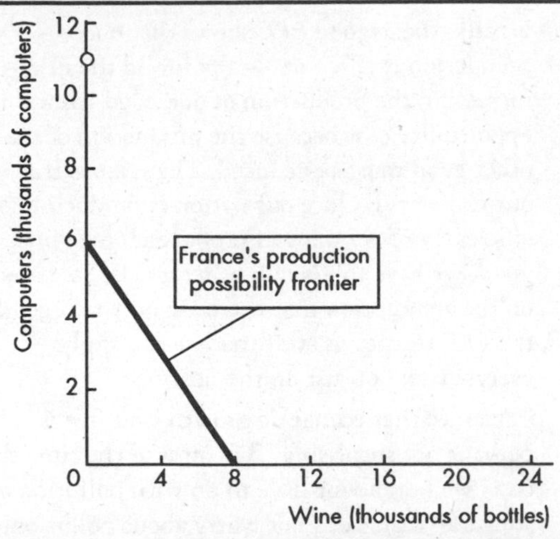

b. Figure 3.16 shows the French *PPF*. The maximum amount of wine is 8,000 bottles and the maximum number of computers that can be produced is 6,000.

c. Table 3.4 shows the opportunity costs for the alternatives. To illustrate how this table was obtained, we can use the opportunity cost of a computer in the United States as an example. To produce a computer in the United States requires that one person work for $\frac{1}{10}$ of an hour at manufacturing computers. Thus, to produce an additional computer, a worker must be switched from the wine industry to the computer industry for $\frac{1}{10}$ of an hour. During this time, the worker could have produced ($\frac{1}{10}$)(20 bottles of wine) or 2 bottles of wine. Hence, to produce one additional computer in the United States, 2 bottles of wine are foregone. Two bottles of wine, then, is the opportunity cost of the computer. The rest of the opportunity costs are calculated similarly.

d. The United States has an absolute advantage in computers and wine because the United States can produce more of both goods with the same inputs as France. Correspondingly, France has no absolute advantage.

Table 3.5 Short Answer Problem 7 (c)

	Opportunity cost of one computer	**Opportunity cost of one bottle of wine**
United States	2 bottles of wine	$\frac{1}{2}$ computer
France	$1\frac{1}{3}$ bottles of wine	$\frac{3}{4}$ computer

e. The United States has a comparative advantage in wine because the opportunity cost of a bottle of wine in the United States — $\frac{1}{2}$ computer — is less than the opportunity cost of a computer in France — $\frac{3}{4}$ computer. France has a comparative advantage in the production of computers, because its opportunity cost — $1\frac{1}{3}$ bottle of wine — is less than that in the United States — 2 bottles of wine.

The key point in parts (d) and (e) is that absolute advantage and comparative advantage are *very* different. A country can have an absolute advantage but that does not mean that it possesses a comparative advantage in producing all goods.

f. In the United States, the shift gains 20 bottles of wine and loses 10 computers. In France, the shift loses 16 bottles of wine and gains 12 computers. On balance, wine production increases by 4 bottles and computer production increases by 2 computers. The fact that world production of wine *and* computers both increase demonstrates that specialization according to comparative advantage can boost world output of all goods.

8. Property rights play a key role in shaping people's incentives to innovate. Innovation — whether a new product or a new, better way to manufacture an old good — benefits society. But innovation is costly; resources, time, and effort, must be devoted to this process. By securing a property right to an innovation, the innovator stands to benefit greatly from the resources expended. But, if the innovator cannot obtain a property right, anyone can copy the new innovation. In that case the innovator's return will either be dissipated when a lot of

people copy the innovation or someone else may reap the rewards. Hence property rights to an innovation, by promising that the innovator will personally benefit from the effort involved, motivate significantly more innovation than would occur in the absence of property rights. Incidentally, this fact may have played a role in the collapse of the former Soviet Union. Under the previous communist system no property rights were offered to innovators. Interestingly, the Soviet Union was falling increasingly behind Western nations in developing new and improved products and methods of production.

9. You have a major problem: You must find a farmer with eggs who wants to be amused. Then, once you find this farmer, you must tailor the size of the joke you will tell to the number of eggs you want. In other words, if you want only 1 egg, perhaps a small joke will do, whereas if you want 4 eggs, a larger joke is necessary. And, if you miscalculate — so that the farmer finds your act more amusing than the number of eggs you want warrants — you must figure out how to get change back from the farmer. As this (humorous and potentially worth 1½ eggs) story illustrates, barter is very cumbersome. In an economy with monetary exchange, you would present your act in the evening in front of people — not necessarily farmers! — who want to be entertained and be paid in the form of money. Then, in the morning, you can use the money to buy the eggs, even from a farmer with no sense of humor.

■ You're the Teacher

1. "*All* economic models vastly simplify an incredibly complex reality. But that is no reason to throw them away. The lessons that can be learned from the simple 2-good *PPF* carry over to the real world. For instance, the 2-good *PPF* shows that there are limits to production. These limits are represented by the *PPF* curve, which divides attainable from unattainable production points. Now, just as you say, in the real world billions of goods are produced. But there are still limits. Regardless of the number of goods produced, every nation faces a limit on how much it can produce, just as in the simple 2-good *PPF* case.

   Moreover, the simple *PPF* model demonstrates that production can be efficient and inefficient. This result is also true in the real world.

   Finally, the 2-good *PPF* shows that once production is efficient — a point on the *PPF* — increasing the production of one good has an opportunity cost because the production of the other good must be reduced. The same is true in our real world. Once our nation is producing efficiently, if we want to produce more of one good, we have to give up other goods. So, based on the assumption that there are only two goods, the *PPF* teaches us stuff that we can apply everywhere, not just on the next test."

2. "The idea that economic growth isn't free is perhaps not surprising. But most of the time the costs we hear about have to do with pollution or stuff like that. Let's not worry about pollution; we haven't studied it yet in class. But even if we don't have any more pollution or such things, economic growth is costly. And that, perhaps, *is* surprising! The idea, actually is simple. Suppose that we increase growth by building more factories and developing better technology to manufacture faster computer chips. The essential point is that resources, such as people and equipment, are required to build more factories or develop new technology. Because these people and resources are building factories and developing technology, they cannot be used to produce other stuff, like more clothes for us to wear games or new video games for us to play. So, the whole deal is that increased economic growth has cost us new clothes and new video games. While the increased growth may be good because we'll be able to get a lot of new clothes or video games after the growth, the growth sure hasn't been free."

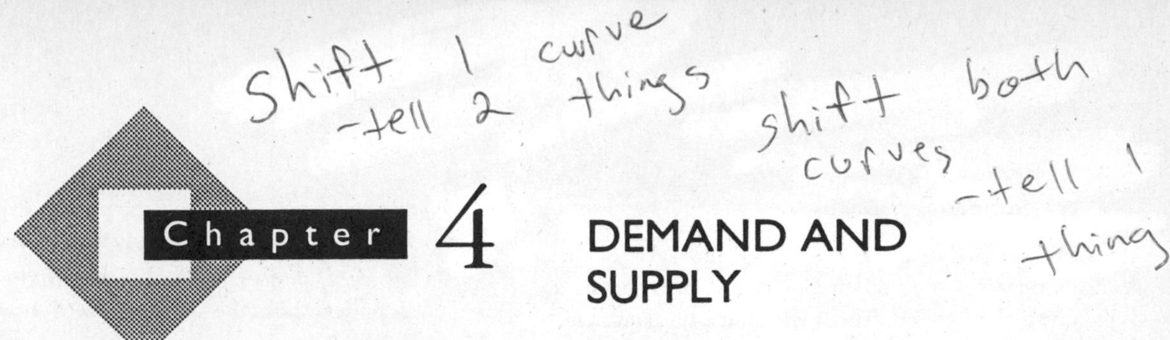

Chapter 4 DEMAND AND SUPPLY

Key Concepts

Opportunity Cost and Price

The ratio of the money price of one good to the money price of another good is the **relative price**. The relative price of a product is the opportunity cost of buying it. The demand for and supply of a product depend, in part, on its relative price.

Demand

The **quantity demanded** of a good is the amount that consumers plan to buy at a particular price in a given time period. The **law of demand** states that "other things remaining the same, the higher the price of a good, the smaller is the quantity demanded." Higher prices decrease the quantity demanded for two reasons:

- *substitution effect* — a higher relative price raises the opportunity cost of buying a good and so people buy less of it.
- *income effect* — a higher relative price reduces the amount of goods people can buy and this effect tends to decrease people's demand for the product that rose in price

The demand curve shows the inverse relationship between the quantity demanded and price, everything else remaining the same.

- Demand curves are negatively sloped, as illustrated in Figure 4.1.
- A change in the price of the good leads to a **change in the quantity demanded** and a **movement along the demand curve**. The higher the price of a good, the lower is the quantity demanded. This relationship is shown in Figure 4.1 with the movement along D_1 from Q_1 to Q_2 in response to a rise in price from P_1 to P_2.

A shift in the demand curve is called a **change in demand**. An increase in demand means that the

FIGURE **4.1**
Demand Curves

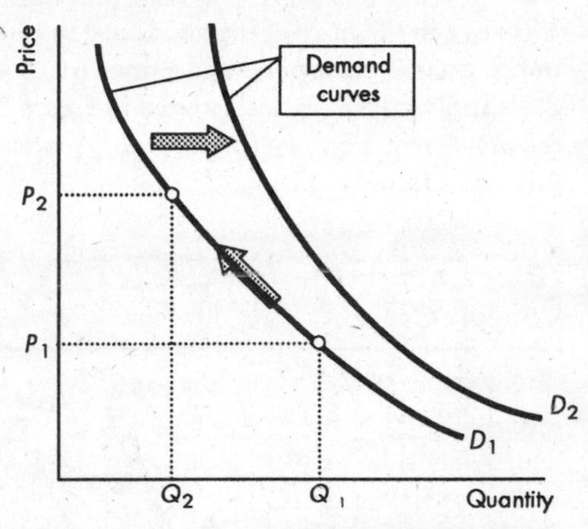

demand curve shifts rightward, such as the shift from D_1 to D_2 in Figure 4.1; a decrease in demand refers to a shift leftward. The demand curve shifts from changes in:

- *prices of related goods* — A rise in the price of a **substitute** shifts the demand curve rightward; a rise in the price of a **complement** shifts the demand curve leftward.
- *income* — An increase in income shifts the demand curve for a **normal** good rightward; an increase in income shifts the demand curve for an **inferior** good leftward.
- *expected future prices* — If a product's price is expected to rise in the future, the demand for it shifts rightward.
- *population* — An increase in population shifts the demand curve rightward.
- *preferences* — If people decide they "like" a good more, its demand curve shifts rightward.

Supply

The **quantity supplied** is the amount of a good that producers plan to sell at a particular price during a given time period. The **law of supply** states that "other things remaining the same, the higher the price of a good, the greater is the quantity supplied." Supply curves show the positive relationship between the price of a product and the quantity supplied.

- Supply curves are positively sloped, as shown in Figure 4.2.
- A change in the price of the good causes a **change in the quantity supplied and a movement along the supply curve.** It is illustrated in Figure 4.2 as the movement along S_1 from Q_1 to Q_2 when the price rises from P_1 to P_2.

FIGURE **4.2**
A Supply Curve

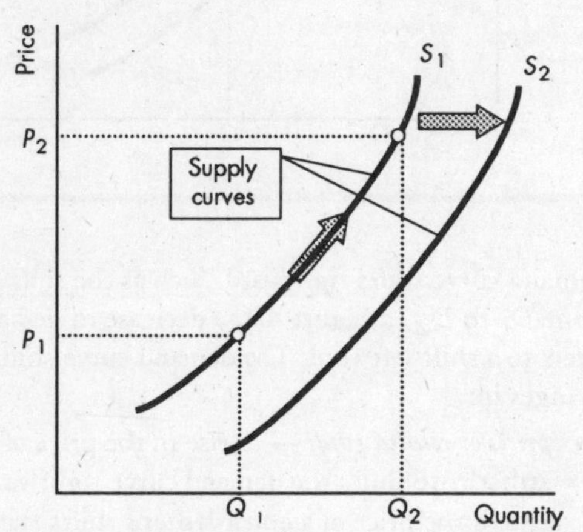

A **change in supply** is a shift in the supply curve. An increase in supply is a shift rightward in the supply curve, shown in Figure 4.2 as the shift from S_1 to S_2; a decrease in supply is a leftward shift in the supply curve. The supply curve shifts in response to changes in:

- *prices of factors of production* — A rise in the price (cost) of an input shifts the supply curve leftward.
- *prices of other goods produced* — A rise in the price of a substitute in production shifts the supply curve leftward; a rise in the price of a complement in production shifts the supply curve rightward.
- *expected future prices* — If the price is expected to rise in the future, the supply shifts leftward.
- *number of suppliers* — An increase in the number of suppliers shifts the supply curve rightward.
- *technology* — An advance in technology shifts the supply curve rightward.

Price Determination

The **equilibrium price** is determined by the intersection of the demand and supply curves. The **equilibrium quantity** is the quantity bought and sold at the equilibrium price. Figure 4.3 shows the equilibrium price, *P*, and the equilibrium quantity, *Q*.

FIGURE **4.3**
The Equilibrium Price and Quantity

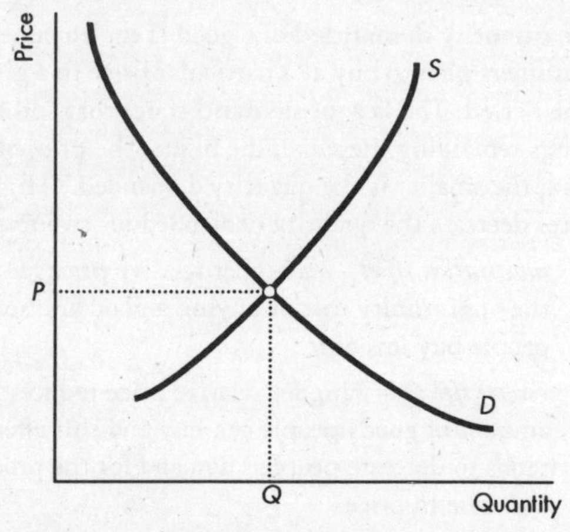

Below the equilibrium price, a shortage exists and the price will rise. Above the equilibrium price, a surplus exists and the price will fall. Only in equilibrium does the price to remain the same.

Predicting Changes in Price and Quantity

When one of the demand and supply curves shifts, the effect on both the price (*P*) and quantity (*Q*) can be determined:

- An increase in demand (a shift rightward in the demand curve) raises *P* and increases *Q*.
- A decrease in demand (a shift leftward in the demand curve) lowers *P* and decreases *Q*.

- An increase in supply (a shift rightward in the supply curve) lowers *P* and increases *Q*.
- A decrease in supply (a shift leftward in the supply curve) raises *P* and decreases *Q*.

When both the demand and supply curves shift, the effect on the price *or* the quantity can be determined, but without information about the relative sizes of the shifts, the effect on the other variable is ambiguous.

- If both the demand and supply curves increase (shift rightward) the quantity increases but the price may rise, fall, or remain the same.
- If the demand decreases (shifts leftward) and the supply increases (shifts rightward) the price falls but the quantity may increase, decrease, or not change.

Helpful Hints

1. When you are first learning about demand and supply, thinking in terms of concrete examples helps build overall understanding. Have some favorite examples in the back of your mind. This procedure is easiest for demand because we are all experienced demanders of products. For instance, when you hear "complementary goods" (goods used together) think about hot dogs and hot dog buns because few people eat hot dogs without using a hot dog bun. For "substitute goods" (things that take each other's place) think about hot dogs and hamburgers, because they are obvious substitutes. Using similar concrete examples is a bit trickier when you are considering supply because you probably aren't a business owner. However, an easy and concrete way to identify with suppliers is to think of "profit": Anything that increases the profit from producing a product increases the supply and shifts the supply curve rightward, whereas anything that decreases profit decreases the supply and shifts the supply curve leftward. Thus, when studying the effect from a rise in the price of a factor of production, you could think about a rise in the wage rate paid to workers. That lowers the firm's profit, thereby shifting the supply curve leftward.
2. The benefit of using the demand and supply model is that it allows us systematically to sort out the influences on price and quantity of anything that can affect them. A key feature of this sorting is the fact that things that shift the demand curve — such as income or people's preferences — generally do *not* shift the supply curve. Changes in any of the influences affecting demand shift the demand curve and move us up or down the given supply curve. Similarly, changes in the influences affecting supply usually shift only the supply curve and move us up or down the given demand curve.
3. Do not make the common error of believing that an increase in demand — that is, a shift rightward in the demand curve — causes an increase in supply — a shift rightward in the supply curve. Use Figure 4.4 as an example. Television sets are a normal good, so an increase in income shifts the demand curve rightward, as shown. This shift in the demand curve causes the equilibrium price of a television to rise (from P_1 to P_2) and also causes the equilibrium quantity to increase (from Q_1 to Q_2). But note that the shift in the demand curve does not cause the supply curve to *shift*. Instead, there is a movement *along* the unchanging supply curve.

FIGURE **4.4**

The Effect From An Increase in Demand

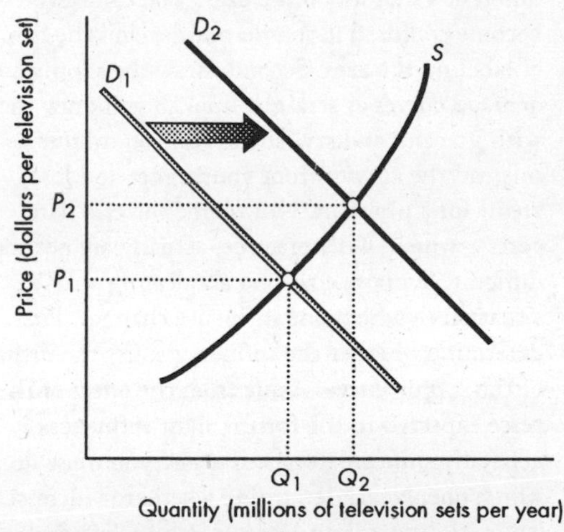

The supply curve shifts in response to a change in anything that affects the supply *except* the price of the product itself. (These influences include the prices of factors of production, the prices of other goods produced, expected future prices, the number of suppliers, and technology). Why doesn't the price of the product shift the supply curve? Because the effect on the supply from a change in the price of the good is captured by the slope of the supply curve. If the price of the product rises, say, from P_1 to P_2, firms respond by increasing the quantity they supply, in Figure 4.4, from Q_1 to Q_2, and so they move up along the supply curve.

Remember: Shifts in demand and supply curves cause the market price to change. Changes in the market price do NOT cause demand and supply curves to shift.

4. The safest way to solve any demand and supply problem is always to draw a graph, even if it is just a small graph in the margin of a true/false/uncertain or multiple choice problem. Graphical representation is an efficient way to visualize what happens. As you become comfortable with graphs, you will find that they are an effective way to organize your thinking.

   Because graphs are such a useful way of answering any question dealing with supply and demand, learning a few mechanical rules can make their use easy and is worthwhile. First, when you draw a graph, be sure to label the axes. As the course progresses, you will encounter many graphs with different variables on the axes. You can easily become confused if you do not develop the habit of labeling the axes. Second, draw the supply and demand curves as straight lines. If you draw them with graceful and stylish curves, you might misread the answer from your figure and lose credit for a problem. Now come the two hard parts—which, with practice, actually are not too difficult. Suppose that you are dealing with a situation in which one influence changes. First, determine whether the influence shifts the demand or the supply curve. Aside from the effect of the price expected in the future, most influences generally shift only one curve and you must decide which one. Next, determine whether it increases (shifts rightward) or decreases (shifts leftward) the curve that is affected. From here on, it's easy: Take the figure you have already drawn, shift the appropriate curve, and read off the answer.

   Do not make the common mistake of thinking that a problem is so easy that you can do it in your head, without drawing a graph. Using a supply and demand graph is so easy that spending the time necessary to master it is time well spent.

5. Failing to distinguish correctly between a shift in a curve and a movement along a curve can lead to error and lost points on examinations. This distinction applies both to demand and supply curves. Many questions in this lesson are designed to reinforce your understanding of this distinction, and you can be sure that your instructor will test you heavily on it. The difference between "shifts in" versus "movement along" a curve is crucial for systematic thinking about the factors influencing demand and supply, and for understanding the determination of the equilibrium price and quantity.

   Consider an example of the demand curve. The quantity of a good demanded depends on its own price, the prices of related goods, income, expected future prices, population, and preferences. The term "demand" refers to the relationship between the price of the good and the quantity demanded, holding constant all other factors on which the demand depends. This demand relationship is represented graphically by the demand curve. Thus the effect of a change in price on the quantity demanded is already reflected in the slope of the demand curve. Thus, if the price is the only factor that affects the demand that changes, there is a movement along the demand curve. This result is referred to as a change in quantity demanded.

   But, if one of the other factors affecting the quantity demanded changes, the demand curve itself shifts; that is, the quantity demanded at each price changes. This shift of the demand curve is referred to as a change in demand. The important point to remember is *that a change in the price of a good does not shift the demand curve;* it causes a movement along the demand curve.

   Distinguishing between shifts in the supply curve and movement along the supply curve is just as important. The supply curve shifts if some relevant factor that affects the supply, *other than the price of the good,* changes. A change in the price of the good causes a movement along the supply curve.

Questions

True/False/Uncertain and Explain

1. The law of demand states that, as the price of a good rises, the quantity demanded decreases.
2. A decrease in income shifts the demand curve leftward.
3. The fact that a rise in the price of a product decreases the quantity demanded means that there can never be a situation with both the product's equilibrium price rising and equilibrium quantity increasing.
4. A rise in the price of chicken feed shifts the supply curve of chickens leftward.
5. If both the demand and supply curves shift rightward, the equilibrium quantity increases.
6. If both the demand and supply curves shift rightward, the equilibrium price rises.
7. A rise in the price of popcorn shifts the demand curve for popcorn rightward.
8. A supply curve shows the maximum price for which the last unit will be supplied.
9. If the expected future price of a good that can be stored rise, its current price rises.
10. A shortage occurs when the actual price is higher than the equilibrium price.
11. "An increase in demand" means a movement down and rightward along a demand curve.
12. New technology for manufacturing computer chips is developed. That shifts the demand curve for computer chips rightward.
13. A rise in the price of orange juice shifts the demand curve for orange juice leftward.
14. Once a market is at its equilibrium price, unless something changes, the price will not change.
15. If there is a surplus of a good, its price will fall.

Multiple Choice

1. A rise in the price of bowling a game shifts the
   a. demand curve for bowling balls leftward.
   b. demand curve for bowling balls rightward.
   c. supply curve for bowling balls leftward.
   d. supply curve of bowling balls rightward.
2. A decline in the price of a good causes producers to decrease the quantity of the good supplied. This result illustrates
   a. the law of supply.
   b. the law of demand.
   c. a change in supply.
   d. the nature of an inferior good.
3. If there is a shortage of a good, the quantity demanded ____ the quantity supplied and the price will ____.
   a. is less than; rise
   b. is less than; fall
   c. is greater than; rise
   d. is greater than; fall
4. If a rise in the price of gasoline lowers the demand for large cars,
   a. gasoline and large cars are substitutes in consumption.
   b. gasoline and large cars are complements in consumption.
   c. gasoline is an inferior good.
   d. large cars are an inferior good.

For the next five questions, suppose that the price of paper used in books rise and simultaneously more people decide they want to read books.

5. The rise in the price of paper shifts the
   a. demand curve for books rightward.
   b. demand curve for books leftward.
   c. supply curve for books rightward.
   d. supply curve for books leftward.
6. The fact that more people want to read books shifts the
   a. demand curve for books rightward.
   b. demand curve for books leftward.
   c. supply curve for books rightward.
   d. supply curve for books leftward.

7. The equilibrium quantity of books
   a. definitely increases.
   b. definitely does not change.
   c. definitely decreases.
   d. might increase, not change, or decrease.

8. The equilibrium price of a book
   a. definitely rises.
   b. definitely does not change.
   c. definitely falls.
   d. might rise, not change, or fall

9. Suppose that the demand shift is larger than the supply shift. In this case, the equilibrium quantity of books
   a. definitely increases.
   b. definitely does not change.
   c. definitely decreases.
   d. might increase, not change, or decrease.

10. Gruel is an inferior good. Hence, an increase in people's incomes
   a. decreases the supply of gruel.
   b. increases the quantity supplied of gruel.
   c. shifts the demand curve for gruel rightward.
   d. shifts the demand curve for gruel leftward.

11. How does an unusually cold winter affect the market for anti-freeze?
   a. It increases the supply of anti-freeze.
   b. It decreases the supply of anti-freeze.
   c. It increases the demand for anti-freeze.
   d. It decreases the demand for anti-freeze.

12. How does an unusually cold winter affect the equilibrium price and quantity of anti-freeze?
   a. It raises the price and increases the quantity.
   b. It raises the price and decreases the quantity.
   c. It lowers the price and increases the quantity.
   d. It lowers the price and decreases the quantity.

13. Farmland can be used to produce either cattle or corn. If the demand for cattle increases, the
   a. demand for corn will increase.
   b. supply of corn will increase.
   c. demand for corn will decrease.
   d. supply of corn will decrease.

14. Tea is a normal good if
   a. a rise in the price of sugar, a complement, causes the demand for tea to decrease.
   b. an increase in income causes the demand for tea to increase.
   c. a rise in the price of coffee, a substitute, causes the demand for tea to increase.
   d. it satisfies the law of demand.

15. If the market for twinkies is in equilibrium, then
   a. twinkies must be a normal good.
   b. producers would like to sell more at the current price.
   c. consumers would like to buy more at the current price.
   d. the quantity supplied equals the quantity demanded.

16. To a consumer, in-line skates and conventional roller skates are likely
   a. products with upward sloping demand curves.
   b. unrelated goods.
   c. complements.
   d. substitutes.

17. Some sales managers are talking shop. Which of the following quotations refers to a movement along the demand curve?
   a. "Since our competitors raised their prices our sales have doubled."
   b. "It has been an unusually mild winter; our sales of wool scarves are down from last year."
   c. "We decided to cut our prices, and the increase in our sales has been remarkable."
   d. None of the above

18. Suppose that there is a new baby boom, so that the number of babies drastically increases. How does the baby boom affect the equilibrium price and quantity of diapers?
   a. It raises the price and increases the quantity.
   b. It raises the price and decreases the quantity.
   c. It lowers the price and increases the quantity.
   d. It lowers the price and decreases the quantity.

19. Which of the following could cause the shift in the demand curve illustrated in Figure 4.5?
    a. An increase in the supply curve.
    b. A rise in the price of a substitute good.
    c. A rise in the price of a complement.
    d. A fall in the price of the product.

FIGURE **4.5**

Multiple Choice Question 19

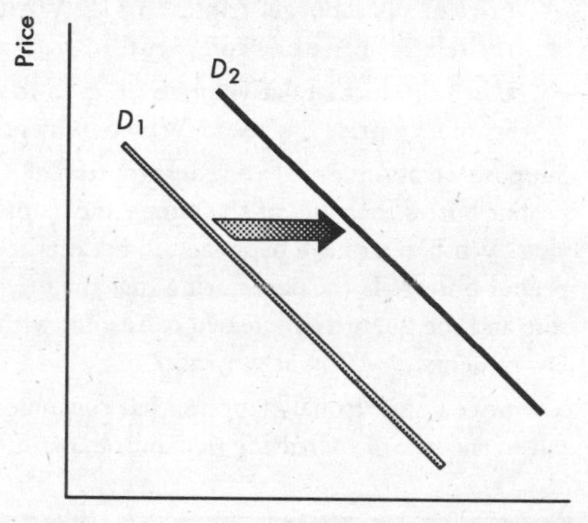

20. You notice that the price of wheat rises and the quantity of wheat increases. This set of observations can be the result of the
    a. demand for wheat curve shifting rightward.
    b. demand for wheat curve shifting leftward.
    c. supply of wheat curve shifting rightward.
    d. supply of wheat curve shifting leftward.

21. An influence that shifts the supply curve rightward
    a. always shifts the demand curve rightward.
    b. generally does not shift the demand curve..
    c. always shifts the demand curve leftward.
    d. is usually offset by a countervailing shift in the supply curve.

22. To say that "supply increases" means there is a
    a. movement rightward along a supply curve.
    b. movement leftward along a supply curve.
    c. shift rightward in the supply curve.
    d. shift leftward in the supply curve.

23. Which of the following influences does NOT shift the supply curve?
    a. A rise in the wages paid workers.
    b. Development of new technology.
    c. People deciding that they want to buy more of the product.
    d. A decrease in the number of suppliers.

24. The price of jet fuel rises, causing the
    a. demand for airplane trips to increase.
    b. demand for airplane trips to decrease.
    c. supply of airplane trips to increase.
    d. supply of airplane trips to decrease.

25. In Figure 4.6 at price *P* there is a
    a. shortage and the price will rise.
    b. shortage and the price will fall.
    c. surplus and the price will rise.
    d. surplus and the price will fall

FIGURE **4.6**

Multiple Choice Question 25

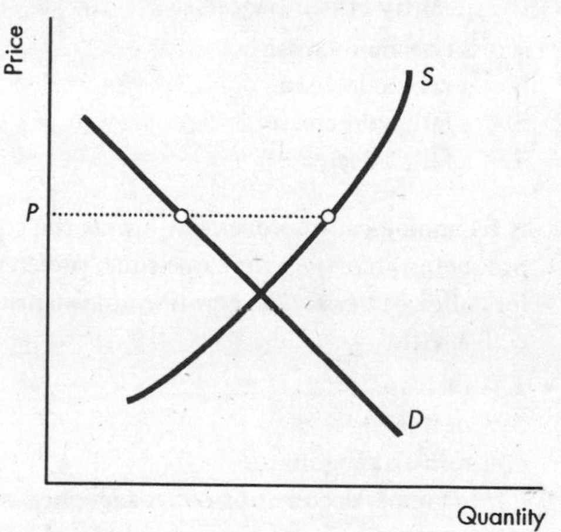

26. Which of the following definitely causes a rise in the equilibrium price?
    a. An increase in both demand and supply.
    b. A decrease in both demand and supply.
    c. An increase in demand combined with a decrease in supply.
    d. A decrease in demand combined with an increase in supply.

27. Some producers are chatting over dinner. Which of the following quotations refers to a movement along the supply curve?
    a. "Wage hikes have forced us to raise our prices."
    b. "Our new, sophisticated equipment will enable us to undercut our competitors."
    c. "Raw material prices have skyrocketed; we will have to pass it on to our customers."
    d. "We anticipate a big increase in demand. Our product price should rise, so we are planning for an increase in output."

28. A normal good is one
    a. with a downward sloping demand curve.
    b. for which demand increases when the price of a substitute rises.
    c. for which demand increases when income increases.
    d. None of the above.

29. For consumers, pizza and hamburgers are substitutes. A rise in the price of a pizza causes ____ in the price of a hamburger and ____ in the quantity of hamburgers.
    a. a rise; an increase
    b. a rise; a decrease
    c. a fall; an increase
    d. a fall; a decrease

30. A technological improvement lowers the cost of producing coffee. At the same time, preferences for coffee decrease. The equilibrium quantity of coffee will
    a. increase.
    b. decrease.
    c. remain the same.
    d. increase, decrease, or not change, depending on the relative shifts of the demand and supply curves.

Short Answer Problems

1. a. This year the price of a hamburger is $2 and the price of a compact disc is $12. In terms of hamburgers, what is the relative price of a compact disc? In terms of hamburgers, what is the opportunity cost of buying a compact disc?
   b. Next year the (money) price of a compact disc doubles to $24 and the (money) price of a hamburger remains at $2. Now what is the relative price of a compact disc?
   c. The following year the (money) price of a compact disc stays at $24 and the (money) price of a hamburger doubles to $4. What is the relative price of a compact disc?
   d. In the next year, the (money) price of a compact disc doubles to $48 and the money price of a hamburger triples to $12. What is the relative price of a compact disc?
   e. Can a product's relative price fall even though its money price has risen? Why or why not?

2. Suppose we observe that the consumption of peanut butter increases at the same time its price rises. What must have happened in the market for peanut butter? Is the observation that the price rose and the quantity increased consistent with the law of demand? Why or why not?

3. The price of a personal computer has continued to fall in the face of increasing demand. Explain.

Table 4.1 Demand and Supply Schedules

Price (per comic book)	Quantity demanded (per month)	Quantity supplied (per month)
$2.50	14,000,000	8,000,000
3.00	13,000,000	10,000,000
3.50	12,000,000	12,000,000
4.00	11,000,000	13,000,000
4.50	10,000,000	14,000,000

4. a. Table 4.1 presents the demand and supply schedules for comic books. Graph these demand and supply schedules in Figure 4.7 (on the next page). What is the equilibrium price? The equilibrium quantity?
   b. Suppose that the price of a movie, a substitute for comic books, rises so that at every price of a comic book consumers now want to buy 2,000,000 more comic books than before. Plot this new demand curve in Figure 4.7. What is the new equilibrium price? The new equilibrium quantity?

FIGURE **4.7**
Short Answer Problem 4

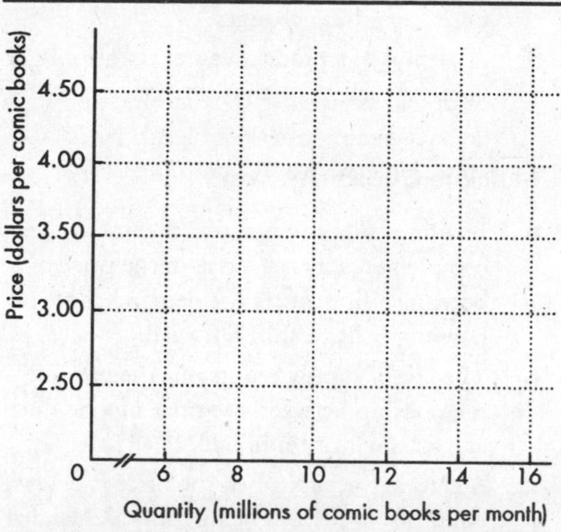

5. Suppose that the wages paid oil workers fall. Use a supply and demand diagram to determine the effect this action has on the equilibrium price and quantity of gasoline.
6. Chemical companies discover a new, more efficient technology for producing benzene. Use a supply and demand model to determine the impact that this new method has on the equilibrium price and quantity of benzene.
7. a. When drawing a demand curve, what five influences are assumed not to change?
   b. If any of these influences change, what happens to the demand curve?
   c. When drawing a supply curve, what five influences are assumed not to change?
   d. If any of these influences change, what happens to the supply curve?
8. Used records and used compact discs are substitutes. Use a supply and demand diagram to determine what happens to the equilibrium price and quantity of used records when the price of a used compact disc falls because of an increase in the supply of used discs.
9. New cars are a normal good. Suppose that the economy enters a period of strong economic expansion so that people's incomes increase substantially. Use a supply and demand diagram to determine what happens to the equilibrium price and quantity of new cars.
10. a. The market for chickens initially is in equilibrium. Suppose that eating buffalo wings (which, contrary to the name, are made from chicken wings) becomes so stylish that people eat them for breakfast, lunch and dinner. Use a supply and demand diagram to determine how the equilibrium price and quantity of chicken change.
    b. Return to the initial equilibrium, before eating buffalo wings became stylish. Now, suppose that a heat wave occurred and caused tens of thousands of chickens to die or commit suicide. Keeping in mind that dead chickens cannot be marketed, use a supply and demand diagram to determine what happens to the equilibrium price and quantity of chicken.
    c. Now assume that both the heat wave and fad strike at the same time. Use a supply and demand diagram to show what happens to the equilibrium price and quantity of chicken. (Hint: Can you tell for sure what happens to the price? The quantity?)

■ You're the Teacher

1. When you and a friend are studying Chapter 4, the friend says to you, "I really don't understand the difference between a 'shift in a curve' and a 'movement along' a curve. Can you help me; what's the difference?" Explain the difference to your friend.
2. "This supply and demand model is nonsense. It says that if demand for some product decreases, the price of that good falls. But, come on — how many times have you actually seen a price fall? Prices *always* rise, so don't try telling me that that they fall." The supply and demand model is sound; it is this statement that is nonsense. Show the speaker the error in that analysis.

Answers

True/False Answers

1. **T** The law of demand points out the negative relationship between a product's price and the quantity demanded.
2. **U** Demand decreases for normal goods but increases for inferior goods.
3. **F** The negative relationship between the price and quantity demanded holds along a fixed demand curve. But, if the demand curve shifts rightward, the equilibrium price rises and the equilibrium quantity increases.
4. **T** Chicken feed is a factor used to produce chickens, so a rise in the price of chicken feed shifts the supply curve of chickens leftward.
5. **T** The equilibrium quantity definitely increases but the price may rise, fall, or stay the same, depending on which shift is bigger.
6. **U** The price rises if the demand is shift is larger than the supply shift; but if the shifts are the same size, the price does not change and if the supply shift is larger, the price falls.
7. **F** A rise in the price of popcorn causes a movement along the demand curve for popcorn; it does not shift the demand curve.
8. **F** The supply curve shows the minimum price that suppliers must receive in order to produce the last quantity supplied.
9. **T** The rise in the future price shifts the demand curve rightward and the supply curve leftward, unambiguously raising the current price.
10. **F** If the price exceeds the equilibrium price, there is a surplus not a shortage.
11. **F** The term "increase in demand" refers to a shift in the demand curve.
12. **F** Technology is a factor that shifts the supply curve; new technology shifts the supply curve rightward.
13. **F** The rise in the price of orange juice creates a movement along the demand curve to a lower quantity demanded (that is, to the northwest), but it does not shift the demand curve.
14. **T** Once at the equilibrium price, because the opposing forces of supply and demand are in balance, the situation can persist indefinitely until something changes.
15. **T** A surplus of a product causes its price to fall until it reaches the equilibrium price.

Multiple Choice Answers

1. **a** Bowling balls and bowling a game are complements; hence a rise in the price of bowling a line causes the demand curve for bowling balls to shift leftward.
2. **a** The law of supply points out the positive relationship between the price of a product and the quantity supplied.
3. **c** A shortage occurs when the price is below the equilibrium price. The quantity demanded exceeds the quantity supplied and the resulting shortage causes the price to rise to its equilibrium level.
4. **b** The definition of complementary goods is that a rise in the price of one decreases the demand for the other.
5. **d** Paper is an input — a factor of production — in the manufacture of books, so a rise in the price of paper shifts the supply curve of books leftward.
6. **a** When people's preferences change so that they want to read more books, the demand curve for books shifts rightward.
7. **d** The equilibrium quantity increases if the demand shift is larger than the supply shift, decreases if the supply shift is larger, and does not change if the shifts are the same size.
8. **a** Both the increase in demand and decrease in supply cause the price to rise, so the equilibrium price rises unambiguously.
9. **a** If the size of the demand shift exceeds the size of the supply shift, the equilibrium quantity increases. This result is illustrated in Figure 4.8 (on the next page), where the quantity goes from Q_1 to Q_2.

FIGURE 4.8
Multiple Choice Question 9

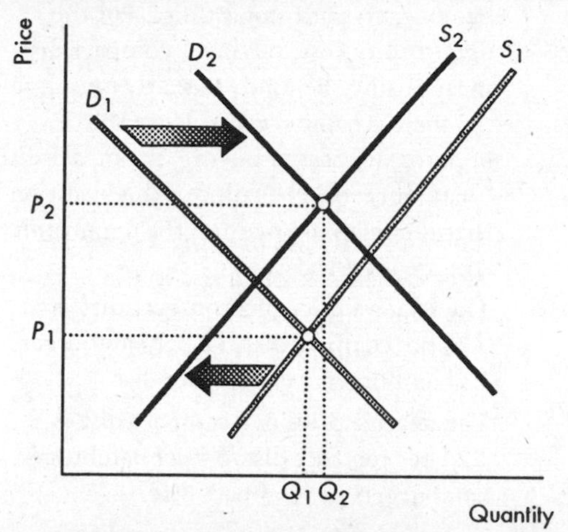

10. **d** An increase in income decreases the demand — shifts the demand curve leftward — for an inferior good.
11. **c** Consumers demand more anti-freeze to keep their car engines from being severely damaged by freezing.
12. **a** The cold winter shifts the demand curve rightward; the supply curve does not shift. As a result, the equilibrium price rises and the quantity increases.
13. **d** Cattle and corn are substitutes in production. Thus an increase in the demand for cattle gives farmers the incentive to switch land to cattle grazing, thereby decreasing the supply of corn.
14. **b** By definition, an increase in income increases the demand for a normal good.
15. **d** At equilibrium, consumers and suppliers are simultaneously satisfied insofar as the quantity consumers are willing to buy matches the quantity producers are willing to sell.
16. **d** In-line skates and roller skates can take each other's place and so are substitutes.
17. **c** A reduction in the price of a product causes a movement along the demand curve.
18. **a** The baby boom increases the demand for diapers; that is, the demand curve for diapers shifts rightward. This shift raises the equilibrium price of a diaper and increases the equilibrium quantity.
19. **b** A rise in the price of a substitute shifts the demand curve rightward.
20. **a** Figure 4.9 shows that an increase in the demand for wheat raises the price of wheat and increases its quantity.

FIGURE 4.9
Multiple Choice Question 20

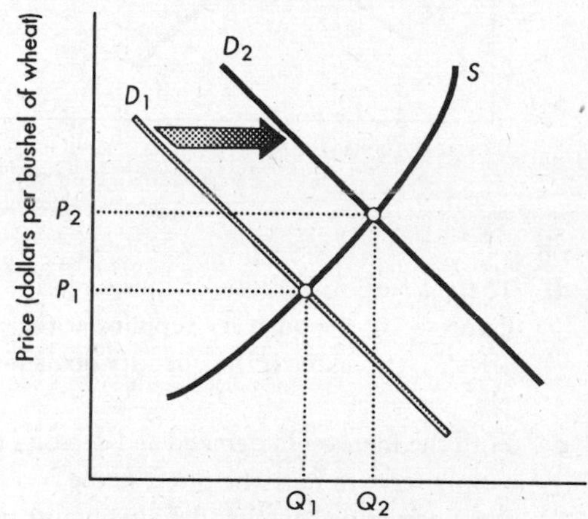

21. **b** Generally an influence that shifts the supply curve does not shift the demand curve and vice versa.
22. **c** An "increase in supply" means that the supply curve shifts rightward; a "decrease in supply" means the supply curve shifts leftward.
23. **c** A change in preferences shifts the demand curve, not the supply curve.
24. **d** Jet fuel is an input in producing airplane trips, so a rise in the price of this factor of production decreases (shifts leftward) the supply of airplane trips.

FIGURE **4.10**
Multiple Choice Question 25

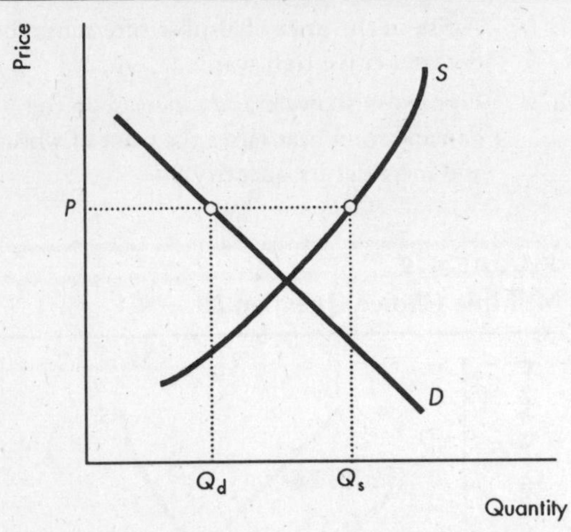

25. **d** There is surplus because, as illustrated in Figure 4.10, the quantity supplied at the price P, Q_s, exceeds the quantity demanded, Q_d.
26. **c** Both the increase in demand and decrease in supply serve to raise the price, so the two of them occurring together definitely must raise the price.
27. **d** In this case the producers are responding to the rise in price by moving along their supply curve and increasing the quantity they supply.
28. **c** This is the definition of a "normal good."
29. **a** The rise in the price of a pizza increases the demand for hamburgers, which results in a rise in the price of a hamburger and an increase in the quantity of hamburgers.
30. **d** The technological improvement increases the supply, which increases the quantity. However, the increase is offset by the change in preferences, which decreases the demand and decreases the quantity. The net effect on the quantity depends on which influence is larger.

■ Answers to Short Answer Problems

1. a. The money price of a compact disc is $12 per compact disc; the money price of a hamburger is $2 per hamburger. The relative price of a compact disc is the ratio of the money prices, $12 per compact disc/$2 per hamburger, or 6 hamburgers per compact disc. For the opportunity cost, buying 1 compact disc means using the funds that otherwise could purchase 6 hamburgers. Hence the opportunity cost of buying 1 compact disc is 6 hamburgers. The point of this question is that the relative price and the opportunity cost are identical.
   b. The relative price of a compact disc is $24 per compact disc/$2 per hamburger, or 12 hamburgers per compact disc.
   c. The relative price of a compact disc is $24 per compact disc/$4 per hamburger, or 6 hamburgers per compact disc.
   d. The relative price of a compact disc is $48 per compact disc/$12 per hamburger, or 4 hamburgers per compact disc.
   e. Yes, a product's relative price can fall even though its money price rises. Part (d) gives an example of how that can occur: If a good's money price rises by less than the money price of other goods, then the product's relative price falls. Keep this relationship in mind when you use the supply and demand model because, when the model predicts that the equilibrium price will fall, it means that the *relative* price and not necessarily the money price falls.
2. In order for both the equilibrium price of peanut butter to rise and the equilibrium quantity to increase, the demand for peanut butter must have shifted rightward. This increase in demand will lead to a rise in the price and an increase in the quantity of peanut butter. The observation that both the price rose and the quantity increased is not at all inconsistent with the law of demand. The law of demand states that "other things remaining the same, the higher the price of a good, the smaller is the quantity demanded." A key part of this law is the "other things remaining equal" clause. When the demand for peanut butter shifts rightward, something else that increased the demand for peanut butter has changed. Hence "other things" have not remained the same and by changing have resulted in a higher price and increased quantity of peanut butter.

FIGURE **4.11**

Short Answer Problem 3

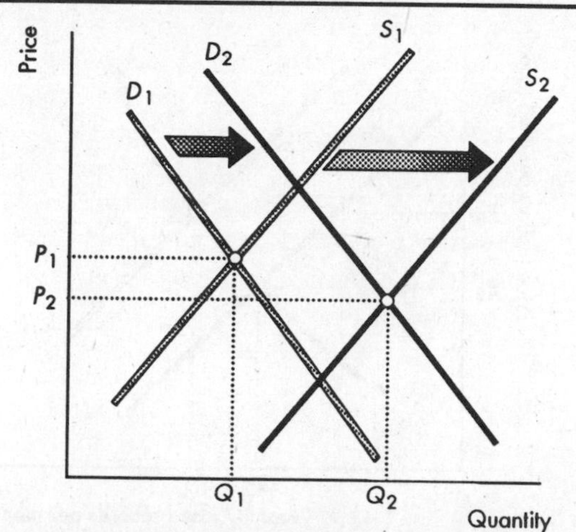

3. Personal computers have fallen in price although the demand for them has increased because the supply has increased even more rapidly. Figure 4.11 illustrates this situation. From one year to the next the demand curve increased from D_1 to D_2. But over the year the supply curve increased from S_1 to S_2. Because the supply curve has increased more than the demand curve, the price of a personal computer fell from P_1 to P_2.

FIGURE **4.12**

Short Answer Problem 4

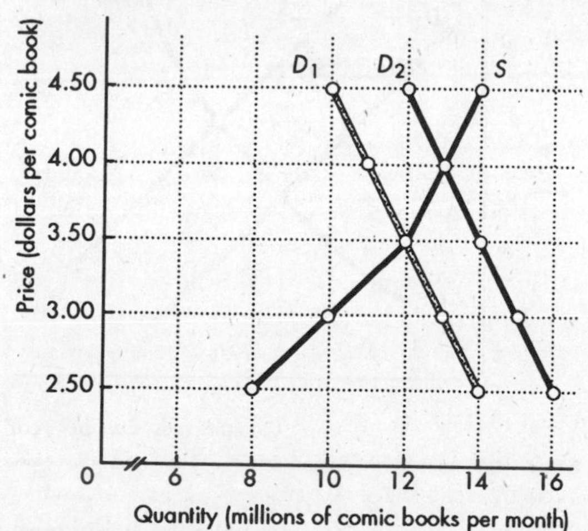

4. a. Figure 4.12 shows the graph of the supply and demand schedules as S and D_1. The equilibrium price is \$3.50 a comic book, and the equilibrium quantity is 12,000,000 comic books.

   b. The new demand curve is plotted in Figure 4.12 as D_2. The new equilibrium price is \$4.00, and the new equilibrium quantity is 13,000,000.

FIGURE **4.13**

Short Answer Problem 5

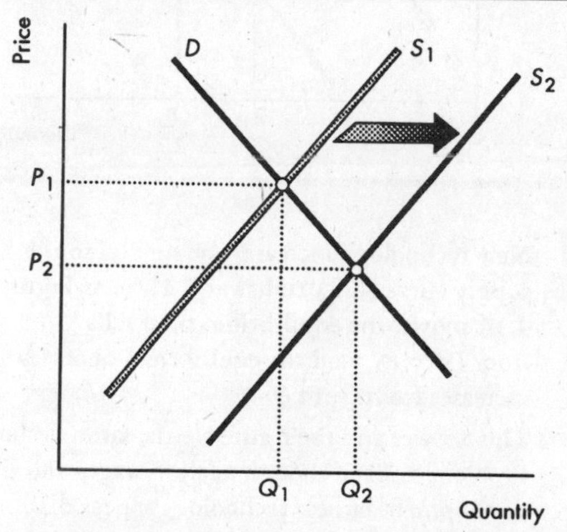

5. Lower wages reduces the price of a factor (labor) used to produce gasoline. As a result, the supply curve of gasoline increases. This change is illustrated in Figure 4.13, where the supply curve shifts rightward from S_1 to S_2. The shift in the supply curve lowers the equilibrium price of gasoline (from P_1 to P_2) and increases the equilibrium quantity (from Q_1 to Q_2).

FIGURE **4.14**

Short Answer Problem 6

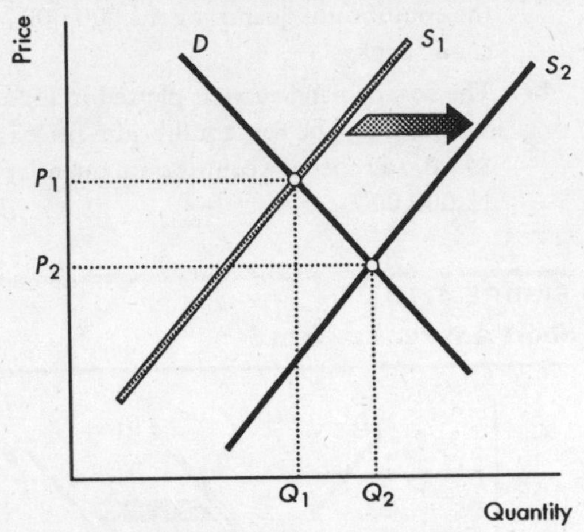

FIGURE **4.15**

Short Answer Problem 8

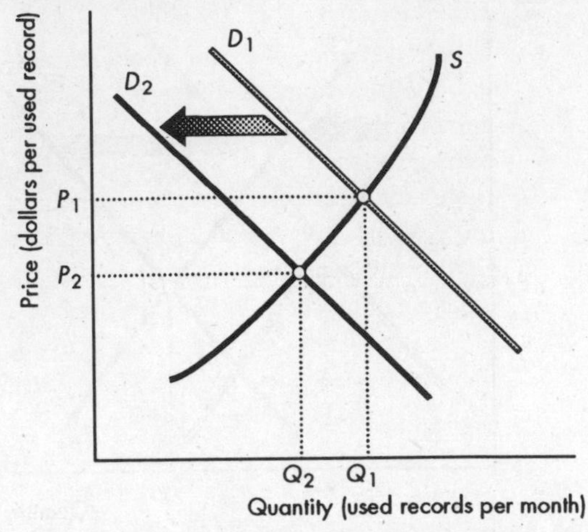

6. New technology increases the supply, so the supply curve shifts rightward. Then, as Figure 4.14 shows, the equilibrium price falls from P_1 to P_2, and the equilibrium quantity increases from Q_1 to Q_2.

   This answer and the figure are the same as those in Problem 5. Even though a fall in wages and the development of new technology appear dissimilar, the demand and supply model reveals that both have the same effect on the price and quantity of the product. This model can easily accommodate these (quite) different changes. For this reason the demand and supply model is a very important economic tool.

7. a. The five influences that do not change along a demand curve are prices of related goods, income, expected future prices, population, and preferences.

   b. If any of these factors change, the demand curve shifts.

   c. The five influences that are held constant when you draw a supply curve are prices of factors of production, prices of other goods produced, number of suppliers, expected future prices, and technology.

   d. If any of these influences change, the supply curve shifts.

8. The fall in the price of a used compact disc, a substitute for used records, decreases the demand for used records. This change causes the demand curve for used records to shift leftward, as shown in Figure 4.15. As a result of this change, the price of a used record falls and the quantity decreases.

FIGURE **4.16**

Short Answer Problem 9

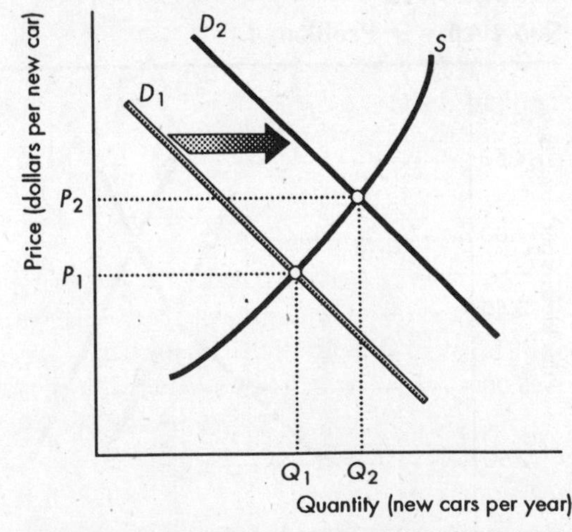

9. Because new cars are a normal good, an increase in income increases the demand for them. Hence the

demand curve shifts rightward, as shown in Figure 4.16. As a result, the equilibrium price rises from P_1 to P_2 and the equilibrium quantity also increases, from Q_1 to Q_2.

10. a. With the change in people's preferences — so that they want more chicken wings and hence more chickens — the demand for chickens increases. Figure 4.17, where the demand curve for chickens shifts rightward, shows this change. As Figure 4.17 demonstrates, the equilibrium price rises and the equilibrium quantity of chickens increase. (Note how this diagram is similar to Figure 4.16. Together they show how both increases in income for a normal good and a change in preferences increase the demand for products and thereby have the same qualitative effect on the price and quantity.)

b. The heat wave decreases the number of chickens that can be supplied. This change shifts the supply curve for chickens leftward, as Figure 4.18 shows. Hence the heat wave raises the price of a chicken (from P_1 to P_2) and decreases the quantity (from Q_1 to Q_2).

c. If the demand increases *and* the supply decreases, the equilibrium price of a chicken rises. But the effect on the quantity is ambiguous. Figures 4.19 and 4.20 (on the next page) reveal the nature of this ambiguity. In Figure 4.19, the demand shift is larger than the supply shift, and the equilibrium quantity increases. But in Figure 4.20, the magnitude of the shifts is reversed, and the supply shift exceeds the demand shift. Because the supply shift is larger, the equilibrium quantity decreases. Thus, unless you know which shift is larger, you cannot determine whether the quantity increases (when the demand shift is larger), decreases (when the supply shift is larger), or stays the same (when both shifts are the same size).However, regardless of the relative sizes, Figures 19 and 20 show that the price will unambiguously rise.

FIGURE **4.17**
Short Answer Problem 10 (a)

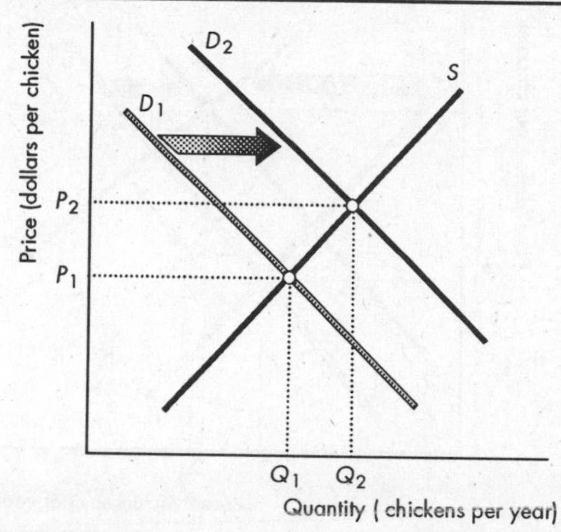

FIGURE **4.18**
Short Answer Problem 10 (b)

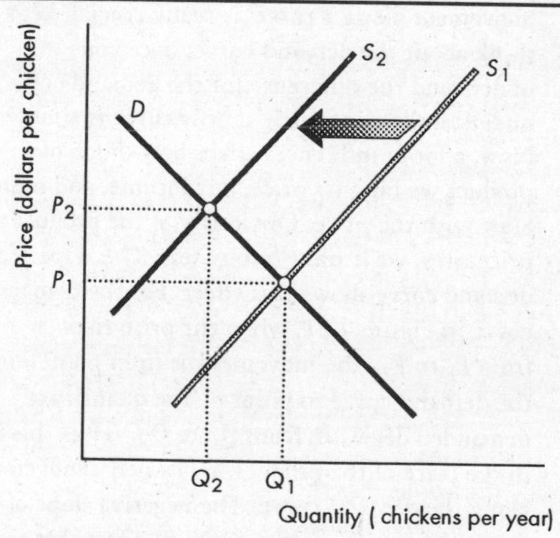

FIGURE 4.19
Short Answer Problem 10 (c)

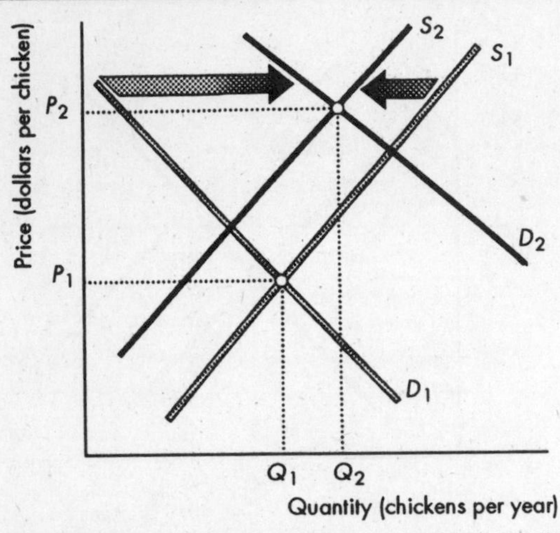

FIGURE 4.20
Short Answer Problem 10 (c)

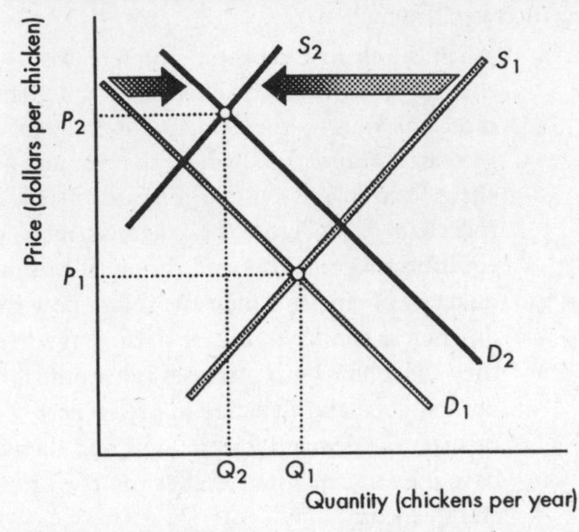

You're the Teacher

1. "The distinction between a 'shift in a curve' and a 'movement along a curve' is really crucial. Let's think about the demand curve; once you understand the difference for the demand curve, understanding it for the supply curve is simple. Now, a lot of influences affect how much of a product we buy: its price, our income, and soon. Start with the price. Obviously, if the product's price rises, we'll want to buy less. The slope of a demand curve shows this effect. For the demand curve in Figure 4.21, when the price rises from P_1 to P_2, the movement is from point *a* on the demand curve to point *b*. The quantity demanded decreases from Q_1 to Q_2. Thus this rise in the price of the product has caused a movement along the demand curve. The negative slope of the demand curve shows the negative effect that higher prices have on the quantity demanded.

"Now, let's suppose that our incomes fall and that as a result we're going to buy less of this product. The demand curve's slope can't show us this effect because the slope indicates the relationship between the price and the quantity demanded. Instead, the whole demand curve is going to shift. That is at any price we'll buy less. Look at Figure 4.22 (on the next page), for instance. If the price stays at P_1 the quantity we demand decreases

FIGURE 4.21
You're the Teacher Question 1

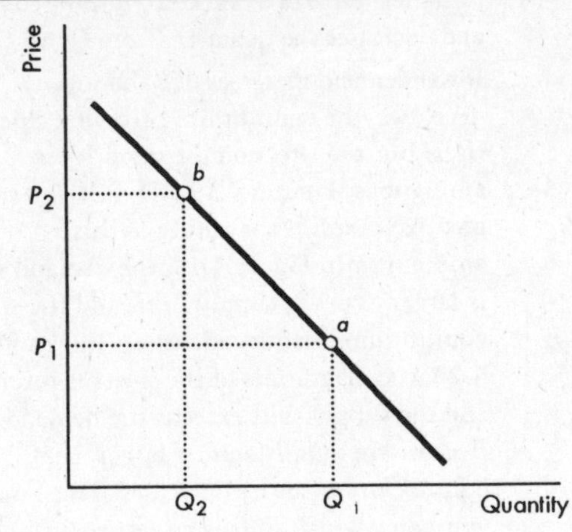

from Q_1 to Q_1'. But the same is true if the price is P_2: if the price stays at P_2, the quantity we demand decreases from Q_2 to Q_2'. Now, I don't mean to say that the price has to stay at P_1 or at P_2. All I'm saying is that at any possible price, the amount that we're going to buy has decreased and I'm just using P_1 and P_2 as examples. Thus we're going to decrease the quantity demanded not

FIGURE 4.22
You're the Teacher Question 2

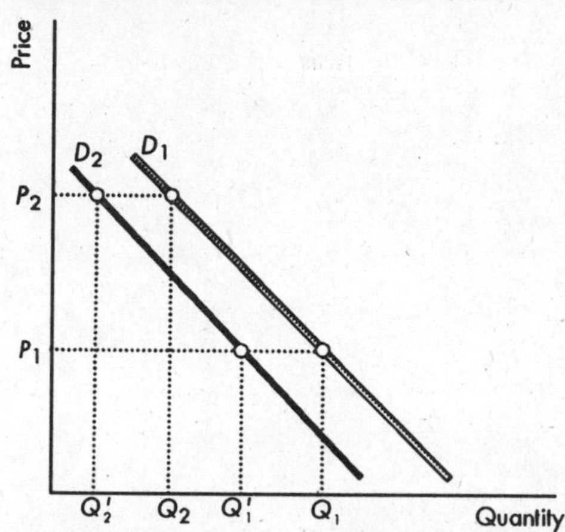

only at P_1 and at P_2, but at every possible price. That means that we can draw a new demand curve (D_2)to show how much we demand at every price after our incomes fall. So, the drop in income has shifted the demand curve from D_1 to D_2. And, that's all there is to the difference between a 'movement along the demand curve' and a 'shift in the demand curve.' "

2. "You're missing a key point about the demand and supply model. This model predicts what happens to *relative* prices, not *money* prices. You're certainly right when you say that we don't often see a money price fall. We live in inflationary times and most money prices usually rise. But when the demand and supply model says that the price falls, it means that the *relative* price falls. A good's relative price can fall even though its money price rises. For instance, if the money price of some product rises by 5 percent when the money prices of all other goods are rising by 10 percent, the first product's relative price has fallen. That is, its money price relative to every other money price is lower. If you think about it, relative prices change all the time, and at least half the time relative prices fall. Drops in relative prices aren't rare; they're common. So, don't be too hasty to throw away the demand and supply model. Not only are we going to see it on our test in this class, but it also works well to help us understand what happens to a product's (relative) price and quantity whenever there's a change in a relevant factor."

Chapter 5 ELASTICITY

Key Concepts

Price Elasticity of Demand

The price elasticity of demand measures the *responsiveness* of the quantity demanded to a change in the price of the good.

- The price elasticity of demand is a units-free measure of responsiveness.

The elasticity of demand equals the magnitude of:

$$\frac{\%\Delta \text{ quantity demanded}}{\%\Delta \text{ price}} = \frac{\Delta Q / Q_{ave}}{\Delta P / P_{ave}}.$$

Elasticity is *not* equal to the slope of the demand curve. Along a linear demand curve the slope ($\Delta P/\Delta Q$) is constant but the elasticity decreases as P_{ave} falls, thereby increasing Q_{ave}.

When	*Demand is*
elasticity = ∞	perfectly elastic (horizontal)
1 < elasticity < ∞	elastic
elasticity = 1	unit elastic
0 < elasticity < 1	inelastic
elasticity = 0	perfectly inelastic (vertical)

The price elasticity of demand depends on:

- *substitutability* — the more close substitutes there are for the good, the larger is its price elasticity.
- *proportion of income spent on the product* — the greater the proportion of income spent on a good, the higher is its price elasticity of demand.
- *time elapsed since the price change* — the more time that has passed since the price changed, the greater is its price elasticity of demand.

- Price elasticity and total revenue ($P \times Q$):

When demand is	*A price cut causes*
inelastic (elasticity < 1)	a drop in total revenue
unit elastic (elasticity = 1)	no change in total revenue
elastic (elasticity > 1)	a rise in total revenue

Income Elasticity of Demand

The income elasticity of demand measures the responsiveness of the quantity demanded to a change in income.

The income elasticity of demand equals:

$$\frac{\%\Delta \text{ quantity demanded}}{\%\Delta \text{ income}}.$$

When	*The good is*
income elasticity > 1	normal and demand is income elastic
0 < income elasticity < 1	normal and demand is income inelastic
income elasticity < 0	inferior

Cross Elasticity of Demand

The cross elasticity of demand measures the responsiveness of the quantity demanded of good A to a change in the price of good B.

The cross elasticity of demand equals:

$$\frac{\%\Delta \text{ quantity demanded of good A}}{\%\Delta \text{ price of good B}}.$$

When	*Then*
cross elasticity > 0	the goods are substitutes
cross elasticity < 0	the goods are complements

Elasticity of Supply

The elasticity of supply measures the responsiveness of the quantity supplied to a change in its price.

The elasticity of supply equals

$$\frac{\%\Delta \text{ quantity supplied}}{\%\Delta \text{ price}}.$$

The elasticity of supply depends on:

- the ease with which additional factors can be substituted into the production process.
- the time since the price change. (The elasticity increases from the momentary to short-run to long-run supply.)

Helpful Hints

1. There are many elasticity formulas in this chapter. It is very easy to become overwhelmed by trying to memorize all of them and lose sight of their intuition. *All* the elasticity formulas merely measure how strongly a relationship responds to some change. The price elasticity of demand, for instance, indicates how strongly a change in a product's price affects the quantity demanded of the product. If demanders react strongly so that, say, a drop in price causes a large increase in the quantity demanded, the demand is elastic. But, if demanders hardly change the quantity demanded even in the face of large price changes, the demand is inelastic. Keeping this explanation in mind will help you whenever you face a question dealing with elasticity.
2. Elasticities are calculated using percentages. This method can cause confusion, but a moment's thought shows that percentages actually are the most natural way to determine the importance of a change in price, income, or quantity. For example, which seems larger: a $1 rise in the price of a Big Mac served at the local McDonald's or a $1 rise in the price of the least expensive BMW sold at the nearest BMW dealer? Clearly, the $1 rise in the price of the Big Mac is larger because it represents approximately a 50 percent boost. With the least expensive BMW selling for more than $20,000, a $1 rise in its price is minuscule, less than a 0.005 percent rise. Many consumers would respond to a $1 change in the price of a Big Mac; few would to a $1 change in the price of a BMW. Thus, rather than being "mysterious," use of percentages to determine the size of a price change actually is easy to understand.
3. The formula for the price elasticity of demand between two points on the demand curve is to take the magnitude of:
$$\frac{\%\Delta \text{ quantity demanded}}{\%\Delta \text{ price}} = \frac{\Delta Q / Q_{ave}}{\Delta P / P_{ave}}.$$
Taking the magnitude of this expression is the same as taking its absolute value. Why do we want the magnitude? Because the law of demand assures us that the relationship between the price change and the quantity demanded is negative. For instance, a rise in the price of the product decreases the quantity demanded. Therefore the price elasticity always will be a negative number. By taking the magnitude (absolute value) of the elasticity we ignore the (meaningless) negative sign.
4. Easy to forget is whether the percentage change in the quantity demanded or the percentage change in the price goes in the numerator for the price elasticity of demand. If you think of a "kewpie doll," the sort of doll that is (or was) given away at carnivals for a display of an otherwise fairly useless talent, you should be able to keep the formula straight. The word "kewpie" is pronounced "q-p", thereby telling us that "*q*" goes first (in the numerator) and that "*p*" goes second (in the denominator).
5. One of the most practical uses for the price elasticity of demand is to determine how a change in price affects total revenue. Businesses are quite frequently interested in whether a price hike (or price cut) will increase or decrease their total revenue. Recall that total revenue is price times quantity. To see intuitively how the price elasticity of demand tells us whether a price change increases or decreases total revenue, think about a price rise. A price hike has two separate effects on total revenue. First, a higher price directly raises total revenue. Second, however, consumers respond to the higher price by decreasing the quantity they buy. Hence the higher price results in a decrease in the quantity sold and this "indirect" effect reduces total revenue. Which effect is larger? That depends on

the price elasticity of demand. If demand is elastic, the percentage decrease in the quantity demanded exceeds the percentage rise in price. Thus in this case the effect from the decreased quantity exceeds the impact from the higher price and total revenue falls. But, if demand is inelastic, the percentage decrease in the quantity demanded is less than the percentage rise in the price. In this situation, the effect of the higher price dominates that of the decreased quantity, and total revenue rises. Finally, if demand is unit elastic, the percentage decrease in the quantity demanded just equals the percentage rise in price. The two effects offset each other, with no change in total revenue.

For a price drop, the results are just the reverse. A price reduction raises total revenue if demand is elastic and lowers it if demand is inelastic.

6. Two other key demand elasticities are the cross elasticity of demand and the income elasticity of demand. The income elasticity of demand equals:

$$\frac{\%\Delta \text{ quantity demanded}}{\%\Delta \text{ income}},$$

and the cross elasticity of demand equals:

$$\frac{\%\Delta \text{ quantity demanded of good A}}{\%\Delta \text{ price of good B}}.$$

Unlike for the price elasticity of demand, for the income elasticity and the cross elasticity do we not use the magnitude; that is, for neither elasticity do we use the absolute value. The reason is that the sign of these elasticities is important and we don't want to lose it. We know that the price elasticity of demand always is negative. The income and cross elasticities, however, can be either negative or positive. For instance, a negative income elasticity indicates that the product is an inferior good. As people's incomes rise, they buy less of this particular product. A positive income elasticity signifies that the product is a normal good. Higher incomes lead to increased purchases. The sign of the cross elasticity also is important. A negative cross elasticity indicates that the two goods are complements, but a positive cross elasticity means that the two goods are substitutes. Thus, because the signs of the income elasticity and cross elasticity convey information, we retain the sign rather than discard it.

Questions

True/False/Uncertain and Explain

1. The price elasticity of demand is the same as the slope of the demand curve.
2. Moving downward and rightward along a linear demand curve, the price elasticity of demand does not change.
3. The price elasticity of demand ranges from 0 to ∞.
4. The demand for Exxon gasoline is likely to be elastic.
5. If a company wants to increase its total revenue, it should raise the price of its product.
6. If the price elasticity of demand is positive, the demand is considered to be "elastic."
7. The more that demanders respond to a price change, the larger is the price elasticity of demand.
8. As more time passes after a price change, the price elasticity of demand becomes smaller.
9. As more time passes after a price change, the elasticity of supply generally increases.
10. A product whose demand is "elastic" has an income elasticity of demand that exceeds 1.0.
11. The price elasticity of demand for food is highest in poor nations.
12. The cross elasticity of demand between hot dogs and hot dog buns is negative.
13. If you spend more on rent than on soap, your price elasticity of demand for housing is likely to be larger than your price elasticity of demand for soap.
14. If your local Domino's Pizza outlet estimates that the price elasticity of demand for its pizzas is 4.00

and if it raises the price it charges for its pizzas, its total revenue will increase.

15. An inferior good has an income elasticity of demand that is negative; a normal good has an income elasticity of demand that is positive.

Multiple Choice Questions

1. If the price elasticity of demand equals 1.0, then as the price falls the
   a. quantity demanded decreases.
   b. total revenue falls.
   c. quantity demanded does not change.
   d. total revenue does not change.

2. Suppose that a 10 percent hike in the price of a textbook decreases the quantity demanded by 2 percent. Then the elasticity of demand for textbooks is
   a. 0.2.
   b. 2.0.
   c. 5.0.
   d. 10.0.

3. The income elasticity of the demand for food is likely to be
   a. larger in high-income countries than in low income countries.
   b. negative.
   c. nonexistent because people always need food.
   d. below 1.0.

4. A product whose demand curve is vertical has a price elasticity of demand that
   a. equals 0.
   b. is greater than 0 but less than 1.0.
   c. equals to 1.0.
   d. is negative.

5. A 10 percent increase in income decreases the demand for beans by 3 percent. Then the income elasticity of demand for beans is
   a. –0.3.
   b. 3.3.
   c. 0.3.
   d. 10.0

6. Suppose that the short-run price elasticity of demand for oil is 0.1. Then, in order to boost the price of oil by 20 percent, the quantity of oil must be
   a. decreased by 200 percent.
   b. decreased by 20 percent.
   c. decreased by 2 percent.
   d. decreased by 0.2 percent.

7. Two points on the demand curve for volleyballs are shown in Table 5.1. What is the price elasticity of demand between these two points?
   a. 2.5.
   b. 2.0.
   c. 0.5.
   d. 0.4.

Table 5.1 Multiple Choice Question 7

Price per volleyball	Quantity demanded
$19	55
21	45

8. A product with perfectly elastic demand has a demand curve that
   a. is vertical.
   b. is horizontal.
   c. has a 45° slope.
   d. is a rectangular hyperbola.

9. The elasticity of supply generally is larger along the
   a. momentary supply curve.
   b. short-run supply curve.
   c. long-run supply curve.
   d. long-run supply curve for substitutes and momentary supply curve for complements.

10. For which of the following is the cross elasticity of demand positive?
    a. Tennis balls and tennis rackets.
    b. Videotapes and laundry detergent.
    c. Airline trips and textbooks.
    d. Beef and chicken.

11. The supply of new cars increases by 8 percent. If the price elasticity of demand for new cars is 2.00, the price of a new car will
    a. fall by 0.25 percent.
    b. fall by 2 percent.
    c. fall by 4 percent.
    d. fall by 8 percent.

12. The demand for a good is more price inelastic if
    a. its price is higher.
    b. the percentage of income spent on it is larger.
    c. it is a luxury good.
    d. it has no close substitutes.

13. A normal good has
    a. an income elasticity of demand greater than 1.0.
    b. a price elasticity of demand greater than 1.0.
    c. a positive price elasticity of demand.
    d. a positive income elasticity of demand.

14. A rise in the price of a product increases the total revenue from the product if the
    a. income elasticity of demand exceeds 1.
    b. good is an inferior product.
    c. demand for the product is inelastic.
    d. demand for the product is elastic.

15. Suppose that the *income* elasticity of demand for apartments is –0.2. This value indicates that
    a. the demand for apartments is price inelastic.
    b. the demand for apartments is unit elastic.
    c. a rise in the rent for apartments lowers the total revenue from renting apartments.
    d. apartments are an inferior good.

16. 39,000,000 CDs per year are supplied when the price of a CD is $13. When the price is $15, 41,000,000 CDs per year are supplied. What is the elasticity of supply for CDs?
    a. 2.86.
    b. 0.35.
    c. 0.14.
    d. 0.05.

17. Which of the following is likely to have the highest price elasticity of demand?
    a. An automobile.
    b. A new automobile.
    c. A new Ford automobile.
    d. A new Ford Mustang.

18. A 10 percent increase in the price of a Pepsi increases the demand for Coca Cola by 50 percent. Thus the cross elasticity of demand between Pepsi and Coca Cola is
    a. 50.
    b. 10.
    c. 5.
    d. 0.20.

19. IBM discovers that, when it lowers the price of its personal computers, the total revenue it obtains from the sale of personal computers rises. This result means that the
    a. supply of IBM personal computers is elastic.
    b. demand for IBM personal computers is elastic.
    c. supply of IBM personal computers is inelastic.
    d. demand for IBM personal computers is inelastic.

20. Business people often speak about price elasticity without actually using the term. Which of the following statements describes an elastic demand for a product?
    a. "A price cut won't help me. It won't increase my sales, and I'll just get less money for each unit that I was selling before."
    b. "I don't think a price cut will help my bottom line any. Sure, I'll sell a bit more, but what I may gain by selling more, I'll more than lose because the price will be lower."
    c. "My customers are real shoppers. Since I cut my prices just a few cents below those my competitors charge, customers have been flocking to my store and sales are booming."
    d. "The economic expansion has done wonders for my sales. With more people back at work, my sales are taking off and I don't even have to reduce my prices!"

21. A fall in the price of X from $6 to $4 causes an increase in the quantity of Y demanded from 900 to 1,1000 units. What is the cross elasticity of demand between X and Y?
   a. 0.5.
   b. −0.5.
   c. 2.0.
   d. −2.0.

22. A movement downward (rightward) along a linear demand curve cause the price elasticity of demand to
   a. fall.
   b. not change.
   c. rise.
   d. first rise and then fall.

23. Beans are an inferior good; chicken is a normal good. Hence, when people's incomes rise, the demand for beans ____ and the demand for chicken ____.
   a. increases; increases
   b. increases; decreases
   c. decreases; increases
   d. decreases; decreases

24. If the long-run supply of wheat is perfectly elastic,
   a. as people's incomes rise, the quantity of wheat supplied decreases.
   b. as the price of corn falls, the quantity of wheat demanded decreases.
   c. in the long run, a large rise in the price of wheat causes no change in the quantity of wheat supplied.
   d. in the long run, a small fall in the price of wheat means that no wheat will be supplied.

25. If a 4 percent rise in the price of peanut butter causes total revenue from sales of peanut butter to fall by 8 percent, the demand for peanut butter
   a. is elastic.
   b. is inelastic.
   c. is unit elastic.
   d. is elastic and has an elasticity of 2.0.

■ Short Answer Problems

1. Why does the elasticity of supply generally increase as more time passes after a price change?
2. You are the manager of a local restaurant. You notice that when you lower the price of your meals, your total revenue rises. What conclusion can you draw about the demand for your restaurant's meals?
3. Assume that the price elasticity of demand for oil is 0.2 in the short run and 0.8 in the long run. To raise the price of oil by 10 percent in the short run, what must be the decrease in the quantity of oil? In the long run, to have a 10 percent rise in the price of oil, what must be the decrease in the quantity of oil?
4. The demand for a product permanently increases. When will the price of the product rise the most: Immediately after the demand change or in the long run? When will the quantity increase the most? Draw a graph to illustrate your answers.
5. Why is the price elasticity of demand for food greater in poor nations than in rich nations?
6. In Figure 5.1, which demand is more elastic between prices P_1 and P_2? (Hint: Use the elasticity formula.)

FIGURE 5.1
Short Answer Problem 6

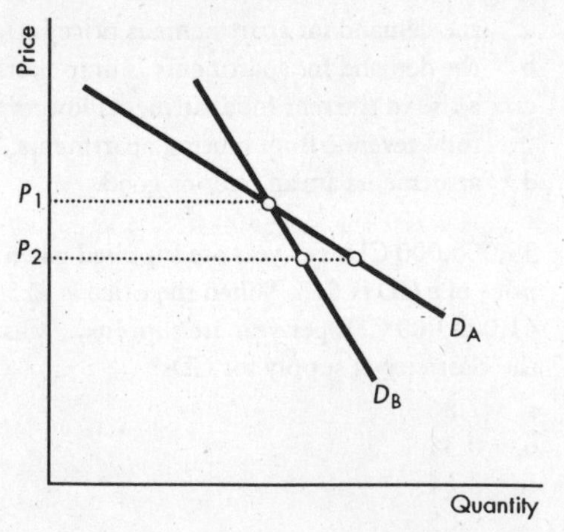

7. Table 5.2 gives eight points on a demand curve for burritos.
   a. Graph this demand curve.
   b. Calculate the price elasticity of demand between $1 and $2, $2 and $3, $3 and $4, $4 and $5, $5 and $6, $6 and $7, and $7 and $8.
   c. In Table 5.2, complete the "Total revenue per week" column.
   d. Based on your answer to part (b), how does the price elasticity of demand change for a movement downward along this demand curve? How does this change relate to your answers in part (c) for total revenue at the different prices?

Table 5.2 The Demand for Burritos

Price (dollars per burrito)	Quantity demanded (burritos per week)	Total revenue per week
$1	100	____
2	90	____
3	80	____
4	70	____
5	60	____
6	50	____
7	40	____
8	30	____

8. Table 5.3 gives eight points on a demand curve for slices of pizza.
   a. Graph this demand curve.
   b. Calculate the price elasticity of demand between $1 and $2, $2 and $3, $3 and $4, $4 and $5, $5 and $6, $6 and $7, and $7 and $8.
   c. Complete the "Total revenue per week" column in Table 5.3.
   d. Based on your answers to parts (b) and (c), how does the total revenue per week relate to the price elasticity of demand at the different prices?

Table 5.3 The Demand For Pizza

Price (dollars per slice of pizza)	Quantity demanded (slices of pizza per week)	Total revenue per week
$1	100	____
2	50	____
3	33.3	____
4	25	____
5	20	____
6	16.7	____
7	14.3	____
8	12.5	____

9. Perhaps because of a rise in costs, suppose that the supply curve for paperback books shifts vertically upward by $1; that is, for every possible quantity, the new supply curve lies above the old supply curve by $1.
   a. If the demand for paperback books is perfectly elastic, by how much does the price of a paperback book rise? Draw a figure to illustrate your answer. (Hint: You do *not* need to know the initial equilibrium price of a paperback book to answer this question.)
   b. If the demand for paperback books is perfectly inelastic, by how much does the price of a paperback book rise? Draw a figure to illustrate this situation. (Hint: Again, you do *not* need to know the initial equilibrium price of a paperback book to answer this question.
   c. Based on your answers to parts (a) and (b), when will a rise in costs raise the price of a product the most: When demand is elastic or when it is inelastic? When will it decrease the quantity the most: When demand is elastic or inelastic?

10. Explain what perfectly elastic demand for a product represents. Sketch an example of a demand curve for such a product. When will the demand for a product be perfectly elastic? Be sure to use the notion of substitutes in your answer.

11. Sketch a typical set of momentary, short-run, and long-run supply curves. Explain why the elasticity of supply is different along each curve.

■ You're the Teacher

1. "How can I use the price elasticity of demand formula to calculate the price elasticity of demand? Also, how can I determine how much a decrease in quantity boosts the price or how much a price change affects the quantity demanded?"

2. "The whole idea of 'elasticity' is unnecessarily complicated! Take the price elasticity of demand; it tries to measure how strongly demanders respond to a price change. But the slope of the demand curve shows us that. The flatter the demand curve, the more consumers react to a price change. Clearly, economists should just use the slope of the demand curve as their measure of 'elasticity.' " Correct the error in this analysis.

Answers

True/False Answers

1. **F** The slope of the demand curve equals $\Delta P/\Delta Q$, whereas the price elasticity of demand equals $(\Delta Q/Q_{ave})/(\Delta P/P_{ave})$.
2. **F** Moving down the demand curve the price elasticity of demand falls.
3. **T** The smallest value for the price elasticity of demand, 0, reflects perfectly inelastic demand; the largest, ∞, indicates perfectly elastic demand.
4. **T** Other brands of gasoline, such as Shell or Amoco, are close substitutes for Exxon gasoline, so the demand for Exxon gasoline is likely to be elastic.
5. **U** If the price elasticity of demand for the product is inelastic, to raise total revenue the price should be raised; however, if it is elastic, the price should be lowered.
6. **F** Demand is elastic when the price elasticity of demand exceeds 1.0.
7. **T** This is the intuitive meaning of elasticity. The stronger the response to a price change, the greater is the elasticity.
8. **F** As more time passes, more changes in demand can occur, so demand becomes *more* elastic.
9. **T** The elasticity of supply generally is largest for the long-run supply curve and smallest for the momentary supply curve.
10. **F** To be elastic, the *price* elasticity of demand must exceed 1.0.
11. **T** In poor nations food takes a larger portion of consumer spending, so the price elasticity of demand is larger.
12. **T** Hot dogs and hot dog buns are complements, so the cross elasticity of demand is negative.
13. **T** Generally, the larger the total budget share spent on a product, the greater is the price elasticity of demand.
14. **F** The demand for Domino's Pizza is elastic, so rising the price decreases the quantity by so much that total revenue declines.
15. **T** An increase in income decreases the demand for inferior goods and increases it for normal goods.

Multiple Choice Answers

1. **d** If the demand is unit price elastic, a change in the price of the product creates an offsetting change in the quantity demanded so that total revenue does not change.
2. **a** The price elasticity of is demand equal to $(\%\Delta Q_D)/(\%\Delta P)$, or $2\%/10\% = 0.2$.
3. **d** Food is a normal good, so its income elasticity is positive but less than 1.0.
4. **a** A product whose demand curve is vertical is a product with perfectly inelastic demand, that is, with a price elasticity of demand of zero.
5. **a** The income elasticity of demand equals $(\%\Delta Q_D)/(\%\Delta Y)$, where Y is income. In this case it equals $-3\%/10\%$ or -0.3.
6. **c** The price elasticity of demand equals 0.1, or in terms of a formula $(\%\Delta Q_D)/(\%\Delta P) = 0.1$. The $\%\Delta Q_D$ must equal the change in the quantity supplied, so rearranging this gives: $\%\Delta Q = (0.1)(\%\Delta P) = (0.1)(20\%) = 2\%$.
7. **b** The price elasticity of demand between two points equals $(\Delta Q/Q_{ave})/(\Delta P/P_{ave})$. In this case we get $(10/50)/(\$2/\$20) = 2$.
8. **b** "Perfectly elastic" means that a very small rise in the price causes the quantity demanded to decrease to 0, which is the situation with a horizontal demand curve.
9. **c** As time passes, substituting additional factors into the production process becomes easier, so supply becomes more elastic.
10. **d** The cross elasticity of demand is positive for substitutes. Beef and chicken are substitutes, so their cross elasticity of demand is positive.
11. **c** Price elasticity of demand equals $\%\Delta Q/\%\Delta P$. Rearranging this formula gives: $\%\Delta P = (\%\Delta Q)/(\text{elasticity of demand})$. Thus $\%\Delta P$ equals $(8\%)/(2.0) = 4.00\%$.
12. **d** If there are no close substitutes, demanders continue to buy the product even if its price is boosted substantially, which means that the demand is inelastic.
13. **d** An increase in income increases the demand for a normal good.
14. **c** If the demand is inelastic, the percentage rise in price exceeds the percentage decrease in the quantity demanded, so total revenue from sales of the good increases.

15. **d** If the income elasticity is negative, the product is an inferior good.
16. **b** Analogous to the price elasticity of demand, the elasticity of supply is defined as $(\Delta Q/Q_{ave})/(\Delta P/P_{ave})$, or (2,000,000/40,000,000)/($2/$14)= 0.35.
17. **d** There are many more substitutes for a new Ford Mustang than for the other goods. This answer is an example of the proposition that the more narrowly defined a good, the larger is its price elasticity of demand.
18. **c** The cross elasticity of demand is defined as $\%\Delta Q/\%\Delta P$ where the "quantity" refers to Coca Cola and the "price" to Pepsi. Hence the cross elasticity of demand equals 50%/10% = 5.0.
19. **b** When the demand is elastic, the percentage increase in the quantity demanded exceeds the percentage drop in the price, so total revenue rises.
20. **c** This statement describes a situation whereby a small cut in price increased the quantity demanded substantially, which means that the demand is elastic.
21. **b** The cross elasticity of demand is calculated as $(\Delta Q/Q_{ave})/(\Delta P/P_{ave})$, in which the "quantity" refers to good Y and the "price" to good X. Hence (200/1,000)/(–$2/$5) = –0.5.
22. **a** Moving down a linear demand curve, the price elasticity of demand falls in value.
23. **c** For an inferior good an increase in income decreases demand; for a normal good an increase in income increases demand.
24. **d** Perfectly elastic supply implies that small changes in price have *huge* changes in the quantity supplied, so a small drop in price decreases the quantity of wheat supplied to 0.
25. **a** When demand is elastic, a rise in the price of the product decreases the quantity demanded so much that total revenue falls.

Answers to Short Answer Problems

1. The elasticity of supply increases as time passes after a price change because substituting additional factors into the production process becomes easier. For instance, to meet a permanent increase in the demand for automobiles, initially automakers may only be able to add an additional shift of workers at existing factories. But, with the passage of time, the companies can make larger changes, such as building more factories. As more capacity is added, more cars will be manufactured, increasing the elasticity of supply.
2. The demand for your restaurant's meals is elastic. Why? When the demand is elastic, a fall in price raises total revenue, which is precisely what you have observed.
3. Price elasticity of demand = $(\%\Delta Q)/(\%\Delta P)$, or by rearranging this formula, we see that (Price elasticity of demand)$(\%\Delta P) = (\%\Delta Q)$. The desired price rise is 10 percent, so we calculate the amount by which the quantity must be restricted in the short run as (0.2) × (10%) = 2%. Thus, in the short run, supply must be decreased by (only) 2%. In the long run, the price elasticity of demand is 0.8, so the decrease in the supply is (0.8) × (10%) = 8%. In order to raise the price by 10%, the long-run decrease in supply must be four times the short-run decrease.

FIGURE **5.2**

Short Answer Problem 4

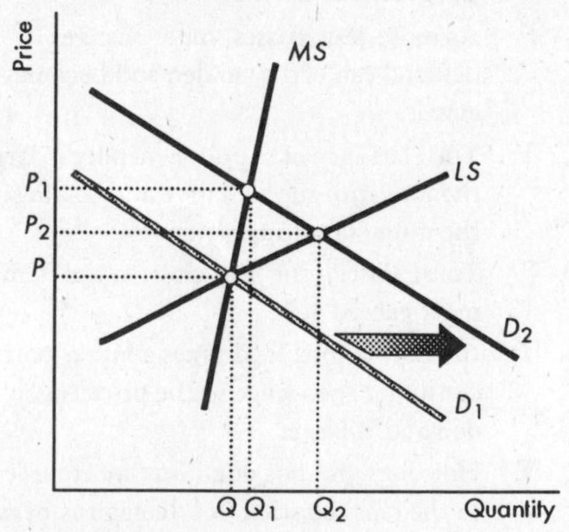

4. The price of the product rises the most immediately after the increase in demand, and the quantity increases the most in the long run. These changes are illustrated in Figure 5.2. Here the demand curve increases from D_1 to D_2. Immediately after the increase, the price rises from

P to P_1 and the quantity increases from Q to Q_1. In the long run, supply becomes more elastic and so the price rises ultimately only to P_2 and the quantity all the way to Q_2.

5. The larger the fraction of their income consumers spend on a product, the greater the price elasticity of demand. People in poor nations spend a larger proportion of their income on food than do people in wealthy nations, so the price elasticity of demand for food is larger in poor nations.

6. D_A is more elastic than D_B. To see why, recall the formula for the price elasticity of demand:

$$\frac{\%\Delta \text{ quantity demanded}}{\%\Delta \text{ price}}$$

Along both demand curves, the percentage change in the price from P_1 to P_2 is the same. But Figure 5.3 shows that the percentage change in the quantity demanded is greater along D_A where the quantity demanded increases from Q to Q_A, whereas along D_B the quantity demanded increases only to Q_B. Because the percentage increase in the quantity demanded is greater along D_A the price elasticity of demand over this price range is larger for D_A.

FIGURE 5.3
Short Answer Problem 6

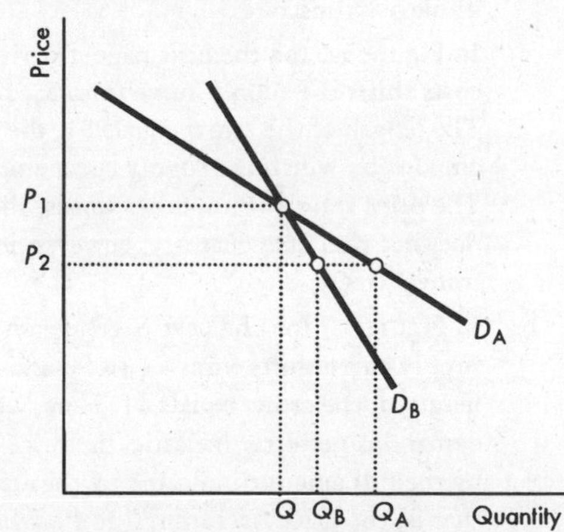

7. a. Figure 5.4 shows the demand curve.

b. Table 5.4 contains the price elasticities of demand. Take the elasticity between \$1 and \$2 as an example. The elasticity of demand is $(\Delta Q/Q_{ave})/(\Delta P/P_{ave})$, which in this case gives (10/95)/(\$1/\$1.50) = 0.16.

c. The total revenues are given in Table 5.5. For

FIGURE 5.4
Short Answer Problem 7 (a)

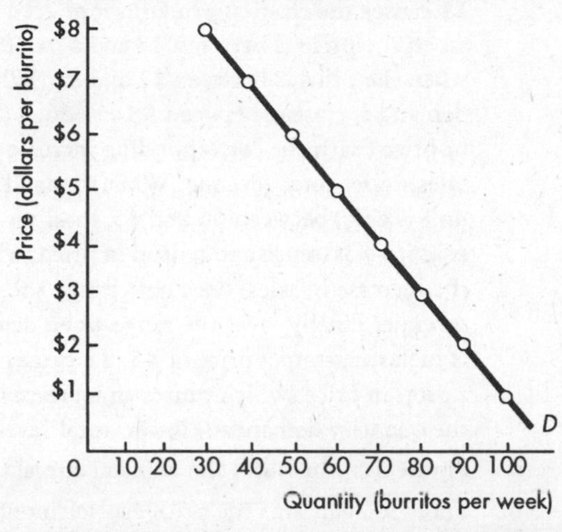

Table 5.4 Short Answer Problem 7 (b)

Prices	Elasticity
\$1 to \$2	0.16
2 to 3	0.29
3 to 4	0.47
4 to 5	0.69
5 to 6	1.00
6 to 7	1.44
7 to 8	2.14

Table 5.5 Short Answer Problem 7 (c)

Price	Total Revenue
\$1	\$100
2	180
3	240
4	280
5	300
6	300
7	280
8	240

example, at a price of $6 total revenue equals $P \times Q$, so $6 × 50 = $300.

d. Moving down the demand curve from $8 to $1 causes the elasticity to fall, from 2.14 when the price is between $8 and $7 to 0.16 when the price is between $2 and $1. When demand is elastic, between $8 and $6, a drop in price (with the corresponding increase in sales) raises total revenue. When demand is unit elastic, between $6 and $5, total revenue is at its maximum and a drop in price (with the increase in sales) does not change the total revenue. Finally, over the range when demand is inelastic, from a price of $5 to a price of $1, a drop in price (which causes an increase in the quantity demanded) lowers total revenue.

8. a. Figure 5.5 illustrates the demand curve.

b. Table 5.6 contains the price elasticities of demand. For example at a price of between $4 and $5, the price elasticity of demand, $(\Delta Q/Q_{ave})/(\Delta P/P_{ave})$, equals (5/22.5)/($1/$4.50) = 1.00.

c. Total revenues are in Table 5.7. Total revenue equals $P \times Q$. Thus, to calculate the total revenue at a price of, say, $2, multiply the price times the quantity, or ($2)(50) = $100.

d. This price elasticity of demand along this demand curve always equals 1.00. In other words, this demand is always unit elastic.

FIGURE 5.5
Short Answer Problem 8 (a)

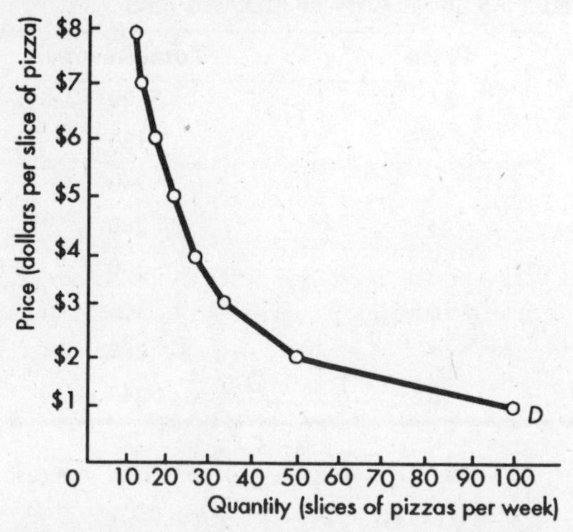

Table 5.6 Short Answer Problem 8 (b)

Prices	Elasticity
$1 to $2	1.00
2 to 3	1.00
3 to 4	1.00
4 to 5	1.00
5 to 6	1.00
6 to 7	1.00
7 to 8	1.00

Table 5.7 Short Answer Problem 8 (c)

Price	Total Revenue
$1	$100
2	100
3	100
4	100
5	100
6	100
7	100
8	100

With unit elasticity, changes in price do not change total revenue, which is precisely what Table 5.7 illustrates.

9. a. In Figure 5.6 (on the next page) the rise in costs shifts the supply curve from S_A to S_B. The length of the arrow equals $1, the amount by which the supply curve shifts up. The price stays at P; in other words, the price does not rise. The quantity, however decreases from Q to Q_B.

b. In Figure 5.7 (on the next page), again the supply curve shifts from S_A to S_B and the length of the arrow equals $1. Here, when the demand is perfectly inelastic, the price rises by the full amount indicated by the arrow; that is, the price rises from P to P_B which is a rise of exactly $1. The quantity, however, remains constant at Q.

c. As Figures 5.6 and 5.7 show, the rise in costs raises the price the most when demand is inelastic. When demand is perfectly inelastic, the price rises by the full amount of the rise in costs. Then, as demand becomes more

FIGURE 5.6
Short Answer Problem 9 (a)

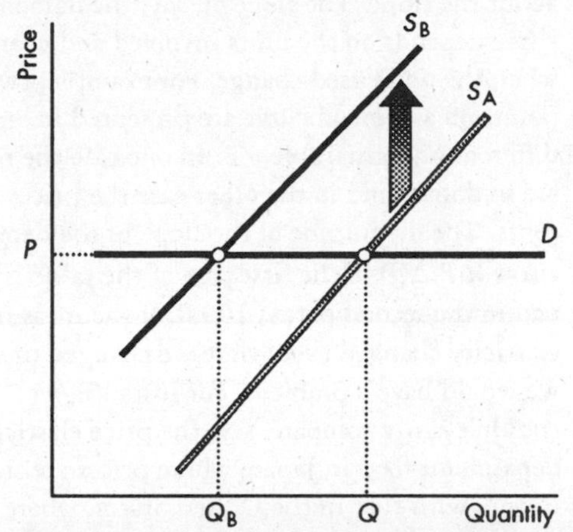

FIGURE 5.7
Short Answer Problem 9 (b)

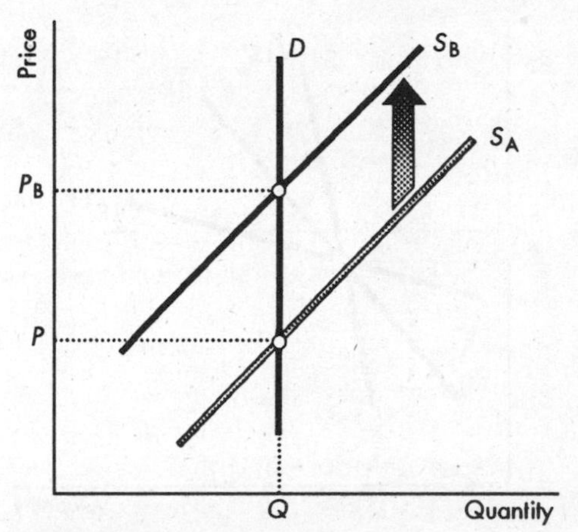

elastic, the price rises by less. At the other extreme, when demand is perfectly elastic, the price does not rise. The quantity decreases most when demand is perfectly elastic. As demand becomes less elastic, the size of the change in the quantity shrinks.

10. A perfectly elastic demand is illustrated in Figure 5.8. Demand is perfectly elastic when demanders can find perfect substitutes for a product. For example, consider corn grown by one farmer. Other farmers' corn is a perfect substitute for the first farmer's corn. If there are perfect substitutes for the product, even the smallest rise in the price of the product causes the quantity demanded to decrease to 0. The horizontal line in Figure 5.8 indicates that any boost in the price above *P* will decrease the quantity demanded to 0.
11. Figure 5.9 (on the next page) shows a typical set of momentary (*MS*), short-run (*SR*), and long-run (*LR*) supply curves. The elasticity of supply is the smallest along the momentary supply curve and greatest along the long-run supply curve. These curves illustrate the point that, as more time passes after a price change, introducing additional factors into the production process is easier. Immediately after a price hike from *P* to P_A, firms find it very hard to change the amount of inputs they use, so the quantity supplied does not change by much, as shown by the relatively inelastic momentary supply curve. But as more time passes, more and different inputs can be utilized or constructed, so the quantity supplied increases. Hence, as shown in the diagram, the short-run supply curve is more elastic than the momentary supply curve, and the long-run supply curve is the most elastic.

FIGURE 5.8
Short Answer Problem 10

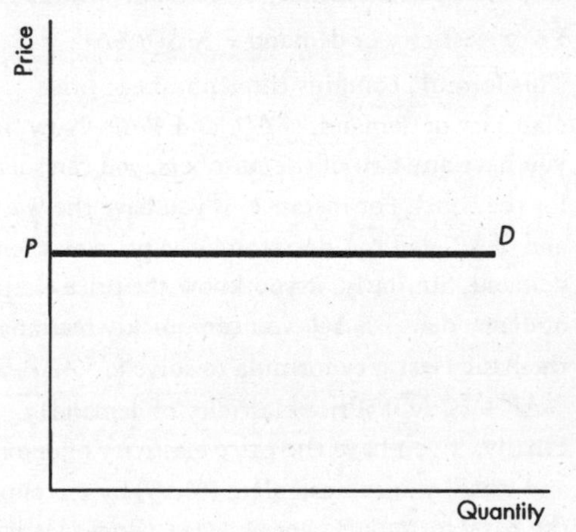

FIGURE **5.9**

Short Answer Problem 11

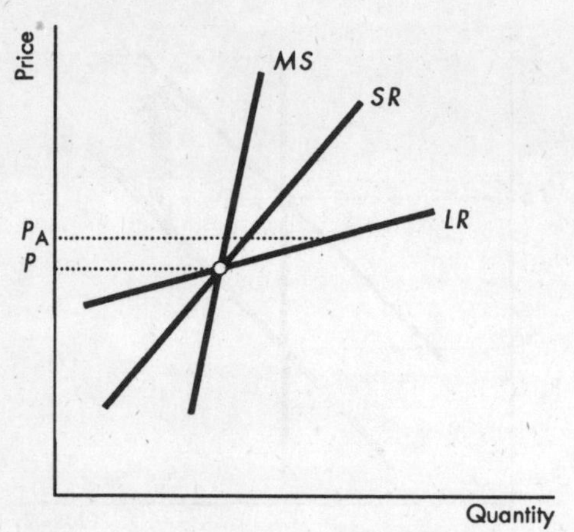

You're the Teacher

1. "This not so hard if you think about it the right way! The price elasticity of demand formula is:

   Price elasticity of demand = $\%\Delta Q/\%\Delta P$.

   This formula contains three numbers: price elasticity of demand, $\%\Delta Q$, and $\%\Delta P$. Now, if you have any two of the numbers, you can solve for the third. For instance, if you have the $\%\Delta Q$ and $\%\Delta P$, you can determine the price elasticity of demand. Similarly, if you know the price elasticity of demand and $\%\Delta Q$, you can quickly rearrange the basic elasticity formula to solve for $\%\Delta P$, as $\%\Delta P = (\%\Delta Q)$/(Price elasticity of demand). Finally, if you have the price elasticity of demand and $\%\Delta P$, you can calculate ($\%\Delta Q$) by rearranging the basic formula to get $\%\ \Delta Q$ = (Price elasticity of demand) × ($\%\ \Delta P$). That's all there is to it!"

2. "You're right: All 'elasticity' tries to do is measure how strongly a relationship responds to some sort of change, but you're missing an important point about the slope. The slope of, say, the demand curve depends on the units involved and changes when the units used change. For example, two points on a demand curve are presented in different units in Table 5.8. In one case the prices are in dollars and in the other case the prices are in cents. The magnitude of the slope of the demand curve ($\Delta P/\Delta Q$) in the first part of the table is 1.00 and in the second part is 100.0. If the measure of elasticity changed every time we changed units, we would have a problem. For instance, we couldn't easily compare, say, the price elasticity of demand for food in Japan, where prices are stated in yen, with that in the United States, where they are stated in dollars. Using percentages, however, avoids this problem. In each of the two columns, the price elasticity of demand is the same: 0.14. That's why percentages are used in the elasticity formulas."

Table 5.8 You're the Teacher Question 2

Price	Quantity	Price	Quantity
$1.00	10	100¢	10
2.00	11	200	11

Chapter 6 MARKETS IN ACTION

Key Concepts

Housing Markets and Rent Ceilings

The response of the housing market to shocks depends on whether the market is regulated. Suppose that the supply decreases, perhaps because of an earthquake. In an unregulated market:

- In the short run the equilibrium rent rises and there is no shortage. This outcome is demonstrated in Figure 6.1, which shows what happened in San Francisco after the 1906 earthquake. Rents rose from $16 to $20 and the equilibrium quantity of apartments decreased to 74,000 units.

FIGURE **6.1**
The Housing Market in San Francisco

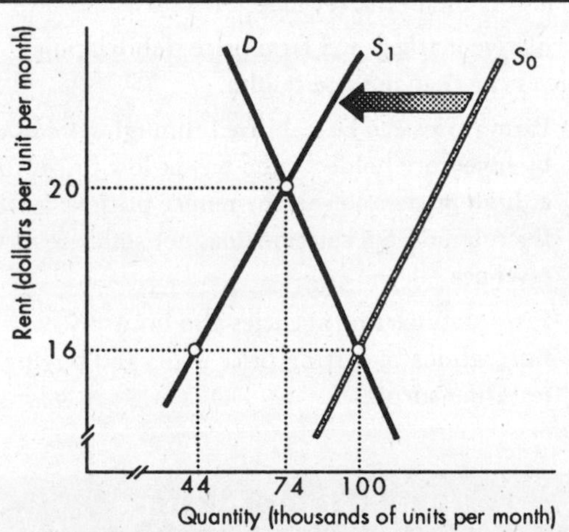

The higher rent encourages building activity, so as time passes the supply curve shifts rightward.

- In the long run the rent and quantity of apartments rented return to their original levels.

In a regulated housing market, a rent ceiling makes raising rents illegal.

- In the short run, rent stays at $16 and a shortage of 56,000 units (100,000 demanded minus 44,000 supplied) emerges.
- There is no incentive to build new housing, so in the long run the shortage persists.

Shortages cause

- *search activity* — renters look for available apartments.
- *black markets* — illegal payments in excess of rent ceilings.

The total cost of housing in regulated markets includes the cost of search and any payments made on the black market.

The Labor Market and Minimum Wages

In an unregulated labor market a decrease in the demand for labor results in a lower wage rate.

Labor markets can be regulated with **minimum wage laws**. Minimum wage laws make hiring workers below the specified wage rate illegal.

In a regulated labor market, when the demand for labor decreases:

- Minimum wage laws create an excess supply of labor.
- The quantity of workers hired is less than in an unregulated labor market.
- Unemployed workers search for work paying the minimum wage and persistent unemployment results.
- Minimum wage laws contribute to high unemployment among low-skilled and younger workers.

Taxes

A sales tax on a good shifts its supply curve vertically upward by a distance equal to the amount of the tax. The equilibrium price, including the tax, rises and the equilibrium quantity decreases, as illustrated in Figure

6.2. After the tax is imposed, the equilibrium quantity decreases to Q_t and the equilibrium price paid by buyers rises to P_t (sellers keep P_t minus the tax).

FIGURE **6.2**
Effect of a Tax

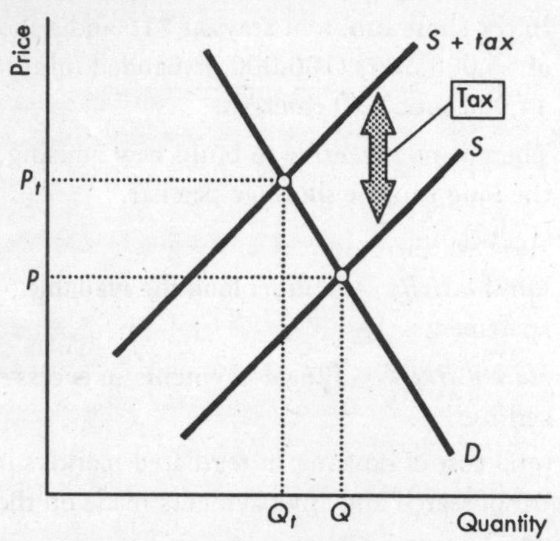

The question of who pays the tax depends on the elasticities of supply and demand. The more inelastic the demand, the more demanders pay of the tax:

- Perfectly inelastic demand — buyers pay all the tax.
- Perfectly elastic demand — sellers pay all the tax.

The more inelastic the supply, the more sellers pay of the tax:

- Perfectly inelastic supply — sellers pay all the tax.
- Perfectly elastic supply — buyers pay all the tax.

Generally, products with inelastic demands are heavily taxed because the tax does not reduce the quantity purchased by as much as if goods with elastic demands are taxed.

Markets for Prohibited Goods

The purchase and sale of some goods is prohibited. Penalties can be levied on sellers and/or buyers.

If sellers are penalized:

- The cost of selling the product rises, so the supply curve shifts leftward.
- These penalties boost the price and reduce the quantity.

If buyers are penalized:

- The perceived benefits from the product fall, so the demand curve shifts leftward.
- These penalties cause a fall in the price and a decrease in the quantity.

If buyers and sellers are each penalized:

- Both the demand and supply curve shift leftward.
- The quantity definitely falls. The price rises if the supply curve shift is larger and falls and the demand curve shift is larger.

A policy of decriminalizing and then taxing the product may be able to achieve same consumption levels as prohibition. Problems with this policy are:

- The required tax rate may be high, leading to substantial tax evasion.
- Legalization may send the wrong signal to potential consumers.

Stabilizing Farm Revenue

The demand for farm products is inelastic; hence variations in the harvest can cause wide price and revenue swings. In an unregulated market, a poor harvest leads to a large rise in price and raises total farm revenue; a bumper crop causes a large fall in price and lowers total farm revenue.

Speculative markets and farm price stabilization policies can change these results.

- Farm prices can be stabilized through *speculation* by inventory holders, who buy at low prices to sell at high prices and thereby reduce price fluctuations. Speculation does not stabilize farm revenues.
- Farm stabilization agencies also limit price fluctuations by setting price floors and buying any resulting surpluses.

Helpful Hints

1. Governments often attempt to regulate markets by imposing price constraints of one form or another. Studying government regulation leads to a deeper appreciation of how markets work when, by contrast, the government does not affect the normal operation of markets.

Whenever some influence disturbs an equilibrium in an unregulated (free) market, the differing desires of buyers and sellers are brought back into balance by price movements. If prices are controlled by government regulation, however, the price mechanism no longer can serve this purpose. Thus balance must be restored in some other way. In the case of price ceilings, black markets are likely to emerge. If black markets cannot develop because of strict enforcement of the price ceiling, demanders will be forced to bear the costs of increased search activity, waiting in line, or some other activity.

Economists have made the point that price ceilings, by creating increased search and other unproductive allocation schemes, waste society's scarce resources. For instance, with rent controls, would-be apartment dwellers, fruitlessly driving around the city searching for an apartment accomplish nothing from a social perspective. The time and energy that these people dissipate in futile search activity creates nothing socially useful.

In addition, economists also have pointed out that price ceilings deliver the wrong signals to suppliers. In particular, rent controls mean that apartment owners receive the wrong signals. In a free market, a shortage of apartments causes rents to be driven higher. Higher rents give apartment owners the incentive to increase the number of apartments they rent, which helps overcome the initial shortage.

With effective rent controls, however, rents do not rise. Instead, unsuccessful search activity on the part of renters occurs. Apartment owners do not profit from this increased search. As a result, they have no incentive to increase the scale of their operations and so they do nothing to help eliminate the initial shortage. Thus rent controls cause apartment shortages to persist indefinitely.

2. This chapter discusses government price constraints in three specific markets: rental housing, labor, and farm products. The principles raised in these discussions, however, can be generalized to other markets.

   In *any* market with a legal price ceiling set below the market-clearing price, a shortage will occur because the price cannot rise to eliminate it. Consequently, consumers are willing to engage in costly activities such as search, waiting lines, and black market transactions in order to obtain the good. Lines (queues) were a common sight in the former Soviet Union where prices were controlled by the government at artificially low levels. Furthermore, allowing the price to rise in response to a decrease in supply or an increase in demand, as occurs in a free market, yields incentives for suppliers to produce more and demanders to purchase less. In the short run, these effects are the movements along the supply and demand curves that eliminate any shortage or surplus. In the long run, these effects drive the market to a new long-run equilibrium; that is, these are the incentive effects that shift the demand and/or supply curves to their new long-run positions. Thus the examples in the text do not apply only to housing, labor, and agricultural markets. They are general in nature and apply to any market with government intervention of the type discussed here.

3. The division of who pays a sales tax is called *tax incidence*. Who pays a sales tax imposed on producers depends on the elasticities of demand and supply. As the textbook makes clear, the general principles of tax incidence are:

   - The more inelastic the demand, the more consumers pay.
   - The more elastic the demand, the more producers pay.
   - The more inelastic the supply, the more producers pay.
   - The more elastic the supply, the more consumers pay.

   While you should remember these results, the intuition behind them may prove powerful. Let's first consider how the demand elasticity affects the division of the tax. Suppliers always want to pass all of the tax along to buyers in the form of a higher price. But, if the demand for the product is very elastic, consumers can easily find good substitutes for the product being taxed. So, if producers tried to stick demanders with a large part of the tax, buyers would immediately substitute other products and suppliers would find themselves unable to sell anything. In this case, suppliers are going to absorb a large portion of the tax. However, if the demand for the good is inelastic, demanders cannot readily find anything to take the product's place. Producers therefore are able to raise the price and demanders, unable to locate a substitute, continue to buy the good. In this situation, consumers are going to pay a large part of the tax.

Similar reasoning applies to the elasticity of supply. If the supply is very elastic, producers can readily find other products to produce. Hence, if buyers want to consume the good being taxed, they will have to pay most of the tax. However, if the supply is inelastic, producers cannot easily switch to producing another product. Buyers, never eager to pay any of the tax, do not have to pay much in this case because suppliers can't find anything else to produce.

Thus, in general, the more elastic the demand, the more flexible are consumers and the less tax they have to pay. Similarly, the more elastic the supply, the more flexible are producers and the less tax they have to pay.

Questions

True/False/Uncertain and Explain

1. In an unregulated housing market, higher rents increase the quantity of housing supplied.

2. The more elastic demand is for a product, the larger is the fraction of a sales tax paid by consumers.

3. With a rent ceiling, there is no way to allocate apartments among potential renters.

4. Suppose that price controls are holding the price of elbow grease below its equilibrium level. When controls are abolished and the price rises, the quantity of elbow grease sold decreases.

5. If demand for a farm product is inelastic, in the absence of speculation or government programs, a crop failure lowers farmers' total income.

6. Imposing penalties on both buyers and sellers of an illegal product causes its price to rise.

7. If the minimum wage is above the equilibrium wage, raising the minimum wage decreases the number of workers employed.

8. Levying a sales tax on a product shifts its supply curve downward by the amount of the tax.

9. Decriminalizing a product may send the message that its use is now officially approved.

10. In an unregulated labor market, a decrease in the demand for low-skilled labor causes a fall in the wage rate for low-skilled workers.

11. If the demand for Exxon gasoline is perfectly elastic, imposing a tax on Exxon gasoline causes a rise in the price of Exxon gasoline.

12. If the current price is higher than a speculator's expected future price, the speculator sells goods from inventory.

13. Farm stabilization agencies generally create large shortages of farm products.

14. Time spent searching is part of the opportunity cost of buying a product.

15. Buyers always pay a larger fraction of a sales tax than sellers.

Multiple Choice

1. The short-run supply curve for rental housing is positively sloped because
   a. the supply of housing is fixed in the short run.
   b. the current stock of buildings will be used more intensively as rents rise.
   c. the cost of constructing new buildings rises as the number of buildings increases.
   d. new buildings will be constructed as rents rise.

FIGURE **6.3**
Multiple Choice Question 2

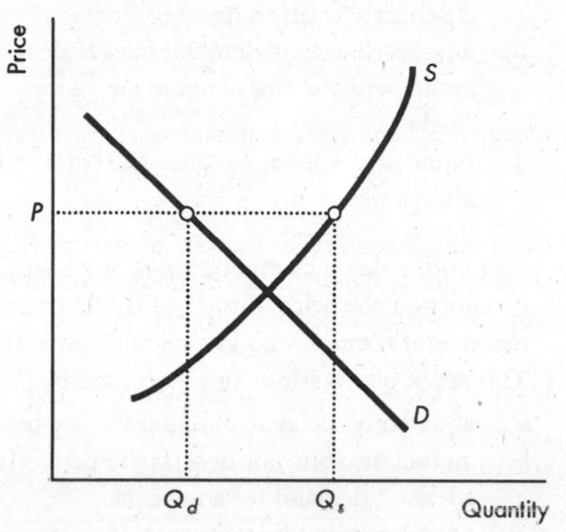

FIGURE **6.4**
Multiple Choice Questions 5, 6, and 7

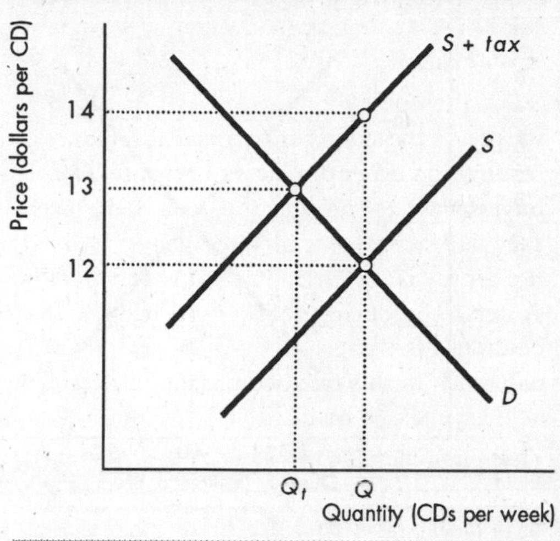

2. Refer to Figure 6.3. By setting a price floor of *P*, the government causes a
   a. shortage equal to $Q_s - Q_d$.
   b. shortage equal to Q_d.
   c. surplus equal to $Q_s - Q_d$.
   d. surplus equal to Q_s.

3. Speculators try to buy when the current price is
   a. higher than the future expected price.
   b. equal to the future expected price.
   c. lower than the future expected price.
   d. None of the above because the future expected price has nothing to do with when speculators buy.

4. Suppose that the government sets a price ceiling on pizza that is below the equilibrium price of a pizza. Then, there is
   a. a shortage of pizza.
   b. a surplus of pizza.
   c. no shortage of pizza because the existing firms will expand their production to meet the increased quantity demanded.
   d. no shortage of pizza because new firms will enter the market to meet the increase in the quantity demanded.

5. In Figure 6,4, what is the amount of the tax on CDs?
   a. $14 per CD.
   b. $13 per CD.
   c. $2 per CD.
   d. $1 per CD.

6. In Figure 6.4, how much of the tax is paid by demanders?
   a. $14 per CD.
   b. $13 per CD.
   c. $2 per CD.
   d. $1 per CD.

7. In Figure 6.4, how much of the tax is paid by suppliers?
   a. $14 per CD.
   b. $13 per CD.
   c. $2 per CD.
   d. $1 per CD.

8. If sanctions are imposed on sellers but not users of a prohibited good, the
   a. price falls and the quantity decreases.
   b. price rises and the quantity increases.
   c. price rises and the quantity decreases.
   d. price falls and the quantity increases.

FIGURE **6.5**
Multiple Choice Questions 9 and 10

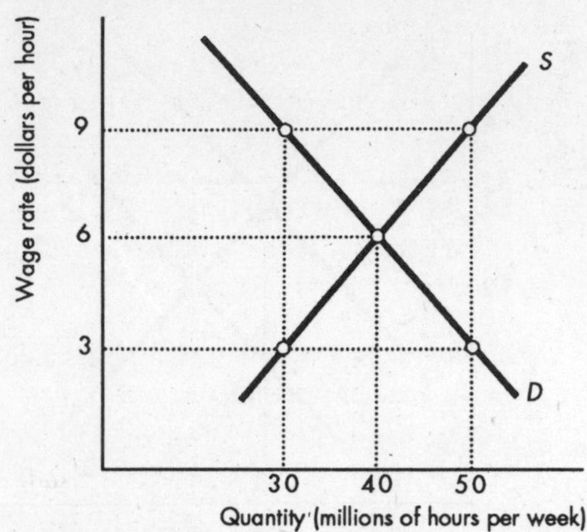

9. In Figure 6.5, if the minimum wage is set at $3 per hour, what is the level of unemployment in millions of hours?
   a. 50.
   b. 40.
   c. 20.
   d. 0.

10. In Figure 6.5, if the minimum wage is set at $9 per hour, what is the level of unemployment in millions of hours?
    a. 50.
    b. 40.
    c. 20.
    d. 0.

11. In an unregulated market, which of the following will <u>NOT</u> happen as result of the sudden destruction of a large proportion of the stock of housing?
    a. Higher rental prices.
    b. A shortage of rental housing.
    c. More basement apartments offered for rent.
    d. More families sharing living quarters.

12. Suppose that the government imposes a $1 tax on Frisbees and that the price of Frisbees does not change. This outcome is consistent with
    a. a perfectly elastic supply of Frisbees.
    b. a perfectly elastic demand for Frisbees.
    c. an upward sloping demand curve for Frisbees.
    d. None of the above because the price will always rise.

13. You notice that a bumper crop of soy beans has no effect on the price of soy beans and that the incomes of farmers who grow soy beans increase. This set of observations can be caused by
    a. a perfectly inelastic demand for soy beans.
    b. an inelastic but not necessarily perfectly inelastic demand for soy beans.
    c. speculators holding inventories of soy beans.
    d. soy beans and soy sauce being joint products.

14. The tax incidence on consumers is largest when
    a. demand is perfectly elastic.
    b. demand is inelastic but not perfectly inelastic.
    c. demand is perfectly inelastic.
    d. supply is perfectly inelastic.

15. Which of the following is <u>NOT</u> a likely outcome of rent ceilings?
    a. A black market for rent-controlled housing.
    b. Long waiting lists of potential renters of rent-controlled housing.
    c. A short-run shortage of housing.
    d. Black market rents below the ceiling rent.

16. The European Union countries have been accumulating butter mountains and wine lakes. These surpluses are caused by
    a. floor prices for agricultural products that are below equilibrium market prices.
    b. floor prices for agricultural products that are above equilibrium market prices.
    c. ceiling prices for agricultural products that are below equilibrium market prices.
    d. ceiling prices for agricultural products that are above equilibrium market prices.

FIGURE 6.6
Multiple Choice Questions 18 and 19

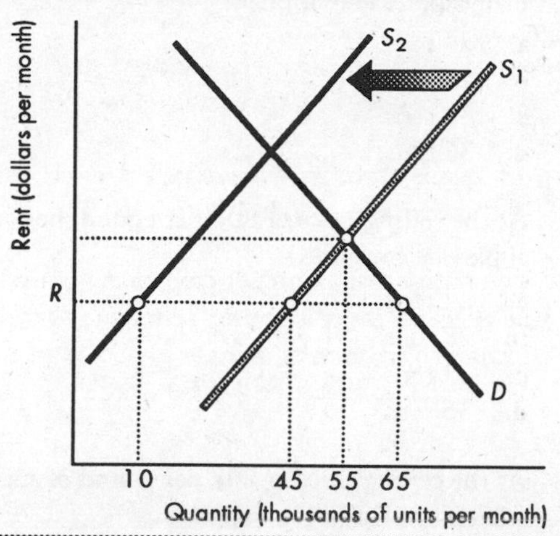

17. In Figure 6.6, with the supply curve of housing S_1 and with a rent ceiling of R, there is a
   a. surplus of 20,000 units a month.
   b. shortage of 65,000 units a month.
   c. shortage of 55,000 units a month.
   d. shortage of 20,000 units a month.

18. In Figure 6.6, a disaster strikes so that the supply curve shifts to S_2. If the rent ceiling remains at R, there is a
   a. shortage of 65,000 units a month.
   b. shortage of 55,000 units a month.
   c. shortage of 20,000 units a month.
   d. shortage of 10,000 units a month.

19. Which of the following types of labor would be most significantly affected by a rise in the legal minimum wage?
   a. Professional athletes.
   b. Young, low-skilled workers.
   c. Skilled union workers.
   d. University professors.

20. What is a black market?
   a. A market where legal transactions take place at prices lower than the government imposed price ceiling.
   b. A market where illegal transactions take place at prices higher than the government imposed price ceiling.
   c. A legal market where buyers and sellers search for each other.
   d. A market where the lights are not turned on.

21. Which of the following combinations would yield the greatest price fluctuation?
   a. Large supply shifts and inelastic demand.
   b. Large supply shifts and elastic demand.
   c. Large supply shifts and perfectly elastic demand.
   d. Small supply shifts and elastic demand.

22. Suppose that the government imposes a minimum wage that is *above* the equilibrium wage rate for low-skilled workers. When will more workers be employed?
   a. When the minimum wage is in effect.
   b. When the minimum wage is NOT in effect.
   c. The level of employment is the same regardless of the presence or absence of this minimum wage.
   d. The question cannot be answered without knowledge of the actual amounts of the minimum wage and equilibrium wage rate.

23. The more elastic the supply, the
   a. more likely the government is to tax the product.
   b. more likely the government is to impose a price ceiling.
   c. smaller the fraction of any tax imposed on the product will be paid by the suppliers.
   d. more elastic is the demand.

24. Speculation
   a. always raises the price paid by consumers of the product.
   b. always lowers the price received by supplier of the product.
   c. can help limit fluctuations in the price of the product.
   d. Both answers (a) and (b) are correct.

25. Suppose that the government wants to discourage the use of cigarettes. If it imposes a tax on cigarettes, the equilibrium quantity falls the most when the elasticity of demand equals
   a. 2.00.
   b. 1.00.
   c. 0.50.
   d. 0.

For the next five questions, use Table 6.1, which shows the supply and demand schedules for apples.

Table 6.1 Multiple Choice Questions 26, 27, 28, 29, 30

Price (dollars per pound)	Quantity demanded (tons per year)	Quantity supplied (tons per year)
$1.20	20	32
1.10	24	30
1.00	28	28
0.90	32	26
0.80	36	24
0.70	40	22

26. What is the equilibrium price of an apple?
   a. $1.20 per pound.
   b. $1.00 per pound
   c. $0.80 per pound.
   d. $0.60 per pound.

27. What is the equilibrium quantity of apples?
   a. 24 tons.
   b. 28 tons.
   c. 32 tons.
   d. 36 tons.

28. Suppose that the government imposes a price ceiling of 80¢ per pound. At this price, how many apples are supplied?
   a. 24 tons.
   b. 28 tons.
   c. 32 tons.
   d. 36 tons.

29. At the ceiling price of 80¢ per pound, how many apples are consumed?
   a. 24 tons.
   b. 28 tons.
   c. 32 tons.
   d. 36 tons

30. At the ceiling price of 80¢ per pound of apples, what is the shortage of apples?
   a. 0 tons.
   b. 12 tons.
   c. 24 tons.
   d. 36 tons.

Short Answer Problems

1. You have been placed in charge of combating illegal drug use in the United States. You must decide between two policies: imprison users of illegal drugs or imprison sellers of drugs. (You can't do both; there isn't space in the jails.)
   a. If you decide to imprison users, what effect do you expect this policy to have on the price and quantity of illegal drugs?
   b. If you decide to imprison sellers, what effect do you think this policy will have on the price and quantity of illegal drugs?
   c. Without knowing which type of policy is being followed, can changes in the price of illegal drugs alone determine the success or failure of a policy designed to reduce the consumption of illegal drugs?

2. Suppose that policymakers decide that the price of a pizza is too high and that not enough people can afford to buy pizza. As a result, they impose a price ceiling on pizza that is below the current equilibrium price. When are consumers able to buy more pizza: before the price ceiling or after? Use a demand and supply diagram to support your answer.

3. Suppose that there is a significant decrease in the supply of timber. Explain how an unregulated market adjusts. What induces consumers to decrease their consumption of timber?
4. Suppose that demand for a good that can be stored is subject to unpredictable fluctuations. Explain how inventories help reduce the price variability of the good.
5. The supply of oranges is subject to unpredictable fluctuations. Why does the price of a fresh orange fluctuate much more than the price of frozen orange juice?

Table 6.2 Short Answer Problems 6, 7, 8

Price (dollars per bushel)	Quantity demanded (millions of bushels per year)	Quantity supplied (millions of bushels per year)
$4.20	30	42
4.10	34	40
4.00	38	38
3.90	42	36
3.80	46	34
3.70	50	32

6. Table 6.2 presents the demand and supply schedules for corn.
   a. Plot these values in Figure 6.7.
   b. What is the equilibrium price of corn? The equilibrium quantity?
   c. Suppose that the government imposed a price ceiling of $3.90 per bushel. On your diagram, show the quantities demanded and supplied and identify any shortage or surplus.
7. Use the demand and supply schedules in Table 6.2. Suppose that the government decides to impose a tax of 30¢ a bushel.
   a. Plot the demand and supply curves in Figure 6.8 and show how the tax affects the supply curve.
   b. After the tax is imposed, what is the equilibrium price of corn? The equilibrium quantity?

FIGURE 6.7
Short Answer Problem 6

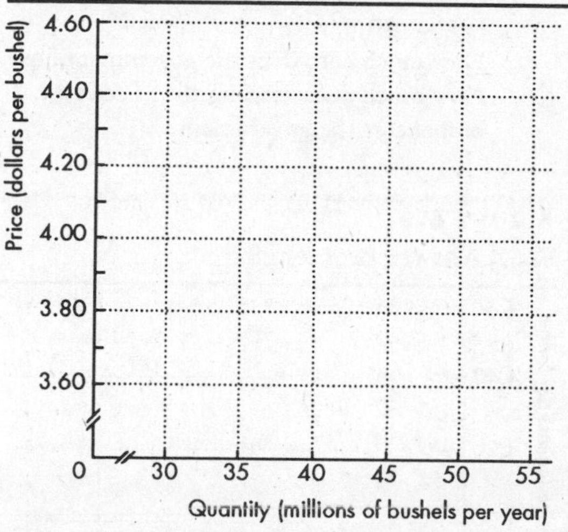

FIGURE 6.8
Short Answer Problem 7

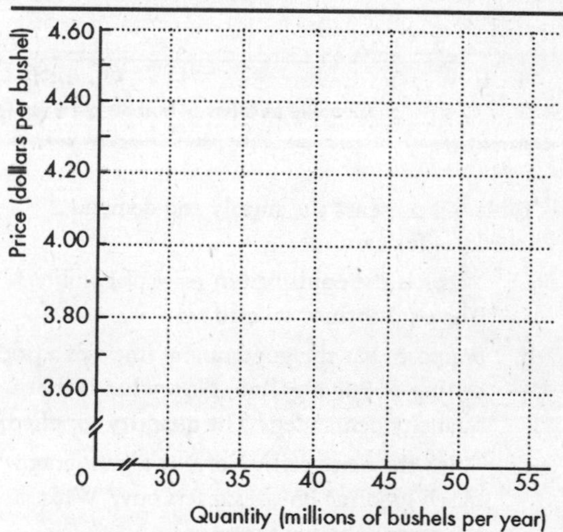

8. Making one more attempt to alter the equilibrium in the corn market, for the demand and supply schedules in Table 6.2, the government decides to impose a price floor of $4.10. It does so by promising farmers that it will buy the amount of corn necessary to keep the price pegged at no less than $4.10 a bushel.
   a. In Figure 6.9, plot the demand and supply schedules and the price floor.

b. With the price floor in place, what is the equilibrium amount of corn consumed by private demanders? How much corn do farmers grow?

c. How much corn does the government buy? How much does keeping the price at $4.10 a bushel cost the government?

FIGURE 6.9

Short Answer Problem 8

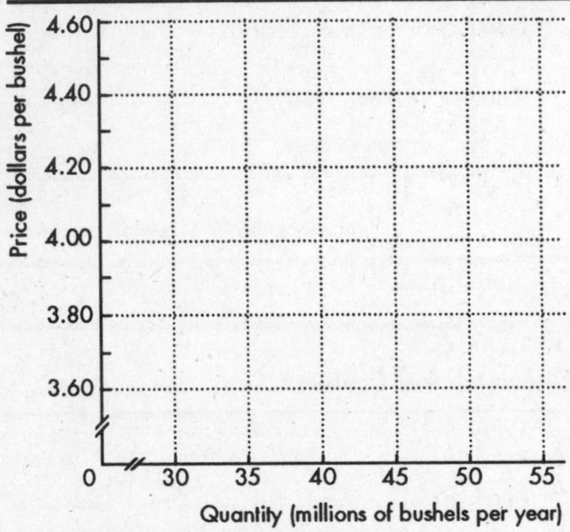

9. Table 6.3 presents the supply and demand schedules for gasoline.
   a. What is the equilibrium price of gasoline? The equilibrium quantity?
   b. Suppose that the government imposes a price ceiling of 90¢ a gallon. Now what is the quantity demanded? The quantity supplied?
   c. With the price ceiling of 90¢ a gallon, how much gasoline do consumers buy? What is the amount of the shortage?

10. Suppose that the supply of gasoline suddenly decreases, perhaps because of events occurring in the Middle East. In particular, suppose that at every possible price of gasoline, the quantity supplied is now 8 million gallons less per year.
    a. If the government did not impose any price controls, what is the new equilibrium price of gasoline? The new equilibrium quantity? How is the gasoline allocated among potential consumers?

Table 6.3 Short Answer Questions 9, 10

Price (dollars per gallon)	Quantity demanded (millions of gallons per year)	Quantity supplied (millions of gallons per year)
$1.40	8	24
1.30	10	22
1.20	12	20
1.10	14	18
1.00	16	16
90	18	14

    b. Suppose that the government imposed a price ceiling of 90¢. Now what is the quantity demanded? The quantity supplied?
    c. With a price ceiling of 90¢ in place, how much gasoline do consumers buy? What is the amount of the shortage? How is gasoline allocated among potential consumers?
    d. When are demanders able to consume more gasoline: when the price is controlled at 90¢ a gallon or when the price is left free to reach its equilibrium? Explain.

11. After graduating, you land a plush job advising the president on economic matters. One day the president asks you for your suggestions about products to tax.
    a. At first, the president asks you to produce a list of items to be taxed that will yield substantial tax revenue to the government and whose tax incidence will fall most heavily on consumers. Without trying to name specific products, what is the general characteristic of the demand curves for the products that you will suggest be taxed? Why?
    b. After you discuss this first list with the president, the president realizes that this year is an election year. As a result, the president changes your assignment a bit. Now the president asks you for a list of products that will still yield a lot of revenue for the government, but whose tax incidence will fall more heavily on producers. Again without trying to name specific products, what is the general characteristic of the supply curves of the products that would comprise your second list? Why?

12. Assume that you still have the job discussed in Problem 11. Another of the president's advisors states that "we think we're winning the war on drugs. Recently, the price of cocaine has climbed, which indicates that we are cutting off the supply of cocaine smuggled into the country. Unfortunately, we have no statistics on the amount of cocaine being sold." The president asks your advice on whether this claim of victory in the war on drugs should become a centerpiece of the president's re-election campaign. How would you respond?

You're the Teacher

1. "I really don't get this stuff about how suppliers and demanders split the sales tax. Every time *I* go to the store and buy something, I get to pay *all* the sales tax. I have never seen a store that offered to split the tax with me. So, how can our text say that suppliers usually have to pay part of a tax? I'm really lost; can you help me out?" Even though helping your befuddled classmate might hurt your grade (especially if your teacher grades on the curve) nonetheless point your befuddled friend in the right direction.

Answers

True/False Answers

1. **T** The supply curve has a positive slope: As the rent rises, the quantity supplied of apartments increases.
2. **F** The more elastic the demand, the more suppliers pay of the tax.
3. **F** Lines and payments on the black market are devices that help allocate apartments among potential renters.
4. **F** With the price control, there was a shortage of elbow grease; when the price rises, suppliers produce more elbow grease and demanders are able to buy more.
5. **F** The crop failure raises the price of the crop and, because the demand for it is inelastic, boosts farmers' total revenue.
6. **U** The price rises if the penalties are more severe on sellers and falls if they are more severe on buyers.
7. **T** By raising the wage that firms must pay, firms decrease the quantity of workers they demand.
8. **F** The supply curve shifts vertically *upward* by the amount of the tax.
9. **T** This outcome is a potential drawback to legalizing and then taxing currently illegal products.
10. **T** The fall in the wage rate signals workers to substitute other endeavors where the demand for their effort has not decreased.
11. **F** If the demand for a product is perfectly elastic, a tax has no effect on its price.
12. **T** The speculator will sell to take advantage of the temporarily higher price.
13. **F** Stabilization programs almost always result in large surpluses, not shortages.
14. **T** The time spent searching for a product has alternative uses, so search time has an opportunity cost.
15. **F** The fraction paid by buyers depends on the relative elasticities of demand and supply.

Multiple Choice Answers

1. **b** As rents rise, building owners are motivated to make more space available for use as apartments.
2. **c** At the price floor, the quantity supplied, Q_s, exceeds the quantity demanded, Q_d, so there is a surplus of $Q_s - Q_d$.
3. **c** By purchasing when the price is currently low, speculators expect to profit by selling when the price rises in the future.
4. **a** When a price ceiling is below the equilibrium price, the quantity demanded exceeds the quantity supplied and a shortage results.
5. **c** The supply curve shifts vertically upward by the amount of the tax; the vertical shift in Figure 6.4 is $2, so this amount is the tax.
6. **d** The total price paid by consumers rises from $12 to $13, so demanders pay $1 of the tax.
7. **d** The receipts per CD fall from $12 to $11, so suppliers pay $1 of the tax.
8. **c** The sanctions shift the supply curve leftward, thereby raising the price and decreasing the quantity.
9. **d** A minimum wage of $3 falls below the equilibrium wage, so no unemployment is created.
10. **c** If the minimum wage is raised to $9, the quantity of labor supplied, 50 million hours, exceeds the quantity demanded, 30 million hours, by 20 million hours.
11. **b** Any incipient shortage is eliminated by the higher rents that result.
12. **b** Only in the extreme cases of a perfectly elastic demand or a perfectly inelastic supply does a tax not raise the price of a product.
13. **c** Speculators buy a large part of the crop, so the price does not fall, and their purchases boost the incomes of soy bean farmers.
14. **c** When demand is perfectly inelastic, the price of the product rises by the entire amount of the tax.
15. **d** Black market prices will be above the rent ceiling.

16. **b** The floor price being above the market equilibrium price gives producers the incentive to increase their production of butter and wine. Meanwhile, demanders have the incentive to decrease their consumption. This result is illustrated in Figure 6.10. In this wine market there is a price floor of P_f. With this floor, Q_s worth of wine is produced but only Q_d is consumed, rather than the amount Q that would be produced and consumed were the market unregulated.

FIGURE **6.10**
Multiple Choice Question 16

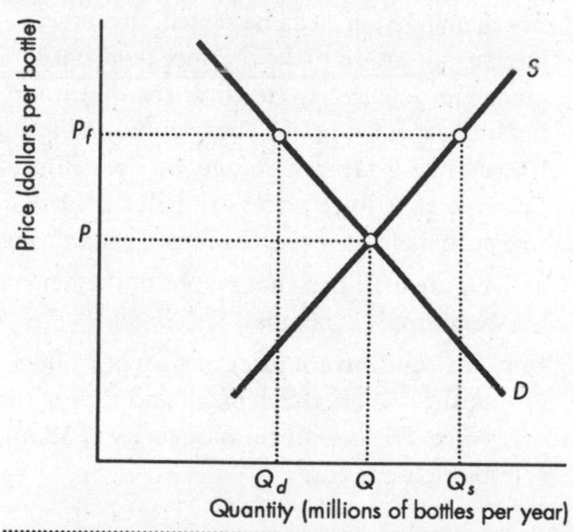

17. **d** The shortage equals the quantity demanded at the ceiling price (65,000) minus the quantity supplied at that price (45,000).
18. **b** The shortage increases because the quantity demanded remains at 65,000 while the quantity supplied falls to 10,000.
19. **b** The minimum wage has its largest effect on relatively low-skilled workers whose wages in an unregulated market would be below the minimum wage.
20. **b** Black markets are illegal markets wherein people conduct transactions at prices forbidden by the government.
21. **a** This set of factors describes the situation in many agricultural markets, so in the absence of regulation, agricultural prices would be subject to large fluctuations.
22. **b** The fact that the minimum wage rate exceeds the equilibrium wage rate means that firms will decrease the quantity of employment that they demand, thereby decreasing employment.
23. **c** The more elastic the supply, the greater is the share of any tax consumers pay.
24. **c** Speculators buy when the current price would otherwise be low and sell when the current price otherwise would be high.
25. **a** The greater the elasticity of demand, the more the tax reduces the equilibrium quantity consumed.
26. **b** At this price, the quantity supplied of apples equals the quantity demanded.
27. **b** When apples are $1.00 per pound, 28 tons of apples are demanded and supplied.
28. **a** At a price of 80¢ a pound, the supply schedule shows that producers supply 24 tons per year.
29. **a** Although consumers demand 36 tons of apples, only 24 tons are produced, so only 24 tons can be consumed.
30. **b** The shortage equals the quantity of apples demanded, 36 tons, minus the quantity of apples supplied, 24 tons.

Answers to Short Answer Problems

1. a. Imposing sanctions on consumers shifts the demand curve for illegal drugs leftward. That lowers the price and decreases the quantity of illegal drugs consumed.

   b. If sellers are penalized, the supply curve shifts leftward. In this case, the price of illegal drugs rises and the quantity consumed decreases.

   c. The answers to parts (a) and (b) illustrate that the price of illegal drugs alone cannot be used to judge the success of a policy against drugs. For instance, if the price rises when sanctions are imposed against sellers the policy is effective. However, if the price rises when sanctions are imposed against users, the policy is failing.

2. Figure 6.11 illustrates the pizza market before and after the price ceiling has been imposed. Before the price ceiling of P_c is imposed, the

equilibrium price is P and the equilibrium quantity produced and consumed is Q. With the price ceiling, P_c, suppliers are willing to produce only Q_s. Consumers would like to buy more pizza, but they cannot buy what is not produced. Thus only Q_s pizza is consumed after the price ceiling. So, even though the price ceiling may have been imposed to allow more consumers to afford to buy pizza, in aggregate more pizza is consumed without the price ceiling than with it.

FIGURE **6.11**
Short Answer Problem 2

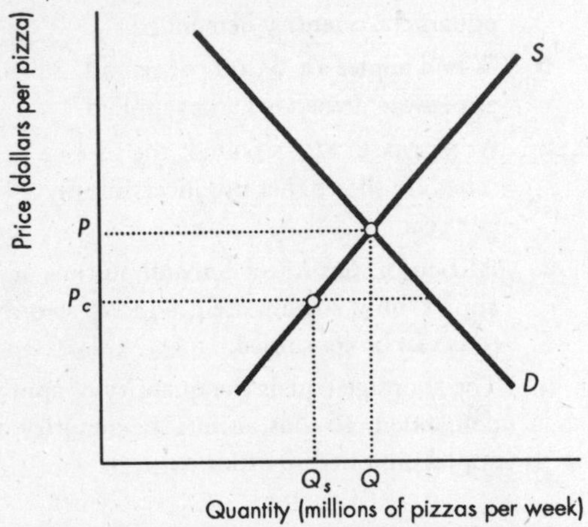

3. If the market for timber is in equilibrium initially and there is a significant decrease in supply, an excess quantity will be demanded at the existing price. As a result, the price of timber rises, which causes movements along the new supply curve and the demand curve. The rising price causes a price-induced increase in the quantity supplied and a price-induced decrease in the quantity demanded. The price continues to rise until the excess quantity demanded is eliminated. The price rise causes consumers to reduce their desired consumption of timber and substitute other products, such as brick or plaster.
4. Inventories are held to exploit any potential profit opportunities, such as selling goods from inventories if the current price is higher than the expected future price or buying goods to be added to inventories if the current price is below the expected future price. The first profit opportunity — selling when the current price is higher than the expected future price — reduces the current price. The second profit opportunity — buying when the current price is lower than the expected future price — raises the current price. Selling, if the price is above, or buying, if the price is below the expected future price, means that the price will not deviate much from the expected future price. Thus inventories help reduce price fluctuations.
5. The key difference between the two goods is that fresh oranges cannot be stored effectively, whereas frozen orange juice can be stored easily. Without storage, inventory speculation is difficult, and the price of a fresh orange fluctuates widely with variations in the momentary supply curve. As frozen orange juice can be stored, inventory holders operate to make the supply of frozen orange juice perfectly elastic at the inventory holders' expected price. Thus supply-induced price fluctuations for frozen orange juice are eliminated. Frozen orange juice prices can still fluctuate if the inventory holders' expected future price changes.
6. a. Figure 6.12 presents graphs of the demand and supply schedules.
   b. The equilibrium price of corn is \$4.00 a bushel, where the demand and supply curves cross. The equilibrium quantity is 38 million bushels per year.

FIGURE **6.12**
Short Answer Problem 6

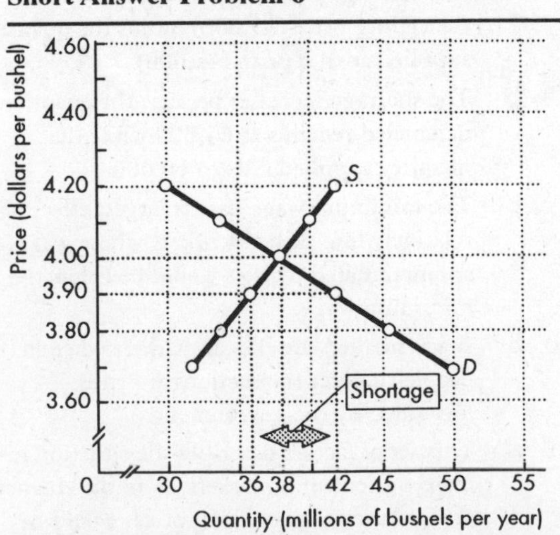

c. Figure 6.12 shows that, with a price ceiling of \$3.90, the quantity demanded is 42 million bushels of corn and the quantity supplied is 36 million bushels of corn. Thus the shortage is 6 million bushels of corn.

7. a. Figure 6.13 illustrates the demand schedule and the supply schedule (with and without the tax). The tax shifts the supply curve vertically upward by the amount of the tax, or 30¢ a bushel.

b. As Figure 6.13 shows, the equilibrium price after the tax is imposed is \$4.10 a bushel because the demand curve and the supply plus tax curve cross at this price. The equilibrium quantity is 34 million bushels.

FIGURE **6.13**

Short Answer Problem 7

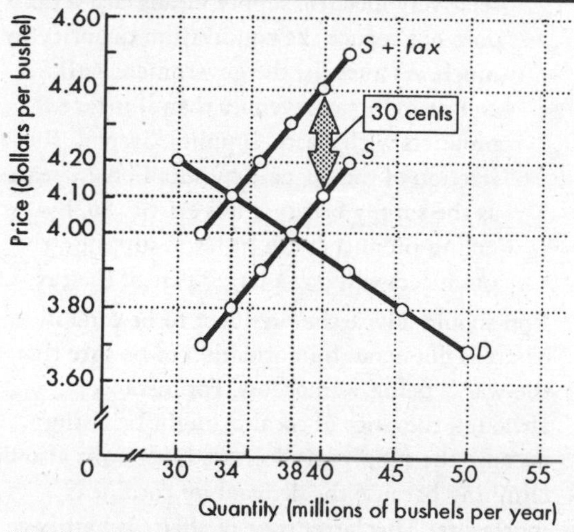

8. a. Figure 6.14 shows the market with the price floor of \$4.10 a bushel.

b. With the price floor in place, private demanders buy only 34 million bushels of corn, but farmers supply 40 million bushels.

c. Without any government action, a price of \$4.10 a bushel would create a surplus of 6 million bushels of corn. To keep the price at \$4.10 a bushel, the government must buy this surplus. Hence the government spends (\$4.10/bushel) (6 million bushels), or \$24,600,000.

FIGURE **6.14**

Short Answer Problem 8

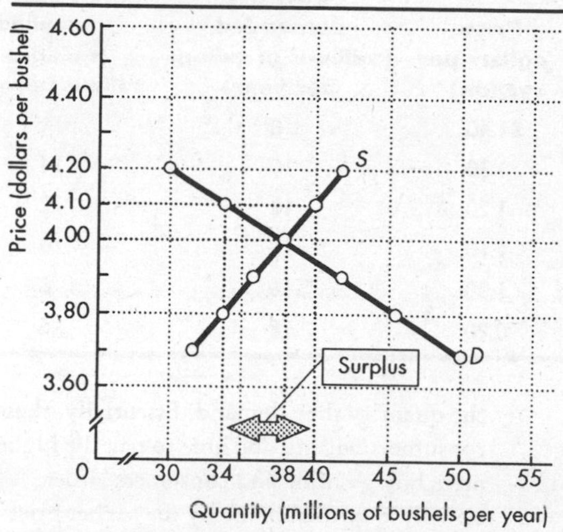

9. a. The equilibrium price of gasoline is \$1.00 a gallon because that price equates the quantity supplied to the quantity demanded. The equilibrium quantity is 16 million gallons a year.

b. If the government imposes a price ceiling of 90¢ a gallon, the demand schedule shows that consumers demand 18 million gallons of gasoline a year. At the ceiling price, the supply schedule indicates that producers supply 14 million gallons of gasoline a year.

c. With the price ceiling, only 14 million gallons of gasoline are available. Thus, even though consumers would be willing to purchase 18 million gallons, all they can actually buy is 14 million gallons. The shortage equals the amount consumers are willing to buy (18 million gallons) minus the amount actually available (14 million gallons), or 4 million gallons.

10. a. Table 6.4 (on the next page) makes answering this question easier. Table 6.4 shows the new supply schedule after the decrease in supply. Note that the demand schedule is unchanged. The new equilibrium price is \$1.20 a gallon, and the new equilibrium quantity is 12 million gallons a year. The gasoline is allocated among consumers by price. Faced with the higher price, consumers will decrease

Table 6.4 Short Answer Question 10

Price (dollars per gallon)	Quantity demanded (millions of gallons per year)	New quantity supplied (millions of gallons per year)
$1.40	8	16
1.30	10	14
1.20	12	12
1.10	14	10
1.00	16	8
0.90	18	6

the quantity they demand. Essentially, those consumers willing and able to pay the higher price buy gasoline and consumers either unwilling or unable to pay the higher price do not.

b. If the government imposes a price ceiling of 90¢ a gallon, the demand schedule shows that the quantity demanded remains at 18 million gallons. The quantity supplied at the ceiling price is 6 million gallons.

c. With the price ceiling, consumers are able to purchase only the amount of gasoline actually made available. That is, consumers can buy only 6 million gallons of gasoline, and there is a shortage of 6 million gallons (12 million gallons – 6 million gallons). Because the price cannot allocate gasoline among consumers, other mechanisms come into play. Long lines will exist at gasoline stations, so people willing and able to wait in the lines will buy gasoline. Black markets, where bribes and other side payments are made to suppliers by consumers, will spring up. Thus consumers willing and able to participate in black markets will buy gasoline.

d. When the price is left free to reach its equilibrium, consumers can buy and use 12 million gallons of gasoline. With the price ceiling, consumers can buy only 6 million gallons of gasoline. Hence, as a group, consumers are able to consume more gasoline when the market is left unregulated.

11. a. You want to find products for which the demand is relatively inelastic. Taxing products with inelastic demands has two effects. First, the reduction in the equilibrium quantity is less than it would be if a good with an elastic demand were taxed; and, second, the amount of the tax paid by consumers is higher for goods with inelastic demands. Because the president wants the taxes to fall most heavily on consumers, the second effect directly achieves the president's second goal. In addition, the president also wants to generate substantial tax revenues. Because the equilibrium quantity is not decreased much, more of this product will be bought and sold. Thus, with more transactions, the government will collect more tax. So, the first effect means that the government will collect significant tax revenues, the president's first goal.

b. You will recommend that the government tax products with relatively inelastic supplies. A relatively inelastic supply means that a tax does not reduce the equilibrium quantity by much. As a result, the government will collect more tax revenues than if it taxed products with elastic supplies. Second, the fraction of the tax paid by suppliers increases as the supply becomes less elastic. So, by taxing products with inelastic supplies, the producers will pay a larger part of the tax.

12. You should advise the president to be careful. There is not enough information to be sure that the war is being won or lost. For instance, although the price of cocaine might be rising because the supply has decreased, it might also be climbing because the demand for cocaine is increasing. This latter state of affairs is hardly a sign of victory. To be certain of which is the case, data on the quantity of cocaine is required.

■ You're the Teacher

1. "You're getting a bit confused. It's easiest to explain this concept with a concrete example; I'm hungry so let's think about pizza. Suppose that the government did not tax pizza and that the equilibrium price was $11 per pizza. Okay, now suppose that the government slaps a $2 per pizza tax on pizza. What our textbook has shown me is that this tax will raise the price, say, to $11.50 per pizza. In other words, the price — *including* the

tax — will be $11.50 per pizza. That also means that the price without the tax falls to $9.50 per pizza. So, when we call the people at the pizza shop on the phone, they tell us that the price of a pizza is $9.50 plus $2 tax, or $11.50. So, it looks like we're getting stuck with the entire $2 tax. But we're not. Actually, after the tax is imposed, we pay only $0.50 more because the price we pay rises only from $11.00 to $11.50. The pizza makers wind up paying $1.50 of this tax: Before the tax they got to keep $11.00 per pizza but after the tax they get to keep only $9.50 per pizza. The moral here is that appearances can be deceiving and that you need to study your economics some more!"

Part Review 1

HOW MARKETS WORK

Reading Between the Lines

YOUR CHEAP STEAK POISON TO CATTLEMEN

When the hot dogs and hamburgers are finished this weekend, there will likely be something else left over besides a little macaroni salad: more money.

A surge in the cattle supply has pushed down the price of beef. And in the height of the cookout season, that's particularly good news for consumers, but tough for Florida ranchers to swallow.

Reporting on its monthly 19-city survey of supermarkets, the National Cattlemen's Association in Denver said that the average retail price of six cuts of beef on July 14 was $3.10 a pound, the third consecutive monthly decline. The price last July was $3.28.

The decline in retail beef prices is driven by a 2 percent to 3 percent increase in the beef supply, said Gary Mills, a beef analyst in Dodge City, Kan., for the U.S. Department of Agriculture.

Mills said that retail grocery chains may feature beef later this summer to entice shoppers to buy beef at lower prices.

"We think that it will be cheaper in stores for at least a few weeks," Mills said.

■ Analyze It

It is clear from the story that cattle ranchers faced a problem in the form of lower prices for beef. We can analyze why the price of beef fell using a standard supply and demand diagram.

1. Draw a supply and demand figure showing why the price of beef fell between the two years. Then, use the data in the problem to calculate the price elasticity of demand for beef.
2. According to the data in the article, is the demand for beef elastic or inelastic?
3. What does this estimate of the elasticity mean for the total revenue collected by ranchers: Between the years covered in the article, did the total revenue go up or go down?

Mid-Term Examination

1 Willy makes $25 an hour as a carpenter. He must take two hours off from work (unpaid) to go to the dentist to have a tooth pulled. The dentist charges $60. The opportunity cost of Willy's visit to the dentist is

a. $25.
b. $50.
c. $60
d. $110.

2 A company produces 100 units of a good at a cost of $400 or produces 101 units of the same good at a cost of $415 dollars. The $15 difference is

a. the marginal benefit of producing 101 units.
b. the marginal cost of producing the 101st unit.
c. the marginal cost of producing the first unit.
d. less than the average cost.

3 Positive statements are statements about

a. prices.
b. quantities.
c. what is.
d. what ought to be.

4 The branch of economics that studies individual markets within the economy is called

a. macroeconomics.
b. microeconomics.
c. Keynesian economics.
d. open economics.

5 A time-series graph displays the price of copper. The slope of the line is positive for periods when the

a. price of copper is rising.
b. price of copper is falling.
c. quantity of copper is rising.
d. quantity of copper is falling.

6 On the x-axis, smaller values will be

a. directly above larger values.
b. directly below larger values.
c. farther to the right than larger values.
d. farther to the left than larger values.

7 A positive relationship between two variables is shown by

a. an upward-sloping line.
b. a horizontal or vertical line.
c. a downward-sloping line.
d. a steeply sloping line.

8 Along a curved line, the slope at the minimum

a. is greater than zero.
b. is less than zero.
c. is zero.
d. may be greater than, less than, or equal to zero.

9 Output combinations beyond the production possibility frontier

a. result in more rapid growth.
b. are associated with unused resources.
c. are attainable only with the full utilization of all resources.
d. are unattainable.

10 The *PPF* shifts inward as a result of

a. a decrease in the production of consumption goods.
b. an increase in R&D expenditure.
c. an increase in population.
d. the destruction of a portion of the capital stock.

11 Whenever a person can produce less of all goods than anyone else, that person

a. should specialize in nothing.
b. has a comparative advantage in something.
c. should be self-sufficient.
d. has a comparative advantage in nothing.

12 To obtain all the gains available from comparative advantage, individuals or countries must do more than trade, they must also

a. specialize.
b. save.
c. invest.
d. engage in research and development.

13 As the opportunity cost of a good rises, people buy

a. less of that good and also less of its complements.
b. less of that good but more of its complements.
c. more of that good but less of its complements.
d. more of that good and also more of its complements.

14 The law of demand states that, other things remaining the same, the higher the price of a good, the

a. smaller will be the demand for the good.
b. larger will be the demand for the good.
c. smaller will be the quantity of the good demanded.
d. larger will be the quantity of the good demanded.

15 A surplus causes the

a. demand curve to shift to the left.
b. supply curve to shift to the right.
c. price to fall.
d. price to rise.

16 When supply increases, the equilibrium quantity

a. increases and the price rises.
b. decreases and the price falls.
c. increases and the price falls.
d. decreases and the price rises.

17 If a shift of the supply curve to the right causes a 5 percent decrease in price and a 10 percent increase in quantity, then the price elasticity of demand is

a. 0.50.
b. 2.0.
c. 5.0.
d. 10.0.

18 If the price elasticity of demand exceeds 1, then demand is

a. elastic.
b. unit elastic.
c. inelastic.
d. positively related to the price of the product.

19 The elasticity of demand for Pizza Hut pizza is

a. lower than the elasticity of demand for pizza in general and probably inelastic.
b. larger than the elasticity of demand for pizza in general and probably inelastic.
c. larger than the elasticity of demand for pizza in general and probably elastic.
d. lower than the elasticity of demand for pizza in general and probably elastic.

20 A fall in the price of rutabagas from $10.50 to $9.50 a bushel raises the quantity demanded from 19,2000 bushels to 20,800 bushels. The price elasticity of demand in this part of the demand curve is

a. 0.80.
b. 1.20.
c. 1.25.
d. 8.00.

21 A good has an upward sloping supply curve and a perfectly elastic demand curve. Imposing a sales tax on this good shifts the supply curve

a. upward and the buyer bears the cost of the tax.
b. downward and the buyer bears the cost of the tax.
c. downward and the seller bears the cost of the tax.
d. upward and the seller bears the cost of the tax.

22 Outlawing buying drugs shifts the demand curve

a. left and lowers the price.
b. left and raises the price.
c. right and lowers the price.
d. right and raises the price.

23 If demand is inelastic, a shift of the supply curve to the right will

a. decrease total revenue.
b. increase total revenue.
c. have no effect on total revenue.
d. reduce the demand for the product.

24 A short-run supply curve is

a. less elastic than a momentary supply curve.
b. more elastic than a momentary supply curve.
c. more elastic than a long-run supply curve.
d. None of the above.

Answers

Reading Between the Lines

In the news story, Gary Mills pointed out that the supply of beef increased by 2 to 3 percent. This means that the supply curve of beef shifted rightward, as Figure 1 illustrates with the shift from S to S_A. As a result, the price of beef fell, from $3.28 to $3.10.

Intuitively we see that a small increase in the supply of beef created a relatively large decline in the price of beef. We can formalize this observation by calculating the price elasticity of demand. Split the difference between the two estimates of the increase in the quantity and assume that the quantity increased by 2.5 percent. The percentage fall in the price of beef is given by $(\Delta P / P_{ave})$ or (.18)/(3.19) = 5.6 percent. Hence, the price elasticity of demand equals (2.5)/(5.6) = 0.45. Because the elasticity is less than one, according to the article the demand for beef is inelastic.

Because the demand for beef is inelastic, when the quantity of beef increases and the price of beef falls, the total revenue collected by ranchers falls. Hence, between the years covered in the article, the total revenue earned by ranchers declined. Indeed, this is the fundamental problem faced by ranchers: The increased supply of beef translates into lower total revenue.

FIGURE 1
The Market For Beef

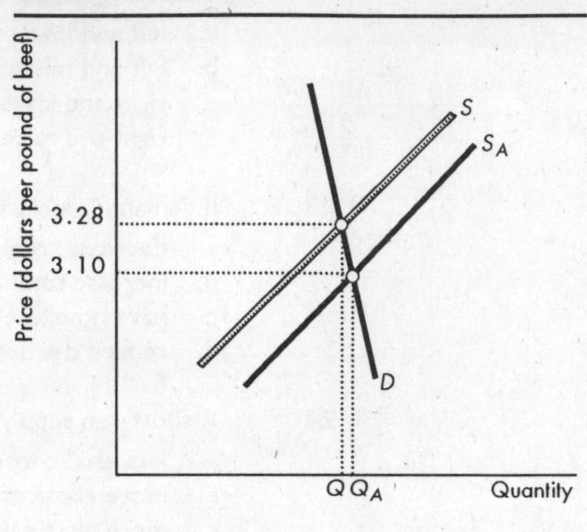

Mid-Term Exam

1 d; 2 b; 3 c; 4 b; 5 a; 6 d; 7 a; 8 c; 9 d; 10 d; 11 b; 12 a; 13 a; 14 c; 15 c; 16 c; 17 b; 18 a; 19 c; 20 b; 21 d; 22 a; 23 a; 24 b

Chapter 7 UTILITY AND DEMAND

Key Concepts

Household Consumption Choices

Consumption choices are determined by the interaction of the household's budget constraint and preferences.

- **Budget constraint** — The household's purchases are limited by its income and by the prices of the goods and services. A *budget line*, as illustrated in Figure 7.1, shows the limits to what the household can purchase.
- **Preferences** — Preferences are an individual's likes and dislikes. They are measured by **utility**.

Utility is the benefit or satisfaction from consumption.

- **Total utility** is the *total* benefit or satisfaction from consumption of goods and services.
- **Marginal utility** (*MU*) is the *change* in total utility from a one-unit increase in the quantity of one good consumed. *MU* is positive, but because of **diminishing marginal utility**, falls as the consumption of the good increases.

Maximizing Utility

Consumers strive to obtain the most total utility possible; that is, they maximize their utility. A **consumer equilibrium** occurs when the consumer's income is allocated between different products so that the combination of products consumed maximizes the consumer's total utility.

Total utility is maximized when:

- all the consumer's income is spent; and
- the marginal utility per dollar spent is equal for all goods. In terms of a formula, for the choice between sodas and movies, this requirement is:

$$\frac{MU_m}{P_m} = \frac{MU_s}{P_s}$$

with MU_m the marginal utility from an additional movie, P_m the price of a movie, and MU_s and P_s the analogous variables for soda.

Equating the marginal utilities divided by price is an example of *marginal analysis*.

FIGURE 7.1
A Budget Line

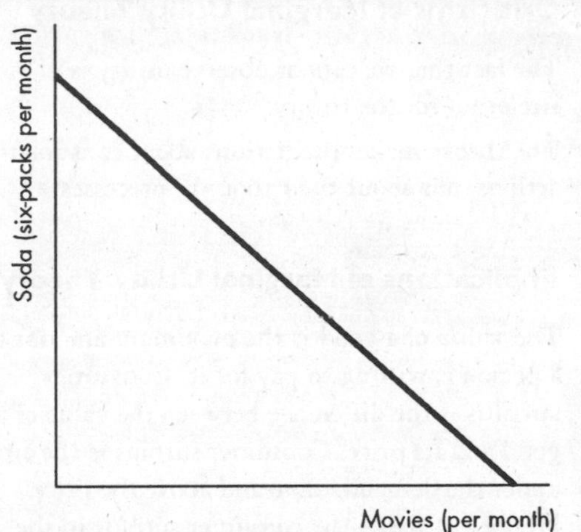

Predictions of Marginal Utility Theory

- *Ceteris paribus*, a fall in the price of a movie increases the quantity of movies viewed as consumers substitute movies for sodas. The movement along the demand curve for movies is downward, and the demand curve for soda, a substitute for movies, shifts leftward.
- *Ceteris paribus*, a rise in the price of soda causes a decrease in the quantity of sodas consumed. The movement along the demand curve for soda is upward and the demand curve for movies, a substitute for soda, shifts rightward.

- Movies and soda are normal goods. Hence, *ceteris paribus*, an increase in income increases the consumption of both movies and soda and thereby causes rightward shifts in both demand curves.

If the marginal utility for a product declines in large steps, the demand for the product is price and income inelastic; if it declines in small steps the demand is price and income elastic.

- **Individual demand** — the relationship between the price of an item and the quantity demanded by one individual.
- **Market demand** — the relationship between the price of an item and the total quantity demanded.

The market demand curve is the horizontal sum of the individual demand curves.

Criticisms of Marginal Utility Theory

- The fact that we cannot observe utility is irrelevant for the theory.
- The theory makes predictions about consumers' actions, not about their thought processes.

Implications of Marginal Utility Theory

- The value of a good is the maximum amount that a person is willing to pay for it. **Consumer surplus** is the difference between the value of a good and its price. Consumer surplus is the area under the demand curve and above the price. Figure 7.2 shows the consumer surplus in the market for movies when the price of a movie is P_m.
- The distinction between total utility and marginal utility solves the diamond-water paradox of value. Diamonds are less useful than water (that is, they have lower total utility) but they have a higher price because most people have only a few diamonds, if any, so diamonds have higher *marginal* utility. Water is more useful (it has higher total utility) but has a lower price because it has a lower *marginal* utility, as so much water is already consumed.

FIGURE **7.2**
Consumer Surplus

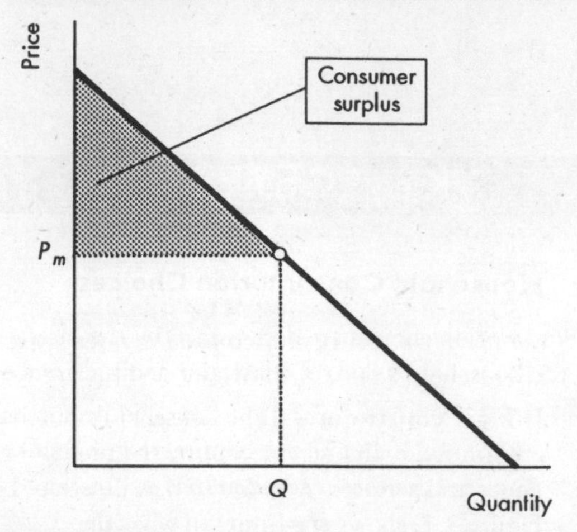

Helpful Hints

1. Utility is an extremely useful abstract concept that allows us to think more clearly about consumer choice. Do not be confused by the fact that arbitrary units are used to measure utility. The only important requirement of marginal utility theory is that you be able to judge whether the additional satisfaction per dollar spent on good X is greater or less than the additional satisfaction per dollar spent on Y. If it is greater, you will decide to consume an additional unit of X. How much greater is irrelevant for the decision.
2. This chapter introduces another equilibrium condition, namely, the consumer equilibrium requirement that the marginal utility of each good divided by its price must equal the marginal utility of other goods divided by their prices. What does consumer equilibrium mean? Recall that the general definition of equilibrium is a situation "where opposing forces balance." When that occurs, there is no incentive for any changes. In the supply and demand model, equilibrium is attained at the price where the quantity supplied equals the quantity demanded because at that price neither demanders nor suppliers have an incentive to change their behavior. Consumer equilibrium is similar. When it is not met, the

consumer will adjust the amounts consumed because a change can increase the consumer's total utility. (This condition is discussed in the next hint.) However, when the equilibrium condition is satisfied, the consumer has no incentive to change the combination of goods consumed. At this point, the consumer has the most total utility that can be attained. As a result, the consumer won't change the consumption bundle and so an equilibrium — with no incentive to change — is reached.

3. The condition for consumer equilibrium is that the marginal utility of each good divided by its price equal the marginal utility of the other goods divided by their price. In terms of a formula, for two goods, X and Y, the requirement is that the consumer allocate income so that

$$\frac{MU_X}{P_X} = \frac{MU_Y}{P_Y}.$$

Why is this condition necessary for consumer equilibrium? Let's find out by using marginal analysis. First, note that the term MU_X/P_X is the marginal utility per dollar spent on good X. In other words, it is the utility gained if an extra dollar is spent on X or the utility lost if spending on X is decreased a dollar. MU_Y/P_Y gives us similar information about Y.

Now, suppose that the equilibrium equality did not hold; in particular, suppose that $MU_X/P_X > MU_Y/P_Y$. In this case, the consumer will reduce spending on Y and increase spending on X. Why? Use marginal analysis and consider reducing spending on Y by a dollar. By so doing, the consumer will lose MU_Y/P_Y worth of utility because less Y is consumed. But the consumer can now use the dollar to buy an extra dollar's worth of X. By so doing, the consumer gains MU_X/P_X worth of utility. The gain in utility from more X — MU_X/P_X — exceeds the loss in utility from less Y — MU_Y/P_Y — so the consumer's total utility increases from this rearrangement. *Anytime* there is an inequality between the marginal utilities divided by their prices, the consumer can gain by buying less of the product with the low MU/P and buying more of the good with the high MU/P. Thus only when the marginal utilities per dollar are equal does the consumer not want to rearrange the consumption bundle and thus only when this equality holds is the consumer in equilibrium.

Questions

True/False/Uncertain and Explain

1. The market demand curve is the horizontal sum of all individual demand curves.

2. Utility measures a consumer's level of satisfaction.

3. Because consumers must pay for almost everything they consume, consumer surplus is rarely encountered.

4. An individual demand curve shows the total market demand for an individual product.

5. The principle of diminishing marginal utility means that as consumption of a good increases, total utility rises but at a decreasing rate.

6. Economists assume that households try to maximize their marginal utility per dollar spent.

7. A household is maximizing its utility if the marginal utility per dollar spent is equal for all goods and the household spends all its income.

8. Marginal utility theory shows that goods with high prices (such as diamonds) must have high total utilities.

9. If the marginal utilities from consuming two goods are equal, the consumer must be in equilibrium.

10. If the marginal utility per dollar spent on good X exceeds the marginal utility per dollar spent on good Y, total utility rises by increasing consumption of X and decreasing consumption of Y.

11. In order for marginal utility theory to "work," we must be able to measure consumers' utilities.

12. The principle of diminishing marginal utility means that, as more of a product is consumed, the total utility from the good diminishes.

13. Marginal utility measures the *additional* utility from consuming an *additional* unit of a good.

14. A budget line shows the different combinations of goods and services that a consumer can afford to buy.

■ Multiple Choice

1. As more of a good is consumed,
   a. both the marginal utility and total utility from the good rise.
   b. the marginal utility from the good rises and the total utility falls.
   c. the marginal utility from the good falls and the total utility rises.
   d. both the marginal utility and total utility from the good fall.

2. Andrew finds that the marginal utility from a BMW exceeds that from a slice of pizza. This condition means that Andrew
   a. is not maximizing his utility.
   b. is maximizing his utility.
   c. must increase his income in order to maximize his utility.
   d. may be maximizing his utility, but we cannot tell without more information

3. Robert buys only soda and pizza and is buying the amounts that maximize his utility. The marginal utility from a soda is 10, and the price of the soda is $1. The marginal utility from a slice of pizza is 20. The price of a slice of pizza must be
   a. $20.
   b. $2.
   c. $1.
   d. some amount that cannot be calculated without more information.

4. Courtney buys only soda and pizza and is buying the amounts that maximize her utility. The marginal utility from a soda is 30 and the price of the soda is $1. The marginal utility from a slice of pizza is 60. The price of a slice of pizza must be
   a. $20.
   b. $2.
   c. $1.
   d. some amount that cannot be calculated without more information

5. Economists assume that consumers aim to
   a. maximize their total utility.
   b. maximize their marginal utility.
   c. maximize their income.
   d. None of the above.

6. The marginal utility from the first burrito that Brian can consume is less than the marginal utility from the last taco that Brian can consume. As a result,
   a. burritos are an inferior good for Brian.
   b. Brian will never consume any burritos.
   c. Brian will consume a burrito only if the price of a burrito is less than the price of a taco.
   d. burritos and tacos are substitute goods for Brian.

7. When Kelly maximizes her utility, the
   a. marginal utility of each good she buys is as high as possible.
   b. marginal utility of each good she buys is equal.
   c. amount of each good she buys is the same.
   d. marginal utility of a good divided by its price is equal for each good she buys.

8. Marginal utility theory predicts that a rise in the price of a banana causes
   a. the demand curve for bananas to shift rightward.
   b. the demand curve for bananas to shift leftward.
   c. a movement upward along the demand curve for bananas.
   d. a movement downward along the demand curve for bananas.

9. Consumer surplus
    a. equals the total quantity of a product consumed multiplied by its price.
    b. equals the difference between the value of a good and its the price.
    c. is undefined for products that are essential for life, such as water.
    d. is always less than the price of the product.

10. Consumer surplus in Figure 7.3 is the area marked
    a. *A*.
    b. *B*.
    c. *C*.
    d. None of the above.

FIGURE 7.3
Multiple Choice Question 10

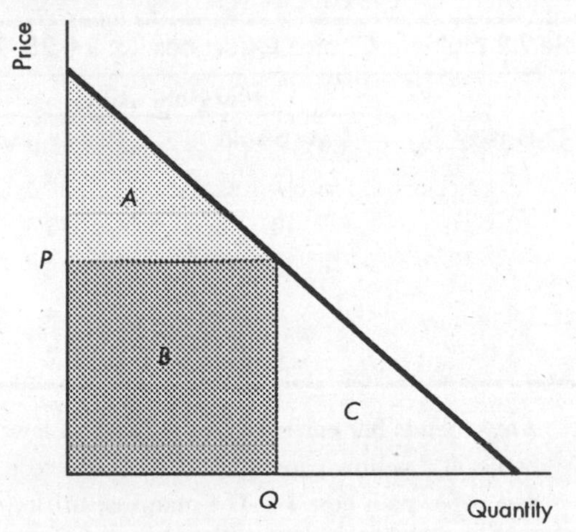

11. Ben thinks that playing another round of a video game is worth $1.50; to play another round costs $0.50. Ben's consumer surplus from playing this video game is
    a. $1.50.
    b. $1.00.
    c. $0.50.
    d. None of the above.

12. Michael consumes only steak and lobster. Suppose that the price of a steak rises. After Michael is back at equilibrium, compared to the situation when steak was cheaper, the marginal utility from the last steak will
    a. have increased.
    b. have not changed.
    c. have decreased.
    d. not be comparable with the marginal utility from before the price hike.

13. The marginal utility from gasoline diminishes very rapidly. As a result, the
    a. demand curve for gasoline is upward sloping.
    b. demand for gasoline is price inelastic.
    c. demand for gasoline is price elastic.
    d. consumer surplus from gasoline is likely to be nonexistent.

14. Lisa finds that the marginal utility from a compact disc is 30 and that the marginal utility from an audiocassette is 20. The price of a compact disc is $15 and the price of an audiocassette is $10. To maximize her utility, Lisa should
    a. increase her consumption of compact discs.
    b. increase her consumption of audiocassettes.
    c. not change her consumption of compact discs and audiocassettes.
    d. lower the price of an audiocassette.

15. The principle of diminishing marginal utility means that the consumer surplus from the second slice of pizza is
    a. greater than that from the first.
    b. equal to that from the first.
    c. less than that from the first.
    d. not comparable to that from the first.

16. Which of the following is <u>NOT</u> an assumption of marginal utility theory?
    a. People derive utility from their consumption.
    b. More consumption yields more total utility.
    c. Marginal utility diminishes with more consumption.
    d. Utility can be measured.

17. Sergio is maximizing his utility and consumes only beef and bubble gum. If the price of a pound of beef is greater than the price of stick of bubble gum,
    a. Sergio buys more beef than bubble gum.
    b. Sergio buys more bubble gum than beef.
    c. the marginal utility of the last pound of beef purchased is greater than the marginal utility of the last pack of bubble gum purchased.
    d. the marginal utility of the last pack of bubble gum purchased is greater than the marginal utility of the last pound of beef purchased.

18. Chuck and Barry have identical preferences but Chuck has a much higher income. If each is maximizing his utility,
    a. they will have equal total utilities.
    b. Chuck will have lower marginal utility than Barry for most goods.
    c. Chuck will have higher marginal utility than Barry for most goods.
    d. they will have equal marginal utilities for most goods.

19. If Soula is maximizing her utility, when two goods have the same price she will
    a. buy only one.
    b. buy equal quantities of both.
    c. get the same marginal utility from each.
    d. get the same total utility from each.

20. A household's consumption choices are determined by
    a. prices of goods and services.
    b. its income.
    c. its preferences.
    d. all of the above.

21. The fact that rubies are more expensive than milk reflects the fact that for most consumers
    a. the total utility from rubies exceeds that from milk.
    b. the marginal utility from rubies equals that from milk.
    c. more milk is consumed than rubies.
    d. a quart of rubies is prettier than a quart of milk.

22. Jack's demand schedule for squid is given in Table 7.1. If the price of a pound of squid is $2, what is his consumer surplus from squid?
    a. $15.
    b. $8.
    c. $6.
    d. $4.

Table 7.1 Multiple Choice Question 22

Price (dollars per pound of squid)	Quantity demanded (pounds of squid)
$5	1
4	2
3	3
2	4
1	5

Use the following table for the next four questions.

Table 7.2 Multiple Choice Questions 23, 24, 25, 26

	Marginal utility	
Quantity	Law books	Paper pads
1	12	16
2	10	12
3	8	8
4	6	4
5	4	2

23. Amy spends her entire income of $10 on law books and yellow paper pads. Law books cost $2 and paper pads cost $4. The marginal utility of each good, given in Table 7.2, is independent of the amount consumed of the other good. If Amy is maximizing her income, how many yellow paper pads does she buy?
    a. 0.
    b. 1.
    c. 2.
    d. 3.

24. Continuing with Question 23, what is Amy's total utility?
    a. 82.
    b. 48.
    c. 46.
    d. 40.

25. Amy's income rises to $16. She continues to buy only law books and yellow paper pads and she continues to maximize her utility. How many yellow paper pads does she buy after her income increases?
   a. 0.
   b. 1.
   c. 2.
   d. 3.

26. After Amy's income rises to $16, what is her total utility?
   a. 82.
   b. 64.
   c. 40.
   d. 36.

27. Which of the following is NOT consistent with the assumption of diminishing marginal utility?
   a. As more of a good is consumed, its marginal utility falls.
   b. As less of a good is consumed, its marginal utility rises.
   c. As more of a good is consumed, its total utility rises.
   d. As less of a good is consumed, its total utility rises.

Short Answer Problems

1. Loren is in equilibrium, spending her income of $200 buying 2 video games at a price of $40 each and 8 compact discs at a price of $15 each. Then, inflation causes the price of a compact disc and a video game to double (to $80 and $30, respectively) while Loren's income also doubles (to $400). What happens to Loren's purchases of video games and compact discs: Do both increase, decrease, not change, or change in some direction that cannot be determined?

2. Jake consumes only asparagus and broccoli. He is initially maximizing his utility so that:

$$\frac{MU_A}{P_A} = \frac{MU_B}{P_B}$$

with MU_A the marginal utility from asparagus, P_A the price of asparagus, MU_B the marginal utility from broccoli, and P_B the price of broccoli. The price of asparagus rises as a result of the shift in the supply curve shown in Figure 7.4. Use the condition for utility maximization to explain how Jake will move to a new utility-maximizing equilibrium. Show the connection between your explanation and the change in the figure.

FIGURE 7.4
Short Answer Problem 2

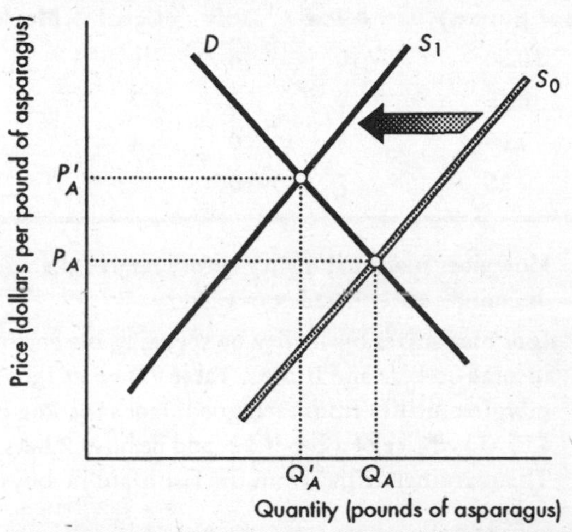

3. Lori has $40 a week that she spends on playing tennis and buying comic books. A set of tennis costs $1 and a comic book costs $2. One week when Lori spent all her income, she found that the marginal utility from the last set of tennis was 16 and that the marginal utility from the last comic book was 20.
   a. How can we show that Lori's choice of how many sets of tennis to play and how many comic books to buy was not optimal?
   b. To increase her utility, which good should Lori consume more of and which less?

4. Explain how the consumer equilibrium condition and the principle of diminishing marginal utility can be used to derive the law of demand.

5. Table 7.3 (on the next page) shows Alice's, Bob's, and Carol's demand schedules for rutabagas (a potato-like vegetable that is one of Canada's main exports).
   a. Assume that Alice, Bob, and Carol comprise the entire market and complete the table by calculating the market demand schedule.

b. On a single diagram, draw the individual demand curves for Alice, Bob, and Carol, as well as the market demand curve.

Table 7.3 Short Answer Problem 5

Price (dollars per pound)	Quantity demanded (pounds per week) Alice	Bob	Carol	Market
$0.50	10	4	10	___
0.75	9	2	7	___
1.00	8	0	4	___
1.25	7	0	1	___

6. How does marginal utility theory resolve the diamond / water paradox of value?
7. Igor maximizes his utility by spending his entire income on bats and lizards. Table 7.4 gives Igor's marginal utility from each good. Igor's income is $16. The price of a bat is $2, and he buys 2 bats. The marginal utility from the last lizard he buys is 36.
   a. Calculate the price of a lizard *two* ways.
   b. What is Igor's total utility?
   c. Igor could buy 4 lizards. If he did so and also purchased the maximum number of bats possible given his income, what would be his total utility?
   d. The marginal utility of even the fourth lizard exceeds the marginal utility from the first bat; yet when maximizing his utility, Igor nonetheless buys some bats. Explain why Igor buys some bats. (Hint: Igor is not batty.)

Table 7.4 Short Answer Problem 7

Quantity	Marginal utility Bats	Lizards
1	20	50
2	18	44
3	14	36
4	8	26

8. Tables 7.5 and 7.6 give Liz's utility from her consumption of popcorn and candy.
   a. Complete Tables 7.5 and 7.6.

Table 7.5 Liz's Utility from Popcorn

Bags of popcorn	Total utility	Marginal utility from last bag
0	0	XX
1	20	20
2	36	16
3	50	___
4	___	12
5	72	___
6	80	___

Table 7.6 Liz's Utility from Candy Bars

Candy bars	Total utility	Marginal utility from last bar
0	0	XX
1	14	14
2	26	12
3	___	10
4	44	___
5	51	___
6	57	___

Table 7.7 Liz's Marginal Utilities per Dollar

Bags of popcorn	*MU/P*	Candy bars	*MU/P*
1	___	1	___
2	___	2	___
3	___	3	___
4	___	4	___
5	___	5	___
6	___	6	___

   b. Suppose that the price of a bag of popcorn is $1 and that the price of a candy bar is $0.50. Use the information in Tables 7.5 and 7.6 and complete Table 7.7. There, *MU/P* means marginal utility divided by price, which is equivalent to marginal utility per dollar spent.
   c. Liz's weekly allowance is $4. If she spends her entire allowance on popcorn and candy, how

much popcorn and how many candy bars will Liz consume each week?

d. In part (c), what is Liz's total utility?

e. Instead of your answer to part (c), suppose that Liz consumed 3 bags of popcorn and 2 candy bars. Explain why she would not be maximizing her utility. Be sure to compare her total utilities for the two consumption bundles — your answer to part (c) and the 3 bags of popcorn, 2 candy bars used in this question. Also use the MU/P terms to explain why consuming 3 bags of popcorn and 2 candy bars is not optimal.

9. Suppose that Liz's preferences remain as they were in Problem 7 but the price of a candy bar doubles to $1.

a. Construct a new table (similar to Table 7.7) of MU/P for popcorn and candy bars.

b. Liz's allowance continues to be $4. After the price change, how much popcorn and how many candy bars will she consume each week?

c. Are popcorn and candy bars substitutes or complements for Liz? Why?

d. Based on the information you have obtained, draw Liz's demand curve for candy bars.

10. What is the relationship between price elasticity and the speed with which marginal utility diminishes? Why does this relationship exist?

11. Figure 7.5 shows the market demand curve for wrist watches. The price of a wrist watch is P. Use the figure to illustrate the consumer surplus in this market and then explain the meaning of consumer surplus.

FIGURE 7.5
Short Answer Problem 11

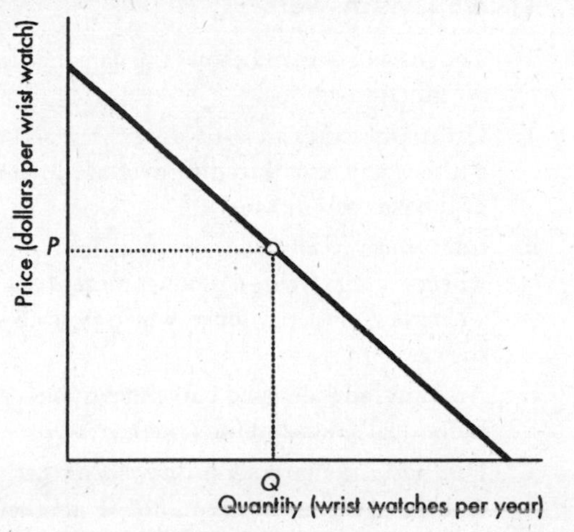

You're the Teacher

1. "This whole idea of marginal utility is stupid. I mean after all, who goes into a store and calculates the marginal utility from something before deciding to buy it? No one I know does this, so why do I have to learn this stuff?" What response do you make to your classmate? (*Don't* agree!)

2. "One thing I don't understand about all this material dealing with consumers and their choices is how I am supposed to think about products like apartments. Suppose that the rent in my apartment goes up. Marginal utility theory says that I will consume fewer apartments. But what does this mean? I'll still rent *one* apartment. And, if rent goes down, I sure won't go out and rent two! How does marginal utility theory account for this fact?" Your friend has come up with a good question; provide an equally good explanation to help your friend understand this point.

Answers

True/False Answers

1. **T** The market demand shows the demand from *all* individuals.
2. **T** Utility measures an individual's satisfaction without any regard to the prices of the items or the person's income.
3. **F** Consumers receive consumer surplus whenever they value a product more than what they must pay for it, which typically is the case.
4. **F** An individual demand curve shows one individual's demand for a product.
5. **T** Diminishing marginal utility means that the additional utility from consuming another unit of a product falls as more of the product is consumed.
6. **F** Economists assume that households maximize their total utility.
7. **T** These are the two conditions necessary for a household to maximize its utility.
8. **F** Products with high prices must have high marginal utilities, not necessarily high total utilities.
9. **F** To be in equilibrium, the marginal utilities divided by the prices, MU/P, must be equal.
10. **T** In this case, the gain in utility from consuming one dollar more of X exceeds the loss in utility from consuming one dollar less of Y.
11. **F** Marginal utility theory is an abstraction that helps us understand events in the real world.
12. **F** The principle of diminishing marginal utility implies that the *marginal* utility from additional units declines.
13. **T** As this definition stresses, marginal utility is the extra utility from an extra unit of a good.
14. **T** The budget line shows the limits to what a consumer can afford to purchase.

Multiple Choice Answers

1. **c** The marginal utility diminishes and, as a result, total utility increases but by less as each additional unit of the good is consumed.
2. **d** If Andrew is maximizing his utility, $MU_{\text{pizza}}/P_{\text{pizza}} = MU_{\text{BMW}}/P_{\text{BMW}}$. But without information about the prices of BMWs and pizzas, we cannot determine whether this condition is satisfied.
3. **b** To maximize his utility, Robert must set $MU_{\text{soda}}/P_{\text{soda}} = MU_{\text{pizza}}/P_{\text{pizza}}$. Because $MU_{\text{soda}}/P_{\text{soda}} = 10/1 = 10$, in order for $MU_{\text{pizza}}/P_{\text{pizza}}$ also to equal 10, with $MU_{\text{pizza}} = 20$, $P_{\text{pizza}} = \$2$.
4. **b** The same reasoning outlined in the answer to Question 3 applies and $P_{\text{pizza}} = \$2$. Even though Robert's and Courtney's marginal utilities are not the same, nonetheless to maximize their utility, both set $MU_{\text{soda}}/P_{\text{soda}} = MU_{\text{pizza}}/P_{\text{pizza}}$.
5. **a** By maximizing their total utilities, people make themselves as well off as possible.
6. **c** Because $MU_{\text{burrito}} < MU_{\text{taco}}$, if Brian consumes any burritos (so that we know $MU_{\text{burrito}}/P_{\text{burrito}} = MU_{\text{taco}}/P_{\text{taco}}$), then $P_{\text{burrito}} < P_{\text{taco}}$.
7. **d** To maximize her utility, Kelly consumes the amounts of the different goods that cause equality between the marginal utilities of each good divided by its price.
8. **c** With a higher price for a banana, consumers decrease the quantity they consume, which raises the marginal utility of bananas.
9. **b** This is the definition of consumer surplus.
10. **a** The answer to Question 9 gave the definition of consumer surplus, and the answer to this question illustrates consumer surplus by using the demand curve and the price paid.
11. **b** Consumer surplus equals the value of the product ($1.50) minus its price ($0.50).
12. **a** Michael consumes fewer steaks, so the marginal utility from the last steak he consumes is higher.
13. **b** Consider a large drop in the price of gasoline. To bring $MU_{\text{gas}}/P_{\text{gas}}$ back to equality with MU/P for other goods, more gasoline will be consumed, which lowers MU_{gas}. If the marginal utility schedule declines rapidly, only a little more gasoline is consumed before

MU_{gas} falls enough that MU_{gas}/P_{gas} equals MU/P for everything else. Hence the large drop in the price of gasoline causes only a small increase in the quantity demanded.

14. **c** $MU_{CDs}/P_{CDs} = MU_{cassettes}/P_{cassettes}$. Hence Lisa is already maximizing her utility.
15. **c** Because the second slice of pizza is valued less than the first, consumer surplus from the second slice is less than that from the first.
16. **d** Utility cannot be measured, so this requirement is not an assumption of marginal utility theory.
17. **c** With $P_{beef} > P_{gum}$, in order to have $MU_{beef}/P_{beef} = MU_{gum}/P_{gum}$, of necessity $MU_{beef} > MU_{gum}$.
18. **b** Chuck generally consumes greater quantities of each good, so the *MU* of these goods is lower.
19. **c** Because *MU*/*P* is equal for all goods, if two products have the same *P*, they must have the same *MU*.
20. **d** A household's consumption is determined by the interplay of its preferences, its income, and the prices of the products.
21. **c** Because more milk is consumed, the *MU* from milk is lower than the *MU* from rubies.
22. **c** For the first pound, Jack would pay $5 but actually pays only $2, thereby receiving $3 of consumer surplus for this pound. Similarly, for the second pound, Jack gets $2 of consumer surplus because he would pay $4, but actually pays only $2. The third pound gives $1 in consumer surplus, and the fourth pound has no consumer surplus. The total consumer surplus is $6.
23. **b** When Amy buys 1 yellow paper pad, she can buy 3 law books. With this consumption bundle, $MU_{pad}/P_{pad} = 4$ and $MU_{book}/P_{book} = 4$.
24. **c** Amy receives utility of 16 from yellow paper pads and 30 (12 + 10 + 8) from law books, for total utility of 46.
25. **c** Amy now buys 2 paper pads and 4 law books because this combination of pads and books uses all her income and sets $MU_{pad}/P_{pad} = MU_{book}/P_{book} = 3$
26. **b** Amy has utility of 28 (16 + 12) from yellow paper pads and 36 (12 + 10 + 8 + 6) from law books for total utility of 64.
27. **d** As less of a good is consumed, its total utility falls.

Answers to Short Answer Problems

1. After the inflation Loren still purchases 2 video games and 8 compact discs. Loren buys the combination of games and CDs that maximizes her utility, spending all her income and setting $MU_{games}/P_{games} = MU_{CDs}/P_{CDs}$. After (and before) the inflation, buying 2 video games and 8 compact discs uses up all of Loren's income, so the first criteria is met. For the second requirement, before the inflation the combination of 2 games and 8 CDs maximized Loren's utility so that it was the case that $MU_{games}/P_{games} = MU_{CDs}/P_{CDs}$. After the inflation, the marginal utilities do not change but the prices double. So, MU/P for games equals $MU_{games}/(2 \times P_{games})$ and the ratio for CDs equals $MU_{CDs}/(2 \times P_{CDs})$. Thus the *MU*/*P* for video games is half what it was before, as is the *MU*/*P* for compact discs. Because they were equal before the inflation, dividing each by 2 does not change their equality; that is, after the inflation the second condition for utility maximization is still met. Hence the combination of 2 games and 8 CDs continues to maximize Loren's utility, so that is the combination she will purchase.
2. When the price of asparagus rises,

$$\frac{MU_A}{P_A} < \frac{MU_B}{P_B}.$$

Jake no longer is in equilibrium. To restore the equilibrium condition (equality), Jake must change his consumption to make MU_A rise and MU_B fall. Because marginal utility diminishes with increases in the quantity consumed, Jake decreases his consumption of asparagus and increases his consumption of broccoli. Jake's decreased consumption of asparagus moves him upward and leftward on the demand curve, from the initial intersection of D and S_0 to the intersection of D and S_1. In the new consumer equilibrium, equality is restored between the MU/P for asparagus and the MU/P for broccoli.

3. a. Lori is not maximizing her utility because the marginal utility per dollar spent on the set of tennis ($16/\$1 = 16$) is not the same as the marginal utility per dollar spent on comic books ($20/\$2 = 10$).
   b. To equate the marginal utilities per dollar spent (and thus increase utility), Lori should increase her consumption of tennis and decrease her consumption of comic books. To show that this change raises her utility, we use marginal analysis. By cutting back a dollar on comic books, Lori loses 10 units of utility; by then spending the dollar on tennis, Lori gains 16 units. Hence, on net, Lori gains 6 units of utility by changing her consumption bundle.
4. Suppose that an individual in consumer equilibrium consumes only two goods, X_0 units of good X and Y_0 units of good Y with the prices of X and Y given by P_X and P_Y, respectively. Hence, at consumption levels X_0 and Y_0, the marginal utility per dollar spent on X equals the marginal utility per dollar spent on Y. If the price of X rises, how does the consumer respond? The marginal utility per dollar spent on X declines and thus is now less than the marginal utility per dollar spent on Y. To restore equilibrium, the consumer must increase the marginal utility of X and decrease the marginal utility of Y. From the principle of diminishing marginal utility we know that the only way to do so is to decrease the consumption of X and increase the consumption of Y. This action demonstrates the law of demand because a rise in the price of X causes a decrease in the consumption of X to restore consumer equilibrium.
5. a. Table 7.8 gives the market demand. For an example of how to calculate these answers, at the price of \$0.50 per pound, the market demand is 24, with 10 demanded by Alice plus 4 demanded by Bob plus 10 demanded by Carol.
   b. Figure 7.6 shows the three individual demand curves and the market demand curve.

Table 7.8 Short Answer Problem 5

Price (dollars per pound)	Market demand
\$0.50	24
0.75	18
1.00	12
1.25	8

FIGURE 7.6
Short Answer Problem 5

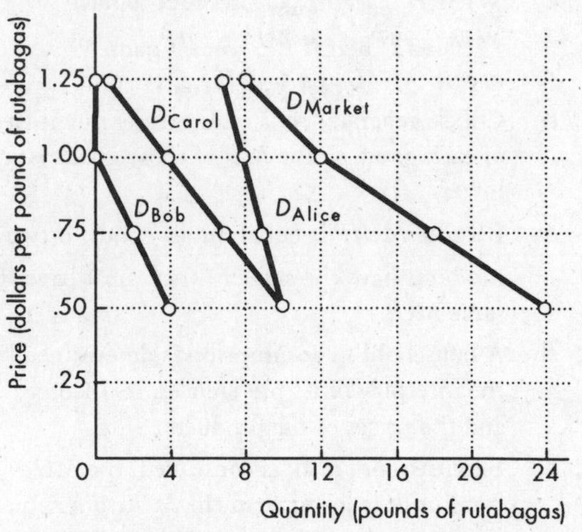

6. We resolve the paradox of value by recognizing that, although the total utility from consumption of water is large, the marginal utility from the last unit of water is small. The total utility from the consumption of diamonds is small, but the marginal utility of the last unit of diamonds is large. In consumer equilibrium, because the marginal utility per dollar spent is the same for water and diamonds, the price of water must be low and the price of a diamond must be high.
7. a. There are two methods for calculating the price of a lizard. One method is based on the fact that Igor spends all his income on bats and lizards. This fact means that:

$$Y = P_b \times Q_b + P_l \times Q_l$$

where Y is income, P_b is the price of a bat, Q_b is the quantity of bats bought, P_l is the price of a lizard, and Q_l is the quantity of lizards purchased. We know that $Y = \$16$, $P_b = \$2$, $Q_b = 2$, and, if the marginal utility of the last lizard is 36, that $Q_l = 3$. Substituting these values, we solve for P_l:

$$\$16 = \$2 \times 2 + P_l \times 3$$
$$\$12 = P_l \times 3$$
$$\$4 = P_l$$

The second way to determine the price of a lizard uses the condition for utility maximization, namely,

$$\frac{MU_l}{P_l} = \frac{MU_b}{P_b}.$$

We know that $MU_l = 36$, $P_b = \$2$, and, if Igor buys 2 bats, that $MU_b = 18$. Substituting these values, we solve for P_l:

$$\frac{36}{P_l} = \frac{18}{\$2}$$
$$\frac{36}{9} = P_l$$
$$\$4 = P_l$$

b. Igor receives total utility of 38 from his bats (20 + 18) and total utility of 130 from his lizards (50 + 44 + 36). Igor's overall total utility from bats and lizards is 168.

c. If Igor buys 4 lizards, because each lizard costs \$4, he spends all his income and so can purchase no bats. In this case, Igor's total utility is 156 (50 + 44 + 36 + 26).

d. Even though each bat returns less marginal utility than a lizard, bats are less expensive then lizards. Thus, when Igor is selecting his utility-maximizing combination of bats and lizards, the cheapness of bats means that he will buy some. For example, compare Igor's total utility when he buys 2 bats and 3 lizards, given in part (b) as 168, with his total utility when he buys 0 bats and 4 lizards, computed in part (c) as 156. Clearly Igor's *total* utility is higher when he buys 2 bats and 3 lizards than when he concentrates solely on lizards by purchasing 4 lizards and 0 bats.

8. a. Tables 7.9 and 7.10 are completed versions of Tables 7.5 and 7.6, respectively.

b. Table 7.11 completes Table 7.7.

Table 7.9 Liz's Utility from Popcorn

Bags of popcorn	Total utility	Marginal utility from last bag
0	0	XX
1	20	20
2	36	16
3	50	14
4	62	12
5	72	10
6	80	8

Table 7.10 Liz's Utility from Candy Bars

Candy bars	Total utility	Marginal utility from last bar
0	0	XX
1	14	14
2	26	12
3	36	10
4	44	8
5	51	7
6	57	6

Table 7.11 Liz's Marginal Utilities per Dollar

Bags of popcorn	MU/P	Candy bars	MU/P
1	20	1	28
2	16	2	24
3	14	3	20
4	12	4	16
5	10	5	14
6	8	6	12

c. 2 bags of popcorn and 4 candy bars. This combination uses up all of Liz's income and also equates the marginal utility per dollar spent on popcorn and candy bars (16).

d. Total utility is the utility from the consumption of 2 bags of popcorn (36) plus the utility from the consumption of 4 candy bars (44) or 80.

e. If Liz consumed 3 bags of popcorn and 2 candy bars, total utility would be 76, which is less than 80, the total utility from the consumption of 2 bags of popcorn and 4 candy bars. For the combination of 3 bags of popcorn and 2 candy bars, *MU/P* for popcorn is 14 and *MU/P* for candy bars is 24. Because *MU/P* is not the same for both goods, this combination does not meet the condition for utility maximization. More specifically, Liz could decrease her consumption of popcorn by a dollar and use the dollar to buy more candy bars and this would raise her total utility. This marginal analysis shows that Liz can increase her total utility by consuming less popcorn and more candy whenever the *MU/P* from popcorn is less than the *MU/P* from candy bars.

9. a. Table 7.12 shows Liz's *MU/P* for candy and candy after the price hike for candy. Keep in mind that the price rise did not change Liz's *MU*s.

b. Liz will consume 3 bags of popcorn and 1 candy bar. This combination of popcorn and candy spends all of Liz's income ($4), and the marginal utility per dollar spent is the same for popcorn and candy bars (14).

Table 7.12 Liz's (New) Marginal Utilities per Dollar

Bags of popcorn	MU/P	Candy bars	MU/P
1	20	1	14
2	16	2	12
3	14	3	10
4	12	4	8
5	10	5	7
6	8	6	6

c. Popcorn and candy bars are substitutes for Liz because a rise in the price of a candy bar causes an increase in the demand for popcorn.

d. Two points on Liz's demand curve have been identified. When the price of a candy bar is $1, 1 candy bar will be demanded, and when the price is $0.50, 4 candy bars will be demanded. The demand curve is a line through these two points, as illustrated in Figure 7.7.

FIGURE 7.7
Short Answer Problem 9

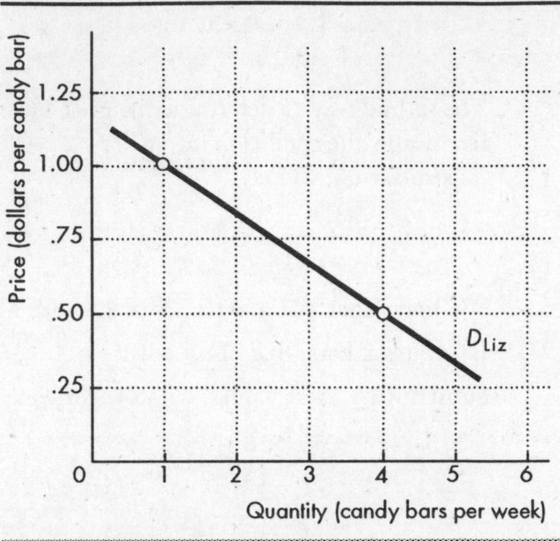

10. The more rapidly the marginal utility from a good diminishes, the less price elastic is the demand for the product. Conversely, the less rapidly the marginal utility diminishes, the more elastic is the demand for the product. For an example, take the case of sugar. The marginal utility of sugar diminishes rapidly as more units of it are consumed. Initially consumers set the *MU/P* from sugar equal to the *MU/P* for all other products. Suppose that the price of sugar falls by a substantial amount. This change causes the marginal utility per dollar spent on sugar — *MU/P* — to rise (a lot) because *P* falls (a lot). In response to the increase in the *MU/P* of sugar, people consume more sugar. This increase in consumption reduces sugar's marginal utility, and the *MU/P* from sugar falls. Enough additional sugar will be consumed so that the *MU/P* from sugar will fall back to equality with the *MU/P* from all other products. How much sugar consumption is required? Because the marginal utility from sugar falls rapidly as more sugar is consumed, not very much more sugar must be consumed in order to reduce substantially the *MU/P* of sugar. Thus, when the marginal utility from a good diminishes rapidly, a large price change causes only a small change in the quantity

demanded. In other words, the demand for the product is price inelastic.

11. Figure 7.8 shows the consumer surplus in the watch market. Consumer surplus equals the difference between the value of a product and its price. The value that consumers assign to different units of a product is equal to the height of the demand curve because this height shows how much someone is willing to pay for a particular unit of the good. The actual price that must be paid is usually less than this maximum amount. Thus the vertical distance between the demand curve and the price is the consumer surplus for any particular unit of the good. As illustrated in Figure 7.8, the area between the demand curve and the price of the product is the total consumer surplus from all units of the good.

FIGURE 7.8
Short Answer Problem 11

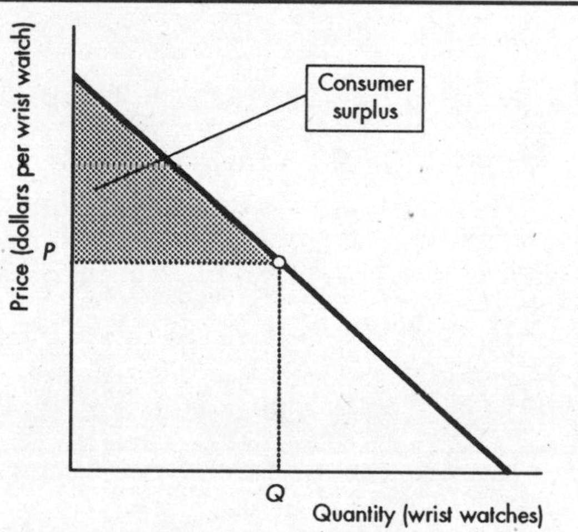

■ You're the Teacher

1. "You're right that no one goes into a store and calculates marginal utility before deciding whether to buy something. But that is missing the point of marginal utility theory. Marginal utility theory is *not* trying to explain how people make decisions about what to buy. Instead, it is based on the assumption that people make themselves as well off as possible — maximize their utility — to explain how people respond to changes in prices and incomes. It's not a theory of people's thoughts. It's a theory of people's actions."

2. "What you are missing is the fact that apartments are not all identical. My apartment is larger than yours. If the price of an apartment rose — rents go up — I'd move to a smaller apartment. Or, if the price went down, I wouldn't rent two apartments but I'd move to a larger one. So, think about it this way: If the price of an apartment goes up, we'll consume 'fewer' apartments by renting smaller apartments; and, if the price goes down, we'll consume 'more' apartments by renting larger ones."

8 POSSIBILITIES, PREFERENCES, AND CHOICES

Key Concepts

Consumption Possibilities

The **budget line** shows the limits to a household's consumption. Figure 8.1 graphs a budget line; the formula for the budget line in this figure is:

$$Q_{soda} = \frac{y}{P_{soda}} - \left(\frac{P_{movies}}{P_{soda}}\right) Q_{movies}$$

- (y/P_{soda}) is the consumer's **real income** in terms of soda. An increase in income (y) shifts the budget line rightward but does not change its slope.
- The magnitude of the slope of the budget line (P_{movies}/P_{soda}) is the **relative price** of a movie in terms of a soda. Changes in the relative price rotate the budget line.

FIGURE 8.1
The Budget Line

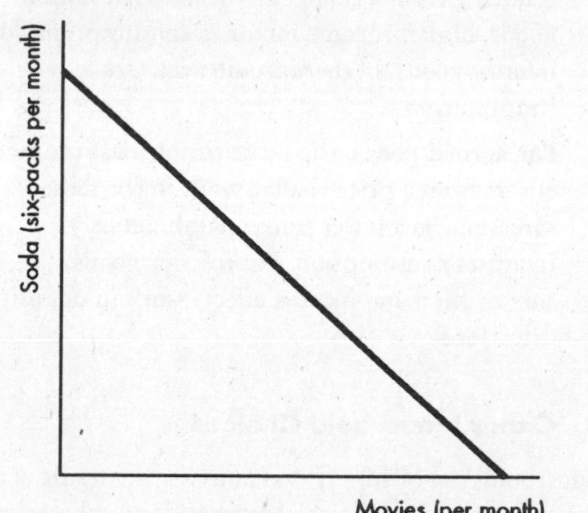

Preferences and Indifference Curves

Preferences are a person's likes and dislikes; they do not depend on price or income. **Indifference curves** map preferences, joining combinations of goods giving equal satisfaction. Figure 8.2 illustrates a family of indifference curves.

FIGURE 8.2
Indifference Curves

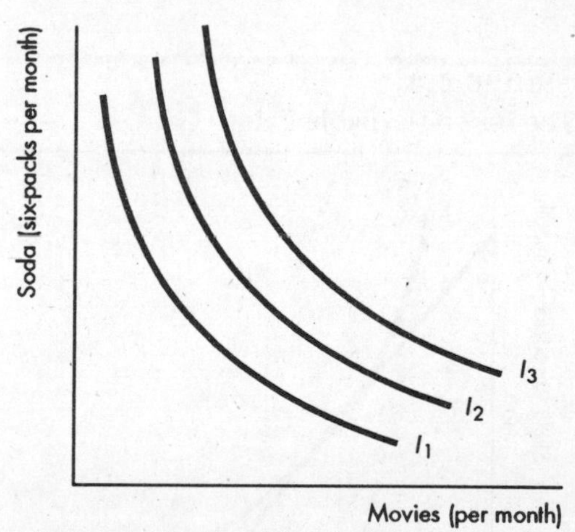

- Indifference curves farther from the origin represent higher levels of satisfaction.
- Indifference curves never intersect.

The **marginal rate of substitution** (**MRS**) is the rate at which the household gives up the good on the vertical axis (soda) for an additional unit of the good on the horizontal axis (movies) and still remains indifferent. The magnitude of the slope of the indifference curve equals the MRS.

- The **diminishing marginal rate of substitution** is the tendency for the MRS to fall in value moving down along an indifference curve. This accounts for the concave shape of indifference curves.

- Products that are good substitutes have straighter indifference curves; goods that are complements have more bowed indifference curves.

The Household's Consumption Choice

A household allocates its income to maximize its satisfaction. The household chooses the best affordable point. This point is a combination that is on the budget line and on the highest possible indifference curve. Figure 8.3 illustrates this, where the household consumes M movies and S soda. At this optimal point:

- The household spends all its income and achieves maximum satisfaction.
- The budget line and indifference curve are tangent and have same slope so that the MRS equals the relative price.

FIGURE 8.3
The Best Affordable Point

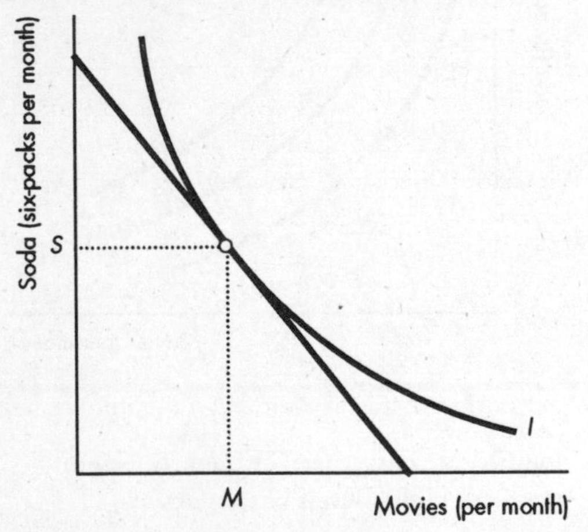

Predicting Consumer Behavior

The price effect is the change in consumption resulting from a change in the price of a good. When the price of a movie falls, the budget line rotates as shown in Figure 8.4 and the consumption of movies increases from M_1 to M_2. This analysis can be used to derive the demand curve for movies. The price effect can be divided into a substitution effect plus an income effect.

- **The substitution effect** is the change in consumption resulting from a change in price accompanied by a (hypothetical) change in income that leaves the household indifferent between the initial and new situations. For both normal and inferior goods, the substitution effect of a price fall increases consumption of the good.

FIGURE 8.4
A Fall in the Price of Movies

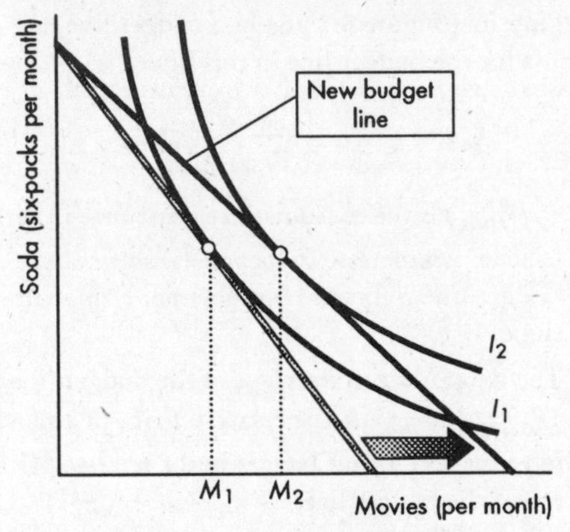

- **The income effect** is the change in consumption resulting from a change in income. For normal goods, higher income increases consumption; for inferior goods, higher income decreases consumption.
- For normal goods, the substitution and income effects from a price change work in the same direction, so a lower price unambiguously increases consumption. For inferior goods, the substitution and income effects work in opposite directions.

Other Household Choices

Households' labor supply decisions are the result of a utility maximizing choice of time allocation between labor and leisure.

- A budget line and indifference curves exist between leisure and consumption of other goods.

- A rise in the wage rate changes the slope of the budget line and creates income and substitution effects. The substitution effect leads to more hours spent working, but the income effect causes hours at work to decline.

Saving is the choice between consuming now and consuming in the future (by saving now).

- The **lifetime budget line** between current and future consumption rotates when the interest rate changes. The substitution effect from this change motivates more saving.

Helpful Hints

1. Although the analysis in this chapter may seem technical, it helps to maintain a broad perspective. All this analysis does is translate into a diagram economists' general view that people strive to make themselves as well off as possible. This assumption — that people try to maximize their utility — is perhaps one concise description of economics!

   Even though people do the best possible, they face constraints. These constraints, which limit the range of possible choices, depend on income and the prices of goods and are represented graphically by the budget line. Doing the best means finding the most preferred outcome consistent with those constraints. In this chapter, preferences are represented graphically by indifference curves. Graphically, the problem is to find the highest indifference curve attainable given the budget line. To make graphical analysis feasible, we restrict ourselves to choices between only two goods, but the same principles apply in the real world to a broader array of choices.

2. The budget equation for soda and movies discussed in the text is:

$$Q_s = \frac{y}{P_s} - \left(\frac{P_m}{P_s}\right) Q_m$$

   This equation is the type of straight line equation ($y = a + bx$) that was discussed in Chapter 2 of this Study Guide. The differences are that Q_s takes the place of y as the dependent variable and Q_m takes the place of x as the independent variable. Note that the budget equation is the same as the equation for a straight line. Thus what you know about a straight line helps you to remember the relevant facts about the budget line. For example, the vertical intercept — where a straight line crosses the vertical axis — is equal to a in the straight line formula. Taking the place of a in the budget equation is y/P_s. Hence the vertical intercept of the budget line is y/P_s! Similarly, in the formula for a straight line, the slope equals b. In the budget equation, the "b" parameter is $-(P_m/P_s)$. Thus $-(P_m/P_s)$ equals the slope of the budget line.

3. The magnitude of the slope of the budget line between movies and soda is (P_m/P_s). This term is the opportunity cost of a movie in terms of sodas; in other words, it tells us how many sodas must be lost to consume an additional movie. It also is the relative price of a movie in terms of soda. That is, the relative price of a movie rises either because the money price of a movie (P_m) rises or because the money price of soda (P_s) falls. Both changes rotate the budget line and make it steeper.

4. It is important to realize that indifference curves plot people's preferences and do not depend on their incomes or the prices of the goods. For example, an indifference curve indicates how much a person likes — or dislikes — lobster without regard to the price of a lobster or the person's income. When the price of a lobster or the person's income changes, the person's budget line changes but the indifference curves do not change. In other words, a person who *really* likes lobster likes it regardless of income. Now, the amount of lobster that the person actually buys does depend on income so that higher income leads to more lobster being consumed. But the reason that more lobster is consumed is because the person's budget line has shifted outward, making more combinations of goods affordable. It is not because the person's indifference curves have moved.

5. Understanding the distinction between the income and substitution effects of a change in the price of a good can be challenging. Consider a fall in the price of a good, perhaps ground beef. There are two effects on the consumption of ground beef. First, the drop in the price of ground beef reduces the relative price of ground beef and, second, it increases real income. The substitution effect is

the answer to the question: How much would the consumption of ground beef change as a result of the relative price decline if we also (hypothetically) reduced income by enough to leave the consumer indifferent between the new and original situations? The income effect is the answer to the question: How much more would the consumption of ground beef change if we (hypothetically) restored the consumer's real income but left relative prices at the new level?

Questions

True/False/Uncertain and Explain

1. The budget line has a negative slope and is linear.
2. For an inferior good, an increase in income shifts the budget line leftward
3. A person's indifference curves do not cross.
4. When the relative price of a good falls, the income effect leads to increased consumption of the good.
5. The magnitude of the slope of a person's indifference curve is the marginal rate of substitution.
6. Both the substitution effect and income effect from higher wages lead to a decrease in the quantity of labor supplied.
7. The best affordable point of consumption is on the budget line and on the highest attainable indifference curve.
8. The substitution effect can be divided into the price effect and income effect.
9. Goods that are perfect substitutes have "L" shaped indifference curves.
10. The marginal rate of substitution falls when moving upward along an indifference curve.
11. The law of demand can be derived from an indifference curve model by tracing the impact of changes in price on the quantity demanded.
12. The indifference curve/budget line approach shows that a rise in the interest rate must decrease people's saving.
13. Indifference curves farther from the origin are associated with higher satisfaction.
14. The best affordable point is on the consumer's highest indifference curve.
15. All points on an indifference curve have the same amount of total satisfaction.

Multiple Choice

1. Which of the following statements best describes a consumer's budget line?
   a. It shows all combinations of goods among which the consumer is indifferent.
   b. It shows the limits to a consumer's set of affordable consumption choices.
   c. It shows the desired level of consumption for the consumer.
   d. It shows the consumption choices made by a consumer.
2. If your local newspaper reported that wearing plaid clothing was a sure way to obtain good grades, students'
   a. budget lines would shift rightward to compensate for the higher price of plaid clothing.
   b. budget lines would rotate so that more plaid clothing would be purchased.
   c. preferences would change in favor of more plaid clothing.
   d. None of the above.
3. If two goods are perfect substitutes, their
   a. indifference curves are positively sloped straight lines.
   b. indifference curves are negatively sloped straight lines.
   c. indifference curves are L shaped.
   d. marginal rate of substitution is infinity.

4. Over the past 100 years, the quantity of labor supplied has decreased as wages have risen. This change indicates that the income effect
   a. and the substitution effect have both discouraged leisure.
   b. and the substitution effect have both encouraged leisure.
   c. encouraging leisure has dominated the substitution effect discouraging leisure.
   d. has not affected the labor–leisure choice.

5. If the indifference curves between two goods are L shaped, the goods are
   a. complementary goods.
   b. substitute goods.
   c. normal goods.
   d. inferior goods

For the next two questions, use Figure 8.5.

FIGURE **8.5**
Multiple Choice Questions 6 and 7

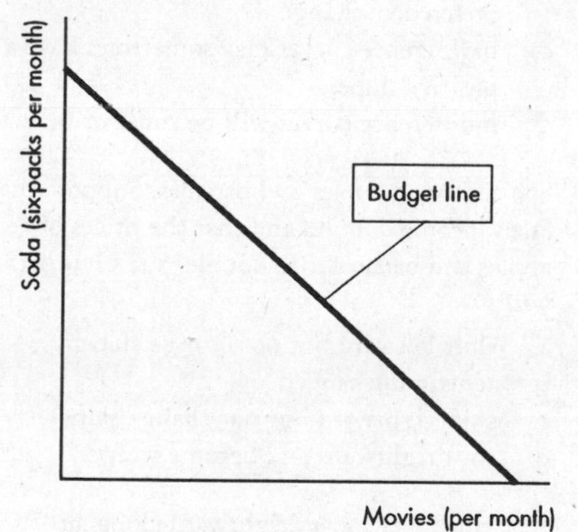

6. Suppose that this consumer's income increased. As a result, the budget line
   a. rotates around the vertical intercept and becomes steeper.
   b. rotates around the vertical axis and becomes shallower.
   c. shift rightward and becomes steeper.
   d. shift rightward and its slope does not change.

7. Suppose that the price of a movie rises. This change causes the budget line to
   a. rotate around the vertical intercept and become steeper.
   b. rotate around the vertical axis and become flatter.
   c. shift rightward and become steeper.
   d. shift rightward and not change its slope.

8. When oranges fall in price, the substitution effect
   a. increases the consumption of oranges only if oranges are a normal good.
   b. increases the consumption of oranges only if oranges are an inferior good.
   c. always increases the consumption of oranges.
   d. always decreases the consumption of oranges.

9. When the price of an orange falls, the income effect
   a. increases the consumption of oranges only if oranges are a normal good.
   b. increases the consumption of oranges only if oranges are an inferior good.
   c. always increases the consumption of oranges.
   d. always decreases the consumption of oranges.

10. The magnitude of the slope of the budget line
   a. is defined as the marginal rate of substitution.
   b. equals the relative price of the good measured along the horizontal axis.
   c. increases when income increases.
   d. decreases when income increases.

11. The budget line shifts
   a. only when income changes.
   b. only when prices change.
   c. when either income or prices change.
   d. None of the above because changes in income and prices do not shift the budget line.

12. Indifference curves shift
    a. only when income changes.
    b. only when prices change.
    c. when either income or prices change.
    d. None of the above because changes in income and prices do not shift indifference curves.

13. When the price of a normal good falls,
    a. both the income and substitution effects cause an increase in the quantity demanded.
    b. the income effect causes an increase in the quantity demanded and the substitution effect causes a decrease in the quantity demanded.
    c. the income effect causes a decrease in the quantity demanded and the substitution effect causes an increase in the quantity demanded.
    d. both the income and substitution effects cause a decrease in the quantity demanded.

Use Figure 8.6 for the next two questions.

FIGURE 8.6
Multiple Choice Questions 14 and 15

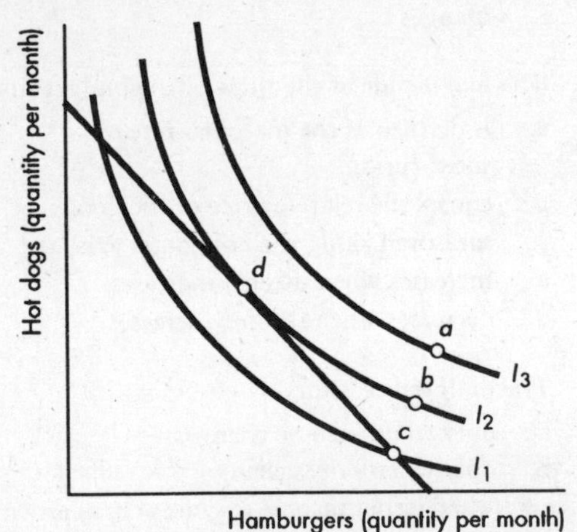

14. Which of the following statements about Figure 8.6 is correct?
    a. Point *a* is preferred to point *d*, but *a* is not affordable.
    b. Points *d* and *c* yield the same utility, but *c* is more affordable.
    c. Point *b* is preferred to point *d* , but *b* is not affordable.
    d. Points *a* and *d* cost the same, but *a* is preferred to *d*.

15. The best affordable point of consumption is point
    a. *a*.
    b. *b*.
    c. *c*.
    d. *d*.

16. Diminishing marginal rate of substitution means that
    a. the budget line has a negative slope.
    b. the budget line does not shift when people's preferences change.
    c. indifference curves may sometimes have a positive slope.
    d. indifference curves will be concave.

17. Sue consumes apples and bananas. Suppose that Sue's income doubles and that the prices of apples and bananas also double. Sue's budget line will
    a. shift leftward but not change slope.
    b. remain unchanged.
    c. shift rightward but not change slope.
    d. shift rightward and become steeper.

18. As a consumer moves rightward along an indifference curve, the
    a. consumer's total satisfaction does not change.
    b. consumer's total satisfaction generally decreases.
    c. income required to buy the combinations of the goods always increases.
    d. relative price of both goods falls.

19. Jack and Jill have different preferences about bread and water but have the same income. As a result,
    a. the amount of bread and water they consume is the same.
    b. their indifference curves between bread and water are identical.
    c. we cannot compare the amount of bread and water they consume.
    d. the amount of bread and water they consume is different

20. Which of the following statements is true?
    a. The law of diminishing marginal rate of substitution means that indifference curves are convex (bowed out).
    b. A demand curve can be derived from the indifference curve/budget line analysis.
    c. Demand curves and indifference curves measure the same things.
    d. Demand curves and indifference curves have negative slopes for the same reason.

Use Figure 8.7 for the next three questions.

FIGURE 8.7

Multiple Choice Questions 21, 22, and 23

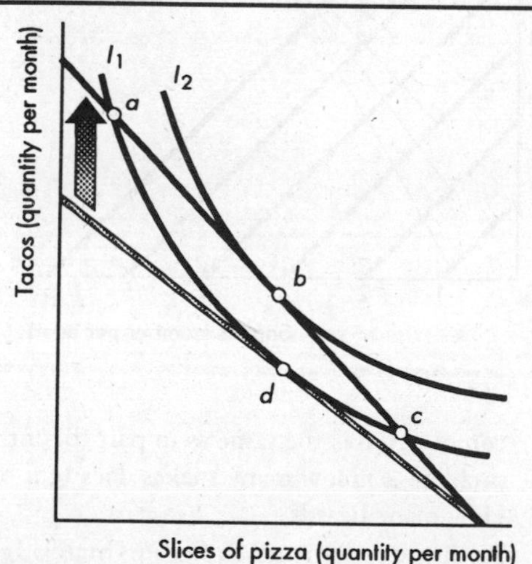

21. The change in the budget line shown in Figure 8.7 is the result of a
    a. fall in the price of a slice of pizza.
    b. fall in the price of a taco.
    c. increase in income.
    d. None of the above

22. The consumer's real income measured in units of tacos
    a. definitely increased.
    b. definitely decreased.
    c. did not change.
    d. may have changed, but it is impossible to tell from the figure.

23. The new consumer equilibrium is at point
    a. *a*.
    b. *b*.
    c. *c*.
    d. *d*.

24. The substitution effect from a rise in the interest rate
    a. decreases saving.
    b. increases current consumption.
    c. has the same effect on saving as does the income effect.
    d. increases saving.

25. Which of the following is NOT true when the consumer is at the best affordable point?
    a. The point is on the budget line and highest attainable indifference curve.
    b. The slope of the budget line equals the slope of the indifference curve.
    c. The *MRS* equals the relative price.
    d. All of the above are true at the best affordable point.

26. When you examine the effect from a change in price while (hypothetically) changing income to keep the consumer on the same indifference curve, you are examining the
    a. price effect.
    b. income effect.
    c. substitution effect.
    d. *ceterus paribus* effect.

27. People's labor supply decisions
    a. can be analyzed by using an indifference curve/budget line approach.
    b. are unrelated to their preferences.
    c. are irrelevant because people must work 40 hours a week.
    d. None of the above.

28. An inferior good
    a. has a substitution effect opposite that of a normal good.
    b. has an income effect opposite that of a normal good.
    c. has a price effect opposite that of a normal good.
    d. is one that breaks after its first use.

29. A consumer is in equilibrium when the consumption point is on
    a. the budget line.
    b. an indifference curve.
    c. the highest indifference curve that just touches the budget line.
    d. None of the above.

Short Answer Problems

1. Why do indifference curves have negative slopes?
2. As illustrated by his indifference curves in Figure 8.8, Igor thinks that snakes and lizards are perfect substitutes.
    a. Suppose that the price of a snake is $10, the price of a lizard is $20, and Igor has $60 to spend on snakes and lizards. Draw his budget line in Figure 8.8. How many snakes does Igor buy? How many lizards?
    b. Suppose that the price of a snake rises to $30 while the price of a lizard does not change. If Igor's income stays at $60, draw his new budget line in Figure 8.8. Now how many snakes does Igor buy? How many lizards?
    c. When is Igor's total satisfaction highest: before or after snakes go up in price? How can you tell?
3. Figure 8.9 again shows Igor's indifference curves. Snakes and lizards are still perfect substitutes.
    a. Snakes cost $30, lizards cost $20, and Igor's income is $60. Draw Igor's budget line in Figure 8.9. (Hint: This price/income combination is the same as in part (b) of the problem 2.) How many snakes does Igor buy? How many lizards?
    b. For his superior work in finding brains, Igor's master gives Igor a raise to $120. In Figure 8.9 draw Igor's new budget line. After the raise, how many snakes does Igor buy? How many lizards?
    c. When is Igor's total satisfaction the highest: Before or after his raise? How do you know?

FIGURE 8.8
Short Answer Problem 2

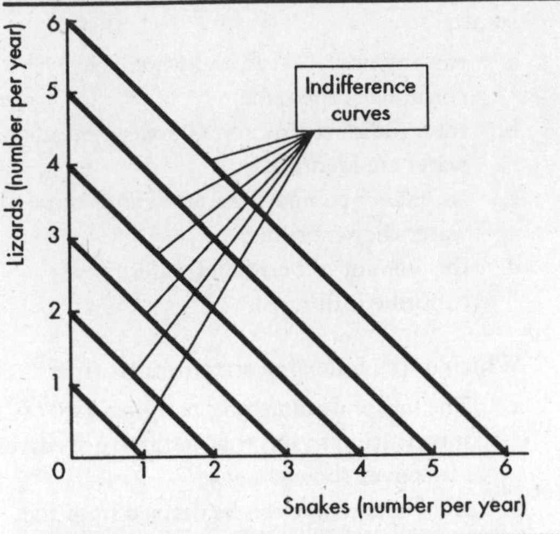

FIGURE 8.9
Short Answer Problem 3

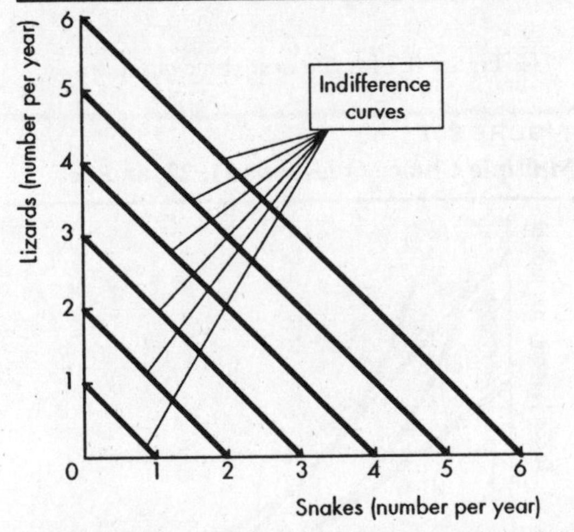

4. Jan and Dan both like bread and peanut butter and have the same income. Because they face the same prices, they have identical budget lines. Currently, Jan and Dan consume the same quantities of bread and peanut butter; they have the same best affordable consumption point. Jan, however, views bread and peanut butter as close (though not perfect) substitutes, whereas Dan considers bread and peanut butter to be quite (but not perfectly) complementary. On the same diagram, draw a budget line and representative indifference curves for Jan and Dan. (Measure the quantity of bread on the horizontal axis.)

5. In Figure 8.10, indicate the initial hours of leisure this person enjoys. Now, suppose that the wage rate rises so that the person moves to another of the indifference curves already in the figure; that is, the budget line rotates so that another indifference curve is now optimal. Draw the new budget line and show the new equilibrium amount of leisure. How did the amount of labor supplied change as the wage rate rose?

FIGURE 8.10
Short Answer Problem 5

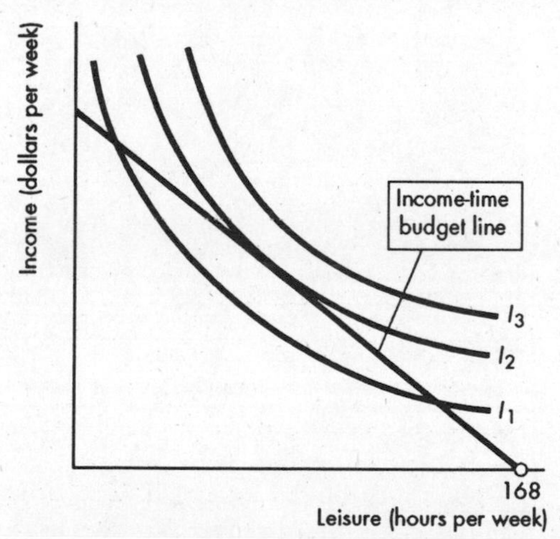

6. Ms. Muffet consumes both curds and whey. The initial price of curds is \$1 per unit, and the price of whey is \$1.50 per unit. Ms. Muffet's initial income is \$12.
   a. What is the relative price of curds?
   b. Derive Ms. Muffet's budget equation and draw her budget line on a graph. (Measure curds on the horizontal axis.)
   c. On your graph, draw an indifference curve so that the best affordable point corresponds to 6 units of curds and 4 units of whey.
   d. What is the marginal rate of substitution of curds for whey at this point?
   e. Show that any other point on the budget line is inferior.

7. For the initial situation described in problem 6, suppose that Ms. Muffet's income now increases.
   a. Illustrate graphically how the consumption of curds and whey are affected if both goods are normal. (Numerical answers are not necessary. Just show whether consumption increases or decreases.)
   b. Draw a new graph showing the effect of an increase in Ms. Muffet's income if whey is an inferior good.

8. Return to the initial circumstances described in Problem 6. Now, suppose that the price of curds doubles to \$2 a unit while the price of whey remains at \$1.50 per unit and income remains at \$12.
   a. Draw the budget line before and after the price change.
   b. Why is the initial best affordable point (label it point *a*) no longer the best affordable point?
   c. Use your graph and show the new best affordable point and label it *d*. What has happened to the consumption of curds?

9. Figure 8.11 (on the next page) illustrates Caroline's indifference map between bread and wine.
   a. Initially, the price of a bottle of wine is \$2, and the price of a loaf of bread is \$1. Caroline has \$6 to spend on bread and wine. In Figure 8.11 draw her budget line. How many bottles of wine does Caroline buy?
   b. The price of a bottle of wine falls to \$1. The price of a loaf of bread remains at \$1, and Caroline's income is constant at \$6. Draw her new budget line. How many bottles of wine does Caroline now buy?

c. Assume that Caroline's demand curve is linear. In Figure 8.12 draw Caroline's demand curve for wine.

FIGURE 8.11
Short Answer Problem 9 (a) and 9 (b)

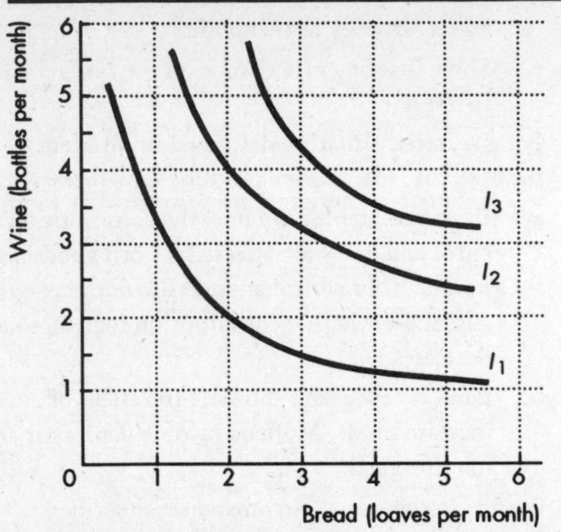

FIGURE 8.12
Short Answer Problem 9 (c)

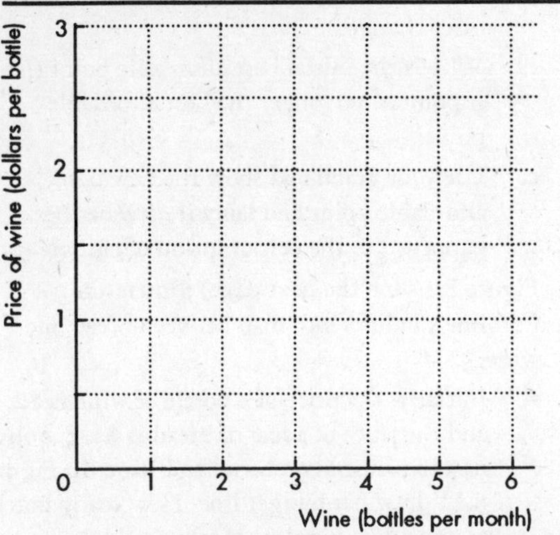

You're the Teacher

1. "I see that we can use this indifference curve/budget line approach to derive demand curves. But why bother? I mean after all, why not just use the demand curves like we've been doing all along and not worry about this other stuff?" This question is reasonable. Tell your friend why this other stuff is worth bothering about.
2. "I finally understand this chapter: Indifference curves and demand curves are the same thing! My studying is beginning to pay off." Actually your friend is not studying enough. Help your friend by explaining why indifference curves and demand curves are not the same.

Answers

True/False Answers

1. **T** The budget line is straight; indifference curves are concave (bowed toward the origin).
2. **F** The budget line shifts out, but the equilibrium amount consumed decreases.
3. **T** If an individual's indifference curves crossed there would be combinations of consumption that were considered both better than other combinations *and* equal to the other combinations, an evident contradiction.
4. **U** The income effect leads to increased consumption for normal goods and decreased consumption for inferior goods.
5. **T** The statement is how the marginal rate of substitution is calculated from graphs of indifference curves.
6. **F** The income effect decreases the quantity of labor supplied, but the substitution effect increases the quantity.
7. **T** This is the definition of the best (on the highest indifference curve) affordable (on the budget line) point.
8. **F** The price effect equals the sum of the substitution effect and the income effect.
9. **F** Goods that are complements have L shaped indifference curves.
10. **F** The marginal rate of substitution is the magnitude of the slope of an indifference curve, so the principle of diminishing marginal rate of substitution means that it increases while moving upward along an indifference curve.
11. **T** This is how a demand curve can be derived.
12. **F** Theoretically, a rise in the interest rate may either increase or decrease saving; as a practical matter, it increases saving just a bit.
13. **T** Indifference curves farther from the origin have more potential consumption of *all* goods and services and so have higher total satisfaction.
14. **F** The best affordable point is on the highest indifference curve that can be reached given the consumer's income, not on the highest overall indifference curve.
15. **T** This definition is why a consumer is indifferent between any point on a particular indifference curve.

Multiple Choice Answers

1. **b** The budget line illustrates the different combinations of consumption an individual can afford. In this sense it is like a menu, showing what can be purchased.
2. **c** Preferences change because now students "like" plaid clothing more than before.
3. **b** The more closely two goods substitute for each other, the more closely their indifference curves approach being straight lines.
4. **c** The income effect from a higher wage rate encourages people to spend less time at work and more at leisure; the substitution effect is the opposite, encouraging more time at work and less at leisure.
5. **a** Perfect complements have L shaped indifference curves.
6. **d** Changes in the relative price rotate the budget line; changes in income shift it in a parallel fashion.
7. **a** A rise in the price of a movie does not change the vertical intercept (y/P_{soda}) but the magnitude of the slope (P_{movies}/P_{soda}) increases.
8. **c** The substitution effect from a drop in price *always* motivates an increase in the consumption of the relatively cheaper good.
9. **a** The income effect of a lower price motivates an increase in the consumption of normal goods only.
10. **b** The slope indicates how many units of the good measured on the vertical axis must be given up in order to gain another unit of the good measured on the horizontal axis.
11. **c** Income and price changes shift the budget line, not indifference curves.
12. **d** Only changes in the individual's preferences shift the indifference curves.
13. **a** For normal goods, both the substitution and income effects from a lower price increase the quantity demanded.

14. **a** Point *a* is preferred because it is on a higher indifference curve, but it is not affordable because it lies beyond the budget line.

15. **d** Point *d* is on the highest indifference curve that is affordable.

16. **d** The diminishing marginal rate of substitution means that an indifference curve becomes flatter while moving rightward along it.

17. **b** The relative price of bananas and apples does not change because both prices doubled, so the slope of the budget line is unchanged. In addition, the intercepts do not change because higher income matches the higher prices.

18. **a** A movement in any direction along an indifference curve does not change the consumer's total satisfaction.

19. **d** Owing to the different preferences, each has a different combination of bread and water that yields the maximum satisfaction.

20. **b** In other words, demand curves are the result of people's maximization of their satisfaction.

21. **b** When the price of a taco falls, the maximum amount of tacos that can be purchased increases but the maximum amount of slices of pizza that can be purchased does not change.

22. **a** Real income increased because more tacos can be purchased.

23. **b** After the price change point *b* is on the highest affordable indifference curve.

24. **d** The substitution effect encourages an increase in saving.

25. **d** All the statements accurately characterize consumer equilibrium.

26. **c** This question defines the substitution effect.

27. **a** Similar to the choice about what to consume, economists assume that an individual's choice about the quantity of labor to supply reflect the person's effort to maximize satisfaction.

28. **b** Increases in income increase the demand for a normal good and decrease the demand for an inferior good.

29. **c** The consumption bundle represented by the point on the budget line where the highest indifference curve touches the budget line is the best affordable consumption bundle.

Answers to Short Answer Problems

1. An indifference curve shows how much the consumption of one good must increase as the consumption of another good decreases in order to leave the consumer indifferent (no better or worse off). It has a negative slope because both goods are desirable. In order to not be made worse off, as the consumption of one good decreases, consumption of the other good must increase. This relationship implies a negative slope.

2. a. Figure 8.13 shows the budget line as the lighter line. The point with the highest attainable utility is indicated by the circle on the horizontal axis, where the budget line touches the highest possible indifference curve. At this point Igor buys 6 snakes and 0 lizards.

   Igor selects the "corner" solution — 6 snakes and 0 lizards — because snakes and lizards are perfect substitutes. If they were not perfect substitutes, Igor's indifference curves would not be linear and Igor would buy both snakes and lizards.

FIGURE **8.13**

Short Answer Problem 2 (a)

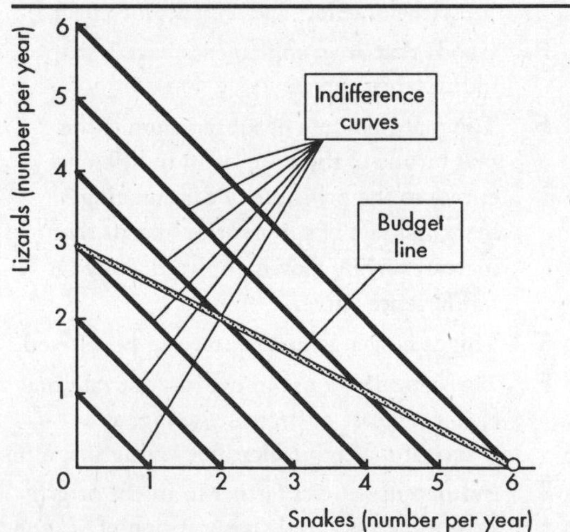

b. Figure 8.14 illustrates Igor's new (and old) budget line. After the price hike for snakes, Igor buys 0 snakes and 3 lizards.

c. Igor's total satisfaction was highest before the price of a snake rose. A comparison of Figures 8.13 and 8.14 reveals that Igor was on a higher indifference curve before the price of a snake rose, so his total satisfaction was higher at that time.

FIGURE **8.14**

Short Answer Problem 2 (b)

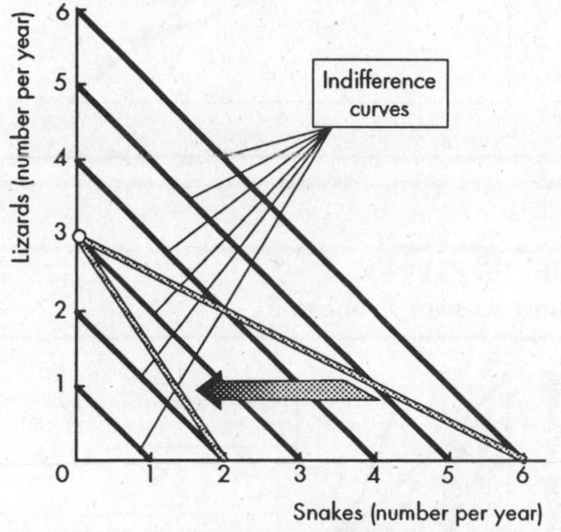

3. a. Figure 8.15 show's Igor's budget line as the lighter line. The point of maximum affordable satisfaction is on the vertical axis, where Igor buys 0 snakes and 3 lizards.

b. The increase in income shifts Igor's budget line, as indicated in Figure 8.16. After his increase in income, Igor continues to buy 0 snakes but now buys 6 lizards.

c. Igor's total satisfaction is higher after his raise because he is able to reach a higher indifference curve.

FIGURE **8.15**

Short Answer Problem 3 (a)

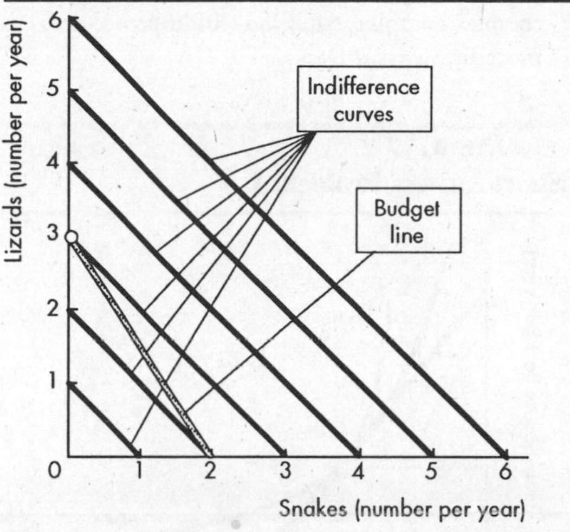

FIGURE **8.16**

Short Answer Problem 3 (b)

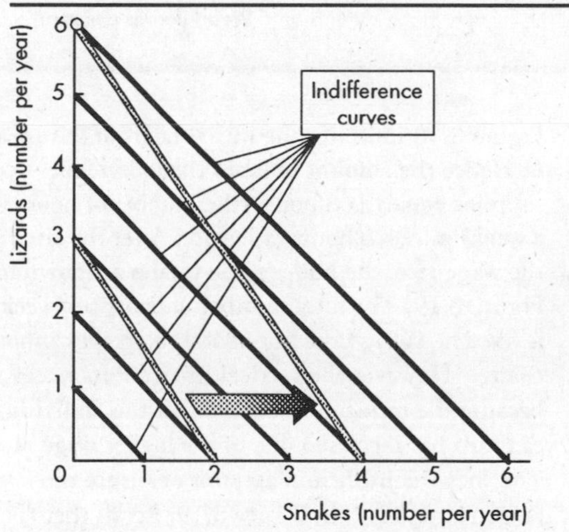

4. Figure 8.17 shows Jan and Dan's budget line and their indifference curves. Because Jan views bread and peanut butter as substitutes and Dan views them as complements, Jan's indifference curve is more linear than Dan's.

FIGURE **8.17**
Short Answer Problem 4

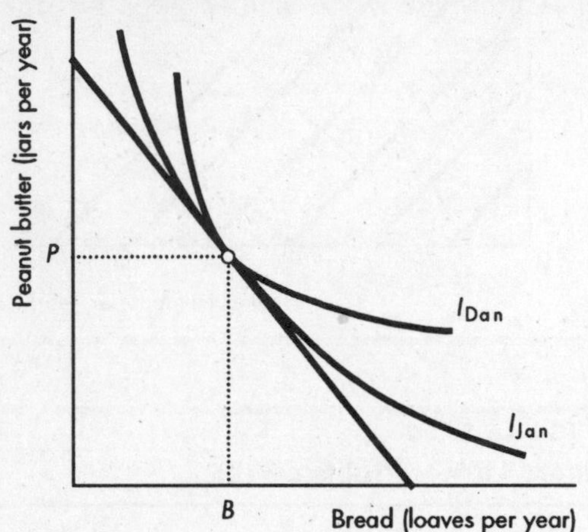

5. Figure 8.18 indicates the initial hours of leisure as *L*. Hence the amount of labor the individual supplies equals 168 hours (the number of hours in a week) minus *L* hours of leisure. After the rise in the wage rate, the budget line rotates as shown in Figure 8.19. The total number of hours per week is fixed at 168, so the horizontal intercept cannot change. However the vertical intercept increases because the maximum income that this individual can earn has increased due to the higher wage rate. The "new" equilibrium amount of leisure the person enjoys is *L* in Figure 8.19. Recall that the impact on leisure is the net result of two forces working in opposing directions: the income effect encourages an increase in leisure, whereas the substitution effect motivates a decrease in leisure. In Figure 8.19, these effects exactly offset each other because the amount of leisure does not change; it remains equal to *L*. Because the time spent at leisure did not change, neither did this person's labor supply. In other words, the higher wage did not change the quantity of labor supplied by this individual.

FIGURE **8.18**
Short Answer Problem 5

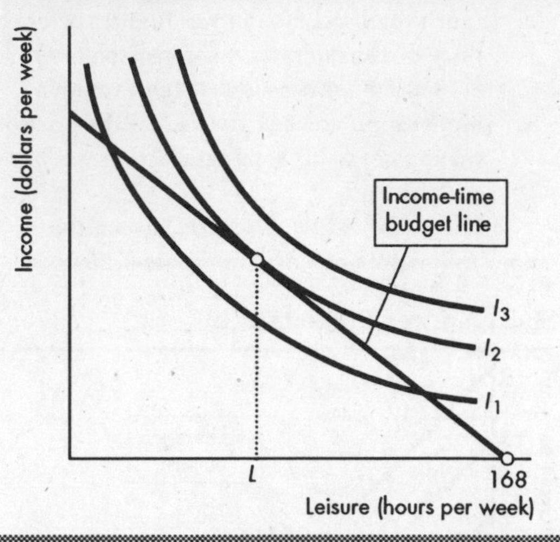

FIGURE **8.19**
Short Answer Problem 5

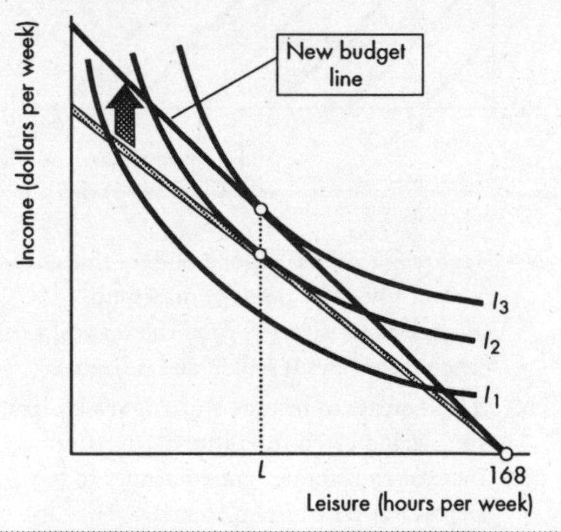

6. a The relative price of curds is the money price of curds divided by the money price of whey: (\$1 per unit of curds)/(\$1.50 per unit of whey) or ⅔ whey per curd.

b. Let P_c = the price of curds, P_w = the price of whey, Q_c = quantity of curds, Q_w = quantity of whey, and y = income. The budget equation, in general form, is:

$$Q_w = \frac{y}{P_w} - \left(\frac{P_c}{P_w}\right) Q_c$$

Because P_c = \$1, P_w = \$1.50, and y = \$12, Ms. Muffet's budget equation is specifically given by:

$$Q_w = 8 - \frac{2}{3} Q_c$$

The graph of this budget equation, the budget line, is given in Figure 8.20.

FIGURE 8.20
Short Answer Problem 6

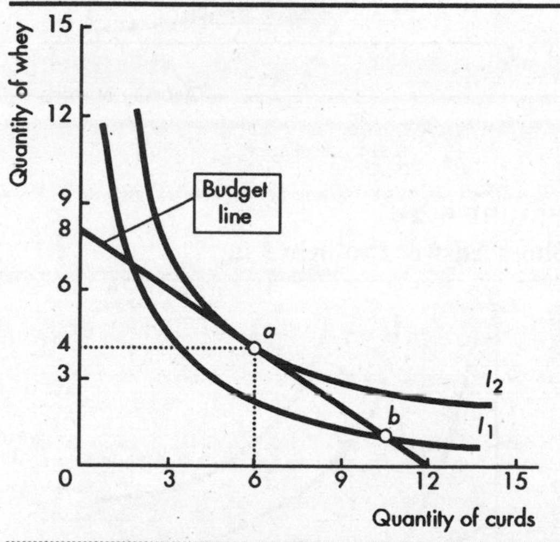

c. Indifference curve I_2 is the indifference curve tangent to the budget line so that Ms. Muffet's best affordable point, point *a*, is 6 units of curds and 4 units of whey.

d. The marginal rate of substitution is the magnitude of the slope of the indifference curve at point *a*. We do not know the slope of the indifference curve directly, but we can easily compute the slope of the budget line. At the best affordable point *a*, the indifference curve and the budget line have the same slope. So we can obtain the marginal rate of substitution of curds for whey by using the slope of the budget line. Because the slope of the budget line is −2/3, the marginal rate of substitution is 2/3. For example, Ms. Muffet is willing to give up 2 units of whey in order to receive 3 additional units of curds and still have the same total satisfaction.

e. Because indifference curves cannot intersect each other and because indifference curve I_2 lies above the budget line (except at point *a*), every other point on the budget line is on a lower indifference curve. For example, point *b* lies on indifference curve I_1. Thus every other point on the budget line is inferior to point *a*.

7. a. An increase in income causes a parallel rightward shift of the budget line, as shown in Figure 8.21. If both curds and whey are normal goods, Ms. Muffet moves to a point such as *c*, at which the consumption of both goods has increased.

FIGURE 8.21
Short Answer Problem 7 (a)

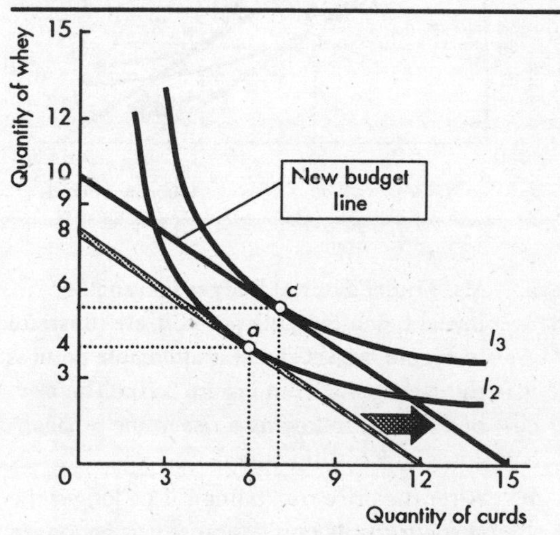

b. If whey is an inferior good, its consumption decreases as income increases, as illustrated in Figure 8.22. Again, the budget line shifts rightward, as in part (a), but Ms. Muffet's preferences are such that her new consumption point is given by a point such as *d*, where the consumption of whey has declined.

FIGURE **8.22**
Short Answer Problem 7 (b)

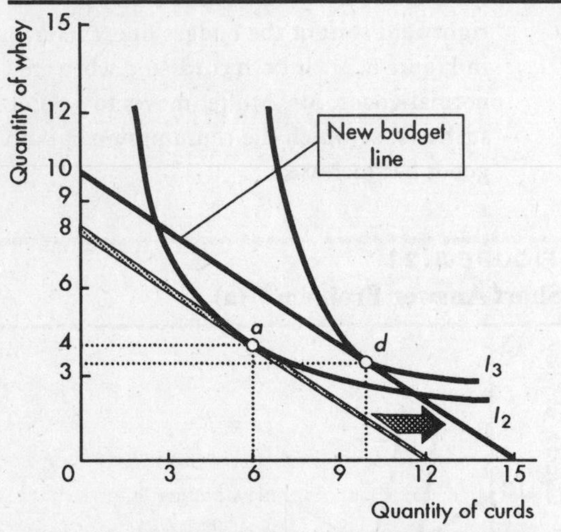

8. a. Ms. Muffet's initial budget line and her initial best affordable point, *a*, are illustrated in Figure 8.23. (The best affordable point is the same point as in Figure 8.20.) The new budget line following a rise in the price of curds to $2 is illustrated.

b. After the price rise, point *a* is no longer the best affordable point because it is no longer affordable.

c. The new best affordable point (labeled *d* in Figure 8.23) indicates a decrease in the consumption of curds. That is as expected because the price of curds rose.

9. a. Figure 8.24 shows Caroline's budget line. In this figure Caroline's best attainable point is labeled *a*. She consumes 2 bottles of wine per month.

FIGURE **8.23**
Short Answer Problem 8

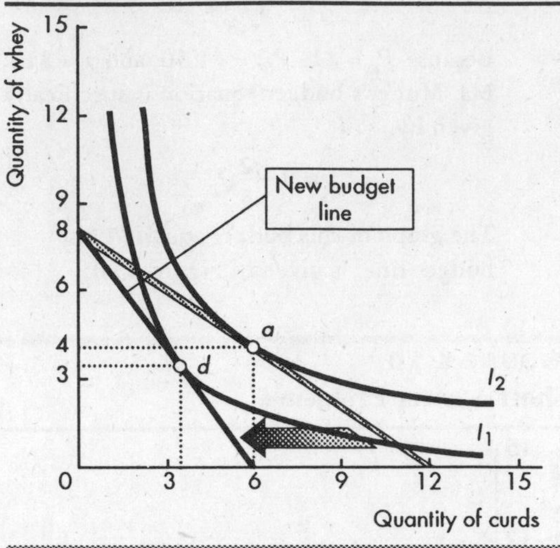

FIGURE **8.24**
Short Answer Problem 9 (a)

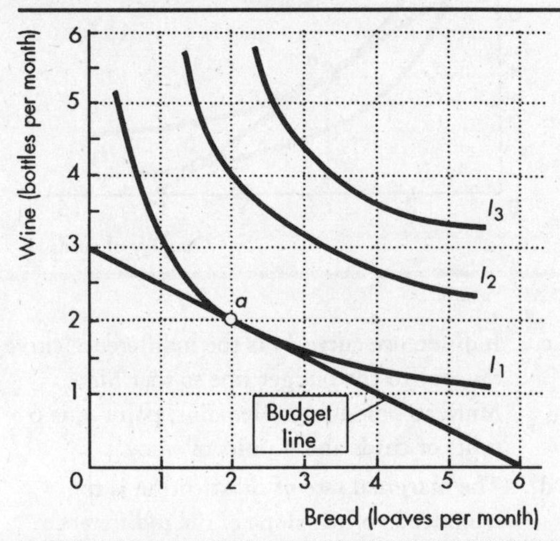

b. The reduction in the price of a bottle of wine rotates Caroline's budget line higher, as illustrated in Figure 8.25 (on the next page). Here her best attainable point is *b* and she consumes 4 bottles of wine per month. Note that indifference curve I_3 continues to remain unaffordable.

FIGURE 8.25
Short Answer Problem 9 (b)

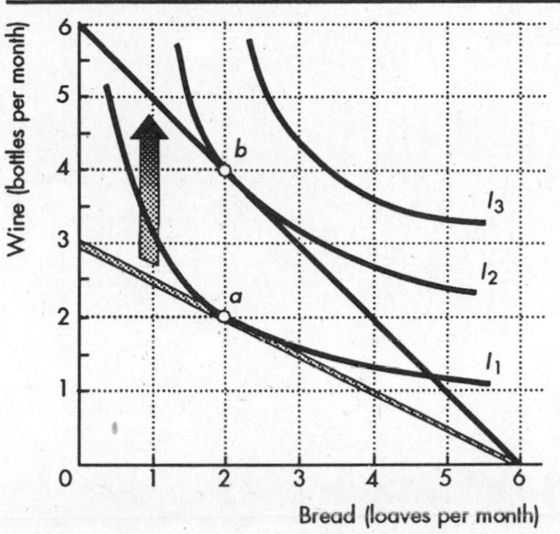

c. When the price of wine is $2 a bottle, part (a) indicates that Caroline buys 2 bottles of wine. When the price of wine falls to $1 a bottle, part (b) shows that Caroline buys 4 bottles. These two points on her demand curve are illustrated in Figure 8.26, and her (assumed linear) demand curve is drawn through these points.

FIGURE 8.26
Short Answer Problem 9 (c)

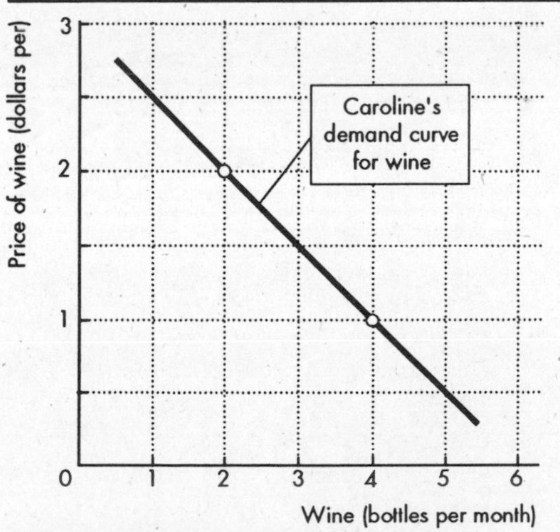

You're the Teacher

1. "It's certainly true that one of the main goals of budget line/indifference curve analysis is deriving the demand curve. There are a couple of reasons for doing so. First, it's 'nice' to see that we can derive a demand curve by just assuming that people try to obtain the maximum possible satisfaction. The idea that people attempt to make themselves as well off as possible is the hallmark of economics. This idea represents the basic world view of an economist; if you think it's a reasonable assumption, maybe you ought to major in economics!

   Second, the indifference curve/budget line approach allows us to think about income and substitution effects. These concepts help clarify some important household choices. For instance, without these ideas understanding why the quantity of labor people supply has declined as wages rose would be difficult. If we didn't know about the income effect, we'd probably think that people were either irrational or stupid for decreasing the quantity of their labor supplied when wage rates rose. So, this approach gives us some new insights into how economists view the world and the factors that affect people's choices."

2. "Look, you're wrong about this. I know that both indifference curves and demand curves slope downward, but indifference curves and demand curves really are different. In fact, we use indifference curves to help derive demand curves. But, to see the difference, think about a demand curve. It shows us how the price of a good affects how much we will buy. For instance, your demand curve for frozen yogurt cones tells us how much frozen yogurt you'll buy if a cone is $1.50 or how much you'll buy if one is $2.00. Indifference curves are different. They don't give us the relationship between a good's price and how much you'll buy. Indifference curves show us different combinations of two goods that give a consumer the same amount of total satisfaction. You have indifference curves between frozen yogurt cones and ice cream cones. This type of indifference curve shows us all the combinations of yogurt and ice cream cones that will give you the same total satisfaction. So, you see, these aren't the same, so don't make this mistake."

Chapter 9 ORGANIZING PRODUCTION

Key Concepts

■ The Firm and Its Economic Problem

A **firm** is an institution that hires factors of production and then uses these factors to produce and sell output. Uncertainty about the future and incomplete information cause firms to devise incentives that raise productivity and spread risk.

The **principal–agent problem** arises when agents (people employed by others) do not act in the best interests of the principals (the individuals who employ the agents). Giving managers partial ownership of the company, using incentive pay, and long-term contracts help overcome the principal–agent problem.

There are three forms of business organization:

- **Proprietorship** — single owner with unlimited liability.
- **Partnership** — two or more owners with unlimited liability.
- **Corporation** — owned by limited liability stockholders.

There are more proprietorships than any other type of business; corporations account for the lion's share of total business revenue.

■ Business Finance

- The funds an owner invests in the business are **equity**. Corporations raise equity by selling stock.
- Companies also raise funds by issuing **bonds**. Bonds are debts of the issuing company; they are legally enforceable obligations to pay specified sums of money at future dates.

The **present value** of a future amount of money is the amount of money that, if invested today, will grow to be as large as the future amount, including earned interest. In terms of a formula, the present value of an amount of money to be received one year in the future is:

$$\text{Present Value} = \frac{\text{Future Value}}{(1 + r)}$$

The present value of money to be received n years in the future is:

$$\text{Present Value} = \frac{\text{Future Value}}{(1 + r)^n}$$

In both present value formulas, r is the interest rate. If the net present value from borrowing a dollar is positive, the firm increases its profit by borrowing.

■ Opportunity Cost and Economic Profit

A firm's opportunity costs can be separated into explicit costs (costs for which an actual payment is made) and implicit costs. There are three main implicit costs:

- **Cost of capital** — The **economic depreciation** of capital is the change in its market value. (Accountants use conventional depreciation schedules to determine depreciation.) The forgone interest on funds used to buy capital is another opportunity cost of capital.
- **Cost of inventories** — The cost of using an item from inventory is the replacement cost of the item. (Accountants often use "last in, first out" (LIFO) or "first in, first out" (FIFO) to calculate the cost of using an item from inventory.)
- **Cost of owners' resources** — Owners supply entrepreneurial ability to the business. Their compensation for this input is the **normal profit**.

Economic profit = Total revenue – Opportunity cost

A business earning an economic profit is earning a profit that exceeds the normal profit.

Economic Efficiency

- **Technological efficiency** — when producing more output without using more inputs is not possible.
- **Economic efficiency** — when producing an output at a lower cost is not possible.

If a firm is economically efficient, it must be technologically efficient, but technological efficiency does not necessarily imply economic efficiency.

Firms and Markets

Firms coordinate economic activity when they perform the task more efficiently than markets. Firms often have advantages in the form of lower transactions costs, economies of scale, and economies of team production.

Helpful Hints

1. The concept of present value is fundamental in thinking about the value today of an investment that pays off in the future. It gives a method of comparing investments that have payments occurring at different times. The idea behind present value is that a dollar today is worth more than a dollar in the future because today's dollar can be invested to earn interest. To calculate the value today of an amount of money that will be paid in the future, we must discount that future amount to compensate for the forgone interest that cannot be earned because the dollar is not yet in hand. As a result, the present value of a future amount of money is the amount that, if invested today, with interest will grow as large as the future amount.
2. In this chapter, we again meet our old friend opportunity cost. Here we look at the costs that firms face, with a special emphasis on the differences between cost measures used by accountants and opportunity cost measures used by economists. Accountants usually include only explicit, out-of-pocket costs. Opportunity cost, which is the cost relevant to people's decisions, includes explicit *and* implicit costs. Because accountants and economists measure costs differently, these differences in costs lead to differences in how profit is measured. Profit equals revenues minus costs. Accountants and economists use the same measure for revenue. Hence accounting profit equals revenue minus accounting costs and economic profit equals revenue minus economic costs. Economic costs generally exceed accounting costs. As a result, economic profit usually is less than accounting profit
3. The idea of a normal profit is important. A normal profit is the (implicit) cost of buying an owner's entrepreneurial ability — for instance, the owner's ability to make sound business decisions. In other words, the normal profit is the average profit paid for such entrepreneurial ability.

   Normal profit is part of the firm's opportunity cost of doing business, in the same way that paying workers' wages or interest on debt are opportunity costs to the firm. One natural way to view normal profit as an opportunity cost that the firm must pay is to think of costs as liabilities that *must* be paid; if a company fails to meet its liabilities it will (eventually) close. For example, if a business cannot pay its workers their wages or its debt holders the interest due to them, the firm will have to shut down. Similarly, if the firm cannot return at least a normal profit to its owners to compensate them for their talents in running the business, eventually the firm will close as the owners take up other endeavors that promise to pay them at least a normal profit.

   Economists define "economic profit" as revenue minus all opportunity costs. Because a normal profit is already embedded in opportunity costs, an economic profit signifies a profit over and above the normal profit; that is, viewing the normal profit as the average profit, an economic profit is an *above-average* profit.

Questions

True /False/Uncertain and Explain

1. A sales associate working in the sportswear department at JCPenny is an example of an "agent."

2. A firm's residual claimant is the last individual or institution to loan money to the firm.

3. If a proprietorship fails, the owner is responsible for *all* the firm's debts.

4. If the interest rate is 10 percent a year, the present value of $100 received in one year is $110.

5. Only corporations have equity funds.

6. A firm's normal profit is part of the opportunity costs of running the business.

7. Money to be received in the future is worth less than the same amount of money received today.

8. A firm's opportunity costs include both its explicit and implicit costs.

9. If the net present value of borrowing a dollar is positive, borrowing the dollar decreases the firm's profits.

10. The opportunity cost of producing output is lower if a firm uses its own machine rather than renting one.

11. The opportunity cost of using inventories is the current replacement cost.

12. The opportunity cost of using inventories can be measured either by the FIFO or the LIFO method.

13. The implicit rental rate of using a piece of capital equipment is almost always lower than the explicit rental rate.

14. If a firm is economically efficient, it must be technologically efficient.

15. Markets likely will coordinate economic activity in situations where there are economies of scale.

16. If you own a bond issued by General Electric, you are a partial owner of General Electric.

17. Giving top executives of large corporations stock in their companies often is a method of handling a principal–agent problem.

18. The economic depreciation of a piece of capital equipment is less than the depreciation calculated by an accountant.

19. A major advantage of the corporate form of business organization is limited liability.

20. A major disadvantage of the corporate form of business organization is that corporations' profits are taxed twice.

Multiple Choice

1. Which of the following types of firms has limited liability?
   a. Only proprietorships.
   b. Only partnerships.
   c. Only corporations.
   d. Both partnerships and corporations.

2. Economists and accountants agree when it comes to measuring a firm's
   a. revenues.
   b. costs.
   c. profit.
   d. All of the above.

3. The term *sunk cost* refers to the
   a. past economic depreciation of capital.
   b. current economic cost of using capital.
   c. future accounting depreciation yet to be charged for a firm's capital.
   d. cost of building and then running a mine.

4. The major *disadvantage* of the corporate form of business organization is its
   a. limited liability for its owners.
   b. unlimited liability for its owners.
   c. ability to be run by professional managers.
   d. profits are taxed twice.

5. The present value of $100 to be received in one year is
   a. less the lower the interest rate is.
   b. less the higher the interest rate is.
   c. not at all related to the interest rate.
   d. related, though in no consistent manner, to the interest rate

Use the following table for the next three questions.

Table 9.1 Multiple Choice Questions 6, 7, and 8

Method	Quantities of Inputs Labor	Capital
1	5	10
2	10	7
3	15	5
4	20	5

6. Which is a technologically inefficient method of making a photon torpedo?
   a. Method 1 only.
   b. Method 2 only.
   c. Method 3 only.
   d. Method 4 only.

7. If labor costs $10 per unit and capital $20 per unit, which is an economically efficient method of making a photon torpedo?
   a. Method 1 only.
   b. Method 2 only.
   c. Method 3 only.
   d. All four methods are economically efficient.

8. If labor costs $10 per unit and capital falls to $15 per unit, which is an economically efficient method of making a photon torpedo?
   a. Method 1 only.
   b. Method 2 only.
   c. Method 3 only.
   d. All four methods are economically efficient.

9. A form of business that is simple to set up, whose profits are taxed only once, and is run by a single owner is a
   a. proprietorship.
   b. partnership.
   c. corporation.
   d. either a proprietorship or partnership, depending on other information.

10. Which of the following is an implicit cost of operating a business?
   a. The wages paid to the workers.
   b. The salary paid to the owners.
   c. The interest not earned on funds used to buy capital equipment.
   d. The interest paid on a bank loan the owners incurred to help finance the company.

11. On January 1, Tommy's store, the Video Game Empire, had in inventory 100 copies of a hit video game, "Mortal Kong." The market price was $60 per game. On February 1, Tommy had the same 100 games in inventory and the market price was $10 per game. The opportunity cost of the inventory in January was
   a. $6,000.
   b. $5,000.
   c. $1,000.
   d. None of the above.

12. A normal profit is
   a. an explicit opportunity cost of the company.
   b. a cost that is always measured by an accountant.
   c. the amount of profit an accountant calculates for a company.
   d. not the same as the company's economic profit.

13. The possibility that an employee may not work hard is an example of the
   a. problem of opportunity cost.
   b. principle of scarcity.
   c. limited liability doctrine.
   d. principal–agent problem.

14. Economies of scale exist when
   a. transactions costs are high.
   b. transactions costs are low.
   c. hiring additional inputs does not raise the price of the inputs.
   d. the cost of producing a unit of output falls as more output is produced.

15. Most firms are
   a. proprietorships.
   b. partnerships.
   c. corporations.
   d. Proprietorships and corporations are tied.

16. If the interest rate is 5%, the present value of $100 to be received in one year is
    a. $105.00.
    b. $100.00.
    c. $95.24.
    d. $95.00.

17. If the interest rate is 10%, the present value of $100 to be received in one year is
    a. $110.00.
    b. $100.00.
    c. $90.91.
    d. $90.00.

18. If the interest rate is 10%, the present value of $100 to be received in two years is
    a. $121.00.
    b. $120.00.
    c. $100.00.
    d. $82.64.

19. Which of the following types of firms issue(s) shares of stock?
    a. Proprietorship.
    b. Partnership.
    c. Corporation.
    d. Not-for-profit.

For the next two questions, suppose that Tracy and Pat start a business. Because of a series of bad decisions by Tracy, the company goes bankrupt, owing a total of $50,000. Tracy is penniless and Pat is a multimillionaire.

20. If the company were organized as a partnership, Pat would be responsible for
    a. $100,000 of debt.
    b. $50,000 of debt.
    c. $25,000 of debt.
    d. $0 of debt.

21. If the company were organized as a corporation, Pat would be responsible for
    a. $100,000 of debt.
    b. $50,000 of debt.
    c. $25,000 of debt.
    d. $0 of debt.

22. The present value of a future payment of money is higher the
    a. higher the interest rate or the farther in the future the payment.
    b. lower the interest rate or the farther in the future the payment.
    c. higher the interest rate or the nearer the date of the future payment.
    d. lower the interest rate or the nearer the date of the future payment.

Short Answer Problems

1. Give the meaning of present value by explaining (in words) why $110 received one year from now has a present value of $100 if the interest rate is 10 percent per year.
2. The standard tip in a restaurant is 15%. Restaurants *could* raise their prices 15%, set a policy of no tipping, and then give their servers the extra 15%. Use the concept of the principal–agent problem to explain why most restaurants do not do so.
3. Compare the accounting and opportunity cost approaches to
    a. depreciation cost.
    b. the firm borrowing money to finance purchasing its capital.
    c. the firm using its own funds rather than borrowing to purchase its capital.
    d. the value of the business owner's inputs.
4. Distinguish between technological efficiency and economic efficiency.
5. Markets and firms are alternative ways of coordinating economic activity. Why do both firms and markets exist?
6. Kathryn's Kat Kottage is considering borrowing money in order to invest in new cat kennels. If Kathryn borrows $30,000 from Bank A, she must pay $2,000 in interest in one year and $34,000 in two years. Alternatively, if Kathryn borrows from Bank B, she must pay $3,000 in interest in a year and $33,000 in two years. Using an interest rate of 10%, what is the present value of the two bank loans? Which loan should she take?
7. A year ago, Frank, a bricklayer, decided to start a business manufacturing doll furniture. Frank has

two sisters; Angela is an accountant and Edith is an economist. (Both sisters are good with numbers, but Edith doesn't have enough personality to be an accountant.) Each of the sisters uses the following information to compute Frank's costs and profit for the first year.

1) Frank's revenue for his first year is $100,000.
2) Frank took no income from the firm. He has a standing offer to return to work full time as a bricklayer for $30,000 per year.
3) Frank rents his machinery for $9,000 a year.
4) Frank owns the garage in which he produces but could rent it out at $3,000 per year.
5) To start the business, Frank used $10,000 of his own money from a savings account that paid 10 percent per year interest. Frank also borrowed $30,000 at 10 percent per year.
6) Frank hires one employee at an annual salary of $20,000.
7) The cost of materials during the first year is $40,000.
8) No inventory was used during the year.
9) Frank's entrepreneurial services are worth $20,000 to his business.

a. Set up a table indicating how Angela and Edith would compute Frank's cost. What is Frank's cost as computed by Angela? by Edith?

b. What is Frank's profit (or loss) as computed by Angela? by Edith?

8. Complete Table 9.2.

Table 9.2 Present Values

	Present Value of	
Interest rate	**$100 received in one year**	**$100 received in two years**
5%	____	____
10%	____	____

You're the Teacher

1. "I don't understand the difference between a 'normal profit' and an 'economic profit'. And, what's more, why should I care? After all, a profit is a profit is a profit!" Help explain to this student the difference and why the difference matters.
2. Answer the question: "How can a situation be technologically efficient and not economically efficient?"
3. "I purchased 100 shares of IBM stock when it was $150 a share. It's now selling for only $70 a share. I simply can't afford to sell my shares." Correct this unlucky investor's reasoning. Be sure to mention the role played by sunk costs when explaining why this reasoning is flawed.

ANSWERS

True/False Answers

1. **T** The sales associate is (indirectly) hired by the shareholders of JCPenny to help sell sportswear. The associate is an agent for the owners, who are the principals.
2. **F** The residual claimant is the individual who receives the firm's profits and, up to the limits of his or her liability, is responsible for the firm's losses.
3. **T** The owners of proprietorships and partnerships face unlimited liability for their companies' debts.
4. **F** The present value equals $100/(1.10) = $90.91.
5. **F** All companies have equity funds, funds contributed to the firm by its owner(s).
6. **T** The normal profit is the payment (implicitly) accruing to an owner for the owner's entrepreneurial ability.
7. **T** Money received in the present can be immediately saved and earn additional interest, an opportunity not available today with money received in the future.
8. **T** Opportunity costs include *all* the costs of running a business.
9. **F** If the net present value is positive, the return from the dollar exceeds its cost, so borrowing the dollar and investing it increases the company's profits.
10. **F** If the firm rents the machine, it pays an explicit rental rent; if it uses its own machine, it pays an implicit rental rate, and market forces drive the implicit and explicit rental rates to equality.
11. **T** The opportunity cost of using an item from inventory is whatever replacing the item in inventory currently costs.
12. **F** As the answer to question 11 pointed out, the opportunity cost is the *current* replacement cost, not the cost based on what the item cost sometime in the past.
13. **F** Market forces cause implicit and explicit rental rates to be equal.
14. **T** Economic efficiency means that the firm is technologically efficient; technologic efficiency, however, does not necessarily mean that the firm is economically efficient.
15. **F** When there are economies of scale — so that the cost of producing an item falls as more are produced — firms will coordinate the activity because they can capture these economies of scale.
16. **F** If you own a bond issued by General Electric, General Electric owes you money; shares of General Electric stock convey ownership in the company.
17. **T** Because the price of a share of stock generally rises when the company increases its profits, giving executives stock in the company presents them with an incentive to maximize the company's profit.
18. **U** An accountant uses a depreciation formula based on the initial cost of the equipment; this cost may be more than, less than, or equal to the change in the market value of the equipment, which is the measure of economic depreciation.
19. **T** Limited liability means that owners of corporations are not liable for its debts if the company goes bankrupt.
20. **T** Corporate profits are taxed once as income to the corporation. Then, when given to owners in the form of dividends, they are taxed again as part of the owners' incomes.

Multiple Choice Answers

1. **c** Owners of proprietorships and partnerships have unlimited liability for *all* the firm's debts.
2. **a** Revenues are measured in the same way; costs differ and hence profit — which equals revenues minus costs — differs.
3. **a** The past economic depreciation of an asset is no longer relevant to determining what should be done with it, which is why it is called "sunk."
4. **d** The income is taxed when the corporation earns it and also when it is received by the corporation's owners.

5. **b** The present value is $\$100/(1+r)$, so the higher is r, the lower is the present value.
6. **d** Method 4 uses more labor and the same capital as method 3; hence it is technologically inefficient.
7. **b** Method 2 costs $240 to produce a photon torpedo, whereas methods 1 and 3 cost $250.
8. **a** With the change in input prices, method 1 costs $200, which is less than method 2 ($205) and method 3 ($225).
9. **a** Answers b and d are incorrect because partnerships (which are easy to set up and whose profits are taxed only once) have more than one owner.
10. **c** By using the funds to buy capital equipment, interest on the funds is forgone, so this lost interest is an opportunity cost of running the business.
11. **b** The market value on January 1 was $6,000; on February 1 the market value is $1,000. The difference of $5,000 is the opportunity cost of owning the inventory for the month of January.
12. **d** Economic profit is any profit over and above normal profit.
13. **d** By loafing, the agent — the employee — takes an action that is not in the best interests of the principal — the owner.
14. **d** This is the definition of economies of scale.
15. **a** Proprietorships are the most numerous type of business organization.
16. **c** The present value equals $\$100/(1+r)$, with r the interest rate, so the present value is $\$100/(1+0.05) = \$95.24$
17. **c** Comparing this answer with the answer to question 16 shows that the higher the interest rate, the lower is the present value of funds to be received in the future.
18. **d** The present value is $\$100/(1+r)^2$, or $\$100/(1.10)^2$. Comparing questions 17 and 18 shows that the longer the time until a sum of money is received, the lower is its present value.
19. **c** Stock is how corporations raise equity.
20. **b** As a partnership, Pat has *unlimited* liability for all the firm's debts.
21. **d** If the company is a corporation, Pat's liability is limited to the initial amount invested, so Pat has no additional liability for the $50,000 debt.
22. **d** The present value formula is: present value = (future value)/$(1 + r)^n$ Clearly, the lower the interest rate (r) or the shorter the time until the funds are received (n), the larger is the present value.

Answers to Short Answer Problems

1. The present value of $110 received one year from now is the amount that, if invested today at the market rate of interest, would grow to be $110 in one year. The interest rate is 10 percent, so $100 invested grows to $110 in one year. Thus $100 is the present value of $110 in one year.
2. Restaurants are faced with a classic principal–agent problem because servers may provide poor service to the customers. Rather than attempt to have the manager closely monitor each server, delegating the monitoring to customers is more efficient. If the server gives good service, the customer will tip the server 15 percent or more; if the server provides poor service, the customer will easily note this fact and tip less than 15 percent. Hence the server has the incentive to be a good agent and provide prompt, good service, which is precisely what the principal — the restaurant's owner — wants.
3. a. Under the accounting cost approach, depreciation cost is computed as a prespecified percentage of the original purchase price of the capital good, with no reference to current market value. The opportunity cost approach measures economic depreciation cost, change in the market value of the capital good over the period in question.
   b. If a firm borrows money, the accounting and opportunity cost approaches are the same; both include the explicit interest payments.
   c. If a firm uses its own funds rather than borrowing, the accounting and opportunity cost approaches differ. The accounting cost is zero because there are no explicit interest payments. The opportunity cost approach recognizes that those funds could have been

loaned and thus the (implicit) interest income forgone is the opportunity cost.

d. If the owner forgoes the opportunity for other employment, this loss is not part of the accounting costs even though it is an opportunity cost. If the owner draws a salary, it will be captured as both an opportunity cost and an accounting cost. In addition, whether or not the owner took money from the business, the cost of the entrepreneurial talent the owner provides to the business is always an opportunity cost — the firm's normal profit.

4. A method is technologically efficient if increasing output without increasing inputs is not possible. A method is economically efficient if the cost of producing a given level of output is as low as possible. Technological efficiency is independent of prices, but economic efficiency depends on the prices of inputs. An economically efficient method of production is always technologically efficient, but a technologically efficient method is not necessarily economically efficient.

5. As demonstrated in the example in the text, car repair can be coordinated by the market or by a firm. The institution (market or firm) that actually coordinates in any given case is the one that is more efficient. In cases where there are significant transactions costs, economies of scale, or economies of team production, firms are likely to be more efficient and firms will dominate the coordination of economic activity. But the efficiency of firms is limited, and there are many circumstances where market coordination of economic activity dominates because it is more efficient. Essentially, if coordination by firms is more efficient, the number of firms increases because doing business with them is cheaper than relying on a market. Conversely, if coordination by the market is more efficient, firms will not be able to compete successfully because doing business with them would be more expensive then relying on a market.

6. The present value of the loan is calculated by adding the present value of the loan payments. Thus, for the loan from Bank A, the present value equals:

$$\frac{\$2{,}000}{(1+.10)}+\frac{\$34{,}000}{(1+.10)^2}=\$29{,}917.36.$$

The present value of the loan from Bank B is

$$\frac{\$3{,}000}{(1+.10)}+\frac{\$33{,}000}{(1+.10)^2}=\$30{,}000.00.$$

The present value of the loan from Bank B exceeds that from Bank A. Hence, Kathryn should take the loan from Bank A because it is less expensive.

7. a. Table 9.3 shows how Angela, the accountant, and Edith, the economist, calculate Frank's cost and revenue for each item listed.

b. Accounting profit equals revenue minus accounting cost, and economic profit equals revenue minus opportunity cost. The accounting cost is the sum of the accounting costs listed for items 2 – 9, or \$69,000, and the opportunity cost is the sum of the economic costs listed for items 2 – 9, or \$123,000. Hence Frank's accounting profit is \$31,000 and his economic profit actually is an economic loss of –\$23,000.

Table 9.3 Short Answer Problem 7

Item	Accounting cost (Angela's costs)	Economic cost (Edith's costs)
1 (Revenue)	\$100,000	\$100,000
2 (Alternative job)	0	30,000
3 (Rent)	9,000	9,000
4 (Garage)	0	3,000
5 (Invested funds)	3,000	4,000
6 (Employee)	20,000	20,000
7 (Materials)	40,000	40,000
8 (Inventory)	0	0
9 (Entrepreneurial services)	0	20,000

8. The completed table is shown as Table 9.4 (on the next page). Each answer is an application of the present value formula. For instance, take the present value of \$100 received in one year when the interest rate is 5 percent. The formula for this is \$100/(1.05) or \$95.24. Then, the present value of the \$100 received in two years when the interest rate is 5 percent is given by $\$100/(1.05)^2$ which equals \$90.70. The calculations for the present value with the interest rate equal to 10 percent are calculated similarly.

There are two important points easily visible in Table 9.4. First, the farther in the future before a given sum of money is to be received, the lower is its present value. Second, the higher the interest rate, the lower the present value of a given sum of money.

Table 9.4 Short Answer Problem 8

	Present Value of	
Interest rate	**$100 received in one year**	**$100 received in two years**
5%	$95.24	$90.70
10%	$90.91	$82.64

■ You're the Teacher

1. "The difference between a 'normal profit' and an 'economic profit' is important; and it's also not too difficult. Every business owner supplies some inputs to the business. One of these inputs is entrepreneurial talent — the decisions, leadership, and possibly insight that the owner provides. Normal profit is the payment for these services. Because this payment (perhaps implicitly) is for services rendered, a normal profit is part of the firm's opportunity costs. Essentially, you should think of the normal profit as the standard — average — payment owed to a business's owner. An economic profit equals the firm's revenues minus its opportunity costs. Because opportunity costs already include normal profit, an economic profit is a profit over-and-above a normal profit. Basically, an economic profit is an above-average profit."

2. "Technological efficiency merely reflects a firm's inputs and resulting output. A situation is technologically efficient when producing more output without using more inputs is impossible. The converse is that technological efficiency occurs whenever decreasing the amount of an input used decreases the amount of output produced. In other words, the firm is not wasting resources.

   Economic efficiency occurs when the cost of producing a given amount of output is as low as possible. Clearly, if a firm is wasting resources — reducing an input without decreasing the amount produced is possible — the business is not economically efficient because decreasing an input will reduce the firm's costs. Hence, if a firm is economically efficient, it must be technologically efficient, too. But it can be technologically efficient and not economically efficient if it uses the 'wrong' mix of inputs. For instance, the local McDonald's could hire brain surgeons rather than students to cook its burgers. This move would be technologically efficient because someone is required to cook the burgers. But it would not be economically efficient because the students would work for about $20,000 a year, whereas the brain surgeons command at least $500,000 a year."

3. "We are going to ignore any issues dealing with taxes. With this simplification, I want to tell you that you are making a fundamental error in thinking about the shares. The fact that each share has lost $80 in value is a sunk cost. It should have no bearing on what you decide to do with them at the present. For instance, you should hang onto them if you think that the price will rise from $70. But, if you think that the share price will drop from $70, you ought to sell them. The key point is that your decision about what to do with this stock hinges on the stock's *current* price, $70 a share. The fact that you paid more is irrelevant and that you lost $80 a share is regrettable, but that is a sunk cost and so should have no influence on your current decision."

Chapter 10 OUTPUT AND COSTS

Key Concepts

The Firm's Objective and Constraints

- The firm's objective is profit maximization.
- The firm faces market constraints — the conditions under which it buys its inputs and sells its output — and technology constraints — limits as to how much output can be produced from its inputs.

Firms have two planning horizons:

- Short run — at least one input is fixed and the other inputs are variable.
- Long run — all inputs are variable.

Short-Run Technology Constraint

A firm's short-run technology constraint is described by the:

- total product curve (*TP*) — the maximum attainable output with a fixed quantity of capital as the quantity of labor is varied.
- marginal product curve (*MP*) — the change in the total product resulting from a one-unit change in a variable input.
- average product curve (*AP*) — the total product per unit of an input.

Figure 10.1 illustrates the *MP* and *AP* curves for labor. It shows the (general) relationship between the marginal product and average product:

- When the $MP > AP$, the *AP* rises.
- When the $MP < AP$, the *AP* falls.
- When $MP = AP$, the *AP* is at its maximum.

The product curves have the shapes shown in Figure 10.1 because production usually has increasing marginal returns followed by diminishing marginal returns. The law of diminishing returns states that, with the amount of the fixed inputs not changing, as a firm uses more of a variable input the *MP* of the variable input eventually diminishes.

FIGURE 10.1

The Average and Marginal Products

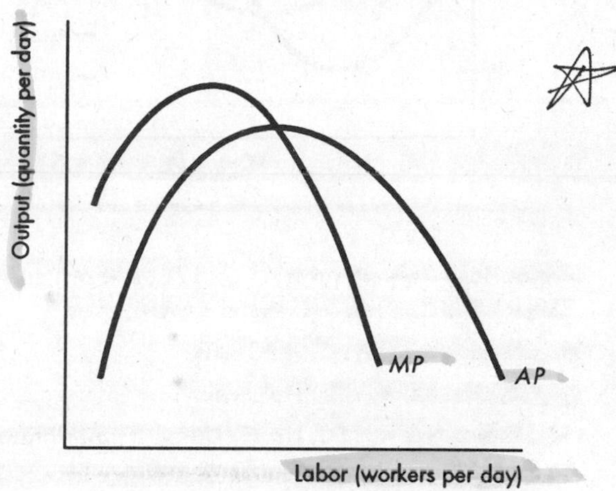

Short-Run Cost

The important cost concepts are:

- total cost (*TC*) — cost of all inputs used. Average total cost (*ATC*) is TC/q.
- total fixed cost (*TFC*) — cost of fixed inputs. Average fixed cost (*AFC*) is TFC/q.
- total variable cost (*TVC*) — cost of variable inputs. Average variable cost (*AVC*) is TVC/q.

Two relationships between these costs are:

$TC = TFC + TVC$ and $ATC = AFC + AVC$.

- marginal cost (*MC*) — the change in total cost resulting from one-unit change in output or, in terms of a formula, $MC = \Delta TC/\Delta q$.

FIGURE 10.2
Average and Marginal Cost Curves

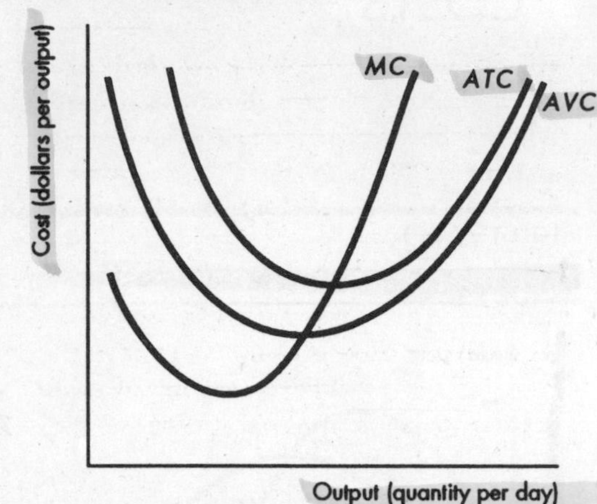

Figure 10.2 shows typical *AVC*, *ATC*, and *MC* curves. The *AVC*, *ATC*, and *MC* curves are U-shaped.

- When $MC < ATC$, ATC falls.
- When $MC > ATC$, ATC rises.
- When $MC = ATC$, the ATC is at its minimum.

The same marginal/average relationship holds between *MC* and *AVC*.

The *MC* and *MP* curves are related.

- Over the range of output where the *MC* curve falls, the *MP* curve rises
- At the level of output where the *MC* curve is at its minimum, the *MP* curve is at its maximum
- Over the range of output where the *MC* curve rises, the *MP* curve falls.

An increase in technology shifts the firm's product curves upward and shifts its cost curves downward. A rise in factor prices shifts the firm's cost curves.

Plant Size and Cost

- **Long-run cost** — cost of production when all inputs, including plant size, are adjusted to their economically efficient levels.
- **Production function** — shows the relationship between the maximum attainable output and the quantities of all inputs.

In the long run, returns to scale are important. **Returns to scale** are the changes in output resulting from changing all inputs by the same percentage. Returns to scale are different from diminishing returns because diminishing returns apply to the case where only *one* input changes. The three possibilities for returns to scale are:

- **increasing returns to scale.** The percentage change in the firm's output is greater than the percentage change in inputs.
- **constant returns to scale.** The percentage change in the firm's output equals the percentage change in inputs.
- **decreasing returns to scale.** The percentage change in the firm's output is less than the percentage change in inputs.

The **long-run average cost curve** (*LRAC*) traces a U-shaped relationship between the lowest attainable *ATC* and output when all inputs are variable. In the long run, all costs are variable costs.

- **Economies of scale** — the range of output over which the *LRAC* falls.
- **Diseconomies of scale** — the range of output over which the *LRAC* rises.

Producing at Least Cost (Appendix)

- **Isoquant** — A curve showing the different combinations of labor and capital that can produce a fixed quantity of output. With labor measured on the horizontal axis and capital on the vertical axis, the magnitude of the slope of an isoquant is the **marginal rate of substitution of labor for capital.**
- **Isocost line** — A line showing combinations of labor and capital than can be bought for a given total cost. With labor measured on the horizontal axis and capital on the vertical axis, the magnitude of the slope of an isocost line equals the relative price of labor in terms of capital.
- The **least-cost technique** is the combination of inputs that minimizes the total cost of producing a given amount of output.

FIGURE 10.3
The Least-Cost Combination

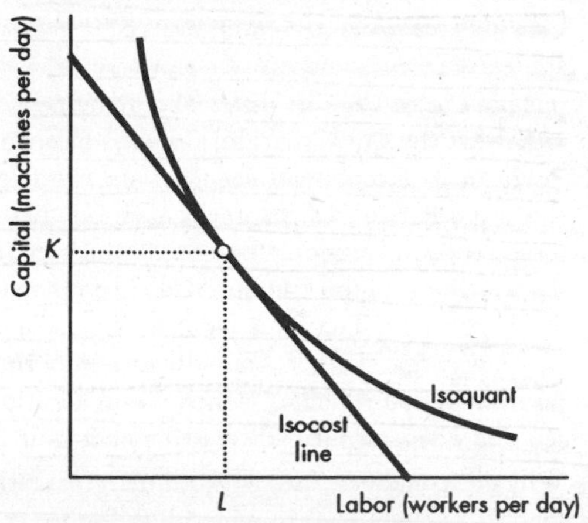

The least-cost technique occurs where an isocost line for the lowest cost is tangent to the isoquant for the given quantity of output. At this point, the marginal rate of substitution equals the relative price of labor in terms of capital. Figure 10.3 illustrates the least-cost combination of capital, *K*, and labor, *L*.

- At the least-cost combination of capital and labor, the marginal cost of increasing output by using additional capital equals the marginal cost of increasing output by using more labor.

Helpful Hints

1. This chapter introduces many new concepts and graphs and may at first appear overwhelming. Don't get lost among the trees and lose sight of the forest. The relationship between production and cost functions is simple.

   The chapter begins with the concepts of total product, marginal product, and average product. They are followed by the short-run cost function and the concepts of total cost, marginal cost, average variable cost, and average total cost.

   All of these seemingly disparate concepts are related to the law of diminishing returns. It states that as a firm uses additional units of a variable input, while holding constant the quantity of fixed inputs, the marginal product of the variable input will eventually diminish. This law explains why the marginal product and average product curves eventually fall and why the total product curve becomes flatter. Then, when productivity falls, costs rise, and so the law also explains the eventual upward slope of the marginal cost curve. The marginal cost curve, in turn, explains the U-shape of the average variable cost and average total cost curves. When the marginal cost curve is below the average variable (or total) cost curve, the average variable (or total) cost curve is falling. When the marginal cost curve is above the average variable (or total) cost curve, the average variable (or total) cost curve is rising. The marginal cost curve intersects the average variable (or total) cost curve at the minimum point on the average variable (or total) cost curve.

   Another key point to realize is that all of the concepts presented are not equally important. Pay the most attention to the average total cost and marginal cost concepts because they are used the most in later chapters to analyze the behavior of firms.

FIGURE 10.4
Average and Marginal Cost Curves

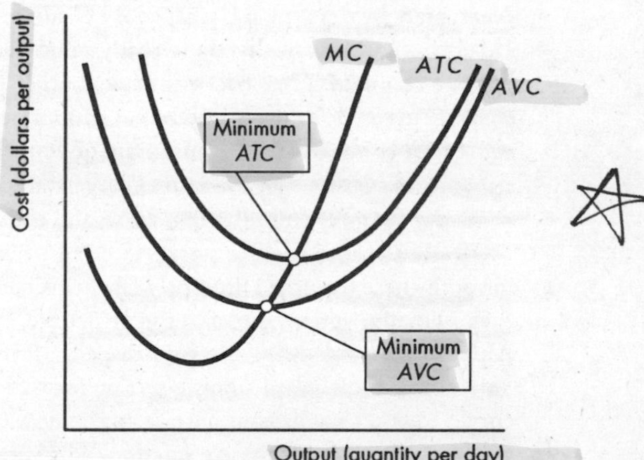

2. Be sure you understand Figure 10.4 thoroughly. Not only is it is the most important graph in the chapter, it is one of the most important graphs in all of microeconomics. You will see it repeatedly in the next several chapters.

You should know four important points about Figure 10.4. First, both the *ATC* and *AVC* curves are U-shaped. The *MC* curve also is U-shaped, but the portion that slopes upward is the most important. Second, because total cost include both fixed and variable costs, the *ATC* curve lies above the *AVC* curve. The vertical distance between the two shrinks as output increases because the difference, *AFC*, decreases as output rises. Third, the *MC* curve intersects the *ATC* and *AVC* curves at their minimum points. In other words, when the *MC* equals the *ATC*, the *ATC* is at its minimum. Fourth, following the conventional relationship between a marginal and an average, when the *MC* curve is below the *ATC* or *AVC* curves, the *ATC* or *AVC* fall. Similarly, when the *MC* curve is above the *ATC* or *AVC* curves, the *ATC* or *AVC* curves rise.

3. You will probably draw a graph like the one in Figure 10.4 at least a hundred times in this course. Aside from learning the points mentioned in the preceding helpful hint, here are some additional hints on drawing the graph quickly and easily.

   Be sure to label the axes; the quantity of output, *q*, goes on the horizontal axis and dollars (of cost) go on the vertical axis.

   Next, start by drawing a U-shaped *ATC* curve. Label this curve immediately so that you do not become confused. Then below it draw another U-shaped curve. Move the minimum of this curve somewhat to the left of the minimum of your first curve. Also be sure that the second curve starts vertically far away from the first curve and ends up vertically closer to the first curve. (See Figure 10.4 for both these features.) Promptly label this curve *AVC*. Finally, you need to add the *MC* curve. Although the *MC* curve also is U-shaped, draw only a small downward sloping section for this curve. In other words, concentrate on the upward sloping part of the curve. As you draw this part of the curve, the crucial point to remember is that it *must* pass through the minimum points of the two curves that you have previously drawn. Be absolutely certain that this curve passes through both minimums. Label this last curve *MC* and you are done.

   Whenever a test question (including those following in this Study Guide as well as on your exams in class) asks about these curves, draw a graph before you answer.

4. Be certain that you understand the difference between "marginal cost" and "average cost." These are *very* different concepts. An easy way to remember that they are different is to keep in mind that the word "marginal" always means "additional." Economists use the word marginal this way a lot. In this chapter, you already have seen it used in "marginal product," which means the additional output produced when employment of a factor of production is increased by one unit. In the next few chapters you will encounter the term "marginal revenue," which means additional revenue when output is increased by one unit.

   Why do economists use the word marginal rather than additional? That is, why call the added cost from increasing output "marginal cost" rather than "additional cost"? One reason may be to sound scientific; after all, the term "marginal cost" sounds much more precise and scientific than "additional cost." Another, more serious reason *is* the added precision: Marginal cost means the added cost from producing *one* more unit of output. The term "additional cost" is simply not as precise. But, regardless of the rationale, marginal cost means added cost. It is *not* the same as average cost!

5. The later sections of the chapter explain the long-run production function and cost function when the plant size — that is, the capital stock — varies. As the law of diminishing returns is the key to understanding short-run costs, the concept of returns to scale is the key to understanding long-run costs. Returns to scale are the increase in output relative to the increase in inputs when *all* inputs are increased by the same percentage; diminishing returns are what happens when only *one* factor of production is changed, with the rest of the factors being kept constant. Returns to scale can be increasing, constant, or decreasing. Returns to scale are related to economies and diseconomies of scale. Indeed, if factor prices do not change as a firm changes its output, increasing returns to scale correspond to the downward-sloping part of the *LRAC*, constant returns to scale to the horizontal part, and decreasing returns to scale to the upward-sloping part.

Returns to scale are different from diminishing returns. It is possible — and in some industries likely — for a firm to have both increasing returns to scale and diminishing returns to factors of production at the same time. To understand this idea, think about your local Mexican restaurant. If the owner hired another worker, the added worker would have to fit in the existing restaurant, work with a fixed number of ovens, a fixed number of tables and so on. Essentially, adding the worker means that more labor is working with a fixed amount of capital and land, that is, a fixed scale of operations. Most likely adding the worker would increase the owner's output of Mexican food but by less than the previous worker — diminishing returns. Now suppose that the owner hired more of all the factors of production used to produce Mexican food. In other words, the owner adds another worker, increases the size of the restaurant, increases the number of ovens, boosts the number of tables, and so on. In this case the amount of food that can be produced is likely to increase proportionally more than the increase in the amount of inputs used. If this outcome occurs, the owner experiences increasing returns to scale. Thus the restaurant business can have both diminishing returns by employing more labor while at the same time have increasing returns to scale by employing more of all factors of production.

Questions

True/False/Uncertain and Explain

1. Variable costs are greater than fixed costs.

2. If the marginal product of labor exceeds the average product of labor, the average product of labor rises.

3. Increasing returns to scale occur when an increase in the amount of workers employed increases total output.

4. Total cost equals fixed cost plus variable cost.

5. Marginal cost is always greater than average total cost.

6. The average total cost curve, like the average product of labor curve, has an upside-down U shape.

7. Total costs first fall and then rise as the firm expands its output.

8. The law of diminishing returns implies that the marginal product of a factor of production eventually falls as more of the factor is used.

9. The *ATC* curve always passes through the minimum point of the *MC* curve.

10. When the *LRAC* curve is rising, the firm is experiencing economies of scale.

11. Marginal cost equals total cost divided by total output.

12. A firm's goal is to maximize its sales.

13. In the long run, all costs are variable costs.

14. No part of any short-run average total cost curve lies below the long-run average total cost curve.

Multiple Choice

1. The long run is a time period in which
   a. one year or less elapses.
   b. all inputs are variable.
   c. all inputs are fixed.
   d. there is at least one fixed input and at least one variable input.

2. The change in total cost from producing another unit of output equals the
   a. average total cost.
   b. variable cost.
   c. average variable cost.
   d. marginal cost.

3. Which curve intersects the *ATC* curve at its minimum point?
   a. The *MC* curve.
   b. The *AVC* curve.
   c. The *AFC* curve.
   d. The *MP* curve.

4. When a firm is experiencing economies of scale,
   a. the *MP* curve is rising.
   b. the *LRAC* curve is falling.
   c. diminishing returns to labor have been suspended.
   d. the *MC* curve is falling.

5. When the marginal product of labor curve is below the average product of labor curve,
   a. the average product of labor curve is rising.
   b. the average product of labor curve is falling.
   c. the total product curve has a negative slope.
   d. the firm experiences decreasing returns to scale.

6. Often business people state that "I like to produce more because then I can spread my costs over more output." To interpret this statement, which cost always falls as output increases?
   a. Total cost.
   b. Marginal cost.
   c. Average total cost.
   d. Average fixed cost.

7. A farmer discovers that the total cost of growing 50 acres of eggplant is $50,000 and that the total cost of growing 51 acres of eggplant is $52,000. The marginal cost of the 51st acre of eggplant is
   a. $52,000.
   b. $50,000.
   c. $2,000.
   d. $1,000.

8. A technological advance
   a. shifts the total product curve upward.
   b. does not shift the total product curve.
   c. shifts the total product curve downward.
   d. cannot occur without raising the firm's average total costs.

9. The cost of a variable input, such as the wage paid to workers, rises. This change shifts the
   a. total fixed cost curve upward.
   b. marginal product of labor curve downward.
   c. average variable cost curve upward.
   d. marginal product of labor curve upward.

10. Pat's Catering finds that when it caters 10 meals a week, its total cost is $3,000. If Pat has a total variable cost of $2,500, what is Pat's fixed cost?
   a. $250.
   b. $300.
   c. $500.
   d. $3,000.

Use Figure 10.5 for the next four questions.

FIGURE **10.5**

Multiple Choice Questions 11, 12, 13, and 14

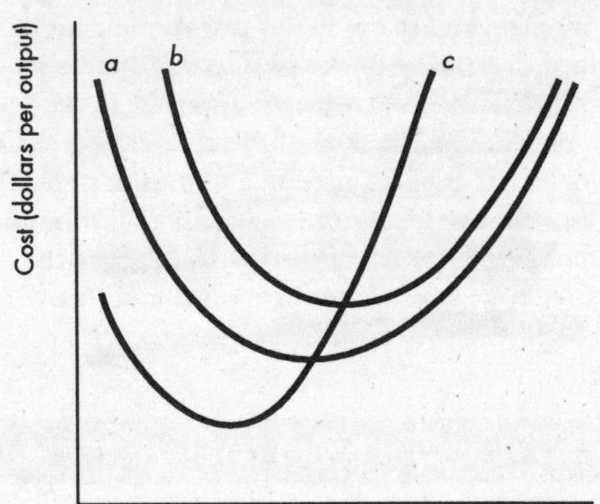

11. In Figure 10.5, the *MC* is curve
   a. *a*.
   b. *b*.
   c. *c*.
   d. None of the curves is the *MC* curve.

12. In Figure 10.5, the *ATC* is curve
   a. *a*.
   b. *b*.
   c. *c*.
   d. None of the curves is the *ATC* curve.

13. In Figure 10.5, the *AVC* is curve
    a. *a.*
    b. *b.*
    c. *c.*
    d. None of the curves is the *AVC* curve.

14. In Figure 10.5, the *AFC* is curve
    a. *a.*
    b. *b.*
    c. *c.*
    d. None of the curves is the *AFC* curve.

15. The average variable cost curve shifts upward if
    a. fixed costs rise.
    b. technological advances are made.
    c. the cost of a variable input rises.
    d. the price of output rises.

16. Constant returns to scale means that as all inputs are increased,
    a. total output remains constant.
    b. average total cost rises.
    c. average total cost rises at the same rate as do the inputs.
    d. total output increases in the same proportion as all inputs have been increased.

17. Over the range of output where the *MP* curve is rising, the
    a. *MC* curve is falling.
    b. *AFC* curve is rising.
    c. firm is experiencing increasing returns to scale.
    d. *TC* curve is falling.

18. If the *ATC* curve is falling, the *MC* curve must be
    a. rising.
    b. falling.
    c. above *ATC*.
    d. below *ATC*.

19. In the long run,
    a. only the scale of plant is fixed.
    b. all inputs are variable.
    c. all inputs are fixed.
    d. a firm must experience decreasing returns to scale.

Use Table 10.1 for the next three questions.

Table 10.1 Multiple Choice Questions 20, 21, and 22

Output	Total variable cost	Total cost
3	$15	$21
4	18	24

20. The marginal cost of producing the fourth unit is
    a. $6.
    b. $5.
    c. $3.
    d. $2.

21. The average total cost of the fourth unit is
    a. $6.
    b. $5.
    c. $3.
    d. $2.

22. The average *fixed* cost of the third unit is
    a. $6.
    b. $5.
    c. $3.
    d. $2

23. The marginal product of labor equals the average product of labor when
    a. the average product of labor is at its maximum.
    b. the average product of labor is at its minimum.
    c. the marginal product of labor is at its maximum.
    d. None of the above because the marginal product of labor never equals the average product of labor.

24. If the company produces no output, it must pay
    a. no costs.
    b. a small amount of variable cost.
    c. its fixed cost.
    d. its owners a normal profit.

25. The *LRAC* curve
   a. equals the minimum points on all the short-run *ATC* curves.
   b. equals the lowest possible *MC* of producing the different levels of output.
   c. equals the lowest attainable average total cost for all levels of output when all inputs can be varied.
   d. generally lies above the short-run *ATC* curves.

The next five questions come from the appendix.

26. Which of the following is <u>NOT</u> a characteristic of the least-cost technique of production?
   a. The marginal rate of substitution of labor for capital equals the ratio of the price of labor to the price of capital.
   b. The slope of the isoquant equals the slope of the isocost line.
   c. Increasing output by boosting the amount of capital has the same marginal cost as increasing output by boosting the amount of labor.
   d. The marginal product of labor equals the marginal product of capital.

27. An isocost shows combinations of labor and capital that
   a. have the same marginal product.
   b. can produce a given amount of output.
   c. can be bought for given total cost.
   d. cannot be changed without decreasing the level of output.

28. Jim finds that the *MC* of increasing his production of mountain bikes is cheaper when he increases his capital stock than when he hires more workers. This result means that
   a. the marginal product of capital exceeds the marginal product of labor.
   b. capital is cheaper than labor.
   c. Jim's production is not based on the least-cost technique.
   d. Jim is producing where an isocost curve is tangent to an isoquant curve.

FIGURE **10.6**
Multiple Choice Question 29

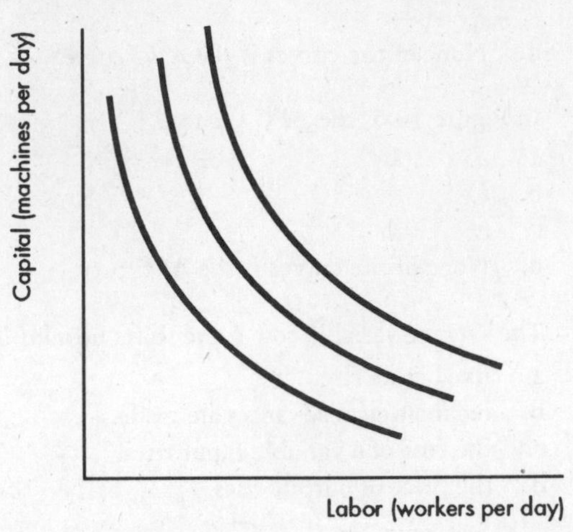

29. Figure 10.6 shows
   a. how the *MP* of workers declines as more workers are employed.
   b. a series of isocosts.
   c. diminishing marginal product of labor and capital.
   d. a series of isoquants.

30. A technological innovation that raises the marginal product of capital
   a. changes the marginal rate of substitution of capital for labor.
   b. shifts the isocost curves rightward.
   c. shifts the isocost curves leftward.
   d. has no effect on the least-cost technique.

■ Short Answer Problems

1. Where does the marginal product curve intersect the average product curve? Why?
2. What is the difference between diminishing returns and decreasing returns to scale?
3. a. Table 10.2 gives the total weekly output of turkeys at Al's Turkey Town. Complete this table. (The marginal product is entered midway between rows to emphasize that it is the result of changing inputs — moving from one row to the next. Average product corresponds to a fixed quantity of labor and so is entered on the appropriate row.)

Table 10.2 Production of Turkeys

Labor	Quantity (turkeys per week)	Average product of labor (*AP*)	Marginal product of labor (*MP*)
0	0	XX	
			100
1	100	100	
			___
2	300	___	
			___
3	450	___	
			110
4	___	___	
			___
5	630	___	
			___
6	___	110	

FIGURE 10.8
Short Answer Problem 3 (c)

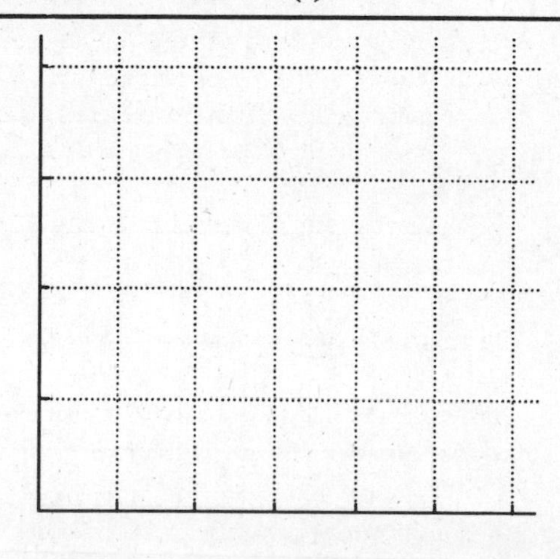

b. In Figure 10.7, label the axes and draw a graph of the total product curve (*TP*).

c. In Figure 10.8, label the axes and draw a graph of the marginal product (*MP*) and the average product (*AP*). (As in Table 10.2, plot the marginal products midway between the units of labor and the average products directly above the units of labor.) Where do the *AP* and *MP* curves cross?

FIGURE 10.7
Short Answer Problem 3 (b)

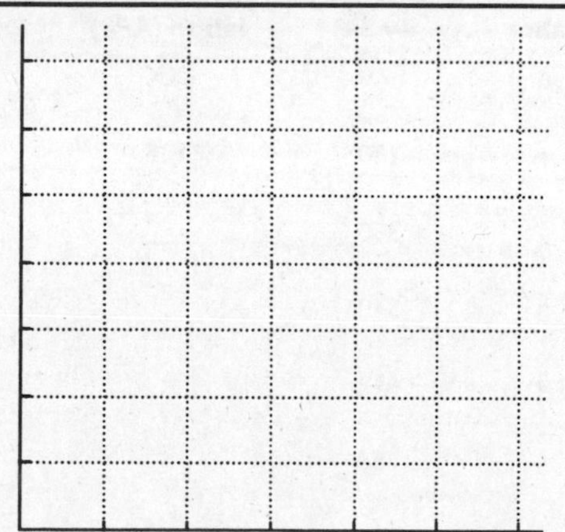

4. a. Now let's examine Al's short-run cost of growing turkeys. The first two columns of Table 10.2 are reproduced in the first two columns of Table 10.3. The cost of 1 worker (the only variable input) is $2,000 per month. Total fixed cost is $4,000 per month. Complete Table 10.3 by using your answers from Table 10.2 and by computing total variable cost and total cost.

Table 10.3 Total Cost of Growing Turkeys

Labor	Quantity (turkeys per week)	Total variable cost (*TVC*)	Total cost (*TC*)
0	0	___	$4,000
1	100	2,000	___
2	300	___	___
3	450	___	___
4	___	___	12,000
5	630	___	___
6	___	12,000	___

FIGURE **10.9**
Short Answer Problem 4 (b)

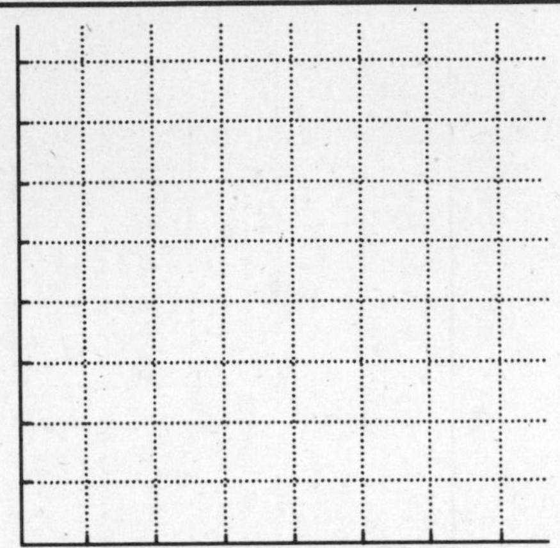

FIGURE **10.10**
Short Answer Problem 4 (d)

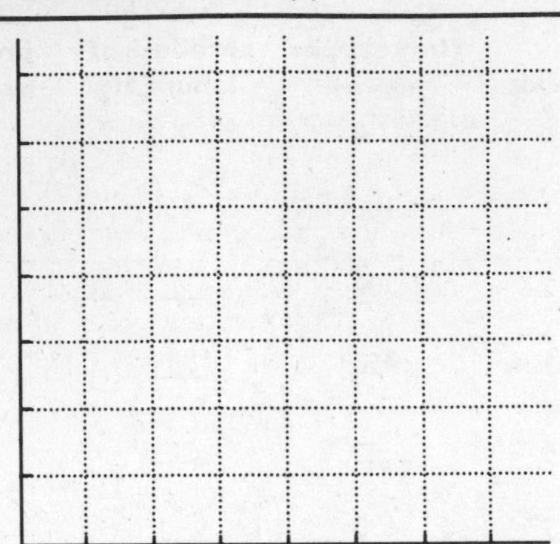

b. In Figure 10.9, label the axes and draw the *TC* and *TVC* curves. What is the relationship between these two curves?

c. Table 10.4 contains spaces for the average total cost (*ATC*), average variable cost (*AVC*), and marginal cost (*MC*). Complete this table using your answers from Table 10.3.

d. In Figure 10.10, label the axes and draw the *ATC*, *AVC*, and *MC* curves. Be sure to plot the values for the *MC* between the relevant levels of output. What is the relationship between the *ATC* and *AVC* curves? Between the *MC* and *AVC* curves?

5. a. Suppose that Al discovers new technology that boosts the productivity of his workers so that more turkeys can be grown than before. Table 10.5 presents some production data with the new technology. Complete the table.

Table 10.4 Other Costs of Growing Turkeys

Quantity (turkeys per week)	Average variable cost (AVC)	Average total cost (ATC)	Marginal cost (MC)
0	XX	XX	
			$20.00
100	$20.00	___	
			___
300	___	___	
			___
450	___	___	
			___
___	___	21.43	
			___
630	___	___	
			66.67
___	___	___	

Table 10.5 New Technology

Labor	Quantity (turkeys per week)	Average product of labor (APL)	Marginal product of labor (MPL)
0	0	XX	
			120
1	120	120	
			___
2	360	___	
			___
3	540	___	
			___
4	672	___	
			___
5	756	___	
			___
6	792	___	

b. Al's fixed cost remains at \$4,000, and he can continue to hire workers at a wage rate of \$2,000. Use the new technology production data to complete Table 10.6, which has the total cost, and Table 10.7, which has (some of) the average costs and the marginal cost.

Table 10.6 New Technology and Total Costs

Labor	Quantity (turkeys per week)	Total variable cost (*TVC*)	Total cost (*TC*)
0	0	___	___
1	120	___	___
2	360	___	___
3	540	___	___
4	672	___	___
5	756	___	___
6	792	___	___

Table 10.7 New Technology and Other Costs

Quantity (turkeys per week)	Average variable cost (*AVC*)	Average total cost (*ATC*)	Marginal cost (*MC*)
0	XX	XX	
			___
120	___	___	
			___
360	___	___	
			___
540	___	___	
			___
672	___	___	
			___
756	___	___	
			___
792	___	___	

c. In Figure 10.11, plot the ATC and MC curves you just entered in Table 10.7. Also draw the ATC and MC curves you plotted in Figure 10.10 (before the technology changed). Be sure to plot MCs midway between the corresponding units of output. Label the old ATC curve ATC_1 and the old MC curve MC_1; label the new ATC curve ATC_2 and the new MC curve MC_2. How do the old and new ATC curves compare? The old and new MC curves?

FIGURE **10.11**
Short Answer Problem 5 (c)

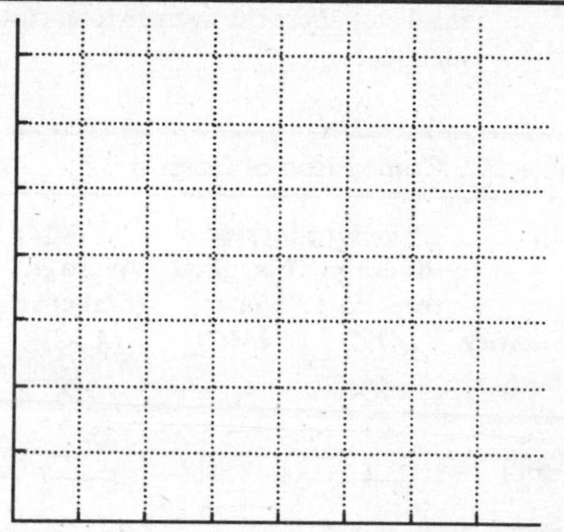

6\. a. Return to the old technology for growing turkeys, worked out in problems 3 and 4. Suppose that the cost of Al's fixed inputs double, to \$8,000. The cost of the variable input — labor — stays the same at \$2,000 per worker. Complete Table 10.8. For the two missing quantities, copy your answers from Table 10.2.

Table 10.8 A Change in Fixed Cost

Labor	Quantity (turkeys per week)	Total variable cost (*TVC*)	Total cost (*TC*)
0	0	___	\$8,000
1	100	2,000	___
2	300	___	___
3	450	___	___
4	___	___	16,000
5	630	___	___
6	___	12,000	___

b. To compare the effect of the rise in fixed cost on the average total cost and marginal cost, complete Table 10.9. (Hint: Copy the "before increase" *ATC* and *MC* values from Table 10.4; work out the "after increase" *ATC* and *MC* values from the just completed Table 10.8.) From Table 10.9, how did the rise in fixed cost affect the average total cost? The marginal cost?

Table 10.9 Comparison of Costs

	Before increase		After increase	
Quantity	**Average total cost (*ATC*)**	**Marginal cost (*MC*)**	**Average total cost (*ATC*)**	**Marginal cost (*MC*)**
0	XX		XX	
		___		___
100	___		___	
		___		___
300	___		___	
		___		___
450	___		___	
		___		___
___	___		___	
		___		___
630	___		___	
		___		___
___	___		___	

7. a. Return again to the old technology for growing turkeys, worked out in problems 3 and 4. Suppose that the cost of Al's fixed inputs remain at $4,000, as they were in problem 3. Now, however, the cost of his variable input, labor rises. Specifically, suppose that workers now receive $3,000. Complete Table 10.10. For the two missing quantities, again copy your answers from Table 10.2

b. To compare the effect of the rise in variable cost on the average total cost and marginal cost, complete Table 10.11. (Hint: As before, copy the "before increase" *ATC* and *MC* values from Table 10.4; work out the "after increase" *ATC* and *MC* values from Table 10.10.) From Table 10.11, how did the rise in variable costs affect the average total cost? The marginal cost?

c. Compare your answers to part (b) of problem 6 and part (b) of this problem. The rise in fixed cost and the rise in variable cost affected the marginal cost differently. Explain this difference.

Table 10.10 A Change in Variable Costs

Labor	Quantity (turkeys per week)	Total variable cost (*TVC*)	Total cost (*TC*)
0	0	___	$4,000
1	100	3,000	___
2	300	___	___
3	450	___	___
4	___	___	16,000
5	630	___	___
6	___	18,000	___

Table 10.11 Comparison of Costs

	Before increase		After increase	
Quantity	**Average total cost (*ATC*)**	**Marginal cost (*MC*)**	**Average total cost (*ATC*)**	**Marginal cost (*MC*)**
0	XX		XX	
		___		___
100	___		___	
		___		___
300	___		___	
		___		___
450	___		___	
		___		___
___	___		___	
		___		___
630	___		___	
		___		___
___	___		___	

The next two questions draw on material from the appendix.

8. a. Figure 10.12 shows Michelle's isoquant for producing 1 ton of wheat per hour. If using a unit of capital (one machine) for one hour costs $20 and hiring a worker for one hour also costs $20 an hour, what combination of capital and labor will Michelle use to produce 1 ton of wheat? Draw the relevant isocost line in Figure 10.12 when answering this question. What is the marginal rate of substitution? What is Michelle's total cost of producing this ton of wheat?

FIGURE 10.12

Short Answer Problem 8

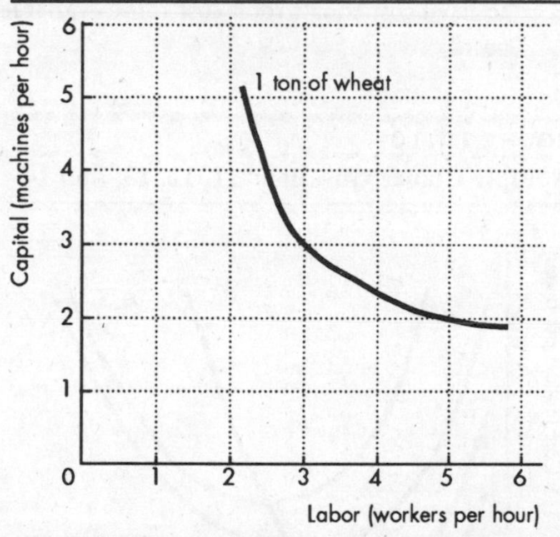

b. The cost of using a unit of capital (a machine) rises to $100 per hour. The cost of a worker does not change. Again, draw the relevant isocost line in Figure 10.12. Now what combination of capital and labor does Michelle use? How does Michelle respond to the rise in the cost of capital? What is Michelle's total cost of producing a ton of wheat now?

9. Explain what a cost-minimizing firm should do if it finds that, for the technique it is currently using, the ratio of the marginal product of labor, MP_L, to the marginal product of capital, MP_K, is greater than the ratio of the price of labor, P_L, to the price of capital, P_K.

■ You're the Teacher

1. "This chapter has a lot to say about firms: production, costs, and stuff like that. But I don't really see the purpose. In real life, firms are a lot more complicated than this chapter says. Workers are different, different companies make different goods, and what have you. What's the use of this chapter?" This student is missing an essential point about economic theories. Can you help straighten out the student?
2. "I get the idea that marginal cost is important, but I don't know why. You have any ideas about it?" Your friend is asking you for your ideas; you have a chance to help your friend, so explain why you think marginal cost is important.

Answers

True/False Answers

1. **U** The amount of variable cost and the amount of fixed cost are not necessarily related, except that in the long run all costs are variable costs.
2. **T** This result is a reflection of the relationship between marginals and averages.
3. **F** Increasing returns to scale occur when a proportionate increase in *all* inputs increases output by a larger proportion.
4. **T** Total cost is the sum fixed cost and variable cost.
5. **F** Marginal cost usually starts below average total cost and then rises above it.
6. **F** The average total cost curve has a "right-side-up" U shape.
7. **F** As output increases, total cost always rises.
8. **T** This is the definition of diminishing returns.
9. **F** The *MC* curve always passes through the minimum point of the *ATC* curve.
10. **F** When the *LRAC* curve is rising, the firm is experiencing diseconomies of scale.
11. **F** Marginal cost equals the *additional* total cost divided by the *additional* output.
12. **F** A firm's goal is to maximize its profit.
13. **T** In the long run, all inputs can be varied so all costs are variable costs.
14. **T** The long-run average cost curve shows the least possible cost to produce any level of output.

Multiple Choice Answers

1. **b** This is the definition of the long run.
2. **d** Marginal cost shows the added cost from producing an added unit of output.
3. **a** The *MC* curve intersects both the *ATC* and the *AVC* curves at their minimums.
4. **b** Economies of scale means that increases in output lower the firm's long-run average costs.
5. **b** This answer reflects the average/marginal relationship that when the marginal is below the average, the average falls.
6. **d** Because the total fixed cost, *TFC*, is constant, as output, *q*, expands the average fixed cost — which equals *TFC*/*q* — must fall.
7. **c** The marginal cost equals the change in total cost ($52,000 – $50,000, or $2,000) divided by the change in output (51 acres of eggplant – 50 acres of eggplant, or 1 acre of eggplant). Thus the marginal cost equals $2,000 per acre of eggplant.
8. **a** By shifting the total product curve upward, the technological advance generally shifts the average total cost curve downward.
9. **c** Wages are a variable cost and so a rise in the wage rate shifts the average variable cost curve upward.
10. **c** Total cost equals fixed cost plus variable cost, so fixed cost equals total cost minus variable cost.

FIGURE **10.13**

Multiple Choice Questions 11, 12, 13, and 14

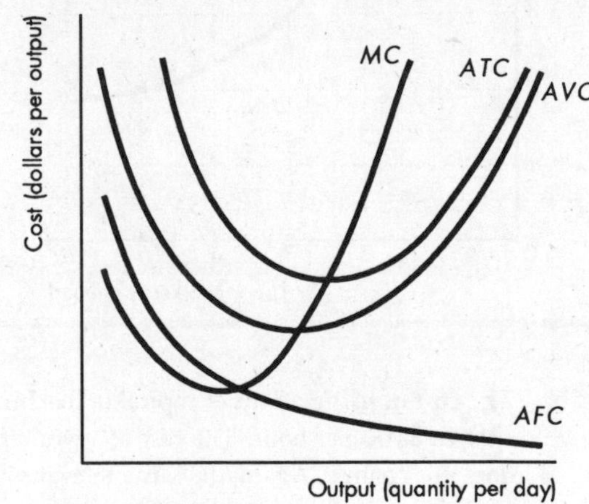

11. **c** Figure 10.13 identifies the *MC* curve. Note that it goes through the minimum points of both the *ATC* and *AVC* curves.
12. **b** Again, Figure 10.13 identifies the *ATC* curve.
13. **a** Figure 10.13 shows that the *AVC* curve is the U-shaped curve that lies below the U-shaped *ATC* curve.

14. **d** None of the curves in the original figure was the *AFC* curve, but Figure 10.13 shows the *AFC* curve.
15. **c** The rise in the cost of a variable input raises average variable costs and so shifts the *AVC* curve upward.
16. **d** This is the definition of constant returns to scale.
17. **a** When the *MP* curve is rising, each additional variable input produces more additional output than the previous unit of the input. Hence the added cost of producing the added units falls — that is, the *MC* curve is falling — because each variable unit has the same additional cost but produces more additional output.
18. **d** When the marginal cost is less than the average cost, the average cost falls as output expands.
19. **b** The long run is the amount of time until all inputs become variable.
20. **c** The marginal cost equals the difference in total cost ($24 − $21 = $3) divided by the change in output (4 − 3 = 1), so the marginal cost is $3.
21. **a** Average total cost equals total cost divided by total output, that is, $24/4 or $6.
22. **d** Because total cost equals total fixed cost plus total variable cost, total fixed cost equals $6. Then, average fixed cost is total fixed cost divided by total output so that average fixed cost equals $6/3 = $2.
23. **a** When *MP* > *AP*, the average product rises; when *MP* < *AP*, the average product falls; and when *MP* = *AP*, the average product is at its maximum.
24. **c** Fixed cost remains the same regardless of the level of output, that is, whether the firm produces a million units of output or no units of output.
25. **c** The *LRAC* curve shows the lowest possible average total cost for producing any level of output.
26. **d** The marginal products divided by the prices are the same, but the marginal products are not necessarily the same.
27. **c** Isocosts show the different combinations of capital and labor that have the same total cost.
28. **c** With the least-cost technique, the marginal cost of increasing output is the same regardless of which factor of production is increased.
29. **d** Note the similarity between isoquants and indifference curves.
30. **a** By changing the marginal product of capital, the isoquants — but not the isocosts — are affected.

Answers to Short Answer Problems

FIGURE **10.14**
Short Answer Problem 1

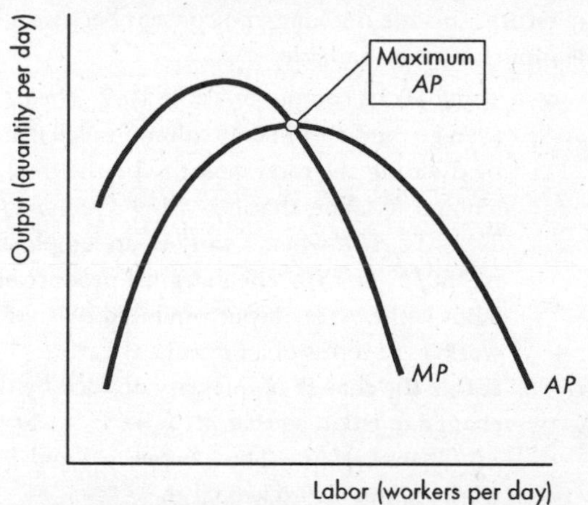

1. The marginal product curve intersects the average product curve where the average product is at its maximum. To understand why, look at Figure 10.14. To the left of the maximum point, *MP* > *AP*. That means that an additional worker produces more additional output than the average of the previously employed workers. As a result, the average product increases. Thus, as long as the *MP* exceeds the *AP*, the average product must be increasing. Now look to the right of the maximum point. Here *MP* < *AP*. Thus each new worker produces less additional output than the average of the previously employed workers, so the average product falls. As long as the *MP* is less

than the AP, the average product must decrease. That means that whenever the marginal product is larger than the average product, the average product increases; whenever the marginal product is less than the average product, the average product falls. Hence, when the marginal product equals the average product, the average product does not change, and the average product is at its maximum.

2. The law of diminishing returns states that as a firm uses additional units of a variable input, while holding constant the quantity of fixed inputs, the marginal product of the variable input will eventually diminish. Decreasing returns to scale occur when a firm increases all of its inputs by an equal percentage, and this increase results in a smaller percentage increase in output. Diminishing (marginal) returns is a short-run concept because there is a fixed input. Decreasing returns to scale is a long-run concept because all inputs must be variable.

3. a. Table 10.12 completes Table 10.2. The average product of labor column is calculated by dividing the total quantity by the total amount of labor; that is, $APL = \text{Quantity}/L$. Thus the APL when 2 workers are employed is $300/2$, or 150. The marginal product of labor is the extra output produced by an extra worker. In terms of a formula, the MPL equals the change in quantity divided by the change in labor, so that $MPL = (\Delta \text{ Quantity})/\Delta L$. Thus, between 2 and 1 workers, the MPL is equal to $(300-100)/(2-1) = 200$. Because the MPL equals the additional output when another unit of labor is employed, the quantity when 4 workers are employed equals the total quantity produced when 3 workers are employed (450) plus the additional amount the 4th worker produces, 110, or 560. Finally, for the total quantity when 6 workers are used, multiply the average product of labor, 110, by the total number of workers employed, 6, to get the total quantity of 660.

   b. Figure 10.15 shows the graph of the firm's total product curve.

Table 10.12 Short Answer Problem 3 (a)

Labor	Quantity (turkeys per week)	Average product of labor (*AP*)	Marginal product of labor (*MP*)
0	0	XX	
			100
1	100	100	
			200
2	300	150	
			150
3	450	150	
			110
4	560	140	
			70
5	630	126	
			30
6	660	110	

FIGURE **10.15**
Short Answer Problem 3 (b)

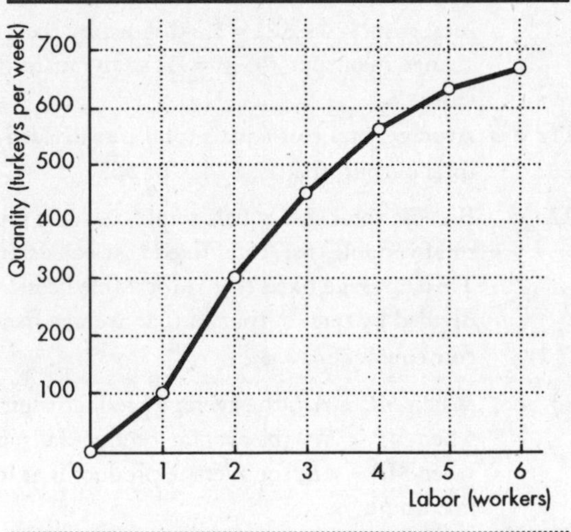

FIGURE **10.16**
Short Answer Problem 3 (c)

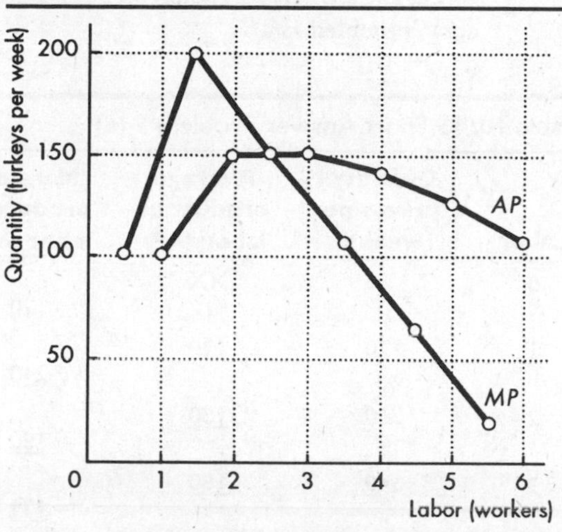

c. Figure 10.16 shows the firm's *AP* and *MP* curves. The *MP* curve crosses the *AP* curve when the *AP* is at its maximum.

4. a. Table 10.13 shows the total cost for each quantity of labor. Total variable cost equals the number of workers (the variable input) multiplied by $2,000 per worker; hence the total variable cost when 3 workers are employed is (3 workers)($2,000) or $6,000. Total cost then equals the total variable cost plus the total fixed cost, which is given in the problem as $4,000.

Table 10.13 Short Answer Problem 4 (a)

Labor	Quantity (turkeys per week)	Total variable cost (*TVC*)	Total cost (*TC*)
0	0	$0	$4,000
1	100	2,000	6,000
2	300	4,000	8,000
3	450	6,000	10,000
4	560	8,000	12,000
5	630	10,000	14,000
6	660	12,000	16,000

b. Figure 10.17 shows the firm's total cost (*TC*) and total variable cost (*TVC*) curves. The *TC* curve always lies $4000 above the *TVC* curve.

FIGURE **10.17**
Short Answer Problem 4 (b)

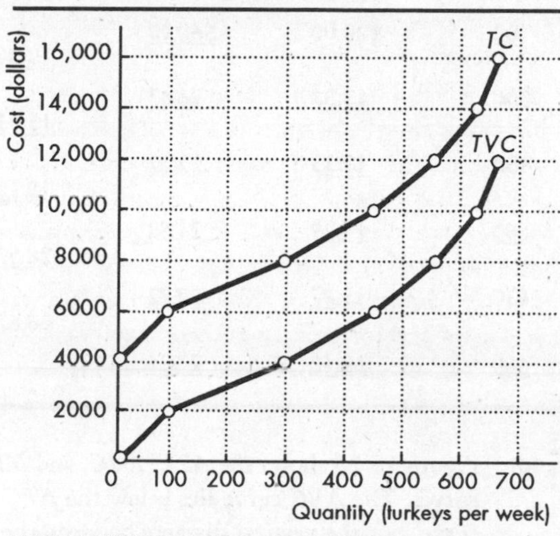

c. Table 10.14 (on the next page) completes Table 10.4. In Table 10.14, the average variable cost column was calculated by dividing total variable cost by the total quantity produced. Thus the *AVC* when 300 turkeys are produced is $4,000/300 = $13.33. Similarly, the average total cost column is calculated by dividing total cost by the total quantity produced. Finally, marginal cost equals the change in total cost divided by the change in quantity, that is, $MC = (\Delta TC)/\Delta q$. Hence the *MC* between 300 and 100 turkeys per week is ($8,000 – $6,000)/(300 – 100), or $10.00.

Table 10.14 Short Answer Problem 4 (c)

Quantity (turkeys per week)	Average variable cost (AVC)	Average total cost (ATC)	Marginal cost (MC)
0	XX	XX	
			$20.00
100	$20.00	$60.00	
			10.00
300	13.33	26.67	
			13.33
450	13.33	22.22	
			18.18
560	14.29	21.43	
			28.57
630	15.87	22.22	
			66.67
660	18.18	24.24	

d. Figure 10.18 shows the *ATC*, *AVC*, and *MC* curves. The *AVC* curve lies below the *ATC* curve, but the vertical distance between the two (which equals *AFC*) shrinks as output expands. The *MC* curve crosses the *AVC* curve where the *AVC* is at its minimum. (It also crosses the *ATC* curve where the *ATC* is at its minimum, which is not as easy to see in the figure.)

FIGURE **10.18**
Short Answer Problem 4 (d)

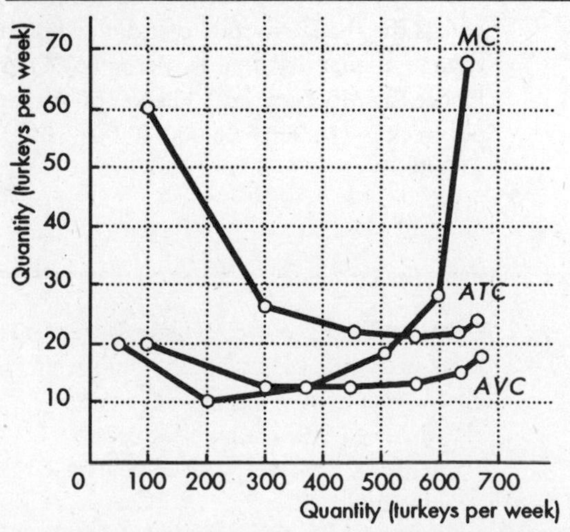

5. a. Table 10.15 shows the new *APs* and *MPs*. These answers were calculated in the same way as the answers in Table 10.12 for short answer problem 3(a).

Table 10. 15 Short Answer Problem 5 (a)

Labor	Quantity (turkeys per week)	Average product of labor (*AP*)	Marginal product of labor (*MP*)
0	0	XX	
			120
1	120	120	
			240
2	360	180	
			180
3	540	180	
			132
4	672	168	
			84
5	756	151.2	
			36
6	792	132	

b. Tables 10.16 and 10.17 show the firm's new costs after the advance in technology. The answers in Table 10.16 are calculated similarly to those in Table 10.13 for short answer problem 4(a); the answers in Table 10.17 correspond to the those in Table 10.14 for short answer problem 4(c).

Table 10. 16 Short Answer Problem 5 (b)

Labor	Quantity (turkeys per week)	Total variable cost (*TVC*)	Total cost (*TC*)
0	0	$0	$4,000
1	120	2,000	6,000
2	360	4,000	8,000
3	540	6,000	10,000
4	672	8,000	12,000
5	756	10,000	14,000
6	792	12,000	16,000

Table 10.17 Short Answer Problem 5 (b)

Quantity (turkeys per week)	Average variable cost (*AVC*)	Average total cost (*ATC*)	Marginal cost (*MC*)
0	XX	XX	
			$16.67
120	$16.67	$50.00	
			8.33
360	11.11	22.22	
			11.11
540	11.11	18.52	
			15.15
672	11.90	17.86	
			23.81
756	13.23	18.52	
			55.55
792	15.15	20.20	

c. Figure 10.19 shows the old and new *ATC* and *MC* curves. The new *ATC* curve generally lies beneath the old *ATC* curve. (The new curve *always* lies below the old curve, but the large discrete changes in output that are plotted make the new *ATC* curve appear to lie a little above the old *ATC* curve at low levels of output.) The new *MC* curve is below the old *MC* curve. Thus, technological advances shift the firm's cost curves downward.

FIGURE **10.19**
Short Answer Problem 5 (c)

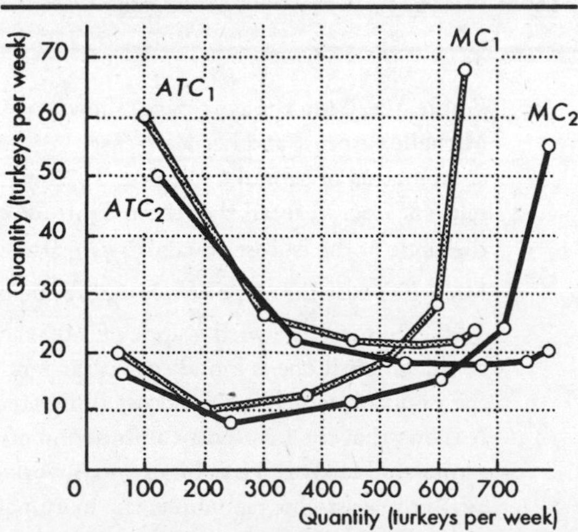

6. a. Table 10.18 shows the total cost after the rise in fixed cost. Comparison with Table 10.13 (the situation before the rise in fixed cost) shows that the total variable cost did not change but that the total cost rose.

Table 10.18 Short Answer Problem 6 (a)

Labor	Quantity (turkeys per week)	Total variable cost (*TVC*)	Total cost (*TC*)
0	0	$0	$8,000
1	100	2,000	10,000
2	300	4,000	12,000
3	450	6,000	14,000
4	560	8,000	16,000
5	630	10,000	18,000
6	660	12,000	20,000

Table 10.19 Short Answer Problem 6 (b)

	Before increase		After increase	
Quantity	Average total cost (*ATC*)	Marginal cost (*MC*)	Average total cost (*ATC*)	Marginal cost (*MC*)
0	XX		XX	
		$20.00		$20.00
100	$60.00		$100.00	
		10.00		10.00
300	26.67		40.00	
		13.33		13.33
450	22.22		31.11	
		18.18		18.18
560	21.43		28.57	
		28.57		28.57
630	22.22		28.57	
		66.67		66.67
660	24.24		30.30	

b. Table 10.19 shows the firm's average total costs and marginal costs before and after the rise in fixed cost. These answers were calculated the same way as the answers in Table 10.14. The rise in fixed cost raised the Al's average total cost, *ATC*. That is, at any level of output, the average total cost is higher after the rise in fixed cost. However, the boost in fixed cost had no effect on Al's marginal cost, *MC*. The marginal cost at any level of output is the same before and after the rise in fixed cost. In terms of a diagram, the increase in fixed cost would shift the firm's *ATC* curve upward but would have no effect on the *MC* curve.

7. a. Table 10.20 completes Table 10.10 and shows Al's total variable cost and total cost after the variable input, labor, rises in cost. The rise in the cost of the variable input raises both the total variable cost and the total cost.

b. Table 10.21 shows the firm's average total cost and marginal cost after the variable cost has risen. The rise in variable cost raises both the average total cost and the marginal cost. In other words, at any level of output, both the average total cost and marginal cost are greater after the rise in variable cost than before. In a diagram, the rise in Al's variable cost would shift both the firm's *ATC* and *MC* curves upward.

c. When the fixed cost rose, the firm's marginal cost did not change; when the variable cost rose, the firm's marginal cost rose. The reason for this difference lies in the definition of marginal cost. Marginal cost measures how total cost changes when output is changed. Fixed cost — by definition and name — is fixed so that it does not change when output changes. Thus, the fixed cost has no influence on the marginal cost. When the fixed cost changes, the total cost changes but the marginal cost is unaffected. However, the variable cost does affect the marginal cost. In particular, to increase output, a firm must hire more variable inputs, labor in this case. Hence changes in the cost of a variable input affect how much the total cost changes when more output is produced. As a result, when the cost of a variable input rises, the firm's marginal cost rises. When the cost of a variable input falls, the marginal cost falls.

Table 10.20 Short Answer Problem 7 (a)

Labor	Quantity (turkeys per week)	Total variable cost (*TVC*)	Total cost (*TC*)
0	0	$0	$4,000
1	100	3,000	7,000
2	300	6,000	10,000
3	450	9,000	13,000
4	560	12,000	16,000
5	630	15,000	19,000
6	660	18,000	22,000

Table 10.21 Short Answer Problem 7 (b)

	Before increase		After increase	
Quantity	Average total cost (*ATC*)	Marginal cost (*MC*)	Average total cost (*ATC*)	Marginal cost (*MC*)
0	XX		XX	
		$20.00		$30.00
100	$60.00		$70.00	
		10.00		15.00
300	26.67		33.33	
		13.33		20.00
450	22.22		28.88	
		18.18		27.27
560	21.43		28.57	
		28.57		42.83
630	22.22		30.16	
		66.67		100.00
660	24.24		33.33	

8. a. Figure 10.20 (on the next page) shows Michelle's isocost and her least-cost combination of capital and labor. To draw the relevant isocost, recall that the magnitude of the slope of the isocost equals P_L/P_K. In Michelle's case the slope equals $\$20/\$20$, or 1.00. Thus isocosts with a slope of 1.00 can be drawn until one is found that is tangent to the isoquant, which is the isocost illustrated. It shows that the least-cost combination of capital and labor is 3 machines and 3 workers. With the least-cost technique, the marginal rate of substitution equals the slope of the

FIGURE 10.20
Short Answer Problem 8 (a)

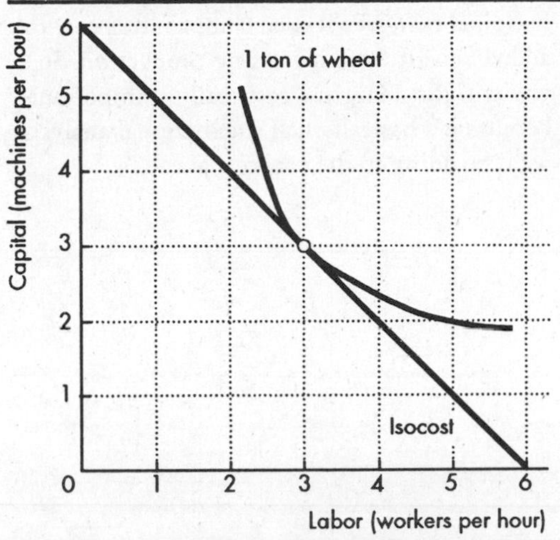

FIGURE 10.21
Short Answer Problem 8 (b)

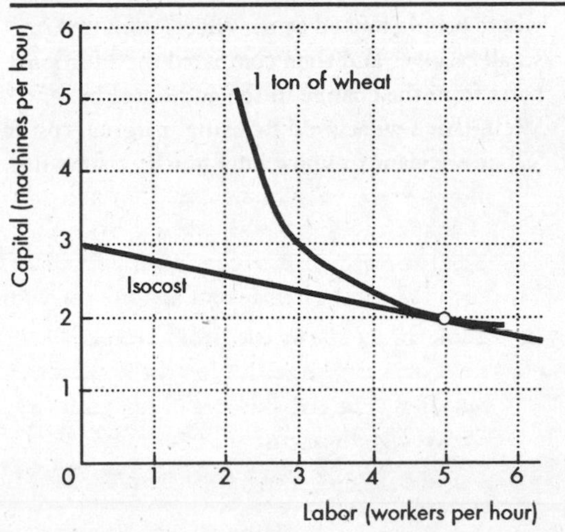

isocost line, so the marginal rate of substitution is 1.00. The total cost of producing this ton of wheat is $120.

b. When capital rises in price to $100, the slope of the isocost lines changes. The magnitude of the slope becomes $20/$100, or 0.20. Figure 10.21 shows a new isocost with this slope that is tangent to the isoquant. It illustrates that the new least-cost technique of production uses 2 machines and 5 workers. Compared to the situation when capital was $20, the rise in the price of a machine caused Michelle to decrease her use of capital (from 3 to 2 machines) and increase her use of labor (from 3 to 5 workers). The total cost of producing a ton of wheat rises to $200.

9. If a firm finds that $MP_L/MP_K > P_L/P_K$, we know that MP_L/MP_K is too large to minimize the firm's cost. This condition implies that the firm should increase the quantity of labor used and decrease the quantity of capital used. Because the marginal product of an input declines as the quantity of the input increases, the increase in labor will decrease MP_L, and the decrease in capital will increase MP_K. This outcome means that MP_L/MP_K will decline, which is the result needed to make the ratio of marginal products equal to the ratio of prices.

■ You're the Teacher

1. "Look, we've talked about this before. Economic theories deliberately abstract; that is, they deliberately do not include all the nitty-gritty detail of the real world. Instead they attempt to focus only on the most important issues. Sure, all companies employ lots of different types of labor — skilled labor, unskilled labor, blue collar workers, white collar workers, sales representatives, and so on. So what? Including this fact in a theory would just give us a bunch more details that don't tell us anything.

It's the same when you say that firms are different. Look, consumers are different too. That didn't stop us from developing useful theories about the factors that affect their demand curves.

The whole idea is that economic theory looks for qualities that are the same. That is what we're doing with firms. For instance, *all* firms hire labor and use capital. And these productive factors are different when we think about how rapidly the firm can change the amounts that it uses. So all firms have to face the difference between fixed and variable factors of production. I don't care if you're talking about General Motors building cars or that Subway place you like making sandwiches. The point is that the theory we're learning can be applied to all types of firms, which gives the theory its power."

2. "You're lucky because I've been reading ahead in the book. Remember the discussion of marginal analysis in one of the earlier chapters? You know, where people looked at the effects from making small changes and then compared the additional costs from the change to the additional benefits? Well, that's what we'll be using marginal cost for. When we want to know how much a firm will produce, we can ask whether it wants to increase its production. By increasing its production, the firm will incur some additional costs — its marginal cost. We'll then compare this cost to the added benefit from increasing production. So, you're right: Marginal cost really is important because it's basically half the marginal analysis we'll be doing in the chapters ahead."

Chapter 11 COMPETITION

Key Concepts

Perfect Competition

The concept of perfect competition is based on the assumptions of many firms, each selling an identical good; many buyers; free entry; no advantage for existing firms over new firms; and complete information.

- Each firm is a price taker.
- The *market* demand curve slopes downward. But each *firm* faces a horizontal — perfectly elastic — demand curve at the market price. Such a demand curve is illustrated in Figure 11.1.

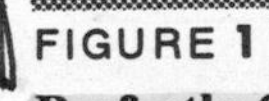

FIGURE 11.1
Perfectly Competitive Firm's Demand Curve

Price

D = AR = MR

Quantity

In the short run, each firm must decide:

- whether to shut down temporarily.
- if it produces, how much to produce.

In the long run, the firm must decide:

- whether to change its plant size.
- whether to exit permanently.

Economic profit equals total revenue minus total opportunity cost. Total revenue equals the price of the output times the number sold, $TR = P \times q$ with P the price and q the amount the firm produces.

- Marginal revenue, MR, equals the change in total revenue divided by the change in output, $(\Delta TR)/\Delta q$.
- In perfect competition $P = MR$.

To maximize profit in the short run, the firm produces the quantity of output at which $MR = MC$. This result is illustrated in Figure 11.2. Maximizing profit by setting $MR = MC$ is an example of marginal analysis.

FIGURE 11.2
A Perfectly Competitive Firm

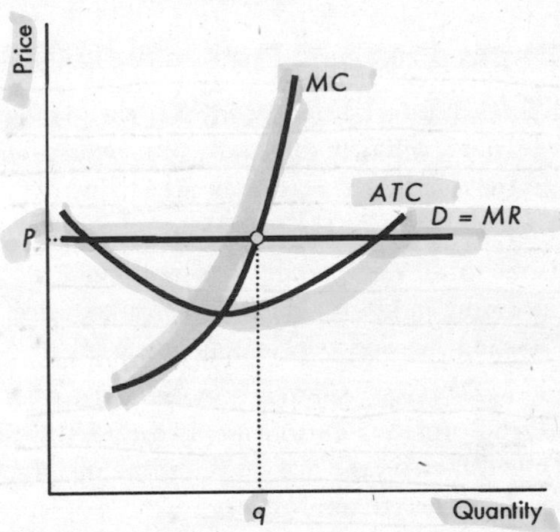

There are three possible short-run profit-maximizing outcomes:

- $P > ATC$ — the firm earns an economic profit. (This case is illustrated in Figure 11.2.)
- $P = ATC$ — the firm earns a normal profit and zero economic profit.
- $P < ATC$ — the firm incurs an economic loss.

A firm incurring economic losses must decide whether to shut down temporarily:

- If $P > AVC$, the firm continues to produce.
- If $P < AVC$, the firm shuts down temporarily. Thus the shutdown point is reached when P equals the minimum AVC.

A perfectly competitive firm's supply curve is its MC curve above the minimum AVC.

Output, Price, and Profit in the Short Run

The **short-run industry supply curve** shows how the total quantity supplied by the industry changes when the market price changes. It is the horizontal sum of each individual firm's supply curve.

- The equilibrium market price and industry equilibrium level of output are determined by the industry demand and supply curves.
- In the short run, perfectly competitive firms can make an economic profit, a normal profit, or suffer an economic loss.
- The number of firms in the industry, and their size, is fixed in the short run.

Output, Price, and Profit in the Long Run

In the long run, the number of firms in the industry and the size of each firm can adjust. Economic profits or losses cause firms to enter or exit the industry.

- Economic profits cause entry by new firms, thereby shifting the industry supply curve rightward and thus reducing the market price. The drop in price reduces economic profits.
- Economic losses lead to exit by existing firms, which shifts the industry supply curve leftward. This shift raises the market price, and the higher price reduces economic losses.
- Firms change their plant size if it increases their profits.

Figure 11.3 illustrates a firm in long-run competitive equilibrium. Three conditions are satisfied:

- $MR (= P) = MC$ — firms maximize their profits.
- P = minimum ATC — economic profit is zero.
- P = minimum $LRAC$ — plant size cannot be changed in order to increase profits.

FIGURE **11.3**
Long-Run Equilibrium

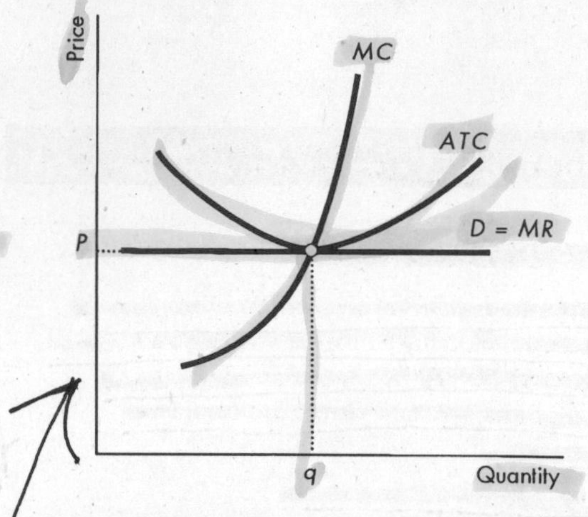

Changing Tastes and Advancing Technology

A permanent decrease in demand causes adjustments:

- The market price falls. Each firm reduces its output, so the equilibrium industry quantity decreases.
- Firms incur economic losses, so some exit the industry. This exit shifts the industry supply curve leftward. As a result, the market price rises and industry quantity decreases.
- Eventually the market price rises to eliminate economic losses. At this point, firms no longer exit and long-run equilibrium is established.

If there are **external economies** — factors that lower firms' costs as the industry output expands — with the contraction in output, the long-run equilibrium market price is higher than the initial price before the decrease in demand. If there are **external diseconomies** — factors that raise firms' costs as industry output increases — the long-run equilibrium price is lower than the initial price. The **long-run industry supply curve** shows how the quantity supplied by an industry varies with changes in the market price after all adjustments have been made.

Technological change also creates adjustments:

- New technology lowers firms' costs and increases their supply. The industry supply curve shifts rightward, thereby lowering the market price and increasing industry output.

- Firms that do not adopt the new technology incur economic losses and exit the industry.
- In the long run, all firms use the new technology and earn only a normal profit.

Competition and Efficiency

Allocative efficiency occurs when no resources are wasted so that no one can be made better off without making someone else worse off. Allocative efficiency requires:

- **producer efficiency.** Firms are technologically and economically efficient. Profit maximization guarantees that these conditions hold, so all points on a supply curve are producer efficient.
- **consumer efficiency.** Consumers are maximizing their utility. This condition is met at all points on a demand curve.
- **exchange efficiency.** When the price equals the **marginal social cost,** ***MSC*****, and marginal social benefit,** ***MSB***. The *MSC* is the cost of additional output, including external costs. The *MSB* is the benefit from additional consumption, including external benefits. If there are no external costs or benefits, perfect competition is exchange efficient.

The presence of external costs or benefits and the existence of monopoly can cause markets to be allocatively inefficient.

Helpful Hints

1. Although perfectly competitive markets are rare in the real world, there are three important reasons for developing a thorough understanding of their behavior.

   First, many markets closely approximate perfect competition. The analysis in this chapter gives direct and useful insights into the behavior of these markets.

   Second, the theory of perfect competition allows us to isolate the effects of competitive forces that are at work in all markets, even in those that do not match the assumptions of perfect competition.

   Third, the perfectly competitive model serves as a useful benchmark for evaluating relative allocative efficiency.

2. In the short run, a perfectly competitive firm cannot change the size of its plant — its capital input is fixed. The firm also is a price taker; it always sells at the market price, which it cannot influence. The only variable that the firm controls is its level of output. The short-run condition for profit maximization is to choose the level of output at which marginal revenue equals marginal cost. This is a general condition, which — as demonstrated in later chapters — applies to other market structures, such as monopoly and monopolistic competition. For the perfectly competitive firm, marginal revenue equals price, so this profit-maximizing condition takes a particular form: Choose the level of output at which price is equal to marginal cost, or $P = MC$.

3. That profit maximization requires producing where $MR = MC$ might seem odd. Producing where $MR > MC$ might seem more reasonable because this situation apparently implies that the firm is making a profit. However, this line of thought is wrong because it ignores how to use marginal analysis. The correct way to view this situation is to start by noting that a firm strives to maximize its *total* profit. To meet this objective, the firm produces any unit of output for which the revenue from the unit exceeds the cost of producing the unit. After all, if the revenue from the unit — the marginal revenue — is greater than the cost of producing it — the marginal cost — the unit adds to the firm's total profit. In other words, as long as $MR > MC$ for a unit of output, producing this unit adds to the firm's total profit. True, some units add more to the profit — those with MR much greater than MC — and others add less — those with MR only slightly larger than MC — but as long as producing the unit of output adds to the firm's total profit, the firm produces it. Comparing the additional revenue from a unit with its additional costs (using marginal analysis) shows that the firm would pass up profit if it produced an amount of output so that $MR > MC$. Only by producing the level of output that gives $MR = MC$ does the firm not forgo some profit, so only at this level of output does the firm maximize its total profit.

4. Another point that may seem odd is why a firm continues to operate even though its economic profit is zero. The key to understanding this situation lies in the definition of the average total cost curve. Recall from Chapter 9 that the economist defines a firm's total cost as all its *opportunity* costs, which include both explicit and implicit costs. Among the implicit costs are the owners' forgone interest on funds invested in the business and the normal profit due the owners for their provision of entrepreneurial talent to the business. When total revenue equals total cost (or, equivalently, when the firm is earning no economic profit), the firm's owners are still receiving a return on their investment that is equal to the return that they could earn elsewhere and are being adequately compensated for their entrepreneurial talent. At this point, the firm earns a "normal profit." As the phrase implies, a normal profit is the profit that could normally be earned in any other industry. Even though the firm's economic profit (sometimes called "extra normal profit") is zero, by earning a "normal profit" it is earning just as much profit as it could anywhere else and its owners therefore are content to continue producing in the same industry.
5. In the long run, the firm can switch industries and change plant size. Economic profit and loss serves as the signal for the movement or reallocation of the firm's resources. Firms move out of industries with economic losses and into industries with economic profits. Only when there is no economic profits or loss is there no tendency for firms to enter or exit industries.

   Without restrictions on entry into the industry, economic profits will be zero and firms will be producing at the minimum of their long-run average cost curves in long-run equilibrium.
6. In long-run equilibrium, three conditions are satisfied for each firm in a perfectly competitive industry:
   - $MR = P = MC$. This equality means that profit is maximized for each firm.
   - $P = ATC$. This equality implies that economic profit is zero and that each firm is just earning a normal profit.
   - P = minimum $LRAC$. This result means that production takes place at the point of minimum long-run average cost.

Questions

True/False/Uncertain and Explain

1. In a perfectly competitive industry, no single firm can significantly affect the market price of the good.
2. The industry demand curve in a perfectly competitive industry is horizontal.
3. A perfectly competitive firm may earn an economic profit, a normal profit, or incur an economic loss in the short run.
4. A perfectly competitive firm may earn an economic profit, a normal profit, or incur an economic loss in the long run.
5. $P = MR$ for a perfectly competitive firm.
6. In the long run, a perfectly competitive firm produces at the minimum $LRAC$.
7. The supply curve of a perfectly competitive firm shows the quantities of output supplied at alternative prices as long as the firm earns an economic profit.
8. If $P > ATC$, the firm is incurring an economic loss.
9. A firm making zero economic profit makes no profit at all.
10. Allocative efficiency occurs when no resources are wasted so that making someone better off without making someone else worse off is impossible.
11. A perfectly competitive firm must decide what price to charge for its goods.
12. If the price is below a firm's minimum ATC, the firm immediately shuts down.
13. If it does not shut down, to maximize its profit a perfectly competitive firm produces the level of output that yields $MR = MC$.

14. A perfectly competitive firm's supply curve is its *ATC* curve.

15. Allocative efficiency requires that the marginal social benefit be greater than the marginal social cost.

Multiple Choice

1. Which of the following is NOT a characteristic of a perfectly competitive industry?
   a. A downward-sloping industry demand curve.
   b. A perfectly elastic demand curve for each firm.
   c. Each firm decides its quantity of output.
   d. Each firm produces a good slightly different from that of its competitors.

2. The short-run industry supply curve is
   a. the horizontal sum of the individual firms' supply curves.
   b. the vertical sum of the individual firms' supply curves.
   c. vertical at the total level of output being produced by all firms.
   d. horizontal at the current market price.

3. Which of the following is necessarily true when a perfectly competitive firm is in short-run equilibrium?
   a. *MR* = *MC*.
   b. *P* = minimum *LRAC*.
   c. *P* = *ATC*.
   d. All of the above are true at short-run equilibrium.

4. Which of the following is necessarily true when a perfectly competitive firm is in long-run equilibrium?
   a. *MR* = *MC*.
   b. *P* = minimum *LRAC*.
   c. *P* = *ATC*.
   d. All of the above are true at long-run equilibrium.

5. In the price range below minimum average variable cost, a perfectly competitive firm's supply curve is
   a. horizontal at the market price.
   b. vertical at zero output.
   c. the same as its marginal cost curve.
   d. the same as its average variable cost curve.

Use the Figure 11.4 for the next two questions.

FIGURE 11.4

Multiple Choice Questions 6 and 7

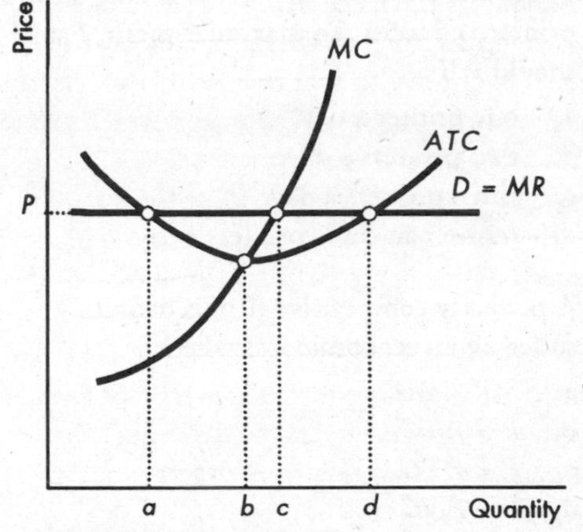

6. The firm illustrated in Figure 11.4 will produce how much output?
   a. *a*.
   b. *b*.
   c. *c*.
   d. *d*.

7. The firm illustrated in Figure 11.4 is
   a. earning an economic profit.
   b. earning a normal profit.
   c. incurring an economic loss.
   d. in long-run equilibrium.

8. In the short run, a perfectly competitive firm can
   a. earn an economic profit.
   b. earn a normal profit.
   c. incur an economic loss.
   d. All of the above are possible.

9. In the long run, a perfectly competitive firm can
   a. earn an economic profit.
   b. earn a normal profit.
   c. incur an economic loss.
   d. All of the above are possible

10. Paul runs a shop that sells printers. Paul's business is a perfect competitor and can sell each printer for a price of $1,000. The marginal cost of selling one printer a day is $800, the marginal cost of selling a second printer is $900, and the marginal cost of selling a third printer is $1050. To maximize profit, Paul should sell
   a. one printer a day.
   b. two printers a day.
   c. three printers a day.
   d. more than three printers a day.

11. A perfectly competitive firm is definitely suffering an economic loss when
   a. $MR < MC$.
   b. $P > ATC$.
   c. $P < ATC$.
   d. $P > AVC$.

12. Of the following, which is most likely to be a perfect competitor?
   a. MCI, one of the three major providers of long distance telephone service in the United States.
   b. The company that provides your local cable TV service.
   c. A tomato grower living in Florida.
   d. DeBeers, the provider of over 80 percent of the rough diamonds in the world.

13. Marginal cost, MC, equals
   a. TR/q.
   b. TC/q.
   c. $(\Delta TC)/\Delta q$.
   d. $(\Delta ATC)/(\Delta AVC)$.

14. A perfectly competitive firm's demand curve
   a. is less elastic than the market demand curve.
   b. has the same elasticity as the market demand curve.
   c. is more elastic than the market demand curve.
   d. is not comparable to the market demand curve.

FIGURE 11.5
Multiple Choice Question 15

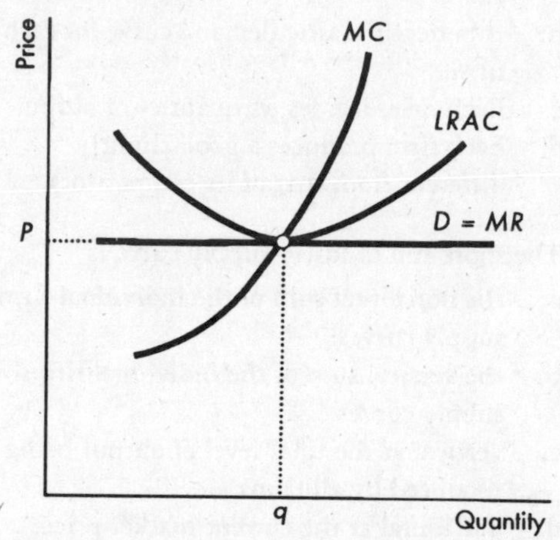

15. In Figure 11.5, the firm is producing q. Which of the following statements is correct?
   a. This level of production cannot be the long-run equilibrium because the firm is not maximizing its profit.
   b. This level of production cannot be the long-run equilibrium because the firm is earning an economic profit.
   c. This level of production cannot be the long-run equilibrium because the firm is incurring an economic loss.
   d. This level of production is the long-run equilibrium.

16. If a perfectly competitive firm is incurring an economic loss, it
    a. always shuts down immediately.
    b. continues to operate until either the price rises or its costs fall so that it no longer has an economic loss.
    c. shuts down only if $P > AVC$.
    d. shuts down only if $P < AVC$.

17. For a perfectly competitive firm, *MR* always equals
    a. *ATC*.
    b. *P*.
    c. *AVC*.
    d. None of the above because *MR* is not always equal to the same thing.

18. Which of the following is NOT necessary for allocative efficiency?
    a. The presence of external benefits.
    b. Producer efficiency so that firms are economically efficient.
    c. Consumer efficiency so that consumers cannot increase their total satisfaction by rearranging their consumption.
    d. Exchange efficiency so that the price equals marginal social benefit and marginal cost.

19. Suppose that firms in a perfectly competitive industry are earning economic profits. Over time,
    a. other firms enter the industry so that the price rises and economic profits fall.
    b. some firms leave the industry so that the price rises and economic profits fall.
    c. other firms enter the industry so that both price and economic profits fall.
    d. Nothing happens because there are no incentives for change.

20. If demand for a good decreases permanently, in the short run the market price
    a. falls and each firm produces more output to make up for the lower price.
    b. falls and each firm produces less output.
    c. does not change but some firms shut down.
    d. does not change because each firm produces less output.

21. If firms in an industry are incurring an economic loss, then as some exit, the market price
    a. rises and the existing firms' economic losses do not change.
    b. rises and the existing firms' economic losses fall.
    c. falls and the existing firms' economic losses rise.
    d. falls and the existing firms' economic losses fall.

22. In the short run, which of the following is false?
    a. Perfectly competitive firms can possibly earn an economic profit.
    b. The number of firms is fixed.
    c. To maximize its profit, a perfectly competitive firm produces enough output so that $MR = MC$.
    d. Perfectly competitive firms necessarily produce at the minimum *ATC*.

23. New technology in an industry means that
    a. all firms in the industry permanently earn economic profits regardless of whether they adopt the technology.
    b. firms that adopt the new technology permanently earn economic profits.
    c. firms that do not adopt the new technology permanently earn economic profits.
    d. firms that adopt the new technology temporarily earn economic profits.

24. When will new firms want to enter an industry?
    a. When $MR = MC$ for the existing firms in the industry.
    b. Anytime the price of the good has risen.
    c. When the new firms can earn economic profits.
    d. When the new firms think that there are external economies in the industry.

25. The term "external economies" refers to the
    a. situation in which the firm's *MC* curve slopes downward as more output is produced.
    b. case in which the firm's *ATC* curve shifts upward as more output is produced.
    c. fact that a firm's *ATC* curve slopes down at low levels of output.
    d. situation in which increases in an industry's output lower the costs of the firms in the industry.

26. For a perfectly competitive firm, which curve is perfectly elastic?
    a. The firm's demand curve.
    b. The *ATC* curve.
    c. The market demand curve.
    d. The *MC* curve.

27. Owing to a rise in the wage rate that it must pay, a perfectly competitive firm's marginal costs rise but its demand curve does not change. As a result, the firm
    a. decreases the amount of output it produces and raises its price.
    b. increases the amount of output it produces and lowers its price.
    c. decreases the amount of output it produces and does not change its price.
    d. None of the above.

Table 11.1 Multiple Choice Question 28

Quantity	Price (dollars)
100	$5.00
101	5.00

28. Refer to Table 11.1. What is the marginal revenue from selling 101 units of output rather than 100?
    a. $5.00.
    b. $500.00.
    c. $505.00.
    d. The marginal revenue cannot be calculated without more information.

29. A perfectly competitive firm produces a good that is
    a. unique.
    b. somewhat different from that of its competitors.
    c. identical to that of its competitors.
    d. sometimes identical to and sometimes slightly different from that of its competitors.

30. If there are external diseconomies in an industry, after a permanent increase in demand, in the long run the market price
    a. is higher than initially.
    b. is the same as initially.
    c. is lower than initially.
    d. may be higher or lower depending on whether the firms' are earning economic profits.

Short Answer Problems

1. Why will a firm in a perfectly competitive industry choose not to charge a price either above or below the market price?
2. Why will economic profits tend to zero at long-run equilibrium in a perfectly competitive industry?
3. Suppose that a perfectly competitive industry is at long-run equilibrium when there is a permanent decrease in demand for the industry's good. There are no external economies or diseconomies. How does the industry adjust to its new long-run equilibrium? Be sure to discuss what happens to the firms' profits and the number of firms in the industry. Draw two diagrams showing what happens to the price and quantity during the adjustment process.
4. a. Draw a diagram illustrating the case of a perfectly competitive firm that is earning an economic profit. In the diagram, show the amount of the economic profit.
   b. In a diagram, show the case of a perfectly competitive firm that is earning only a normal profit — that is, it is not incurring an economic loss nor making an economic profit.
   c. Draw a diagram to illustrate the case of a perfectly competitive firm that is incurring an

economic loss but is continuing to operate. Be sure to include the *AVC* curve. Show the amount of the economic loss.

Table 11.2 Rudy's Total Cost and Revenue

Quantity (acres)	Total cost (dollars)	Total revenue (dollars)
1	$1,000	$2,000
2	2,500	4,000
3	5,000	6,000
4	8,500	8,000
5	13,000	10,000
6	18,500	12,000

5. Rudy runs a rutabaga farm. (Rutabagas are potato-like vegetables that in some nations take the place of potatoes.) Rudy relishes the idea of maximizing his profit, so he must decide how many acres to farm. He receives $2,000 per acre of rutabagas farmed. Table 11.2 shows Rudy's total cost and total revenue for different numbers of acres farmed.
   a. Based on Table 11.2, how many acres of rutabagas should Rudy farm? What is his total economic profit ?
   b. Complete Table 11.3, which gives Rudy's marginal cost and marginal revenue schedules. (Note that both marginal costs and marginal revenues relate to changes in production, so they are located between the quantity of acres farmed.)
   c. In Figure 11.6, draw Rudy's marginal cost and marginal revenue curves.
   d. Based on Table 11.3 and Figure 11.6, how many acres should Rudy farm? Why?
   e. Are your answers to parts (a) and (d) different? If so, why?
6. a. More people in more nations decide that they like french fried rutabagas with hamburgers. As a result, the revenue from growing rutabagas rises to $4,000 an acre. Rudy's costs do not change from those in Table 11.2. Draw Rudy's new *MC* and *MR* curves in Figure 11.7. (On the next page.)

Table 11.3 Rudy's Marginal Cost and Revenue

Quantity (acres)	Marginal cost (dollars)	Marginal revenue (dollars)
1		
	___	___
2		
	___	___
3		
	___	___
4		
	___	___
5		
	___	___
6		

FIGURE 11.6
Rudy's *MC* and *MR*

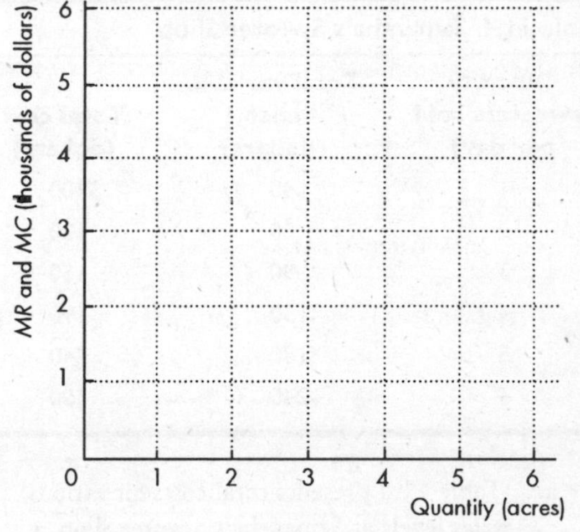

   b. How does Rudy respond to the rise in the price of a rutabaga; that is, how many acres of rutabagas does Rudy now grow?
   c. If all rutabaga farmers have the same cost schedule as Rudy's, does your answer in part (b) represent the long-run equilibrium? Why or why not?

FIGURE 11.7
Rudy's New *MC* and *MR*

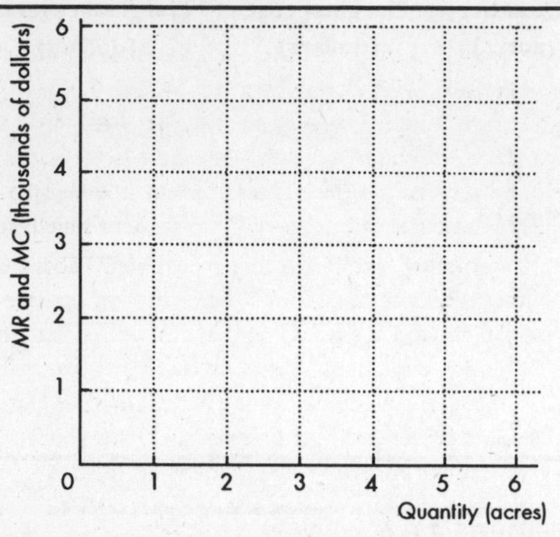

Table 11.4. Samantha's Sweater Shop

Quantity (sweaters sold per day)	Total variable cost (dollars)	Total cost (dollars)
1	$40	$100
2	60	120
3	90	150
4	130	190
5	180	240
6	240	300

7. a. Table 11.4 presents total costs for various sales levels at Samantha's Sweater Shop, a perfectly competitive firm. Use these cost figures to complete Table 11.5.
   b. In Figure 11.8, draw Samantha's *MC* curve.
   c. Use the costs from Table 11.5 and the graph in Figure 11.8 to determine Samantha's supply schedule in Table 11.6.
   d. In addition to the *MC* curve you have already drawn, draw Samantha's supply curve in Figure 11.8.

Table 11.5. Samantha's Average and Marginal Costs

Quantity (sweaters sold per day)	Average variable cost (dollars)	Average total cost (dollars)	Marginal cost (dollars)
1	___	___	
			___
2	___	___	
			___
3	___	___	
			___
4	___	___	
			___
5	___	___	
			___
6	___	___	

FIGURE 11.8
Samantha's *MC* Curve and Supply Curve

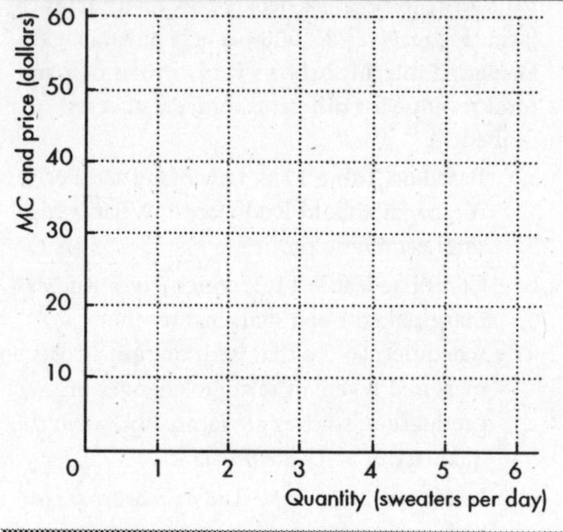

Table 11.6 Samantha's Supply Curve

Price (dollars per sweater)	Quantity (sweaters per day)
$25	___
35	___
45	___
55	___

8. Suppose that a firm can use three levels of capital. Figure 11.9 shows the ATC curves for each level; ATC_1 uses the least amount of capital and ATC_3 the most. Carefully draw the firm's $LRAC$. The level of output indicated by q can be produced by using all three levels of capital. In the long run, which amount of capital will the firm use to produce this level of output?

FIGURE 11.9
Short Answer Problem 8

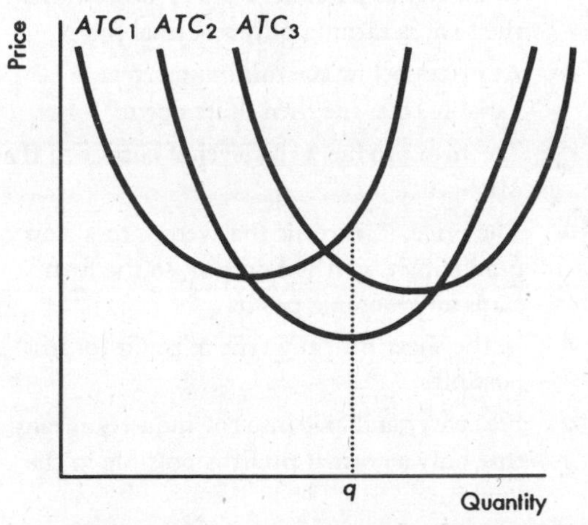

9. Suppose that output in an industry is such that the marginal social benefit is greater than the marginal social cost. Explain why this level of output is allocatively inefficient.

You're the Teacher

1. "I really don't get why a perfectly competitive firm wants to produce so that $MR = MC$. I mean, the goal of the firm is to earn the most profit possible. Why does it produce so that $MR = MC$? I think that it ought to want to produce so that $MR > MC$; that is, so that revenues exceed costs and it earns a profit." This student is making a fundamental error. Correct the student's analysis.
2. "You know, one thing that seems weird about this chapter is the claim that a business will operate even though it's losing money. I'd think that the moment a business started to incur an economic loss, unless there was some chance that the loss would be reversed in the future, the business would shut down." This student is right: A business operating even though it incurs an economic loss *does* seem weird. Can you explain why this situation happens?

Answers

True/False Answers

1. **T** Each firm is a price taker.
2. **F** The *firm's* demand curve is horizontal, but the *industry* demand curve slopes downward.
3. **T** In the short run, depending on market demand and the firm's costs, a perfectly competitive firm may earn an economic profit, incur an economic loss, or earn a normal profit.
4. **F** In the long run, the process of entry and exit means that a perfectly competitive firm earns only a normal profit.
5. **T** Because a perfectly competitive firm can sell however much output it wants at the market price, P, the market price is the MR from selling another unit of output.
6. **T** In the long run, the overwhelming competition within a perfectly competitive industry forces each firm to produce as efficiently as possible.
7. **F** The supply curve shows the amount that will be produced regardless of whether the firm earns an economic profit or not.
8. **F** If $P < ATC$, the firm suffers an economic loss.
9. **F** A firm making zero economic profit earns a normal profit that is sufficient to compensate its owners adequately for their entrepreneurial inputs.
10. **T** This statement conveys the general meaning of allocative efficiency.
11. **F** A perfectly competitive firm is a price taker, like a wheat farmer who can charge only the market price for the wheat grown.
12. **U** If $P < ATC$, the firm suffers an economic loss but it continues to operate as long as $P > AVC$.
13. **T** Produce the level of output so that $MR = MC$ is the rule followed to maximize profits.
14. **F** The firm's supply curve is its MC curve above its AVC curve.
15. **F** Allocative efficiency requires that the level of output be such that the marginal social benefit equals the marginal social cost.

Multiple Choice

1. **d** In perfect competition, each firm produces a good identical to that of its competitors.
2. **a** At any price, the quantity supplied by the industry equals the sum of the amounts that each firm produces.
3. **a** The condition $MR = MC$ is necessary for the firm to be maximizing its profit.
4. **d** $MR = MC$ means that the firm is maximizing its profit; $P =$ minimum $LRAC$ is because which competition forces firms to produce as efficiently as possible; $P = ATC$ means that the firm is earning only a normal profit.
5. **b** At prices below the minimum average variable cost, the firm shuts down.
6. **c** The firm produces the level of output so that $MR = MC$.
7. **a** The price, P, exceeds the average total cost of producing c worth of output, so the firm earns an economic profit.
8. **d** In the short run, any type of profit (or loss) is possible.
9. **b** Free entry and exit into the industry means that only a normal profit is possible in the long run.
10. **b** The second printer adds $100 to Paul's total profit and so will be sold; however, the third printer would lower Paul's total profit by $50 and so is not sold.
11. **c** When $P < ATC$, the firm incurs an economic loss.
12. **c** The other possibilities describe industries with only a few firms, so they cannot be perfectly competitive firms.
13. **c** Marginal cost equals the *additional* cost caused by producing *additional* output.
14. **c** The firm's demand curve is perfectly elastic, whereas the market demand curve is not perfectly elastic.
15. **d** Figure 11.5 illustrates the long-run equilibrium for a perfectly competitive firm.
16. **d** As long as $P > AVC$, the firm's losses are smaller if it operates than if it shuts down.
17. **b** Because a perfectly competitive firm can always sell another unit of output at the going market price, the market price is the firm's marginal revenue.

18. **a** The presence of external benefits means that a perfectly competitive industry will not be allocatively efficient.

19. **c** The entry of new firms lowers the price and economic profits, thereby driving the industry toward its long-run equilibrium.

20. **b** When the price falls, each firm moves down its *MC* curve and produces less. This response — each firm producing less — accounts for the reduction in the quantity supplied along the market supply curve when the price falls.

21. **b** Firms continue to leave as long as they incur an economic loss.

22. **d** In the long run, perfectly competitive firms produce at the minimum *ATC*, but that is not necessarily the case in the short run.

23. **d** The fact that new technology creates economic profits gives other firms the incentive to adopt the technology. The increased competition from these firms ultimately eliminates any economic profits.

24. **c** The possibility of earning an economic profit is the incentive that encourages entry into an industry.

25. **d** This answer is the definition of external economies.

26. **a** The firm's demand curve is horizontal, which means that it is perfectly elastic.

27. **c** When the marginal costs rise, the *MC* curve shifts upward. In response, the firm decreases the amount it produces. The firm's demand curve did not change, which indicates that the (market) price is constant.

28. **a** $MR = (\Delta TR)/\Delta q$ so in this case $MR =$ (\$505 – \$500)/(101 – 100) = \$5. More directly, for a perfectly competitive firm, marginal revenue equals price.

29. **c** A perfectly competitive firm produces a good that is precisely the same as that of its (many) competitors.

30. **a** The diseconomies mean that, as the industry expands its output, firms' costs rise, so in the long run the price — which equals the (higher) average total cost — is higher.

Answers to Short Answer Problems

1. If a firm in a perfectly competitive industry charged a price even slightly higher than the market price, it would lose all of its sales. Thus it will not charge a price above the market price. Because it can sell all it wants at the market price, the firm would not be able to increase sales by lowering its price. Thus it would not charge a price below the market price because such a price would lower total revenue and profits.

2. In a perfectly competitive industry, the existence of positive economic profits attract the entry of new firms. Entry shifts the industry supply curve rightward, causing the market price to fall and firms' profits to decline. Entry continues as long as there are positive economic profits. Similarly, the existence of economic losses causes firms to exit from the industry. Exit shifts the industry supply curve leftward, causing the market price to rise and (surviving) firms' losses to decline. Exit continues as long as losses are being incurred. Thus only when economic profits and losses are zero is there no tendency for firms to enter or exit the industry. So, when economic profits are zero, the industry is in long-run equilibrium.

3. In the short run, the decrease in demand causes the market price to fall. In response to the fall in price, each firm produces less, so the market quantity also decreases. These changes are illustrated in Figures 11.10 and 11.11 (on the next page) as the fall in price from P to P_{sr} and the decrease in quantity from Q to Q_{sr} at (short-run) time T_{sr}.

   In the initial long-run equilibrium, each firm was earning zero economic profit. As a result, the fall in price means that firms now incur economic losses. Because the decrease in demand is permanent, these losses induce some firms to leave the industry. This exit shifts the industry supply curve leftward, causing a rise in the market price. The rising price reduces the economic losses for the remaining firms. Firms continue to exit until the economic losses are totally eliminated. Costs have not been affected by the decrease in demand, so if there are no external economies or diseconomies, the price must continue rising

FIGURE 11.10

Short Answer Problem 3

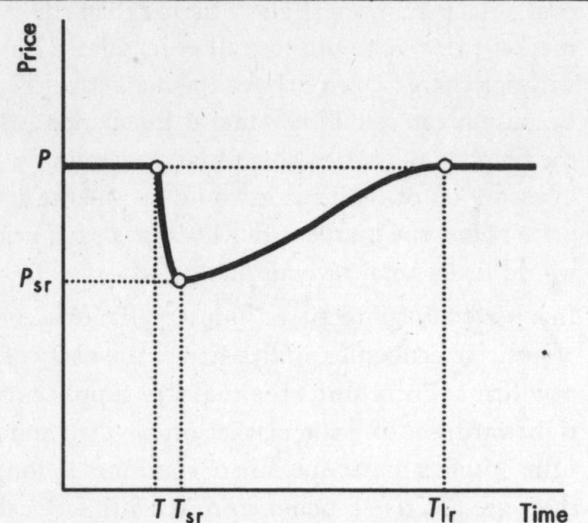

FIGURE 11.11

Short Answer Problem 3

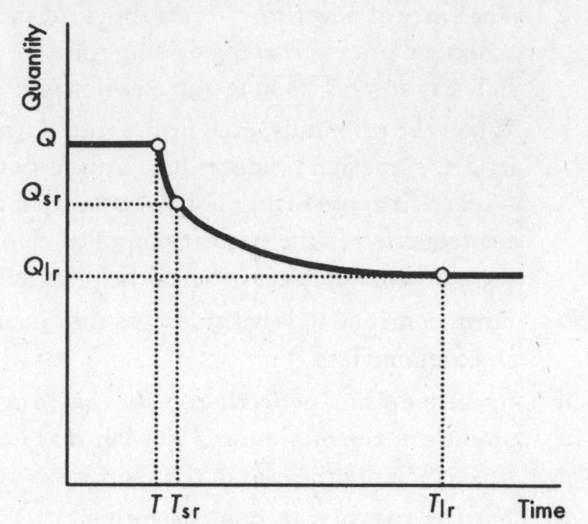

until, as shown in Figure 11.10, it reaches its original level in the new long-run equilibrium at time T_{lr}. The output of each firm also will equal its original level, but as shown in Figure 11.11 the equilibrium quantity at the industry level will be less than initially (Q versus Q_{lr}) because the number of firms in the industry has declined.

4. a. Figure 11.12 shows the case in which the firm earns an economic profit. To maximize its profit, the firm produces the level of output such that $MR = MC$. Because $P > ATC$, the firm is earning an economic profit, as shown in the figure.

FIGURE 11.12

Short Answer Problem 4 (a)

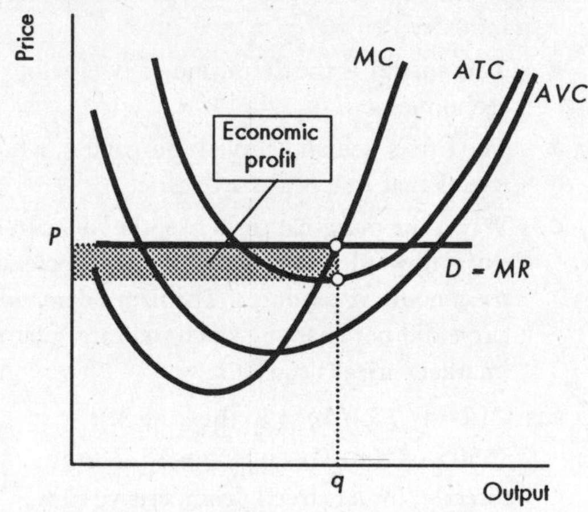

FIGURE 11.13
Short Answer Problem 4 (b)

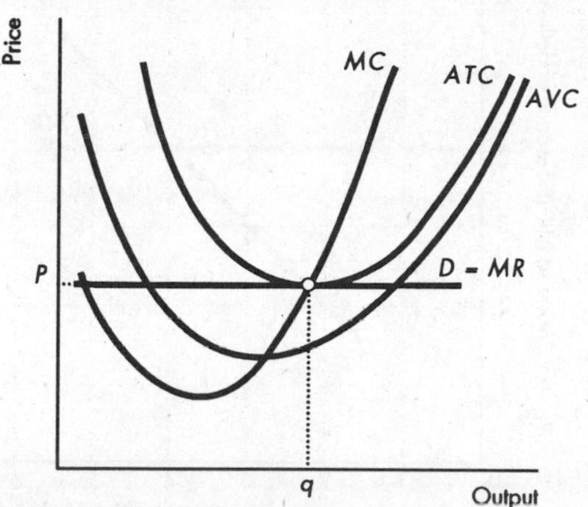

FIGURE 11.14
Short Answer Problem 4 (c)

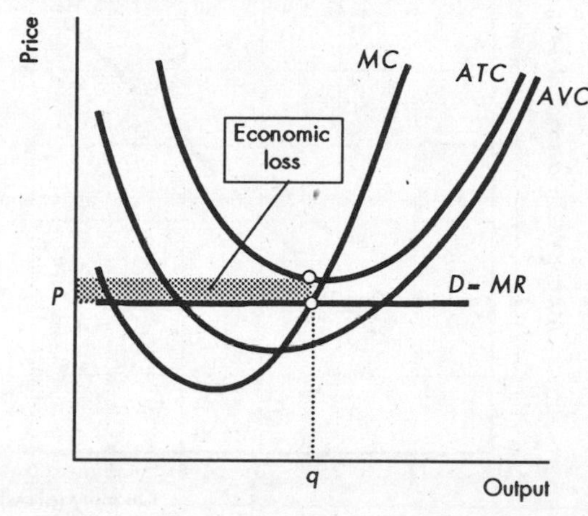

b. A perfectly competitive firm earning only a normal profit is illustrated in Figure 11.13. As always, to maximize its profit the firm produces q, the level of output that makes MR and MC equal. Then, because $P = ATC$, the firm is earning only a normal profit.

c. Figure 11.14 illustrates the case of a firm that incurs an economic loss but continues to operate. The firm suffers an economic loss (as shown in the figure) because, at the profit-maximizing (loss-minimizing) level of output q, $P < ATC$. But the firm minimizes its loss by operating because $P > AVC$.

5. a. Table 11.2 shows that Rudy's profit-maximizing quantity of rutabagas is 2 acres. Rudy's economic profit when growing 2 acres of eggplant is $1,500 (Rudy's total revenue of $4,000 minus his total cost of $2,500), which exceeds his economic profit at any other level of production.

b. Table 11.7 shows the marginal cost and marginal revenue schedules. Marginal cost is defined as $(\Delta TC)/\Delta q$, with ΔTC the change in total cost and Δq the change in quantity. Thus the marginal cost going from 1 to 2 acres farmed is $(\$2{,}500 - \$1{,}000)/(2-1)$, or $1,500.

Table 11.7 Short Answer Problem 5 (b)

Quantity (acres)	**Marginal cost (dollars)**	**Marginal revenue (dollars)**
1		
	$1,500	$2,000
2		
	2,500	2,000
3		
	3,500	2,000
4		
	4,500	2,000
5		
	5,500	2,000
6		

Marginal revenue can be calculated two ways. First, for a perfectly competitive firm, marginal revenue equals price. Hence marginal revenue is $2,000. Alternatively, the definition of marginal is $(\Delta TR)/\Delta q$, with ΔTR the change in total revenue. Using this definition, the marginal revenue from 1 to 2 acres is $(\$4{,}000 - \$2{,}000)/(2-1) = \$2{,}000$.

FIGURE 11.15
Short Answer Problem 5 (c)

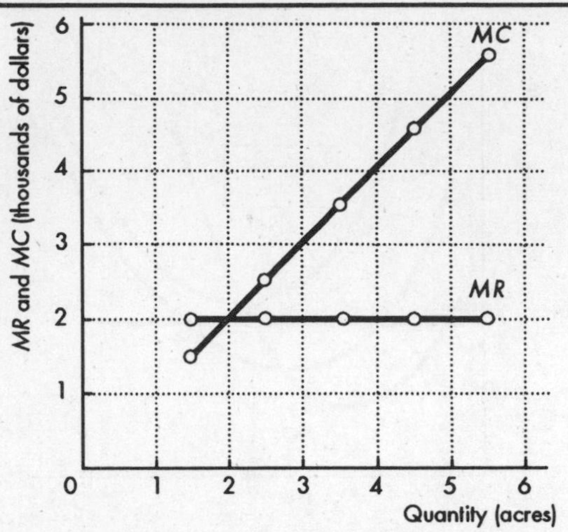

FIGURE 11.16
Short Answer Problem 6 (a)

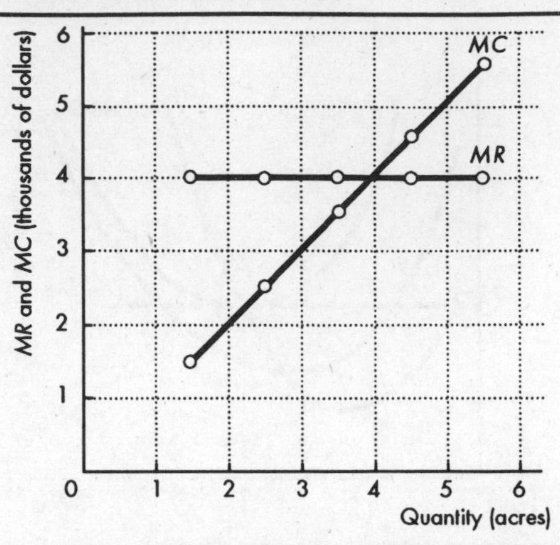

c. Figure 11.15 shows the *MC* and *MR* curves.

d. Table 11.7 shows that Rudy should grow 2 acres of rutabagas. The marginal cost of increasing from 2 acres to 3 acres is $2,500, which exceeds the marginal revenue of the increase. Thus increasing from 2 to 3 acres would reduce Rudy's profit. Similarly, Figure 11.15 shows that the marginal revenue and marginal cost curves intersect at 2 acres, indicating also that Rudy should grow 2 acres of rutabagas.

e. The answers in parts (a) and (d) are the same: Rudy grow 2 acres of rutabagas. Note how the analysis based on ***marginal*** revenue and cost (in part d) gives the same answer as the analysis based on ***total*** revenue and cost (in part a).

6. a. Figure 11.16 shows Rudy's "new" *MC* and new *MR* curves. The marginal cost curve does not change. Rudy's marginal revenue equals the price of a rutabaga. The rise in the price to $4,000 shifts Rudy's *MR* curve (which is the same as Rudy's demand curve) upward to $4,000.

b. As Figure 11.16 shows, with the higher price of a rutabaga, Rudy increases the acres of rutabagas he grows to 4 acres.

c. The answer in part (b) cannot be the long-run equilibrium. When Rudy grows 4 acres of rutabagas, his total revenue is $16,000 and his total cost (from Table 11.2) is $8,500. Rudy is earning an economic profit of $7,500. The presence of an economic profit attracts new farmers to the rutabaga market. As new farmers begin to grow rutabagas, the market supply curve for rutabagas shifts rightward, lowering the price of a rutabaga and eliminating some of the economic profit. New farmers enter and the price of a rutabaga falls as long as an economic profit exists. Only when the economic profit is entirely eliminated is the long-run equilibrium attained.

7. a. Table 11.8 (on the next page) contains Samantha's average costs and marginal cost. Average variable cost equals $(TVC)/q$, where TVC is total variable cost and q is quantity. Hence average variable cost when Samantha sells 3 sweaters a day is $\$90/3$ or $30. Average total cost is computed in a similar fashion, namely $(TC)/q$, with TC total cost. Thus, for the sale of 3 sweaters per day, average total cost is $\$150/3$, or $50.

Table 11.8 Short Answer Problem 7 (a)

Quantity (sweaters sold per day)	Average variable cost (dollars)	Average total cost (dollars)	Marginal cost (dollars)
1	$40.00	$100.00	
			$20.00
2	30.00	60.00	
			30.00
3	30.00	50.00	
			40.00
4	32.50	47.50	
			50.00
5	36.00	48.00	
			60.00
6	40.00	50.00	

Finally, marginal cost is $(\Delta TC)/\Delta q$. Using this formula, the marginal cost of going from 2 to 3 sweaters sold per day equals $(\$150 - \$120)/(3-2)$, or $30.

b. Figure 11.17 shows the *MC* curve.

c. Table 11.9 contains Samantha's supply schedule. The supply curve is the same as her marginal cost curve above the average variable cost curve. Thus, when the price of a sweater is $25, Figure 11.17 shows that Samantha would supply 2 sweaters except for the fact that this price is below the average variable cost. Hence, when the price is $25, Samantha shuts down and does not supply any sweaters. At $35, Figure 11.17 shows that Samantha supplies 3 sweaters. Because this price is above her average variable cost, Samantha supplies 3 sweaters. The rest of Samantha's supply curve is obtained from Figure 11.17 in a similar manner.

d. Figure 11.18 is a plot of Samantha's supply curve. At prices above $30 — that is, at prices above the minimum average variable cost — the supply curve is identical to Samantha's marginal cost curve. For prices below $30, Samantha supplies no sweaters.

FIGURE 11.17
Short Answer Problem 7 (b)

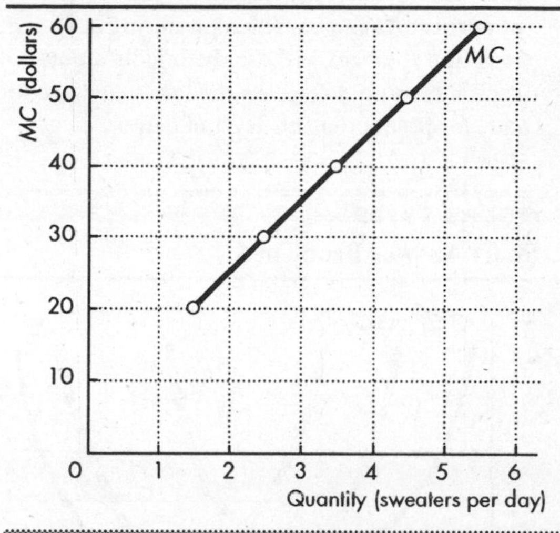

Table 11.9 Short Answer Problem 7 (c)

Price (dollars per sweater)	Quantity supplied (sweaters per day)
$25	0
35	3
45	4
55	5

FIGURE 11.18
Short Answer Problem 7 (d)

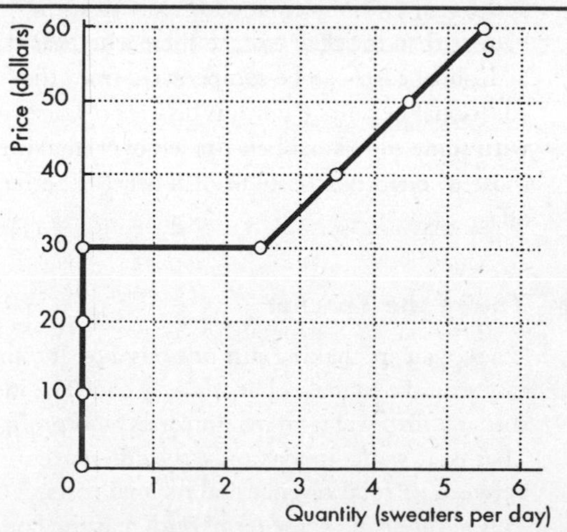

8. The dark line in Figure 11.19 is the *LRAC* curve. Note that it is constructed from the *ATC* curve that has the lowest average total cost for each level of output. As shown, when producing *q*, in the long run the firm will use the middle amount of capital because ATC_2 has the lowest average total cost for producing this level of output.

FIGURE **11.19**

Short Answer Problem 8

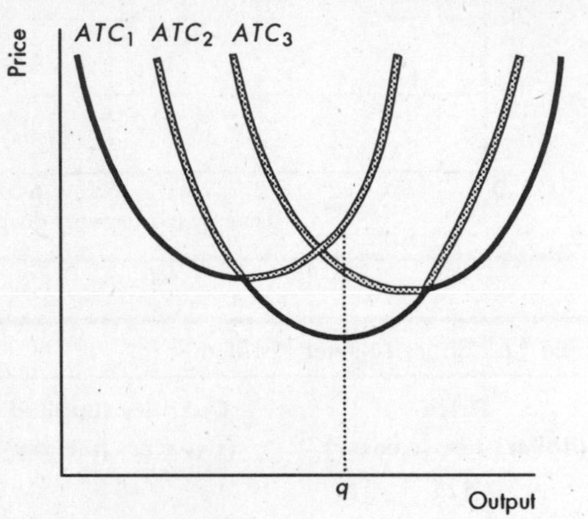

9. A level of output at which the marginal social benefit is greater than the marginal social cost is allocatively inefficient because some people can be made better off without making anyone worse off if more is produced. The production of an additional unit of output adds more to social benefit than to social cost, so those who bear the additional costs can be compensated from the additional benefits (and thus be left no worse off) with some additional benefits left over (making those who receive the additional benefits better off).

■ You're the Teacher

1. "Look, you are making just one mistake. It's an easy mistake to make, but it's a *big* one! The idea is that a firm wants to maximize its *total* profit. That is, it wants to maximize the difference between its total revenue and its total costs. You're confusing these terms with marginal revenue and marginal cost. Remember that the word "marginal" means 'additional'. So, marginal revenue means additional revenue, and marginal cost means additional cost. Now, suppose that *MR* is larger than *MC*. For instance, suppose that a wheat farmer finds that the marginal revenue from growing an additional acre of wheat is $5,000 and that the marginal cost of doing so is only $3,000. Then, growing the additional acre of wheat adds more to the farmer's revenue than it adds to the cost and so this acre will add to the farmer's total profit. In particular, this acre adds $2,000 (marginal revenue of $5,000 minus marginal cost of $3,000) to the farmer's total profit. The farmer will want to grow this additional acre of wheat. Now, suppose that the next acre still has a marginal revenue of $5,000 but that it has a marginal cost of $4,000. *MR* still is larger than *MC*, so this acre will continue to add to the farmer's total profit. It adds less (only $1,000), but the key point is that it adds. So, the farmer will plant this acre, too.

   Now look, I know that the added profit from the second acre isn't as much as the added profit from the first acre. But, who cares? As long as the acre adds to the profit, the farmer, who wants to get the maximum possible total profit will still grow the second acre of wheat. The deal is that as long as the acre adds to total profit, the farmer will grow more wheat. In other words, as long as *MR* > *MC*, the additional acre adds additional profit, so the farmer will put the acreage into production. Only when *MR* = *MC* does the additional acre not add to profit. The farmer simply stops adding acres when *MR* = *MC*."

2. "At first thought, it does seem weird that a firm would continue to produce even though it's losing money. I couldn't get the point, either, until I thought about it a bit. Here's the idea: Whenever the price of output falls below the break-even point (the minimum average total cost) but remains above the shutdown point (the minimum average variable cost), the firm continues to produce even though it's incurring an economic loss. The key here is that the firm's owner, when suffering an economic loss, wants to make the loss as small as possible.

   Now, if the owner shuts down, the firm still must pay its fixed costs. (Recall that fixed costs are independent of output; whether the firm produces

10 million units or 0 units, fixed costs remain the same.) Thus, if the owner shuts down, the total loss will equal the total fixed cost. The owner compares this loss to the loss incurred by operating. If the price exceeds the average variable cost, the owner loses less by operating the business. When $P > AVC$, the firm earns enough revenue to pay all its variable costs and have some revenue left over to cover part of its fixed costs. In this case, by operating the business, the owner loses less than the total amount of the fixed costs. The loss is smaller than would be incurred by shutting down, so the owner will operate the business as long as $P > AVC$. But, if $P < AVC$, the loss from running the business exceeds the total fixed cost because the business's revenue isn't sufficient to cover all of the variable costs. Hence, when the average variable costs exceed the price, the owner will close the business."

12 MONOPOLY

Key Concepts

How Monopoly Arises

Monopoly is an industry with one supplier of a product that has no close substitutes. Monopoly results from **barriers to entry** — impediments protecting the existing firm from competition by new entrants.

- Legal barriers to entry, such as public franchise, government license, or patent, create **legal monopolies**.
- Control over a key resource is a barrier to entry that can create a monopoly.
- Natural barriers to entry occur when economies of scale (which create a downward sloping *ATC* curve) are so large that one firm can supply the market at lower cost than two or more firms. This situation can create a **natural monopoly**.

Single-Price Monopoly

A single-price monopoly charges the same price for every unit of output.

- The monopoly firm's demand curve is the industry demand curve.
- Marginal revenue for a monopoly is less than its price ($MR < P$).

In moving down the monopoly's demand curve:

- when demand is elastic, *MR* is positive and total revenue rises with output.
- when demand is unit elastic, *MR* is zero and total revenue is at its maximum.
- when demand is inelastic, *MR* is negative and total revenue falls with output.

A monopoly's cost curves are similar to those of a competitive firm. A profit-maximizing monopoly produces the level of output at which $MR = MC$. (This rule is the same one used by a competitive firm). The monopoly uses the demand curve to charge the maximum price that consumers are willing to pay for this quantity of output. Figure 12.1 shows a monopoly's profit-maximizing level of output, *Q*, and price, *P*.

FIGURE **12.1**

A Single-Price Monopoly

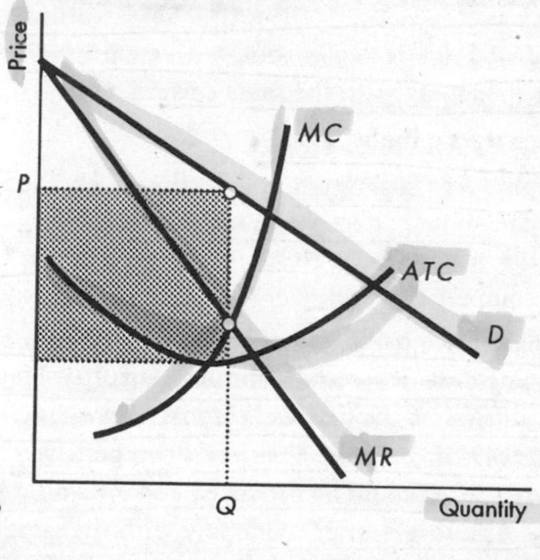

- As Figure 12.1 shows, *P* always exceeds *MC* for a monopoly.
- Because $P > ATC$, the monopoly in Figure 12.1 is earning an economic profit, equal to the area of the dark rectangle.

Price Discrimination

Price discrimination is charging some customers a lower price than others for the identical good or charging an individual consumer a lower price for larger purchases even though the selling costs of each good are the same.

- *Perfect price discrimination* charges each consumer the maximum price that he or she is willing to pay for each unit of output purchased.

- Price discrimination transfers consumer surplus away from consumers and to the monopoly, thereby benefiting the monopoly and harming consumers.

Price discrimination requires:

- groups of consumers with different elasticities of demand.
- the members of each group are easily identified.
- no resales of the good from one group to another.

With price discrimination, the group with the high elasticity of demand pays a low price and the group with the low elasticity of demand pays a high price. The firm's profit rises.

Comparing Monopoly and Competition

Compared to a perfectly competitive industry, a single-price monopoly with the same costs:

- charges a higher price.
- produces less output and is allocatively inefficient. The more perfectly a monopoly can price discriminate, the closer its output is to the competitive level.

A single-price monopoly creates a **deadweight loss** by reducing **consumer and producer surplus.** Figure 12.2 illustrates the deadweight loss from a single-price monopoly. If this were a perfectly competitive industry, Q_C would be produced and P_C would be the price. As a single-price monopoly with the same costs, Q_M is produced and P_M is the price.

A perfectly price-discriminating monopoly eliminates the consumer surplus but is allocatively efficient and does not cause a deadweight loss.

The costs of a monopoly are:

- The deadweight loss it creates.
- Resources used in **rent seeking,** the activity of searching for a monopoly.

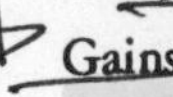

Gains from monopoly:

- Monopolies may be able to capture **economies of scale,** when an increase in output lowers average total cost, or **economies of scope,** when an increase in the range of goods produced lowers average total cost.
- Monopolies may increase the incentive to innovate, but the empirical evidence on this possible gain is mixed.

FIGURE **12.2**

A Single-Price Monopoly's Deadweight Loss

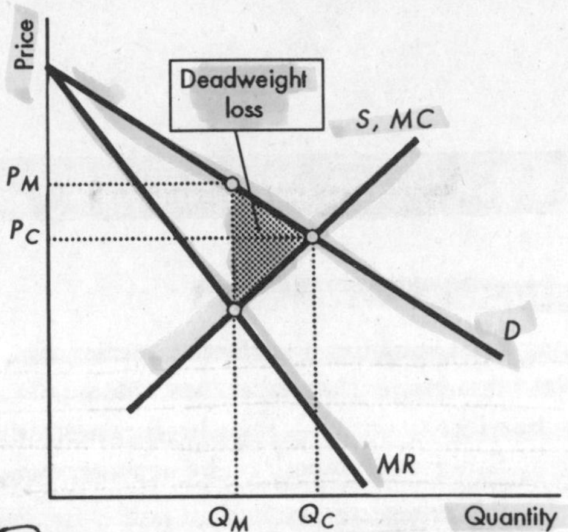

Helpful Hints

1. The opposite extreme from perfect competition is monopoly. In perfect competition there are many firms that can decide only the quantity they produce but not the price to be charged. In contrast, a monopoly is a single firm with the ability to set both quantity and price. In the real world, neither industry structure is likely to appear in its pure form. For instance, of the few monopolies that exist, most are regulated by the government and, as you will see in Chapter 20, regulation can have an impact on their behavior. Nonetheless, thoroughly understanding the differences between perfect competition and monopoly is valuable because these two industry structures are the ends of the competition spectrum. Thus, as competition within an industry heats up, the industry moves closer to behaving like a perfectly competitive industry; however, if competition dries up, the industry's output and price approach those of a monopoly.
2. In a monopoly, there is only one firm. Hence the industry demand curve also is the firm's demand curve. Facing a negatively sloped demand curve, if a single-price-monopoly wants to sell one more unit of output, it must lower its price. Selling

another unit has two effects on revenue:

- First, the sale of an additional unit raises revenue by the amount of the (new, lower) price. If this effect was the sole effect, the marginal revenue would equal the price. (Indeed, this effect *is* the only one for a perfectly competitive firm, and so for these firms marginal revenue equals the price.)
- Second, because the firm also must lower the price on all the units it had previously sold, revenue from them falls. (This effect is absent from a perfectly competitive firm because this firm does not need to lower its price in order to sell an additional unit of output.)

By itself, the first effect would yield marginal revenue equal to the price. But the second effect subtracts from the first. As a result, the net change in revenue, the marginal revenue, is less than the price. Therefore, for a monopoly, the marginal revenue curve lies below the demand curve.

3. To maximize its profit, a monopoly produces the level of output such that $MC = MR$. This rule is the same rule followed by a perfectly competitive firm. It is the same because the firms share the same objective: To maximize their profits. Profit-maximizing firms will produce a unit of output if $MR > MC$ because the added revenue from this unit — the marginal revenue — exceeds the added cost — the marginal cost. As a result, producing this unit adds to the firm's total profit. Similarly, a profit-maximizing firm will not produce a unit of output if $MR < MC$ because producing this unit reduces the firm's total profit. Hence, regardless of whether the firm is a monopoly or perfectly competitive, it produces at the level of output that sets $MR = MC$.

4. Price discrimination can be profitable for a monopoly only if different consumer groups have different elasticities of demand for the good. If such differences exist, the price-discriminating monopolist treats the groups as different markets. The profit maximization rule for a price-discriminating monopoly is to find the quantity of output where $MR = MC$ in each market. Then, in each market the firm charges the maximum price that the consumer group is willing to pay for the amount of output the firm produces. With different elasticities of demand between groups, this rule yields different prices in the markets.

Which group gets charged the lower price? A high elasticity of demand means that demanders can easily find good substitutes for the product. To keep this group of demanders as customers, the monopoly charges them the lower price. The group with the low elasticity of demand — which indicates that they cannot find good substitutes for the product — gets stuck with the higher price.

If the elasticities of demand in the two markets are equal, marginal revenues are equal and the prices corresponding to the marginal revenues are also equal. There is no point in charging different prices, and so the profit-maximizing rule for price discrimination collapses back into the rule for a single-price monopoly.

Questions

True/False/Uncertain and Explain

1. A difference between a perfectly competitive firm and a monopoly is that the monopolist's output decisions can affect the price of the good.

2. To maximize their profits, both monopolies and perfectly competitive firms produce the level of output that gives $MR = MC$.

3. For a monopoly, marginal revenue, MR, equals price, P.

4. A monopoly may earn an economic profit in the long run.

5. Price discrimination is an attempt by a monopolist to capture the producer surplus.

6. A single-price monopoly charges each consumer the highest single price the consumer will pay.

7. Barriers to entry are necessary to create a monopoly.

8. Monopolies reduce the deadweight loss due to perfectly competitive industries.

9. When a single-price monopoly is maximizing its profit, $P > MC$.

10. If a monopoly can successfully price discriminate, it can raise its profit.

11. Rent seeking is a cost that monopoly imposes on society.

12. Compared to a single-price monopoly, a price-discriminating monopoly reduces the amount of consumer surplus.

13. Patents grant the patent owner a legal monopoly.

14. Price discrimination works only for goods that can be resold.

15. In moving from perfect competition to single-price monopoly, all the surplus lost by consumers is captured by the monopoly.

Multiple Choice

1. Which of the following is a *natural* barrier to the entry of new firms in an industry?
   a. Licensing.
   b. Economies of scale.
   c. Issuing a patent.
   d. Granting a public franchise.

2. In a small town, Marilyn's Christmas tree lot has a monopoly on sales of Christmas trees. To increase her sales from 100 trees to 101 trees, she must drop the price of all her trees from $28 to $27. What is the marginal revenue?
   a. $2,800
   b. $28
   c. $27
   d. –$73

3. Suppose that a monopolist finds that the marginal revenue from producing another unit of output exceeds the marginal cost of the unit. Then, to maximize its profit, the monopolist will
   a. produce the unit.
   b. not produce the unit but not cut back its production at all.
   c. not produce the unit and cut back its production by at least one unit.
   d. None of the above.

4. Four monopolists were overheard talking at an expensive restaurant. Which of their statements contains a correct strategy for maximizing profits?
   a. "In my company, we don't increase output unless we know that the larger output will raise total revenue."
   b. "I think cost minimization is the sole key to maximizing profits."
   c. "We try to make the most of our equipment by producing at maximum capacity."
   d. "Each month I'm making a profit, so I don't approve any additional business deals unless they increase my revenue more than they raise my costs."

5. Activity for the purpose of creating monopoly is
   a. not legal in the United States.
   b. called rent seeking.
   c. called price discrimination.
   d. called legal monopoly.

6. Which of the following is <u>NOT</u> true for a single-price monopoly?
   a. Price always exceeds marginal cost.
   b. Price always exceeds marginal revenue.
   c. The monopoly always earns an economic profit.
   d. None of the above because all the statements are true.

Use Figure 12.3 for the next two questions.

FIGURE 12.3
Multiple Choice Questions 7 and 8

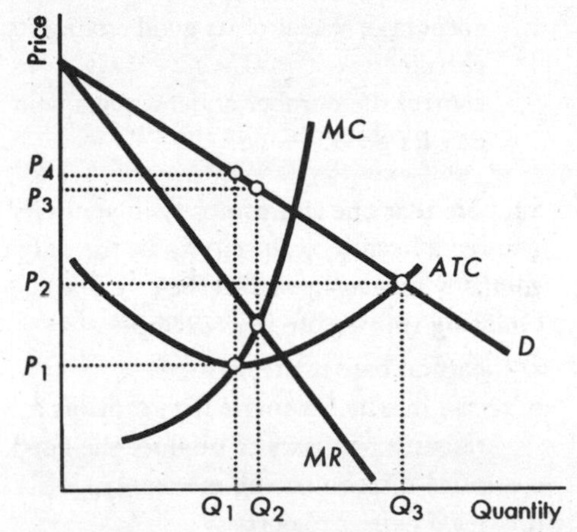

7. In Figure 12.3, a profit-maximizing single-price monopoly will produce
   a. Q_1.
   b. Q_2.
   c. Q_3.
   d. None of the above.

8. In Figure 12.3, a profit-maximizing single-price monopoly will set a price of
   a. P_1.
   b. P_2.
   c. P_3.
   d. P_4.

9. Compared to that of a perfectly competitive industry, the output of a single-price monopoly with the same costs is
   a. more than the competitive industry.
   b. the same as the competitive industry.
   c. less than the competitive industry.
   d. not comparable to the competitive industry.

10. Compared to a perfectly competitive industry, the price charged by a single-price monopoly with the same costs is
    a. more than the competitive industry.
    b. the same as the competitive industry.
    c. less than the competitive industry.
    d. not comparable to the competitive industry.

11. The deadweight loss is largest for
    a. a perfectly competitive industry.
    b. a single-price monopoly.
    c. any price-discriminating monopoly.
    d. a perfectly price-discriminating monopoly.

12. The elasticity of demand for watching movies is lower at 8 P.M. than at 5 P.M. As a result, if a monopoly movie theater wants to price discriminate, it charges
    a. a higher price at 8 P.M.
    b. the same price at 5 P.M. as at 8 P.M.
    c. a lower price at 8 P.M.
    d. None of the above is consistently correct.

13. Price discrimination allows a monopoly to
    a. lower its marginal cost.
    b. reduce its producer surplus.
    c. raise its total revenue.
    d. charge all customers a higher price.

14. Because of a rise in labor costs, a monopoly finds that its *MC* and *ATC* have risen. Presuming that the monopoly does not shut down, it will
    a. raise its price, *P*, and increase the quantity it produces, *Q*.
    b. raise its price, *P*, and decrease the quantity it produces, *Q*.
    c. lower its price, *P*, and increase the quantity it produces, *Q*.
    d. lower its price, *P*, and decrease the quantity it produces, *Q*.

15. A single-price monopolist will maximize profits if it produces the amount of output such that
    a. price equals marginal cost.
    b. price equals marginal revenue.
    c. marginal revenue equals marginal cost.
    d. price equals average total cost.

Figure 12.4 shows a single-price monopoly. Use this figure for the next three questions.

FIGURE **12.4**

Multiple Choice Questions 16, 17, and 18

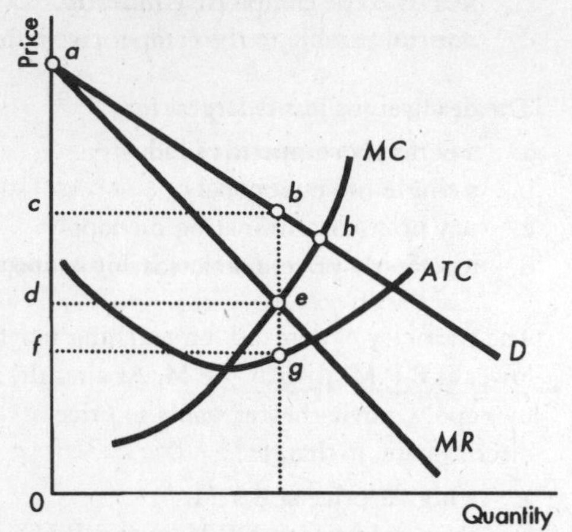

16. The deadweight loss in Figure 12.4 is the area
    a. *abc.*
    b. *bcde.*
    c. *bcfg.*
    d. *beh.*

17. The consumer surplus in Figure 12.4 is the area
    a. *abc.*
    b. *bcde.*
    c. *bcfg.*
    d. *beh.*

18. The economic profit in Figure 12.4 is the area
    a. *abc.*
    b. *bcde.*
    c. *bcfg.*
    d. *beh.*

19. A monopoly has economies of scope if
    a. average total cost declines as output decreases.
    b. average total cost declines as output increases.
    c. total profit declines as output increases.
    d. average total cost declines as the number of different goods produced increases.

20. In order to successfully price discriminate, a firm must be able to
    a. reduce its *MC*.
    b. distinguish between customers who have different elasticities of demand.
    c. encourage resales of its good among its customers.
    d. control the number of demanders who will buy its good.

21. Suppose that one taxi company in your city is granted a license by the city to be the only cab company operating within the city limits. Granting this license is an example of a
    a. natural barrier to entry.
    b. case in which a single firm controls a resource necessary to produce the good.
    c. price-discriminating monopoly.
    d. legal barrier to entry.

22. Which of the following may be a gain from monopoly?
    a. Monopolies do not waste resources trying to innovate.
    b. Monopolies may be able to capture economies of scale.
    c. Monopolies may be able to price discriminate, thereby boosting consumer surplus.
    d. Monopolies may earn an economic profit in the long run.

23. A monopoly that is able to perfectly price discriminate
    a. charges everyone the lowest price that they want to pay for each unit purchased.
    b. produces less output than it would were it a single-price monopoly.
    c. eliminates consumer surplus.
    d. creates a larger deadweight loss than it would if it were a single-price monopoly.

24. Taking rent-seeking activity into account, the maximum social cost of monopoly is equal to the
    a. deadweight loss from monopoly.
    b. economic profit.
    c. deadweight loss plus economic profit.
    d. consumer surplus lost plus producer surplus lost.

25. Business travelers usually pay higher airline fares than families on a vacation. The higher fares indicate that
    a. business travelers are not maximizing their utility.
    b. business travelers have a lower elasticity of demand than vacation travelers.
    c. the *MC* of serving vacation travelers is lower than that of serving business travelers.
    d. vacation travelers have a higher demand curve than business travelers.

26. If a profit-maximizing monopoly is producing a level of output such that marginal cost exceeds marginal revenue, it
    a. should raise its price and decrease its output.
    b. should lower its price and increase its output.
    c. should lower its price and decrease its output.
    d. is incurring an economic loss.

27. If a perfectly competitive industry becomes a monopoly and costs do not change, which of the following allocations of costs and benefits is correct?
    a. The producer benefits; demanders and society are harmed.
    b. The producer and society are harmed; demanders benefit.
    c. The producer, demanders, and society are harmed.
    d. The producer is harmed; demanders and society benefit.

28. If a monopoly is broken up so that it becomes a perfectly competitive industry and costs do not change, which of the following statements describing the costs and benefits is correct?
    a. The producer benefits; demanders and society are harmed.
    b. The producer and society are harmed; demanders benefit.
    c. The producer, demanders, and society benefit.
    d. The producer is harmed; demanders and society benefit.

29. In the short run a monopoly can
    a. earn only an economic profit.
    b. earn an economic profit or a normal profit.
    c. earn only a normal profit.
    d. earn an economic profit or a normal profit, or incur an economic loss.

30. In the long run a monopoly can
    a. earn only an economic profit.
    b. earn an economic profit or a normal profit.
    c. earn only a normal profit.
    d. earn an economic profit or a normal profit, or incur an economic loss.

Short Answer Problems

1. Why is marginal revenue less than price for a single-price monopoly?
2. Explain why the output of a perfectly competitive industry is greater than the output of the same industry if it is a single-price monopoly.

FIGURE **12.5**
Short Answer Problem 3

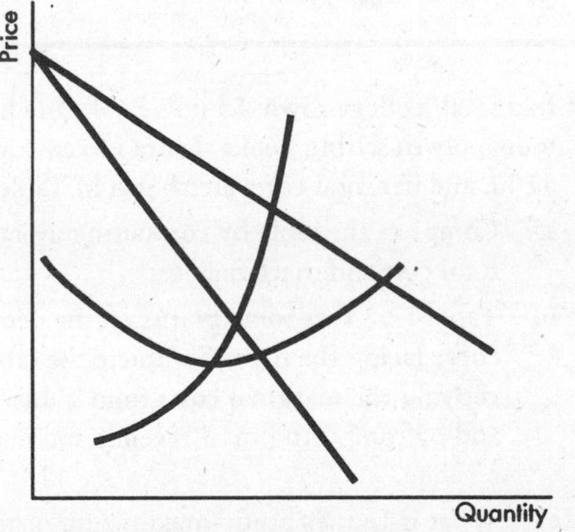

3. In Figure 12.5, label the curves. Show the amount this single-price monopolist will produce and the price it will charge. Indicate the firm's economic profit and show the deadweight loss created.

Table 12.1 Short Answer Problem 4 (a)

Quantity (books sold per hour)	Total cost	Average total cost (*ATC*)	Marginal cost (*MC*)
9	$247.00	$27.44	
			$9.00
10	256.00	____	
			____
11	267.00	____	
			____
12	280.00	____	
			____
13	295.00	____	
			____
14	312.00	____	
			____
15	331.00	____	
			____
16	352.00	____	
			____
17	375.00	____	
			____
18	400.00	____	
			____
19	427.00	____	
			____
20	456.00	____	
			____
21	487.00	____	

Table 12.2 Short Answer Problem 4 (b)

Quantity (books per hour)	Price	Total Revenue	Marginal Revenue (*MR*)	Marginal Cost (*MC*)
9	$57.00	$513.00		
			$47.00	$9.00
10	56.00	____		
			____	____
11	55.00	____		
			____	____
12	54.00	____		
			____	____
13	53.00	____		
			____	____
14	52.00	____		
			____	____
15	51.00	____		
			____	____
16	50.00	____		
			____	____
17	49.00	____		
			____	____
18	48.00	____		
			____	____
19	47.00	____		
			____	____
20	46.00	____		
			____	____
21	45.00	____		

4. In a small college town, Laura's Bookstore has a monopoly in selling books. Laura's fixed costs are $100, and her total costs are shown in Table 12.1.
   a. Complete the table by computing average total cost and marginal cost.
   b. Table 12.2 lists some points on the demand curve facing the firm. Complete the table by copying the marginal costs from Table 12.1 and by computing total revenue and marginal revenue.
   c. What is Laura's profit-maximizing quantity of output? At what price will she sell her books? What is her total economic profit?
   d. In Figure 12.6, plot the demand curve and the *MR*, *ATC*, and *MC* curves corresponding to the data in parts (a) and (b). Show the equilibrium output and the area of economic profit on your diagram.

FIGURE 12.6
Short Answer Problem 4

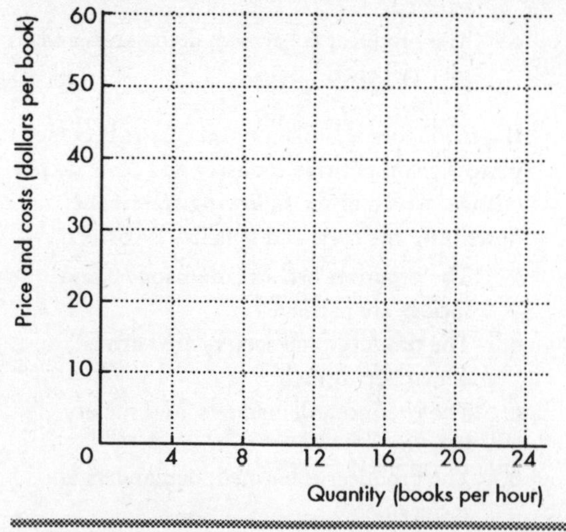

Table 12.3 Short Answer Problem 4 (e)

Quantity (books per hour)	Price	Total Revenue	Marginal Revenue (MR)	Marginal Cost (MC)
9	$24.50	$220.50		
			$19.50	$9.00
10	24.00	___		
			___	___
11	23.50	___		
			___	___
12	23.00	___		
			___	___
13	22.50	___		
			___	___
14	22.00	___		
			___	___
15	21.50	___		
			___	___
16	21.00	___		
			___	___
17	20.50	___		
			___	___
18	20.00	___		
			___	___
19	19.50	___		
			___	___
20	19.00	___		
			___	___
21	18.50	___		

e. Laura's cost curves are unchanged, but now consumers decrease their demand. Table 12.3 lists some points on the new demand curve. Complete the table by copying the marginal costs from Table 12.1, and by computing the new total revenue and marginal revenue.

f. What is Laura's new profit-maximizing quantity of output? At what price does she now sell her books? What is her total profit? Explain your answers.

5. Suppose that three industries have the same market demand and identical cost curves. Industry A is perfectly competitive, industry B is a single-price monopoly, and industry C is a monopoly able to perfectly discriminate.

FIGURE 12.7
Short Answer Problem 5

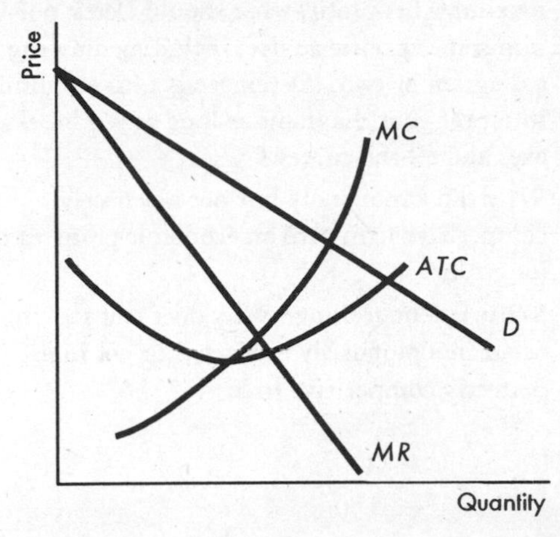

a. In Figure 12.7, identify how much each industry produces by labeling the outputs as Q_A, Q_B, and Q_C for industry A, B, and C, respectively.

b. In which industry structure or structures is consumer surplus the largest? The smallest?

c. In the long run, in which industry structure or structures is the total economic profit the largest? The smallest?

d. Which industry structure or structures are allocatively efficient?

6. Suppose that your city grants one pizza delivery service a legal monopoly on delivering pizzas; all other pizza delivery services must close.

a. What will happen to the price and quantity of delivered pizzas?

b. What will happen to the profit of the owner who has been granted the monopoly?

c. Suppose that the owner offers to sell the pizza delivery company to you. Would you be able to earn an economic profit? Be careful when you answer this question; think about the price the previous owner will charge you for the business.

7. Derek is the owner of the only movie theater in town. He is determined to maximize his profit. By hiring several well-trained economists, Derek learns that the people watching movies after 8

P.M. have a much lower elasticity of demand than people watching at 5 P.M. The costs of showing a movie are identical at 5 P.M. and 8 P.M. To maximize his profit, what should Derek do? Give him some specific advice, including drawing him a diagram or two. (Derek can get his economists to interpret your diagrams as long as you label all the axes and all the curves.)

8. Why can a monopoly but not a perfectly competitive firm earn an economic profit in the long run?
9. What is rent seeking? Why does rent seeking occur in a monopoly industry but not in a perfectly competitive industry?

■ You're the Teacher

1. "I don't really understand how monopoly firms decide how much to produce and what price to charge. Can you give me some help? I'd really like just a rule or two to remember." Because you have studied this material, you are in a position to help this student. Offer a couple of rules that this student can use to determine, first, how much is produced, and second, what price is charged.
2. "How does price discrimination reduce the amount of consumer surplus?" This question is short, so give a good answer to it!

Answers

True/False Answers

1. **T** Because the monopolist is the only producer in the market, the monopolist's decisions about how much to produce determine the market price.
2. **T** If $MR > MC$, a firm's profit increases — no matter what its industry structure — by increasing its output.
3. **F** For a monopoly, $MR < P$.
4. **T** Barriers to entry limit the competition faced by the monopoly, so it is able to earn an economic profit permanently.
5. **F** Price discrimination captures consumer surplus, not producer surplus.
6. **F** A single-price monopoly charges each consumer the same price.
7. **T** Without barriers to entry, other firms will enter the industry so that it no longer is a monopoly.
8. **F** A monopoly creates deadweight loss; it does not reduce it.
9. **T** A single-price monopoly produces at $MR = MC$. Because $P > MR$, the equality between MR and MC means that $P > MC$.
10. **T** This motivation lies behind price discrimination.
11. **T** Rent seeking refers to the use of resources to establish, be granted, or protect a monopoly.
12. **T** Effectively, the price-discriminating monopolist converts consumer surplus into additional economic profit.
13. **T** Patents legally prohibit anyone else from producing the same good.
14. **F** Price discrimination works for goods that cannot be resold.
15. **F** Single-price monopolists create deadweight loss, part of which is the consumer surplus lost to everyone in society.

Multiple Choice Answers

1. **b** The other possibilities listed are legal barriers to entry.
2. **d** Total revenue when 100 trees are sold is $2,800; when 101 trees are sold, it is $2,727. Hence, the marginal revenue from the 101st tree is –$73.
3. **a** As long as MR exceeds MC, producing the unit adds to the firm's total profit because it adds more to revenue than cost.
4. **d** This owner is stating that projects must have a marginal revenue that exceeds their marginal costs.
5. **b** This answer illustrates one type of rent seeking.
6. **c** Like any firm, if demand for its good declines or its costs rise, in the short run a monopoly may earn a normal profit or incur an economic loss.
7. **b** The firm produces the level of output that sets $MR = MC$.
8. **c** As noted in the answer to question 7, the firm produces Q_2 of output. The highest price the firm can charge and still sell this amount of output is P_3.
9. **c** The point that a single-price monopoly produces less output is the essential reason why single-price monopolies create deadweight losses.
10. **a** By producing less output, the company is able to boost the price it charges.
11. **b** Perfectly competitive industries and perfectly price-discriminating monopolies do not create deadweight losses.
12. **a** Customers with a low elasticity of demand are charged a higher price than those with a high elasticity of demand.
13. **c** The monopoly raises its total revenue by capturing some consumer surplus.
14. **b** The upward shift in the MC curve causes the firm to decrease the quantity it produces and raise the price it charges.
15. **c** *All* firms maximize their profit by producing where $MR = MC$.
16. **d** The deadweight loss is caused because a single-price monopoly produces less than a perfectly competitive industry. If it produced these units, its cost would be less than the value consumers place on them, and this difference is the deadweight loss.

17. **a** The consumer surplus is the area between the demand curve and the price.
18. **c** The economic profit is the rectangle whose height is the difference between *P* and *ATC* and whose length equals the quantity produced.
19. **d** The answer is the definition of economies of scope.
20. **b** The monopoly must be able to distinguish between high- and low-elasticity customers in order to determine who should be charged the low price and who should be charged the high price.
21. **d** The taxi company has been granted a legal monopoly.
22. **b** If enough economies of scale are present, a monopoly may produce more than a competitive industry.
23. **c** Any price discrimination eliminates some consumer surplus and perfect price discrimination eliminates it all.
24. **c** The loss to society equals the amount spent on rent seeking plus the deadweight loss. The maximum that will be expended on rent seeking is the amount of the economic profit, so the maximum loss to society equals the deadweight loss plus the economic profit.
25. **b** Airlines can price discriminate and charge business travelers, who have a low elasticity of demand, more than vacation travelers, who have a high elasticity of demand.
26. **a** Output should be reduced because the last units produced lower the firm's profit and, by reducing output, the firm can raise its price.
27. **a** The producer benefits because the monopoly can earn an economic profit; consumers lose because of the reduction in consumer surplus; and society loses due to the deadweight loss.
28. **d** This answer is the reverse of the previous answer and shows that society benefits from breaking up a monopoly.
29. **d** In the short run, depending on demand and cost, any firm can earn an economic profit or a normal profit, or incur an economic loss.
30. **b** A monopoly generally can earn an economic profit, but, depending on its demand and costs, it might be able to earn only a normal profit.

Answers to Short Answer Problems

1. To sell an additional unit of output, a monopoly must drop its price. The lower price has two effects on revenue: one positive, and the other negative. Marginal revenue is the net effect.

   The additional unit sold at the new lower price adds an amount to revenue equal to the price. But a single-price monopoly must also lower the price to previous customers who would have paid more. Marginal revenue equals the new revenue — the price — minus the loss of revenue from lowering the price to previous customers. Thus, marginal revenue must necessarily be less than the price.

2. A perfectly competitive industry produces the level of output at which the industry's marginal cost curve intersects the industry's demand curve. A single-price monopoly produces the level of output at which the industry's marginal cost curve intersects the monopoly's marginal revenue curve. Because the marginal revenue curve lies below the demand curve, the monopoly industry produces less. More intuitively, compared to a perfectly competitive industry, a single-price monopoly restricts its output in order to raise its price and generate an economic profit.

FIGURE **12.8**
Short Answer Problem 3

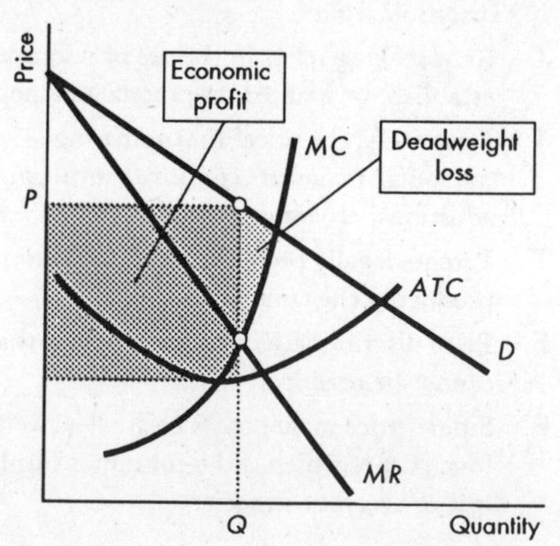

3. All the curves are labeled in Figure 12.8. Also illustrated is the economic profit (the darker

rectangle) and the deadweight loss (the lighter triangular area).

4. a. Table 12.4 shows the average total costs and marginal costs. The average total costs are calculated by dividing the total costs by the total outputs. For instance, the average total cost when 10 books are sold is \$256/10, or \$25.60. The rest of the *ATC*s are calculated similarly. Marginal cost equals the change in the total cost divided by the change in output. For example, the marginal cost going from 10 to 11 units of output is (\$267 – \$256)/(11 – 10), which equals \$11.00. The remainder of the *MC*s are calculated in the same way.

Table 12.4 Short Answer Problem 4 (a)

Quantity (books sold per hour)	Total cost	Average total cost (*ATC*)	Marginal cost (*MC*)
9	\$247.00	\$27.44	
			\$9.00
10	256.00	25.60	
			11.00
11	267.00	24.27	
			13.00
12	280.00	23.33	
			15.00
13	295.00	22.69	
			17.00
14	312.00	22.29	
			19.00
15	331.00	22.07	
			21.00
16	352.00	22.00	
			23.00
17	375.00	22.06	
			25.00
18	400.00	22.22	
			27.00
19	427.00	22.47	
			29.00
20	456.00	22.80	
			31.00
21	487.00	23.19	

Table 12.5 Short Answer Problem 4 (b)

Quantity (books sold per hour)	Price	Total Revenue	Marginal Revenue (*MR*)	Marginal Cost (*MC*)
9	\$57.00	\$513.00		
			\$47.00	\$9.00
10	56.00	560.00		
			45.00	11.00
11	55.00	605.00		
			43.00	13.00
12	54.00	648.00		
			41.00	15.00
13	53.00	689.00		
			39.00	17.00
14	52.00	728.00		
			37.00	19.00
15	51.00	765.00		
			35.00	21.00
16	50.00	800.00		
			33.00	23.00
17	49.00	833.00		
			31.00	25.00
18	48.00	864.00		
			29.00	27.00
19	47.00	893.00		
			27.00	29.00
20	46.00	920.00		
			25.00	31.00
21	45.00	945.00		

b. Table 12.5 gives the total revenue and marginal revenue. In this table, total revenue equals (Quantity)(Price). So, by way of example, the total revenue at the quantity of 10 books sold is (10)(\$56) = \$560. After finishing with the total revenues, the marginal revenues can be calculated as the change in total revenues divided by the changes in output. Take the marginal revenue going from 10 to 11 books sold per hour as an example. This marginal revenue equals (\$605 – \$560)/(11 – 10), or \$45. The rest of the marginal revenues are computed the same way

c. To maximize her profit, Laura produces at $MR = MC$. Between 18 and 19 books the marginal revenue is \$29 and between 19 and 20 it is \$27. Thus at 19 books the marginal revenue is \$28. Similarly, the marginal cost is \$27 between 18 and 19 books and \$29 between 19 and 20 books, which indicates that at 19 books the marginal cost is \$28. Marginal revenue equals marginal cost at an output of 19 books, so this quantity is the profit-maximizing level of output.

The data for the demand curve show that Laura can sell 19 books at a price per book of \$47.00. Thus the equilibrium price is \$47.00 per book. (Note that the price, \$47, is greater than the marginal cost, \$28.) Laura's economic profit equals her total revenue minus her total cost. From Table 12.5, the total revenue when selling 19 books is \$893, and, from Table 12.4, the total cost of selling 19 books is \$427. Thus Laura's total economic profit is \$893 – \$427 = \$466.

d. Figure 12.9 shows the demand, *MR*, and cost curves. The area of the darkened rectangle equals her economic profit.

e. Table 12.6 shows the total revenue, marginal revenue, and marginal cost after the decrease in demand. The total and marginal revenue schedules are calculated similarly to those in Table 12.5.

f. After the decrease in demand, Laura finds that *MR* = *MC* when she sells 13 books per hour. (The *MR* equals \$16, the same as the *MC*.) Thus 13 books is the profit-maximizing level of sales.

When Laura sells 13 books per hour, the (new) demand schedule shows that she can charge \$22.50 per book and sell all 13. Hence the new profit-maximizing price is \$22.50 per book.

Laura's economic profit equals her total revenue of \$292.50 minus her total cost of \$295.00. Hence her "profit" is –\$2.50; that is, with the decrease in demand, Laura actually incurs an economic loss of \$2.50. Table 12.6 indicates that this loss is the minimum possible loss. Laura will continue to operate in the short run because this loss is less than her shut-down loss, which would be \$100, the amount of the business's fixed cost.

FIGURE **12.9**
Short Answer Problem 4 (d)

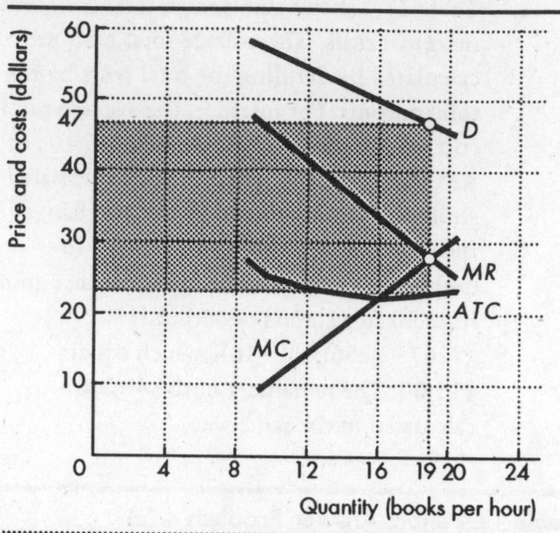

Table 12.6 Short Answer Problem 4 (e)

Quantity (books sold per hour)	Price	Total Revenue	Marginal Revenue (*MR*)	Marginal Cost (*MC*)
9	\$24.50	\$220.50		
			\$19.50	\$9.00
10	24.00	240.00		
			18.50	11.00
11	23.50	258.50		
			17.50	13.00
12	23.00	276.00		
			16.50	15.00
13	22.50	292.50		
			15.50	17.00
14	22.00	308.00		
			14.50	19.00
15	21.50	322.50		
			13.50	21.00
16	21.00	336.00		
			12.50	23.00
17	20.50	348.50		
			11.50	25.00
18	20.00	360.00		
			10.50	27.00
19	19.50	370.50		
			9.50	29.00
20	19.00	380.00		
			8.50	31.00
21	18.50	388.50		

FIGURE 12.10
Short Answer Problem 5

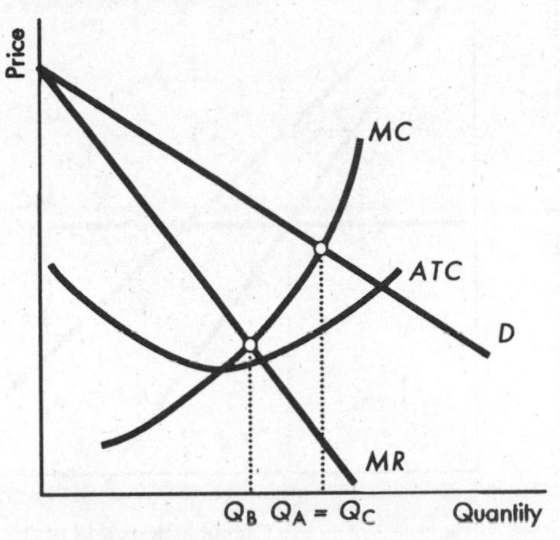

5. a. Figure 12.10 shows the level of output for each industry structure. The single-price monopoly produces the least. Both the perfectly competitive industry and the monopoly able to perfectly price discriminate produce the same amount, which is more than that produced by the single-price monopolist.
   b. The consumer surplus is largest in the perfectly competitive industry; it is smallest with the perfectly price-discriminating monopoly.
   c. The total economic profit is largest for the monopoly able to perfectly price discriminate because this monopoly converts all the potential consumer surplus to economic profit. It is smallest for the perfectly competitive industry because in the long run firms in this industry cannot earn economic profits.
   d. Both the perfectly competitive industry and the perfectly price-discriminating monopoly produce the allocatively efficient amount.
6. a. When the one firm has a monopoly on pizza delivery, it boosts its price and thereby reduces its output. Predictably, the price of a pizza will rise, and the quantity of pizzas delivered will decrease.
   b. The owner of the (new) monopoly pizza delivery service will earn an economic profit.
   c. Perhaps surprisingly, you will not be able to earn an economic profit. Why not? Think of the selling price the pizza owner will charge. The selling price must compensate the owner for all the economic profit that he or she will lose in the future by not owning the business. Hence the price of the business will rise with the economic profit that it is earning, both now and in the future. The fact that the price of the business rises means that you will be able to earn only a normal profit on the funds that you use to buy the business. Thus, if you want to earn an economic profit, you must be in on the ground floor: Buying into a business after it is already earning an economic profit will not work because the higher price of buying in eliminates the economic profit.
7. In order to maximize his profits, Derek should charge a lower price for his 5 o'clock movies and a higher price for his 8 o'clock movies. In other words, Derek should price discriminate. Price discrimination is possible because this situation easily fulfills its requirements. First, Derek can readily distinguish between customers with a high elasticity of demand and those with a low elasticity of demand by noting when they want to see the movie. Second, to resell the good is impossible; that is, people attending at 5 P.M. are not going to be able to resell viewing the movie to those who want to attend at 8 P.M.

   Why does price discrimination increase Derek's profit? Figures 12.11 and 12.12 (on the next page) shed some light on this question. The marginal cost of showing a movie at 5 P.M. or at 8 P.M. is assumed to be constant. In order to maximize his profit in the 5 o'clock market, Derek equates *MR* to *MC* and sells Q_H ("H" for "high elasticity") tickets by charging P_H. In the low-elasticity, 8 P.M. market, Derek sells Q_L ("L" for "low elasticity") tickets by charging P_L per ticket. By charging a lower price at 5 P.M. and a higher price at 8 P.M., Derek is able to convert into economic profit some of the consumer surplus that would result if he charged both classes of customers the same price. Thus price discrimination raises Derek's economic profit.

FIGURE 12.11
Short Answer Problem 7

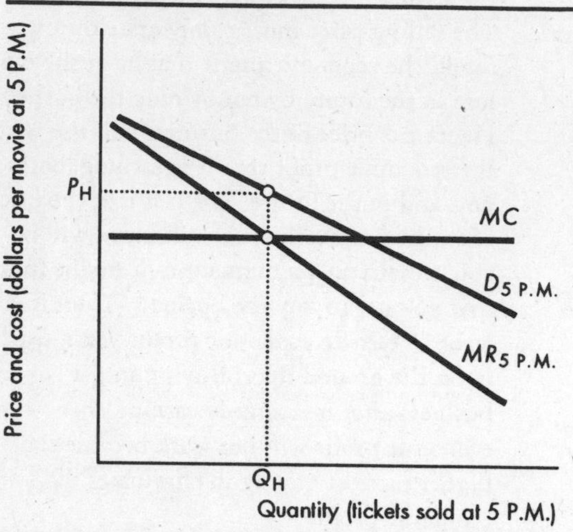

FIGURE 12.12
Short Answer Problem 7

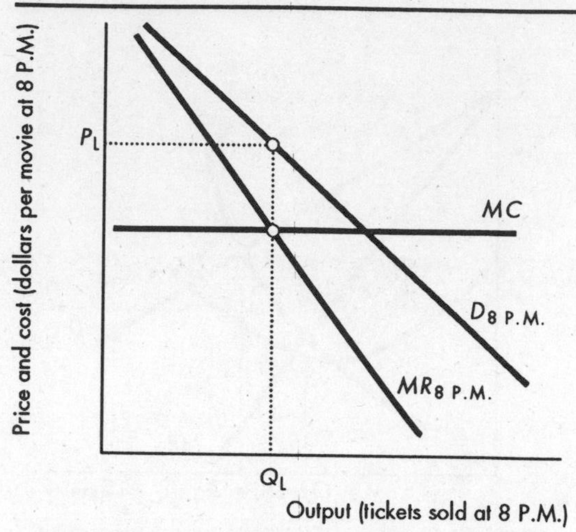

8. The fundamental reason that monopolies are able to earn an economic profit in the long run is that they are protected from competition by barriers to entry. Essentially when the monopolist is earning an economic profit, other firms would like to enter that market. However, they are precluded from doing so by the existence of barriers to entry — some feature of the market, be it economies of scale or perhaps a patent, that prevents new firms from entering the industry. Perfectly competitive firms are not protected by barriers to entry. If they are earning an economic profit, new competitors will enter the market and, by so doing, compete away the economic profit.
9. Rent seeking refers to the attempt to create a monopoly. People are motivated to rent seek because, if they can create a monopoly, they stand to earn an economic profit persistently. Rent seeking occurs in a monopoly industry precisely because monopolies can earn economic profits. It does not occur in perfectly competitive industries because firms in these industries cannot earn a long-lasting economic profit. Hence the incentive to rent seek does not exist for a perfectly competitive industry.

■ You're the Teacher

1. "A couple of mechanical rules may be helpful when we're studying how a monopoly selects its output and determines its price. First, decide how much the firm produces. Second, determine the price charged. To find the profit-maximizing quantity, use the *MR* and *MC* curves. The equilibrium quantity is where these curves cross: Draw a vertical line down to the horizontal axis and read the quantity. Then, to find the profit-maximizing price, continue this vertical line up to the demand curve. From the intersection of the demand curve and your vertical line, draw a horizontal line over to the price axis. Where this line meets the price axis is the profit-maximizing price. Use these rules and we'll be okay."
2. "Look, the whole idea of price discrimination is that a monopoly wants to charge you a price for the good that more closely reflects how much you value it. If you value it a lot, the monopoly wants to stick you with a really high price; if you don't value it too much, the monopoly will let you buy it for a lower price. Now, the idea behind consumer surplus is that it measures the difference between how much you value a good and how much you have to pay for it. By price discriminating, the monopoly can reduce this difference: Customers who value it a lot, pay a lot, and customers who don't value it as much don't pay as much. Thus a price-discriminating monopoly moves the price closer to how much the good is valued, and so the monopoly reduces consumer surplus."

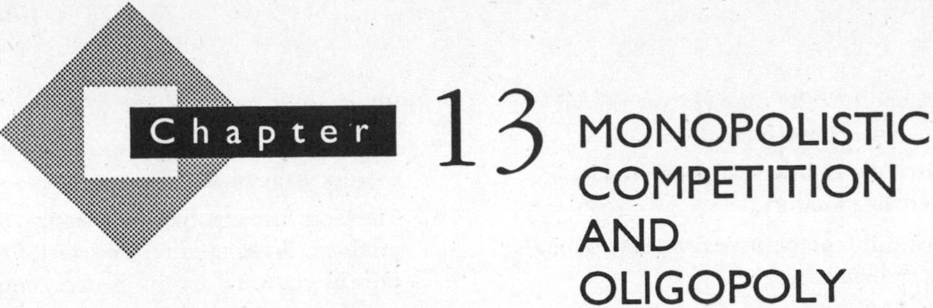

Chapter 13 MONOPOLISTIC COMPETITION AND OLIGOPOLY

Key Concepts

Varieties of Market Structure

The market structure of most industries lies between the extremes of perfect competition and monopoly.

- **Monopolistic competition** is a market structure in which many firms compete through *product differentiation*; that is, they make similar but slightly different products.
- **Oligopoly** is a market structure in which a few firms compete.

Economists use two measures of industrial concentration:

- **Four-firm concentration ratio** — the percentage of an industry's sales made by its four largest firms.
- **Hirschman–Herfindahl Index (HHI)** — the sum of the squared market shares of the 50 largest firms in the industry.
- A low value for the measure of concentration indicates the presence of extensive competition.

There are problems with concentration ratios:

- They are calculated for the national market, but the relevant market for some goods is local and for others is international in scope.
- They give no indication of the existence or absence of entry barriers.
- Often the relevant market does not correspond to an industry as defined in the measures.
- Many firms operate in several industries.

Monopolistic Competition

Monopolistic competition requires:

- a large number of firms.
- that firms are free to enter or exit the industry.
- that the firms produce goods that are close but not perfect substitutes for their competitors' goods.

A monopolistically competitive firm faces a downward sloping demand curve. The marginal revenue curve lies below the demand curve. In the short run:

- The firm maximizes its profit by producing the level of output such that $MR = MC$.
- The firm can earn an economic profit. If does, free entry means that competitors enter the industry.

In the long run:

- The firm maximizes its profit by producing the amount of output that sets $MR = MC$.
- The firm does not earn an economic profit, so $P = ATC$.

Figure 13.1 shows the long-run equilibrium.

FIGURE 13.1
The Long Run in Monopolistic Competition

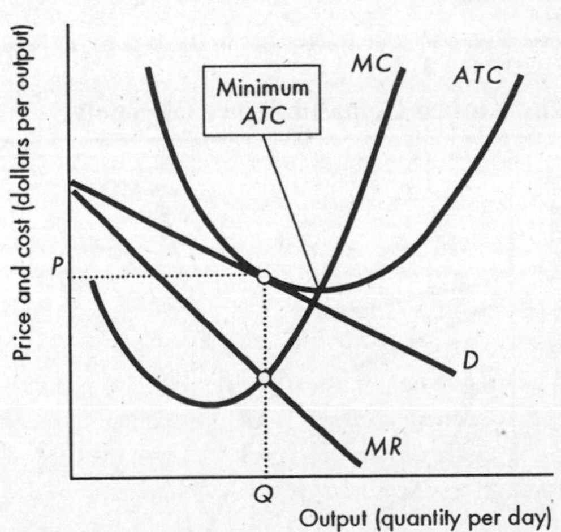

A monopolistically competitive firm has *excess capacity* because, as Figure 13.1 shows, in the long run it does not produce at the minimum ATC. From a social standpoint monopolistically competitive firms are not allocatively efficient. However:

- Monopolistically competitive firms produce a large variety of a product.
- Monopolistically competitive firms have strong incentives to innovate.
- Monopolistically competitive firms often have high selling costs, which sometimes provide services, such as information, that are valuable to consumers.

Oligopoly

In oligopoly a few firms compete. Each firm considers the effects of its actions on the behavior of the others and the actions of the others on its own profit.

The **kinked demand curve model**:

- The firm believes that, if it raises its price, no competitors will follow but that, if it lowers its price, all its competitors will follow. Thus the firm faces a kinked demand curve, with the kink at the current price and quantity, as illustrated in Figure 13.2.
- The kink causes a break in the *MR* curve. As long as the *MC* curve remains within this break, the firm's price and quantity do not vary.
- The model fails to tell how the current price and quantity were determined or what happens if firms discover that their beliefs are incorrect.

FIGURE **13.2**

The Kinked Demand Curve Oligopoly

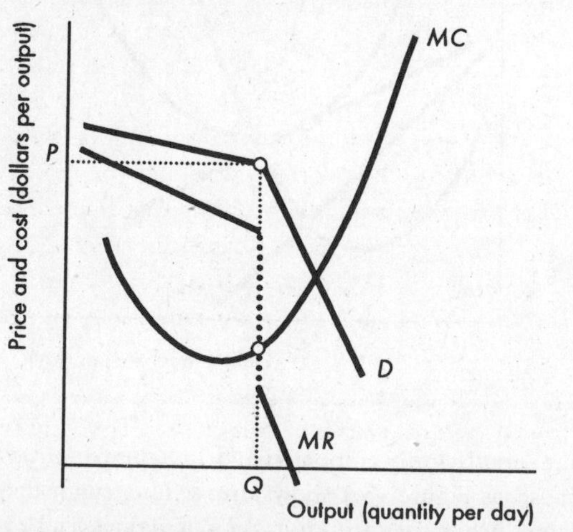

The **dominant firm oligopoly model**:

- One large firm has a substantial cost advantage over its many small competitors.
- The large firm acts like a monopoly and sets its profit-maximizing price. The small firms take this price as given and act like perfect competitors.
- This model applies only to the case of one large firm with a cost advantage over its competitors.

Game Theory

Game theory analyses strategic behavior. Games have rules, strategies, and payoffs:

- *Rules* specify permissible actions by players.
- *Strategies* are actions, such as raising or lowering price, output, advertising, or product quality.
- *Payoffs* are the profits and losses of the players. A payoff matrix relates the payoffs to the strategies.

A "prisoners' dilemma" is a two-person game. In a one-time prisoners' dilemma game, each player has a dominant strategy of cheating, that is, confessing.

- **Dominant strategy** — a unique best strategy independent of the other player's action.
- **Dominant strategy equilibrium** — the equilibrium determined when each player uses its dominant strategy.
- **Nash equilibrium** — A takes the best possible action given the action of B, and B takes the best possible action given the action of A.

Oligopoly Game

Duopoly is a market with two competitors. In a **duopoly game**, each firm can comply with a **cartel** agreement to lower output and raise price or can cheat on the agreement. In a one-time game, a prisoners' dilemma solution emerges, in which each firm has the dominant strategy of cheating. In a repeated game, other strategies can create a **cooperative equilibrium**, and each firm complies with the cartel agreement.

- A "tit-for-tat" strategy consists of taking the same action the other player took last period.
- A trigger strategy cooperates until the other player cheats and then cheats forever.

Price wars can occur when new firms enter an industry and the industry finds itself in a prisoners' dilemma game.

Other decisions of a firm — how much to spend in research and development, how much to spend on advertising, and so on — can often be analyzed using game theory.

A contestable market comprises only a few existing firms and has no barriers to entry, so the existing firms face perfect competition from potential entrants. The firms in the market may play an entry-deterrence game:

- In an **entry-deterrence game** the firm in the market sets a low price and earns a normal profit to keep a potential competitor from entering the market.
- **Limit pricing** refers to the situation in which a firm charges a price lower than the monopoly price (and earns less than the monopoly profit) to keep potential competitors out of the market.

Helpful Hints

1. Most industries are neither perfectly competitive nor pure monopolies; they lie somewhere between these two extremes. This fact does not mean that the last two chapters have been wasted. By examining firms under these market conditions, we are now able to discuss the wide range of industries between the extremes in a single chapter. Moreover, the assumptions of the models of perfect competition and monopoly allow us to isolate the impact of important forces, such as profit maximization, and important constraints, such as competition and market demand. These forces and constraints also operate in the market structures analyzed in this chapter. Isolating these forces and constraints beforehand, rather than attempting immediately to analyze "realistic" market structures such as monopolistic competition and oligopoly, avoided a confusing jumble of details and possible outcomes. To have jumped right in would have been like driving in a strange, large city without a road map.
2. Common to firms in any type of market structure is the rule to maximize profit: Produce the level of output that sets $MC = MR$. This rule applies not only in perfect competition and monopoly, but also in monopolistic competition, kinked demand curve, and dominant firm oligopolies. The essential reason for its widespread applicability is that the rule does not depend on industry structure. The framework of the $MR = MC$ rule is marginal analysis: As long as another unit of output adds more to the firm's revenue than to its cost (e.g., as long as $MR > MC$), producing more output adds to the firm's total profit. However, if producing another unit of output adds less to the firm's revenue than to its cost ($MR < MC$), producing more output subtracts from the firm's total profit. (Indeed, in this case, the firm's total profit will rise if the level of output is decreased.)

   The fact that $MR = MC$ applies to all industry structures has two ramifications. First, it reflects the importance of marginal analysis. Second, and more pragmatically, it means that you do not have to remember a separate profit-maximizing rule for each type of industry structure.
3. Free entry leads to zero long-run economic profits both in perfect competition and monopolistic competition. If a monopoly is earning an economic profit, other firms would like to enter the monopoly's industry, but barriers to entry keep them out. Hence the question of whether a firm can earn an economic profit in the long run revolves around the presence or absence of barriers to entry.
4. This chapter uses elementary game theory to explain oligopoly. The prisoners' dilemma game illustrates the most important game theory concepts (rules, strategies, and payoffs), which are then used in more complex game theory models such as those of repeated games.

   Learning how to find the equilibrium of a prisoners' dilemma–type game is important. Take the example of players A and B. Each player has to choose between two strategies — confess or deny. First, set up the payoff matrix. Then look at the payoff matrix from A's point of view. A does not know whether B is going to confess or deny, so A asks two questions: (1) Assuming that B confesses, do I get a better payoff if I confess or deny? (2) Assuming that B denies, do I get a better payoff if I confess or deny? If A's best strategy is to confess, regardless of whether B confesses or denies, confessing is A's dominant strategy.

   Next, look at the payoff matrix from B's point of view. Let B ask the equivalent two questions, and determine whether B has a dominant strategy. The combination of A's dominant strategy and B's dominant strategy comprises the equilibrium outcome of the game.

5. The key insight of the prisoners' dilemma game is the tension between the equilibrium outcome (in which both players' best strategy is to confess because they can't trust each other) and the fact that both players could make themselves better off if only they would cooperate. This tension helps explain complex events that we see in the real world.

   The Organization of Petroleum Exporting Countries (OPEC) provides the classic example of this tension. OPEC is a cartel that controls a large fraction of the world's oil. Looking at OPEC as a whole, to restrict the supply of petroleum and keep the price of petroleum high is in OPEC's interest. Keeping the price of petroleum high — perhaps near $40 a barrel, which was the price about 15 years ago — would maximize the total revenues and profits of the OPEC nations. But, when the price is this high, the *individual* interest of each nation lies in pumping more oil than the amount allocated to it under the OPEC agreement. Each nation figures that if it — and it alone — cheats on the output restriction imposed by the cartel agreement, the effect on the world price of oil would be small but the positive impact on its profit from selling more oil would be large. Thus each nation is tempted to cheat on the cartel. Widespread cheating by OPEC member nations is exactly what occurred!

Questions

True/False/Uncertain and Explain

1. A low concentration ratio indicates a low degree of competition.

2. Monopolistically competitive firms can earn an economic profit in the long run.

3. Game theory is used to analyze the behavior of monopolistically competitive firms.

4. A monopoly firm in a contestable market may be unable to earn an economic profit.

5. The kinked demand curve model of oligopoly predicts that the firm's price will change infrequently.

6. Free entry is the basic reason that monopolistically competitive firms have excess capacity.

7. If oligopolistic firms are able to sustain an output-restricting, price-increasing cartel, they will be producing the allocatively efficient level of output.

8. Like a monopoly firm, a monopolistically competitive firm has a downward sloping demand curve.

9. The four-firm concentration ratio is the sum of the squared market shares of the four largest firms in an industry.

10. Repeated games are more likely to have a cooperative equilibrium than one-time only games.

11. In the short run, to maximize its profit, a monopolistically competitive firm produces the level of output that sets $P = ATC$.

12. Product differentiation gives each monopolistically competitive firm a downward sloping demand curve.

13. Monopolistically competitive firms are allocatively inefficient.

14. An oligopolist will consider the reactions of other firms before it decides to cut its price.

15. In a one-time only prisoners' dilemma game, the best strategy for a prisoner is to confess only if the prisoner believes that the other player will confess.

Multiple Choice

1. The four-firm concentration ratio measures the share of the largest four firms in total industry
   a. profits.
   b. sales.
   c. cost.
   d. capital.

2. What type of industry structure has many firms, each producing a slightly different good, with no barriers to entry or exit?
   a. Perfect competition.
   b. Monopolistic competition.
   c. Oligopoly.
   d. Monopoly.

Figure 13.3 represents a monopolistically competitive firm in the short run. Use it for the next four questions.

FIGURE 13.3
Multiple Choice Questions 3, 4, 5, and 6

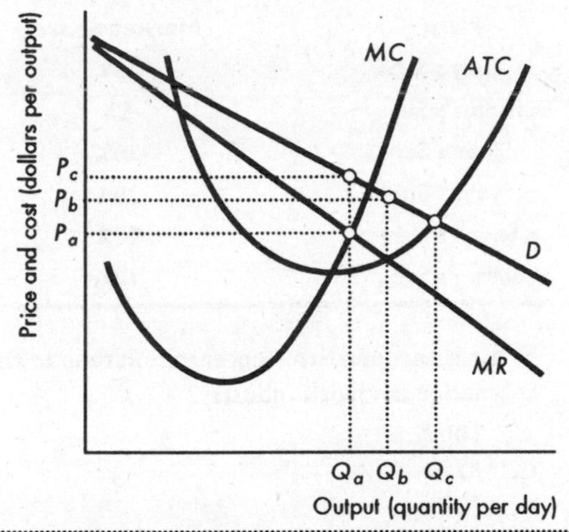

3. How much output does the firm produce?
   a. Q_a.
   b. Q_b.
   c. Q_c.
   d. None of the above.

4. What price does the firm charge?
   a. P_a.
   b. P_b.
   c. P_c.
   d. None of the above

5. The firm is
   a. earning an economic profit.
   b. earning only a normal profit.
   c. incurring an economic loss.
   d. Without more information, determining whether it is earning an economic profit or a normal profit, or suffering an economic loss, is impossible.

6. In the long run,
   a. new firms will enter, and each existing firm's demand shifts leftward.
   b. new firms will enter, and each existing firm's demand shifts rightward.
   c. existing firms will leave, and each remaining firm's demand shifts leftward.
   d. existing firms will leave, and each remaining firm's demand shifts rightward.

7. In the dominant firm model of oligopoly, the smaller firms act like
   a. oligopolists.
   b. monopolists.
   c. monopolistic competitors.
   d. perfect competitors.

8. A strategy in which a firm takes the same action that the other firm did in the last period is a
   a. dominant strategy.
   b. trigger strategy.
   c. tit-for-tat strategy.
   d. wimp's strategy.

9. A firm that has a kinked demand curve assumes that, if it raises its price, _____ of its competitors will raise their prices and that, if it lowers its price, _____ of its competitors will lower their prices.
   a. all; all
   b. none; all
   c. all; none
   d. none; none

10. A monopolistically competitive firm has excess capacity because in the
   a. short run $MR = MC$.
   b. short run ATC does not equal the minimum ATC.
   c. long run ATC does not equal the minimum ATC.
   d. long run it cannot earn an economic profit.

11. In the prisoners' dilemma game,
   a. one prisoner confesses and the other does not.
   b. neither prisoner confesses.
   c. both prisoners confess.
   d. any confession is thrown out of court.

12. Which of the following is NOT a problem with concentration ratios as a measure of industry competitiveness?
    a. Concentration ratios are national measures, but firms in some industries operate in regional markets.
    b. Concentration ratios are national measures, but firms in some industries operate in international markets.
    c. Concentration ratios tell us nothing about the size of barriers to entry in the industry.
    d. Concentration ratios tell us nothing about how cost varies among firms in the industry.

13. Limit pricing refers to
    a. the fact that a monopoly firm always sets the highest price possible.
    b. a situation in which a firm may lower its price to keep potential competitors from entering its market.
    c. how the price is determined in a kinked demand curve model of oligopoly.
    d. None of the above.

14. In an oligopoly with a collusive cartel agreement, when can the *industry-wide* profit be as large as possible?
    a. When all firms comply with the agreement.
    b. When one firm cheats on the cartel and the other firms do not.
    c. When all firms cheat on the agreement.
    d. The answer is indeterminate because it depends on the industry's *MR* curve.

15. In an oligopoly with a collusive cartel agreement, when can *one firm* have the maximum possible profit?
    a. When all firms comply with the agreement.
    b. When the one firm cheats on the cartel agreement and all the other firms do not cheat.
    c. When all firms cheat on the agreement.
    d. The answer is indeterminate because it depends on the firm's *MR* curve.

16. Under monopolistic competition, long-run economic profits are zero because of
    a. product differentiation.
    b. the lack of barriers to entry.
    c. excess capacity.
    d. the downward-sloping demand curve of each firm.

Use Table 13.1, which presents market shares for the submarine sandwich industry, for Question 17.

Table 13.1 Market Shares

Firm	Market Share
Sally's Subs	15%
Samantha's Subs	5%
Susan's Subs	30%
Sydna's Subs	20%
Sheryl's Subs	20%
Shirley's Subs	10%

17. What is the four-firm concentration ratio in the submarine sandwich industry?
    a. 100%.
    b. 85%.
    c. 70%.
    d. 30%.

18. Price wars can be the result of
    a. a cooperative equilibrium.
    b. a firm playing a tit-for-tat strategy in which last period the competitors complied with a cartel agreement.
    c. new firms entering the industry and immediately agreeing to abide by a cartel agreement.
    d. new firms entering an industry and all firms then finding themselves in a prisoners' dilemma.

Firms A and B are in a duopoly game, so they can either comply with a cartel agreement or cheat on the agreement. For the next 5 questions, use the following payoff matrix that shows the firms' economic profits.

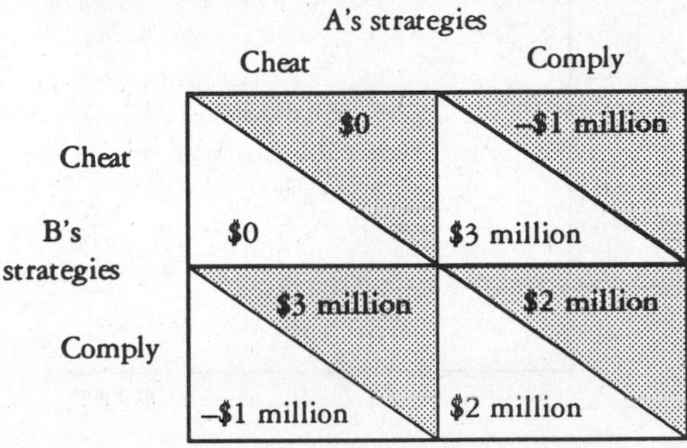

19. If Firm A cheats on the cartel and Firm B complies with the agreement, Firm A's profit is
    a. $3 million.
    b. $2 million.
    c. $0.
    d. –$1 million.

20. If Firm A cheats on the cartel and Firm B complies with the agreement, Firm B's profit is
    a. $3 million.
    b. $2 million.
    c. $0.
    d. –$1 million

21. If this game is played only once,
    a. both firms A and B will cheat.
    b. firm A will cheat and firm B will not cheat.
    c. firm A will not cheat and firm B will cheat.
    d. neither firm A nor firm B will cheat.

22. The equilibrium in question 23 is called a
    a. credible strategy equilibrium.
    b. dominant strategy equilibrium.
    c. duopoly equilibrium.
    d. cooperative equilibrium.

23. If this game is played repeatedly and both firms adopt trigger strategies so that the cooperative equilibrium emerges,
    a. both firms A and B will cheat.
    b. firm A will cheat and firm B will not cheat.
    c. firm A will not cheat and firm B will cheat.
    d. neither firm A nor firm B will cheat.

24. If a cartel agreement in a duopoly maximizes profit,
    a. each firm must produce the same amount.
    b. the industry level of output is allocatively efficient.
    c. industry marginal revenue must equal industry marginal cost at the level of total output.
    d. total output will be greater than without collusion.

25. In the "Incredible Electrical Conspiracy," which of the following did NOT occur?
    a. The firms conspired to fix prices on different types of electrical equipment.
    b. The conspiracy was undertaken in secrecy because such cartel agreements are illegal in the United States.
    c. The Justice Department eventually cracked the conspiracy.
    d. The conspiracy ran smoothly, with all firms remaining as members for the entire period.

26. In classifying markets, the Justice Department uses the
    a. Nash principle.
    b. extent of barriers to entry.
    c. four-firm concentration ratio.
    d. Hirschman–Herfindahl index.

27. In the long run, a firm in monopolistic competition
    a. has a perfectly elastic demand curve.
    b. earns an economic profit.
    c. produces less than the quantity that minimizes *ATC*.
    d. produces the quantity that minimizes *ATC*.

28. A monopolistically competitive firm is like a monopoly firm insofar as
    a. both have perfectly elastic demand curves.
    b. both can earn an economic profit in the long run.
    c. both have *MR* curves that lie below their demand curves.
    d. neither is protected by high barriers to entry.

29. A monopolistically competitive firm is like a perfectly competitive firm insofar as
    a. both have perfectly elastic demand curves.
    b. both can earn an economic profit in the long run.
    c. both have *MR* curves that lie below their demand curves.
    d. neither is protected by high barriers to entry.

30. A dominant strategy equilibrium is most likely to emerge when
    a. a monopolistically competitive industry is dominated by a dominant firm.
    b. an oligopolistic industry faces a repeated game.
    c. a monopoly is forced to compete repeatedly with an oligopolistic industry.
    d. an oligopolistic industry plays a game once.

Short Answer Problems

1. Considering the geographic scope of markets, how might a concentration ratio understate the degree of competitiveness in an industry? How might it overstate the degree of competitiveness?
2. Compare the advantages and disadvantages of perfect competition and monopolistic competition in terms of how they benefit society.
3. In Figure 13.4, draw a diagram illustrating a monopolistically competitive firm that is earning an economic profit in the short run. Identify the area that equals the economic profit.
4. In Figure 13.5, draw the long-run equilibrium for a monopolistically competitive firm. What conditions must be satisfied for long-run equilibrium?

FIGURE 13.4
Short Answer Problem 3

FIGURE 13.5
Short Answer Problem 4

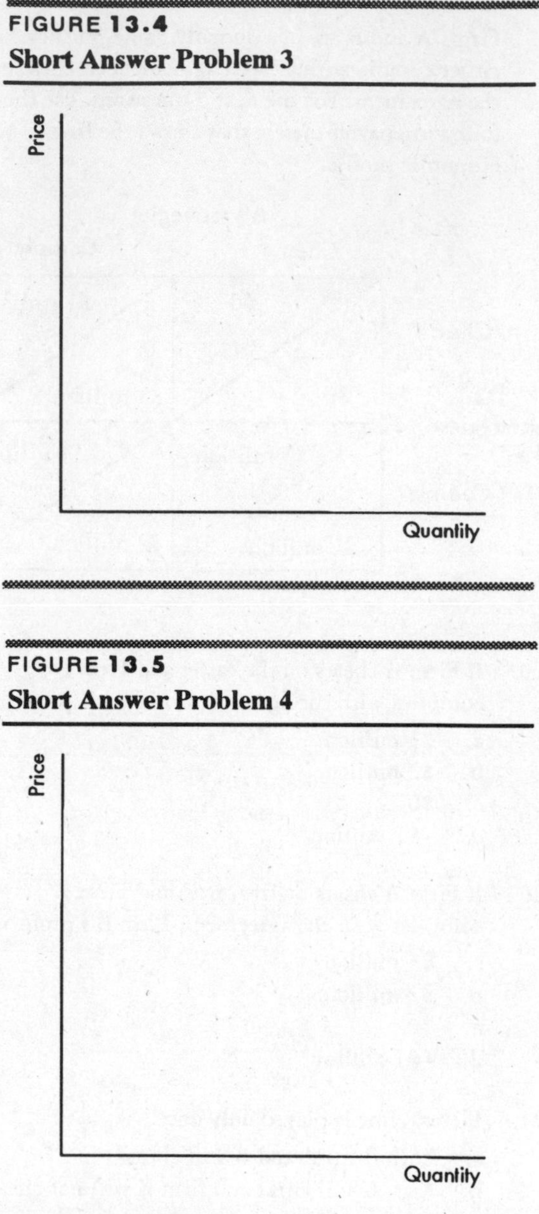

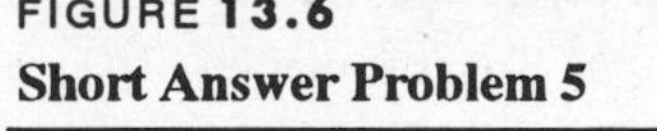

FIGURE 13.6
Short Answer Problem 5

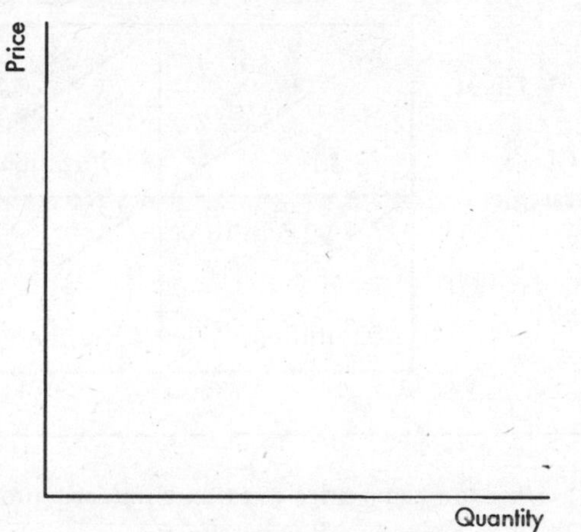

FIGURE 13.7
Short Answer Problem 6

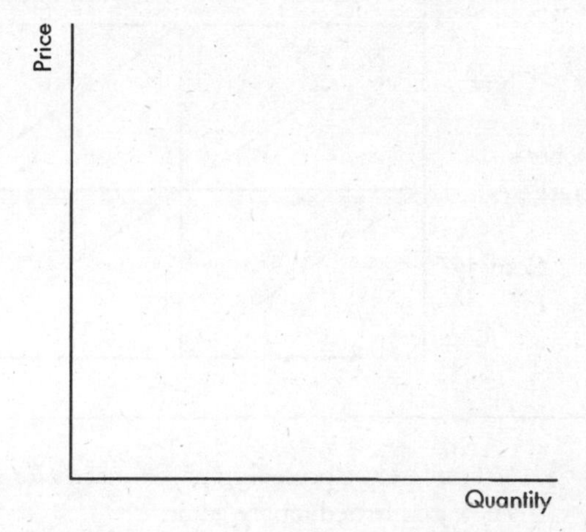

5. Suppose that a monopolistically competitive firm is initially in long-run equilibrium and it succeeds in further differentiating its product. As a result, the demand for its good increases. In Figure 13.6, show what happens to this firm in the short run. Without drawing a diagram, describe what happens in the long run.
6. In Figure 13.7, draw a diagram showing a kinked demand curve oligopoly. Indicate the range between which the marginal cost can vary and still leave the firm's output and price the same.
7. Two firms — Tom's Taxis and Chet's Cabs — are the only two taxi cab companies in a small college town. These firms are engaged in a duopoly game. If they both adhere to a collusive cartel agreement to restrict the number of their cabs and raise their price, each can earn an economic profit of $2 million. However, if one company cheats and the other complies with the agreement, the former earns an economic profit of $2.5 million and the latter suffers an economic loss of $1 million. If both cheat, both earn $0 economic profit; that is, both earn a normal profit.
   a. Use the description of the situation to complete the payoff matrix in the right-hand column. Put Tom's payoffs in the darker triangles and Chet's in the other triangles.
   b. If this game is played only once, what is Tom's best strategy? What is Chet's best strategy? What will be the equilibrium outcome?
   c. When is the *industry's* total profit the largest? When is Tom's profit the largest? Chet's profit?

Payoff Matrix for Short Answer Problem 7

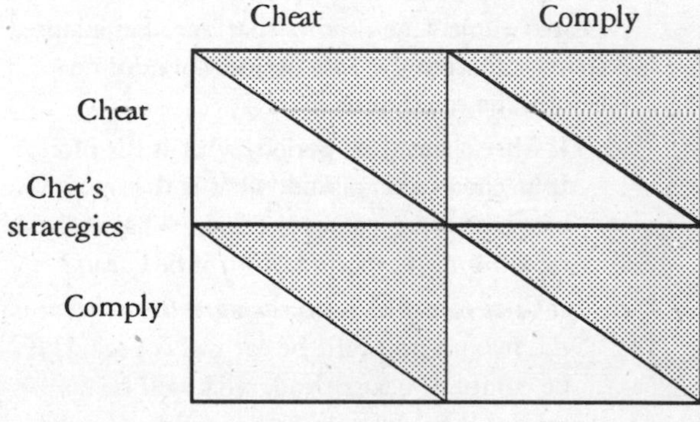

8. Suppose that the taxi firm duopoly game played in problem 7 changes: The payoffs are the same as before except when one player cheats and the other does not. Now the cheating player earns an economic profit of $2.5 million, and the player abiding by the agreement earns an economic profit of $0.5 million.

Payoff Matrix for Short Answer Problem 8

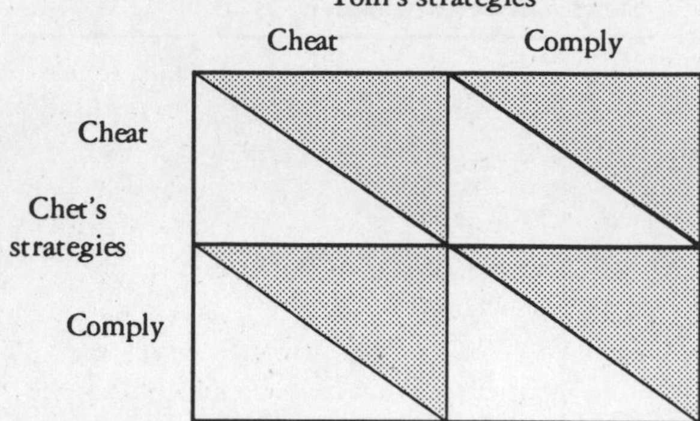

a. Complete the preceding payoff matrix for the new taxi firm duopoly game.

b. Does Tom have a clear-cut best strategy? Does Chet? Is there a clear outcome in this game?

9. The taxi market changes again so that the payoff matrix is as shown in the right-hand column. Chet and Tom now see that they will be playing a repeated game. Chet knows that Tom has adopted a tit-for-tat strategy. Last period Chet did not cheat on the cartel agreement.

   a. If Chet cheats this period, what is his profit? If he cheats this period, what is the maximum profit he can earn next period? What is the maximum two-period profit if he cheats?

   b. If Chet complies with the agreement, what is the maximum profit he earns this period? If he complies next period, what will be his profit? If he does not cheat in either period, what is the two-period total profit he earns?

   c. Is Chet likely to cheat this period? Why or why not?

Payoff Matrix for Short Answer Problem 9

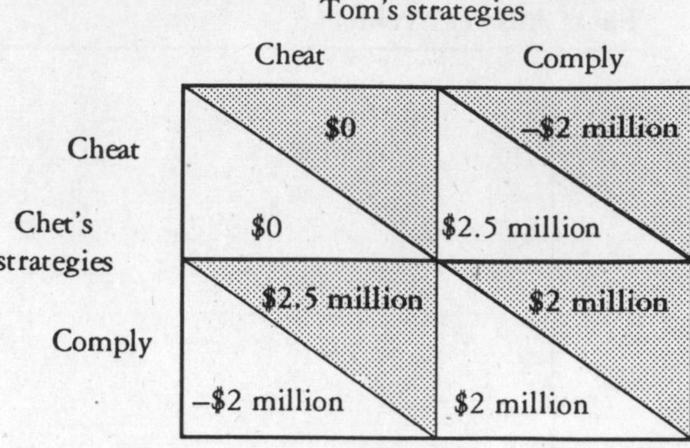

10. How can a price war that eliminates profits be explained with game theory?

■ You're the Teacher

1. "You know, I've really been studying the book and this study guide and now a lot of this stuff is making sense. I liked the helpful hint that pointed out that firms in all types of industries actually had only one profit-maximization rule, what it called the $MR = MC$ rule. It sure makes it easy if we don't have to memorize different rules for different industries! Can you think of any other rules that are the same across all industries?" This student is correct: Common rules ease your work. There is another rule that is common across all types of industries; it deals with when a firm earns an economic profit. With this hint, explain the other rule to the student.

Answers

True False Answers

1. **F** A low concentration ratio indicates a high degree of competition.
2. **F** The firms cannot earn an economic profit in the long run because of the absence of barriers to entry.
3. **F** Game theory is used to analyze the behavior of oligopolistic firms.
4. **T** In a contestable market, if the firm tries to earn a monopoly profit, competitors enter the market.
5. **T** Shifts in the *MC* curve that do not move it beyond the vertical section of the *MR* curve have no effect on the price that the firm charges nor on the quantity it produces.
6. **F** Monopolistically competitive firms have excess capacity because they produce differentiated goods.
7. **F** The cartel described in the problem reduces output below its allocatively efficient level.
8. **T** Both firms are price setters not price takers.
9. **F** The four-firm concentration is the sum of the market shares of the four largest firms.
10. **T** Repeated games have strategies — such as the tit-for-tat or trigger strategy — that can support the cooperative equilibrium and that are absent from games played only once.
11. **F** Like all firms, it will produce so that its *MR* equals its *MC*.
12. **T** By making its product different from those of its competitors, each monopolistically competitive firm has a downward-sloping demand curve.
13. **T** Monopolistically competitive, like monopolies, are allocatively inefficient.
14. **T** This mutual interdependence makes oligopoly such a difficult industry structure to analyze.
15. **F** In a prisoners' dilemma game, the dominant strategy is to confess; that is, regardless of the other players' action, each player will confess.

Multiple Choice Answers

1. **b** This is the definition of the four-firm concentration ratio.
2. **b** Monopolistic competition is similar to perfect competition insofar as there are many firms with no barriers to entry or exit. It is dissimilar in that each firm produces a unique but closely related good.
3. **a** This monopolistically competitive firm produces so that $MR = MC$.
4. **c** With the firm producing Q_a output, the demand curve shows that a price of P_c is the highest price that can be charged and still sell all that is produced.
5. **a** The firm earns an economic profit because, at output of Q_a, $P > ATC$.
6. **a** New firms enter because they, too, want to earn an economic profit. As these firms enter, they reduce the demand for the existing firms' goods.
7. **d** The smaller firms are unable to affect the price charged by the large firm.
8. **c** Tit-for-tat implies that "I'll do to you what you did to me."
9. **b** With this set of assumptions, the firm believes that it will lose a large amount of sales if raises its price but pick up only a small amount if it lowers its price.
10. **c** The firm produces less output than the level that minimizes its long-run *ATC*.
11. **c** Both players confess even though it is in their joint interest for neither to confess.
12. **d** Cost conditions probably indirectly affect the degree of competition, but concentration ratios try to measure the extent of competition directly.
13. **b** Limit pricing can occur in contestable markets when the firm plays an entry deterrence game.
14. **a** The interest of the industry as a whole is to maintain the cartel.
15. **b** Each firm's individual interest is to be the lone cheater on the cartel agreement. Compare this answer to the answer of question 15.
16. **b** If firms in the industry are earning an economic profit, the absence of barriers to entry means that new firms can enter the

industry and compete away the economic profit.

17. **b** Add the market shares of the four largest firms.

18. **d** Neither the new firms nor the old firms want a price war, but a prisoners' dilemma game may make a price war inevitable.

19. **a** Firm A's profits are in the darkened triangle in the square at the lower left.

20. **d** Firm B's profits are in the white triangle in the square at the lower left.

21. **a** Both firms have a dominant strategy of cheating.

22. **b** A dominant strategy equilibrium occurs when both players have a dominant strategy.

23. **d** The cooperative strategy maximizes each firm's profit over the long haul.

24. **c** To maximize its profit, the industry behaves as a monopoly, which means that it produces the level of output needed for $MR = MC$.

25. **d** Firms often dropped out of the conspiracy whenever it was in their individual interest to do so.

26. **d.** If the Hirschman–Herfindahl index is less than 1,800, the market is considered competitive; if it is greater than 1,800, it is considered concentrated.

27. **c** By producing less than the amount that minimizes the long-run ATC, the firm has excess capacity.

28. **c** Both have downward-sloping demand curves, so both have MR curves that lie below their demand curves.

29. **d** The absence of high barriers to entry accounts for the large number of firms in each industry.

30. **d** In one-time only games, a dominant strategy for each firm may be to cheat, so this strategy emerges as the dominant strategy equilibrium.

■ Answers to Short Answer Problems

1. Concentration ratios are calculated from a national geographic perspective. If the actual scope of the market is not national, the concentration ratio will likely misstate the degree of competitiveness in an industry. If the actual market is global, the concentration ratio will understate the degree of competitiveness. A firm may have a concentration ratio of 100 as the only producer in the nation, but may face a great deal of international competition. For instance, this situation closely resembles the case of certain types of computer memory chips. When the scope of the market is regional, the concentration ratio will overstate the degree of competitiveness. The concentration ratio includes firms elsewhere in the nation that are not real competitors in the region. Newspapers provide the classic example: A paper published in Maine is hardly a competitor for a newspaper published in San Francisco.

2. An advantage of perfect competition is that it leads to production at minimum average total cost, whereas monopolistic competition leads to a higher average total cost with reduced output. Another advantage of perfect competition is that a perfectly competitive industry is allocatively efficient; it produces the level of output that sets the marginal social benefit equal to the marginal social costs. A monopolistically competitive industry, however, is not allocatively efficient because the price of the product (which equals the marginal social benefit) exceeds the marginal social cost (which equals the marginal cost).

   The advantage of monopolistic competition is that it leads to greater product variety, which consumers value, whereas in a perfectly competitive industry all firms produce a single, identical good. In addition, monopolistically competitive firms have a greater incentive to innovate new and improved products and methods of production. Monopolistically competitive firms must do more advertising and sales promotion than perfectly competitive firms. To the extent that these activities provide valued services to consumers, they benefit society.

   Thus the loss in allocative efficiency and the higher ATC that occurs in monopolistic competition has to be weighed against the gain of greater product variety, greater incentives to innovate, and potentially valuable promotional activity.

FIGURE 13.8
Short Answer Problem 3

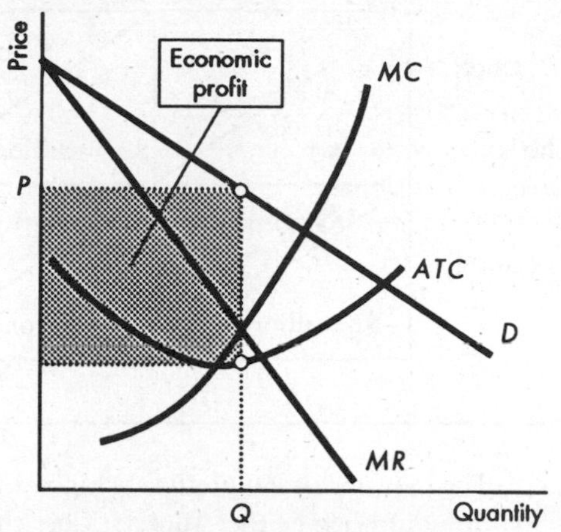

3. Figure 13.8 shows the short-run equilibrium of a monopolistically competitive firm. To maximize its profit, the firm produces so that $MR = MC$. At this level of output, $P > ATC$, so the firm earns an economic profit, as illustrated by the darkened rectangle. This diagram is identical to that of a monopoly firm earning an economic profit. Both firms face downward-sloping demand curves, both firms produce so that $MR = MC$, and, as long as $P > ATC$, both firms earn an economic profit.
4. Figure 13.9 shows the long-run equilibrium for a monopolistically competitive firm. Two conditions must be satisfied for this diagram to show the long-run equilibrium. Think of these requirements as a *firm condition* and a *market condition*. For the firm to be satisfied, it must maximize its profit, which requires that it be producing the amount of output so that $MR = MC$. Then, for there to be long-run equilibrium in the market, firms must have no incentive to either or exit the industry. As a result, there can be no economic profit, so $P = ATC$. (This second condition is not a choice of the firm; the firm would rather earn an economic profit. But, for the market to be in long-run equilibrium, it is required.) Both conditions — production at $MR = MC$ and $P = ATC$ — are met in Figure 13.9.

FIGURE 13.9
Short Answer Problem 4

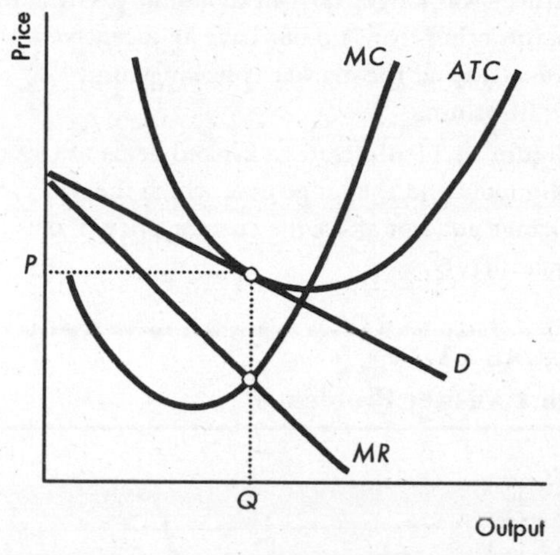

FIGURE 13.10
Short Answer Problem 5

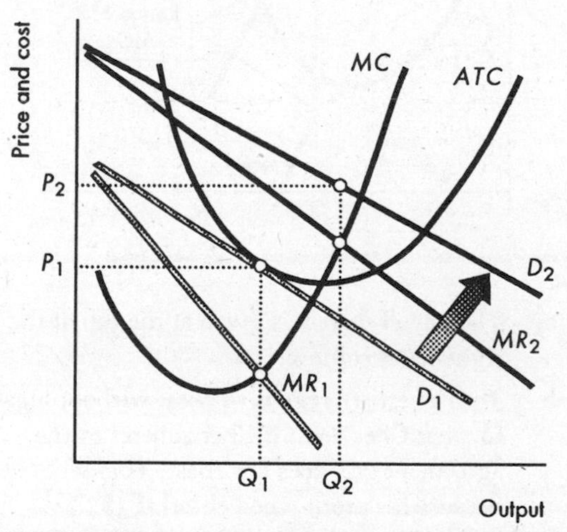

5. Figure 13.10 shows the effect when a monopolistically competitive firm succeeds in further differentiating its good. The demand for this firm's good increases, thereby shifting the demand curve and the MR curve rightward. As a result, the firm increases its output from Q_1 to Q_2 and raises its price from P_1 to P_2. The firm earns an economic profit.

In the long run, other firms copy its product. As they copy, the demand for the initial firm's good falls; that is, the demand curve and *MR* curve shift leftward. Ultimately, demand decreases enough that the pioneering firm — and all other, "copier" firms —no longer earn an economic profit. At this point, other firms do not have an incentive to copy the good and the market is in long-run equilibrium.

6. Figure 13.11 illustrates a kinked demand curve oligopoly and the range over which the *MC* can change and not affect the current price, *P* or quantity, *Q*.

FIGURE **13.11**
Short Answer Problem 6

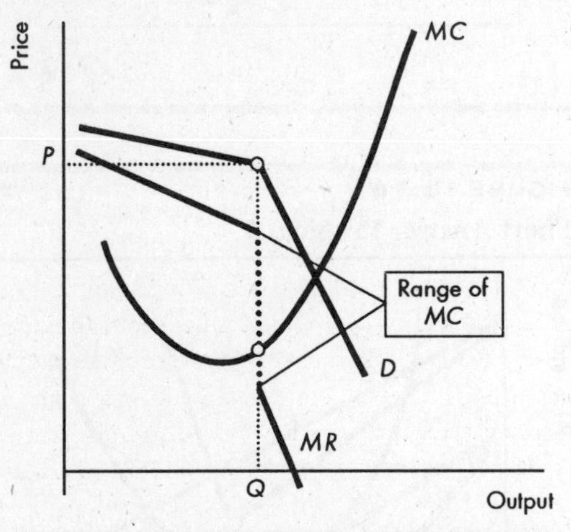

7. a. The payoff matrix is given at the top of the right-hand column.

   b. Tom's best strategy is to cheat without regard to what Chet does. If Chet adheres to the agreement and does not cheat, Tom will cheat because his profit when cheating ($2.5 million) exceeds his profit when he does not cheat ($2 million). And, if Chet cheats, Tom also will cheat because his profit when cheating ($0) is higher than the loss he would incur by not cheating (–$1 million). Thus Tom has a dominant strategy: Cheat. Chet also has a dominant strategy of cheating.

   In exactly the same way, Chet's profits are higher if he cheats regardless of what Tom does. The equilibrium outcome is for both Tom and Chet to cheat on the cartel agreement.

Short Answer Problem 7 (a)

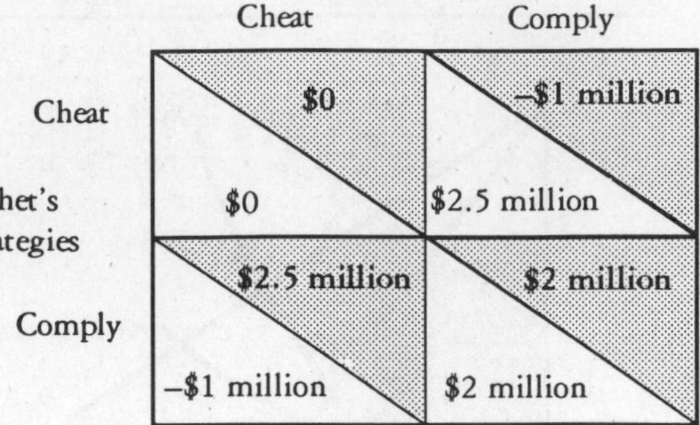

		Tom's strategies: Cheat	Tom's strategies: Comply
Chet's strategies	Cheat	$0 / $0	–$1 million / $2.5 million
	Comply	$2.5 million / –$1 million	$2 million / $2 million

   c. The industry's total profits are highest ($4 million) when neither Tom nor Chet cheat. Tom's profit is largest if he cheats and Chet does not. Similarly, Chet's profit is greatest if he alone cheats. Though each player's *individual* interest is to cheat on the cartel, their *joint* interest is to comply with the agreement.

Short Answer Problem 8 (a)

		Tom's strategies: Cheat	Tom's strategies: Comply
Chet's strategies	Cheat	$0 / $0	$.5 million / $2.5 million
	Comply	$2.5 million / $0.5 million	$2 million / $2 million

8. a. The new payoff matrix is given above.

   b. Tom (and Chet) no longer has a dominant strategy. In particular, if Chet complies with the agreement, Tom wants to cheat because in this case his profit by cheating ($2.5 million) exceeds his profit by complying ($2 million). But, if Chet cheats on the agreement, Tom will want to comply. If Chet is cheating, Tom earns a profit of $0.5 million by complying but \$0 by cheating. Hence, Tom's best strategy depends on what Chet does. Chet is in the same situation: His best strategy depends on what Tom does. Unlike the situation in problem 8, the outcome is not clear-cut. The equilibrium depends on which strategy Chet and Tom decide to pursue. Thus, as this problem demonstrates, there is not always a dominant strategy equilibrium.

9. a. Last period Chet did not cheat, so Tom's tit-for-tat strategy means that Tom will not cheat this period. Because Tom will comply with the cartel agreement, Chet's profit this period by cheating is \$2.5 million. Next period Tom will cheat because Chet cheated this period. Therefore next period the most profit that Chet can earn is \$0 by also cheating. (If Chet complied with agreement and Tom cheated, Chet loses –\$2 million.) Over the two periods, Chet's total profit if he cheats in the first period is \$2.5 million.

   b. If Chet does not cheat this period, this period he will earn \$2 million. Because Chet complied with the agreement this period, Tom's tit-for-tat strategy means that next period Tom will comply with the agreement. Then, if Chet also complies next period, he will earn \$2 million. By complying each period Chet earns a total of \$4 million.

   c. Chet is not likely to cheat this period. If he cheats, his total profits over the two periods are significantly less than if he complies over the two periods. This question illustrates that players in a repeated game are more likely to reach the cooperative equilibrium than players in a one-time game.

10. Game theory explains price wars as the consequence of firms in a colluding industry responding to the cheating of a firm or as the response to new firms entering the industry. If one firm cheats by cutting its price, all other firms will cut their prices, and a price war ensues. After the price has fallen sufficiently, (perhaps to the zero profit level), the firms again have a strong incentive to rebuild their collusion. Alternatively, if new firms (or even just one firm) enter an industry, the old and new firms may find themselves playing a prisoners' dilemma game. Neither set of firms wants the price to fall and profits to shrink, but they may be unable to collude successfully to keep the price and profit high.

■ You're the Teacher

1. "One other rule works for a firm in any type of industry structure. In particular, if $P > ATC$, the firm earns an economic profit; if $P = ATC$, the firm earns a normal profit; and if $P < ATC$, the firm suffers an economic loss. The reason that this rule works is straightforward. Let's take the case of $P > ATC$ and find out why it means that the firm earns an economic profit. If we multiply both sides of the inequality by q, the amount of output the firm produces, we get $Pq > (ATC)q$. Now, Pq, or the price times the amount produced, equals the firm's total revenue. And $ATC = TC/q$, so multiplying ATC times q gives TC, the firm's total cost. Hence $P > ATC$ means that total revenue exceed total cost. Because the firm's normal profit is already included in its total cost, the fact that the firm's total revenue exceeds its total cost means that the "extra" profit is an economic profit.

   But look, the main point of what I am saying is that we really do have it easy: Here's another case where we don't have to memorize a bunch of different rules. If *any* firm finds that P exceeds ATC, it's earning an economic profit."

Part Review 2 MARKETS FOR GOODS AND SERVICES

Reading Between the Lines

De BEERS'S DOMINANCE IN DIAMOND FIELD FACES CHALLENGES FROM RUSSIA, CANADA

The Central Selling Organization, through which South Africa's De Beers Consolidated Mines Ltd. controls world-wide sales of rough diamonds, is confident it can overcome what some analysts are calling one of the sternest challenges in the organization's 60-year history.

The analysts believe the London-based CSO faces a threat to its dominance of the diamond trade, primarily from the recent flood of unauthorized sales of Russian diamonds outside CSO's control, but also from the prospect of significant diamond output from Canada's Northwest Territories.

But De Beers insists it can overcome these obstacles.

"Russia's interest in maintaining the value of its diamond inventory ... prevent [it] from ruining the diamond business," said Gary Ralfe, CSO managing director.

De Beers Centenary AG, the Switzerland-based De Beers affiliate that runs the CSO, estimates that about $350 million of Russian diamonds — about 8% of De Beer's own diamond sales — were sold last year outside the CSO.

That provides a potent threat to the CSO, which limits diamond sales when demand is weak in order to maintain world rough-diamond prices...

De Beers itself supplies about 50% of the world's diamonds, but through the CSO arrangements it has marketing control over 80% of the total rough-diamond trade.

One leading South African diamond analyst is also optimistic. "I am convinced the Russians need De Beers as much as De Beers needs them." Negotiations will lead to a win-win outcome, even if De Beers wins less than the Russians, he said.

Meanwhile, the CSO faces the challenge of a surge in Canadian diamond supply over which it has no control yet.

Matthew Curtin, "DeBeer's Dominance in Diamond Field Faces Challenges from Russia, Canada," May 19, 1994, p. A10. Reprinted by permission of The Wall Street Journal,

■ Analyze It

The story illustrates one of the perils of a cartel. We can analyze this situation using the figures we have used to illustrate firms' behavior and also game theory.

1. Assuming that De Beers is a monopoly, draw a diagram showing how it determines the price of a diamond and the quantity produced. Illustrate De Beers's economic profit in the diagram.
2. De Beers's near monopoly results from its cartel agreements with the Russians, among others. When is Russia's profit from diamonds the largest?

How does this result affect Russia's actions and its negotiations with De Beers?

3. What game theory equilibrium might result if Russia, Canada, and De Beers do not reach agreement?

Mid-Term Examination

1 Diminishing marginal utility means that

a. Ralph will enjoy his first hamburger more than his second.
b. the utility from one hamburger exceeds the utility from two hamburgers.
c. the price of two hamburgers is twice the price of one hamburger.
d. beyond a certain point, total utility falls as income rises.

2 As Sean's consumption of rice goes down, his

a. average utility from consuming rice falls.
b. total utility from consuming rice falls.
c. marginal utility from consuming rice falls.
d. elasticity of utility from consuming rice falls.

3 Inga's graph of her consumption possibilities boundary has apples per week on the vertical axis and loaves of bread per week on the horizontal. An increase in the price of apples shifts the

a. horizontal intercept left.
b. horizontal intercept right.
c. vertical intercept down.
d. vertical intercept up.

4 Jenny buys sodas and popcorn. Sodas sell for $1 and popcorn sells for $2 a bag. Currently she is in consumer equilibrium with the marginal utility from her last dollar spent on popcorn equal to 50. The marginal utility from her last dollar spent on sodas is

a. 10.
b. 15.
c. 25.
d. 50.

5 A budget line is drawn on a diagram with bus tokens on the horizontal axis and gasoline on the vertical axis. Bus tokens are an inferior good while gasoline is normal. As income rises, the best affordable point moves

a. down and left.
b. down and right.
c. up and left.
d. up and right.

6 Movies are \$6 a ticket and videotape rentals are \$3 a tape per day. With tapes on the vertical axis, the magnitude of the slope of the budget line is

a. 0.5.
b. 2.
c. 3.
d. 6.

7 Consumers equate the relative price of two goods to

a. their money income.
b. their real income.
c. their marginal rate of substitution.
d. relative quantities.

8 For inferior goods, an increase in income

a. increases purchases.
b. decreases purchases.
c. does not change the amount purchased.
d. changes the slope of the budget line.

9 Partners of a partnership have

a. limited liability. So do shareholders in a corporation.
b. limited liability. Shareholders in a corporation have unlimited liability.
c. unlimited liability. So do shareholders in a corporation.
d. unlimited liability. Shareholders in a corporation have limited liability.

10 Suppose the interest rate is 10 percent per year. The present value of \$220 to be received one year from today is

a. \$200.00.
b. \$220.00.
c. \$230.00.
d. \$242.00.

11 An electrician quits her current job, which pays \$30,000 per year. She can take a job with another firm for \$40,000 per year or work for herself. The opportunity cost of working for herself is

a. \$10,000.
b. \$30,000.
c. \$40,000.
d. \$70.000.

12 In their relation to a firm's managers, shareholders act

a. as agents.
b. as principals.
c. in loco parentis.
d. as a cabinet for advice.

13 If a firm's marginal product of labor is greater than its average product of labor, than an increase in its use of labor necessarily will

a. reduce its total product.
b. raise its average product of labor.
c. raise its marginal product of labor.
d. not change its average product of labor.

14 An economically efficient method of production

a. is always technologically efficient.
b. lies below the production function.
c. lies below the supply curve.
d. may not always be technologically efficient.

15 In general, decreasing returns to scale occur

a. as output expands at low levels of production.
b. through the entire range of production.
c. as output expands at high levels of output.
d. whenever the slope of the total product curve is positive.

16 The intersection of the *MC* and *ATC* curves is the point at which

a. average total cost is minimized.
b. average variable cost is minimized.
c. average fixed cost is minimized.
d. total product is maximized.

17 In perfect competition, which is <u>NOT</u> the case?

a. No firm can influence the price of the good.
b. There are few sellers.
c. There are no restrictions on entry.
d. All firms sell at the same price.

18 A firm should contract output as long as its

a. average total revenue exceeds its average total cost.
b. average total revenue exceeds its average variable cost.
c. marginal cost exceeds its marginal revenue.
d. marginal revenue exceeds its marginal cost.

19 At a firm's shutdown point, its average variable cost equals its

a. average total cost.
b. average fixed cost.
c. price.
d. None of the above.

20 A perfectly competitive firm finds that at its current output, $MR = MC$ and $P > ATC$. Then this firm will

a. expand its output and lower its price.
b. reduce its output and raise its price.
c. shut down.
d. not change its production nor its price.

21 Public franchises are

a. legal barriers to entry. So are patents.
b. legal barriers to entry. Patents are natural barriers to entry.
c. natural barriers to entry. So are patents.
d. natural barriers to entry. Patents are legal barriers to entry.

22 The demand curve for a monopoly

a. lies above its marginal revenue curve.
b. lies on its marginal revenue curve.
c. lies below its marginal revenue curve.
d. is horizontal.

23 When a single-price monopoly is maximizing its profit, then the level of output it produces is

a. efficient because profit is maximized.
b. inefficient because $P > MC$.
c. efficient because $MR = MC$.
d. efficient because costs are minimized.

24 Which of the following occurs with <u>BOTH</u> a perfect price discriminating monopoly and a single-price monopoly?

a. The level of output is inefficient.
b. All consumer surplus goes to the monopoly.
c. Both create deadweight loss.
d. There is a redistribution of surplus to the monopoly.

25 A high concentration ratio indicates

a. a high degree of monopolization.
b. a high degree of competition.
c. that wages are a low share of costs.
d. that wages are a high share of costs.

26 When firms in an industry that is monopolistically competitive incur an economic loss, firms will

a. enter the industry, and demand will increase for the original firms.
b. exit the industry, and demand will increase for the remaining firms.
c. exit the industry, and demand will decrease for the remaining firms.
d. enter the industry, and demand will decrease for the original firms.

27 In the dominant firm model of oligopoly, the dominant firm acts as if it was a

a. perfect competitor.
b. monopolistic competitor.
c. oligopoly.
d. monopoly

28 The cooperative strategy in the prisoners' dilemma game would cause

a. both players to win.
b. both players to lose.
c. the first player to take an action to win.
d. the last player to take an action to win.

Answers

Reading Between the Lines

Figure 1 shows De Beers's situation as a monopoly. As a monopoly, De Beers will produce where $MR = MC$, which means it sells Q diamonds and charges the highest price possible for this level of production, namely P dollars per diamond. De Beers almost certainly earns an economic profit, which also is illustrated in Figure 1.

FIGURE 1

De Beers as a Monopoly

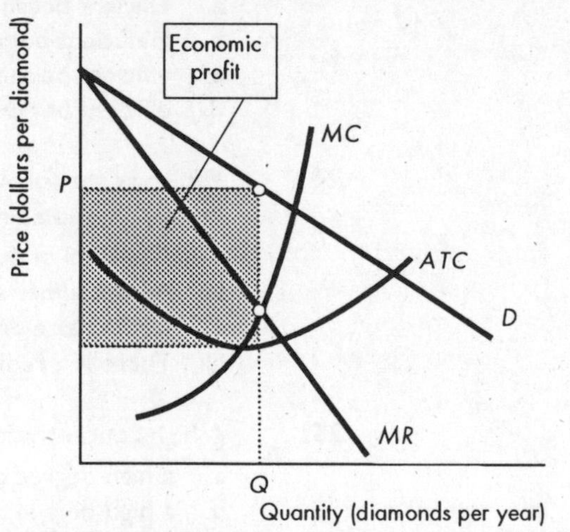

Russia's agreement with De Beers gives Russia some of this economic profit. But, Russia's economic profit is larger still if it cheats on the cartel agreement by selling more diamonds than the agreement allowed. De Beers's problem is exactly the fact that Russia is cheating on the agreement. Hence, the price of rough diamonds is lower than what it would otherwise be, P in Figure 1. Thus, as De Beers and Russia renegotiate their agreement, Russia's goal is to get a larger fraction of the total economic profit; De Beers's goal is to limit the amount the Russians obtain. The South African analyst believes that an agreement will be reached and that likely Russia will receive more than before.

Why is an agreement likely to occur? If it does not, De Beers, Russia, and Canada might find themselves playing a prisoners' dilemma game, in which the price of a rough diamond is driven lower because the producers are unable to cooperate to maintain the high price. Although this situation would make society as a whole better off, it would harm all the producers and so this is why the analyst characterized an agreement as "win-win" for both De Beers and Russia.

Mid-Term Exam

1 a; 2 b; 3 c; 4 d; 5 c; 6 b; 7 c; 8 b; 9 d; 10 a; 11 c; 12 b; 13 b; 14 a; 15 c; 16 a; 17 b; 18 c; 19 c; 20 d; 21 a; 22 a; 23 b; 24 d; 25 a; 26 b; 27 d; 28 a.

Chapter 14 PRICING AND ALLOCATING FACTORS OF PRODUCTION

Key Concepts

■ Factor Prices and Incomes

Factors of production (**labor, capital, land, and entrepreneurship**) are used to produce output. Demand and supply in factor markets determine the prices for the first three factors (wage rate, interest rate, and rental rate). The income earned by a factor equals the factor price times the quantity employed.

- An increase in the demand for a factor raises the factor's price and income.
- A decrease in the demand for a factor lowers the factor's price and income.
- An increase in the supply of a factor lowers the factor's price. If demand is inelastic, it lowers the factor's income, whereas if demand is elastic it raises the factor's income.
- A decrease in the supply of a factor raises the factor's price. If demand is inelastic, the decrease in supply raises the factor's income and if demand is elastic it reduces the factor's income.

■ Demand for Factors

Firms' demand for factors is a **derived demand,** stemming from their objective of maximizing their profits.

- **Marginal factor cost** (*PF*) is the addition to the firm's cost from hiring an additional unit of a factor.
- **Marginal revenue product** (*MRP*) is the extra revenue from employing one more unit of factor.

A profit-maximizing firm hires additional units of a factor up to the point at which the **marginal factor cost equals the marginal revenue product,** or $PF = MRP$. The **firm's demand curve for a factor is the same as the factor's marginal revenue product curve.**

The marginal product of labor (*MP*) is the added output produced by hiring an additional worker. The marginal revenue product from hiring another worker equals the marginal product of labor times marginal revenue. In terms of a formula,

$$MRP = MP \times MR.$$

Profit-maximizing firms hire labor to the point where the wage rate equals the marginal revenue product. A firm's demand curve for labor shifts rightward when:

- the price of output rises.
- the prices of other substitute factors rise.
- technological change increases the marginal product of labor.

The **market demand curve for labor** is the sum of the quantities of labor demanded by all the firms at each wage rate.

The elasticity of demand for labor equals the magnitude of

$$\frac{\%\Delta \text{ quantity of labor demanded}}{\%\Delta \text{ wage rate}}.$$

The elasticity of demand for labor depends on:

- *Labor intensity* — the greater the proportion of the total cost accounted for by wages, the larger is the elasticity of demand for labor.
- *Speed that the marginal product diminishes* — the more rapidly the marginal product of labor diminishes, the smaller the elasticity of demand for labor.
- *Elasticity of demand for the final product* — the larger the elasticity of demand for the final product, the larger is the elasticity of demand for labor.
- *Substitutability of capital for labor* — the more readily capital can be substituted for labor, the larger the elasticity of demand for labor.

Supply of Factors

The supply of factors is determined by households' decisions.

The **supply of labor:**

- Households allocate time between market activity (labor supply) and nonmarket activity (leisure, nonmarket production).
- At wage rates above a household's **reservation wage**, the household supplies labor.
- The **substitution effect** from a higher wage rate increases the quantity of labor supplied.
- The **income effect** from a higher wage rate decreases the quantity of labor supplied and increases the amount of time spent at leisure.
- As Figure 14.1 shows, an individual household **labor supply curve bends backward** when the income effect outweighs the substitution effect.

FIGURE **14.1**

A Household's Supply Curve of Labor

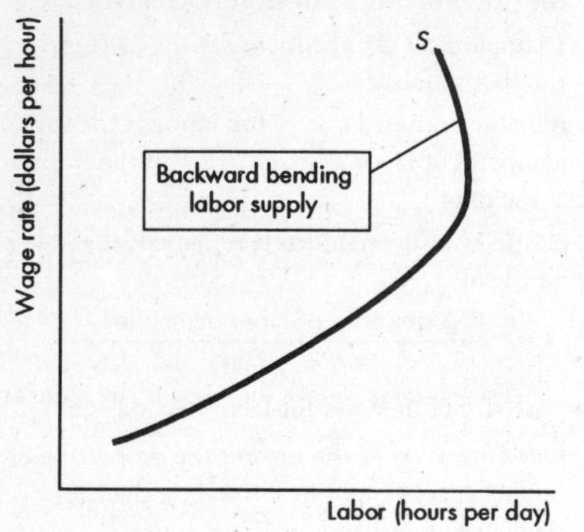

- The **market supply curve of labor** is the horizontal sum of all household supply curves and slopes upward over the normal range of wage rates.

Concerning the **supply of capital:**

- The supply of capital is determined by households' saving decisions. Households supply financial capital to firms who buy the actual (physical) capital.
- Changes in the interest rate affect households' saving and thereby affect the supply of capital.
- In the short run, the supply curve of capital might be zero elastic (vertical); the long-run supply curve is more elastic.

Concerning the **supply of land:**

- The *aggregate* quantity of land is fixed, so its supply is perfectly inelastic.
- The supply of land to an individual perfectly competitive firm is perfectly elastic.

Incomes, Economic Rent, and Transfer Earnings

Economic rent is any income received by a factor owner above the amount required to induce the quantity supplied of the factor. Income required to induce the quantity supplied is called **transfer earnings.** Figure 14.2 illustrates economic rent and transfer earnings.

FIGURE **14.2**

Economic Rent and Transfer Earnings

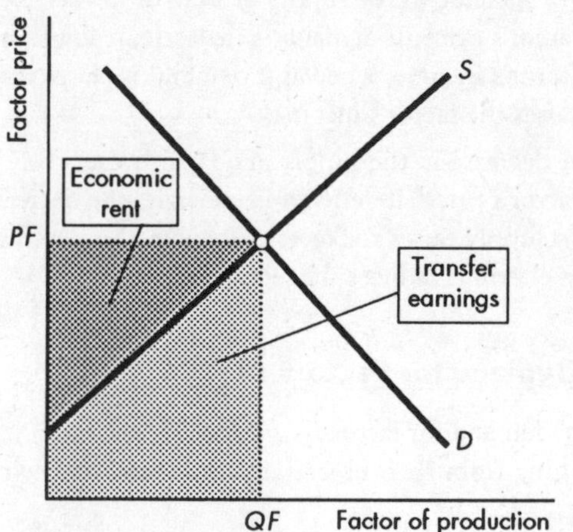

- A factor's total income is the sum of transfer earnings and economic rent.
- The more inelastic the supply of a factor, the larger is the fraction of its income that is economic rent.

Helpful Hints

1. This chapter gives an overview of characteristics that are common to the markets for all factors of production. For example, the assumption that firms are profit maximizers implies that they hire each factor of production up to the point at which the marginal revenue product equals the marginal cost of the factor. This result holds regardless of whether the factor of production is labor, land, or capital. In the next several chapters we examine these factor markets in more detail.
2. Distinguish carefully between the marginal revenue product of a factor of production and the marginal revenue of a unit of output. As noted in the text, the marginal revenue product of a factor of production is calculated by multiplying marginal revenue and marginal product ($MRP = MP \times MR$). In other words, marginal product tells us how much more output we receive from using more of a factor, and marginal revenue tells us how much more revenue we receive from selling each unit of that additional output. Therefore *MP* times *MR* tells us how much more revenue we receive from using more of the factor (the *MRP*).

   When deciding whether to hire another unit of a factor, profit-maximizing firms compare this added revenue to the cost of hiring the factor. As long as the additional revenue from hiring the factor exceeds the additional cost, hiring the factor is profitable. However, if the added revenue falls short of the added cost, hiring the factor reduces the firm's profit. The maximum profit is reached by hiring the amount of the factor necessary to equalize the marginal revenue product and the factor's cost.
3. The most important graph in this chapter appears in the text's Figure 14.4. Using Max's Wash 'n' Wax as an example, it demonstrates that a firm's demand curve for labor is the same as its marginal revenue product curve of labor.

   Why is the *MRP* curve the same as a firm's demand curve for labor? We construct the demand curve for labor by asking the question: "How much labor is a firm willing to hire at alternative wage rates?" Because firms are profit maximizers, they will want to hire labor up to the point at which the marginal revenue product of labor equals the wage rate. For example, if the wage rate is $10 per hour and the marginal revenue product is $10 when three workers are hired, the firm will hire three workers. Other points on the labor demand curve can be obtained in similar fashion. The result is that the demand curve for labor is the same as the *MRP* curve.

   Why is this result so important? Because we know that the demand curve for labor is the same as the marginal revenue product curve, we also know that anything that shifts the marginal revenue product curve therefore shifts — in an identical manner — the demand curve for labor. Now, the marginal revenue product for labor equals the marginal product of labor times the marginal revenue; that is, $MRP = MP \times MR$. Thus anything that changes either the marginal product of labor, *MP*, or the marginal revenue from selling the product, *MR*, changes the marginal revenue product and thereby shifts the marginal revenue product curve. Moreover, if these changes increase either the marginal product of labor or the marginal revenue, the demand curve for labor increases, that is, it shifts rightward. If the changes decrease either the marginal product of labor or the marginal revenue, the demand curve for labor decreases so that it shifts leftward.

Questions

■ True/False/Uncertain and Explain

1. A firm's demand curve for labor is the same as its marginal revenue product of labor curve.

2. When the supply curve of labor bends backward, an increase in the demand for labor raises the equilibrium wage rate and increases the equilibrium quantity of labor employed.

3. The greater the labor intensity of a production process, the smaller is the elasticity of demand for labor.

4. An increase in the supply of a factor lowers the factor's price.

5. An increase in the supply of a factor lowers the factor's income.

6. The aggregate supply of land is perfectly elastic.

7. A supply curve of labor bends backward when the substitution effect is larger than the income effect.

8. The higher the interest rate, the less saving households undertake.

9. If Pearl Jam would be willing to play a concert for $25,000 but instead receive $125,000, they earn an economic rent of $100,000.

10. To maximize its profits, a firm hires the amount of a factor that sets $PF = MRP$.

11. A household supplies no labor when the wage rate is above its reservation wage rate.

12. A factor's price cannot rise while its total income is falling.

13. The long-run supply curve of capital is more elastic than the short-run supply curve of capital.

14. Only land earns economic rent.

Multiple Choice

1. If the income effect from a higher wage rate exceeds the substitution effect, the higher wage rate
   a. increases the quantity of labor supplied.
   b. decreases the quantity of labor supplied.
   c. shifts the supply curve of labor leftward.
   d. shifts the supply curve of labor rightward

2. Increasing the supply of a factor of production
   a. increases the factor's income if the elasticity of factor demand is less than 1.
   b. decreases the factor's income if the elasticity of factor demand is less than 1.
   c. increases the factor's income if the elasticity of factor supply is less than 1.
   d. decreases the factor's income if the elasticity of factor supply is less than 1.

3. Which of the following statements about a firm's demand curve for labor is correct?
   a. The demand curve for labor is the same as the *MRP* curve only for a perfectly competitive firm.
   b. The demand curve for labor is the same as the *MRP* curve only for a monopoly.
   c. The demand curve for labor is the same as the *MRP* curve for both a perfectly competitive and a monopoly firm.
   d. The demand curve for labor is not the same as the *MRP* curve for either a monopoly or a perfectly competitive firm.

4. Suppose that the supply of land is perfectly inelastic. Then
   a. its price is determined only by its supply curve.
   b. all its income is transfer income.
   c. all its income is economic rent.
   d. the demand curve for land must be perfectly elastic.

5. Data show that a rise in the interest rate
   a. slightly increases saving.
   b. increases saving quite strongly.
   c. decreases saving quite strongly.
   d. slightly decreases saving.

6. A worker's reservation wage is the
   a. highest wage rate before the income effect starts to dominate the substitution effect.
   b. lowest wage rate before the income effect starts to dominate the substitution effect.
   c. the lowest wage rate for which the worker will supply labor.
   d. wage rate paid to head waiters at fine restaurants who are involved in taking reservations.

7. The price of the good produced by a perfectly competitive firm falls. As a result, the
   a. supply of labor to the firm decreases.
   b. supply of labor to the firm increases.
   c. demand for labor by the firm increases.
   d. demand for labor by the firm decreases.

8. Economic rent is the
   a. price paid for the use of an acre of land.
   b. price paid for the use of a unit of capital.
   c. income required to induce a given quantity of a factor of production to be supplied.
   d. income received above the amount required to induce a given quantity of a factor of production to be supplied.

9. The supply curve of labor facing an individual *firm* in a perfectly competitive labor market
   a. only slopes upward.
   b. first slopes upward and then bends backward as the wage rate rises.
   c. is vertical.
   d. is horizontal.

10. Which of the following increases the elasticity of the demand for labor?
    a. A rapid decline in the marginal product schedule.
    b. A decrease in the elasticity of demand for the final good.
    c. An increase in the proportion of total cost paid to labor.
    d. A reduction in the substitutability of capital for labor.

11. An example of derived demand is the demand for
    a. sweaters derived by an economics student.
    b. sweaters produced by labor and capital.
    c. labor used in the production of sweaters.
    d. sweater brushes.

12. Suppose that the price and *MR* of oranges fall. As a result, the
    a. supply of orange pickers increases.
    b. supply of orange pickers decreases.
    c. demand for orange pickers increases.
    d. demand for orange pickers decreases.

13. The change in total revenue resulting from employing an additional unit of capital is the
    a. marginal product of capital.
    b. marginal revenue of capital.
    c. marginal revenue cost of capital.
    d. marginal revenue product of capital

14. A company finds that, when it hires the next worker, the worker's *MRP* exceeds the cost of the worker. In this case the company should
    a. definitely hire the worker.
    b. perhaps hire the worker, depending on the relationship between the company's *MC* and *MR*.
    c. definitely not hire the worker.
    d. perhaps not hire the worker, depending on the relationship between the company's *MC* and *MR*.

15. Jennifer will supply 40 hours of labor as a lawyer for $2,000. She actually receives $2,400 for her 40 hours at work. Jennifer's transfer income for the 40 hours is
    a. $2,400.
    b. $2,000.
    c. $400.
    d. undefined.

16. Jennifer will supply 40 hours of labor as a lawyer for $2,000. She actually receives $2,400 for her 40 hours at work. Jennifer's economic rent for the 40 hours is
    a. $2,400.
    b. $2,000.
    c. $400.
    d. undefined.

17. The supply curve of capital
    a. bends back at low interest rates.
    b. is determined by the marginal revenue product of using another piece of capital equipment.
    c. bends back when the interest rate rises.
    d. is more elastic in the long run than in the short run.

18. The marginal product of labor used to produce hubcaps diminishes rapidly. As a result, workers in this industry find that
    a. the demand for labor is inelastic.
    b. their supply of labor bends backward at a low wage.
    c. most of their income is transfer income.
    d. an increase in demand for their labor lowers their total income.

19. Suppose that the supply of airline pilots is very elastic. Then an increase in demand for airline pilots causes a
    a. large increase in employment and a small rise in the wage rate.
    b. large increase in employment and a large rise in the wage rate.
    c. small increase in employment and a small rise in the wage rate.
    d. small increase in employment and a large rise in the wage rate.

20. A firm's marginal revenue product of labor curve is the same as its
    a. supply curve of labor.
    b. demand curve for labor.
    c. marginal cost curve.
    d. marginal revenue curve.

21. Unions in the oil refining industry succeed in raising the wage rate paid their workers. Capital and labor are substitute inputs. As a result, the
    a. demand curve for labor from oil refining companies shifts leftward.
    b. demand curve for labor from oil refining companies shifts rightward.
    c. demand curve for capital from oil refining companies shifts leftward.
    d. demand curve for capital from oil refining companies shifts rightward.

22. *MRP* equals
    a. $MP \times MR$.
    b. $MR \times MC$.
    c. MR/MP.
    d. None of the above.

23. A technological change that causes an increase in the marginal product of labor shifts
    a. the demand curve for labor rightward.
    b. the demand curve for labor curve leftward.
    c. the supply curve of labor leftward.
    d. the supply curve of labor rightward.

24. Which of the following statements about the supply curve of land is correct?
    a. The aggregate supply curve is perfectly elastic, so all income earned by land is transfer income.
    b. The aggregate supply curve is perfectly inelastic, so all income earned by land is economic rent.
    c. The aggregate supply curve of land is perfectly inelastic in the short run and perfectly elastic in the long run.
    d. Land has no supply curve.

25. If the wage rate rises, the substitution effect gives a household the incentive to
    a. raise its reservation wage.
    b. increase its nonmarket activity and decrease its market activity.
    c. increase its market activity and decrease its nonmarket activity.
    d. increase both market and nonmarket activity.

26. If the wage rate rises, the income effect gives a household the incentive to
    a. raise its reservation wage.
    b. increase its nonmarket activity and decrease its market activity.
    c. increase its market activity and decrease its nonmarket activity.
    d. increase both market and nonmarket activity.

27. Which of the following leads to a high price for a factor?
    a. High *MRP* and high supply.
    b. High *MRP* and low supply.
    c. Low *MRP* and high supply.
    d. Low *MRP* and low supply.

28. In the long run, capital
    a. receives no transfer earnings.
    b. receives no economic rent.
    c. can receive both transfer earnings and economic rent.
    d. can never take the place of labor.

29. When a firm is maximizing its profit, which of the following will NOT be true?
    a. $MR = MC$.
    b. $PF = MRP$.
    c. $MC = MRP$.
    d. None of the above because all the conditions will be true.

30. You notice that a factor's price and income rise. This set of events can be the result of the
    a. demand curve for the factor shifting leftward along an elastic supply curve.
    b. demand curve for the factor shifting rightward along an elastic supply curve
    c. demand curve for the factor shifting leftward along an inelastic supply curve.
    d. None of the above because this can never happen since higher factor prices decrease the quantity of the factor firms demand.

Short Answer Problems

1. Why isn't the factor price for capital the price of the specific pieces of capital equipment that the firm buys?
2. Why does the supply curve of labor bend backward? In your answer, be sure to discuss the role played by the substitution and income effects.
3. In Boca Raton, Florida, land prices are extremely high. So, too, is the price of a condominium. Are land prices high because condominium prices are high, or are condominium prices high because land prices are high?
4. Table 14.1 shows part of the marginal product of labor schedule for Christopher's Cookies, a perfectly competitive store owned by Christopher that, unsurprisingly, sells cookies.
    a. Based on Table 14.1, if Christopher can sell a cookie for $1.00, complete the first *MRP* column of Table 14.2.
    b. If Christopher must pay workers $6 an hour, how many workers does Christopher hire? If the wage rate rises to $11 an hour, how many workers will Christopher employ?

Table 14.1 Christopher's Cookies

Quantity of labor (*L*)	Quantity of cookies per hour (*Q*)	Marginal product of labor (*MP*)
3	550	
		30
4	580	
		10
5	590	
		5
6	595	
		2
7	597	

Table 14.2 Christopher's Marginal Revenue Product

	Cookies @ $1.00	Cookies @ $1.50
Quantity of labor (*L*)	Marginal revenue product (*MRP*)	Marginal revenue product (*MRP*)
3		
	___	___
4		
	___	___
5		
	___	___
6		
	___	___
7		

    c. Now suppose that the price of a cookie rises to $1.50. Complete the second *MRP* column in Table 14.2.
    d. If Christopher must pay workers $6 an hour, how many workers does Christopher hire now? If the wage rate rises to $11 an hour, how many does he hire?
    e. In Figure 14.3 (on the next page), draw Christopher's demand curve for labor when the price of a cookie is $1.00 and when the price is $1.50. How does the rise in the price of a cookie affect Christopher's demand for labor?

FIGURE 14.3
Short Answer Problem 4 (e)

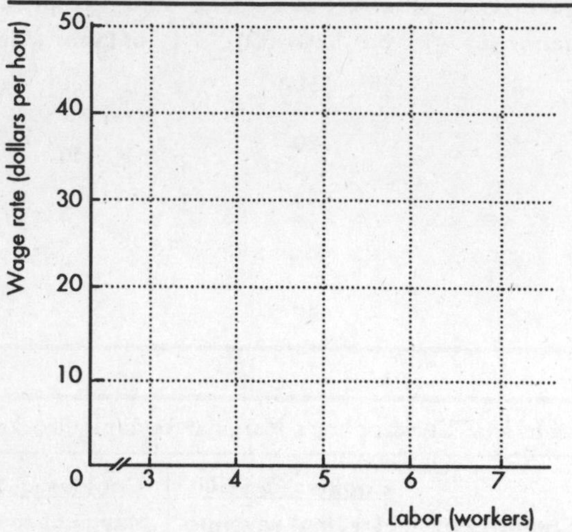

FIGURE 14.4
Short Answer Problem 6

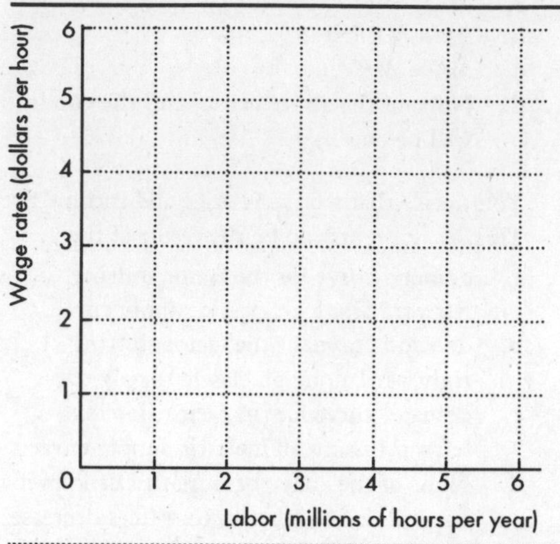

5. Suppose that a new shopping center on the outskirts of town raises the *MRP* of the surrounding land. What happens to the rental rate for this land? Does the land's *economic* rent rise or fall? Does its transfer earnings rise or fall? Draw a diagram to help explain your answers.

Table 14.3 Labor Demand and Supply

Wage rate (dollars per hour)	Quantity of labor demanded (millions of hours)	Quantity of labor supplied (millions of hours)
$0	4.5	0.0
1	4.0	1.0
2	3.5	2.0
3	3.0	3.0
4	2.5	4.0
5	2.0	5.0
6	1.5	6.0

6. The demand and supply schedules for labor in a developing nation are given in Table 14.3.

 a. Draw the demand and supply curves in Figure 14.4. What is the equilibrium wage? The equilibrium quantity of employment?

 b. What is the total income earned by these workers? Show the total income earned in your figure. How much of the total income is transfer earnings? How much is economic rent?

Table 14.4 The Market for Capital

Interest rate	Short-run quantity of capital supplied (billions)	Long-run quantity of capital supplied (billions)	Quantity of capital demanded (billions)
1%	$1000	$900	$1100
2	1000	950	1050
3	1000	1000	1000
4	1000	1050	950
5	1000	1100	900

7. The short-run and long-run supply schedules for capital and the demand schedule for capital is given in Table 14.4.

 a. What is the equilibrium interest rate? The equilibrium quantity of capital?

 b. Owing to technological change that increases the marginal product of capital, the demand schedule for capital increases so that, at every interest rate, firms now demand $100 billion more capital than shown in Table 14.4. What is the new short-run equilibrium interest rate? The new short-run quantity of capital?

c. After the increase in demand, what is the long-run equilibrium interest rate? The long-run equilibrium quantity of capital?

d. When is the supply curve more elastic: In the short run or the long run? When is the change in the interest rate the largest: In the short run or the long run? Is the change in quantity largest in the short run or long run?

8. In the short run, what effect does a lower price have on the quantity of output that a perfectly competitive firm produces? What effect does it have on the quantity of employment? (In both cases, assume that the firm does not shut down.) How do these two effects correspond?

You're the Teacher

1. "I really don't get the whole idea about the supply of labor. People don't have a choice about how much labor to supply: Once you get out of school, you either work 40 hours a week or you don't work. But the book talks like people got a choice about how many hours to work. That really seems silly." While your friend is laughing, take a moment to explain why the idea of a "supply of labor" is perhaps not as funny as it seems to your friend.

Answers

True/False Answers

1. **T** The firm's demand curve for any factor of production is the same as the factor's *MRP* curve.
2. **F** The wage rate rises, but the equilibrium quantity of labor decreases.
3. **F** The greater the labor intensity, the larger is the proportion of the costs accounted for by labor, which increases the elasticity of the demand for labor.
4. **T** When the supply curve shifts rightward, the factor's price falls.
5. **U** This depends on the elasticity of demand: If demand is elastic, total income rises but, if demand is inelastic, total income falls.
6. **F** The aggregate supply of land is perfectly inelastic, not perfectly elastic.
7. **F** The supply curve bends back when the income effect — which encourages an increase in nonmarket activities and hence a reduction in the quantity of labor supplied — is larger than the substitution effect.
8. **F** Data show that a rise in the interest rate has a small positive effect on the amount of saving.
9. **T** Economic rent is the difference between how much an input (Pearl Jam) receives minus the amount that is just enough to have the factor supplied.
10. **T** This condition is analogous to the profit-maximization requirement that a firm produce the level of output that gives $MR = MC$.
11. **F** The household supplies labor whenever the wage rate exceeds its reservation wage.
12. **F** If the supply of a factor decreases and demand is elastic, the factor's price rises and its total income falls.
13. **T** In the short run, the supply of capital may be close to perfectly inelastic.
14. **F** Any factor earns economic rent as long as its supply is not perfectly elastic.

Multiple Choice Answers

1. **b** A higher wage rate has an income effect that motivates a decrease in the quantity of labor supplied and a substitution effect that encourages an increase in the quantity of labor supplied.
2. **b** The increase in supply lowers the factor's price and, if demand is inelastic, does not increase the quantity employed by proportionally as much as the price falls. Hence the total income paid to the factor decreases.
3. **c** The demand curve for labor and the *MRP* curve are the same for perfectly competitive and monopoly firms.
4. **c** The more inelastic the supply of a factor, the larger is the proportion of its income that is economic rent.
5. **a** A higher interest rate has a small, positive effect on saving.
6. **c** This is the definition of the reservation wage.
7. **d** The demand curve is the same as the firm's *MRP* curve. Marginal revenue product for a perfectly competitive firm equals $P \times MP$, so the fall in price decreases the demand curve for labor.
8. **d** This is the definition of economic rent. Note that it says nothing specifically about land; any factor of production can receive economic rent.
9. **d** A firm in a perfectly competitive labor market can hire whatever amount of labor it wants at the going wage rate.
10. **c** As labor accounts for a greater proportion of a firm's total cost, the firm's demand for labor becomes more elastic.
11. **c** The demand for any input is derived from the final product that the input helps produce.
12. **d** The demand for orange pickers equals their *MRP* and the drop in the price and *MR* of oranges reduces the pickers' *MRP*.
13. **d** This is the definition of the marginal revenue product of capital.
14. **a** The worker will add to the firm's total profit (because of the additional revenue, the *MRP* exceeds the additional cost) and should be hired.

15. **b** Transfer income is the amount necessary to have the factor supplied, namely, $2,000.

16. **c** Economic rent is the difference between the factor's total income ($2,400) and its transfer earnings ($2,000).

17. **d** In the short run, the supply may be perfectly inelastic but it becomes more elastic in the long run.

18. **a** When the marginal product diminishes rapidly, the demand for labor is inelastic because even a small change in the quantity of labor employed has a large effect on the marginal product.

19. **a** When the supply is elastic, an increase in demand causes a small rise in the factor price and a large increase in the quantity, as illustrated in Figure 14.5.

FIGURE **14.5**
Multiple Choice Question 19

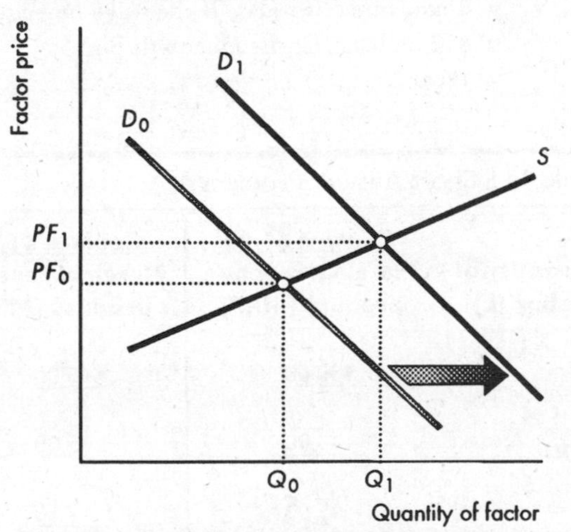

20. **b** The *MRP* of labor curve shows how many workers a firm hires for any wage rate, which means that it is the same as the firm's demand curve for labor.

21. **d** Oil refining companies substitute capital for labor.

22. **a** The *MRP* equals the added output produced by a factor (the factor's *MP*) times the amount of added revenue (the *MR*) that this output returns.

23. **a** By raising the marginal product from hiring workers, firms respond by increasing their demand for workers.

24. **b** If any factor has a perfectly inelastic supply curve, all its income is economic rent.

25. **c** By increasing the opportunity cost of nonmarket activity, the substitution effect of a higher wage rate encourages households to substitute away from these activities and toward supplying labor.

26. **b** By raising a household's income, the income effect of a higher wage rate encourages a household to "buy" more normal goods, such as nonmarket activity, and thereby decrease its labor supply.

27. **b** High *MRP* means a high demand curve; low supply means a low supply curve. Both raise the factor's price.

28. **c** The supply curve of capital is neither perfectly elastic nor perfectly inelastic, so capital receives both transfer income and economic rent.

29. **c** *MC* does not equal *MRP* when a firm maximizes its profit.

30. **b** Regardless of whether the supply is elastic or inelastic, an increase in demand raises both a factor's price and its total income.

■ Answers to Short Answer Problems

1. Factor prices represent the opportunity cost to the firm of using that factor of production. Wages are the cost of using labor, and rent is the cost of using land. The cost of using a piece of capital equipment bought by the firm is the interest that must be paid (explicitly or implicitly) on the funds tied up in the purchase of the equipment. Capital equipment lasts for a long period of time. The cost of capital during any one period is not the purchase price of the equipment. Rather, it is the cost of the funds tied up in the equipment over the period, that is, the interest rate.

FIGURE 14.6
Short Answer Problem 2

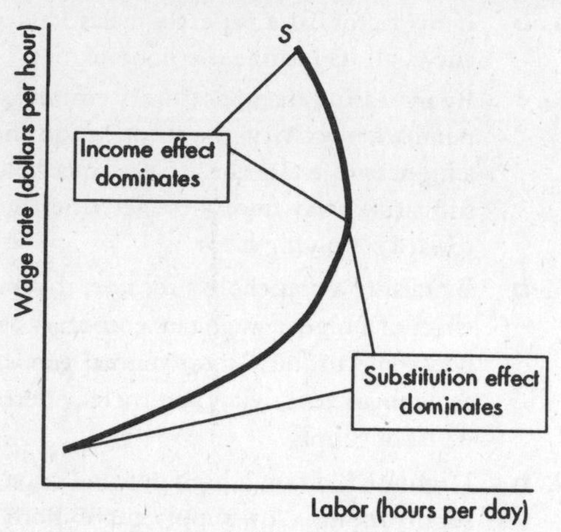

2. Suppose that the wage rate rises. As a result, the opportunity cost of leisure increases so households have a tendency to shift from leisure to work. This shift is the substitution effect, which encourages an increase in the quantity of labor supplied. The higher wage rate also increases the household's income and thus causes the household to increase its demand for leisure and other normal goods. This result is the income effect, which encourages a decrease in the quantity of labor supplied. As Figure 14.6 illustrates, at low wage rates, the substitution effect dominates the income effect, so the supply curve of labor slopes upward. At high wage rates, the income effect is larger and the supply curve of labor bends backward.
3. Although this may seem like a "chicken and egg" problem, actually land prices are high because condominium prices are high. Land is a necessary input into the production of condominiums, so the demand for land is derived from the demand for the final product, condominiums. The demand for condominiums in Boca Raton is quite high because of the attributes of the area. Hence the high demand for condominiums means that the price of a condominium is high. As a result, the *MRP* of land used to produce condominiums is high, which causes the price of land to be high. If the demand to live in Boca Raton decreased, the price of a condominium would fall and this would cause the price of land to drop.
4. a. Table 14.5 has the completed marginal revenue product. To calculate these answers, recall that the marginal revenue product equals marginal revenue times the marginal product; that is, $MRP = MR \times MP$. Because Christopher's Cookies is a perfect competitor, $MR = P$. Thus, $MR = \$1.00$. Using this value, the *MRP* between 3 and 4 workers is (\$1.00)(30), or \$30. The rest of the marginal revenue product schedule is computed in the same way.

   b. If the wage rate is \$6 an hour, Christopher will hire 5 workers. Hiring a sixth worker is not profitable because that worker costs \$6 an hour but contributes only \$5 an hour in revenue. If the wage rate rises to \$11 an hour, Christopher will hire 4 workers.

   c. The *MRP*s are calculated the same way as outlined for part (a), using a *MR* of \$1.50 per cookie rather than \$1.00.

   d. At a wage rate of \$6 an hour, Christopher will now hire 6 workers. If the wage rate rises to \$11 an hour, Christopher will hire 5 workers.

Table 14.5 Short Answer Problem 4

Quantity of labor (*L*)	Cookies \$1.00 Marginal revenue product (*MRP*)	Cookies \$1.50 Marginal revenue product (*MRP*)
3		
	\$30.00	\$45.00
4		
	10.00	15.00
5		
	5.00	7.50
6		
	2.00	3.00
7		

FIGURE 14.7
Short Answer Problem 4 (e)

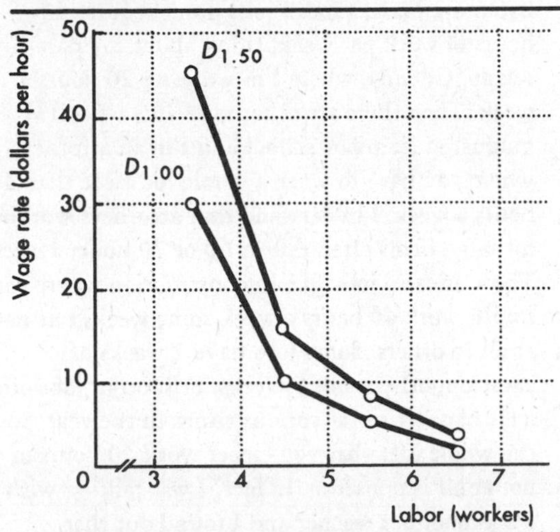

FIGURE 14.8
Short Answer Problem 5

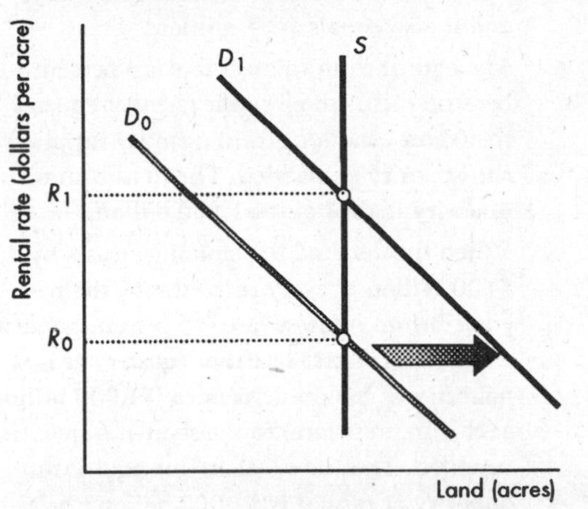

e. The demand curves for labor are the same as the marginal revenue product schedules. Figure 14.7 shows both demand curves. The demand curve when cookies are $1.00 is labeled $D_{1.00}$ and when cookies are $1.50 is labeled $D_{1.50}$. The rise in the price (and marginal revenue) of a cookie shifts Christopher's demand curve for labor rightward.

5. Figure 14.8 illustrates how the increase in the *MRP* affects the rental rate on this land. The supply of land is perfectly inelastic, so the supply curve is vertical. Then, the increase in the *MRP* shifts the demand curve from D_0 to D_1. As a result, the rental rate rises from R_0 to R_1. Because the supply is perfectly inelastic, *all* the income is economic rent. Hence all the rise in income is a rise in economic rent. There is no transfer income, so none of the rise is transfer income.

6. a. Figure 14.9 plots the demand and supply schedules. The equilibrium wage rate is $3 an hour, and the equilibrium quantity of employment is 3.0 million hours.

b. Workers are paid a wage rate, *W*, of $3 an hour. Employment, *L*, in aggregate is 3.0 million hours. The total income earned by all the workers is the wage rate times the hours employed, or $W \times L$, or $9.0 million. In Figure 14.9, the total income is the area of

FIGURE 14.9
Short Answer Problem 6

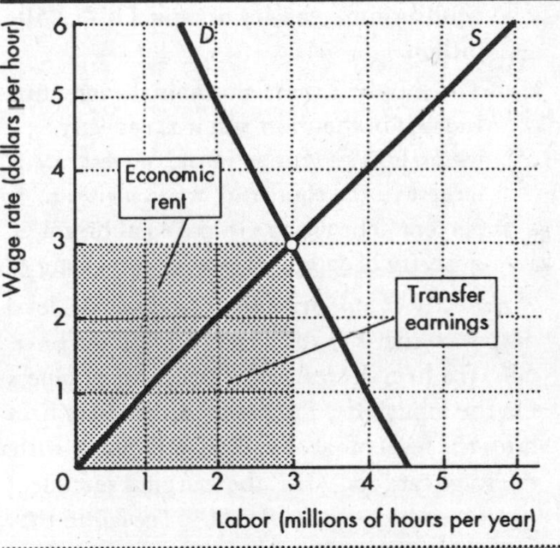

the shaded rectangle. The transfer earnings are the area of the shaded triangle below the supply curve of labor, and the economic rent is the area of the shaded triangle above the supply curve of labor.

Thus, to calculate the amount of transfer earnings, calculate the area of its triangle, or ½ times the base times the height. The base is 3.0 million hours and the height is $3.

Thus the area is $(\frac{1}{2})$(3.0 million hours)(\$3) so that transfer earnings equal \$4.5 million. Economic rent can be calculated similarly, and it also equals \$4.5 million.

7. a. The equilibrium interest rate is 3 percent because this is the interest rate that equates the (short- and long-run) quantity supplied to the quantity demanded. The equilibrium quantity of capital is \$1,000 billion.

   b. When the demand for capital increases by \$100 billion at every interest rate, the new equilibrium interest rate is 5 percent because this is the interest rate that equates the new quantity of capital demanded (\$1,000 billion at this interest rate) to the short-run quantity supplied. The "new " short-run equilibrium quantity of capital is \$1,000 billion, the same as the initial quantity.

   c. The long-run equilibrium interest rate is 4 percent. At this interest rate the new quantity demanded of \$1,050 billion equals the long-run quantity supplied. Hence the long-run equilibrium quantity of capital is \$1,050 billion.

   d. The supply is more elastic in the long run. Indeed, in the short run it is perfectly inelastic. The change in the interest rate is largest in the short run, when it rises to 5 percent. The change in the equilibrium quantity of capital is largest in the long run.

8. A perfectly competitive firm produces the level of output so that $P = MC$. Hence, when the price falls, the firm decreases the amount it produces. On the input side, a perfectly competitive firm hires the level of labor so that $W = MRP$, with W the wage rate and MRP the marginal revenue product, which equals $P \times MP$. The fall in the price lowers the MRP and, as a result, the firm decreases its level of employment

   These two effects — reducing output and reducing employment — correspond perfectly. If the firm produces less output, it needs less employment, and if the firm has less employment, it can produce less output.

■ You're the Teacher

1. "You're missing the point, so quit laughing and listen up. First, a lot of jobs don't require 40 hours of work per week; think about my part-time job at JCPenny, where I'm working 20 hours a week. Then there are other jobs, like when I've graduated from law school and I'm an attorney, where you have to work a whole lot more than 40 hours a week. I understand that attorneys working for large firms often put in 60 or 70 hours a week! There are also jobs like in construction where you might work 40 hours a week some weeks but not at all in others. Some jobs have 2 weeks of vacation, others 4 or 5 weeks. Still other jobs offer a lot of overtime at various times in the year. So the whole idea that you either work 40 hours or not at all is nonsense. In fact, I was talking with our economics teacher and I found out that nowadays the average person in the United States works about 34 hours a week! So, it makes sense to think about a supply of labor because people can decide what sort of jobs they want to look for and can decide how many hours they will be putting in at work."

Chapter 15 LABOR MARKETS

Key Concepts

Skill Differentials

Differences in wages and earnings can be a result of skill differentials. High-skilled labor has higher wages and earnings because:

- Demand — high-skilled labor has a higher marginal revenue product than low-skilled labor, so the demand for high-skilled labor is higher.
- Supply — skills are costly to acquire, so the supply of high-skilled labor is less than that of low-skilled labor; **human capital** is the skills and knowledge of human beings.

Union–Nonunion Wage Differentials

A **labor union** is an organized group of workers:

- **Craft union** — a group of workers with similar skills working for different companies.
- **Industrial union** — a group of workers with different skills working in the same industry or firm.

Unions' objectives for their members include increasing compensation, improving working conditions, and expanding job opportunities. Methods of achieving these objectives include:

- restricting the supply of labor.
- raising the demand for union labor and/or making it more inelastic.

Unions try to increase the demand for their members' labor by encouraging import restrictions, supporting minimum wage laws and immigration restrictions, increasing the demand for the product produced, and raising the marginal product of their members.

Unions can have the following effects:

- In unionized markets, the increased demand and decreased supply raise union members' wages and incomes.
- In nonunionized markets, the supply of labor increases, and so the wage rate falls.

After allowing for differences in skills, the union–nonunion wage differential is between 10 and 25 percent.

A **monopsony** is a market structure in which there is a single buyer. A firm that is the only employer in town is a monopsonist in the labor market.

- To hire more labor, a monopsonist must pay a higher wage. As illustrated in Figure 15.1, the marginal cost of labor curve (*MCL*) for the monopsonist slopes upward and lies above the market supply curve (*S*) of labor.

FIGURE **15.1**
A Monopsonist

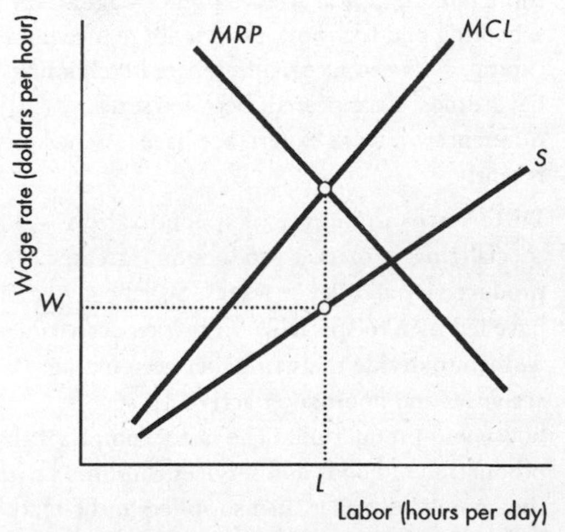

The profit-maximizing rule for a monopsonist is to (1) hire the quantity of labor indicated by the intersection of the *MCL* curve and the *MRP* curve, and (2) then use the supply curve of labor to offer the lowest wage rate possible that allows it to hire the quantity of labor it wants. Figure 15.1 shows that the monopsonist hires *L* and pays *W*.

- With a monopsonist, employment and the wage rate are lower than in a competitive labor market.
- A minimum wage law can affect the outcome in a monopsony market. The minimum wage makes the *MCL* curve perfectly elastic at the minimum wage. In response, the monopsonist hires more labor and pays a higher wage rate.
- If the monopsonist faces a union, the labor market is characterized as a **bilateral monopoly**. In this case the wage rate is determined by the relative bargaining strengths of the firm and the union.

■ Wage Differentials Between Sexes and Races

The positive analysis of why wages differ between sexes and races focuses on four factors:

- **Job types** — jobs historically dominated by white males have paid more than jobs dominated by others. This factor is diminishing in importance.
- **Discrimination** — those discriminated against receive lower wages and are employed less than others.
- **Differences in human capital** — workers with more human capital receive higher wages. Less schooling and less work experience reduce human capital. Between races, differences in schooling have almost disappeared; between sexes, differences in work experience have lessened recently.
- **Differences in degree of specialization** — specializing in market production increases productivity and hence wages. Social conventions have led men to specialize in market activities and women to divide their time between market activities and nonmarket activities, such as household production. (The latter comprises the production of goods and services consumed within the household rather than supplied to the market.) Never-married men and women, who have similar degrees of market specialization, have wage rates that are more nearly equal than those of men and women in the work force generally.

After allowing for observed differences in human capital and specialization, the male/female wage differential is between 5 and 10 percent.

■ Comparable-Worth Laws

Comparable-worth laws require wage rates to be determined by assessing the value of jobs in terms of objective characteristics rather than what the market will pay. The goal is equal pay for work of equal value. Comparable-worth laws have unintended consequences:

- In markets having a market wage higher than the comparable-worth wage, shortages of labor occur.
- In markets having a market wage lower than the comparable-worth wage, unemployment results. Unemployed workers eventually have to move to other markets to find employment.

Helpful Hints

1. This chapter introduces the concept of a monopsonist, a firm that is the only buyer in a market, such as labor. The monopsonist faces an upward-sloping supply curve of labor. As a result, its marginal cost of labor curve, *MCL*, is different from the labor supply curve.

   There is a close parallel between (a) the relationship between the labor supply curve and the *MCL* curve for the monopsonist and (b) the already familiar relationship (Chapter 12) between the demand curve and the marginal revenue curve, *MR*, for the monopolist. Both sets of relationships stem from the assumption of market power; that is, a monopsony determines the wage it pays and a monopoly determines the price it charges.

   The monopolist, as the only seller in an output market, faces a downward-sloping demand curve. The marginal revenue from the sale of an additional unit of output is less than the selling price because the monopolist must lower the price on all previous units as well. Thus the *MR* curve lies below the demand curve for the single-price monopolist.

   For the monopsonist in a labor market, the marginal cost of hiring an additional unit of labor is higher than the wage because the monopsonist must also raise the wage on all previous units of labor. Thus the *MCL* curve lies above the supply curve of labor for the monopsonist.

2. Both monopolies and monopsonies cause allocative inefficiency. And both create this inefficiency for essentially the same reason: Relative to a perfectly

competitive firm and industry, monopolies and monopsonies exploit their market power by restricting their output. Recall from Chapter 12 that a single-price monopoly produces less than a perfectly competitive firm with comparable costs. This chapter describes a similar result for a monopsonist. In particular, compared to a perfectly competitive firm a monopsony hires less labor. Because it hires less labor, it produces less output than a perfectly competitive firm. The amount of output that a perfectly competitive firm produces is allocatively efficient. Hence, by producing less, a monopsony — like a monopoly — causes allocative inefficiency.

Questions

True/False/Uncertain and Explain

1. The marginal revenue product of low-skilled workers is lower than that of high-skilled workers.

2. The demand for low-skilled workers is less than that for high-skilled workers

3. A monopsonist pays a higher wage rate than would a perfectly competitive firm.

4. Unions try to improve the working conditions for their members.

5. If males on average earn more than females, there is discrimination.

6. A closed shop refers to a firm that is not operating because its workers are on strike.

7. Most union members earn about 50 percent more than nonunion members in comparable jobs.

8. Human capital refers to capital equipment that has been constructed by human workers.

9. Comparable-worth laws can create unemployment in some markets.

10. For a monopsony, the marginal cost of hiring another worker is less than the wage it must pay.

11. Minimum wage laws lower employment.

12. Unions support minimum wage laws in part because they raise the cost of low-skilled labor, a substitute for high-skilled union labor.

13. Monopsonists determine the amount of labor they hire by where the *MCL* curve crosses the labor supply curve.

14. Comparable-worth laws advocate that wages should be determined by comparable market wages.

Multiple Choice

1. Which of the following is <u>NOT</u> a reason why the wage of high-skilled workers exceeds the wage of low-skilled workers?
   a. The market for high-skilled workers is more competitive than the market for low-skilled labor.
   b. The marginal revenue product of high-skilled workers is greater than that of low-skilled workers.
   c. The cost of becoming a high-skilled worker is greater than the cost of becoming a low-skilled worker.
   d. High-skilled workers have acquired more human capital than low-skilled workers.

2. For a monopsony, the *MCL* curve
   a. lies above the labor supply curve.
   b. is the same as the labor supply curve.
   c. lies below the labor supply curve.
   d. is the same as the labor demand curve.

3. Unions attempt to do all of the following except
   a. increase the demand for their members' labor.
   b. decrease the supply of labor in their market.
   c. make the demand for their members' labor more elastic.
   d. raise the wage paid their members.

Use Figure 15.2 for the next four questions.

FIGURE **15.2**

Multiple Choice Questions 4, 5, 6, and 7

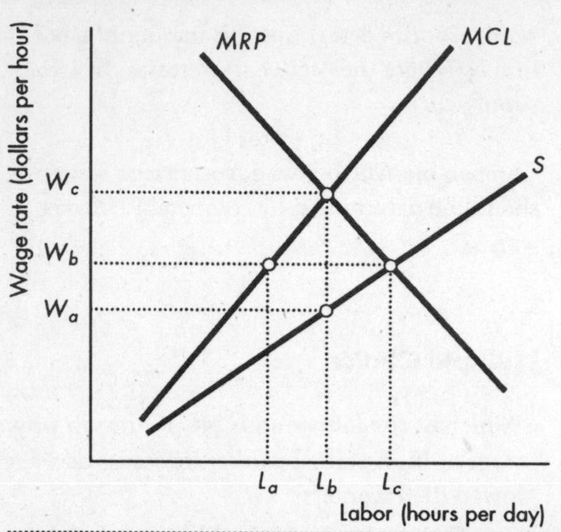

4. If Figure 15.2 illustrates a monopsony industry, the level of employment is
   a. L_a.
   b. L_b.
   c. L_c.
   d. None of the above.

5. If Figure 15.2 illustrates a monopsony industry, the wage rate is
   a. W_a.
   b. W_b.
   c. W_c.
   d. None of the above.

6. If Figure 15.2 illustrates a perfectly competitive labor market, the level of employment is
   a. L_a.
   b. L_b.
   c. L_c.
   d. None of the above.

7. If Figure 15.2 illustrates a perfectly competitive labor market, the wage rate is
   a. W_a.
   b. W_b.
   c. W_c.
   d. None of the above

8. On average, which group receives the highest wage?
   a. White males.
   b. White females.
   c. Black males.
   d. Black females.

9. Which of the following would unions be least likely to support?
   a. Increasing the legal minimum wage.
   b. Restricting immigration.
   c. Encouraging imports.
   d. Increasing demand for the goods that their workers produce.

10. An arrangement in which workers can be employed without joining a union is a (an)
    a. non-union shop.
    b. union shop.
    c. closed shop.
    d. open shop.

11. A bilateral monopoly occurs when a
    a. group of unorganized firms bargain with a group of unorganized workers.
    b. single monopsonist firm bargains with a group of unorganized workers.
    c. group of unorganized firms bargains with a union representing the workers.
    d. monopsonist bargains with a union representing the workers.

12. Which of the following is NOT a potential reason for wage differences by race or sex?
    a. Discrimination.
    b. Differences in human capital.
    c. Differences in the degree of specialization.
    d. All of the above are potential reasons for wage differences by race or sex.

13. A craft union comprises a group of workers who work at
    a. different jobs for the same company or in the same industry.
    b. the same job in different companies or industries.
    c. different jobs in different industries.
    d. craft stores.

14. With competitive labor markets, unions
    a. lower wage rates and decrease employment in unionized markets.
    b. lower wage rates and increase employment in unionized markets.
    c. raise wage rates and decrease employment in unionized markets.
    d. raise wage rates and increase employment in unionized markets.

15. With competitive labor markets, unions
    a. lower wage rates and decrease employment in nonunionized markets.
    b. lower wage rates and increase employment in nonunionized markets.
    c. raise wage rates and decrease employment in nonunionized markets.
    d. raise wage rates and increase employment in nonunionized markets.

16. The higher the cost of acquiring skills, the
    a. closer the demand curve for high-skilled labor is to the demand curve for low-skilled labor.
    b. farther the demand curve for high-skilled labor is from the demand curve for low-skilled labor.
    c. closer the supply curve of high-skilled labor is to the supply curve for low-skilled labor.
    d. farther the supply curve of high-skilled labor is from the supply curve for low-skilled labor

17. A union comprising a group of workers who work at different jobs in the same company is a (an)
    a. craft union.
    b. open union.
    c. shop union.
    d. industrial union.

18. A minimum wage may cause a monopsonist to
    a. lower its wage rate and lower its level of employment.
    b. increase employment.
    c. lower its wage rate and increase its level of employment.
    d. None of the above.

19. Comparable-worth laws do all of the following except
    a. create unemployment in some job markets.
    b. create shortages in some job markets.
    c. determine wages by using objective job characteristics.
    d. increase employment in jobs with low market wages.

20. Comparing the wage rates between never-married men and women, researchers have found that they are
    a. farther apart than the wage rates of other men and women in the labor force generally.
    b. the same as wage rates of other men and women in the labor force generally.
    c. closer together than the wage rates of other men and women in the labor force generally.
    d. not comparable because men and women work at different jobs.

21. In order to hire an additional worker, a monopsonist must pay
    a. a higher wage rate than it paid before.
    b. the same wage rate it paid before.
    c. a lower wage rate than it paid before.
    d. a wage rate that is sometimes higher, sometimes lower, and sometimes the same as before, depending on its supply curve of labor.

For the next two questions, suppose that the market wage of police is higher than the market wage of librarians. A comparable-worth law is passed and these two occupations are deemed to have the same worth. As a result, the wage rate paid librarians is raised and the wage rate paid police is lowered until the two wage rates are equal.

22. After the comparable-worth changes have occurred, there is a
    a. shortage of librarians and more people will become librarians.
    b. shortage of librarians and the wage rate paid librarians will rise.
    c. surplus of librarians and some people will leave this profession.
    d. surplus of librarians and the wage rate paid librarians will fall.

23. After the comparable-worth changes have occurred, there is a
    a. shortage in the market for police.
    b. shortage of police and the wage rate paid police will rise.
    c. surplus of police and some people will leave this profession.
    d. surplus of police and the wage rate paid police will fall.

24. Suppose that the supply of low-skilled labor increases. As a result, if there is not a minimum wage, the wage rate paid to low-skilled labor
    a. rises.
    b. does not change.
    c. falls.
    d. perhaps changes, but whether it does depends on the demand for low-skilled labor.

25. A union successfully makes the demand for its members' labor more inelastic. After this change, how does a rise in the wage rate paid its members affect their employment?
    a. It has no effect on employment.
    b. It decreases employment by less than before.
    c. It decreases employment by more than before.
    d. It increases employment.

26. Consider two people: One specializes in market work, and the other switches from market to nonmarket work. Which of the following is true?
    a. The person who switches is likely to receive a higher wage rate because employers appreciate the versatility.
    b. The person who specializes in market work is likely to receive a higher wage rate because specialization increases productivity.
    c. Both workers are likely to receive the same wage rate because there is no difference in productivity nor versatility.
    d. The person who specializes in market work likely will receive a lower wage rate because his or her supply of labor is greater.

27. If a strike or lockout occurs in a bilateral monopoly situation, it usually is because the
    a. demand for labor is relatively inelastic.
    b. supply of labor is relatively inelastic.
    c. firm is not maximizing its profit.
    d. union or firm has misjudged the bargaining situation.

28. Compared to a perfectly competitive labor market, a monopsonist pays a
    a. higher wage rate and hires more workers.
    b. higher wage rate and hires fewer workers.
    c. lower wage rate and hires more workers.
    d. lower wage rate and hires fewer workers.

29. Which of the following will <u>NOT</u> increase a worker's human capital?
    a. More work experience.
    b. More training.
    c. More schooling.
    d. A higher wage rate.

Short Answer Problems

1. Most members of labor unions earn wages well above the minimum wage. Why, then, do unions support raising the legal minimum wage?

FIGURE **15.3**
Short Answer Problem 2

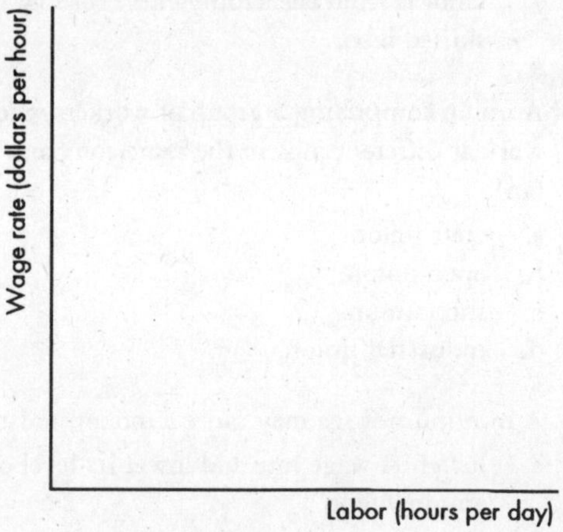

Wage rate (dollars per hour)

Labor (hours per day)

2. Some observers have suggested that reductions in transportation costs and tariffs imposed on goods imported into the United States have made U.S.

companies more likely to produce products manufactured with low-skilled labor in foreign nations. Essentially, this change means that the supply of low-skilled labor has increased. In Figure 15.3 (above), illustrate the effect that this increase in the supply of low-skilled labor has on the wage rate paid to low-skilled workers. How is the relative wage rates paid high-skilled and low-skilled workers affected?

3. Jason and Lisa form a household. They have decided that Lisa will specialize in market activity and Jason will pursue activities both in the job market and in the household. If most households are like Jason and Lisa's, what would be the result?
4. Table 15.1 shows the labor supply curve facing Mark's Mines, the only employer in a small (!) mining town.
   a. Calculate the values for the *MCL* column and complete the table.
   b. Plot the labor demand, labor supply, and *MCL* schedules in Figure 15.4.
   c. How many workers does Mark hire? What wage does Mark pay?
   d. Suppose Mark was a perfect competitor rather than a monopsonist. In this case, how many workers would Mark hire and what wage would he pay them?

Table 15.1 Mark's Mining Monopsony

Wage rate (dollars per hour)	Labor demand (workers)	Labor supply (workers)	Marginal cost of labor, *MCL* (dollars per hour)
$2	10	2	
			___
3	9	3	
			___
4	8	4	
			___
5	7	5	
			___
6	6	6	
			___
7	5	7	
			___
8	4	8	
			___
9	3	9	

FIGURE 15.4
Short Answer Problem 4 (b)

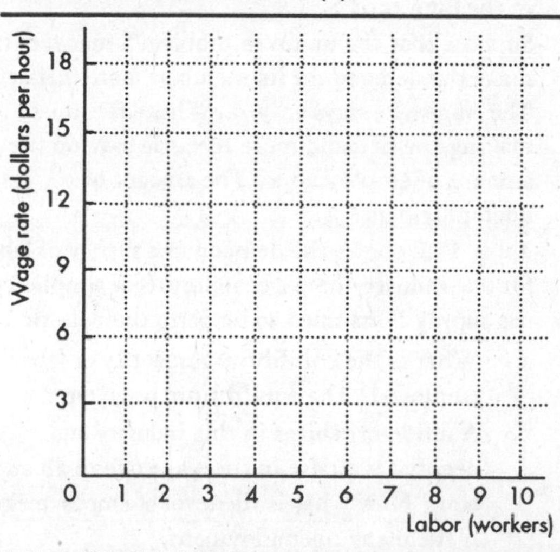

   e. How does the wage rate that Mark pays when he is a monopsonist compare with the wage rate he would pay if he were a perfect competitor? How does the number of workers he hires compare in the two cases?

5. Figure 15.5 shows a competitive labor market. The initial equilibrium wage rate is *W*, and the level of employment is *L*. Suppose that a union organizes and raises the wage rate to W_U. In the figure, illustrate what happens to the level of

FIGURE 15.5
Short Answer Problem 5

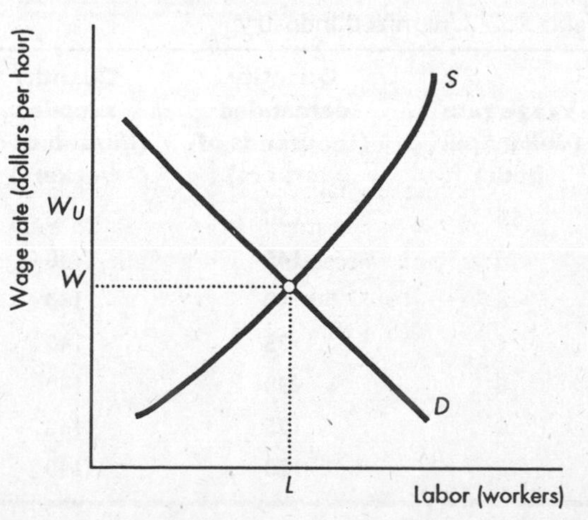

employment. Label the new level of employment L_U. Is there any unemployment? What happens in the long run?

6. Suppose that the union in problem 5 manages to make the demand for its members more inelastic. The wage rate stays at W_U. What effect does making the demand more inelastic have on the amount of employment? The amount of unemployment?
7. Table 15.2 shows the demand and supply of labor for one industry in the economy. (For simplicity, the supply is assumed to be perfectly inelastic.)
   a. What is the equilibrium quantity of labor employed? The equilibrium wage rate?
   b. A union organizes in this industry and negotiates a raise in the wage rate to $8 an hour. Now what is the level of employment? Is there any unemployment?
   c. After the union negotiates the higher wage rate, workers who cannot find employment leave the first industry and switch to a second. The initial labor demand and supply schedules for the second industry are shown in Table 15.3. Complete the table showing the new quantity of labor supplied.
   d. Based on Table 15.3, before the first industry became unionized, what was the equilibrium wage rate in the second industry? After the first industry was unionized, what is the equilibrium wage rate in the second industry?
   e. What is the union–nonunion wage differential between the two industries?

Table 15.2 Unionized Industry

Wage rate (dollars per hour)	Quantity demanded (thousands of workers)	Quantity supplied (thousands of workers)
$4	150	140
5	145	140
6	140	140
7	135	140
8	130	140
9	125	140
10	120	140

Table 15.3 Nonunionized Industry

Wage rate (dollars per hour)	Quantity demanded (thousands of workers)	Initial quantity supplied (thousands of workers)	New quantity supplied (thousands of workers)
$4	150	140	____
5	145	140	____
6	140	140	____
7	135	140	____
8	130	140	____
9	125	140	____
10	120	140	____

8. Industry A is a perfectly competitive industry that has no monopsony power in the input market. Industry B is a monopoly that has no monopsony power in the input market. Industry C is a monopoly in the output market and a monopsony in the input market. The marginal product of labor curves and the market demand curves are identical for all three industries. Which industry hires the most workers? Which hires the least? Why?

■ You're the Teacher

1. "I know that unions try to raise the wages paid their members, but I can't see how they lower wages paid to nonunion members. I mean, why would they want to do this?" Your friend is a bit confused about what unions do and what they want to do. Help set your friend straight by answering the question posed.
2. "Unions ought to be banned. After all, they're just monopolies operating in a labor market! And my bet is that somehow cause allocative inefficiency!" React to the student's statement and then explain how unions do, indeed, cause allocative inefficiency.

Answers

True/False Answers

1. **T** High-skilled workers can produce more products and products with higher prices than low-skilled workers, so the *MRP* of low-skilled workers is less that of high-skilled workers.
2. **T** The demand and *MRP* curves are identical. Then, because the *MRP* of low-skilled workers is less that of high-skilled workers, the demand for low-skilled workers necessarily is less than that of high-skilled workers.
3. **F** A monopsonist exploits its market power by paying a lower wage rate.
4. **T** The statement is one of the union's goals.
5. **U** There may be discrimination, but there are other possibilities — such as differences in the degree of specialization — that can account for wage differentials.
6. **F** A closed shop is a factory or business in which a worker must be a union member in order to work at a particular job.
7. **F** Union members earn about 10 to 25 percent more than nonunion members in comparable jobs.
8. **F** Human capital refers to skills and talents possessed by people.
9. **T** If comparable-worth laws raise wages for some jobs above levels determined by the market, unemployment results.
10. **F** The marginal cost of hiring another worker exceeds the wage rate that must be paid.
11. **U** If a minimum wage is imposed on a monopsony, employment might increase; otherwise, minimum wage laws cause lower employment.
12. **T** By raising the cost of substitute inputs, unions try to increase the demand for their members' labor.
13. **F** The level of employment is determined where the *MCL* curve crosses the *MRP* curve.
14. **F** Comparable-worth laws determine wages by setting equal wages in jobs with comparable characteristics.

Multiple Choice Answers

1. **a** The markets are likely to be equally competitive.

FIGURE 15.6
Multiple Choice Question 2

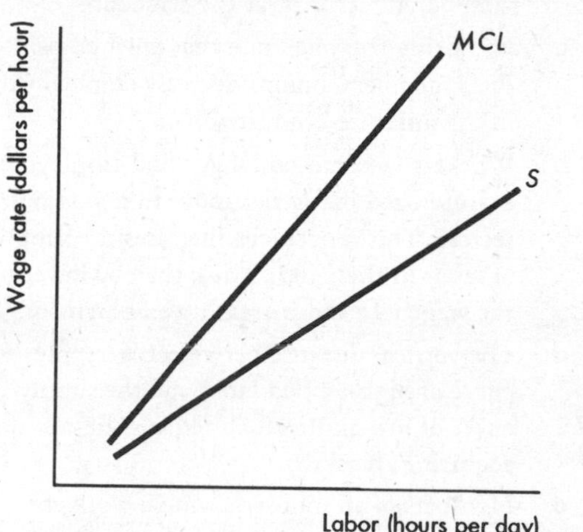

2. **a** As Figure 15.6 shows, the *MCL* curve is above the labor supply curve.
3. **c** Unions strive to make the demand for their members' labor more *inelastic*.
4. **b** A monopsonist determines the level of employment by setting the marginal cost of labor (the *MCL*) equal to the marginal revenue product of labor (the *MRP*).
5. **a** The monopsonist hires L_b labor. The supply curve indicates that the lowest wage rate it can pay and still hire this amount of labor is W_a.
6. **c** In a perfectly competitive labor market, the quantity of labor is determined by the intersection of the supply curve and demand curve, which is the same as the *MRP* curve.
7. **b** The last four answers show that a monopsonist pays a lower wage rate and hires fewer workers then in a perfectly competitive labor market.
8. **a** Compared to white males, other groups in the economy receive lower average wage rates.
9. **c** Imports are produced by foreign labor, which is a substitute for domestic, union labor. Hence unions try to *restrict* imports.

10. **d** Answer (d) defines an open shop.
11. **d** Bilateral monopoly occurs when both the demand side and supply side of a market are monopolies.
12. **d** All of these factors potentially can account for wage differentials.
13. **b** Craft unions join workers who work at the same "craft," that is, at the same job.
14. **c** By raising the wage rate that must be paid their members, unions decrease employment in the unionized industry.
15. **b** Workers who can no longer find employment in unionized industries move to nonunionized sectors. This movement increases the supply of labor in these industries, thereby lowering the wage rate and increasing employment.
16. **d** The vertical distance between the supply curve of high-skilled labor and the supply curve of low-skilled labor equals the cost of acquiring the skill.
17. **d** Members of an industrial union work at different jobs in the same industry or for the same company.
18. **b** In a competitive labor market, a minimum wage decreases employment, but it may increase employment in a labor market dominated by a monopsonist.
19. **d** By raising the wage rate in jobs with low market wages, firms decrease the quantity of employment in these jobs.
20. **c** Never-married men and never-married women have the same degree of specialization in market work, and as a result their wage rates are closer than those of men and women in the work force generally.
21. **a** Because the monopsonist must pay the higher wage to *all* the workers it employs, the marginal cost of hiring another worker exceeds the wage rate.
22. **c** The surplus results from the higher wage rate, as libraries decrease the quantity of librarians they demand. As a result, some unemployed, ex-librarians leave this labor market to search for employment elsewhere.
23. **a** The lower wage rate decreases the number of people willing to work as police.
24. **c** The increased supply lowers the wage rate of low-skilled labor.
25. **b** By making demand more inelastic, unions can achieve higher wage rates with less unemployment.
26. **b** Differences in specialization account for the some of the wage differential between men and women.
27. **d** By misjudging the situation, either the union or firm may make an offer that it does not realize will drive the other to close the company through a lockout or strike.
28. **d** A monopoly exploits its selling power by producing less and charging a higher price; a monopsonist exploits its buying power by buying less and paying a lower price.
29. **d** A higher wage rate is the result of an increase in human capital, not a cause.

Answers to Short Answer Problems

1. A rise in the minimum wage boosts the cost of hiring low-skilled labor. Low-skilled labor can substitute — to an extent — for high-skilled union labor. Hence the rise in the cost of low-skilled labor increases the demand for high-skilled labor and makes sustaining its higher wage easier for the union.

FIGURE **15.7**
Short Answer Problem 2

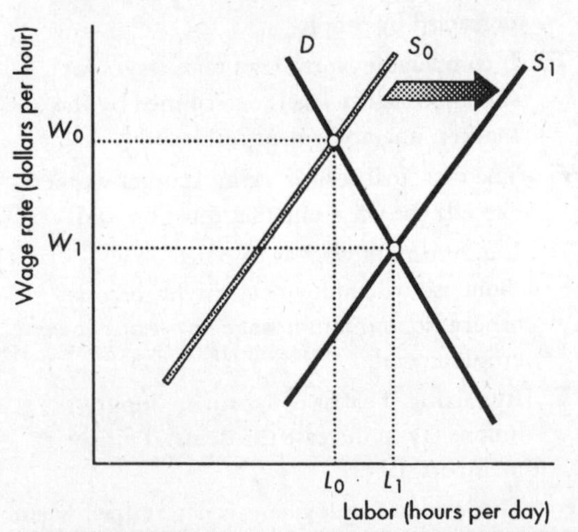

2. The increase in the supply of low-skilled workers shifts the supply curve rightward as shown in Figure 15.7, where the shift is from S_0 to S_1. As a

result, the wage rate falls from W_0 to W_1. The wage rates of high-skilled workers are not directly affected by this change, so the relative wage rate of high-skilled to low-skilled workers rises. Some analysts believe that the changes analyzed in this question have been occurring in the United States for the past decade or so.

3. If Lisa specializes in market activity while Jason is diversified, Lisa's earning ability is likely to exceed Jason's because of the gains from her specialization. If most households followed this pattern of specialization, the income of women would exceed that of men. This difference is the result of the gains from specialization: Lisa's productivity will be higher than Jason's and so Lisa's wage rate will exceed Jason's wage rate.

4. a. Table 15.4 shows the marginal cost of labor, *MCL*. To see how to calculate these values, consider the *MCL* between 2 and 3 workers. The marginal cost of labor equals $(\Delta \text{ total wages})/\Delta L$. Total wages equals the number of workers employed times the wage rate, so for 2 workers it is \$2 times 2 workers, or \$4. Thus the *MCL* between 2 and 3 workers is $(\$9 - \$4)/(3 - 2) = \$5$. The rest of the *MCLs* are calculated similarly.

   b. Figure 15.8 contains plots of the labor demand, labor supply, and *MCL* schedules.

   c. As Figure 15.8 illustrates, Mark hires 4 workers because employing this number of workers sets the marginal cost of labor equal to the marginal revenue product of labor. Expressed differently, this number of workers is the amount determined by the intersection of Mark's *MCL* curve and his demand curve for labor. The supply curve of labor shows that 4 workers will work for \$4 an hour; hence Mark pays a wage rate of \$4 an hour.

   d. If Mark's Mining was a perfectly competitive firm, the intersection of the demand curve for labor and the supply curve of labor would show the amount of labor he would employ. Figure 15.8 indicates that 6 workers would be the equilibrium level of employment and that the equilibrium wage rate would be \$6 an hour.

   e. Mark hires fewer workers and pays them a lower wage when he is a monopsonist.

Table 15.4 Short Answer Problem 4 (a)

Wage rate (dollars per hour)	Labor demand (workers)	Labor supply (workers)	Marginal cost of labor, *MCL* (dollars per hour)
\$2	10	2	
			\$5
3	9	3	
			7
4	8	4	
			9
5	7	5	
			11
6	6	6	
			13
7	5	7	
			15
8	4	8	
			17
9	3	9	

FIGURE 15.8

Short Answer Problem 4 (b)

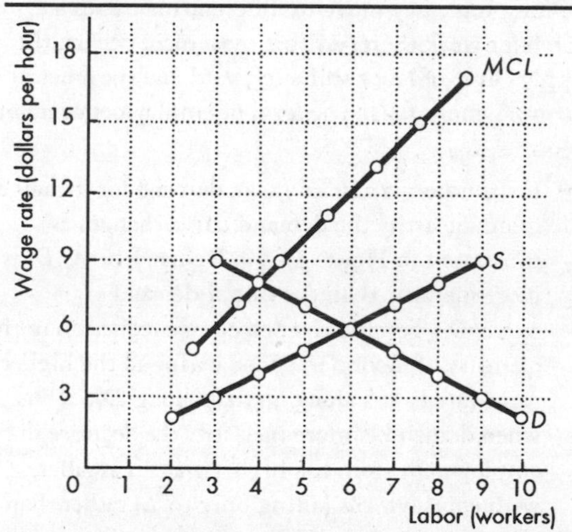

5. Figure 15.9 (on the next page) shows the union's effect on this labor market. After the rise in the wage to W_U, firms in the industry hire only L_U workers. Hence employment falls from L to L_U, and unemployment results. The amount of unemployment will depend on how many workers believe that they will find work at the wage rate W_U. The supply curve of labor shows that, at

FIGURE 15.9
Short Answer Problem 5

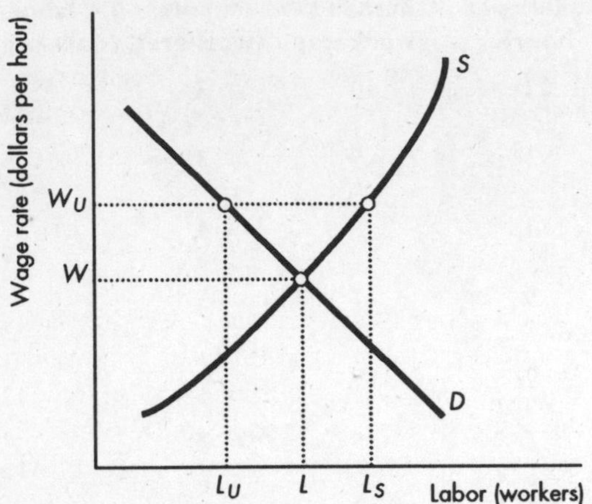

FIGURE 15.10
Short Answer Problem 6

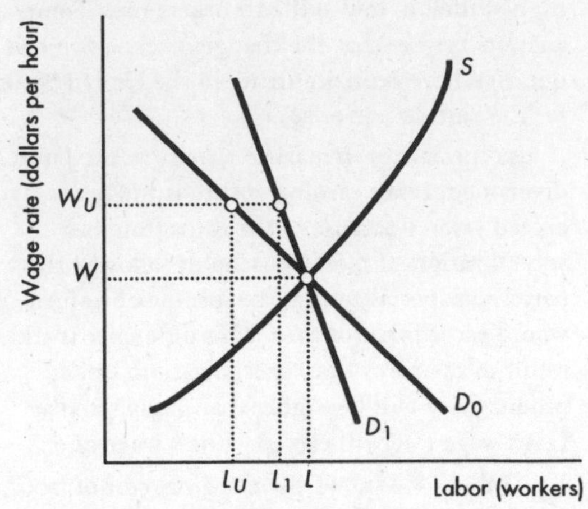

this wage rate, L_S workers supply labor. Hence there can be unemployment up to $L_S - L_U$. But, as time passes, some of the unemployed workers realize that they may never find jobs in this industry. Hence, in the long run, they move to different industries and search for work there. As this movement occurs, the supply curve of labor shifts leftward and the amount of unemployment falls. The level of employment remains the same, L_U.

6. If the union is able to make demand for its labor more inelastic, the demand curve changes as illustrated in Figure 15.10. Demand curve D_1 is more inelastic than the initial demand curve, D_0, because the percentage reduction in the quantity of labor demanded owing to the higher wage rate is less along D_1 than along D_0. Thus when demand is more inelastic, the decrease in employment from the higher wage is smaller, with employment falling only to L_1 rather than all the way to L_U. (The accompanying increase in unemployment from the higher wage also is smaller.) This answer demonstrates why unions strive to make the demand for their members' labor less elastic: It partly offsets the adverse employment effect from the higher union wage rate.

7. a. The equilibrium quantity of labor employed is 140,000 workers and the equilibrium wage rate is $6 an hour.

   b. Once the union negotiates a wage of $8, firms decrease the quantity of employment they demand to 130,000. Hence employment now equals 130,000. Unemployment equals the number of workers willing to work at $8 an hour (140,000) minus the number actually employed (130,000). Therefore unemployment equals 10,000.

Table 15.5 Nonunionized Industry

Wage rate (dollars per hour)	Quantity demanded (thousands of workers)	Initial quantity supplied (thousands of workers)	New quantity supplied (thousands of workers)
$4	150	140	150
5	145	140	150
6	140	140	150
7	135	140	150
8	130	140	150
9	125	140	150
10	120	140	150

   c. Table 15.5 shows the new situation in the nonunionized industry. The 10,000 unemployed workers who could no longer find work in the unionized industry have switched to the nonunionized industry, thereby increasing the supply of labor in this industry.

d. Before the first industry was unionized, the equilibrium wage rate in the second industry was $6 an hour because this wage rate equated the quantity of labor demanded to the (old) quantity of labor supplied. After the first industry became unionized, the wage rate in the second industry falls to $4 an hour because this wage rate equates the quantity demanded of labor to the (new) quantity supplied.

e. The union–nonunion wage differential is $4. This differential includes a $2 rise in the wage rate in the unionized industry and a $2 drop in the wage rate in the nonunionized industry.

8. In all cases, to maximize their profits the firms set the marginal revenue product, *MRP*, of labor equal to the marginal cost of labor, *MCL*.

   Start with the comparison between the perfectly competitive industry A and the monopoly industry B. For both industries the *MCL* equals the wage rate, *W*. For a perfectly competitive firm the *MRP* is $P \times MP$, and for a monopoly the *MRP* is $MR \times MP$, where *P* is the price of the product, *MP* is the marginal product of labor, and *MR* is the marginal revenue. The *MP* curve is assumed to be the same in both industries. But for a monopoly, because $MR < P$, the *MRP* is less than that for the perfectly competitive industry. Hence a monopoly industry hires less labor than a perfectly competitive industry.

   Now compare the situation of the monopoly industry B and the monopoly/monopsony industry C. For these industries, the *MRP*s are the same. But the cost of hiring an additional worker — the *MCL* — is higher for the monopsony. Hence the monopsony hires less labor than does the monopoly.

   Overall, then, the perfectly competitive industry A hires the most labor. The monopsony/monopoly industry C hires the least. The pure monopoly industry B is in-between. Intuitively, the perfectly competitive firms cannot exercise any market power, so they do not restrict their production nor their hiring. The monopoly can use its market power to restrict its output, so it decreases the amount of labor it hires because it produces less output. The monopoly/monopsony, however, can use its market power in both the output market (in which it produces less) and in the input market (in which it buys less). Thus it has two reasons for hiring less labor, and it hires the least amount of labor of all.

■ You're the Teacher

1. "Look, you've confused a couple of things. For one, unions may not *want* to lower wages paid to nonunion members. But, as it turns out, even though they may not want this to happen, it does. Here's how: Suppose that a union organizes some industry. The first thing it does is demand higher wages. Once the companies agree to pay higher wages, the companies have an incentive to cut back on the amount of labor they employ. Perhaps they use more industrial robots or just more computerized automation. Regardless, they will decrease the number of workers they employ. What happens to these workers? Do they stick around? Do they collect unemployment or what? Obviously most people can't afford to be unemployed forever. So, these workers will migrate to other industries, without unions, where they can find work. As that occurs, the supply of labor in these industries increases. The increase in the supply of labor lowers the wage rate paid to workers in these markets. So, by decreasing employment in the unionized sector, unions lower wages in other markets."

2. "Well, it's your view that unions ought to be banned. This is your normative judgment, and I might agree or disagree with it. But I will agree with your positive — not normative — guess that unions create allocative inefficiency. The way to see this result is fairly straightforward. Perfectly competitive firms produce the allocatively efficient level of output. To do so, they have to hire the allocatively efficient level of employment. But unions restrict the level of employment in order to boost their members' wage rates. Hence firms can't hire the 'right' number of workers, and thus they can't produce the 'right' level of output. Therefore unions, like monopolies, create allocative inefficiency and deadweight losses."

16 CAPITAL AND NATURAL RESOURCE MARKETS

Key Concepts

The Structure of Capital Markets

Capital markets link the savings decisions of households and the investment decisions of firms. The price of capital is the interest rate. The three capital markets are:

- **Stock market** — equities of firms are traded.
- **Bond market** — bonds issued by firms are traded.
- **Loans market** — households and firms borrow and lend, usually through a financial intermediary.

Financial assets are paper claims (stocks, bonds, and the like). Physical assets (capital) are buildings, plant, and equipment.

The Demand for Capital

Capital is a *stock*. **Gross investment** is the *flow* purchase of new capital. **Depreciation** is the amount of existing capital that wears out or becomes obsolete. **Net investment** equals gross investment minus depreciation and is the addition to the capital stock.

The demand for capital is determined by firms' profit-maximizing choices.

- The profit-maximizing rule for capital is to use the amount of capital that makes the marginal revenue product of capital equal to price of using capital. *The price of using capital is the interest rate.*

Firms buy additional capital when its net present value (*NPV*) positive.

- A rise in the interest rate lowers the *NPV* from buying capital and thereby decreases the quantity of capital firms demand.

The **demand curve for capital** shows that the price and quantity of capital demanded are inversely related.

- Population growth shifts the demand curve for capital rightward.
- Technological change increases the demand for some types of capital and decreases it for other types.

The Supply of Capital

The supply of capital is determined by households' saving decisions.

- Saving (income minus consumption) is a *flow* addition to a household's wealth, which is the *stock* of accumulated past saving.

A household's saving depends on three factors:

- *income* — the higher the household's income, the more it saves.
- *expected future income* — the higher the household's expected future income, the less it saves.
- *interest rate* — the substitution effect from a higher interest rate encourages more saving. The income effect encourages more saving for a net lender and discourages saving for a net borrower.

The **supply curve for capital** shows a positive relationship between the interest rate and the quantity of capital supplied.

- Increases in income or population shift the supply curve of capital rightward.
- If income becomes distributed more unequally, the supply curve of capital shifts rightward.
- An increase in the fraction of the population that is middle-aged shifts the supply curve of capital rightward.

Interest Rates and Stock Prices

The equilibrium interest rate is determined by equality between the quantity of capital demanded and supplied. Figure 16.1 illustrates this equilibrium.

FIGURE **16.1**
Equilibrium in the Capital Market

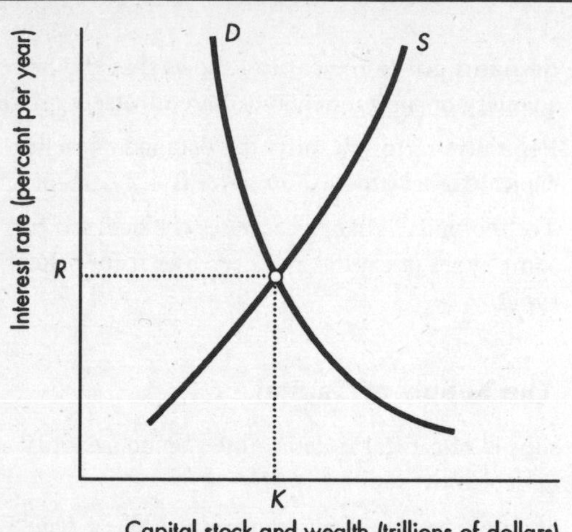

The interest rate on a share of stock is the *stock yield* and equals the stock's dividend divided by the stock's price. The interest rate on a bond is the *bond yield* and equals the bond's coupon payment divided by the price of the bond.

- An increase in the expected future dividends to be paid on a share of stock or a fall in the interest rate raises the price of the stock.
- **Price–earnings ratio** — the ratio of the current price of a share of stock to the current profit per share. The higher the expected future profit compared to the current profit, the higher is the price–earnings ratio.
- The volume of trading increases when there are divergent beliefs about the effect a change will have on a company's profit.
- **Takeover** — when one company buys another company's stock. Takeovers occur when the stock market value of a firm is less than the present value of the expected future profits from operating the firm.

Natural Resource Markets

- **Exhaustible natural resources** are resources that can be used only once and cannot be replaced.
- **Nonexhaustible natural resources** are natural resources that can be used repeatedly and not be depleted.

The *stock* of a natural resource is the total amount that exists; the *flow* is the rate at which it is being used.

The **expected interest rate** from owning a natural resource is its rate of price appreciation plus the rate of economic profit from using it. The **stock demand for a natural resource** is determined by the expected interest rate from owning the resource.

- **Stock equilibrium** for a natural resource occurs when the interest rate from owning the natural resource stock equals the interest rate on assets of comparable risk.
- **Hotelling Principle** — the price of a natural resource will grow at a rate equal to the interest rate on other comparable assets.
- **Choke price** — the price at which use of the natural resource (the flow demand) is zero.

The price and flow use of a natural resource adjust so that, when the current price rises at a rate equal to the interest rate, the price will equal the choke price at the moment that the stock is totally depleted. The current price and flow use depend on:

- **Interest rate** — a rise in the interest rate reduces the current price and increases the use.
- **Demand for the flow** — an increase in the marginal revenue product of the resource raises the current price and increases the current use.
- **Stock of the asset** — the larger the stock, the lower is the current price and the greater is the current use.

The actual price may not equal the expected price because of the arrival of new information about the market for the resource.

Even though a resource eventually may be totally used up, if there are no external costs or benefits, a perfectly competitive market is allocatively efficient.

Helpful Hints

1. A profit-maximizing firm hires an additional unit of a factor as long as the unit's use adds more to revenue than to cost; or, in other words, as long as its marginal revenue product (*MRP*) is greater than its marginal factor cost (*MFC*). The profit-maximizing amount will be the quantity at which the marginal revenue product of a factor is just equal to its marginal factor cost. In a competitive factor market, the marginal factor cost is the price of the factor (*PF*), so this profit-maximizing condition becomes our old friend, *MRP* = *PF*.
2. The *MRP* = *PF* rule covers the situation when a firm considers buying a unit of capital. However, to directly apply the principle, we must modify the profit-maximizing condition. The reason is that capital generally is utilized over more than one period of time and will generate marginal revenue products that are distributed over time. However, the purchase price must be paid now in one lump sum. Thus we must compare the purchase price to the *stream* of marginal revenue products. To make this comparison, we must compute the present value of that stream. (If you need to review the concept of present value, return to Chapter 9.) Then, we can compare the purchase price with the present value of the marginal revenue products and the same general principle will hold: Buy additional units of capital as long as the present value of the marginal revenue products exceeds the purchase price. At the profit-maximizing level of capital, the present value of the marginal revenue products equals the purchase price.

   Recall that the net present value of an investment is defined as the present value of the stream of marginal revenue products minus the price of the unit of capital. Thus profit maximization requires buying capital until the net present value of investment in additional capital is zero.
3. Economists often find the idea of arbitrage useful when thinking about asset prices and returns. Arbitrage is an essential part of the Hotelling Principle. In general, arbitrage refers to the process of buying assets when (or where) they are cheap and selling assets when (or where) they are expensive.

   The Hotelling Principle uses the arbitrage idea that the expected return on two comparable assets must be the same or people will quickly take actions that drive the expected returns to equality. For example, suppose that gold and silver are comparable assets. Suppose further that the current price of gold is $360 an ounce and that the current price of silver is $5.25 an ounce. Finally, suppose that people expect that gold will rise in price to $440 an ounce by next year and that silver will rise in price to $5.50 an ounce. With these expectations, the interest rate expected to be earned on gold is 22.2 percent and the interest rate expected to be earned on silver is 4.7 percent. (Gold is expected to rise in price by $80 and an ounce costs $360, so the expected interest rate is $80/$360 or 22.2 percent. The interest rate on silver is calculated in the same way.) At these expected interest rates, no one wants to hold silver and everyone wants to own gold. People sell silver immediately and use the funds to buy gold. As the supply of silver increases, the current price of silver falls. Conversely, as the demand for gold increases, the current price of gold rises. Thus people are arbitraging by selling the currently expensive asset (silver, whose price will be driven lower) and buying the currently cheap asset (gold, whose price will bid higher). As long as the interest rate expected to be earned on gold exceeds that expected to be earned on silver, people arbitrage by selling silver and buying gold. The process stops when the expected interest rates are equal, perhaps in this example when the current price of gold is driven higher to $400 an ounce and the current price of silver falls to $5.00 an ounce. At these prices, both assets are expected to return 10 percent. Arbitrage no longer is possible, and the market is now in equilibrium.
4. The inverse relationship between the interest rate and asset prices also applies to prices of shares of stock. However, the relationship is more complicated because the annual income from a stock — its dividend — is variable instead of fixed. Nonetheless, *ceteris paribus*, a rise in the interest rate causes stock prices to fall, and vice versa.

Questions

True/False/Uncertain and Explain

1. Natural resources can be used only once and cannot be replaced.

2. If the net present value of investing in a unit of capital is positive, a profit-maximizing firm invests in the unit.

3. The Hotelling Principle states that the price of a natural resource will grow at a rate equal to the interest rate on other comparable assets.

4. A company's price–earning ratio is high if its current profit is large compared to its future expected profits.

5. Markets may efficiently allocate goods that can be replaced or reproduced, but they cannot efficiently allocate exhaustible natural resources.

6. Financial capital and physical capital are the same.

7. A rise in the interest rate lowers the price of a share of stock.

8. An increase in the marginal revenue product of a natural resource raises the choke price of the resource.

9. A rise in the interest rate increases the quantity of investment demanded.

10. If a cheap substitute for oil were developed, the choke price for oil would decline.

11. Timber is a nonexhaustible natural resource.

12. The income effect from a rise in the interest rate encourages more saving.

13. The economic model of exhaustible natural resources implies that the market provides an automatic incentive to conserve as the resource gets closer to being totally depleted.

14. As more of a population becomes middle-aged, the supply of capital increases.

15. A rise in the interest rate raises the current price of an exhaustible natural resource.

Multiple Choice

1. Which of the following is a physical asset?
   a. A shovel.
   b. A share of Microsoft stock.
   c. A General Motors bond.
   d. All of the above.

2. The price–earnings ratio of a company's stock will be high when the company is expected to
   a. raise its dividend in the future because of higher profits.
   b. not change its dividend in the future because profits are not changing.
   c. lower its dividend in the future because of lower profits.
   d. None of the above because the price–earnings ratio has nothing to do with either the future expected dividends or profits.

3. Which of the following statements about a rise in the interest rate is correct?
   a. The substitution effect decreases all people's saving.
   b. The substitution effect increases all people's saving.
   c. The income effect decreases all people's saving.
   d. The income effect increases all people's saving.

4. Net investment equals
   a. the capital stock minus depreciation.
   b. gross investment.
   c. gross investment minus depreciation.
   d. the capital stock minus gross investment.

5. An exhaustible natural resource is
   a. coal.
   b. land.
   c. water.
   d. trees.

6. If the market for a stock of a natural resource is in equilibrium, the price of the resource is
   a. expected to rise at a rate equal to the rate of interest.
   b. expected to fall at a rate equal to the rate of interest.
   c. equal to the choke price of the resource.
   d. equal to the Hotelling price of the resource.

For the next two questions, suppose that the dividend paid on a share of JCPenney stock is $2.00 and is expected to remain at $2.00 forever.

7. If the interest rate is 10 percent, what is the price of a share of JCPenney stock?
   a. $1.00.
   b. $10.00.
   c. $20.00.
   d. $40.00.

8. If the interest rate falls to 5 percent what is the price of a share of JCPenney stock?
   a. $1.00.
   b. $10.00.
   c. $20.00.
   d. $40.00.

9. The net present value of an investment
   a. is always positive as long as the *MRP* from the increased capital stock is positive.
   b. equals the present value of the cost of the capital minus the interest rate.
   c. is negative for a profitable investment.
   d. falls when the interest rate rises.

10. The stock of an exhaustible natural resource
   a. increases with time.
   b. is a fixed amount.
   c. increases when the price of the resource rises.
   d. bends backward when the resource's price is sufficiently high.

11. An increase in the fraction of the population that is middle-aged
   a. raises the interest rate.
   b. has no effect on the interest rate.
   c. lowers the interest rate.
   d. means that more radio stations switch to playing oldies.

12. Bonds issued by a local Boston Market franchise are riskier than bonds issued by McDonald's. Hence the bonds issued by the Boston Market franchise
   a. are not purchased by anyone.
   b. pay the same interest rate as bonds issued by McDonald's.
   c. are higher priced than the bonds issued by McDonald's.
   d. pay a higher interest rate than the bonds issued by McDonald's.

13. Which of the following raise the current price of a natural resource?
   a. A rise in the interest rate.
   b. An increase in the stock of the resource.
   c. An increase in the marginal revenue product from using the resource.
   d. None of the above.

14. Which of the following raises the rate at which the price of a natural resource appreciates?
   a. A rise in the interest rate.
   b. A rise in the choke price.
   c. An increase in the marginal revenue product from using the resource.
   d. None of the above.

15. If the interest rate rises, the
   a. substitution effect encourages more saving only if the household is a net borrower.
   b. substitution effect encourages more saving only if the household is a net lender.
   c. income effect encourages more saving only if the household is a net borrower.
   d. income effect encourages more saving only if the household is a net lender.

16. Wal-Mart unexpectedly raises its dividend and announces that the dividend will remain higher forever. Immediately after this action, the price of a share of Wal-Mart stock will
   a. fluctuate up and down with a high volume of trading.
   b. rise quickly with a low volume of trading.
   c. fall gradually with a high volume of trading.
   d. rise with a high volume of trading.

17. Beth, a junior at your college who is working part-time, expects that her income after graduation will be significantly higher than her current income. As a result, Beth's current saving is likely to be
    a. high because of the substitution effect from the higher future income.
    b. high because of the income effect from the lower current income.
    c. low because of the income effect from the higher future income.
    d. low because her current income is low relative to what she expects to earn in the future.

18. The economic model of an exhaustible natural resource predicts that
    a. the natural resource will never be totally exhausted.
    b. higher prices play no role in encouraging people to conserve on their use of the resource.
    c. at some point the natural resource will be totally depleted.
    d. the price of a natural resource will remain constant until it runs short and then will skyrocket.

19. Last year Ralston Purina earned $4 profit per share and paid a $2 dividend per share. The price of a share of Ralston Purina stock is $40. Ralston Purina's price–earnings ratio is
    a. $40.
    b. 20.
    c. 10.
    d. None of the above

20. You notice that the volume of Marvel Entertainment stock traded has soared but that the price of a share of Marvel's stock has not changed. These observations can reflect an event
    a. that is widely known and widely believed to raise Marvel's future profits.
    b. that is widely known but whose effect on Marvel's profits is controversial.
    c. that is not yet known.
    d. that may or may not be widely known but is believed to raise Marvel's future profits.

21. The yield on a stock of a natural resource is the
    a. rate of interest on the loan used to buy the resource.
    b. marginal revenue product of the resource.
    c. marginal revenue product of the resource divided by its price.
    d. rate of change in the price of the resource plus the rate of economic profit earned by extracting and selling the resource.

22. A rise in the interest rate
    a. increases the quantity demanded of capital if the substitution effect exceeds the income effect.
    b. increases the quantity demanded of capital if the substitution effect is less than the income effect.
    c. has no effect on the quantity demanded of capital.
    d. decreases the quantity demanded of capital.

23. A takeover of a firm is likely to occur when the
    a. stock market value of the firm is higher than the present value of expected future profits from operating the firm.
    b. stock market value of the firm is lower than the present value of expected future profits from operating the firm.
    c. firm's current profit is higher than the present value of expected future profits from operating the firm.
    d. firm's current profit is lower than the present value of expected future profits from operating the firm.

24. Suppose that the dividend paid on a share of stock rises and that the price of a share of the stock does not change. As a result, the
    a. price–earnings ratio rises.
    b. price–earnings ratio falls.
    c. stock's bond yield falls.
    d. stock's yield rises.

25. The choke price of a natural resource is
    a. the price at which the flow demand is zero.
    b. equal to the Hotelling Price.
    c. the current price of the resource.
    d. part of the expected interest rate paid on the resource.

For the next two questions, suppose that on January 1, 1996, Paulette's Pet Palace had a capital stock of $200,000. Over the year, Paulette's gross investment is $50,000 of new capital and depreciation is $30,000.

26. Paulette's net investment during 1996 is
    a. $200,000.
    b. $50,000.
    c. $30,000.
    d. $20,000.

27. At the beginning of 1997, what is Paulette's capital stock?
    a. $250,000.
    b. $230,000.
    c. $220,000.
    d. $200,000.

28. Which of the following causes the supply curve of capital to shift rightward?
    a. An increase in the proportion of young households in the population.
    b. A rise in the interest rate.
    c. An increase in average household income.
    d. An increase in the marginal revenue product of capital.

29. The higher the rate of interest, the
    a. higher is the net present value of an investment.
    b. lower is the present value of the flow of marginal revenue products of an investment.
    c. greater is the quantity of capital demanded.
    d. lower is the marginal revenue product of capital.

30. Which of the following markets helps channel savers' funds to business firms for their investment?
    a. Stock market.
    b. Bond market.
    c. Loans market.
    d. All of the above.

Short Answer Problems

1. Why does the quantity of capital demanded increase when the interest rate falls?
2. Why does the quantity of capital supplied decrease when the interest rate falls?

FIGURE 16.2
Short Answer Problem 3

Interest rate (percent per year)
Capital stock and wealth (trillions of dollars)

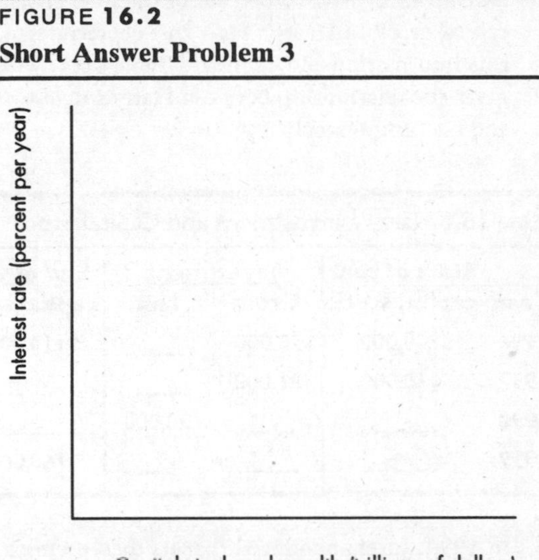

3. In Figure 16.2, show what happens to the interest rate and quantity of capital if people's incomes generally increase.

FIGURE 16.3
Short Answer Problem 4

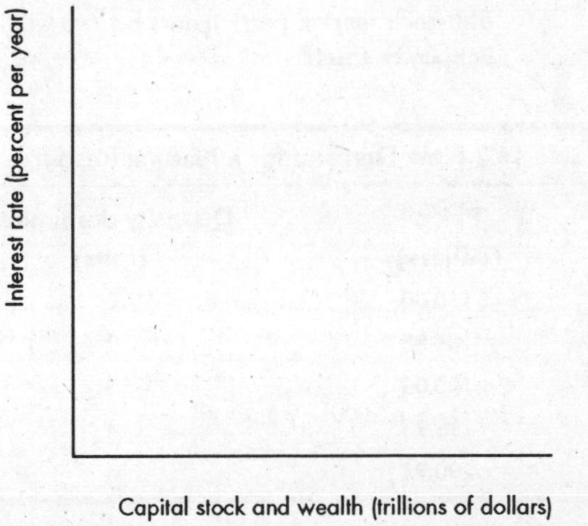

Interest rate (percent per year)
Capital stock and wealth (trillions of dollars)

4. In Figure 16.3, show what happens to the interest rate and capital stock if there are general technological advances that boost the *MRP* from most types of capital.

5. During each year, 10 percent of the start of year capital stock in Harry's Hair Lair depreciates. Use this information and complete Table 16.1, which gives the relationship between Harry's investment and his capital stock.

Table 16.1 Harry's Investment and Capital Stock

Year	Start of year capital stock	Investment Gross	Investment Net	End of year capital stock
1996	$100,000	$20,000	____	$110,000
1997	110,000	31,000	____	____
1998	____	____	20,000	____
1999	____	____	____	160,000

6. In 1994, Intel announced that its then premier chip, the Pentium, had a flaw in it.
   a. Suppose that after the announcement the price of a share of Intel stock fell 10 percent and trading volume was not exceptionally large. If this situation occurred, what did stock market participants' believe would happen to Intel?
   b. Now suppose that the price of a share of Intel stock fell slightly and trading volume was very large. If these changes happened, what did stock market participants believe would happen to Intel?

Table 16.2 Flow Demand for a Natural Resource

Price (dollars)	Quantity demanded (tons)
$110.00	0
104.88	2
100.00	3
95.35	4
90.91	6

7. Table 16.2 shows the flow demand for a natural resource. Nine tons of the resource remain.
   a. What is the choke price?
   b. Suppose that the interest rate is 4.88 percent. What is the current price of the natural resource? Counting the current year, how many years will elapse until the choke price is reached and the resource is completely depleted?
   c. Assume that the interest rate rises to 10 percent. What is the current price of the resource? Counting the current year, how many years are needed for the price to reach the choke price and the asset to be totally exhausted?
   d. In general, how does a rise in the interest rate affect the current price? How does it change the amount of time until the choke price is reached and the resource is totally depleted?

8. Suppose that the rate of economic profit on an exhaustible natural resource does not change. Why will the market for the stock of this resource be in equilibrium only if the price of the resource is expected to rise at a rate equal to the rate of interest?

Table 16.3 Larry's Lawn Care

Number of lawn mowers	*MRP* in first year (dollars)	*MRP* in second year (dollars)
1	100	80
2	80	64
3	72	62

Table 16.4 Short Answer Problem 9 (a)

NPV ($r = 0.05$)	*NPV* ($r = 0.10$)	*NPV* ($r = 0.15$)
____	____	____
____	____	____
____	____	____

9. Larry's Lawn Care is considering the purchase of additional lawn mowers. These lawn mowers have a life of two years and cost $120 each. The marginal revenue products for both years are given in Table 16.3.
   a. Complete Table 16.4 by computing the net present values (*NPVs*) if the interest rate is 5 percent (0.05), 10 percent (0.10), or 15 percent (0,15) per year.

b. How many lawn mowers will Larry's Lawn Care purchase if the interest rate is 15 percent? 10 percent? 5 percent?

c. Construct Larry's demand curve capital in Figure 16.4 by plotting the three points identified in part (b) and drawing a line through them.

FIGURE 16.4

Short Answer Problem 9c

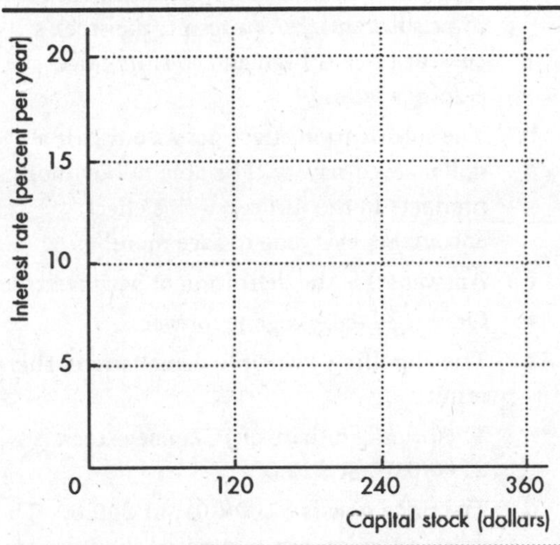

■ You're the Teacher

1. "I really don't understand why a rise in the interest rate lowers the price of a bond. That is really weird! I'd expect just the opposite. I mean, I'd expect that a rise in the interest rate *raises* the price of a bond. Can you help me?" This student truly does need help. And you're probably just the person to supply this assistance! Explain to this student in detail why a higher interest rate lowers the price of a bond.

Answers

True/False Answers

1. **U** Exhaustible resources can be used only once, but nonexhaustible resources can be used any number of times or else can be replaced.
2. **T** As long as the net present value is positive, investing in the unit of capital is profitable.
3. **T** This statement is the definition of the Hotelling Principle.
4. **F** The price–earnings ratio is high if future expected profits — and hence future expected dividends — are large relative to today's profit and dividend.
5. **F** As long as the markets are perfectly competitive, with no external benefits or costs, they will efficiently allocate the use of natural resources.
6. **F** Physical capital is the actual piece of equipment; financial capital represents ownership claims on the capital.
7. **T** If nothing else changes, the higher the interest rate, the lower will be the price of a share of stock.
8. **T** An increase in the marginal revenue product means that the price at which no wants to use the resource — the choke price — must be higher.
9. **F** A rise in the interest rate decreases the quantity of capital demanded and thereby decreases the quantity of investment demanded.
10. **T** The presence of a cheap substitute causes the demand for oil to decrease, which reduces its choke price.
11. **T** Timber can be replaced and thus is a nonexhaustible natural resource.
12. **U** The income effect encourages more saving for net lenders but discourages saving for net borrowers.
13. **T** As the resource gets closer to total depletion, its price rises, which provides an incentive for users to economize on its use.
14. **T** The supply curve of saving shifts rightward, thereby raising the supply of capital.
15. **F** The rise in the interest rate boosts the expected *rate* of price increase but lowers the current price.

Multiple Choice Answers

1. **a** The shovel is an actual piece of capital equipment, so it is physical capital.
2. **a** Essentially, people are willing to pay more for the stock in the current period because they expect the increase in dividends in the future to be substantial. As a result, the stock's current price is high and so is its price–earnings ratio.
3. **b** The substitution effect points out that a dollar saved now will be able to buy more products in the future, so this effect encourages everyone to save more.
4. **c** Answer (c) is the definition of net investment.
5. **a** Once used, coal is gone forever.
6. **a** The Hotelling Principle demonstrates this result.
7. **c** The price of a share of JCPenney stock is $2.00/0.10, or $20.00.
8. **d** The price now is $2.00/0.05, or $40.00. The drop in the interest rate raised the price of a share of stock.
9. **d** The net present value of a unit of capital equals the present value of the current and future *MRP*s minus the cost of the unit of capital. If the interest rate rises, the present value of the *MRP*s falls, which reduces the net present value.
10. **b** The stock is the total amount present.
11. **c** Middle-aged people save more (for retirement). Hence the supply curve of capital shifts rightward and, as a result, the interest rate falls.
12. **d** The higher interest rate compensates the owners of the bond for the increased risk that Boston Market might be unable to meet its obligations to pay interest and repay the principal of the bond.
13. **c** As the *MRP* from using the resource increases, the flow demand increases, which raises the current price of the asset.
14. **a** According to the Hotelling Principle the resource's price appreciates at a rate equal to

the interest rate on an asset of comparable riskiness.

15. **d** The higher interest rate means that net lenders have a positive income effect — that is, their income increases — and so they respond by saving more.

16. **b** Everyone can easily interpret the effect from this announcement, so the price of a share of Wal-Mart stock rises on a low volume of trading.

17. **d** Beth will borrow (rather than save) and plan to repay the loans when her income is higher in the future.

18. **c** The resource will be exhausted just as its price equals the choke price.

19. **c** Ralston's price–earning ratio equals (Price of a share)/(Profit per share). Hence in this case it equals $40/$4, or 10.

20. **b** Because the effect on the profit is controversial, those who expect that it will boost Marvel's profits buy from those who predict that it will lower Marvel's profits.

21. **d** Answer (d) is the definition of the yield from a natural resource.

22. **d** The quantity of capital demanded and the interest rate are inversely related.

23. **b** In this case a profit is to be made by paying the stock market value of the firm to take it over and then running the firm.

24. **d** The stock's yield is defined as (Dividend)/(Price per share). If the dividend goes up and the price does not change, the yield rises.

25. **a** Answer (a) is the definition of the choke price.

26. **d** Net investment equals gross investment minus depreciation, so net investment equals $50,000 – $30,000 = $20,000.

27. **c** The change in the capital stock equals the amount of net investment. Hence Paulette's capital stock increased by $20,000, from $200,000 to $220,000.

28. **c** An increase in income increases saving.

29. **b** As the interest rate rises, the present value of future revenues falls.

30. **d** *All* these markets help move households' saving to business firms for their use as investment.

■ Answers to Short Answer Problems

1. Profit-maximizing firms demand capital as long as the present value of the stream of the future marginal revenue product from the new capital exceeds the price of the new capital; in other words, as long as the net present value is positive. Because a lower interest rate means that the present value of any given future stream of marginal revenue products will be higher, the net present value is positive for a larger number of additional capital goods. Thus more capital will be purchased. Therefore the quantity of capital demanded increases as the interest rate falls. In other words, the interest rate is the price of investment, and this result is like any other: A drop in the price leads to an increase in the quantity demanded.

2. The supply of capital is determined by households' saving. The effect on saving from a fall in the interest rate can be divided into a substitution effect and an income effect. The substitution effect unambiguously decreases saving. Essentially, the lower interest rate reduces the reward from saving because, with a lower interest rate, any amount of saving is able to buy fewer goods in the future. The impact of the income effect depends on whether the household is a net lender or borrower. The lower interest rate reduces lenders' income. As a result, they decrease the amount they save. (This effect reinforces the substitution effect.) Borrowers find that their income rises because they will pay less in interest costs. As a result, borrowers increase their saving. (This outcome offsets the substitution effect.) On balance, data show that a drop in the interest rate slightly decreases the quantity of saving.

3. The increase in income boosts people's saving. As a result, the supply curve of capital shifts rightward. This case is illustrated in Figure 16.5 (on the next page) in which the supply curve shifts from S_0 to S_1. The shift causes the equilibrium interest rate to fall from R_0 to R_1 and increases the capital stock from K_0 to K_1.

FIGURE 16.5
Short Answer Problem 3

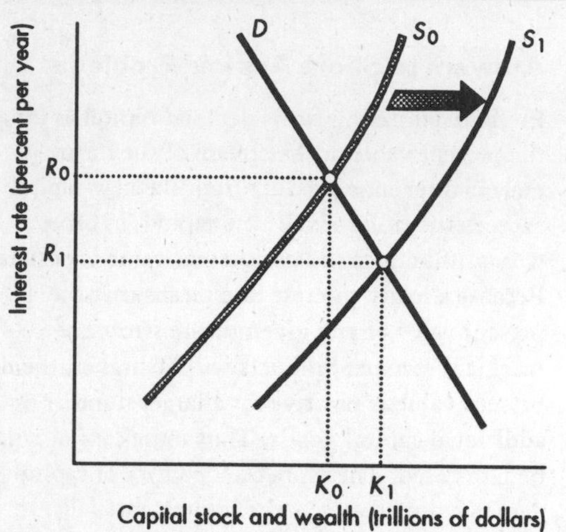

FIGURE 16.6
Short Answer Problem 4

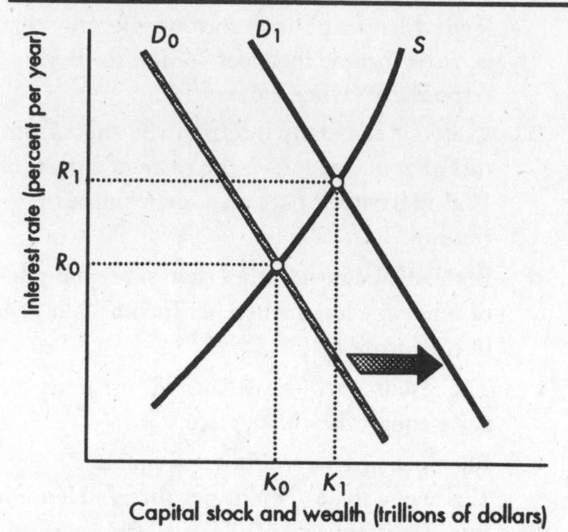

4. When the *MRP* from capital increases, the demand curve for capital shifts rightward (in Figure 16.6 the shift from D_0 to D_1). As a result of this shift, the interest rate rises (from R_0 to R_1) and the capital stock increases (from K_0 to K_1).
5. Table 16.5 shows Harry's capital stock and investment. Working through these answers in order, net investment in 1996 equals gross investment ($20,000) minus depreciation. Depreciation is 10 percent of the initial capital stock, which in this case means that depreciation is $10,000 (10 percent of $100,000). Thus net investment is $20,000 – $10,000 = $10,000. Net investment in 1997 is calculated similarly. The capital stock at the end of 1997 equals the capital stock at the beginning of the year plus gross investment minus depreciation. Gross investment minus depreciation is the same as net investment, so alternatively the capital stock at the end of 1997 equals the capital stock at the beginning of the year, $110,000, plus the net investment, $20,000, during the year. The capital stock at the beginning of 1998 equals the capital stock at the end of 1997, $130,000. Depreciation this year is $13,000, 10 percent of the capital stock of $130,000. Hence gross investment equals net investment of $20,000 plus depreciation of $13,000, or $33,000. The capital stock at the end of 1998 equals the capital stock at the beginning of 1998 plus net investment during the year. Finally, the capital stock at the beginning of 1999 equals the capital stock at the end of 1998. The capital stock at the end of 1999 ($160,000) minus the capital stock at the beginning of 1999 ($150,000) equals the net investment during the year, $10,000. Depreciation is $15,000 (10 percent of $150,000) and, because gross investment equals depreciation plus net investment, gross investment equals $25,000.

Table 16.5 Short Answer Problem 5

Year	Start of year capital stock	Investment Gross	Investment Net	End of year capital stock
1996	$100,000	$20,000	<u>$10,000</u>	$110,000
1997	110,000	31,000	<u>20,000</u>	<u>130,000</u>
1998	<u>130,000</u>	<u>33,000</u>	20,000	<u>150,000</u>
1999	<u>150,000</u>	<u>25,000</u>	<u>10,000</u>	160,000

6 a. A decline in the price of a share of Intel stock with little volume of trade implies a wide consensus among stock market participants that the announcement means a reduction in Intel's future profits and therefore a reduction in the future dividends Intel will pay.

b. A large volume of trade in Intel stock with a small decline implies, at best, a weak consensus about the implications of the announcement for Intel's future profitability. Some investors may forecast a large decline in future profits and dividends, and others may expect a more modest decline. Incidentally, this second description — a small decline (about 3 percent) in the price of a share of stock and a large volume of shares traded — is what occurred after Intel's announcement.

7. a. The choke price is $110.00 a ton because at this price the quantity demanded is 0.

b. If the interest rate is 4.88 percent, the current price is $95.35 a ton. Counting the current year, the choke price will be reached and the stock totally depleted in 3 years.
To derive these results, use the Hotelling Principle. According to the Hotelling Principle the price will grow at the rate of interest, 4.88 percent. So, work backward. Call the price in the year before it reaches the choke price *P*. Now, *P* will grow at a rate of 4.88 percent, and after this year it will equal the choke price, $110.00. In other words, (*P*)(1 + Interest Rate) = $110.00, which means that

$$P = \frac{\$110.00}{1 + \text{Interest rate}}.$$

Hence, *P* equals $110.00/1.0488 so that, in the year before the choke price is reached, the price is $104.88. Continue working backward in the same way: The price in the preceding year is $100.00 and in the year before that is $95.35. How much of the resource will be used along this price path from $95.35 to $100.00 to $104.88 to $110.00? In the first year (when the price is $95.35) 4 tons are used; in the second year (when the price is $100.00 a ton) 3 tons are used; and in the third year (when the price is $104.90) 2 tons are used. (After the third year the price is $110.00 and 0 tons are used.) Thus, over the three years, 9 tons are used, which is precisely the amount of the existing stock. So to reach the choke price and totally exhaust the stock takes 3 years.

c. If the interest rate rises to 10 percent, the current price of the resource falls to $90.91. Now, 2 years will elapse before the resource is completely exhausted and the choke price is reached.
These answers can be calculated the same way as those in part (b). Let's verify these answers. The Hotelling Principle tells us that, if the price starts at $90.91, at the beginning of the next year the price will be ($90.91)(1.10) = $100.00; and, at the beginning of the second year the price will rise to ($100.00)(110), which is the choke price of $110.00. Thus the choke price is reached in 2 years. Then, in the first year, with the price at $90.91, the demand schedule shows that 6 tons are used; in the second year, with the price at $100.00, 3 tons are used. Hence, 9 tons are used along this two-year price path, which is the amount of the initial stock.

d. As this problem shows, a rise in the interest rate lowers the current price and leads to more rapid exhaustion of the total stock.

8. If the rate of economic profit does not change, the yield on the stock of an exhaustible resource is the rate of change in the price of the resource. For the market for the stock of the resource to be in equilibrium, there must be no incentive for movement into or out of the market. This situation occurs only if the yield on the stock of the exhaustible resource is the same as the yield on other assets, which is given by the rate of interest.

Table 16.6 Short Answer Problem 9 (a)

NPV **(r = 0.05)**	***NPV*** **(r = 0.10)**	***NPV*** **(r = 0.15)**
$47.80	$37.02	$27.45
14.24	5.62	–2.04
4.81	–3.31	–10.51

9. a. Table 16.6 shows the *NPV*s. The *NPV* is the present value of the stream of marginal revenue products resulting from an investment minus the cost of the investment. For lawn mowers with a two-year life, the *NPV* is calculated using the following equation:

$$NPV = \frac{MRP_1}{(1+r)} + \frac{MRP_2}{(1+r)^2} - P_m$$

In this formula, MRP_1 and MRP_2 are the marginal revenue products in the first and second years, respectively, and P_m is the price of a lawn mower. The values of MRP_1 and MRP_2 are given in Table 16.3 for the first, second, and third lawn mowers and P_m is $120. The answers for the *NPVs* given in Table 16.6 are obtained by substituting these values into the net present value formula and then evaluating the expression for the alternative interest rates, *r*.

b. If the interest rate is 15 percent, only one additional lawn mower will be purchased because the second lawn mower has a negative net present value. If the interest rate is 10 percent, two lawn mowers will be purchased; if the interest rate is 5 percent, three lawn mowers will be purchased.

c. The demand curve for capital is illustrated in Figure 16.7.

FIGURE 16.7
Short Answer Problem 9 (c)

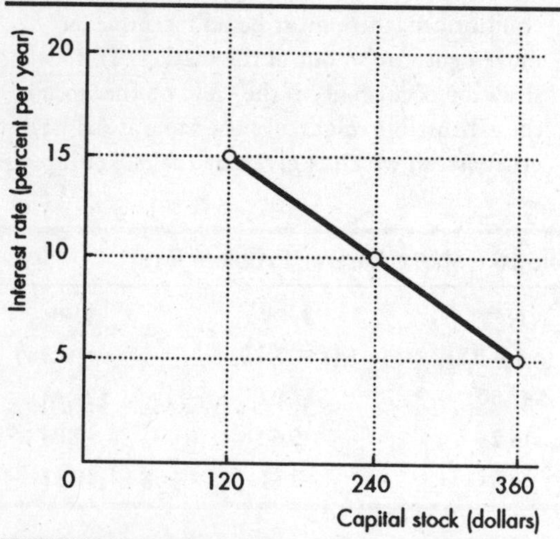

■ You're the Teacher

1. "I agree, this might seem weird at first sight. But actually you're missing a very important point about bonds. The deal is that a bond is a promise to pay a fixed number of dollars in coupon interest per year. In other words, a bond sends you or me a number of dollars that doesn't vary no matter what happens to the interest rate. If the interest rate goes up, the number of dollars paid as coupon interest doesn't change; if the interest rate goes down, the number of dollars paid still doesn't change.

"Once you know this fact, it's not hard to see why the interest rate and bond prices are inversely related. We learned in this chapter that the interest rate on a bond equals the coupon payment divided by the price of the bond, that is,

$$\text{Interest rate} = \frac{\text{Coupon payment}}{\text{Price of bond}}.$$

We can rearrange this equation to get

$$\text{Price of bond} = \frac{\text{Coupon payment}}{\text{Interest rate}}.$$

"Now, suppose that I own a bond that is going to make a coupon payment of $100 a year forever. (I'll pretend that it pays this amount forever so that I don't have to worry about when the bond matures and the principal is repaid.) If the interest rate is 10 percent, the price of this bond is $100/0.10, or $1,000. If the interest rate falls to 5 percent, the price of my bond rises to $100/0.05 = $2,000.

"You can probably see the math, but the idea here is really simple. Let's take the case of my bond paying $100 a year but the interest rate has fallen to 5 percent. Now, suppose you buy a newly issued bond for $1,000 by loaning $1,000 to a company. The price of your new bond is $1,000. With an interest rate of 5 percent, this newly issued bond has a coupon payment of $50 a year because it pays the going interest rate (5 percent) times the amount loaned ($1,000). So, a new bond costs you $1,000 and pays you $50 in interest each year. *My* bond, however, pays $100 in interest each year. In other words, it pays twice what a new bond pays. Hence it is worth twice what a new bond is worth. A new bond sells for $1,000 so my old bond is worth $2,000!

"Turn this around and run it backward to see what happens if the interest rate rises above 10 percent. In this case, new bonds pay more than $100 interest per year, so they are worth more than my old bond. As a result, the price of my bond will fall so that it is less than the price of a new bond, namely, less than $1,000."

Chapter 17 UNCERTAINTY AND INFORMATION

Key Concepts

Uncertainty and Risk

Uncertainty — when more than one event may occur but no one knows which event will occur.

- **Probability** — a number between 0 and 1 that measures the chance of an event occurring.
- **Risk** — when more than one outcome can occur and the probabilities of each outcome can be measured.

Expected utility is the average utility obtained from repeating an action a large number of times. In a risky situation, people maximize expected utility. Expected utility may differ from the person's actual utility, which is the amount of utility the person actually gets.

- **Utility of wealth schedule** — the amount of utility from different amounts of wealth, as illustrated by the utility of wealth curve in Figure 17.1.

FIGURE 17.1
Utility of Wealth and Cost of Risk

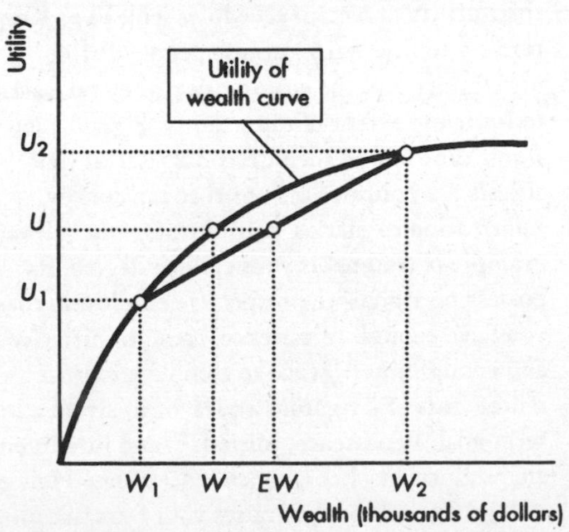

The utility of wealth schedule can be used to measure an individual's cost of risk, that is, the amount by which expected wealth must be increased to give the same expected utility as a no-risk situation. In Figure 17.1 the person faces the risky situation of receiving wealth of W_1 (which yields utility U_1) or W_2 (with utility U_2). The expected wealth is EW, and the expected utility is U. This risky situation has the same utility as receiving certain wealth of W. The difference in wealth between the risky and the sure case, $EW - W$, measures the cost of the risk in this situation to this individual.

- The more risk averse the person, the more rapidly the marginal utility of wealth falls. (The more curved is the utility of wealth curve).
- A risk-neutral person's utility of wealth curve is linear.

Insurance

- People buy insurance to reduce risk.
- Insurance works by pooling a large number of risks so that the total number of adverse outcomes is relatively certain.
- Insurance is profitable because people are risk averse and will pay to reduce their risk. That is, people pay a small sum to be sure that they will not incur a large loss.

Information

Economic information reduces uncertainty. However, gathering information is costly.

Buyers looking for the lowest price search until the expected marginal benefit of further search equals the marginal cost of the additional search and, at that time, buy the product.

- **Reservation price** — the highest price the buyer will pay for a good.

- **Optimal-search rule** — Search until the product is found with a price equal to or lower than the reservation price and then buy it.

Sellers advertise to persuade and to inform.

- Advertising for *search goods* usually informs.
- Advertising for *experience goods* usually persuades.

The effect advertising has on prices is mixed:

- Advertising raises costs, which raises prices.
- Advertising may increase competition, which lowers prices.

Private Information

Private information is information available to one person but too costly for others to discover. Private information creates two problems:

- **Moral hazard** — when after an agreement is made, one party has an incentive to behave in way that benefits him or her at the expense of the other (uninformed) party.
- **Adverse selection** — the tendency for people to accept contracts when they have private information that can be used to their own advantage and to the disadvantage of the other (uninformed) parties to the agreement.

Information problems can be (partially) overcome through signals.

- **Signal** — an action conveying information that can be used by a market.
- An example of a signal is a warranty on a used car.
- In the loan market, banks use signals (e.g., length of time on the job and home ownership) and also ration loans to overcome moral hazard and adverse selection problems.
- A person's past driving record (a signal) and deductible payments limit adverse selection and moral hazard in the insurance market.

Managing Risk in Financial Markets

Risk in financial markets can be lowered through diversification, that is by holding many different assets rather than just one asset.

An efficient market has two characteristics:

- The actual price equals the expected future price and embodies all available information.
- There are no forecastable profit opportunities.

The stock market is an efficient market. Stock prices fluctuate when new information becomes available.

Helpful Hints

1. Until this chapter we have ignored uncertainty and risk when examining firms' and consumers' behavior. That is not to say that uncertainty and risk do not exist; on the contrary, they are pervasive in the real world. Often, however, they do not change what is important about the situation. For instance, the key factor in how a firm chooses its level of output is that the firm maximizes its profit and thereby produces at $MC = MR$. The firm may be uncertain about both its MC and MR, but it still tries to equate MC to MR to maximize its profit. If we had tried to incorporate the role played by uncertainty into our analysis of firms, we could have missed the crucial result that setting MC equal to MR maximizes the firm's profit. Thus the models that we have studied before all ignore uncertainty and risk because including these factors would obscure the important conclusions these models illuminated.
2. As the preceding helpful hint pointed out, risk and uncertainty are not always key players in a situation. But there are times when they are very important. This chapter tackles some of these circumstances. Few people "like" risk and uncertainty, though some do. (Think of big plungers in Atlantic City or Las Vegas. What do their utility of wealth schedules look like? Keep reading to find out.) Because people dislike uncertainty and the ensuing risk, they take actions to limit the extent of uncertainty. Signals play a significant role in such decisions. Recall that signals are nonprice actions that can convey information to market participants. One relevant example of a signal is your college degree. Its possession signals to prospective employers that you have enough persistence, enough initiative, and enough intelligence to complete four (or more) years of a rigorous endeavor to attain a long-term goal. Persistence, initiative, and intelligence are productivity boosting enhancements. Hence a college degree not only raises your human capital in the form of greater knowledge, but it also

provides signals about aspects of your character and personality. (Now, what does the utility of wealth schedule look like for a "risk lover"? A risk-averse person's utility of wealth curve becomes less steep as more wealth is accumulated, and it is concave. A risk-neutral person's utility of wealth curve has the same degree of steepness regardless of the level of wealth, and it is linear. A risk lover has a utility of wealth curve that becomes steeper as wealth increases, and it is convex.)

Questions

True/False/Uncertain and Explain

1. The more rapidly the marginal utility of wealth diminishes, the less risk averse is the person.

2. In a risky situation, people maximize their expected wealth.

3. Advertising increases the prices of the products advertised.

4. A buyer searches until finding the product priced at or below his or her reservation price and at that point buys the item.

5. Predictable profit opportunities abound in an efficient market.

6. A person with a linear utility of wealth curve is very risk averse.

7. Diversification raises the potential return from an investment but at the cost of increasing risk.

8. Traffic tickets are an example of a signal.

9. Adverse selection occurs when one party enters into a contract with private information that shows the agreement will give that party more benefit and the other party to the contract less benefit.

10. Advertising for search goods usually attempts to persuade customers to buy the products.

Multiple Choice

1. In an efficient market,
   a. the current price usually is less than the expected future price.
   b. the current price usually is greater than the expected future price.
   c. the current price and expected future price are not related.
   d. no forecastable profit opportunities exist.

2. Of the following, who is most likely to purchase insurance?
   a. Michael, whose marginal utility of wealth schedule falls very rapidly.
   b. Robin, whose marginal utility of wealth schedule falls slowly.
   c. Richard, whose marginal utility of wealth schedule does not fall at all.
   d. Which one is impossible to determine because the marginal utility of wealth schedule has nothing to do with who buys insurance.

3. Diversification primarily
   a. sends a signal.
   b. increases the return from investments in financial markets.
   c. overcomes a moral hazard problem.
   d. decreases the risk from investments in financial markets.

4. Which of the following is an example of a signal?
   a. Membership in a professional society.
   b. A history of promptly paying bills when they come due.
   c. Informal clothing worn to a formal job interview.
   d. All of the above are signals.

5. Buyers will devote additional resources to searching for information when the expected
   a. marginal benefit of searching is positive.
   b. marginal benefit of searching is less than the marginal cost of searching.
   c. total benefit of searching is greater than the total cost of searching.
   d. marginal benefit of searching is larger than the marginal cost of searching.

6. Goods whose quality can be assessed only after they are bought are called
   a. private information goods.
   b. search goods.
   c. experience goods.
   d. lemons.

Table 17.1 shows the returns per $100 invested in investment A or investment B. The returns for the investments are independent; that is, a $200 return from investment A has an equal chance of being matched with a $400 return from investment B or a $0 return from investment B.

Table 17.1 Multiple Choice Questions 7, 8, and 9

Probability of return	Return on investment A	Return on investment B
50%	$200	$400
50%	60	0

7. What is the expected return from putting $200 in investment A?
   a. $400.
   b. $260.
   c. $120.
   d. $0.

8. What is the expected return from putting $100 in investment A and $100 in investment B?
   a. $1,320.
   b. $400.
   c. $330.
   d. $280.

9. A risk neutral person has $200 to invest in investment A and/or investment B. This person will
   a. invest $200 in investment A.
   b. invest $200 in investment B.
   c. invest $100 in investment A and $100 in investment B.
   d. split the investment between investment A and investment B but not necessarily put $100 in A and $100 in B.

10. Ben becomes more likely to play with matches after he has fire insurance. This situation illustrates
    a. moral hazard.
    b. adverse selection.
    c. the lemon problem.
    d. the "don't play with fire" principle.

11. A buyer's reservation price is
    a. the lowest price the buyer is willing to pay to purchase the product.
    b. lower the more advertising done by the sellers of the product.
    c. unrelated to the amount of searching a buyer undertakes.
    d. the highest price the buyer is willing to pay for the product.

12. If you have private information that you are a riskier driver than your record indicates, you are likely to buy an insurance policy with a (an)
    a. higher than average deductible.
    b. lower than average deductible.
    c. average deductible.
    d. None of the above.

13. JCPenney guarantees to refund a customer's money if the customer returns poorly made clothing. This guarantee is an example of
    a. the adverse selection problem.
    b. the moral hazard problem.
    c. the cost of risk.
    d. a signal.

14. Advertising usually persuades for
    a. signaled goods.
    b. normal goods.
    c. search goods.
    d. experience goods.

15. Banks ration loans because
    a. they are not trying to maximize their profit.
    b. doing so enables them to distinguish between high-risk and low-risk borrowers.
    c. doing so allows them to charge low-risk borrowers a low interest rate and high-risk borrowers a high interest rate.
    d. they are unable to distinguish perfectly between low-risk and high-risk borrowers.

16. If buyers cannot assess the quality of used cars and there are no warranties,
    a. only bad used cars will be sold.
    b. only good used cars will be sold.
    c. good cars will be sold at a higher price than bad cars.
    d. there is no adverse selection problem.

For the next three questions, Dennis is searching for a new computer. The marginal cost of visiting a computer store is $200. His reservation price is $2,000.

17. At the first store Dennis visits, the price of a computer is $2,100. Dennis will
    a. buy the computer at this store.
    b. not buy the computer and continue his search.
    c. be indifferent between buying the computer and continuing his search.
    d. None of the above.

18. Dennis visits a second store, where the price of a computer is $2,150. Dennis will
    a. buy the computer at this store.
    b. not buy the computer at this store but instead return to the first store and buy the computer there.
    c. not buy the computer at this store and not return to the first store but instead continue his search.
    d. None of the above.

19. At a third store Dennis visits, the price of a computer is $1,950. Dennis will
    a. buy the computer at this store.
    b. not buy the computer at this store but instead return to the first store and buy the computer there.
    c. not buy the computer at this store and not return to any of the other stores but instead continue his search.
    d. None of the above.

20. The tendency for a person to make an agreement and then behave after the agreement in a way to increase his or her benefits and harm the other party to the agreement is called
    a. signaling.
    b. adverse selection.
    c. moral hazard.
    d. the cost of contracting.

21. Stock share prices are volatile because
    a. expectations are irrational.
    b. expectations change frequently due to new information.
    c. stock markets are inefficient markets.
    d. shareholders do not behave rationally.

22. You notice that Amy always puts her money into investments with the highest expected payoff regardless of their risk. These actions suggest that Amy is
    a. strongly risk averse.
    b. risk averse but not strongly.
    c. risk neutral.
    d. diversifying her portfolio.

23. If Al is risk averse, as his wealth increases, his total utility of wealth ____ and his marginal utility of wealth ____.
    a. increases; increases
    b. increases; decreases
    c. decreases; increases
    d. decreases; decreases

24. In a risky situation, people maximize their
    a. expected wealth.
    b. diversification.
    c. expected utility.
    d. cost of risk.

Short Answer Problems

1. Larry and Harry have private information about their safety as drivers. Larry is a safe driver; he never speeds and comes to a full stop at every stop sign. Harry believes that speed limit signs give the minimum speed and that yellow lights mean "full speed ahead."
    a. If you owned an automobile insurance company and had to charge everyone the same rate, who would you most want to insure?
    b. You want to sell insurance to safe drivers — like Larry — for $500 a year and to risky drivers — like Harry — for $1,500 a year. In other words, Larry is expected to have accidents costing an average of $500 a year and Harry $1,500 a year. Of course, in any particular year, Larry may have accidents that cost more (or less) than $500 and Harry may

have accidents costing more (or less) than $1,500. Because you cannot determine who is safe and who is risky, you offer both Larry and Harry insurance for $1,000 a year with no deductible. Is Harry likely to buy the insurance? Is Larry? Does Larry's decision depend on whether he can convince another insurance company that he is a safe driver? If he does so, what problem do you face?

c. Suppose that you decide to sell two types of insurance policies: One costs $1,300 a year and has a $100 deductible (so that the car owner pays the first $100 of any claim) and the other costs $300 a year and has a $1,500 deductible. Which type of insurance is Harry most likely to buy? Larry? Why?

d. What do your answers to part (c) tell you about the role played by deductibles?

2. Why do banks often lend more readily to people who have credit cards and have previously borrowed from the bank than to people who have always paid in cash and never borrowed?

3. Will a risk-neutral person be likely to diversify his or her asset holdings? Why or why not?

4. Igor owns a valuable bat worth $100. Unfortunately, this species of bat has a 20 percent annual probability of dying and becoming worthless — even to Igor.

a. Igor's utility of wealth schedule is given in Table 17.2. What is Igor's utility if his bat lives? If it dies? What is Igor's expected utility?

b. It is potentially fortunate for Igor that he is able to purchase bat insurance. Bat Farm Insurance Company is willing to sell him a policy that costs $40 a year and promises to replace his bat if it dies. Might Igor buy insurance from Bat Farm?

c. Is Igor willing to pay $20 for bat insurance? Why or why not?

d. Igor eventually buys insurance from the All Bat Insurance Company. Suppose that Igor knew his bat was already sickly but that All Bat did not know this and so charged Igor the premium that applies to healthy bats. Who expects to gain more than usual from this policy? What does this situation illustrate?

Table 17.2 Igor's Utility of Wealth Schedule

Wealth (dollars)	Utility
$100	400
80	350
60	280
40	200
20	110
0	0

5. What is meant by an efficient market? Explain why the current market price will always equal the expected future price in an efficient market. Why would you expect the stock market to be an efficient market?

6. Figure 17.2 shows Lisa's utility of wealth curve. She is considering an investment that will pay either W_1 with a probability of 50 percent or W_2 with a probability of 50 percent.

a. Identify Lisa's utility if she receives W_1 by labeling this level of utility U_1. Also identify her utility if she receives W_2 by labeling this level U_2. Finally, label Lisa's expected wealth EW and her expected utility U. What does her expected wealth equal?

b. What is the cost of this risk to Lisa? Carefully explain what is meant by "the cost of risk."

FIGURE 17.2
Lisa's Utility of Wealth

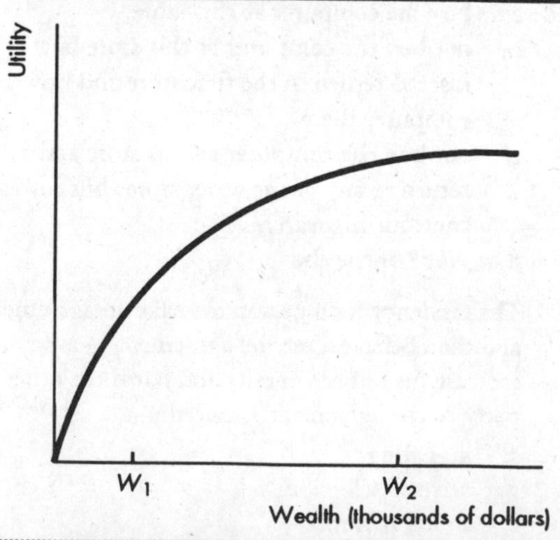

7. Figure 17.3 shows Maria's utility of wealth curve. Maria has the same two opportunities available to her as Lisa, so she can make an investment that will pay either W_1 with a probability of 50 percent or pay W_2 with a probability of 50 percent.
   a. Show Maria's utility if she receives W_1 by labeling this level of utility U_1. Also identify her utility if she gets a payoff of W_2 by labeling this U_2. Finally, label Maria's expected wealth *EW* and expected utility *U*.
   b. What is the cost of this risk to Maria? How does it compare with Lisa's cost for this risk?

FIGURE **17.3**
Maria's Utility of Wealth

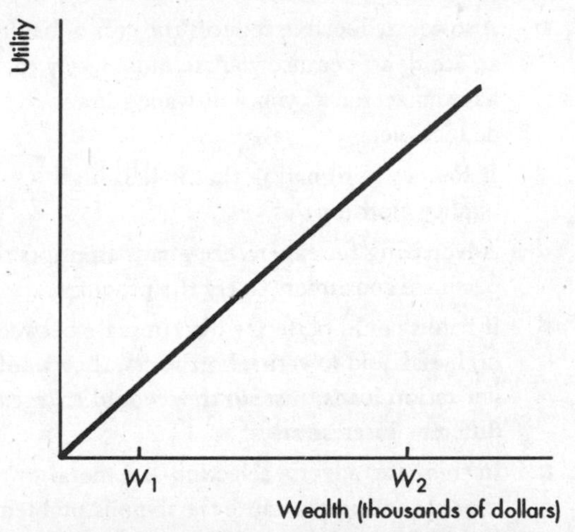

8. Table 17.3 presents Leonard's utility of wealth schedule. Leonard is considering an investment that will pay either $0 or $20,000 with equal probability.
   a. What is Leonard's expected wealth from the investment?
   b. What is Leonard's expected utility?
   c. What is Leonard's cost of risk?
   d. Is Leonard willing to make the investment if it costs him $5,000?

Table 17.3 Leonard's Utility of Wealth

Wealth (dollars)	Utility
$0	0
4,000	52
5,000	60
8,000	79
10,000	87
15,000	98
20,000	104

■ You're the Teacher

1. "I understand all this signaling stuff, but it's just not fair. I mean, the best person should get the job or the loan or whatever, even if he or she doesn't have the best signal." This student raises an interesting point. Comment on the fairness of the role played by signals. Also, comment on the efficiency of using signals.
2. "What does it mean for a market to be 'efficient'? If you can't forecast profit opportunities, how come prices change all the time and how come some stock prices seem to rise all the time? Can't I make a profit from them?" Briefly explain what an efficient market is and then tackle the questions of why prices fluctuate and why profit opportunities can't be predicted.

Answers

True/False Answers

1. **F** The more rapidly the marginal utility of wealth schedule diminishes, the more risk averse is the individual.
2. **F** People maximize their expected utility.
3. **U** Advertising increases costs, which tends to increase the price; however, advertising also may increase competition, which decreases the price. The net effect on price is uncertain.
4. **T** The reservation price is the highest price the demander will pay for the product.
5. **F** An efficient market has no forecastable profit opportunities.
6. **F** An individual with a linear utility of wealth curve is risk neutral, not risk averse.
7. **F** Diversification lowers the risk; it may or may not have affect the potential return.
8. **T** Traffic tickets signal that the person is a riskier driver than someone without the tickets.
9. **T** This is the definition of adverse selection.
10. **F** Advertising for search goods usually conveys some information, such as where the goods can be purchased.

Multiple Choice Answers

1. **d** The current price equals the future expected price, so no forecastable profit opportunities exist.
2. **a** The more rapidly a person's marginal utility of wealth falls, the more risk averse the person is and hence the more likely he or she is to purchase insurance.
3. **d** Diversification is the idea, "Don't put all your eggs in one basket," thereby reducing risk.
4. **d** All are signals because all convey some information about the individual.
5. **d** When the expected benefit of additional search exceeds the expected cost, more search yields net expected benefits.
6. **c** This is the definition of experience goods.
7. **b** The expected return per $100 dollars invested in A is (0.5)($200) + (0.5)($60) = $130. Hence, investing $200 has an expected return of $260.
8. **c** The expected return from $100 invested in B is $200; the expected return from $100 invested in A is $130. Thus the return from investing $100 in both A and B is $330.
9. **b** A risk-neutral individual cares only about the expected return. The expected return from investment B exceeds that from investment A, so a risk-neutral person invests the entire $200 in *B*.
10. **a** Moral hazard exists when, after entering into a contract, one party acts to gain more benefits and thereby lessen the benefits to the other party.
11. **d** This is the definition of the reservation price.
12. **b** A lower deductible reduces the cost of having an accident; because you are more likely to have an accident, you will want a lower deductible.
13. **d** JCPenney is signaling that it sells high quality clothing.
14. **d** Advertising for experience goods attempts to persuade consumers to try the products.
15. **d** If banks could perfectly discriminate between high-risk and low-risk borrowers, they would not ration loans; instead they would charge different interest rates.
16. **a** In this case, adverse selection and moral hazard combine to cause the lemons problem in which only bad used cars are sold.
17. **b** The price exceeds his reservation price, so Dennis continues to search. Note that the cost of going to this store is now sunk; that is, the $200 cost of going to the store has been spent regardless of what Dennis decides to do. Thus, he compares the price of the computer with his reservation price and does not consider the (sunk) cost of visiting the first store when deciding what to do.
18. **c** The price at the second store still exceeds his reservation price, so Dennis continues to search.
19. **a** The price at the third store is less than his reservation price, so Dennis buys the computer and does not search further.
20. **c** This is the definition of moral hazard.

21. **b** New information changes expectations about companies' future prospects and thus changes current prices of stocks.
22. **c** Risk-neutral people care only about the expected return and do not consider the risk of the investment.
23. **b** Increases in wealth raise total utility and reduce the marginal utility of additional wealth.
24. **c** By maximizing their expected utility, people are making themselves as well off as possible if the situation is repeated many times.

Answers to Short Answer Problems

1. a. You most want to sell insurance to Larry because you expect that his policy will be more profitable than Harry's policy.

   b. Harry is likely to buy the policy. If Harry does not buy the policy, he expects to pay $1,500 a year for his accidents. If he buys the policy, he pays only $1,000, a saving — to Harry — of $500. Larry may or may not buy a policy. If he is very risk averse and cannot obtain a lower price from another company, he will buy your insurance. But, if he is only a little risk averse, he may decide to do without insurance. If another company can recognize him as the safe driver he is and therefore offer him a less expensive policy, Larry will buy from your competitor. Indeed, if all safe drivers can find other companies that realize they are safe drivers, you might wind up insuring only risky drivers for $1,000 a year and incurring an economic loss because their claims cost you an average of $1,500 a year.

   c. Harry probably will buy the first policy; Larry likely will buy the second. From Harry's standpoint, the second policy is more expensive than the first. Harry, the risky driver, is likely to have an accident and thereby incur the $1,500 deductible. However, Larry realizes that he is unlikely to have an accident and is not likely to have to pay the deductible. Hence Larry is more likely to opt for the second policy because, if he has no accident, he pays only $300 rather than $1,300 for his insurance.

   d. In general, insurance companies can use deductibles to separate risky and safe drivers. Safe drivers generally will prefer a low premium and high deductible because they realize that they are not likely to have an accident and be forced to pay the deductible. However, risky drivers prefer a high premium and low deductible because they know that an accident is probable and they do not want to be hit with a high deductible payment. High-risk drivers know that they are accident prone and are willing to pay higher premiums for nearly full coverage, but low-risk drivers know that they seldom have accidents and will choose lower premiums with lower coverage. With deductibles, the adverse selection problem of high-risk people driving low-risk people out of the market is less likely to occur. The insurance company can charge differential premiums that reflect the different risks that it is insuring

2. Banks have more information about the ability and willingness to pay of people who have previously borrowed from them or from other financial institutions. A good loan repayment record is evidence (a signal) that the customer is a low-risk borrower. If a customer has never borrowed before, the bank must find other ways to assess whether the customer is a high-risk or a low-risk borrower.

3. A risk-neutral person is not likely to diversify asset holdings. Diversification lowers the risk involved in holding assets, but a risk-neutral person does not care about risk; all that person is interested in is the expected return. Hence, because the individual is not concerned with risk, diversification does not help a risk-neutral person and, to the extent that it lowers the expected return, diversification actually harms a risk-neutral individual.

4. a. If Igor's bat lives, he has utility of 400; if it dies, he has utility of 0. Igor's expected utility equals his utility if the bat lives multiplied by the probability it lives plus his utility if the bat dies multiplied by the probability it dies. Thus the expected utility is $(0.8)(400) + (0.2)(0) = 320$.

   b. If Igor buys insurance from Bat Farm, he is guaranteed wealth of $60 (wealth of $100 minus the insurance payment of $40). Certain wealth of 60 gives Igor utility of 280. That is less than the expected utility Igor gets from being uninsured (320), so Igor will not buy insurance from Bat Farm.

c. Igor is willing to pay $20 for bat insurance. If he pays $20, his wealth is $80 and his utility is 350. This level of utility exceeds the expected utility of 320 when he is uninsured.

d. Igor expects to gain more because the probability of his bat dying exceeds the normal probability of 20 percent. Thus the probability that All Bat will need to pay off on the policy exceeds 20 percent. This situation illustrates the adverse selection problem: The people who most want to buy bat insurance are those who have sickly bats.

5. An efficient market is one in which the actual price embodies all available relevant information. The price thus will equal the next period's expected price so that there are no forecastable profit opportunities; that is, the expected profit rate will be the same as in alternative investments, or the normal rate of profit. The current market price always will equal the expected future price in an efficient market; any deviation would be eliminated immediately because it would provide an expected (economic) profit opportunity. The stock market is likely to be an efficient market because the millions of participants have a great incentive to process efficiently all available relevant information. Everyone tries to be the fastest and most accurate at processing information because everyone understands that if he or she can be the fastest and most accurate, earning a huge income will be the outcome. For instance, if you can understand more rapidly and more accurately the impact of a newly reported change on a company's outlook, you will be the first to take the appropriate action: Buy the stock if the change is expected to raise the company's profit and dividends in the future or sell the stock if the change is expected to lower the profit and dividends. By being the first, your income will soar. Of course, everyone has precisely the same incentive, so the stock market likely is an efficient market.

6. a. Figure 17.4 shows Lisa's utility if she receives W_1 and if she receives W_2. Her expected wealth is EW, and her expected utility is U. Expected wealth equals the probability of receiving wealth W_1 multiplied by W_1 plus the probability of receiving wealth W_2 multiplied by W_2. In this case, each probability is 0.5, so expected wealth equals the average of W_1 and W_2.

b. The cost of risk is illustrated in Figure 17.4 as $EW - W$. The cost of risk reflects the fact that Lisa dislikes uncertainty. The outcome of Lisa's investment is uncertain; it may pay off in a big way (wealth of W_2) or it may pay off only a little (wealth of W_1). The expected — or average — wealth from this investment is EW and the utility is U. But Lisa can achieve the same utility if she receives a certain wealth of W, which is less than EW. Hence the difference between the risky wealth and the sure wealth with the same utility is Lisa's cost of risk.

FIGURE 17.4
Short Answer Question 6

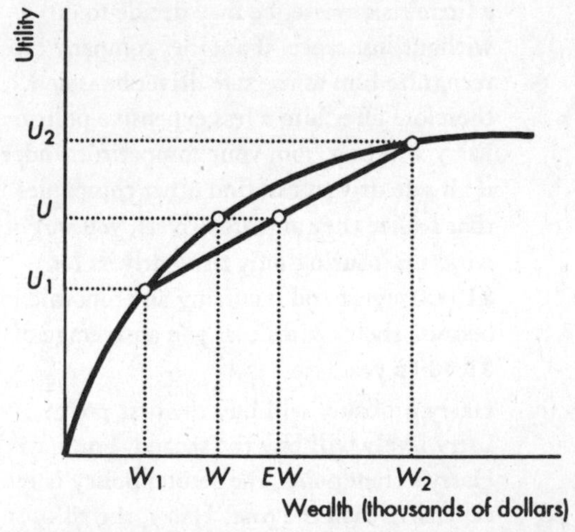

7. a. Figure 17.5 shows that Maria's utility is U_1 if she receives wealth W_1 and that her utility is U_2 if she receives wealth W_2. Her expected wealth and expected utility are labeled EW and U.

   b. The linear utility of wealth curve indicates that Maria is risk neutral, so this risk imposes no cost on her. Certain wealth W gives Maria the same utility, U, as the risky situation with expected wealth EW. But the amount of wealth is the same in both cases; that is, $W = EW$. Compare this result with that in problem 6 for Lisa. For Lisa, a lower amount of sure wealth, W, yielded the same utility as the risky wealth, EW. The difference is Lisa's cost of risk. This outcome shows how Lisa will pay — in the form of lower though certain wealth — and still have the same utility as in the risky situation. For Maria, however, the amount of sure wealth that gives the same utility as the risky wealth is equal to the amount of the risky wealth. Hence Maria has 0 cost of risk. Because risk is costless to Maria, she is unwilling to pay anything — in the form of receiving a lower albeit certain level of wealth — in order to be rid of the uncertainty she faces.

FIGURE 17.5

Short Answer Problem 7

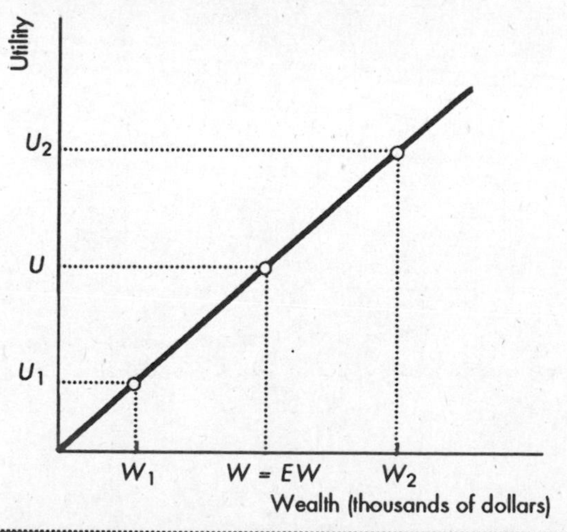

8. a. Leonard's expected wealth is ($20,000)(0.5) + ($0)(0.5) = $10,000.

   b. Leonard's expected utility is (104)(0.5) + (0)(0.5) = 52.

   c. The situation with uncertain wealth of $0 or $20,000 yields expected wealth of $10,000 and expected utility of 52. Table 17.3 shows that certain (no-risk) wealth of $4,000 also yields utility of 52. The cost of risk is $6,000, the amount by which expected wealth must be increased beyond no-risk wealth to give the same utility as the no-risk situation ($10,000 – $4,000).

   d. For Leonard, the forgone utility, 60, of the $5,000 cost of the investment is greater than the expected utility of the risky project, 52. Leonard is not willing to make the investment.

■ You're the Teacher

1. "Well, it's hard to know what's fair. Let's take a concrete example. (This, incidentally, is a true story drawn from the experience of the author of your study guide.) While Mark was an undergraduate, he used to work for a county government. The government used to post job openings on a bulletin board. Certain jobs were open only to college graduates. Mark graduated from college on Saturday. Thus, on Friday before he graduated, he was ineligible for these jobs but on Monday when he returned to work, he was eligible. Had Mark changed over the weekend? Was he suddenly more productive or more intelligent as a result of the graduation ceremony? No; the only difference now was that Mark possessed a signal: that he had graduated from college. So, even though he was the same person, one day he was ineligible and the next day was eligible. Was this fair? At the time, Mark didn't think so. But, suppose that the department advertising the position was forced to accept all applications. Would it have been fair to force the people in the department to look through hundreds or thousands of applications for the possibility that they might find someone without a college degree who could handle the job? Because fairness is a normative issue, the question cannot be answered with certainty.

However, with respect to efficiency, signals and reliance on them seem to enhance efficiency. In particular, the department advertising the opening that required a college degree was guaranteed that a high proportion of the applicants would be qualified to hold the position. Hence the department would not waste time and resources sorting through many applications from people who would not work out in the job. Thus by requiring a college degree — and relying on a signal — the department increased its efficiency and did not squander society's scarce resources."

2. "An efficient market has two characteristics, namely, that the actual price equals the expected future price, that it embodies all the available information, and that there are no forecastable profit opportunities. Almost all economists believe that the stock market is an efficient market.

   So, why do stock prices fluctuate? Stock prices fluctuate when new information becomes available. If new information about a company's future dividends or profit is generated, the stock's price immediately changes to reflect this new information. Forecastable profit opportunities are ruled out because the price immediately changes to reflect the new information. For example, suppose that JCPenney announced that on next Friday it would pay a higher dividend. Further, suppose that the share price didn't increase immediately in response to this announcement; instead, the share price was *forecast* to rise on Friday when the higher dividend was paid. Thus you are able to forecast a profit on the stock by buying it on Thursday knowing that you would be able to sell it for more on Friday. Of course, in this case not only you but everyone else would buy on Thursday! This increase in demand would drive the price up on Thursday, not Friday. Thus the forecasted profit opportunity has moved to Wednesday. Hence you'd buy on Wednesday to take advantage of the forecasted profit caused by the rise in price on Thursday. But, guess what? Everyone else would buy on Wednesday! As a result, the price would rise on Wednesday, not Thursday. This chain of events keeps on going backward in time until the point at which the price rises is immediately after the announcement. By so doing, it eliminates any forecastable profit. So, you see, a forecasted profit opportunity will disappear automatically as everyone rushes to take advantage of it."

Part Review 3 MARKETS FOR FACTORS OF PRODUCTION

Reading Between the Lines

WALL STREET'S COMPLIANCE PROBLEM IS SPOTLIGHTED BY KIDDER'S CASE

As part of its 1987 settlement of civil insider-trading charges, Kidder, Peabody Group Inc. implemented a compliance system designed to help the firm detect the most complex trading crimes.

But Kidder's allegations this week that a top trader executed a series of "phantom" trades that caused it to post $350 million in nonexistent profits raises questions about whether even the most sophisticated compliance program can really work at a Wall Street securities firm.

Kidder, a General Electric Co. unit, said Joseph Jett, a 36-year-old managing director who has run Kidder's government-bond trading desk since 1991, had beat its system for about a year. People close to the firm said Mr. Jett executed thousands of allegedly phony trades before being caught last week.

Kidder has said it believes that Mr. Jett was trying to improve the appearance of his personal trading profits to boost his compensation. Last year, he made $9 million.

"There's a basic assumption that most senior people are honest," said Thomas Russo, a managing director of Lehman Brothers Inc. who is in charge of that firm's compliance and audit department. "Unless you have reason to believe that trades are bogus, the chances of catching fraudulent trades is often random." Because securities firms execute thousands of trades daily, the companies often check them based on small samplings.

Laurie P. Cohen, "Wall Street's Compliance Problem is Spotlighted by Kidder's Case," April 19, 1994, p. A12. Reprinted by permission of The Wall Street Journal,

■ Analyze It

Kidder, like all firms, must determine how much to pay its employees. In some cases, this is easy, but in the case of securities traders, the process is more difficult. Kidder's compensation scheme increased its traders' pay according to how much profit the trader generated.

1. What sort of principal-agent problem did Kidder's compensation scheme attempt to overcome?
2. Kidder's method of compensating its employees caused another problem. Describe the problem in terms of the principal-agent problem it created.
3. Is there an ideal compensation method for Kidder to use?

Mid-Term Examination

1 An increase in the demand for a factor

a. decreases both its price and its factor income.
b. increases both its price and its factor income.
c. decreases its price and increases its factor income.
d. increases its price and decreases its factor income.

2 As the quantity employed of a factor decreases, total product

a. falls and the factor's marginal product falls.
b. falls and the factor's marginal product rises.
c. rises and the factor's marginal product falls.
d. rises and the factor's marginal product rises.

3 Marginal revenue product equals marginal product times the marginal revenue of the product

a. only for perfectly competitive firms.
b. only for monopolistically competitive firms.
c. only for monopoly firms.
d. for all firms.

4 The labor supply curve bends backward if the

a. substitution effect outweighs the income effect.
b. income effect outweighs the substitution effect.
c. demand for labor is elastic.
d. demand for labor is inelastic.

5 Normally, a decrease in the marginal revenue product of labor causes

a. the supply of labor to decrease.
b. wages to decrease.
c. the marginal cost of production to decrease
d. employment to increase.

6 When did 35 percent of the work force belong to unions in the United States?

a. In the 1950s.
b. In the 1960s.
c. In the 1970s.
d. In the 1980s.

7 In comparison to a monopsonist, an employer in a competitive labor market hires

a. fewer workers and produces less.
b. fewer workers and produces more.
c. more workers and produces less.
d. more workers and produces more.

8 With respect to market and non-market production, on average working men are

a. less diversified than women and receive lower pay as a result.
b. less diversified than women and receive higher pay as a result.
c. more diversified than women and receive lower pay as a result.
d. more diversified than women and receive higher pay as a result.

9 Capital

a. and gross investment are flows.
b. and gross investment are stocks.
c. is a flow. Gross investment is a stock.
d. is a stock. Gross investment is a flow.

10 A decrease in the rate of interest raises the

a. marginal revenue product of a machine.
b. net present value of a machine.
c. rate at which a machine becomes obsolete.
d. slope of the firm's demand curve for capital.

11 A decrease in the rate of interest results from a shift of the supply curve for capital

a. leftward or a shift of the demand curve for capital leftward.
b. leftward or a shift of the demand curve for capital rightward.
c. rightward or a shift of the demand curve for capital leftward.
d. rightward or a shift of the demand curve for capital rightward.

12 The price of a firm's stock rises if the expected dividend

a. falls or the interest rate falls.
b. falls or the interest rate rises.
c. rises or the interest rate falls.
d. rises or the interest rate rises.

13 A decrease in wealth brings

a. higher total utility and higher marginal utility.
b. higher total utility but lower marginal utility.
c. lower total utility but higher marginal utility.
d. lower total utility and lower marginal utility.

14 Nicole is indifferent between option A, which gives her $20,000 for sure, and option B, which gives her $10,000 with probability 0.5 or $34,000 with probability 0.5. Nicole's cost of risk for option B is

a. zero.
b. $2,000.
c. $34,000.
d. $44,000.

15 A movie and a new car are

a. search goods, promoted chiefly through informative advertising.
b. search goods, promoted chiefly through persuasive advertising.
c. experience goods, promoted chiefly through informative advertising.
d. experience goods, promoted chiefly through persuasive advertising.

16 In an efficient market, prices change

a. when the demand curve shifts but not when the supply curve shifts.
b. when the supply curve shifts but not when the demand curve shifts.
c. predictably.
d. randomly.

Answers

Reading Between the Lines

Kidder's compensation scheme was an attempt to tie its employees' salaries to the company's profit. By so doing, the owners of the company — the principals —try to give the employees — the agents — the incentive to maximize the company's profit, which is the principals' goal. Thus, employees who shirk or otherwise do not work hard, contribute little to the company's profit and so, receive lower pay than those who work hard and make larger contributions to the profit.

Unfortunately for Kidder, however, this compensation scheme created another principal-agent problem. Specifically, by tying its traders' compensation to the profit created by the trader, the compensation scheme gave each trader the incentive to over-state his or her profit. Thus, the agent wants to report his or her profit being as high as possible, regardless of what it does to the firm's *overall* profit. The story reports that Kidder alleges Mr. Jett's goal was to increase his compensation by reporting that he made a profit of $350 million for Kidder. If this allegation is true, the agent — Mr. Jett — was trying to take advantage of the principals — the upper management and the owners — in order to further the agent's goal. Of course, the truth of the allegation made by Kidder is not yet known and, though not reported in this story, in later stories Mr. Jett has asserted his innocence. There likely is no perfect compensation scheme; every scheme sets up different incentives and so Kidder, like all firms, must be alert for agents responding to these incentives in ways that are perverse for the company. This problem is why Kidder and all brokerage firms have compliance departments, but as Thomas Russo points out, compliance departments cannot be expected to catch every act of malfeasance.

Mid-Term Exam

1 b; 2 b; 3 d; 4 b; 5 b; 6 a; 7 d; 8 b; 9 d; 10 b; 11 c; 12 c; 13 c; 14 b; 15 d; 16 d.

Chapter 18 MARKET FAILURE AND PUBLIC CHOICE

Key Concepts

The Government Sector

- Total spending by all levels of government (federal, state, and local) is 35 percent of U.S. total income; 20 percent of the U.S. labor force is employed by the government sector.
- Government expenditures generally have grown over the past 65 years.

The Economic Theory of Government

Government economic action often stems from market failure and inequality. (Inequality is discussed in Chapter 19.) **Market failure** is the inability of an unregulated market to achieve allocative efficiency. Market failure has three causes:

- **Public goods** — goods or services that can be consumed by everyone and from which no one can be excluded (discussed in this chapter).
- **Monopoly** — monopolies and cartels restrict the amount of output produced (discussed in Chapter 20).
- **Externalities** — when the production or consumption of goods and services create a cost or benefit that falls on someone who did not participate in the transaction (discussed in Chapter 21).

Public Choice and the Political Marketplace

Public choice theory treats the government sector as a political marketplace, analogous to the economic marketplace. Participants in the political marketplace are:

- Voters — the consumers of the outcomes of the political process. They express their demand by voting, lobbying, and making campaign contributions.
- Politicians — the officials elected by voters. Their objective is to get elected and reelected.
- Bureaucrats — officials who work in the government and are appointed by politicians.

A **political equilibrium** occurs when the choices of voters, politicians, and bureaucrats are compatible and no group can make itself better off with a different choice.

- **Public interest theory** — predicts that governments act to eliminate waste and achieve economic efficiency.

Public Goods

A pure public good can consumed by everyone and no one can be excluded. **Public goods** have two features:

- **Nonrivalry** — one person's consumption does not reduce the amount available for anyone else.
- **Nonexcludability** — no one can be excluded from consuming the good.

Nonexcludability means that public goods are subject to **free riding**:

- A **free rider** is someone who consumes a good without paying for it.

Free riding creates the **free-rider problem**, which is the tendency for too little of a public good to be provided if it is produced and sold privately.

The **total benefit** of a public good is the total dollar value placed on it by all citizens. The **marginal benefit** from a public good is the change in the total benefit from a unit change in its quantity. The **net benefit** is the total benefit minus the total cost.

The **efficient scale of provision** of a public good occurs when the net benefit is maximized, which occurs when the marginal benefit of another unit equals the marginal cost of supplying it.

- With private provision, free riding limits the amount produced and results in an inefficiently low level of output.
- Government provision can attain efficiency because free riding is prevented by levying taxes to finance payment for the good.

The amount of the good that is provided by the government depends on the political marketplace and the actions of politicians, bureaucrats, and voters. Politicians often follow the principle of minimum differentiation:

- **Principle of minimum differentiation** — the tendency for competitors (political parties) to be identical in order to appeal to the maximum number of clients or voters.

Bureaucrats try to maximize the budgets of their agencies.

- If voters are well informed, politicians won't allow bureaucrats to expand expenditure beyond the level that maximizes net benefit.
- Voters may be **rationally ignorant**; that is, they decide *not* to acquire information because the personal cost of acquisition is larger than the personal benefit from having the information. If voters are rationally ignorant, politicians, influenced by bureaucrats and lobbyists representing special interests, may allow inefficient over-provision of the public good.

Taxes

In 1994, most of the federal government's revenue came from income taxes. Compared to low-income people, individuals with high income generally pay a larger amount of income tax and receive fewer benefits from the government. High-income people want lower tax rates and fewer benefits; low-income individuals want the reverse. Politicians balance these desires according to the median voter theorem:

- **Median voter theorem** — political parties pursue policies maximizing the net benefit of the median voter.

An **excise tax** is a tax on the sale of particular good.

- An excise tax shifts the supply curve of the good vertically higher by the amount of the tax, as illustrated in Figure 18.1. The amount of tax equals the length of the double headed arrow.
- The tax raises the equilibrium price and lowers the equilibrium quantity. In Figure 18.1 the price including the tax rises the price from P_c to P_t and the quantity falls from Q_c to Q_t.
- A tax creates a **deadweight** loss, which also is shown in Figure 18.1.
- Comparing Figure 18.1 with Figure 18.2 shows that taxes imposed on goods with more elastic demand create larger deadweight losses.

FIGURE 18.1
The Effect of an Excise Tax

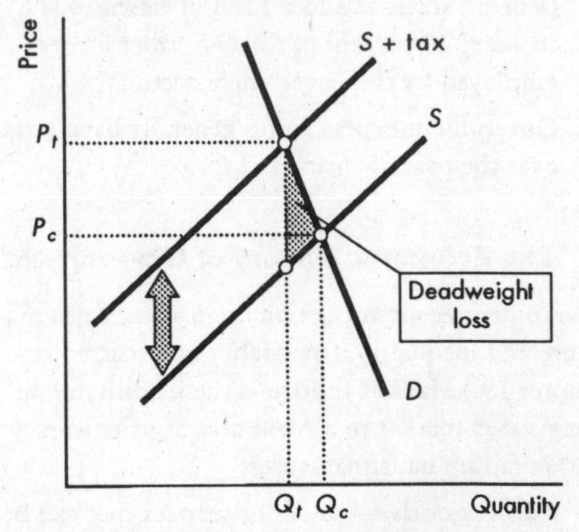

FIGURE 18.2
Deadweight Loss with an Elastic Demand

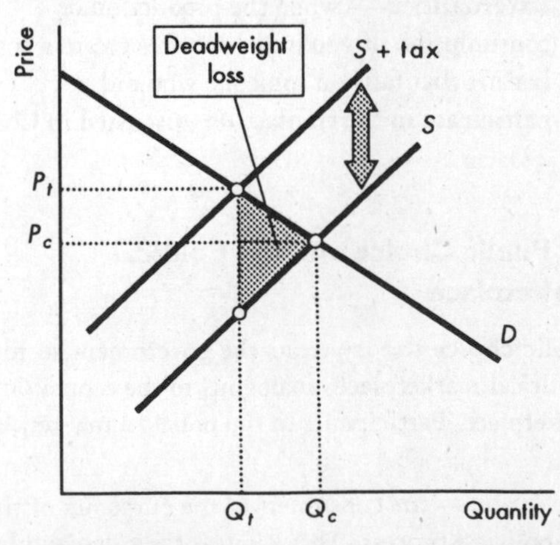

Helpful Hints

1. One of the main criteria that economists use to judge the success of the market (or any other institution, for that matter) is allocative efficiency. Allocative efficiency means that the economy is producing all goods and services up to the point at which the marginal social cost equals the marginal social benefit. In this case, no one can be made better off without making someone else worse off.

   When the market fails to achieve this "ideal" level of efficiency, there is said to be market failure. In this chapter (and throughout this unit of the textbook), you learn that, when governments intervene in the economy, they also may fail to achieve allocative efficiency. This situation is called government failure. Both the market and government can fail by producing either too little (so that the marginal social benefit of the last unit exceeds the marginal social cost) or by producing too much (so that the marginal social cost of the last unit exceeds the marginal social benefit). Because both markets and governments can fail, the relevant economic question in each case is: Which fails less?

2. Contrary to what you might think initially, not all goods provided by the government are public goods. A public good is defined by the characteristics of nonrivalry and nonexcludability, not by whether it is publicly provided. For example, some cities and communities provide swimming pools; others provide utility services such as electricity. None of these are pure public goods even though they are provided by the government. Indeed, in many communities, the same services are provided by the private sector.

3. The properties of nonrivalry and nonexcludability associated with pure public goods imply that the marginal benefit curve for the economy as a whole is different from that for private goods.

   A private good is rival in consumption. Therefore, to obtain the demand curve for the entire economy, we sum the individual marginal benefit (demand) curves horizontally. Here, we ask, "At each possible price, how much will everyone in the economy demand?" Thus, if at a price of $8 you demand 5 units and I demand 5 units, in total we demand 10 units at this price. Because the goods are rival in consumption, none of the 5 units you will consume at this price can be the same as any of the 5 units I will consume. However, for the economy's marginal benefit curve for a public good we sum the individual marginal benefit curves vertically. This procedure is the same as asking, "At every possible level of output, how much will everyone in the economy be willing to pay?" For instance, for 5 units you are willing to pay $8 and I am willing to pay $8, so together we are willing to pay $16 dollars. If 5 units are provided, because the public good is nonrival, the 5 units that you consume are precisely the same as the 5 units that I consume. This key difference — that for a public good we consume the same units but for a private good we must consume different units — is the reason that the marginal benefit curve for evaluating the efficient provision level of a public good is different from that for a private good.

4. Public choice theory provides a theory of the political marketplace that parallels the economic theory of markets for goods and services. Drawing analogies between the operation of political markets and ordinary markets is a good way to grasp their similarities.

   In political markets the demanders are voters, whereas in ordinary markets, the demanders are consumers. In both cases, demanders are concerned about their costs and benefits.

   The suppliers in political markets are politicians and bureaucrats, and in ordinary markets, the suppliers of goods and services are firms.

   In political markets, voters express their demands by means of votes, political contributions, and lobbying. The suppliers (politicians) in this market desire to retain political office. In ordinary markets, consumers express their demands by means of dollars because suppliers are motivated by a desire to maximize profit.

   In both markets, equilibrium is a state of rest. In equilibrium there is no tendency to change because participants cannot become better off by making a different choice or by engaging in an additional transaction.

5. To understand the logic behind the median voter theorem you need to recognize that politicians want to be elected and then remain in office. To do so they must receive a majority of the votes

cast; they must receive at least one more than 50 percent of the votes. Because all politicians realize this fact, the median voter, the "middle" voter, becomes the key voter. A politician who offers a platform that deviates from the preferences of the median voter will lose to a politician who offers a platform closer to those preferences. If voter preferences change so that the median voter changes, the political parties must search for the new median voter. The election of 1994 may be a case in which the median voter changed, and Republicans were better able to capture the preferences of the new median voter. If the median voter has changed, Democrats will respond by reshaping their platform to appeal more to the new median voter. Perhaps by the time you read this passage, the election of 1996 will be over and you will know whether 1994 was a random occurrence or represented a shift in the median voter and, if it did, how successful the Democrats were in trying to recapture the median voter.

Questions

True/False/Uncertain and Explain

1. The government's share of total expenditures has increased since 1929.

2. To be elected, politicians choose platforms that appeal to the median voter.

3. Market failure refers to the situation in which the private market fails to produce the allocatively efficient amount of output.

4. A movie shown in an uncrowded movie theater illustrates a good that is nonexludable and nonrival in consumption.

5. The more inelastic the demand for a good, the larger is the deadweight loss created by an excise tax levied on it.

6. The government provides the efficient amount of a public good.

7. Public goods but not private goods face the free rider problem.

8. The public choice theory of government behavior is based on the assumption that politicians and bureaucrats are motivated primarily by concern for the public interest.

9. Rational ignorance is the situation wherein politicians are uninformed about certain political policies.

10. Any product supplied by government is a public good.

11. According to public choice theory, not only is there possibility of market failure, but there also is the possibility of "government failure."

12. The marginal benefit curve for a public good is obtained the same way as the marginal benefit curve for a private good.

13. Political parties tend to propose fundamentally different policies to give voters a clearer choice.

14. At the efficient level of output, the total net social benefit of a public good is at its maximum.

15. The private, unregulated market tends to produce less than the efficient quantity of pure public goods.

Multiple Choice

1. Which of the following is <u>NOT</u> a source of market failure?
   a. The existence of public goods.
   b. The presence of externalities.
   c. The fact that some goods are rival in consumption.
   d. The existence of monopolies.

2. Which of the following is both nonrival and excludable?
   a. The defense services provided by a new stealth bomber.
   b. A pair of pants.
   c. A beautiful sunset.
   d. An uncrowded theme park such as Walt Disney World.

3. The deadweight loss triangle from an excise tax comprises the loss of
   a. only consumer surplus.
   b. only producer surplus.
   c. consumer surplus plus the loss of producer surplus.
   d. consumer surplus plus the loss of producer surplus minus the tax revenue collected.

4. The idea that political parties will have similar policy proposals reflects
   a. free riding.
   b. rational ignorance.
   c. government failure.
   d. the principle of minimum differentiation.

5. A free rider is someone who
   a. does not pay taxes.
   b. cannot be excluded from consuming a public good even though he or she did not pay for the good.
   c. paid more than his or her fair share for the provision of a public good.
   d. cannot be forced to pay for his or her consumption of a private good.

6. Amy realizes that her personal benefit from becoming an expert on welfare reform is limited, so she does not learn about this issue. Amy's decision reflects
   a. free riding.
   b. the nonexcludability principle.
   c. the median voter theorem.
   d. rational ignorance.

7. According to public choice theory, a voter favors candidates whose political program is
   a. perceived to offer the greatest personal benefit to the voter.
   b. best for the majority of the people.
   c. closest to allocative efficiency.
   d. favored by the median voter.

8. The market demand curve for a private good is obtained by
   a. summing the individual marginal cost curves horizontally.
   b. summing the individual marginal cost curves vertically.
   c. summing the individual marginal benefit curves horizontally.
   d. summing the individual marginal benefit curves vertically.

9. The economy's total demand curve for a public good is obtained by
   a. summing the individual marginal cost curves horizontally.
   b. summing the individual marginal cost curves vertically.
   c. summing the individual marginal benefit curves horizontally.
   d. summing the individual marginal benefit curves vertically.

10. The amount of a public good that maximizes the net benefit to the economy is likely to be provided if
    a. voters are well informed.
    b. rational ignorance is combined with special interest lobbying.
    c. politicians are well informed.
    d bureaucrats are rationally ignorant.

11. To two fishermen, a codfish swimming in mid-ocean is a good that is
    a. nonrival and nonexcludable.
    b. nonrival and excludable.
    c. rival and nonexcludable.
    d. rival and excludable.

12. To two farmers, a steer grazing in the middle of a pasture owned by one of the farmers is a product that is
    a. nonrival and nonexcludable.
    b. nonrival and excludable.
    c. rival and nonexcludable.
    d. rival and excludable

13. Suppose that the demand for wine is not perfectly inelastic and that initially 5 million bottles of wine are produced and consumed in the United States. If the government levies an excise tax of $1 per bottle of wine, the government will collect
   a. more than $5 million in tax revenues.
   b. $5 million in tax revenues.
   c. less than $5 million in tax revenues.
   d. An amount that may be more than, equal to, or less than $5 million in tax revenues, depending on the elasticity of demand.

14. The efficient amount of a public good
   a. is as much as the public demands.
   b. cannot be provided unless the problem of nonexcludability is overcome.
   c. equates total benefit and total cost.
   d. is such that the marginal benefit from another unit equals the marginal cost.

15. Voters are asked to vote for either proposition A or proposition B. Proposition A will win if it
   a. is closer to allocative efficiency.
   b. is supported by bureaucrats.
   c. is preferred by the median voter.
   d. generates greater social benefits than social costs.

16. Governments provide pure public goods such as national defense because
   a. governments know how to produce these goods.
   b. of the free-rider problems that result in underproduction by private markets.
   c. people do not value national defense very highly.
   d. of the potential that private firms will make excess profits.

17. In the political market place, voters do all the following except
   a. support policies that they think will make themselves better off.
   b. fire bureaucrats who do not support efficient policies.
   c. lobby politicians to favor certain policies.
   d. sometimes remain rationally ignorant about a policy.

Figure 18.3 illustrates the effects from an excise tax that has been imposed on compact discs. Use this figure for the next four questions.

FIGURE 18.3
Multiple Choice Questions 18, 19, 20, and 21

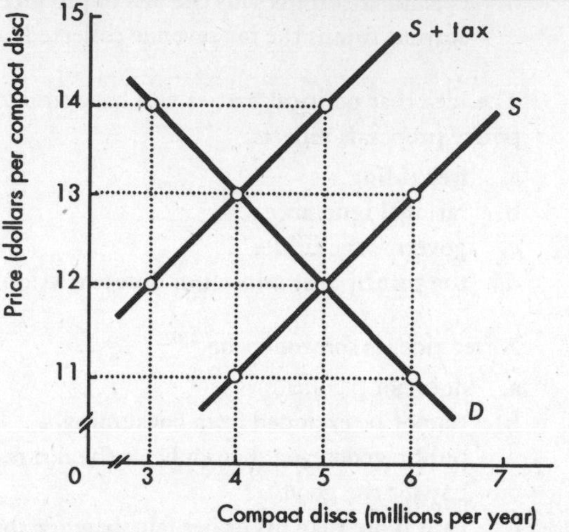

18. The amount of the tax per CD is
   a. $14.
   b. $13.
   c. $12.
   d. $2.

19. The equilibrium price, including the tax, after the tax has been imposed is
   a. $14.
   b. $13.
   c. $12.
   d. $11.

20. The amount of tax revenue the government collects is
   a. $70 million.
   b. $52 million.
   c. $44 million
   d. $8 million.

21. The amount of deadweight loss created is
   a. $12 million.
   b. $8 million.
   c. $6 million.
   d. $1 million.

22. Products with elastic demands often are lightly taxed because
    a. they usually are goods consumed largely by the poor.
    b. the amount of the deadweight loss created is large.
    c. free riders ensure that the government's tax revenue is small.
    d. The premise of the question is wrong because products with elastic demands usually are taxed heavily.

23. Public choice theory
    a. argues that government has a tendency to conduct policies that help the economy move toward allocative efficiency.
    b. argues that politicians and bureaucrats tend to be more concerned about the public interest than individuals in the private sector.
    c. argues that the public choices of government maximize net benefits.
    d. applies economic tools used to analyze markets to the analysis of government behavior.

24. Competition between two political parties will cause those parties to propose policies
    a. that are quite different.
    b. that are quite similar.
    c. that reduce the well-being of middle-income families and increase the well-being of the rich and the poor.
    d. that equate total costs and total benefits.

25. Suppose that the marginal benefit from another unit of a public good exceeds the marginal cost of producing it. Then,
    a. the net benefit from the product is at its maximum, and its provision is at the efficient level.
    b. the net benefit from the product is at its maximum, but the provision of the product is not at its efficient level.
    c. less of the product should be produced because its provision exceeds the efficient level.
    d. more of the product should be produced because its provision is less than the efficient level.

26. Public choice theory is based on the assumption that those involved in the political process generally are motivated by
    a. self-interest.
    b. the desire to achieve allocative efficiency.
    c. public spirit.
    d. the desire for maximum profit.

27. The principle of minimum differentiation can be used to explain all of the following except the reason that
    a. political parties often have platforms that are similar.
    b. fast-food restaurants often locate in the same general area.
    c. students from the same high school often go to the same college.
    d. automobiles often are similar in appearance

■ Short Answer Problems

Table 18.1 Income Tax Rates

Person	Desired income tax rate (percent)
April	80%
Brian	40
Christopher	25
Diane	30
Eric	10

1. Table 18.1 shows the citizens in a (small!) nation and their desired income tax rates. The nation is a democracy, and its political parties are trying to decide which income tax rate to propose as part of their policy packages.
    a. Who is the median voter? What income tax rate will be proposed by the parties? Why?
    b. Before the next election, April changes her mind and decides that she wants an income tax rate of 50 percent. What income tax rate will now be proposed? How does this tax rate compare with that in part (a)? If it is different, why is it different; if it is the same, why is it the same?
    c. April continues to change her mind and before the third election she decides that she wants an income tax rate of 20 percent. Now

what income tax rate will be proposed? How does this tax rate compare with those in parts (a) and (b)? If it is different, why is it different; if it is the same, why is it the same?

2. Explain the nonrivalry and nonexcludability features of a pure public good. Why are both necessary for the good to be a pure public good?
3. Suppose that the demand for a product is perfectly elastic. What effect does a tax imposed on such a product have on its price? What is the deadweight loss from the tax and who pays it? Use a diagram to illustrate your answer.
4. Suppose that the demand for a product is perfectly inelastic. In this case, what effect does a tax imposed on this product have on its price? What is the deadweight loss from this tax? Use a diagram to illustrate your answer.
5. The ships of 10 companies must navigate a particularly treacherous section of coastline. Each year each shipping line incurs $200,000 in shipping costs from ships running aground there. If a lighthouse was built, these costs would fall to 0. Building and maintaining the lighthouse would cost $1,900,000 a year. If it was constructed, all the ships that pass that way would benefit from the lighthouse.
   a. From society's point of view, is building the lighthouse efficient?
   b. From a company's point of view, if each company pays 1/10 the total cost of building a lighthouse, is it profitable?
   c. Suppose that the lighthouse was constructed but that one company did not help pay for it. What is this company's profit from the lighthouse?
   d. Base on your answers to parts (b) and (c), what incentive does each company have?
   e. If one company decides not to pay for the lighthouse, will it be constructed?
   f. What might the government do in this case?
6. Explain why voter ignorance might be rational.
7. Table 18.2 shows the initial demand and supply schedules for shoes.
   a. Based on Table 18.2, what is the initial equilibrium price of a pair of shoes? The equilibrium quantity?
   b. Suppose that the government imposes a tax of $10 per pair of shoes that the supplier must pay. Complete Table 18.3, showing the demand and supply schedules after the tax has been levied.
   c. In Figure 18.4 (on the next page), illustrate the effect of the tax on the market for shoes by drawing the pre-tax and post-tax supply and demand curves.
   d. After the tax is imposed, what is the equilibrium price (including the tax) for a pair of shoes? The equilibrium quantity?
   e. How much of the tax do suppliers pay? Demanders?
   f. What is the amount of deadweight loss from this tax? (Hint: Figure 18.4 should be helpful when answering this question.)

Table 18.2 The Initial Market for Shoes

Price (dollars per pair of shoes)	Quantity of Shoes Supplied (millions)	Quantity of Shoes Demanded (millions)
$55	70	90
60	75	85
65	80	80
70	85	75
75	90	70
80	95	65

Table 18.3 The Market for Shoes After the Tax

Price, Including tax (dollars per pair of shoes)	Quantity of Shoes Supplied (millions)	Quantity of Shoes Demanded (millions)
$55	60	___
60	65	___
65	___	___
70	___	___
75	___	___
80	___	___

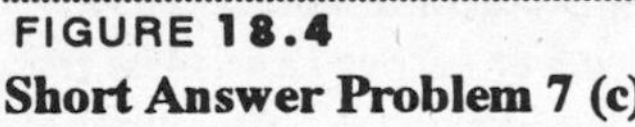

FIGURE 18.4
Short Answer Problem 7 (c)

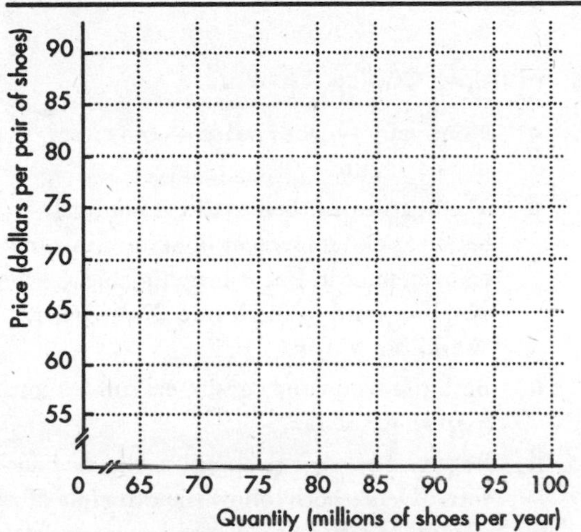

Table 18.4 Security at Parkin Springs Apartments

Number of Guards	Total Cost of Guards (dollars)	Marginal Benefit per Resident (dollars)	Marginal Benefit to All Residents (dollars)
1	$300	$10	$___
2	600	4	___
3	900	2	___
4	1,200	1	___

8. Parkin Springs Apartments has 100 residents who all are concerned about security. Table 18.4 gives the total cost per day of hiring a 24-hour security guard service and the marginal benefit per day to each of the residents.
   a. Why is a security guard a public good for the residents of Parkin Springs Apartments?
   b. Why will no guards be hired if each of the residents must act individually?
   c. Complete the last column of Table 18.4 by computing the marginal benefit of security guards to all the residents combined.

9. Now suppose that the residents form an apartment council that acts as a governing body to address the security issue.
   a. What is the optimal (allocatively efficient) number of guards? What is the net benefit at the optimal number of guards?
   b. Show that net benefit is less for either one less guard or for one more guard than the net benefit for the optimal number of guards.
   c. How might the Apartment Council pay for the guards it will hire?

10. What is the free-rider problem? Why does free riding hinder the private sector in producing the efficient amount of a public good?

You're the Teacher

1. "I don't see why the government would ever do anything that causes inefficiency. Inefficiency hurts the nation and I thought that the government would try to help us." Comment on this student's views and give an example of how the government might take actions that create inefficiency.

Answers

True/False Answers

1. **T** The government's share of total expenditure has increased from 10 percent in 1929 to 35 percent in recent years.
2. **T** By appealing to the median voter, the politician will attract more than half the votes and so win the election.
3. **T** This is the definition of market failure.
4. **F** The movie is nonrival but not nonexcludable because a theater can easily limit the people viewing the movie only to those who paid to see it.
5. **F** The more elastic the demand, the larger is the deadweight loss.
6. **U** Whether government is able to do so depends on whether the provision is in the public interest or whether government failure — as suggested by public choice theory — occurs.
7. **T** Public goods are nonexcludable and thus they face a severe free-rider problem.
8. **F** Public choice theory is based on the assumption that politicians and bureaucrats are motivated by self-interest.
9. **F** Rational ignorance occurs when a voter is uninformed about an issue because the benefit to the voter of becoming informed is less than the cost to the voter.
10. **F** Public goods are characterized by nonrivalry and nonexcludability.
11. **T** Governments and markets "fail" when they do not deliver the allocatively efficient level of output.
12. **F** The marginal benefit curve for a public good is derived by adding *vertically* each individual's marginal benefit curve; the marginal benefit curve for a private good (its demand curve) is derived by adding *horizontally* each person's marginal benefit curve (i.e., each person's individual demand curve).
13. **F** The principle of minimum differentiation points out that political parties tend to propose similar policies.
14. **T** This is a definition of allocative efficiency.
15. **T** The free-rider problem limits the private market to a level of output that is less than the efficient amount.

Multiple Choice Answers

1. **c** Nonrivalry — not rivalry — can create market failure.
2. **d** The uncrowded theme park is nonrival because your enjoyment does not limit my enjoyment of it, but it is excludable as anyone who ever tried to sneak into Walt Disney World can testify.
3. **c** Both producers and consumers suffer a loss from an excise tax.
4. **d** Both parties want to appeal to the median voter. Hence both follow the principle of minimum differentiation and present similar proposals.
5. **b** This is the definition of a free rider.
6. **d** Amy is pursuing her own self-interest and rationally decides not to become an expert on welfare reform.
7. **a** Public choice theory is based on the assumption that people — voters, politician, and bureaucrats — all follow their own self-interest.
8. **c** This procedure shows the quantity that will be demanded by everyone at any particular price.
9. **d** Vertical summation shows the price that everyone is willing to pay for any particular quantity.
10. **a** If voters are well informed, they can ensure that politicians force bureaucrats to provide the efficient amount of the public good.
11. **c** If one fisherman catches the fish, the other cannot, so the codfish is rival; but in the middle of the ocean no fisherman can exclude another from trying to catch the fish, so the codfish is nonexcludable.
12. **d** The farmer who owns the steer can use it but the other farmer cannot, so the steer is rival; in the middle of a pasture, the first farmer can exclude the other farmer from trying to catch the steer. Note the fundamental difference between the steer, which is owned and therefore is both rival and excludable, and the

codfish, which is not owned and therefore is rival but nonexcludable.

13. **c** The new equilibrium quantity of wine is less than 5 million bottles, so the government collects less than $5 million in tax revenue.

14. **d** If the marginal benefit from *any* good equals the marginal cost, the efficient amount is being produced.

15. **c** If the median voter supports proposition A, proposition A will receive a majority of votes and will win.

16. **b** The free-rider problem limits the private market's ability to produce the efficient amount of public goods.

27. **b** Politicians, not voters, fire bureaucrats.

18. **d** The supply curve shifts upward by the amount of the tax. Because the upward shift is $2, the tax is $2.

19. **b** After the tax, the quantity supplied equals the quantity demanded at $13.

20. **d** The equilibrium quantity is 4 million CDs, and the government levies a tax of $2 on each CD. Thus the total tax revenue is $8 million.

FIGURE 18.5
Multiple Choice Question 21

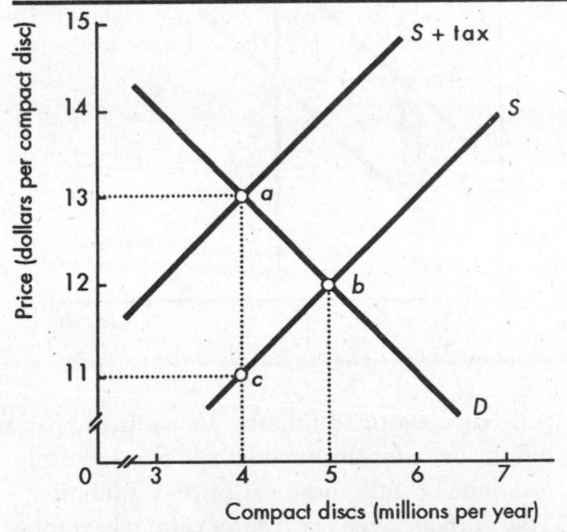

21. **d** The deadweight loss is shown as triangle *abc* in Figure 18.5. The triangle's area is 1/2(1 million CDs)($2 per CD), so the deadweight loss is $1 million.

22. **b** The more elastic the demand for a product, the more a tax reduces the quantity produced and the greater is the deadweight loss.

23. **d** Public choice essentially is the application of economics to the political arena.

24. **b** The parties both want to appeal to the median voter in order to win an election, so they tend to propose similar policies.

25. **d** If one more unit is produced, the gain to society (the marginal benefit) exceeds the cost to society (the marginal cost), so the additional net benefit from the unit is positive.

26. **a** Economists generally assume that self-interest motivates people's behavior.

27. **c** Friendship, tradition, and in-state tuition are more likely to be the reasons that students from the same high school often attend the same college.

■ Answers to Short Answer Problems

1. a. Diane is the median voter: April and Brian want higher tax rates; Christopher and Eric want lower tax rates. The parties will propose the income tax rate that appeals to the median voter, so they will propose an income tax rate of 30 percent. If a party proposed a lower tax rate, it would gain the votes of Eric and Christopher, but the competing party would win votes from April, Brian, and Diane by proposing a 30 percent tax rate. Analogously, if a party proposed a tax rate higher than 30 percent, only April and Brian would vote for it, and the party would lose the election when its competitor proposed a tax rate of 30 percent.

   b. The income tax rate will be 30 percent. This tax rate is the same as in part (a) because Diane is still the median voter. Even with April's change, two voters (April and Brian) still want higher tax rates than Diane, and two voters (Christopher and Eric) want lower tax rates. Note that there is no response to April's switch in this case.

   c. The proposed tax rate will be 25 percent. This tax rate is lower than those in parts (a) and (b). The tax rate is different because the median voter has changed. With April's desire for a lower tax rate, Christopher has become the median voter (April and Eric want lower tax rates, whereas Brian and Diane want higher tax rates), which causes a change in the proposed tax rate. The answers to parts (b) and (c) make the point that the policy proposal is insensitive to changes that do not affect the median voter. However, a change that affects the median voter will alter the policies that are proposed.

2. A good has the nonrivalry feature if its consumption by one person does not reduce the amount available for others. The nonexcludability feature means that if the good is produced and consumed by one person, others cannot be excluded from consuming it.

   Both features are necessary for the good to be a pure public good. A private good, such as a hot dog, is provided to one person for consumption. But the nonrivalry feature of a public good means that everyone can consume the good simultaneously. Limiting the consumption to one person at a time would be inefficient because other people can consume the product without denying it to anyone else. In addition, private goods are sold by firms so that the firms' owners can earn an income and thereby purchase goods and services for themselves. Public goods are nonexcludable, which means that anyone can consume the product regardless of the amount paid. This fact gives people the incentive to free ride. Free riding makes the provision of such goods by private companies unlikely because the firm will not be able to collect any revenue from selling the product.

3. Figure 18.6 shows the effect of a tax when the demand for the product being taxed is perfectly elastic. The price of the product does not rise; that is, the price that includes the tax, P_t, equals the initial price, P. The deadweight loss is solely the reduction in producer surplus. When the demand is perfectly elastic, the price of the product does not rise, and producers are forced to pay the entire tax. Hence suppliers bear the entire deadweight loss.

4. Figure 18.7 shows the impact of a tax when the demand for a product is perfectly inelastic. The price rises by the entire amount of the tax, from P to P_t. Interestingly, there is no deadweight loss from this tax. Theoretically, because demand is perfectly inelastic, consumers are willing to pay an infinite price for this product and so total surplus is infinite because consumer surplus is infinite. Thus, although the tax reduces consumer surplus by some finite amount, both consumer surplus and thus total surplus remain infinite.

   More intuitively, the reason there is no deadweight loss is because the tax does not change the quantity produced. A deadweight loss occurs when a tax causes fewer units of the product to be

FIGURE 18.6
Short Answer Problem 3

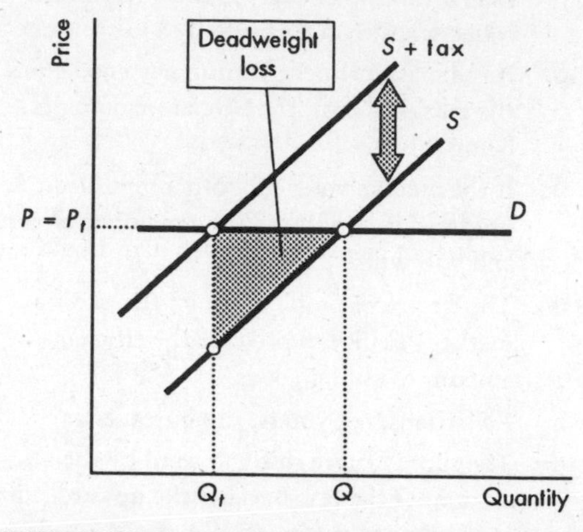

FIGURE 18.7
Short Answer Problem 4

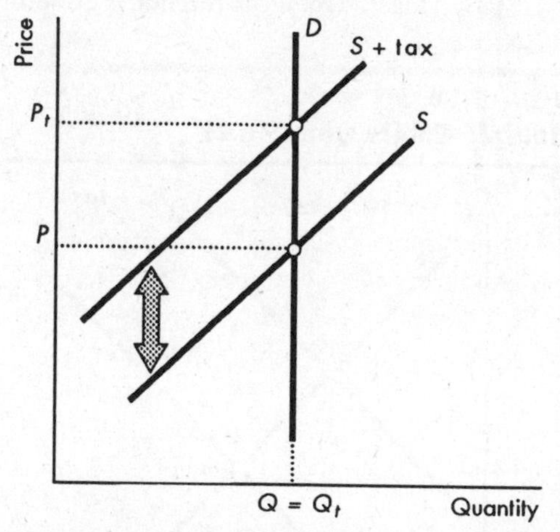

produced. Because consumer and producer surpluses are lost on these units, society suffers a deadweight loss. But, when demand is perfectly inelastic, no fewer units are produced. The higher price merely transfers resources from consumers to the government and so no deadweight loss is imposed on society.

5. a. Yes, building the lighthouse is efficient. The marginal benefit to society from the lighthouse is the saving in shipping costs because of its existence. Each firm would save $200,000 annually, so society as a whole would save $2,000,000 annually. The marginal cost of building and running the lighthouse is $1,900,000 annually, so, on balance, society would be better off by $100,000 a year if the lighthouse was constructed.

   b. Yes, building the lighthouse would be profitable. The company would incur a cost of $190,000, its 1/10 share of the cost. But the company would save $200,000 in shipping costs. So, on balance, each company comes out $10,000 ahead.

   c. After the lighthouse is built, the company would save $200,000 in shipping costs. If the company did not help pay for the lighthouse, its profit would increase by $200,000.

   d. Each company has the incentive to free ride, that is, to not pay for the lighthouse. If the company can avoid payment, its profit increases by $200,000, but if it must pay its 1/10 share of the cost, its profit increases by only $10,000.

   e. If one company decides not to help pay for the lighthouse, the lighthouse will not be constructed. In this case, each of the other companies would have to pay 1/9 the cost of the lighthouse, or $211,111.11 annually. But the lighthouse saves them only $200,000 in shipping costs, so building the lighthouse would not be a profitable venture for the 9 firms that would jointly pay the cost.

   f. Free riding may prevent the lighthouse from being built. Because the lighthouse would be socially efficient, the government might use its taxing powers to tax each company $190,000 and then use the funds to construct and operate the lighthouse.

6. Most issues have only a small and indirect effect on most voters. Thus for a voter to spend much time and effort to become well informed about such issues would be irrational because the additional cost incurred *by the voter* would quickly exceed any additional benefit enjoyed *by the voter*. Only if the voter is significantly and directly affected by an issue does becoming well informed pay. As a result, most voters will be rationally ignorant any specific issue.

7. a. The initial equilibrium price of a pair of shoes is $65, and the initial equilibrium quantity is 80 million pairs of shoes.

Table 18.5 Short Answer Problem 7 (b)

Price, including tax (dollars per pair of shoes)	Quantity of Shoes Supplied (millions)	Quantity of Shoes Demanded (millions)
$55	60	90
60	65	85
65	70	80
70	75	75
75	80	70
80	85	65

   b. Table 18.5 shows the demand and supply schedules after the tax. The tax does not change the demand schedule. Basically, consumers will demand, say, 80 million pairs of shoes if the price is $65 regardless of whether suppliers receive all $65 or if suppliers receive only $55 and $10 is sent to the government as taxes. However, the supply schedule does change. If the price including the tax is $65, suppliers will receive only $55, because they must send $10 to the government. The initial supply schedule indicates that, when suppliers receive $55 per pair, they will produce 70 million pairs of shoes. Hence, when the after-tax price is $65, suppliers — who receive only $55 for themselves — are willing to produce 70 million pairs of shoes. The rest of the answers are calculated similarly.

c. Figure 18.8 shows the effect of the tax. Note that the supply curve shifts vertically higher by $10, the amount of the tax.

FIGURE 18.8
Short Answer Problem 7 (c)

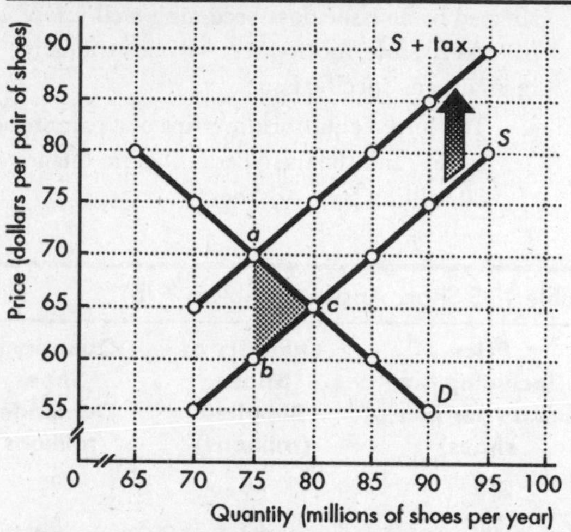

d. From either Figure 18.8 or Table 18.5, the new equilibrium price is $70 and the equilibrium quantity is 75 million pairs of shoes.

e. The price rose from $65 to $70; thus demanders pay $5 of the tax (in the form of a higher price). Suppliers initially received $65 per pair of shoes; after the tax they receive only $60, so they pay $5 of the tax (in the form of lower receipts per shoe).

f. The deadweight loss is the area of the darkened triangle *abc* in Figure 18.8. The height of this triangle is $10 per pair, the amount of the tax. The base of the triangle is 5 million shoes, the reduction in the quantity. Hence the area equals one-half the base times the height, or ½(5 million shoes)($10 per pair) = $25 million.

8. a. A security guard is a public good in this case. The guard has the features of nonrivalry and nonexcludability. Employment of the guard involves nonrivalry because one resident's consumption of the security provided does not reduce anyone else's security. Nonexcludability is involved because, once a security guard is in place, all residents enjoy the increased security and none can be excluded.

b. If each resident must act individually to hire a security guard none will be hired because each resident receives only $10 in benefit from the first guard, who costs $300 per day.

c. The entries in the last column of Table 18.6 show the total marginal benefit. These answers are obtained by multiplying the marginal benefit per resident by the number of residents, 100. This multiplication is the numerical equivalent of summing the individual marginal benefit curves vertically for each quantity of guards.

Table 18.6 Short Answer Problem 8

Number of Guards	Total Cost of Guards (dollars)	Marginal Benefit per Resident (dollars)	Marginal Benefit to All Residents (dollars)
1	$300	$10	$1,000
2	600	4	400
3	900	2	200
4	1200	1	100

9. a. If the apartment council hires each guard for whom the marginal benefit exceeds the marginal cost, they will hire the optimal number of guards. The marginal cost of each additional guard is $300. The marginal benefit of the first guard is $1,000, so this guard is hired. Similarly, the marginal benefit of the second guard is $400, and this guard also is hired.

However, the marginal benefit of the third guard is only $200, which is less than marginal cost. Therefore the allocatively efficient (optimal) number of guards is 2. For 2 guards, the net benefit is $800, or the total benefit ($1,400) minus the total cost ($600).

b. For one guard, the net benefit is $700, or the total benefit ($1,000) minus the total cost ($300). For three guards, the net benefit also is $700, or the total benefit ($1,600) minus the total cost ($900). Thus the net benefit of $800 is greatest for two guards.

c. The apartment council might pay for the optimal number of guards by collecting a security fee of $6 per day from each of the 100 residents in order to hire two security guards.

10. In unregulated markets the free-rider problem results in the production of too little of a pure public good because there is little incentive for individuals to pay for it. The free rider will not pay because that person's payment will likely have no perceptible effect on the amount the person will be able to consume. Hence avoiding payment is rational. This incentive creates a problem for the private sector when it attempts to provide the product. In particular, suppliers produce goods in exchange for payments because the suppliers want to use their receipts to buy goods and services for themselves. If people do not pay for the goods, suppliers receive no income and hence have no incentive to produce the goods.

■ You're the Teacher

1. "The idea that the government won't create inefficiency is called the 'public interest' theory of government. It is based on the assumption that government actions lead to allocative efficiency. However, 'public choice' theories of government suggest that at times government actions can cause inefficiency — that is, can cause government failure. Public choice theories assert that well-informed special interest groups are able to induce the government to undertake programs that do not maximize net benefits because most voters are rationally ignorant. For most voters, being well informed about any particular issue does not pay. As a result, a small, well-informed interest group will have an influence on government programs that greatly exceeds its size relative to all voters.

   "Let me give you an example of how this might work. Suppose that there are three large producers of copper in the United States. If they can convince the government to tax foreign copper $1 per ton, each U.S. copper producer may benefit by $80 million dollars. Meanwhile, this tax might cost each consumer in the United States 80¢. It seems pretty clear to me that the copper producers are going to lobby like crazy for this policy and contribute a lot of dough to candidates' campaigns. But you and I aren't going to care much one way or the other. It sure isn't in our personal interest to study this issue much because we can gain, at most 80¢! So we'll stay rationally ignorant, but the copper producers will lobby hard. As a result, this policy stands a chance of being enacted."

19 INEQUALITY, REDISTRIBUTION, AND HEALTH CARE

Key Concepts

■ Economic Inequality in the United States

- Average family income in 1992 was $39,000.
- The poorest 20 percent of families received less than 5 percent of the total income; the richest 20 percent received almost 45 percent of the total income.

Inequality in income and wealth is measured by the Lorenz curve. The Lorenz curve for income (wealth) graphs the cumulative percentage of income (wealth) against the cumulative percentage of families. Figure 1 illustrates a Lorenz curve.

FIGURE 19.1
The Lorenz Curve

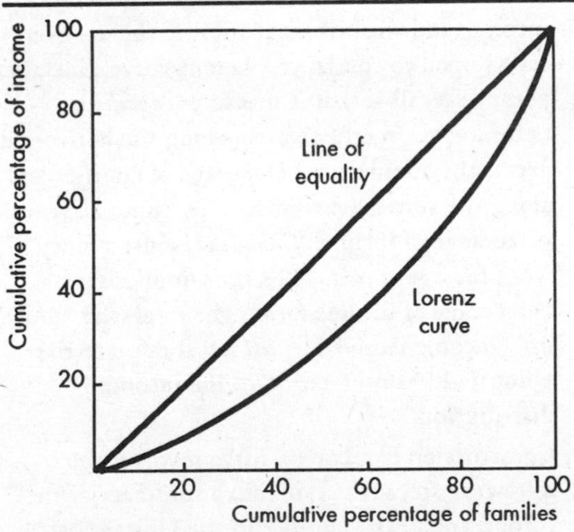

- The "line of equality" shows the (hypothetical) distribution of income (wealth) if everyone had the same income (wealth).
- The farther the Lorenz curve is from the line of equality, the more unequal is the distribution.

From 1950 to 1967, the income distribution became more equal; since 1967, it has become less equal. Poverty exists when families cannot buy adequate food, shelter, and clothing. In 1992, in the United States, 37 million people had incomes below the official poverty level. A disproportionate number of these families were of Hispanic origin or were black.

■ Comparing Like with Like

Wealth is the *stock* of assets owned by an individual. Income is the *flow* of earnings received by an individual from his or her stock of wealth. Wealth includes both human and nonhuman capital.

- The data used to construct the wealth distribution do not include human capital and therefore overstate wealth inequalities.
- The distributions of *annual* income and wealth are more unequal than distributions of *lifetime* income and wealth.

■ Factor Prices, Endowments, and Choices

A family's income depends on the prices of the factors it supplies, on the endowment of the factors that it owns, and on its choices.

- Wage rates — the largest source of income — differ. This is one source of income inequality.
- Endowments of skills differ, but these differences are normally distributed (bell shaped); the income distribution is skewed.
- If the quantity of labor a family chooses to supply increases as the wage rate it receives rises, the distribution of income is less equal than the distribution of wages, and the distribution of income is skewed.

Inequalities can be passed to the next generation through **bequests** (gifts to the next generation) and **assortative mating** (marrying within one's own socioeconomic class).

■ Income Redistribution

Income is redistributed by governments through income taxes, income maintenance programs, and provision of goods and services below cost.

Income taxes can be:

- **Progressive** — the marginal tax rate increases when income increases.
- **Regressive** — the marginal tax rate decreases when income increase.
- **Proportional** — the marginal tax rate does not change when income increases. (This type of tax is also known as a *flat tax.*)

Income maintenance programs include social security, unemployment compensation, and welfare. These programs generate problems, including discouragement of work, encouragement of family breakup, high birth rate of illegitimate children, social tensions, and costly welfare bureaucracy. Reform proposals have suggested placing a limit on the length of time that Aid to Families with Dependent Children (AFDC) can be collected and strengthening the incentive to work.

A **negative income tax** would give every family a guaranteed annual income and then decrease family benefits at specified benefit–loss rates as the family's market income increased. The negative income tax would avoid most of the problems of the other programs, but would be costly.

Provision of goods and services below cost benefit the recipients of the products.

■ Health-Care Reform

- Spending on health care in the United States was 14 percent of total income in 1992 and has been growing rapidly.

Health-care costs have increased rapidly because health care is labor intensive and technological change has concentrated on extending the range of ailments that can be treated. The demand for health care has increased because of higher incomes and because of advances in medical treatment.

Insurance companies face adverse selection (those more likely to require health care are more inclined to buy insurance) and moral hazard (doctors and patients perform tests and procedures because someone else pays for them).

The Clinton health-care plan proposed to expand the role of the government in the health-care market. Under the plan:

- Insurance companies would have been required to offer everyone insurance.
- Costs would have been contained by increasing competition and efficiency and by capping insurance premiums.

The cost containment measures might have provided a one-time fall in prices but would not have stopped the ongoing rise in prices. The premium caps might have created shortages and queues.

Currently, government actions in the health market raise costs and prices. First, the costs of Medicaid and Medicare have risen more rapidly than private health care. Second, "excessive" purchases of health insurance is encouraged because health insurance premiums paid by the employer are sheltered from income taxes.

Helpful Hints

1. The Lorenz curve is the tool used to measure income (and wealth) inequality. If you are ever called upon to construct a Lorenz curve, the crucial point to recall is that it measures *cumulative* percentages. In other words, along the horizontal axis is the cumulative percentage of families and along the vertical axis is, say, the cumulative percentage of income. *Cumulate* is just a fancy word for *sum* or *add.* Thus the cumulative percentage of income means the total (the "added up") income received by *all* families up to the point under consideration in the income distribution.

   Construction of a Lorenz curve involves the following steps. First, obtain a summary of the incomes of all the families in the United States. Then, mark a point representing the 20 percent having the lowest incomes, which is 5 percent of the nation's total income. Next, determine the income for the next 20 percent, which is 11 percent of the nation's total income. Now, add these first two groups to obtain the cumulative percentages. Thus the lowest 40 percent of families in the income distribution has 16 percent of the nation's total income: 5 percent from the lowest 20 percent group plus 11 percent from the second lowest 20 percent group. Then, plot a point representing the cumulative percentage of families, 40 percent, and the cumulative percentage of income, 16 percent. Continue until you reach 100 percent of the families, who will have 100 percent of the nation's total income. Connect the points that you have plotted to get the Lorenz curve.

2. Statistics used to construct Lorenz curves do not always give an accurate picture of income inequality. Understanding why is important. For example, a distribution of wealth that excludes the value of human capital gives a distorted picture relative to the distribution of income. Moreover, the distribution of annual income gives a distorted picture of the distribution of lifetime income.

True/False/Uncertain and Explain

1. Measured income is less equally distributed than measured wealth.
2. The line of equality in a Lorenz curve shows what the income distribution would be if everyone received the same income.
3. The farther the Lorenz curve is from the line of equality, the more equal is the distribution of income.
4. Income is a flow of earnings; wealth is a stock of assets.
5. The life cycle distribution of income is more equal than the annual distribution of income.
6. The fact that people who are more likely to need heath care are therefore more likely to buy health-care insurance reflects adverse selection.
7. Bequests generally make the income distribution more equal.
8. Income in the United States is distributed normally; that is, it has the common bell shape.
9. Spending on health care as a percentage of total income in the United States has been decreasing.
10. Current welfare programs have unintended consequences, such as encouraging families to break up.
11. The poorest 20 percent of U.S. families receive about 15 percent of the nation's total income; the richest 20 percent receive about 25 percent of the nation's total income.

Multiple Choice Questions

1. An example of assortative mating is
   a. a poor woman marrying a rich man.
   b. a rich man marrying a rich woman.
   c. a rich woman marrying a poor man.
   d. something that cannot be expressed in polite society.
2. The farther away a Lorenz curve for income is from the line of equality, the
   a. more equally wealth is distributed.
   b. more equally income is distributed.
   c. less equally income is distributed.
   d. None of the above.
3. In recent years, spending on health care in the United States has been approximately
   a. 5 percent of total income.
   b. 14 percent of total income.
   c. 23 percent of total income.
   d. 52 percent of total income.
4. The wealthiest 1 percent of Americans own what percentage of total measured wealth?
   a. 1 percent.
   b. 10 percent.
   c. 20 percent.
   d. 33 percent.
5. Of the approximate U.S. total population of 280 million people, how many have incomes below the official poverty level?
   a. 13 million.
   b. 37 million.
   c. 59 million.
   d. 93 million.

Use Figure 19.2 for the next two questions.

FIGURE **19.2**

Multiple Choice Questions 6 and 7

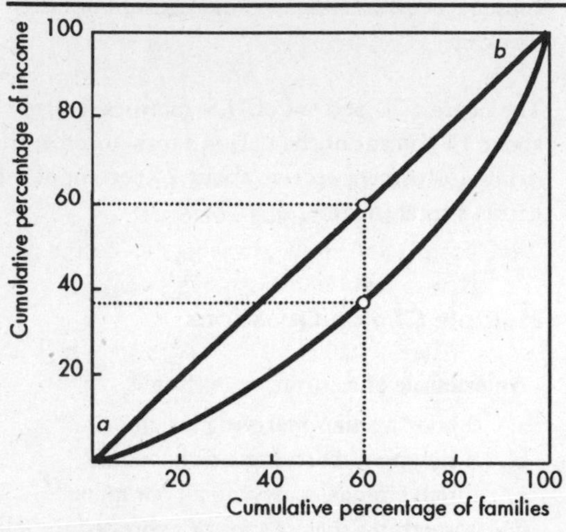

6. In Figure 19.2, the straight line labeled *ab* is the
   a. Lorenz curve.
   b. line of equality.
   c. line of poverty.
   d. line of distribution.

7. In Figure 19.2, the first 60 percent of families have what percent of the nation's total income.
   a. 37 percent.
   b. 60 percent.
   c. 63 percent.
   d. 100 percent.

8. Even if the distribution of wages is symmetric and bell shaped, the distribution of income will be skewed because
   a. abilities are distributed symmetrically.
   b. abilities are distributed asymmetrically.
   c. individuals tend to supply more labor at higher wages.
   d. individuals tend to supply less labor at higher wages.

9. An example of a bequest is
   a. a pair of rich individuals marrying each other.
   b. money given by the government to a person living below the poverty level.
   c. a guaranteed annual income under a negative income tax.
   d. an inheritance left by a deceased parent to a child.

10. A reason for rising health-care prices is
    a. decreased demand owing to higher health-care insurance premiums.
    b. increased supply owing to lower labor costs in the health care industry.
    c. increased demand owing to growth in the number of ailments that can be treated.
    d. increased supply owing to the existence of Medicare.

11. In a Lorenz curve for income, the line of equality shows
    a. the most equitable — fairest — income distribution.
    b. how unequally incomes are distributed.
    c. how much redistribution occurs.
    d. the income distribution if everyone received the same income.

12. Which of the following reduces the inequality of income or wealth relative to the market distribution?
    a. Government payments to the poor.
    b. A regressive income tax.
    c. Large bequests.
    d. Assortative mating.

13. The measured distribution of wealth
    a. understates the degree of inequality because it does not take into account the family's stage in its life cycle.
    b. understates the degree of inequality because it does not take into account the distribution of human capital.
    c. overstates the degree of inequality because it does not take into account the family's stage in its life cycle.
    d. overstates the degree of inequality because it does not take into account the distribution of human capital.

For the next three questions, consider a negative income tax with a guaranteed family income of $12,000. Assume that the benefit–loss ratio is 20 percent.

14. A family that has market earnings of $10,000 has total income of
    a. $10,000.
    b. $12,000.
    c. $20,000.
    d. $22,000.

15. A family with market earnings of $40,000 has total income of
    a. $12,000.
    b. $40,000.
    c. $44,000.
    d. $52,000.

16. What is the break-even level of income; that is, what is the income level at which no payment is given to the family?
    a. $12,000.
    b. $40,000.
    c. $60,000.
    d. $100,000.

17. Suppose that the income tax in the United States was 17 percent of income. This tax is an example of a(n)
    a. regressive tax.
    b. proportional tax.
    c. progressive tax.
    d. efficient tax.

18. If everyone was required to purchase health-care insurance, this policy would limit the
    a. "unequal distribution of insurance" problem faced in the health-care market.
    b. moral hazard problem with health insurance.
    c. adverse selection problem with health insurance.
    d. None of the above.

19. Which of the following statements about the income distribution is correct?
    a. From 1950 to the present, the income distribution has become more equal.
    b. From 1950 to 1967, the income distribution became more equal and since then it has become less equal.
    c. From 1950 to 1967, the income distribution became less equal and since then it has become more equal.
    d. From 1950 to the present, the income distribution has become less equal.

20. On average, which families have the highest incomes?
    a. Black families.
    b. Families of Hispanic origin.
    c. White families.
    d. Families of Hispanic origin and white families are tied for the highest income.

21. In the most recent year for which calculations have been performed, government tax and cash programs
    a. generally redistributed income away from the poor and gave it to the rich.
    b. had no net redistributive effects.
    c. generally redistributed income away from the rich and gave it to the poor.
    d. were dwarfed by the scale of government programs designed to give away goods and services below cost.

22. Which of the following is <u>NOT</u> a problem with current piecemeal income maintenance programs?
    a. They discourage work.
    b. They encourage families to break up.
    c. They are costly to administer.
    d. Most people are unfamiliar with them.

Short Answer Problems

1. What is the difference between wealth and income? If you know one of these for an individual, can you calculate the other?
2. What are the factors that determine a family's income? To what extent are they the result of forces beyond the family's control and to what extent are they the result of choice?
3. Jake has human capital worth $100,000 and tangible capital worth $100,000. James has only human capital worth $200,000. The return on both types of capital is 15 percent.
   a. What is Jake's income? James's income? Who has more income?
   b. Suppose that human capital is not measured. What is Jake's capital? James's capital? According to this measure, who has more capital?
   c. If income can be measured correctly, will Jake's and James's income or capital appear to be less equally distributed?
4. Figure 19.3 shows Lorenz curves for the income distributions of two nations. In which nation is income distributed less equally? How can you tell?

FIGURE 19.3
The Lorenz Curves for Two Nations

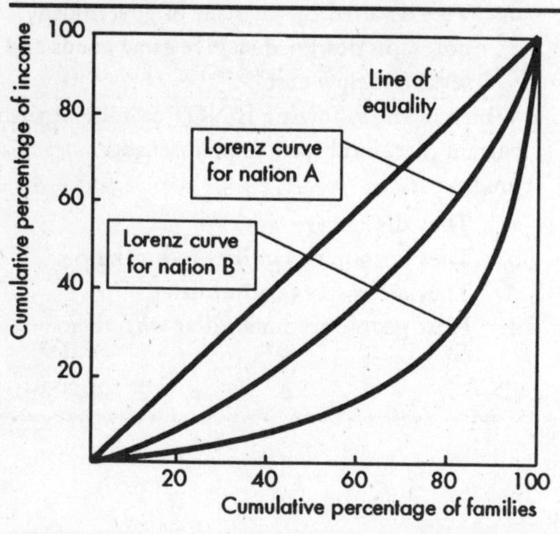

5. Figure 19.4 shows the Lorenz curve for the income distribution of two other nations. In which nation is income distributed less equally? How can you tell?

FIGURE 19.4
The Lorenz Curves for Two Nations

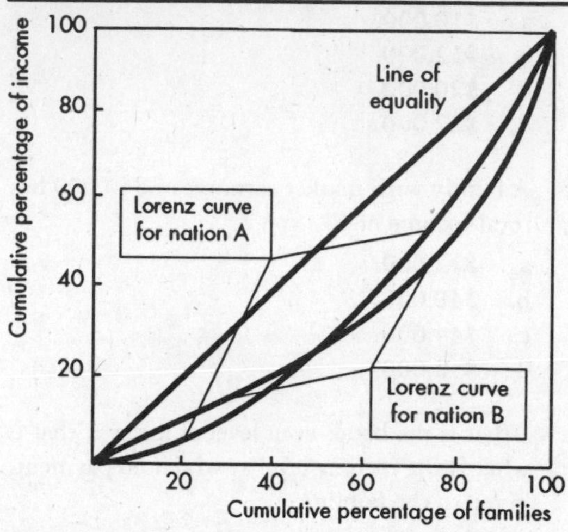

6. Table 19.1 gives information regarding the distribution of market income in Microland, a nation with 100 residents.
   a. Complete the table.
   b. Based on Table 19.1, plot the Lorenz curve for this nation in Figure 19.5 (on the next page).

Table 19.1 Market Income

Families grouped by income	Group income (dollars)	Percentage of total national income	Cumulative percentage
Lowest 20%	**$200,000**	5%	5%
Second lowest 20%	300,000	___	___
Middle 20%	500,000	___	___
Second highest 20%	1,000,000	___	___
Highest 20%	2,000,000	___	___

FIGURE 19.5
Short Answer Problems 6 and 7

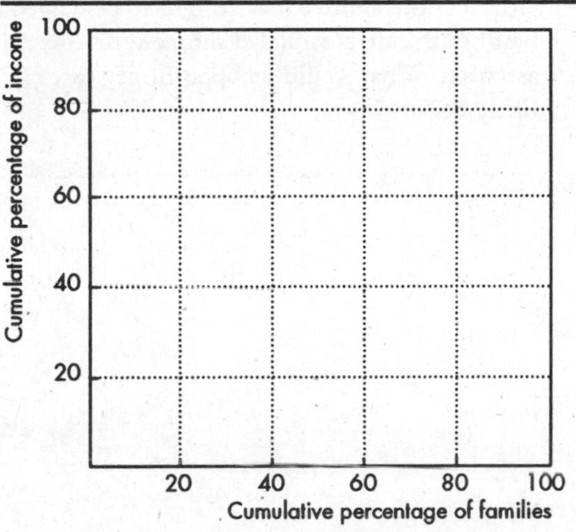

7. The government of Microland imposes a progressive income tax. Only those in the highest 20 percent income bracket pay the tax, and they must pay 30 percent of their income. From the tax receipts, the government gives ⅓ to the lowest 20 percent group, ⅓ to the next lowest, and ⅓ to the next lowest (the middle 20 percent group).
   a. If none of the groups in the economy alter their behavior — so that their market incomes are the same as those in Table 19.1 — complete Table 19.2 for the post-tax, post-transfer income distribution.

Table 19.2 Group Income After Redistribution

Families grouped by income	Group Income (dollars)	Percentage of total national income	Cumulative percentage
Lowest 20%	___	___	___
Second lowest 20%	___	___	___
Middle 20%	___	___	___
Second highest 20%	___	___	___
Highest 20%	___	___	___

   b. In Figure 19.5, draw the new Lorenz curve showing the distribution of income after the government redistribution program has been implemented.
   c. When is income distributed more equally: Before or after the government program? When is it distributed more fairly?

8. Likeland is a nation comprising 100 individuals who are alike in every way except for age. Each resident lives to be 90 years of age and no older. Between birth and the age of 18 years each earns $0 income; between the ages of 18 and 36 each earns an annual income of $30,000; between the ages of 36 and 54 each earns an annual income of $40,000; between the ages of 54 and 72 each receives an annual income of $60,000; and between the ages of 72 and 90 each receives an annual income of $20,000. At any one time 20 individuals are in each of the five age groups. For simplicity we assume that there are no bequests. Table 19.3 summarizes this information.
   a. In Figure 19.6 (on the next page), draw the Lorenz curve for lifetime income in this economy and label it A.
   b. In Figure 19.6 draw the Lorenz curve for annual income in this economy and label it B.
   c. Which method is a better measure of the inequality over a longer time span among individuals in this economy? Why?

Table 19.3 Income Distribution in Likeland

Age Group (years)	Number in Age Group	Annual Income of Age Group (dollars)
0 – 18	20	$ 0
18 – 36	20	30,000
36 – 54	20	40,000
54 – 72	20	60,000
72 – 90	20	20,000

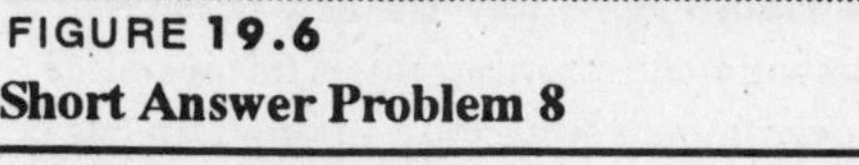
FIGURE 19.6
Short Answer Problem 8

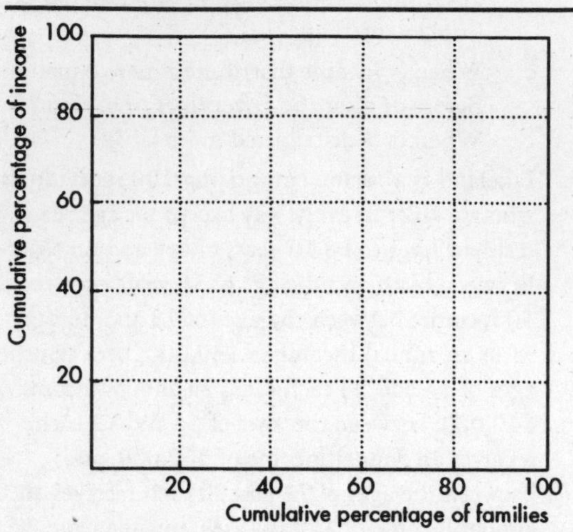

You're the Teacher

1. "Decent health care is a right of all Americans; no citizen of the United States ought to be denied the best health care possible!" Comment on this assertion. What would its opportunity cost of likely be?

Answers

True/False Answers

1. **F** Measured wealth, probably because it excludes human capital, is distributed much less equally than measured income.
2. **T** This is the definition of the line of equality.
3. **F** The *closer* the Lorenz curve to the line of equality, the more equal the income distribution.
4. **T** Income is received over a period of time and so is a flow; wealth is an amount at a point in time and so is a stock.
5. **T** Over people's lifetimes, income is distributed more equally than annual income.
6. **T** This likelihood is called *adverse selection* because the people most apt to select insurance are those most apt to have an adverse outcome and thus need the insurance.
7. **F** Bequests make the income distribution less equal.
8. **F** Income in the United States is skewed, with relatively few people earning above-average incomes and many people earning below-average incomes.
9. **F** As a fraction of income, spending on health care has been increasing, which is one of the reasons that many observers have suggested changes in this market.
10. **T** Other unintended consequences include discouraging work and encouraging a high birth rate of illegitimate children.
11. **F** Income is less equally distributed than the question suggests: The poorest 20 percent receive less than 5 percent of the nation's income, and the richest 20 percent receive 45 percent of the nation's income.

Multiple Choice Answers

1. **b** *Assortative mating* refers to like marrying like.
2. **c** The farther away the Lorenz curve is from the line of equality, the less equally income is distributed.
3. **b** Spending on health care takes about $1 of every $7 of income.
4. **d** As measured, wealth is distributed much less equally than income.
5. **b** According to the government's measure of poverty, 37 million people lived in poverty.
6. **b** The line of equality shows the income distribution if everyone received the same income.
7. **a** Follow the dotted line up from 60 percent of the families to the Lorenz curve and then left to determine that these families have about 37 percent of the nation's total income.
8. **c** By working more hours, high wage earners' incomes are higher for two reasons: Their wage rates are higher *and* they work more hours.
9. **d** Bequests generally make the income distribution less equal.
10. **c** Increases in the demand for health care cause the price of health care to rise.
11. **d** This is the definition of the line of equality.
12. **a** Government payments to the poor raise their income and reduce income inequality.
13. **d** If human capital were included in the measured wealth distribution, the distribution would be more equal.
14. **c** The family's income equals the guaranteed income of $12,000 plus its earned income of $10,000 minus the benefit loss of 20 percent times the earned income of $10,000 (minus $2,000) for a total income of $20,000.
15. **c** The family has total income of the $12,000 guaranteed income plus the $40,000 of earned income minus the benefit loss of 20 percent times $40,000 (minus $8,000), which equals $44,000.
16. **c** The break-even level of income equals $60,000 because at this level of income the loss of benefits (20 percent times $60,000) equals $12,000, which is the same as the amount of the guaranteed level of income.
17. **b** A tax is proportional if everyone pays the same tax rate, or 17 percent in this case.
18. **c** If everyone purchased health-care insurance, the people who are unlikely to use the insurance would buy it along with the people who are more likely to use it.

19. **b** These trends, while present, have not been extreme.
20. **c** White families have the highest average income.
21. **c** These government programs caused income to be distributed more equally than market income.
22. **d** The other factors all are major problems with the current income maintenance system.

Answers to Short Answer Problems

1. Wealth is the stock of assets owned by an individual, whereas income is the flow of earnings received by an individual. The concepts are connected because an individual's income is the earnings that flow from the person's stock of wealth. If we know the person's stock of wealth and rate of return, we can calculate his or her income flow. If we know the person's income flow and the rate of return, we can calculate his or her stock of wealth.
2. A family's income is determined by the market prices for its productive resources and the quantity of resources the family is able and willing to sell at those prices. It also depends on the choices the family makes. These two factors depend on a number of other factors, some of which are (at least partially) under the control of the family and some of which are not.

   The price of labor services, the wage rate, is determined in the market for labor. This factor is not under the immediate control of the family. But, as you learned in Chapters 14 and 15, the wage rate depends on a person's marginal product of labor and the amount of his or her human capital. All these factors are affected by the person's choices about training and education as well as the person's inherent abilities.

   The quantity of labor services supplied depends on personal choices about how to spend time. The quantity of other factors supplied also will depend on personal choices and the family's endowment of the factor. For instance, a family that chooses to save more will be able accumulate more capital than a family that chooses to save less. Alternatively, a family that inherits a large amount of wealth will be able to supply more capital than a family that inherits nothing.
3. a. Jake's income equals the return on capital, 15 percent, times the amount of capital. Hence Jake's income equals $30,000. James's income equals $30,000, so the incomes are the same.

   b. Jake's capital is measured as $100,000. James's capital is measured as $0. Jake seems to have more capital.

   c. Capital *appears* to be less equally distributed. The two measured incomes are equal but the two measured capitals are quite different. This line of reasoning helps explain the difference between the measured income distribution and the measured wealth distribution in the United States.
4. The income distribution in nation B is less equally distributed. The curve for nation B always is farther from the line of equality than is the curve for nation A. For example, the bottom 20 percent of the income distribution in nation B receive a smaller fraction of the country's total income than the bottom 20 percent in nation A. Because the Lorenz curve for nation B is farther from the line of equality, this result is the case for *any* cumulative percentage (other than 100 percent) of B's population compared to A's population.
5. Unlike the situation in question 4, in this case we cannot state that income is distributed less equally in one nation. Figure 19.7 (on the next page) illustrates why. Up to the percentage of families where the curves cross — which appears to be at about 50 percent — income is distributed less equally in nation A; beyond this point, income is distributed less equally in nation B. Take any percentage of families less than 50 percent, say, 20 percent. Compare the bottom 20 percent of the population in nation A to the bottom 20 percent in nation B: the bottom 20 percent in nation A receive a smaller fraction of the nation's total income. Hence income — at this point — is less equally distributed in nation A. Next, select a percentage of families that exceeds 50 percent, say, 80 percent. The bottom 80 percent of families in nation A receive a larger fraction of the nation's income than do the bottom 80 percent in nation B. Therefore, at this point, income in nation A is distributed more equally than in nation B. If the Lorenz curves for two nations cross, you cannot state that income is distributed either more or less equally in one nation relative to the other.

FIGURE 19.7
Short Answer Question 5

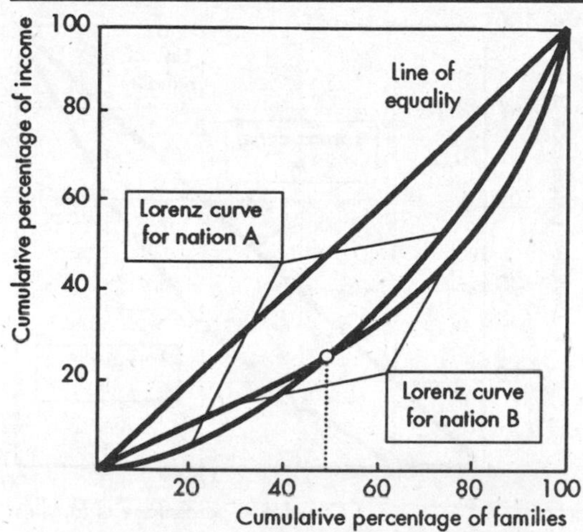

6. a. To calculate the percentages in Table 19.4, first obtain the total income in the nation, which equals $4,000,000, the sum of all groups' incomes. Then, the percentage earned by the second lowest 20 percent equals $300,000/$4,000,000, or 7.5 percent. The cumulative percentage for this group equals the percentage earned by it and all lower groups, which in this case is only the bottom 20 percent group. Hence the cumulative percentage is 5 percent + 7.5 percent = 12.5 percent. The rest of the answers in Table 19.4 are calculated similarly.

   b. Figure 19.8 shows the Lorenz curve for Microland.

7. a. Table 19.5 shows the income distribution after the government redistribution. The richest 20 percent of families are taxed 30 percent of their income, which equals $600,000. Their after-tax income therefore equals $1,400,000. $200,000 (⅓ of the total $600,000) is given to the lowest 20 percent, so their income rises to $400,000; another ⅓ is given to the next lowest group, so their income rises to $500,000; and the final ⅓ is given to the middle group, so their income rises to $700,000. Then, the percentages are calculated in the same way as in problem 6.

Table 19.4 Short Answer Question 6

Families grouped by income	Group income (dollars)	Percentage of total national income	Cumulative percentage
Lowest 20%	$ 200,000	5.0%	5.0%
Second lowest 20%	300,000	7.5	12.5
Middle 20%	500,000	12.5	25.0
Second highest 20%	1,000,000	25.0	50.0
Highest 20%	2,000,000	50.0	100.0

FIGURE 19.8
Short Answer Problem 6

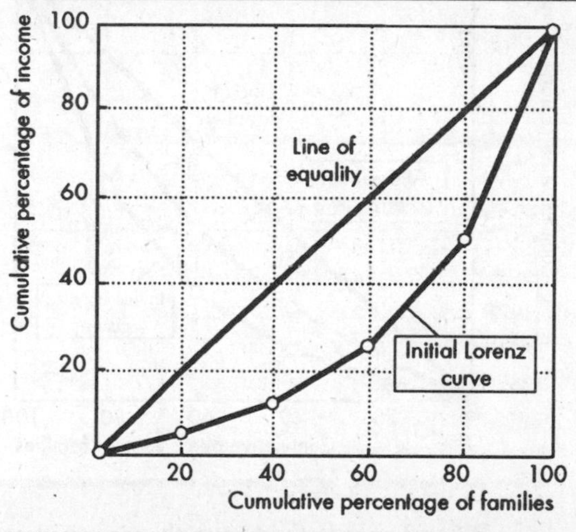

Table 19.5 Short Answer Problem 7

Families grouped by income	Group income (dollars)	Percentage of total national income	Cumulative percentage
Lowest 20%	$ 400,000	10.0%	10.0%
Second lowest 20%	500,000	12.5	22.5
Middle 20%	700,000	17.5	40.0
Second highest 20%	1,000,000	25.0	65.0
Highest 20%	1,400,000	35.0	100.0

b. Figure 19.9 shows the new Lorenz curve and the old Lorenz curve.

c. Income is distributed more equally after the government programs. The Lorenz curve for the income distribution after the government redistribution is closer to the line of equality than the Lorenz curve showing market income before the redistribution. The question of which income distribution is fairer has no clear-cut answer. The question of fairness is inevitably a normative judgment. Hence which income distribution is fairer depends on your views.

FIGURE **19.9**

Short Answer Problems 6 and 7

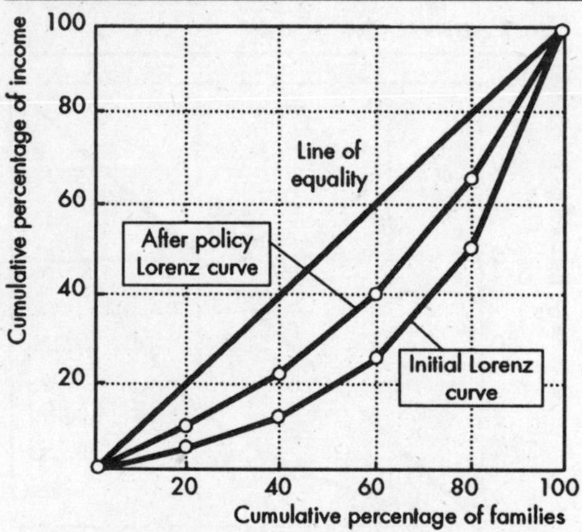

8. a. Because each individual in the economy earns the same lifetime income, the Lorenz curve for lifetime income coincides with the line of equality, labeled A in Figure 19.10.

b. The Lorenz curve for annual income is labeled B in Figure 19.10. It indicates that the poorest 20 percent of the individuals (0–18 years) receive 0 percent of the annual income; the second poorest 20 percent (72–90 years) receive 13 percent of the annual income; the third poorest 20 percent (18–36 years) receive 20 percent of the annual income; the fourth poorest 20 percent (36–54 years) receive 27 percent of the annual income; and the richest 20 percent (54– 72 years) receive 40 percent of the annual income.

FIGURE **19.10**

Short Answer Problem 8

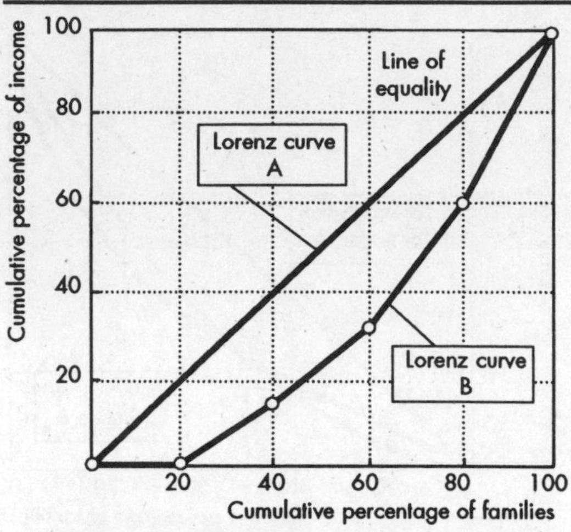

c. The distribution of lifetime income is a better measure of the degree of inequality. In this (imaginary) economy all individuals are totally like each other, a fact that is accurately reflected by equal lifetime incomes. The only reason that the annual income distribution in this economy is not equal is because the individuals are at different stages of identical life cycles.

■ You're the Teacher

1. "The opportunity cost of this policy would be in the goods and services that could no longer be produced and consumed. For instance, an increase in the quantity of health care provided to U.S. citizens may well mean an increase in the number of physicians. Thus someone who otherwise might have been an engineer, designing faster computers, will be a physician. You can see that the opportunity cost to society of having this person working as a doctor is the faster computers that are sacrificed."

Chapter 20 REGULATION AND ANTITRUST LAW

Key Concepts

■ Market Intervention

Two forms of government intervention in monopolistic and oligopolistic markets are **regulation** and **antitrust laws.**

- **Regulation** — rules that determine prices, product standards, and entry conditions. *Deregulation* is the removal of regulation.
- **Antitrust law** — laws that regulate and make illegal monopoly and monopolistic practices.

The total surplus is the sum of *consumer surplus* and *producer surplus*, both of which are illustrated in Figure 20.1. The total surplus is maximized when the market is perfectly competitive and there is no deadweight loss. A (single-price) monopoly increases the producer surplus but reduces the consumer surplus and creates a deadweight loss. Government intervention can affect the surpluses.

FIGURE **20.1**
The Two Surpluses

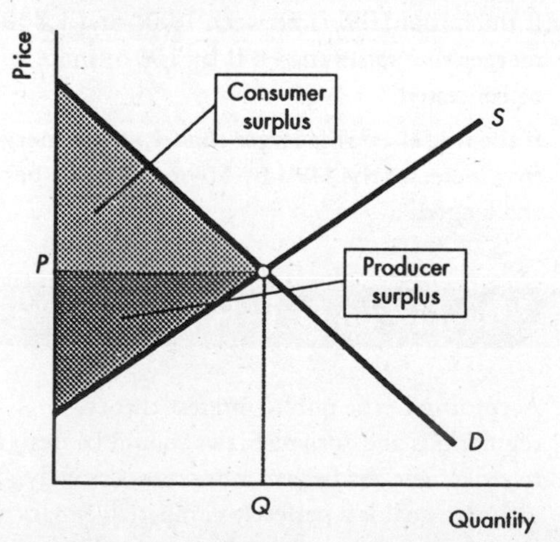

■ Economic Theory of Regulation

Both consumers and producers demand regulation that will be in their interest.

- Consumers' demand for regulation increases when:
  - consumer surplus per buyer increases; and
  - the number of buyers increases.
- Producers' demand for regulation increases when:
  - producer surplus per seller increases; and
  - the number of firms increases.

Regulation is supplied by politicians and bureaucrats.

- The supply increases with increases in:
  - the consumer or producer surplus from the regulation; and
  - the number of people who benefit and know that they have benefited from the regulation.

In political equilibrium, no interest group presses for changes in existing regulations. There are two theories of the political equilibrium:

- **Public interest theory** — predicts that regulation maximizes total surplus.
- **Capture theory** — predicts that regulation maximizes producer surplus.

■ Regulation and Deregulation

From 1887, when the first federal regulatory agency, the Interstate Commerce Commission, was formed until the mid 1970s regulation expanded until about ¼ of the economy was regulated. Since then, there has been gradual deregulation.

Both natural monopolies and cartels are regulated.

Natural monopoly — when one firm can supply the market at lower cost than two or more firms. As illustrated in Figure 20.2 (on the next page), this definition means that the firm's *ATC* curve falls until it is beyond the demand curve.

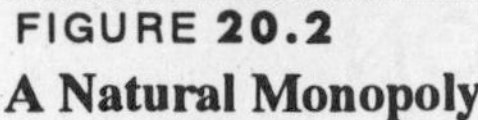

FIGURE **20.2**
A Natural Monopoly

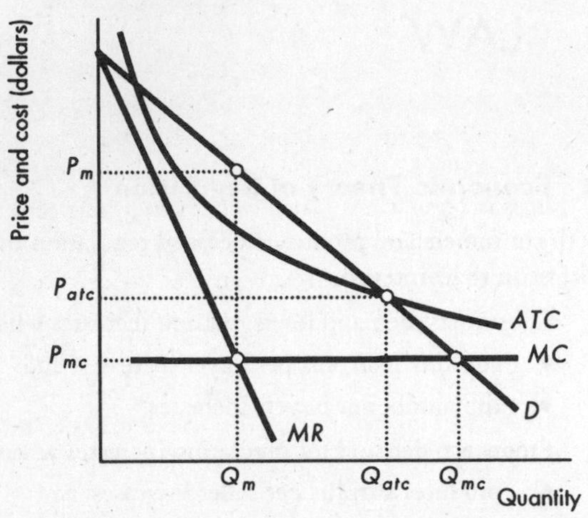

Left unregulated, the firm would produce Q_m and charge P_m. Two methods of regulating a natural monopoly are:

- **Marginal cost pricing** — set the price equal to marginal cost. In Figure 20.2, the price would be P_{mc} and the quantity produced Q_{mc}. This policy maximizes total surplus, but the firm incurs an economic loss.
- **Average cost pricing** — set the price equal to average total cost. In Figure 20.2, the price would be P_{atc} and the quantity produced Q_{atc}. A deadweight loss is created, but the firm does not suffer an economic loss.

Methods used to regulate natural monopolies include rate of return and incentive regulation:

- **Rate of return regulation** — sets the price at a level that lets the company earn a specified target rate of return on its capital. The firm has an incentive to inflate its costs.
- **Incentive regulation** — gives the firm an incentive to operate efficiently. This type of regulation either sets a price cap for the product or allows the firm to earn whatever profit is possible and then, if the profit is high enough, the firm is required to share it with the firm's customers.

The evidence about whether natural monopoly regulation is best characterized by the public interest theory or the capture theory is mixed.

Cartel — a collusive agreement among firms designed to boost the price and decrease the level of output. Public interest theory predicts that oligopolies are regulated to ensure a competitive outcome; the capture theory predicts that regulation will help the producer. Although the evidence is mixed, it tends to favor the capture theory.

Deregulation began in the 1970s. The transportation industry was deregulated in response to higher energy prices; the communications industry was deregulated because of improvements in technology that drastically reduced the cost of telecommunications.

Antitrust Law

- **Sherman Act** — the first federal antitrust law, passed in 1890, prohibited restrictions of trade and monopolization.

Initially, the *rule of reason* was the U.S. Supreme Court's interpretation that only unreasonable acts violated the Sherman Act; eventually this rule was replaced by a view that some acts (e.g., price fixing) are automatically illegal.

Two types of mergers are:

- **Vertical integration** — the joining of a firm with a customer or a supplier.
- **Horizontal integration** — the merger of two firms in the same business.

Merger guidelines used by the U.S. Department of Justice include:

- If the initial Hirschman–Herfindahl Index (HHI) is less than 1,000, a merger will be unopposed.
- If the initial HHI is between 1,000 and 1,800, a merger that raises the HHI by 100 or more will be contested.
- If the initial HHI is larger than 1,800, a merger that increases the HHI by 50 or more will be challenged.

Helpful Hints

1. According to the public interest theory, regulations and antitrust laws should be designed to make markets behave more competitively. The ultimate goal is a perfectly competitive market because, as you have learned, a perfectly

competitive market maximizes the total surplus — the sum of consumer surplus plus producer surplus — enjoyed by society. Markets that behave like monopolies cause economic inefficiency by creating deadweight losses.

The capture theory of regulation points out that regulations may not attempt to maximize the total surplus. The capture theory predicts that regulations generally will be in the producers' interest so that regulations may protect or even create monopoly power in a market.

However, regardless of whether the public interest theory or capture theory is correct, economists agree that there are fewer reasons to regulate markets that are already perfectly competitive. If these markets are regulated, there must be other reasons, such as concern about the distribution of income, for that action.

2. When drawing a graph of a natural monopoly, use as the defining characteristic the point that a natural monopoly's *ATC* slopes downward until it crosses the demand curve. That condition implies that one firm can serve the market with lower costs than two or more firms.

When the *ATC* falls until it crosses the demand curve, why can one firm supply the market at a lower cost than two or more firms? To answer that question, let's suppose that the *ATC* crosses the demand curve at 100 units of output. Thus the *ATC* slopes downward between producing, say, 50 units of output and 100 units, so the *ATC* of producing 50 units is higher than the *ATC* of producing 100. Suppose that the *ATC* of 50 units of output is $15 and that the *ATC* of producing 100 units is $10. If one firm produced 100 units of output, the total cost would be (100)($10) = $1,000. To have two firms produce 100 units, suppose that each produced 50 units. Then, each firm's total cost is (50)($15) = $750. Because there are two firms, the total cost of having 100 units produced by two firms is $750 + $750, or $1,500. Thus the total cost of having two firms produce 100 units of output — $1,500 — exceeds the total cost of having only one firm produce 100 units.

Because one firm can supply the market at lower cost than two or more firms, a tension is created from society's point of view. Having one firm in the industry and thereby reducing costs is good; the lower the cost of producing a product, the more resources available to produce other goods and services. In this regard, allowing the market to be served by one firm is beneficial to society. However, monopolies restrict the level of their output in order to raise their prices and earn economic profits. The restriction of output creates economic inefficiency, and this restriction harms society. The usual result from these countervailing forces is regulation: The government grants the right to one firm to have a monopoly but in exchange the government regulates the company. In this way, society attempts to gain the advantage of lower costs and side-step the disadvantage of monopoly behavior. The capture theory of regulation reminds us that this effort may not be successful, but, to the extent that it is, regulation can improve society's overall welfare.

■ True/False/Uncertain Questions

1. At its profit-maximizing level of output, a monopoly industry maximizes the total surplus.

2. Government regulation moves the economy closer to allocative efficiency.

3. Rate of return regulation gives producers a strong incentive to minimize their costs.

4. The more producer surplus per seller, the greater is producers' demands for regulation.

5. The larger the initial Hirschman–Herfindahl index, the more likely the U.S. Department of Justice is to allow a merger to take place.

6. A natural monopoly regulated using a marginal cost pricing rule may need to be subsidized in order to avoid an economic loss.

7. If top executives of Coca-Cola and Pepsi agree to raise the price of a can of cola to 75¢, the agreement is legal because it does not harm any small producers of soft drinks.

8. Evidence about the regulation of cartels strongly supports the public interest theory of regulation.

9. Any action that increases producer surplus must benefit society by also increasing the total surplus.

10. According to the capture theory, government regulatory agencies eventually capture the profits of the industries they regulate.

11. For a natural monopoly, the *ATC* curve remains below the *MC* curve until after the *ATC* curve crosses the demand curve.

12. The rule of reason was a U.S. Supreme Court interpretation of the Sherman Act that said only "unreasonable" restraints of trade violated the Sherman Act.

13. A natural monopoly regulated according to an average cost pricing rule produces an allocatively inefficient level of output.

14. AT&T gave up its local phone businesses and began competing in its long-distance business as a result of an agreement between it and the U.S. Department of Justice.

15. In recent years an increasingly large share of the U.S. economy has been regulated.

■ Multiple Choice Questions

1. Which of the following statements about the Sherman Act is FALSE?
   a. The Sherman Act was the first federal antitrust law.
   b. The Sherman act prohibited monopolization.
   c. The Sherman Act outlawed natural monopolies.
   d. The Sherman Act made restriction of trade illegal.

2. The difference between the maximum amount that consumers are willing to pay and the amount they actually pay for a given quantity of a good is called
   a. deadweight surplus.
   b. consumer surplus.
   c. producer surplus.
   d. total surplus.

3. A large demand for regulation by consumers will result when there is a
   a. small consumer surplus per buyer.
   b. large consumer surplus per buyer.
   c. small number of buyers.
   d. large producer surplus per firm.

4. Which of the following is most likely to be a natural monopoly?
   a. Burger King, a seller of hamburgers.
   b. Cox Cable, a company supplying cable TV.
   c. Nike, a maker of shoes.
   d. JCPenney, a large department store.

5. When will the output produced by a natural monopoly be the largest?
   a. When the monopoly is left unregulated.
   b. When the monopoly is regulated according to an average cost pricing rule.
   c. When the monopoly is regulated according to a marginal cost pricing rule.
   d. When the monopoly is regulated according to a deadweight loss pricing rule.

6. When will the price charged by a natural monopoly be the lowest?
   a. When the monopoly is left unregulated.
   b. When the monopoly is regulated according to an average cost pricing rule.
   c. When the monopoly is regulated according to a marginal cost pricing rule.
   d. When the monopoly is regulated according to a deadweight loss pricing rule.

7. The capture theory of intervention predicts that government regulation will maximize
   a. producer surplus.
   b. total surplus.
   c. consumer surplus.
   d. deadweight loss.

8. A natural monopoly under rate of return regulation has an incentive to
   a. pad its costs.
   b. produce more than the efficient quantity of output.
   c. charge a price equal to marginal cost.
   d. maximize consumer surplus.

9. Total surplus equals
   a. consumer surplus.
   b. producer surplus.
   c. consumer surplus plus producer surplus.
   d. consumer surplus minus producer surplus.

10. The history of regulation in the U.S. economy shows that from 1880 the extent of regulation generally
   a. increased until about 1975 and since then deregulation has occurred.
   b. increased steadily.
   c. decreased until about 1975 and since then has increased.
   d. None of the above.

11. Economic regulation is imposed by
   a. monopolists.
   b. labor unions.
   c. voters.
   d. politicians and bureaucrats.

12. Regulation that sets a price cap and then allows the regulated company to keep any profit it earns (as long as it is not excessive) is an example of
   a. rate of return regulation.
   b. average cost pricing regulation.
   c. marginal cost pricing regulation.
   d. incentive regulation.

13. If a natural monopoly is required to set its price equal to its marginal cost,
   a. the company earns an economic profit.
   b. the company incurs an economic loss.
   c. competitors will enter the market.
   d. the company will produce more than the efficient level of output.

14. Total surplus is maximized when
   a. producer surplus is maximized.
   b. consumer surplus is maximized.
   c. the deadweight loss is 0.
   d. None of the above.

15. Allocative efficiency is achieved when
   a. consumer surplus is maximized.
   b. producer surplus is minimized.
   c. total surplus is maximized.
   d. total surplus is minimized.

16. Which of the following statements about the "rule of reason" is <u>FALSE</u>?
   a. The U.S. Supreme Court announced the rule of reason as a ruling.
   b. The rule of reason states that only "unreasonable" restraints of trade violate the Sherman Act.
   c. The rule of reason allows mergers among firms that lead to a monopoly as long as the mergers are not "unreasonable."
   d. The rule of reason remains in effect today.

17. An industry in which one firm can serve the market at a lower total cost than two or more firms is known as a(n)
   a. duopoly.
   b. oligopoly.
   c. deadweight loss industry.
   d. natural monopoly.

18. The public interest theory of regulation predicts that the political process seeks to minimize
   a. producer surplus.
   b. consumer surplus.
   c. deadweight loss.
   d. allocative efficiency.

19. Which of the following would be a horizontal merger?
   a. Toys 'R' Us merging with Apple Computer.
   b. General Motors merging with Bridgestone Rubber.
   c. HBO merging with AT&T.
   d. Merck Pharmaceuticals merging with Glaxo Pharmaceuticals

20. The Hirschman–Herfindahl index (HHI) in an industry is 900. A merger is proposed that will raise the HHI to 980. In this case, the
   a. Sherman Act will prohibit the monopoly.
   b. U.S. Department of Justice will challenge the monopoly.
   c. U.S. Department of Justice will not challenge the monopoly.
   d. rule of reason will prevent the monopoly if it represents a horizontal merger

Use Figure 20.3 for the next four questions.

FIGURE **20.3**

Multiple Choice Questions 21, 22, 23, and 24

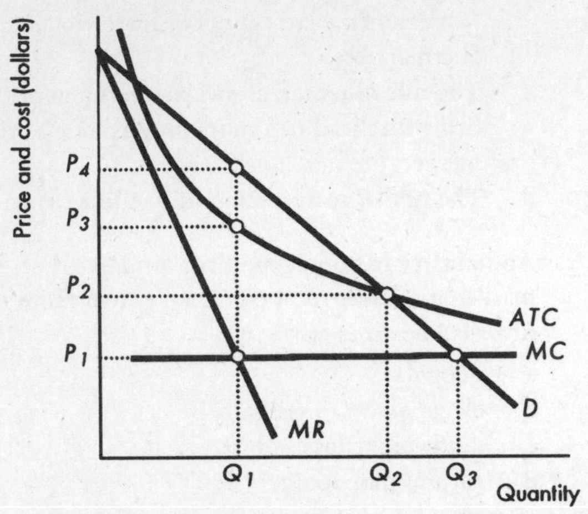

21. In Figure 20.3, total surplus is at its maximum when the quantity is
    a. Q_1 and the price is P_4.
    b. Q_1 and the price is P_3.
    c. Q_2 and the price is P_2.
    d. Q_3 and the price is P_1.

22. In Figure 20.3, producer surplus is at its maximum when the quantity is
    a. Q_1 and the price is P_4.
    b. Q_1 and the price is P_3.
    c. Q_2 and the price is P_2.
    d. Q_3 and the price is P_1.

23. If the natural monopoly in Figure 20.3 is unregulated and operates as a private profit-maximizer, what output will it produce?
    a. 0, because the firm suffers an economic loss when $MR = MC$.
    b. Q_1.
    c. Q_2.
    d. Q_3.

24. If a regulatory agency sets a price just sufficient for the firm to earn a normal profit, what output will it produce?
    a. 0, because the firm suffers an economic loss when $P = MC$.
    b. Q_1.
    c. Q_2.
    d. Q_3.

25. Incentive regulation schemes attempt to give a natural monopoly the incentive to
    a. behave more like an unregulated monopoly.
    b. raise its price to the maximum amount consumers will pay.
    c. pad its costs.
    d. reduce its costs.

■ Short Answer Questions

1. What is a vertical merger? A horizontal merger? Is a vertical merger or a horizontal merger most likely to cause increased market concentration? The U.S. Department of Justice is most likely to contest which type of merger?
2. In Figure 20.4, draw a diagram illustrating a natural monopoly. If the company is regulated under an average cost pricing rule, show the level of production, the price, and the deadweight loss.

FIGURE **20.4**

Short Answer Problem 2

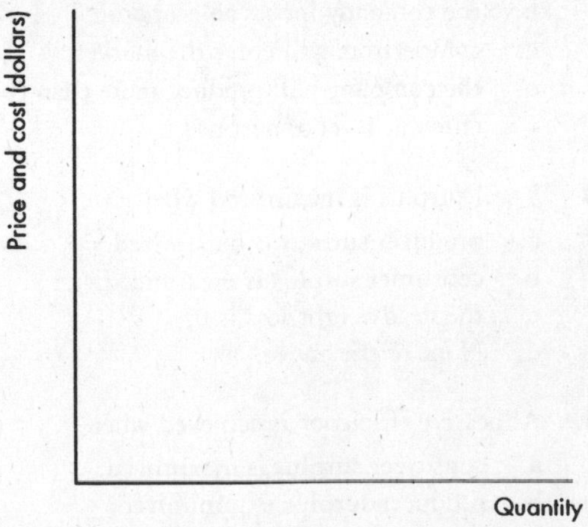

Price and cost (dollars)

Quantity

3. a. How is rate of return regulation of a natural monopoly implemented? What incentive does this type of regulation give companies to reduce their costs?
   b. What are incentive regulation methods? What incentive do companies have to reduce their costs under this type of regulation?
4. Suppose that two electric companies — Watts Up and Power to the People — can serve a residential block. The block has 10 houses on it. To serve the houses a main cable needs to be strung down the street; a main cable costs $100 to maintain. Then, small feeder cables need to be extended to each house; these cost $10 to maintain per house.
   a. Suppose that Watts Up and Power to the People split the market so that each services 5 houses on the street. If both companies string their own main cables and then each extends feeder wires to its customers, what is Watts Up's total cost of supplying power to its 5 customers? Watts Up's average total cost? What are Power to the People's total and average total costs?
   b. When Watts Up and Power to the People split the market evenly, as in part (a), what is the total cost to society of serving these 10 families?
   c. Suppose that only one company — say, Watts Up — supplies power to all the residents of the street. Thus there is one main cable and 10 feeder wires. Now, what is Watts Up's total cost of supplying power to the street's residents? What is its average total cost?
   d. If Watts Up has the monopoly in serving the customers on this street, what are the total costs incurred by society to serve these 10 families?
   e. Is this industry a natural monopoly? Explain your answer.
5. Question 4 reflected a social perspective when exploring the situation of a natural monopoly supplying power to 10 residents on a street. Let's now explore it from the industry's vantage point. Suppose that we have the same costs as in question 4 and again have two companies — Watts Up and Power to the People — competing to supply power to the street's residents.
   a. If both companies string their own main cables and then extend feeder wires to 5 houses each, what is each company's average total cost of servicing a house?
   b. Suppose that Watts Up gains a customer on the street so that it now serves 6 houses and Power to the People serves only 4. What is Watts Up's average total cost? Power to the People's average total cost?
   c. After Watts Up gains its customer, if Watts Up charges its customers a price between $26.67 and $35, does Watts Up earn an economic profit? What is the minimum price that Power to the People can charge and not incur an economic loss? Presuming that the residents on the street can switch power companies, what is likely to happen?
6. We've met Igor in some past chapters. Igor has quit his job with his old master and now works for a new master: The Department of Justice. Igor has been charged with overseeing a merger in the snake market. Currently, the snake market comprises 5 firms of equal size; that is, each firm has a 20 percent market share. Two firms are considering a merger so that after the merger the market will have 4 firms, one with a 40 percent share and 3 with 20 percent shares. Will Igor challenge the merger? Why or why not?

FIGURE **20.5**
Short Answer Problem 7 (a)

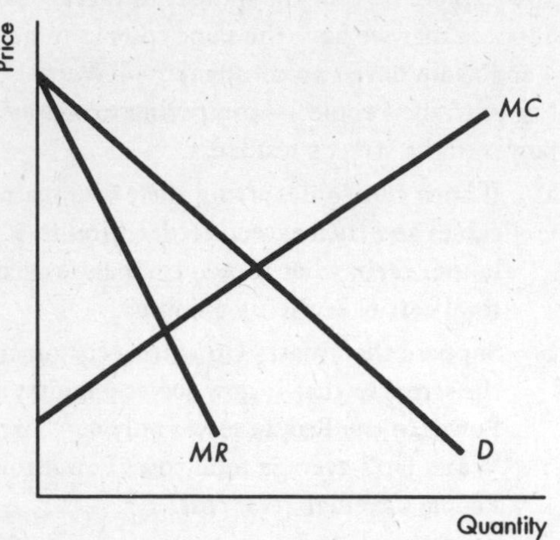

FIGURE **20.6**
Short Answer Problem 7 (b)

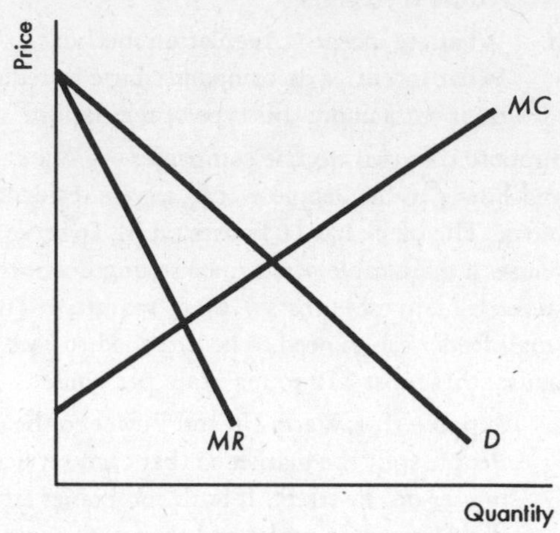

7. Igor's new masters were pleased with his work in the snake market, so they put him to work regulating the bat industry. The bat industry comprises three firms. Figures 20.5 and 20.6 are identical: Both show the market demand for bats, the associated marginal revenue curve for the market demand, and the horizontal sum of the marginal cost curves for the three firms in the bat industry.
   a. Suppose that Igor regulates the bat industry in the public interest. In Figure 20.5, indicate the equilibrium quantity and price of a bat. Show the consumer surplus, the producer surplus, and the total surplus.
   b. Now suppose that the bat industry is able to capture Igor. After being captured, Igor regulates the industry so that the bat producers can earn the maximum possible industrywide profit. In Figure 20.6, show the equilibrium number of bats and their price. Also show the consumer surplus, the producer surplus and indicate the area that is the deadweight loss.

■ You're the Teacher

1. "I just don't get how a natural monopoly happens. I mean, why are some firms natural monopolies and not others? Is it because the government is regulating them that they are natural monopolies?" Your friend is struggling and is confused. Although it would be nice if your friend could sometimes help you, save your friend's grade once again by explaining the origins of a natural monopoly. Be sure to address the (erroneous) idea that it is government regulation that makes an industry a natural monopoly.
2. "I think our teacher sometimes says that allocative efficiency means that helping someone without hurting someone else is impossible. I seem to remember this comment from our book. But does this mean that when there is inefficiency, we can take actions that help everyone?" This student is close to seeing an important point. If you already see it, explain it; if you don't, sneak a look at the answer...

Answers

True/False Answers

1. **F** The monopoly's goal is to maximize its economic profit, but by so doing it creates a deadweight loss.
2. **U** If the regulation is in the public interest, it will increase economic efficiency, but if the industry captures its regulator, regulation can create inefficiency.
3. **F** If the costs rise, the producer knows that the regulators will allow the company to hike its price to offset the higher costs.
4. **T** The more producer surplus there is, the greater the payoff is to an individual producer if regulation is shaped to benefit producers' interests.
5. **F** The lower the initial HHI, the more likely the U.S. Department of Justice will not challenge a merger.
6. **T** The price set under a marginal cost pricing rule is less than the *ATC*, so the firm incurs an economic loss.
7. **F** The Sherman Act outlaws all such price-fixing agreements.
8. **F** The evidence is mixed, but tends to support the capture theory of regulation.
9. **F** If a perfectly competitive industry becomes a monopoly, producer surplus increases but society, overall, is harmed because of the deadweight loss that is created.
10. **F** The capture theory holds that the industry captures the regulator, so the regulator allows the industry to charge (near) the monopoly price and produce (near) the monopoly level of output.
11. **F** The *MC* curve is below the *ATC* curve until the *ATC* curve crosses the demand curve.
12. **T** This is essentially the definition of the rule of reason.
13. **T** The natural monopoly produces the efficient level of output when it is regulated to produce at the level where its price equals its marginal cost.
14. **T** By this accord, AT&T's near monopoly on local and long distance calls was dismantled.
15. **F** In recent years the trend has been toward deregulation.

Multiple Choice Answers

1. **c** Natural monopolies are a result of the technology within an industry and cannot be prohibited.
2. **b** This is the definition of consumer surplus.
3. **b** This increases the potential payoff if demanders can sway regulators to produce regulations in their favor.
4. **b** Most locales have only one cable TV supplier primarily because cable TV is currently close to being a natural monopoly.
5. **c** When regulated according to a marginal cost pricing rule, the natural monopoly produces the allocatively efficient level of output.
6. **c** A marginal cost pricing rule results in the largest level of output. To induce demanders to buy the largest amount of output, the price must be the lowest.
7. **a** By capturing the regulators, producers are able to promote their own interests.
8. **a** This incentive accounts for the recent adoption of incentive regulation methods in many telecommunications markets.
9. **c** This is the definition of total surplus.
10. **a** Why deregulation started to occur in recent years remains somewhat puzzling.
11. **d** Consumers and producers demand regulation; politicians and bureaucrats supply it.
12. **d** Such methods attempt to sharpen regulated firms' incentives to cut costs and have just started to become increasingly common in the telecommunications industry.
13. **b** Because the company suffers an economic loss, it will either need to be subsidized or be allowed to price discriminate in order to earn a normal profit.
14. **c** By setting the deadweight loss to 0, there is no waste, so total surplus is at its maximum.
15. **c** Note the relationship between this answer and the previous answer: When the deadweight loss is 0, allocative efficiency has been achieved.

16. **d** The U.S. Supreme Court backed away from the rule of reason in its decision in the *ALCOA* case. There *ALCOA* was found guilty simply because it was "too big."
17. **d** This is the defining characteristic of an industry that is a natural monopoly.
18. **c** By minimizing deadweight loss, the regulators maximize total surplus.
19. **d** A horizontal merger occurs when firms in the same industry combine.
20. **c** Whenever the initial HHI is below 1,000, the U.S. Department of Justice will not contest a merger in the industry.
21. **d** Total surplus is maximized when the level of output is where the *MC* curve crosses the demand curve because at that point there is no deadweight loss.
22. **a** This is the monopoly level of output and price, which is the combination of output and price that maximizes producer surplus.
23. **b** Left alone, it will operate as a monopoly and maximize its producer surplus.
24. **c** Earning a normal profit means that the company produces so that $P = ATC$, which means it produces Q_2 and charges P_2. This price–output combination is exactly what the company would do under an average cost pricing rule.
25. **d** By reducing its costs, regulators hope to make the firm — and the industry — more efficient.

■ Answers to Short Answer Problems

1. A vertical merger occurs when a firm merges with a customer for its products or with a supplier of its inputs. Microsoft merging with a company that sells it computer discs is an example of a vertical merger. A horizontal merger occurs when a company merges with another company in the same business. Wal-Mart merging with Kmart is an example of a horizontal merger. Horizontal mergers are the most likely to increase market concentration, so the U.S. Department of Justice is most likely to challenge horizontal mergers.
2. Figure 20.7 shows a natural monopoly. The distinguishing characteristic of a natural monopoly is that its *ATC* curve falls until after it crosses the demand curve. Under an average cost pricing rule, the company must set its price equal to its average cost, which means that the price that will be charged is P_{atc} and the level of output is Q_{atc}. (To buy Q_{atc}, consumers are willing to pay P_{atc}, and this price equals the average cost of producing output Q_{atc}.) The deadweight loss is illustrated by the shaded triangle. It equals the loss of consumer and producer surplus on the difference between the efficient level of output Q_{eff} — where the demand (the marginal social benefit) and the marginal cost (the marginal social cost) curves cross — and the amount of output actually produced, Q_{atc}.

FIGURE 20.7
Short Answer Problem 2

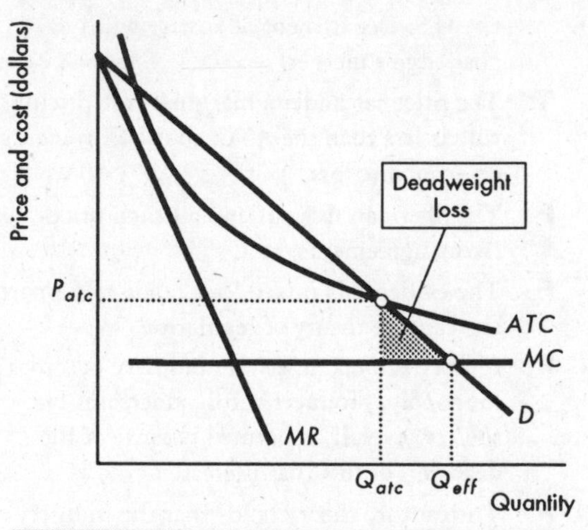

3. a. Rate of return regulation is related to an average total cost price rule. Essentially the regulators try to determine a fair rate of return on the company's capital stock. This rate of return is then multiplied by the total amount of the firm's capital to determine the total "profit" that the regulators consider fair. (Thus, if the company has, say, $10 million in capital and the rate of return is 15 percent, the total amount of "profit" is $1.5 million, $10 million times 15 percent.) This total profit is added to the firm's other costs and the amount becomes the regulators' "target"

for the firm's total revenue. Then, the regulators determine a price that will enable the firm to earn this amount of revenue. Companies have very little incentive to reduce their costs; if costs rise, the regulators will change the price that the company can charge, thus allowing the company to recoup the increased costs.

b. There are two general types of incentive regulation methods. The first sets a price cap and then allows the company to charge whatever price it wishes as long as the price remains under the cap. If the company earns "too much" profit or after some set period of time, the price cap is renegotiated. The second scheme gives the company some freedom to set is own prices, with the restriction that, if its profits rise above a certain level, they must be shared with consumers by reducing the price the company charges. Both methods give the company more incentive to control its costs because, if the company can lower its costs and hence increase its profit, the company will be allowed to keep (at least part of) the higher profit.

4. a. Watts Up strings a main cable, which costs $100, and provides 5 feeder wires, at a cost of $10 each. Thus Watts Up's total cost is $150. It supplies 5 families, so its average total cost is $150 divided by 5 customers, or $30. Power to the People's total cost and average total cost are the same.

b. Watts Up incurs a total cost of $150; Power to the People has the same total cost. Hence the total cost to society is $300.

c. If only Watts Up supplies power, it strings a main cable ($100) and 10 feeder wires ($10 each) for a total cost of $200. Watts Up's average total cost is $20 per customer.

d. With only one company supplying power, the total cost incurred by society is $200, the company's total cost.

e. Yes, this industry is a natural monopoly because the total cost of having one firm supply the market is less than the total cost of two (or more) firms. Another way to see that this industry is a natural monopoly is by noting that the average total cost with 10 customers is less than that with 5 customers. The average total cost declines until the entire market is served, which means that this industry is a natural monopoly.

5. a. As worked out in part (a) of question 4, the average total cost when 5 houses are served is $30.

b. After Watts Up gains a customer, its total cost is $160: $100 for the main cable and $60 for 6 feeder wires. Thus its average total cost is $\$160/6$, or $26.67 per customer. Power to the People's total cost is now $140, or $100 for the main cable and $40 for the 4 feeder wires. Hence Power to the People's average total cost is $\$140/4$, or $35 per customer.

c. For any price greater than $26.67, Watts Up will earn an economic profit because its price will exceed its average total cost. Hence for prices between $26.67 and $35, Watts Up earns an economic profit. Power to the People must charge a price no less than $35 (so that its price is not less than its average total cost) to avoid an economic loss. Thus Watts Up can charge a lower price than Power to the People and still earn an economic profit. Customers are likely to switch from Power to the People — where they pay a higher price — to Watts Up — where they pay a lower price. As this switching occurs, Watts Up's *ATC* continues to fall and Power to the People's *ATC* rises. The ultimate result is likely to be that Watts Up becomes the monopoly supplier of electricity on this street. A key point is how the industry (naturally) evolves into a monopoly.

6. Igor's decision whether to challenge the merger depends on the initial Hirschman–Herfindahl index (HHI) and the effect of the merger on the HHI. Before the merger, HHI = 2,000, from $20^2 + 20^2 + 20^2 + 20^2 + 20^2$. If the merger occurs, HHI = 2,800, or $40^2 + 20^2 + 20^2 + 20^2$. Hence this merger would increase the HHI by 800. If the initial HHI exceeds 1,800, any merger that raises it by 50 or more is contested by the U.S. Department of Justice. Thus Igor will challenge this merger.

FIGURE **20.8**
Short Answer Problem 7 (a)

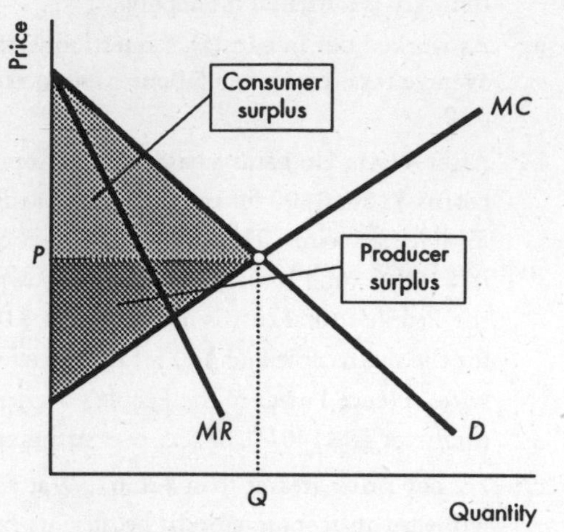

FIGURE **20.9**
Short Answer Problem 7 (b)

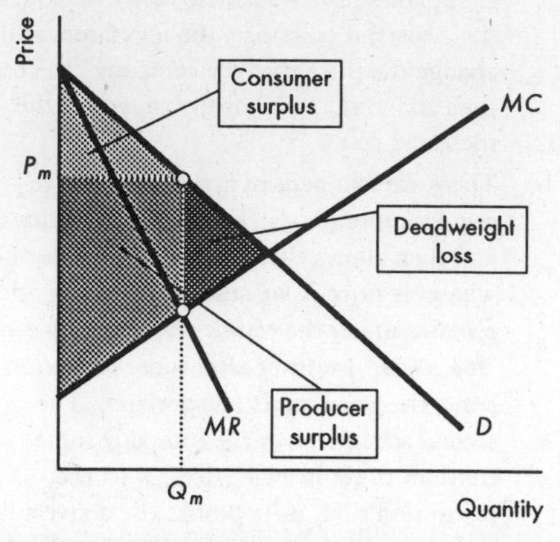

7. a. Figure 20.8 shows the industry output as Q and the price as P when this industry is regulated in the public interest. The consumer and producer surpluses also are shown; the total surplus is the sum of the consumer surplus and the producer surplus.

   b. Once Igor is captured by the industry, it will operate as a monopoly. That is, it will operate at the level where the industry MC equals the market MR, so, as shown in Figure 20.9, it produces Q_m and is allowed to charge P_m. The consumer and producer surpluses also are shown. The total surplus is the sum of the consumer surplus and the producer surplus. Comparing Figure 20.8 with the Figure 20.9 shows that the total surplus is less when the industry is able to capture its regulator. The amount by which it is less is the deadweight loss, also illustrated in Figure 20.9.

■ You're the Teacher

1. "If you're confused about the origin of a natural monopoly, you may be trying to make it too hard. But I finally figured it out. Here's the deal: A natural monopoly occurs when the technology within an industry allows one firm to serve the market at lower cost than more than one firm can. In other words, a natural monopoly just happens; if the technology makes it possible for one firm to serve the market at lower total cost than more than one firm, this industry is a natural monopoly. I used to confuse regulation with the formation of natural monopolies. Natural monopolies are *not* the result of regulation. It's just the opposite: the industries are regulated *because* they are natural monopolies. The type of technology that has been developed determines whether the industry is a natural monopoly."

2. "Yeah, you're right: When there is inefficiency, we can take actions that help everyone! The idea is that inefficiency means a deadweight loss. When we remove the inefficiency, we eliminate the deadweight loss. That serves as a bonus — something that we can spread around and make everyone better off.

   "Look, a numerical example will make this point a lot clearer. Take some industry. Suppose that consumer surplus would be $200 and producer surplus would be $100, for a total surplus of $300 if this industry is perfectly competitive. However, suppose that this industry is a monopoly. Then, consumer surplus is, say, $80 and producer surplus is $150. In this case, the total surplus is $230 and the deadweight loss (the difference between the two total surpluses) is $70.

"Now, if we broke up the monopoly and made the industry perfectly competitive, we'd get a total surplus of $300. It would include a consumer surplus of $200 (so that consumers would gain $120, the new consumer surplus of $200 minus the current consumer surplus of $80) and a producer surplus of $100 (so that producers would lose $50, the difference between the current producer surplus of $150 minus the new producer surplus of $100). But suppose that we took away, say, $75 of the gain from consumers and gave it producers. Then, consumers would still be better off because their new consumer surplus would be $125, as compared to only $80 when the industry was a monopoly. And producers would also be better off because their producer surplus would be $175 versus only $150 as a monopoly. Thus, with this redistribution, *both* consumers and producers can be better off when the industry is perfectly competitive!

"OK, I'll agree that this outcome is unrealistic because we've assumed that we can redistribute the gain as we want. If we didn't do any redistribution and just broke up the monopoly, consumers would gain ($120) and producers would lose ($50). But what this shows is important anyway: Whenever there is allocative inefficiency, inefficiency can be eliminated and *everyone* made better off. You know, now that I think about it, it's my guess that this is why our teacher likes the idea of efficiency so much!"

21 EXTERNALITIES, THE ENVIRONMENT, AND KNOWLEDGE

Key Concepts

Externalities

An **externality** is cost or benefit arising from a transaction that affects someone who is not part of the original activity. Externalities are not taken into account by transactors. Externalities may be negative (from pollution) or positive (from knowledge). Externalities create ***market failure***; that is, the market produces a level of output different from the allocatively efficient amount.

Economics of the Environment

The demand for a clean environment has increased because of higher incomes and increased knowledge about environmental problems. Environmental problems can be divided into air pollution, water pollution, and land pollution.

Externalities exist because of the absence of property rights.

- **Property rights** are social arrangements that set the rules for ownership, use, and disposal of factors of production and goods and services.
- **Coase theorem** holds that, if property rights exist and transactions costs are low, there are no externalities.

The Coase theorem implies that, regardless to whom the property right is given (the polluter or the victim), as long as a property right is granted, the efficient level of pollution results.

When attacking an externality problem, to maximize society's well-being, the government's actions should be aimed at producing the level of output having equal **marginal social cost** (the marginal private cost and any marginal external cost) and **marginal social benefit** (the marginal private benefit and any marginal external benefit). The U.S. Environmental Protection Agency (EPA) has three tools that it can use when taking government action to limit an externality problem:

- **Emission charges** — a price per unit of pollution that the government sets and the polluter pays.
- **Marketable permits** — each polluter is given a pollution limit. If it reduces its pollution below this limit, it can sell the "excess" reduction to other firms who then do not need to reduce their pollution by this amount.
- **Taxes** — the government can levy a tax equal to the marginal externality cost, as shown in Figure 21.1. Initially, the amount produced is Q_0, where the private supply curve (the private marginal cost curve, *MC*) crosses the demand curve. The price is P_0 and the external cost of $SC_0 - P_0$ is ignored. Imposing a tax equal to the marginal external cost shifts the private supply curve upward so that it is the same as the marginal social cost curve, *MSC*. As a result, the efficient level of output, Q_1, is produced.

FIGURE **21.1**

Taxing a Negative Externality

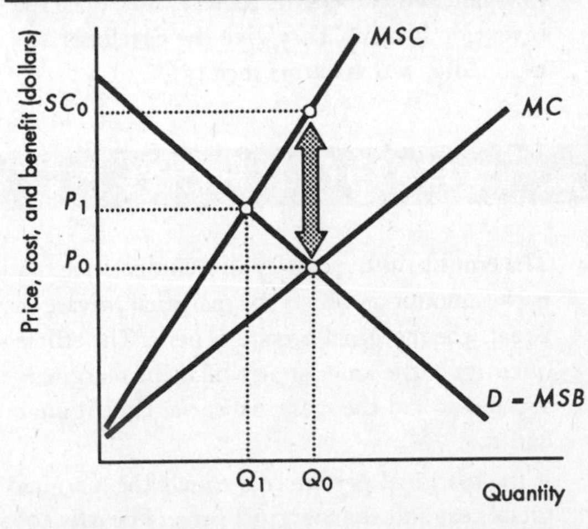

A carbon-fuel tax would limit the addition of carbon dioxide to the atmosphere and potentially limit global warming. There is no such tax because of the scientific uncertainty about the extent to which carbon dioxide contributes to global warming, uncertainty about the costs of global warming, and the fact that the costs of the tax would be paid now and any benefits reaped only in the future. Developed and less-developed nations may be engaged in a prisoners' dilemma game that will lead neither to cut back their emissions of carbon dioxide.

■ Economics of Knowledge

Knowledge creates substantial external benefits, so a private market produces less than the efficient amount of information. Government actions to offset this problem include:

- ♦ **Subsidies** — a payment from the government to the producers of the good that depends on the amount produced, such as subsidizing private colleges or private research.
- ♦ Below-cost provisions — the government may provide the good and charge a price less than the cost of the good, such as relatively low tuition state colleges and universities.
- ♦ **Patents and copyrights** — patents and copyrights grant the inventor of a good, service or new production technique the exclusive property right to the product. Patents and copyrights help ensure that the inventor will personally profit from the invention. They increase the incentive to innovate, which benefits society. But, once the invention is made, they give the developer a monopoly, which harms society.

Helpful Hints

1. The equilibrium quantity in a competitive market is the amount at which the marginal private cost equals the marginal private benefit. The efficient quantity is the amount at which the marginal social cost and the marginal social benefit are equal.

   If the marginal private cost equals the marginal social cost and the marginal private benefit equals the marginal social benefit, the equilibrium amount that is produced equals the efficient amount. This outcome reflects Adam Smith's idea of the invisible hand — that people, seeking to do only what is best for themselves will be led to do what is best for society "as if by an invisible hand."

   In most transactions, there are no affected third parties and so there are no external costs or benefits. In other words, private and social costs along with private and social benefits coincide and competitive markets are efficient.

   But, when third parties are affected, external costs or benefits arise and competitive markets will not be efficient. With external benefits, the marginal private benefit curve lies to the left of the marginal social benefit curve. With external costs, the marginal private cost curve lies to the right of the marginal social cost curve. In both instances, the amount produced in an unregulated market — the level at which the marginal private benefit and private cost curves intersect — is not the efficient amount.

2. If the production of a good or service produces external costs, a competitive market results in a quantity that exceeds the allocatively efficient level. This conclusion makes sense in terms of marginal analysis. People continue an action as long as the marginal benefit from it exceeds the marginal cost. If they ignore some of the marginal costs of the action, they will do "too much" of it; that is, more than the efficient amount of the product is produced. Similarly, with external benefits, some of the marginal benefits from the action are ignored. As a result, too little of the action is undertaken, and less than the efficient amount is produced. If you keep this explanation in mind, you will not go wrong when thinking about the impact of externalities on a private market.

3. Competitive markets with externalities are not efficient because some of the costs or benefits are external. If those costs or benefits could be internalized somehow, the market would be efficient. The chapter discusses two general approaches to internalizing externalities.

   The first is to define property rights clearly and enforce them strictly. Then, costs (or benefits) imposed on (enjoyed by) nonparticipants in a transaction will no longer be external. The affected individual will have a voice in the transaction because some of his or her property is affected and the costs (or benefits) become internal through this voice.

The second is to tax or otherwise charge activities that generate external costs and subsidize or otherwise reward activities that generate external benefits. Charging a tax equal to the external cost makes the entire cost internal. Similarly, paying a subsidy in the amount of the external benefit makes the entire benefit internal.

Both of these general methods strive to ensure that the private marginal cost and private marginal benefit accurately reflect the social marginal cost and social marginal benefit. If the private marginal cost and benefit curves correctly mirror the social marginal cost and benefit curves, the level of the good that will be produced is the efficient amount.

True/False/Uncertain and Explain

1. If negative externalities exist, marginal social cost and marginal external cost are equivalent.

2. Externalities arise from the absence of private property rights.

3. Knowledge is an example of a product with external benefits.

4. Assigning a property right will cure the problem of an externality.

5. The efficient amount of pollution always is no pollution.

6. The private market produces more than the efficient amount of a good having a positive externality.

7. For the EPA to use marketable permits and achieve the efficient level of pollution, the agency must know each firm's marginal benefit from pollution.

8. One reason that there is not a high tax on carbon fuels is that the cost of the tax is incurred now but any benefits from the tax would be obtained in the future.

9. Patents increase the incentive to discover new products and new production techniques.

10. If the production of a good involves no external costs, the marginal social cost equals the marginal private cost.

11. The inefficiency created by an external cost in the production of a good can be overcome if the government subsidizes production of the good.

12. The Coase theorem states that externalities do not exist if property rights are defined and transactions costs are low.

13. Externalities can create market failure.

14. The existence of an external benefit means that the marginal social cost of a product is less than its marginal private cost.

15. When external costs are present, the private market produces less than the allocatively efficient level of output.

Multiple Choice

1. An externality is a cost or benefit arising from an economic transaction that falls on
   a. consumers but not producers.
   b. producers but not consumers.
   c. someone not party to the transaction.
   d. rivals.

2. The production of too many goods with negative externalities is an example of
   a. consumer sovereignty.
   b. producer sovereignty.
   c. public failure.
   d. market failure.

3. A copper ore refiner pollutes the water upstream from a brewery. The transactions costs of reaching an agreement between the two are low. When will the amount of water pollution be at its efficient level?
   a. Only if the property right to the stream is assigned to the ore refiner.
   b. Only if the property right to the stream is assigned to the brewery.
   c. Whenever the property right to the stream is assigned to either the refiner or the brewer.
   d. None of the above because the premise of the question is wrong: There is no such thing as the efficient level of pollution.

4. Suppose that production of rubber for sneakers creates an external cost of $2 per ton of rubber but no external benefits. Then, the efficient amount of rubber will be produced when the government imposes a
   a. subsidy of more than $2 per ton of rubber.
   b. subsidy of $2 per ton of rubber.
   c. tax of more than $2 per ton of rubber.
   d. tax of $2 per ton of rubber.

5. Which of the following illustrates the concept of external cost?
   a. Bad weather decreases the size of the wheat crop.
   b. A reduction in the size of the wheat crop causes the income of wheat farmers to fall.
   c. Smoking harms the health of the smoker.
   d. Smoking harms the health of nearby non-smokers.

6. A reason for not enacting a high carbon-fuel tax in the United States is that
   a. both the cost and benefits from the tax will occur sometime in the future.
   b. less developed nations may not decrease their consumption of fuels.
   c. the costs of global warming have been accurately estimated to be small.
   d. scientific evidence no longer supports the hypothesis that carbon dioxide adds to global warming.

Use the Figure 21.2 for the next five questions.

FIGURE **21.2**
Multiple Choice Questions 7, 8, 9, 10, and 11

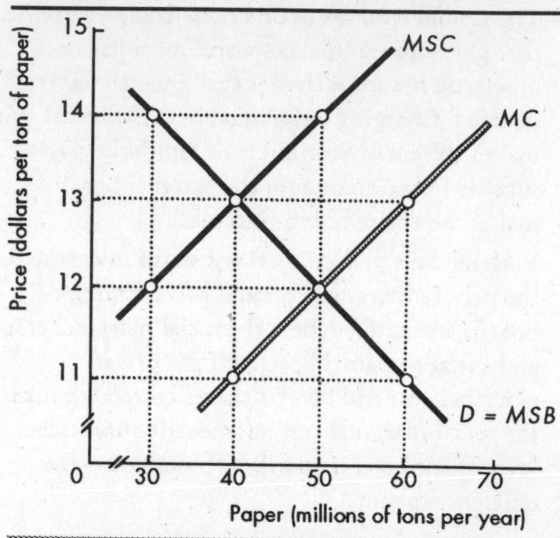

7. As illustrated in Figure 21.2, the production of paper creates
   a. only a positive externality.
   b. only a negative externality.
   c. both positive and negative externalities.
   d. no externalities.

8. The amount of the externality illustrated in Figure 21.2 is
   a. $14 per ton.
   b. $12 per ton.
   c. $2 per ton.
   d. $0 per ton because no externality is produced.

9. In the absence of any government intervention, how many tons of paper are produced in a year?
   a. 60 million tons.
   b. 50 million tons.
   c. 40 million tons.
   d. 30 million tons.

10. The allocatively efficient amount of paper produced in a year is
   a. 60 million tons.
   b. 50 million tons.
   c. 40 million tons.
   d. 30 million tons.

11. What amount of tax is necessary to cause the efficient amount of paper to be produced?
   a. $14 a ton.
   b. $12 per ton.
   c. $2 per ton.
   d. $0 per ton because the efficient amount is produced without any government intervention.

12. The efficient level of pollution is
   a. no pollution.
   b. the level at which the marginal social benefit of pollution is 0.
   c. the level at which the marginal social benefit of pollution equals the marginal social cost of pollution.
   d. the level at which the marginal cost of pollution is 0.

13. An externality is
   a. the amount by which price exceeds marginal private cost.
   b. the amount by which price exceeds marginal social cost.
   c. the effect of government regulation on market price and output.
   d. a cost or benefit that arises from a decision but is not borne by the decision maker.

14. Patents are a solution to the
   a. positive externality from attending college.
   b. positive externality from discovering new knowledge.
   c. negative externality from attending college.
   d. negative externality from discovering new knowledge.

15. Suppose that the government allows firms to emit sulfur dioxide and pollute the air as long as the firms pay the government $70 per ton of sulfur dioxide. This approach is an example of
   a. the Coase theorem.
   b. an emission charge.
   c. a marketable permit.
   d. None of the above.

16. Which of the following transactions is most likely NOT to have an externality associated with it?
   a. Eating a hot dog.
   b. Being vaccinated.
   c. Producing steel.
   d. Discovering a new human gene.

Use the Table 21.1 for the next four questions.

Table 21.1 Multiple Choice Questions 17, 18, 19, and 20

Quantity	Marginal private cost (dollars)	Marginal private benefit (dollars)	Marginal social benefit (dollars)
500	$5	$9	$11
550	6	8	10
600	7	7	9
650	8	6	8
700	9	5	7

17. Table 21.1 represents the market for a good with
   a. only a negative externality.
   b. only a positive externality
   c. both positive and negative externalities.
   d. no externalities.

18. Left alone, the equilibrium amount produced is
   a. 550.
   b. 600.
   c. 650.
   d. 700.

19. The allocatively efficient level of output is
   a. 550.
   b. 600.
   c. 650.
   d. 700.

20. What can the government do to cause the efficient amount to be produced?
   a. Subsidize suppliers $8 per unit.
   b. Subsidize suppliers $2 per unit.
   c. Tax suppliers $2 per unit.
   d. Tax suppliers $8 per unit.

21. Efficiency requires that the marginal social benefit from a good
   a. be as much greater as possible than the marginal social cost of the good.
   b. equal the marginal social cost of the good.
   c. be as much smaller as possible than the marginal social cost of the good.
   d. None of the above because there is no general rule for efficiency.

22. Which of the following is NOT a possible government solution to the problem posed by a positive eternality?
   a. Subsidize the production of the good.
   b. Provide the good below cost.
   c. Tax the consumption of the good.
   d. All of the above are possible solutions.

23. Which of the following statements about property rights is correct?
   a. Property rights have nothing to do with externalities.
   b. The absence of property rights creates negative externalities but has nothing to do with the creation of positive externalities.
   c. Property rights pertain only to the rights of owners of real estate.
   d. Copyrights are a method of assigning intellectual property rights.

24. An unregulated market tends to produce too ___ of a good with a negative externality and too ___ of a good with a positive externality.
   a. much; much
   b. much; little
   c. little; much
   d. little; little

Short Answer Problems

1. At public colleges and universities governments provide education at a price (tuition) less than cost. What economic argument supports this policy?
2. Explain how a tax can be used to achieve efficiency in the face of external costs.
3. What is the marginal social benefit of pollution?
4. In a small town two factories — factory A and factory B — each produce 10 units of pollution so that the total pollution is 20 units. Factory A can decrease its pollution at a constant marginal cost of $50 per unit; factory B can reduce its pollution at a constant marginal cost of $100 per unit.
   a. If both factory A and factory B decrease their pollution by 5 units, what is the total amount of pollution in the town and what is the total cost of attaining this level of pollution?
   b. If factory A decreases its level of pollution by 10 units and factory B does not decrease its pollution, what is the total amount of pollution in the town and what is the total cost of achieving this level of pollution?
   c. From a social standpoint, to obtain a total of 10 units of pollution, which is more desirable: both factories cutting back by 5 units each or A cutting back by 10 units and B not cutting back? Why?
5. Continuing with the situation presented in problem 4, suppose that the EPA determines that the efficient level of pollution is 10 units.
   a. If the EPA requires each factory to decrease its pollution by 5 units, what is the total cost of attaining a total of 10 units of pollution?
   b. Suppose that the EPA introduces marketable permits and allows each firm to produce 5 units of pollution. What is likely to occur? In particular, will factory A or B want to sell its permits to the other factory and is the other factory willing to buy them? What is the price range for the permits?
   c. From a social standpoint, which is more desirable: when the EPA requires equal reductions in pollution or when it introduces marketable permits? Why?
6. Farmer Dave's and farmer Mark's farms are next to each other. They get along well so transactions costs are low, except that Dave's pig, Will, occasionally gets into Mark's corn field and eats the corn. If Will did not roam free, he would eat valueless garbage, not the corn. Property rights to allowing Will to roam or to keep Mark's farm free from Dave's pig have yet to be assigned. Suppose that Will eats $350 of corn per year and that to erect a fence to keep Will off Mark's farm costs $250 per year. Either Dave or Mark can erect the fence and, once the fence is in place, Will eats none of the corn.
   a. Suppose that the property right is given to Dave so that Will can roam free anytime he desires. Will Mark erect a fence?

b. Now suppose that the property right is given to Mark, so that he can charge Dave whenever Will shows up on Mark's farm and eats the corn. Will Dave erect a fence?

c. What general proposition is illustrated in this question?

7. Vaccination creates a positive externality. Use Figure 21.3 to illustrate the market for chicken pox vaccination. Label as Q_0 the doses that will be taken in the absence of any government intervention and as Q_1 the efficient number of doses. How might the government move this market toward allocative efficiency?

FIGURE **21.3**
The Market for Chicken Pox Vaccine

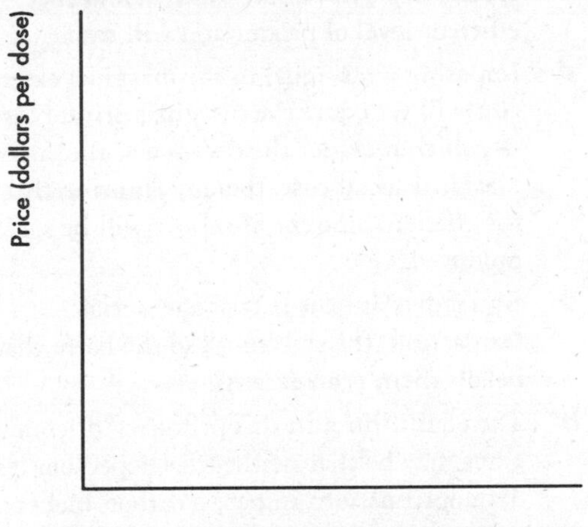

Price (dollars per dose)

Vaccine (million of doses per year)

8. The first two columns of Table 21.2 give the demand schedule for education in Translyvania, and the third column gives the marginal private cost. Because education generates external benefits, the marginal social benefit shown in the last column is greater than marginal private benefit.

a. What equilibrium price and quantity would result if the market for education is unregulated?

b. What is the allocatively efficient quantity of students in Translyvania?

9. In an attempt to address the inefficient level of education in his nation, Igor — the newly appointed minister of education — has decided to provide a low-cost public university, Igor Omphesus (Igor's middle name is Omphesus) University.

a. To attain the efficient level of schooling, what must tuition be at the new university, I.O.U.?

b. What is the marginal cost of schooling the last student at this university?

Table 21.2 Education in Translyvania

Quantity (number of students)	Marginal private benefit (dollars)	Marginal private cost (dollars)	Marginal social benefit (dollars)
1	$500	$200	$800
2	400	250	700
3	300	300	600
4	200	350	500
5	100	400	400
6	0	450	300

You're the Teacher

1. "I just don't understand some of this stuff. I mean, how can our book say that it's 'efficient' to have some pollution. I mean, come on, pollution is bad; we don't want any of it. I mean, the best level of pollution has to be zero, right?" Aside from having a severe "I mean" problem, this student also has a severe problem understanding that the efficient level of pollution is not zero. You probably can't do anything about the "I mean" problem, but you should be able to help the student grasp why zero pollution is not efficient.

2. After you've answered that question, the same student comes up with another: "I mean, I can see now that we don't want zero pollution. But, I mean, how come once we're at this so-called 'efficient' level of pollution, why don't we want to keep on cleaning up pollution?" You haven't been able to help the "I mean" problem, but you have helped the student begin to grasp the concept of an efficient level of pollution. Continue this process by answering this second question.

3. The student listens to your explanation and then asks one last question: "I mean, I can see this! But why don't we clean up less pollution than the efficient amount? I mean, we'd surely save some resources if we cleaned up less pollution!" Answer this final question.

Answers

True/False Answers

1. **F** Marginal social cost equals the marginal private cost plus the marginal externality cost.
2. **T** The fundamental reason for the existence of externalities is that property rights are not well defined.
3. **T** Because knowledge has external benefits, the unregulated private market produces less than the efficient amount.
4. **U** As the Coase theorem points out, assigning property rights will cure the problem of an externality only when transactions costs are low.
5. **F** The efficient amount of pollution is the amount that equalizes the marginal social benefit and cost from pollution.
6. **F** The private market produces *less* than the efficient amount of a good that has a positive externality.
7. **F** The major advantage of marketable permits is that the EPA does not need to know each firm's marginal benefit from pollution.
8. **T** Because the benefits are obtained in the future, to take any actions at present to reap these benefits may not be worthwhile.
9. **T** Patents are one method the government uses to overcome the positive externality problem with knowledge.
10. **T** The marginal social cost equals the marginal private cost plus the marginal externality cost. If there is no marginal externality cost, the marginal social cost equals the marginal private cost.
11. **F** If a good creates a negative externality, to attain allocative efficiency its production needs to be taxed, not subsidized.
12. **T** This essentially is the definition of the Coase theorem.
13. **T** Externalities are a reason for market failure; that is, the private, unregulated, market does not produce the allocatively efficient level of a good.
14. **F** The presence of an external benefit means that the marginal social benefit exceeds the marginal private benefit.
15. **F** The existence of external costs means that the private market produces more than the efficient amount of the good.

Multiple Choice Answers

1. **c** Answer (c) is the definition of an externality.
2. **d** By producing more than the allocatively efficient amount, the private market has failed.
3. **c** The Coase theorem shows that, when transactions costs are low, to whom a property right is assigned makes no difference: The externality will be internalized, and the efficient level of production will result.
4. **d** Imposing a tax equal to the marginal external cost will set equal the marginal private cost — which includes the tax — and the marginal social cost, thereby ensuring that the efficient amount of rubber will be produced.
5. **d** Bystanders are not part of the initial transaction (the smoking), so the harm that befalls them is an external cost.
6. **b** The equilibrium in this prisoners' dilemma game may be that neither developed nor less-developed nations impose a carbon-fuel tax.
7. **b** Because the *MSC* curve is leftward of the *MC* curve, the figure indicates that the good is creating a negative externality.
8. **c** The vertical difference between the *MSC* curve and the *MC* curve is the marginal external cost, which in this case is $2 per ton.
9. **b** In the absence of any intervention, the private market produces where the private demand curve (which is the same as the private marginal benefit curve) crosses the private supply curve (which is the same as the private marginal cost curve).
10. **c** Allocative efficiency requires that production be at the level where marginal social cost, *MSC*, equals marginal social benefit, *MSB*.
11. **c** The tax must shift the private *MC* curve until it is the same as the *MSC* curve. Imposing a $2 tax will shift the *MC* curve higher by the

amount of the tax, $2, which is the amount desired. More generally, by imposing a tax equal to the marginal externality cost, the new marginal private cost, which includes the tax, is the same as the marginal social cost.

12. **c** The efficient level of *anything* is the amount required for its marginal social cost to equal its marginal social benefit.

13. **d** Because the cost or benefit is not borne by the decision maker, the cost or benefit is *external* to the decision maker's choice. Being external, the cost or benefit is ignored by the decision maker.

14. **b** New discoveries often may be used by many people, which is an externality from the point of view of the discoverer.

15. **b** Emission charges allow firms to pollute as long as they pay the fee for the pollution. Emission charges are common in Europe but are less common in the United States.

16. **a** Eating a hot dog is not likely to create either an external cost or an external benefit.

17. **b** At any level of output, the marginal social benefit exceeds the marginal private benefit, which indicates that there must be a positive external benefit.

18. **b** The private market produces the level of output that equalizes the marginal private cost (the private supply curve) and the marginal private benefit (the private demand curve).

19. **c** Efficiency requires that the amount of the good produced equalize the marginal social cost and the marginal social benefit. In this case, efficiency requires that output be 650.

20. **b** If suppliers are granted a $2 per unit subsidy, the marginal private cost schedule drops by $2 at every unit of output. Hence to produce 650 units of output the new marginal private cost becomes $6. This equals the marginal private benefit of 650 units, so the (new) equilibrium price is $6 and the quantity produced is the efficient amount, or 650 units.

21. **b** Efficiency requires the equality of marginal social benefit and marginal social cost.

22. **c** Taxes are a solution to the problem posed by an external cost.

23. **d** Intellectual property rights are a major issue in trade negotiations between the United States and many foreign nations.

24. **b** This summarizes the "bottom line" results about how externalities affect efficiency.

■ Answers to Short Answer Problems

1. The economic argument is that education generates external benefits. In particular, when individuals are educated, society at large receives benefits beyond the private benefits that accrue to those choosing how much education to obtain. The presence of this positive externality means that in the absence of government intervention, the private sector would provide too little education for allocative efficiency. Hence to attain efficiency in the market for education, the government provides below-cost education at public colleges and universities.

2. The existence of external costs means that producers do not take into account all costs when deciding how much to produce. If a tax is levied that is exactly the amount of the external cost, the cost is no longer external. As a result, the producer takes it into account and thus is induced to produce the efficient quantity.

3. The marginal social benefit of pollution is the benefit firms receive from being able to pollute. For instance, by polluting the air, an electric utility reduces its costs because it does not have to install expensive pollution reduction devices, such as scrubbers, to decrease air pollution. Hence society benefits from pollution because firms are part of society. (More basically, the fact that the firm does not need to install pollution reduction devices means that the resources that might have been used to produce these devices can be used to produce other goods and services.) The fact that society benefits from pollution must be balanced against the fact that pollution imposes a cost on society, expressed as the marginal social cost of pollution.

4. a. The total amount of pollution is 10 units, 5 (remaining) units from factory A and 5 (remaining) units from factory B. The total cost of achieving this level of pollution is $750, the cost of $250 incurred by factory A plus the cost of $500 incurred by factory B.

b. The total amount of pollution (again) is 10 units, comprising no pollution from factory A and 10 units from factory B. The total cost of attaining this level of pollution is $500, all incurred by factory A.

c. From a social standpoint, having factory A decrease its pollution by 10 units and factory B do nothing is the most desirable. This solution has the lowest total social cost — $500 versus $750 for an equal reduction at each factory — which means that eliminating the 10 units of pollution have inflicted the lowest possible total cost on society, which certainly is a desirable outcome.

5. a. Similar to the answer in part (a) of problem 4, the total cost is $750.

b. Factory A will sell its permits to factory B. This transaction will occur because decreasing its pollution is less expensive for factory A than it is for factory B. In particular, the price of a permit for a unit of pollution will range between $50 and $100. For any price greater than $50, factory A is willing to sell its permits and reduce its pollution because this transaction is profitable: The cost to A is $50 per unit of pollution eliminated but, as long as the price exceeds $50, factory A gains more revenue than it incurs in costs. Factory B is willing to buy permits for any price less than $100 because buying permits at this price reduces B's costs. For each permit that B can buy, it saves $100 by not having to decrease its pollution. Thus, as long as the price of a permit is less than $100, buying the permits reduces B's costs.

c. The outcome with marketable permits is more efficient. In this case, only factory A decreases its pollution. Factory B does not lower its pollution but instead buys permits from factory A. Thus with marketable permits we obtain, as in part (c) of problem 4, the socially desirable outcome: Factory A decreases its pollution and factory B does not.

6. a. Farmer Mark will erect the fence. Doing so costs him $250 a year but saves him the $350 Will would otherwise eat.

b. Farmer Dave will erect the fence. If he did not do so, Will would eat $350 worth of corn and Mark would bill Dave for the corn. Thus erecting the fence costs Dave $250 a year but saves him $350.

c. These answers illustrate the Coase theorem. Erecting the fence is socially desirable because the cost to society of the fence — $250 — is less than the cost to society of not having a fence — $350 in corn consumed by Will. Thus, as the Coase theorem points out, regardless of whether Dave or Mark is given the property right, the fence is erected and Will dines on valueless garbage rather than valuable corn.

7. Figure 21.4 shows the market for chicken pox vaccine. Because there are no negative externalities, the marginal social cost curve equals the marginal private cost. This curve is labeled $MC = MSC$ in the figure. It also is the private supply curve. However, the presence of the positive externality means that the marginal social benefit (MSB) curve lies rightward of the marginal private benefit curve, which is the same as the private demand curve (labeled $MB = D$). The vertical distance between the curves equals the marginal externality; that is, it is the additional (external) benefit to society over and above the benefit to the private individual. In the absence of government intervention, Q_0 is produced, and the efficient amount is Q_1.

To move this market closer to the efficient level of output, the government might subsidize

FIGURE 21.4
Short Answer Question 7

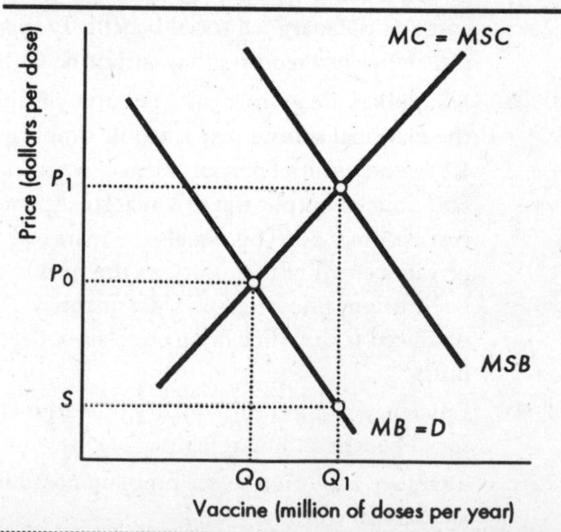

production or use of the vaccine. This policy could take the form of paying producers to produce more vaccine. The aim is to shift the private supply curve rightward so that it intersects the private demand at output Q_1, the efficient amount, and price S. Alternatively, the government might buy Q_1 worth of doses and then resell them to consumers below cost at price S, the price necessary to induce consumers to buy Q_1 doses.

8. a. In an unregulated market, the equilibrium price and quantity are determined by the intersection of the marginal private benefit and cost curves because these are the demand and supply curves, respectively. Thus the equilibrium price is $300, and the equilibrium quantity is 3 students.

   b. Because there are no external costs, the efficient quantity is determined by the intersection of the marginal private cost and marginal *social* benefit curves. This result implies that allocative efficiency is attained at a quantity of 5 students attending college.

9. a. Igor wants 5 students to attend his new university, I.O.U. Five students will attend only when the tuition is $100.

   b. When 5 students attend the university, the marginal cost of the fifth student is $400. By charging the student only $100 in tuition, Igor apparently is losing money on this student. However, the loss is only apparent: Five students are the efficient level of education because the *total* marginal social benefit from the fifth student is $400, which equals the marginal cost of educating this student.

■ You're the Teacher

1. "I agree with you that pollution is bad, but clearly to totally eliminate it isn't optimal. Think about this: Society could get rid of all air pollution by outlawing all cars, all trains, all planes, shutting down all factories, and eliminating all cows. (Cows produce methane.) But, come on, you know we won't do this. And the reason is immediate: It's just too expensive. Sure, we'd like less pollution, but the cost to get to zero pollution is prohibitive — a whole lot more than the benefit! So, anyone that says 'Zero pollution is best' hasn't thought through the issue. In fact, some pollution is good. We get to drive rather than walk, have pizza delivered rather than doing without, air condition our homes rather than perspire, and heat our homes rather than freeze."

2. "Okay, you agree that we don't want to aim for zero pollution. So, our target should be what the book calls the 'efficient' level of pollution. This amount of pollution is the level at which the marginal social cost of pollution reduction equals the marginal social benefit from the reduction. The idea here is not hard, once you see it. Suppose that we're at the point where the marginal social cost of reducing pollution equals the marginal social benefit. If we decreased pollution any more, the marginal social cost would *exceed* the marginal social benefit. In other words, the cost of any further reduction would exceed the benefit from the reduction. You have to agree that it doesn't make sense to do something when the cost of the action is larger than the benefit. Well, this is exactly the situation we're in when we're at the efficient level of pollution: The marginal cost of further reduction is larger than the marginal benefit. We'd use resources cleaning up this pollution and society doesn't value the reduction enough to make use of these resources worthwhile! So, further reduction would harm society."

3. "Look, I'll explain this to you if you knock off the 'I means'! Once we're at the efficient level of pollution, you agree that we don't want to keep going and further decrease pollution. But, once we're at the efficient point, if we cut back and clean up less pollution, we're also going to lose. Why? For all the pollution up to the point where the marginal social benefit equals the marginal social cost, the marginal social benefit from cleaning up the pollution exceeded the marginal social cost of cleaning it up. In other words, for all these 'units' of pollution, society valued cleaning them up more than it cost society to clean them up. We want these units cleaned up because the net benefit (the marginal social benefit minus the marginal social cost) from doing so is positive. Thus, if we cut back, we'd lose this net benefit. Obviously we don't want to do that. So the efficient level of pollution is the amount that makes society as well off as possible. You don't want to clean up more, nor do you want to clean up less!"

Part Review 4 MARKETS AND GOVERNMENT

Reading Between the Lines

SPRINT PUTS PRICE TAG OF UP TO $8 BILLION ON FORAY INTO LOCAL PHONE MARKETS

Sprint Corp. said its bold plan to raid local phone markets with cable-television partners may cost as much as $8 billion over the next several years.

The Sprint team will be fighting the regional Bell giants and AT&T Corp. in most markets for customers using similar pocket-sized portable phones. The U.S. local phone business is a $90 billion lode virtually monopolized by the seven regional Bell giants and GTE Corp. Mr. Grubman (a Salomon Brothers Inc. analyst) figures that monopolies typically lose 20% to 30% of their customer base when competition opens, offering a lucrative upside for the Sprint-cable alliance.

... the cable companies will contribute their ownership of Teleport Communications Group, which has built fiber-optic networks serving businesses in 37 U.S. metropolitan areas and has received authorization to provide local service in nine states, including California, Illinois and New York.

The cable partners are hitched to millions of U.S. subscribers. TCI, Cox, and Comcast together have about 18 million customers, with lines passing 30 million homes.

Sprint also is talking with a number of smaller potential cable affiliates ... about hooking their lines to the new venture's switching centers. These potential affiliates pass an additional 20 million homes, bringing Sprint close to its goal of having a network that could serve half of U.S. homes...

John J. Keller, "Sprint Puts Price Tag of Up to $8 Billion on Foray into Local Phone Markets," March 30, 1995, p. B7. Reprinted by permission of The Wall Street Journal,

■ Analyze It

Local phone service has traditionally been a natural monopoly, regulated by the government. This, however, may be changing as Sprint together with cable-television partners is proposing to enter the market.

1. In a diagram, illustrate the case of a natural monopoly by drawing the industry demand curve and the natural monopoly's *ATC* curve. What is the distinguishing characteristic of a natural monopoly?
2. In a second diagram, show how the costs of providing local phone service have (apparently) changed by using the same demand curve as in your first diagram and drawing one firm's *ATC* and *MC* curves.
3. What caused the cost curves to change?
4. If local phone service is no longer a natural monopoly, what potential benefits await consumers? What fate awaits the existing local phone companies?

Mid-Term Examination

1 The public choice theory of government argues that politicians try to

a. maximize the likelihood of their election and re-election.
b. maximize the amount of their campaign contributions.
c. promote an efficient allocation of resources.
d. None of the above.

2 Nonrivalry is a feature of

a. external goods.
b. nonexcludable goods.
c. private goods.
d. public goods.

3 In general, an excise tax reduces

a. only consumer surplus.
b. only producer surplus.
c. both consumer and producer surplus.
d. neither consumer nor producer surplus.

4 A radio station is a

a. private good, as is access to its broadcast signal.
b. private good, but access to its broadcast signal is a public good.
c. public good, as is access to its broadcast signal.
d. public good, but access to its broadcast signal is a private good.

5 The tendency of people with lower wages to work

a. fewer hours makes the distribution of income less equal.
b. fewer hours makes the distribution of income more equal.
c. more hours makes the distribution of income less equal.
d. more hours makes the distribution of income more equal.

6 If the marginal tax rate rises with income, the tax is

a. a sales tax.
b. an excise tax.
c. a regressive tax.
d. a progressive tax.

7 During recent decades the supply of health care has shifted

a. left slower than the demand has shifted.
b. left faster than the demand has shifted.
c. right slower than the demand has shifted.
d. right faster than the demand has shifted.

8 Distributions of wealth that include human capital

a. are more equal than distributions of wealth that exclude human capital.
b. overstate the degree of income inequality.
c. understate the degree of income inequality.
d. None of the above.

9 The goal of regulators is to maximize producer surplus according to the
a. capture theory of regulation.
b. public interest theory of regulation.
c. consumer surplus theory of regulation.
d. producer surplus theory of regulation.

10 The supply of economic regulation will be smaller whenever
a. consumer surplus per buyer increases.
b. the number of buyers decreases.
c. producer surplus per supplier increases.
d. the total surplus decreases.

11 Price cap regulation
a. and earnings share plans are both incentive regulation schemes.
b. and earnings share plans are not incentive regulation schemes.
c. is an incentive regulation scheme. Earnings share plans are not.
d. is not an incentive regulation scheme. Earnings share plans are.

12 Average cost pricing is equivalent to
a. marginal cost pricing.
b. maximizing consumer surplus.
c. maximizing producer surplus.
d. rate of return regulation.

13 An example of an activity that generates positive externalities is
a. dumping soap suds into a trout stream.
b. planting flowers along an interstate highway.
c. eating an apple.
d. None of the above.

14 Unregulated markets are efficient when there are
a. external benefits and external costs.
b. external benefits but no external costs.
c. external costs but no external benefits.
d. no external benefits nor external costs.

15 The Coase theorem applies when transactions costs are
a. low and property rights have been assigned.
b. low and property rights do not exist.
c. high and property rights have been assigned.
d. high and property rights do not exist.

16 When individuals make decisions about whether to be vaccinated, they
a. undervalue the private benefits that it creates.
b. undervalue the external benefits that it creates.
a. overvalue the private benefits that it creates.
a. overvalue the external benefits that it creates.

Answers

Reading Between the Lines

Figure 1 illustrates the case of a natural monopoly. The distinguishing characteristic of a natural monopoly is that one firm can supply the market at lower cost than two or more firms. This characteristic means that the firm's *ATC* curve slopes downward until after it crosses the industry demand curve, just as illustrated in Figure 1. The fact that the *ATC* curve is downward sloping also implies that the minimum of the *ATC* is located at a point beyond the demand curve. This situation probably accurately describes the cost situation in the local phone market, at least until recently.

FIGURE 1
Local Phone Service as a Natural Monopoly

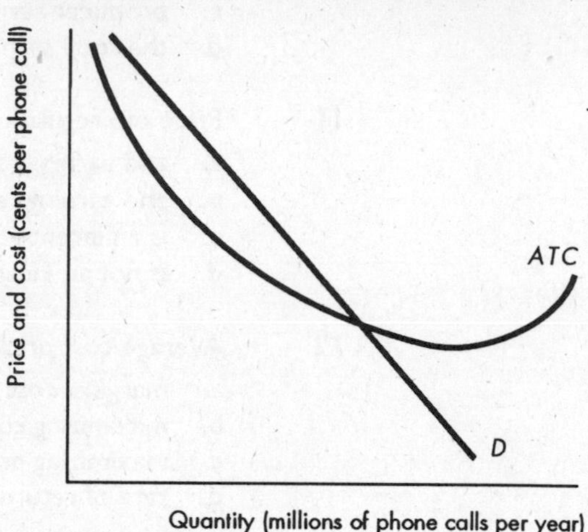

Figure 2 shows how the *ATC* curve of a firm in this industry has apparently changed. The fact that new firms want to enter the market strongly suggests that these firms believe they will be able to earn at least a normal profit from producing in this market. In other words, these firms think that it is no longer the case that one firm can serve the market at a lower cost than with more firms, so that the *ATC* curve now reaches its minimum at a point before it crosses the demand curve. Figure 2 illustrates the situation where the *ATC* reaches its minimum halfway to the demand curve, which suggests that it might be possible for two firms to successfully compete in the market.

FIGURE 2
Local Phone Service After Technology Change

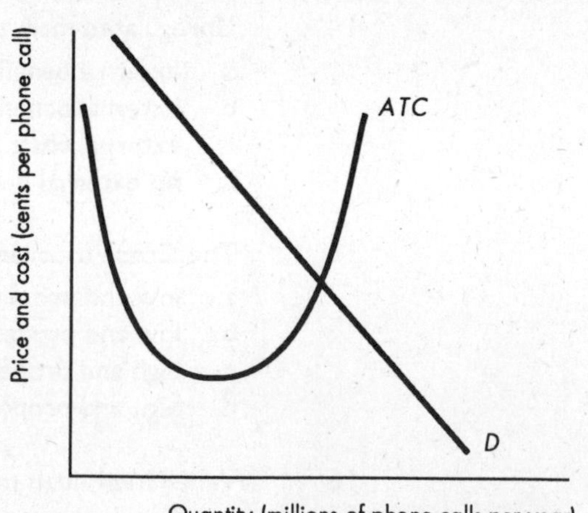

The reason for the change in cost curves is that technology has changed. As the story indicates, technological advances have made it possible to use the fiber-optic wire that brings cable TV to a house also to bring phone service. And, cellular phone service has fallen dramatically in cost due to technological advances.

The benefits to the customer are the usual benefits associated with competitive industries. If the technology has changed so that the market can more closely approximate monopolistic competition, consumers can look forward to a lower price for local phone service and, most likely, a greater variety in service. The local phone companies, however, may find life somewhat more difficult. If the industry can support competitive behavior, there will be increasing calls for deregulation. Thus, the local phone companies may find themselves competing against other producers in the near future.

This future, however, may also bring the local phone companies opportunities. For instance, not reported in this story, is the fact that local phone companies are trying to enter the long distance market as well as provide cable television services.

Mid-Term Exam

1 a; 2 d; 3 c; 4 b; 5 a; 6 d; 7 c; 8 a; 9 a; 10 b; 11 a; 12 d; 13 b; 14 d; 15 a; 16 b.

Chapter 22

TRADING WITH THE WORLD*

Key Concepts

Patterns and Trends in International Trade

The goods we buy from producers in other nations are our **imports**; the goods we sell to people in other nations are our **exports**. Most U.S. exports and imports are manufactured goods. Trade in goods accounts for about 80 percent of U.S. international trade; trade in services (travel and transportation) accounts for about 20 percent. Trade has accounted for an increasingly large fraction of U.S. total output. The balance of trade is the value of exports minus the value of imports.

- If the value of exports exceeds the value of imports, the country is a **net exporter**.
- If the value of imports exceeds the value of exports, the country is a **net importer**.

Throughout the 1980s and 1990s the United States has experienced a large excess of imports over exports.

Opportunity Cost and Comparative Advantage

Countries can produce anywhere on their production possibilities frontier (*PPF*) curve. Figure 22.1 shows a *PPF* for a nation that is producing at point *a*.

- The *PPF*'s slope is (Δ bushels of grain)/(Δ cars), with Δ again meaning "change in." The slope equals the opportunity cost of one more car at point *a*.
- A country has a **comparative advantage** in the production of the good for which it has the lowest opportunity cost.

FIGURE **22.1**

Slope of the *PPF* is the Opportunity Cost

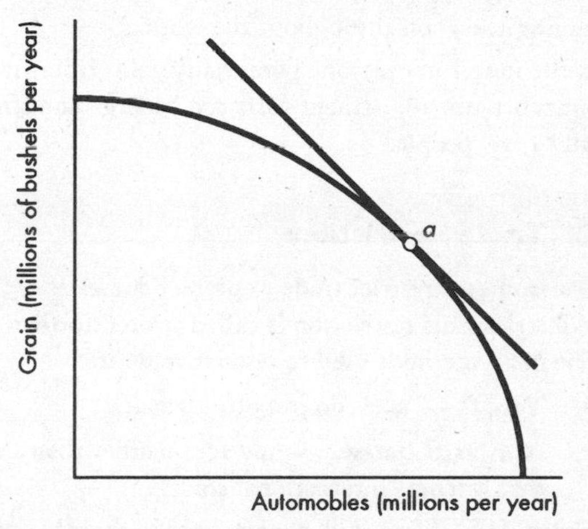

Gains from Trade

A country gains from trade by buying from other nations the goods that the other nations produce at the lowest opportunity cost and selling to the other countries goods it produces at the lowest opportunity cost.

- A nation gains by specializing in production of goods for which it has a comparative advantage and trading for other goods.
- International trade allows all nations to consume *outside* their *PPF*s. This is the gains from trade.
- With international trade, a nation receives a higher relative price for the goods it exports and pays a lower relative price for the goods it imports.
- **Absolute advantage** occurs when a nation's productivity in the production of all goods is greater than that of another country. Absolute advantage does not determine trade; comparative advantage does.

*This is Chapter 35 in *Economics*.

Gains from Trade in Reality

Most trade can be explained by comparative advantage. However, much trade involves similar goods for two reasons:

- Diversified tastes — people demand many similar but slightly different products.
- Economies of scale — average total cost declines with output.

A nation can specialize in the production of one of the similar goods and capture economies of scale by trading the good throughout the world.

In the long run everyone potentially gains from trade, but short-run adjustment costs can be large and affect only a few people.

Trade Restrictions

Governments restrict trade to protect domestic industries; this restriction is called **protectionism.** The main methods used to restrict trade are:

- **Tariffs** — taxes on imported goods.
- **Nontariff barrier** — any action other than a tariff that restricts international trade.

Today, U.S. tariffs are low compared to their historical levels. The **General Agreement on Tariffs and Trade (GATT)** is an international agreement designed to reduce tariffs and increase international trade. The most recent GATT agreement created the World Trade Organization and was ratified by the United States in 1994. The United States, Canada, and Mexico also are signatories of the North American Free Trade Agreement (NAFTA).

Figure 22.2 illustrates the effects of a tariff.

- The tariff shifts the supply curve of imports vertically upward by the amount of the tariff (the length of the arrow).
- The price rises from P_0 to P_1 and the quantity decreases from Q_0 to Q_1. The government gains revenue.
- By decreasing imports to the domestic economy, foreigners can buy less from the domestic economy. Hence the value of domestic exports decreases by an amount equal to the drop in the value of domestic imports.

Nontariff barriers include quotas and voluntary export restraints.

FIGURE **22.2**
The Effect of a Tariff

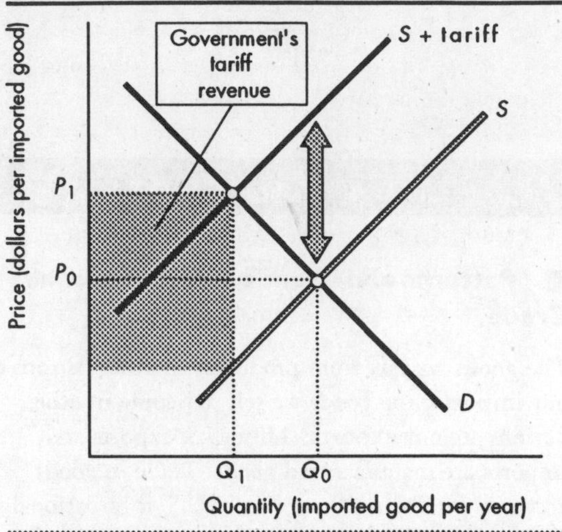

- **Quota** — a quantitative restriction on the amount of a good that can be imported.
- **Voluntary export restraint** — an agreement between governments in which the exporting nation agrees to limit the volume of its exports.

Similar to tariffs, nontariff barriers raise the prices of imported goods and decrease the quantities imported. Unlike a tariff, the government gets no revenue from a nontariff barrier; the revenue from the higher price goes to importers in the case of quotas and to foreign exporters in the case of voluntary export restraints.

The Case Against Protection

Arguments in favor of protection are flawed. The arguments and their errors are:

- *National security* — the nation should protect industries that are necessary for its defense. Error: Virtually every industry may be considered "vital" for defense; increased security must be compared with the cost of lower income; direct subsidies to targeted industries are more efficient than protection from international competition.
- **Infant-industry argument** — the nation should protect a young industry that will reap learning-by-doing gains in productivity and eventually be able to compete successfully in the world market. Error: If the learning-by-doing benefits accrue only to the firms in the industry, this argument

fails because these firms can finance their own start-ups. Direct subsidies are more efficient.

- *Restraining monopoly* — the nation should protect an industry from **dumping** by foreign competitors, who sell goods below cost in order to gain a monopoly.
  Error: Determining when a firm sells below cost is difficult; only global natural monopolies are able to sustain a monopoly; if the firm is a natural monopoly, regulation is the more efficient way to restrain it.
- *Protection saves jobs* — imports cost U.S. jobs.
  Error: Although free trade costs jobs in importing industries, it creates them in exporting industries; tariffs that protect jobs do so at an exceedingly high cost.
- *Cheap foreign labor* — tariffs are necessary to compete with cheap foreign labor.
  Error: U.S. labor is more productive than cheap foreign labor, and U.S. firms compete successfully in industries in which they have a comparative advantage because of their productivity relative to other nations.
- *Diversity and stability* — nations specialized in the production of one good may be subject to severe economic fluctuations.
  Error: Such specialization is not the case for the United States; nations that are specialized can gain by such specialization and then diversify by investing abroad.
- *Lax environmental standards* — protection is needed to compete against nations with weak environmental standards.
  Error: Not all poor nations have weak standards; their concerns about the environment will increase when they grow richer through trade.
- *Rich nations exploit developing countries* — protection prevents developed nations from forcing people in poor nations to work for slave wages.
  Error: By allowing poor nations to trade with rich nations, wages in poor nations rise because of the increased demand for labor.

International trade is restricted because some people lose from it. Losers lobby politicians to limit free trade.

Helpful Hints

1. This chapter applies the fundamental concepts of opportunity cost and comparative advantage discussed in Chapter 3 to the problem of trade between nations. The basic principles are the same for trade between individuals in the same country and between individuals in different countries.

   Many people involved in debates about trade seem confused by the concept of comparative advantage, partially because they implicitly consider absolute advantage as the sole reason for trade. A country has an absolute advantage if it can produce all goods using less inputs than another country. However, such a country can still gain from trade. Consider California and Saskatchewan. California has a better climate and with widespread irrigation has an absolute advantage in the production of all agricultural products. Indeed, California frequently has more than one harvest a year. This fact would seem to imply that California has no need to trade with Saskatchewan. However, Saskatchewan has a comparative advantage in the production of wheat. Therefore California will specialize in fruits and vegetables and trade them for wheat. California could easily grow its own wheat, but the opportunity cost would be too high — the lost fruit crops. By specializing and trading, both California and Saskatchewan gain.

2. The argument that protection saves jobs is popular but incorrect. As you learned in this chapter, imposing a tariff on imports costs jobs in export industries. We lose jobs because foreigners, unable to sell as much to us, are thus unable to buy as much from us. Because they cannot buy as much, our export industries shrink, or fail to grow as much as otherwise.

   The claim that protection saves jobs continues to be made largely because the jobs saved by tariffs are highly visible but the job losses are invisible. Factories that are in operation only because the goods they produce are favored with a tariff or other form of protection from foreign competition may be visited. However, visiting factories that would have been built had an exporting industry been able to expand is not possible. This asymmetry makes arguing that tariffs protect U.S. jobs easy, but this argument is incorrect.

3. The chapter noted that tariffs save jobs in protected industries but do so only at a high cost. For example, each U.S. textile job saved costs the United States $221,000 a year. This cost is far greater than the annual salary for the average job saved. Moreover, protection in the automobile industry costs $105,000 per job; in dairy products $220,000 per job; and in steel, $750,000 per job. Clearly these costs greatly exceed the amounts in wages that these jobs pay. Hence protection winds up costing the country more than it benefits the nation.
4. Be sure that you understand the political economy point made in the last section of the chapter. If, as stressed in this chapter, gains from free trade can be considerable, why do countries tend to impose trade restrictions? The key is that, although free trade creates overall benefits to the economy as a whole, there are both winners and losers. The winners gain more in total than the losers lose, but the latter tend to be concentrated in a few industries.

   Because of this concentration, free trade is resisted by some acting on the basis of rational self-interest. Even though trade restrictions benefit only a small minority while the overwhelming majority are hurt, their implementation is not surprising. The cost of a particular trade restriction to each of the majority individually is quite small, but the benefit to each of the few individually large. Thus the minority has a strong incentive to have a restriction imposed, whereas the majority has little incentive to expend time and energy in resisting a trade restriction.

Questions

True/False/Uncertain and Explain

1. If a nation has an absolute advantage in producing a good, it will export the good.

2. Only the nation exporting a good gains from trade.

3. Trade allows a nation to consume combinations of products that lie beyond its *PPF*.

4. Tariffs in the United States are at an all time high.

5. Voluntary export restraints reduce the amount of a good imported into a nation but quotas do not.

6. A quota and a voluntary export restraint on an imported good both raise its price.

7. U.S. workers can compete with lower paid foreign workers in industries in which the United States has a comparative advantage.

8. When governments impose tariffs, they increase their consumers' welfare.

9. Free international trade benefits some citizens and harms others.

10. A nation may have both an absolute advantage in the production of all goods and services and a comparative advantage in the production of all goods and services.

11. Throughout the 1980s and 1990s the United States has been a net importer.

12. The United States is a net exporter of agricultural products.

13. Economists generally agree that high tariffs improve a nation's standard of living.

Multiple Choice Questions

1. International trade based on comparative advantage may allow each country to consume
   a. more of the goods it exports, but less of the goods it imports.
   b. more of the goods it imports, but less of the goods it exports.
   c. more of the goods it exports and imports.
   d. less of the goods it exports and imports.

2. A tariff is
   a. a limit on the amount of a good that can be exported from a nation.
   b. a limit on the amount of a good that can be imported into a nation.
   c. a tax on a good imported into a nation.
   d. an agreement between governments to limit exports from a nation.

3. Which of the following is a sound reason for protecting an industry?
   a. The industry is unable to compete with low-wage foreign competitors.
   b. The industry is necessary to diversify the nation's production.
   c. The protection keeps a richer nation from exploiting the workers of poorer countries.
   d. None of the above is a sound reason for protection.

4. To produce a bottle of wine in Portugal requires 4 hours of labor; in England it requires 6 hours of labor. Labor is the only input. As a result, you can conclude that
   a. Portugal has a comparative advantage in producing wine.
   b. England has a comparative advantage in producing wine.
   c. Both Portugal and England have a comparative advantage in producing wine.
   d. None of the above because not enough information is available to determine which nation possesses a comparative advantage in producing wine.

5. The combination of diversified tastes and economies of scale can account for
   a. a nation importing and exporting similar products.
   b. the fact that for the United States nontariff barriers are a greater impediment to free trade than tariffs.
   c. specialization according to comparative advantage.
   d. the result that free trade allows nations to consume at points beyond their *PPF*.

6. International trade allows a nation to
   a. produce and consume at a point beyond its *PPF*.
   b. produce at a point beyond its *PPF* but not consume at a point beyond its *PPF*.
   c. consume at a point beyond its *PPF* but not produce at a point beyond its *PPF*.
   d. neither produce nor consume at a point beyond its *PPF*.

7. Suppose that the United States imports only textiles from Mexico and exports only computers to Mexico. If the United States imposes a tariff on Mexican textiles, the U.S. textile industry ____ and the computer industry ____.
   a. expands; expands
   b. expands; does not change
   c. expands; contracts
   d. contracts; expands

8. If the United States has an absolute advantage in producing all goods and services, it will
   a. still import some goods and services.
   b. import no goods and services.
   c. export no goods and services.
   d. None of the above.

9. When does the domestic government gain the most revenue?
   a. When it imposes a tariff.
   b. When it imposes a quota.
   c. When it negotiates a voluntary export restraint.
   d. The amount of revenue it gains is the same with a tariff and a voluntary export restraint.

10. Who benefits from a tariff on a good?
    a. Domestic consumers of the good.
    b. Domestic producers of the good.
    c. Foreign governments.
    d. Foreign producers of the good.

11. Quotas ____ jobs in the import-competing industries and ___ jobs in the exporting industries.
    a. increase; increase
    b. increase; have no effect on
    c. increase; decrease
    d. decrease; decrease

12. Selling a product in a foreign nation at a price less than its cost of production is called
    a. infant industry exploitation.
    b. absolute advantage.
    c. dumping.
    d. net exporting.

Figures 22.3 and 22.4 show production in two nations, Solaris and Chaff. Production is taking place at point *a* in Solaris and at point *b* in Chaff. Use these figures for the next four questions.

FIGURE **22.3**
Production in Solaris

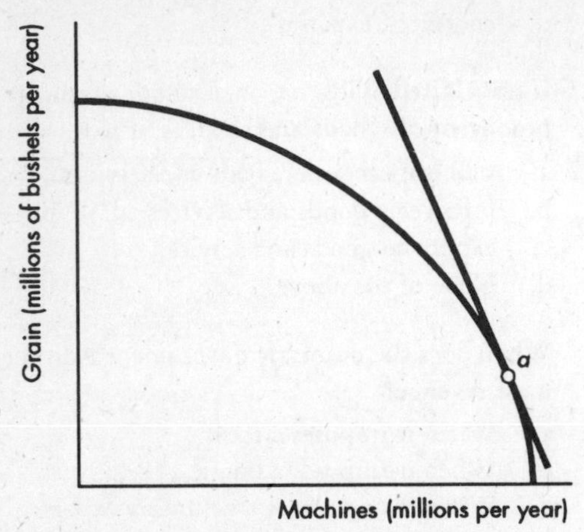

FIGURE **22.4**
Production in Chaff

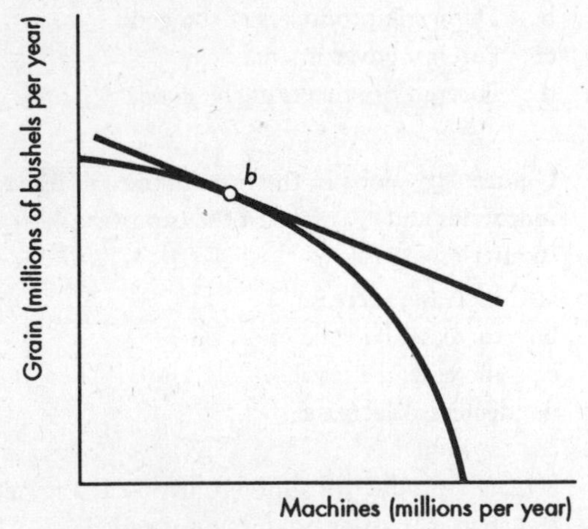

13. The slope of the *PPF* at point *a* in Solaris is 200 bushels of grain per machine; the slope of the *PPF* at point *b* in Chaff is 15 bushels of grain per machine. Without trade between the nations, what is the relative price of a machine in Solaris?
    a. 200 bushels of grain.
    b. $1/200$ bushels of grain.
    c. 15 bushels of grain.
    d. $1/15$ bushel of grain.

14. Without trade between the nations, what is the relative price of a machine in Chaff?
    a. 200 bushels of grain.
    b. $1/200$ bushels of grain.
    c. 15 bushels of grain.
    d. $1/15$ bushel of grain.

15. Solaris has a comparative advantage in ____ and Chaff has a comparative advantage in ____.
    a. machines; grain
    b. grain; machines
    c. machines and grain; neither good
    d. neither good; machines and grain.

16. Once Solaris and Chaff begin to trade, Solaris exports ____ to Chaff and Chaff exports ____ to Solaris.
    a. machines; grain
    b. grain; machines
    c. machines and grain; neither good
    d. neither good; machines and grain

17. In recent years
    a. trade in services has accounted for about 50 percent of total U.S. exports.
    b. the United States has become a large net importer of agricultural products.
    c. the U.S. government rejected the NAFTA treaty.
    d. U.S. imports have been substantially greater in value than U.S. exports.

18. Which of the following does not raise the domestic price of an imported good?
    a. A tariff imposed on the good.
    b. A quota imposed on the good.
    c. A voluntary export restraint for the good.
    d. None of the above because they all raise the domestic price of an imported good.

19. Suppose that Musicland and Videoland produce two goods — CDs and videos. Musicland has a comparative advantage in the production of CDs if
   a. fewer videos must be given up to produce 1 CD than in Videoland.
   b. less labor is required to produce 1 CD than in Videoland.
   c. less capital is required to produce 1 CD than in Videoland.
   d. less labor and capital are required to produce 1 CD than in Videoland.

20. The (false) idea that an industry should be protected because of learning-by-doing until it is large enough to compete successfully in world markets is the _____ argument for protection.
   a. absolute advantage
   b. infant industry
   c. dumping
   d. diversity

21. Which of the following statements about the gains from international trade is correct?
   a. Everyone gains.
   b. Some people gain from international trade and some lose, though overall the gains exceed the losses.
   c. Some people gain and some people lose from international trade; overall the losses exceed the gains.
   d. Everyone loses.

22. Which of the following is a U.S. service export?
   a. A U.S. citizen buys dinner while traveling in Switzerland.
   b. A Canadian buys a dinner while traveling in Canada.
   c. A Swiss citizen buys a computer made in the United States.
   d. A Mexican citizen spends the night in a motel while visiting the United States.

23. Nations often trade similar goods because of
   a. comparative advantage.
   b. nontariff barriers.
   c. different opportunity costs.
   d. economies of scale and diversified tastes.

24. When a rich nation buys a product made in a poor nation, in the poor nation the demand for labor _____ and the wage rate _____.
   a. increases; rises
   b. increases; falls
   c. decreases; rises
   d. decreases; falls

Short Answer Problems

FIGURE 22.5
Short Answer Problem 1

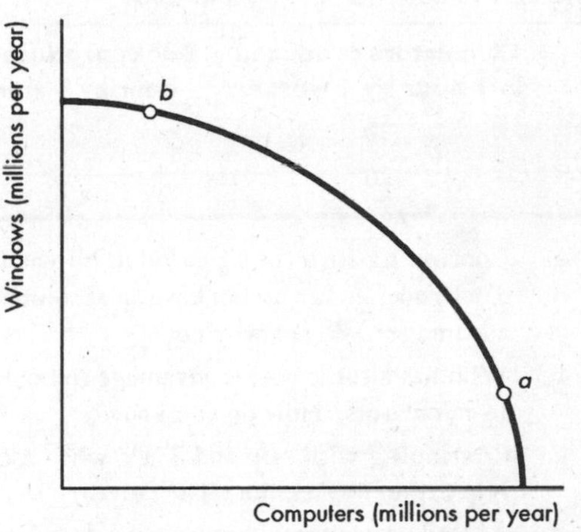

1. Two nations, Microsloth and Notell, have the same *PPF*. Both produce only two goods, windows and computers. Figure 22.6 shows their current production points: Microsloth at point *a* and Notell at point *b*.
   a. In which nation is the opportunity cost of a window lowest? In which is the opportunity cost of a computer lowest? Explain how you arrived at your answer.
   b. Which nation has a comparative advantage in producing windows? In producing computers? Why?
   c. If Microsloth and Notell were to trade, which nation would export windows? Which would export computers? Why?

2. Table 22.1 shows the amount of books and calculators that can be produced by one worker in one hour in the nations of Nip and Tuck. Labor is the only input used, and these are the only products produced in Nip and Tuck.

a. What the opportunity cost of producing a book in Nip? In Tuck?
b. What is the opportunity cost of a calculator in Nip? In Tuck?
c. What is the relative price of a book in Nip? In Tuck?
d. What is the relative price of a calculator in Nip? In Tuck?
e. What is the relationship between your answers to parts (a) and (b) compared to your answers to parts (c) and (d)?

Table 22.1 Production in Nip and Tuck

	Calculators produced in 1 hour by 1 worker	Books produced in 1 hour by 1 worker
Nip	30	20
Tuck	20	5

3. a. Continuing with the situation in Nip and Tuck, does either nation have an absolute advantage? Why or why not?
   b. Who has a comparative advantage in books? In calculators? How do you know?
4. a. Continuing with Nip and Tuck, what does Nip export? What does Tuck export?
   b. As trade continues, in what good does Nip specialize in producing? Tuck?
   c. Suppose that 100 workers in Nip switch to producing books and 200 workers in Tuck switch to calculators. Complete Table 22.2, which shows the effect of this switch on books and calculators in Nip, in Tuck, and in the world.
   d. What general principle does your result for the world production of books and calculators illustrate?

Table 22.2 Changes in Production

Country	Change in calculators	Change in books
Nip	___	___
Tuck	___	___
World	___	___

5. How does a tariff on a particular imported good affect the domestic price of the good, the quantity imported, and the quantity of the good produced domestically?
6. How does a quota on an imported good affect the domestic price of the good, the quantity imported, and the quantity produced domestically?
7. How does a tariff on imports affect the exports of the country?

Table 22.3 Market for Watches in Norolex

Price (dollars per watch)	Quantity demanded (millions of watches)	Quantity supplied (millions of watches)
$20	65	15
25	60	20
30	55	25
35	50	30
40	45	35
45	40	40
50	35	45

8. Table 22.3 gives the domestic supply and demand schedules for watches for the nation of Norolex.
   a. Draw the supply and demand schedules in Figure 22.6.
   b. What is the equilibrium price?
   c. How many watches are produced in Norolex? How many are purchased by consumers in Norolex?

FIGURE 22.6
Short Answer Problems 8 and 9

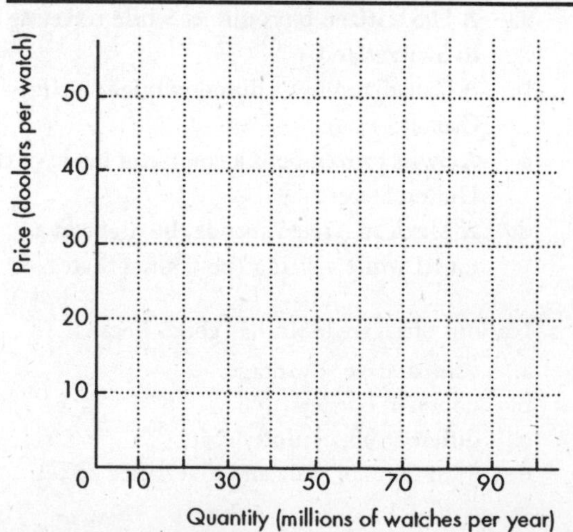

9. Norolex now trades with another nation, Switch. Switch exports watches to Norolex. Switch's export supply schedule is in Table 22.4 along with Norolex's domestic supply schedule.
   a. Complete Table 22.4 by determining the total supply schedule of watches.
   b. Graph the total supply schedule in Figure 22.6, which already contains the domestic supply and demand schedules.
   c. What is the new equilibrium price of a watch?
   d. How many watches are produced in Norolex? How many are purchased by consumers in Norolex? How many are imported?

Table 22.4 Supply Schedule of Watches with Trade

Price (dollars per watch)	Quantity supplied in Norolex (millions of watches)	Quantity supplied by Switch (millions of watches)	Total quantity supplied (millions of watches)
$20	15	20	___
25	20	25	___
30	25	30	___
35	30	35	___
40	35	40	___
45	40	45	___
50	45	50	___

10. The watch industry in Norolex is not happy with the situation after trade with Switch has occurred. The watch industry lobbies the government to impose a $15 per watch tariff on imports from Switch.
   a. Complete Table 22.5, which shows how the tariff affects imports from Switch.
   b. Using your answers from Table 22.5, complete Table 22.6, which shows the new total supply schedule after the tariff has been imposed.
   c. After the tariff is imposed, what is the equilibrium price of a watch in Norolex?
   d. How many watches are produced in Norolex? How many watches are purchased by consumers in Norolex? How many watches are imported?
   e. Relative to the situation in problem 9, explain who has gained from the tariff and who has lost? Explain why the gainers gained and the losers lost.

Table 22.5 Short Answer Problem 10 (a)

Price (dollars per watch)	Pre-tariff quantity supplied by Switch (millions of watches)	Post-tariff quantity supplied by Switch (millions of watches)
$20	20	5
25	25	10
30	30	15
35	35	___
40	40	___
45	45	___
50	50	___

Table 22.6 Short Answer Problem 10 (b)

Price per watch	Quantity supplied in Norolex (millions of watches)	Quantity supplied by Switch (millions of watches)	Total quantity supplied (millions of watches)
$20	15	5	___
25	20	10	___
30	25	15	___
35	30	___	___
40	35	___	___
45	40	___	___
50	45	___	___

■ You're the Teacher

1. "I understand the stuff in this chapter about comparative advantage and it makes sense. But I still can't see how the U.S. can compete with nations like Mexico, where the wages are so low. I think the only way we can protect our high wages is to keep Mexican products out of our markets." Your friend may think that he or she understands comparative advantage but actually is missing the essential idea. Have informed friends is better than having ignorant ones, so help your friend understand comparative advantage by explaining how U.S. firms are able to compete with Mexican companies.

2. After you explain your friend's error in question 1, your friend makes another mistake: "Well, thanks to you, now I can see how U.S. firms can compete. But, still, international trade can't be good. After all, if this trade helps Mexico, we must lose. So I think that international trade should be banned." Explain to your friend how international trade benefits both the U.S. and Mexico.

Answers

True/False Answers

1. **U** The nation may export the good but only if it has a *comparative* advantage in its production.
2. **F** All nations engaged in international trade gain from the trade.
3. **T** By allowing consumption to occur beyond the limits expressed by the *PPF*, the nation gains from trade.
4. **F** Tariffs in the United States are near an all-time low.
5. **F** Tariffs, quotas, and voluntary export restraints all limit the quantity of imports.
6. **T** As the answer to question 5 pointed out, tariffs, quotas, and voluntary export restraints all limit the quantity of imports and thus all raise the price of imports.
7. **T** In industries with a comparative advantage, higher U.S. productivity more than offsets the higher U.S. wages, so U.S. firms can successfully compete.
8. **F** By raising the price of imported goods, tariffs harm consumers.
9. **T** Free trade benefits consumers and harms workers and firms in import-competing industries.
10. **F** A nation can have an absolute advantage in all goods, but it cannot have a comparative advantage in all goods.
11. **T** Indeed, the extent to which the United States has been a net importer has been large in the 1980s and 1990s.
12. **T** The U.S. has a comparative advantage in agricultural products.
13. **F** Economists agree that tariffs reduce a nation's standard of living.

Multiple Choice Answers

1. **c** By specializing in the product with a comparative advantage and trading with other nations, the nation can consume more of both the goods it imports and the goods it exports.
2. **c** Answer (c) is the definition of a tariff.
3. **d** All of the reasons offered for protection are faulty.
4. **d** To determine who has a comparative advantage in wine, you need to know the relative price of a bottle of wine, which requires that you know the cost in both nations of producing another good.
5. **a** By specializing in the production of one good that is similar to another and then exporting the good, a firm can capture economies of scale and satisfy people's desires for its particular variation of the good.
6. **c** Producing at points beyond the *PPF* is impossible, but trade allows consumption to occur at points beyond the *PPF*.
7. **c** The textile industry gains from the tariff, and the computer industry loses.
8. **a** International trade depends on comparative advantage — not absolute advantage —so the United States will import the goods in which it has a comparative disadvantage.
9. **a** Quotas and voluntary export restraints yield no revenue for the domestic government.
10. **b** Domestic producers gain because the price of the product rises.
11. **c** Quotas, tariffs, and voluntary export restraints all limit trade, thereby increasing jobs in import-competing industries but decreasing jobs in exporting industries.
12. **c** Although often alleged, dumping is difficult to prove because determining whether a firm actually is selling a good below cost is difficult to prove.
13. **a** The relative price equals the slope of the *PPF* because the slope is the opportunity cost, in terms of grain, of producing 1 more machine.
14. **c** For the reason outlined in the answer to question 13, the opportunity cost of a machine in Chaff is 15 bushels of grain.
15. **b** The relative price of grain is less in Solaris, and the relative price of a machine is less in Chaff.
16. **b** Each nation exports the good in which it has a comparative advantage.
17. **d** The value of U.S. imports has exceeded the value of U.S. exports by a wide margin in recent years.

18. **d** All protectionist measures raise the price of imported goods.
19. **a** The opportunity cost of a good is the number of other goods that must be sacrificed to increase production of the first good.
20. **b** The description in the problem is the definition of the infant industry argument for protection.
21. **b** Because the overall gains exceed the overall loses, in principle the losers from international trade can be compensated so that, on balance, everyone gains from the trade.
22. **d** The Mexican resident has purchased a service — lodging — from a U.S. firm.
23. **d** The combination of economies of scale and diversified tastes means that nations often import and export similar goods.
24. **a** By increasing the demand for the goods produced in the poor nation, the demand for labor rises, thereby raising the wage rate in that nation.

Answers to Short Answer Problems

1. a. The opportunity cost of a window is lowest in Microsloth. The opportunity cost of a computer is lowest in Notell. Figure 2.7 demonstrates this result. The opportunity cost of a computer equals the magnitude of the slope of the line tangent to the *PPF*. In Figure 22.7, the magnitude of the slope of the line tangent at point *b* is less than the magnitude of the line tangent at point *a*. Hence the opportunity cost of a computer is less at point *b*, which is the level at which Notell produces. The opportunity cost of a window equals the inverse of the slopes of these lines, so the opportunity cost of a window is less at point *a*, Microsloth's production point.

   b. Microsloth has a comparative advantage in producing windows because its opportunity cost of producing a window is less than Notell's opportunity cost. Similarly, Notell has a comparative advantage in producing computers.

   c. Microsloth would export windows and Notell would export computers because these are the goods for which each nation has a comparative advantage. Alternatively, windows are relatively cheaper in Microsloth, so Microsloth will export them. Computers are relatively less expensive in Notell, so Notell exports computers.

FIGURE **22.7**
Short Answer Problem 1

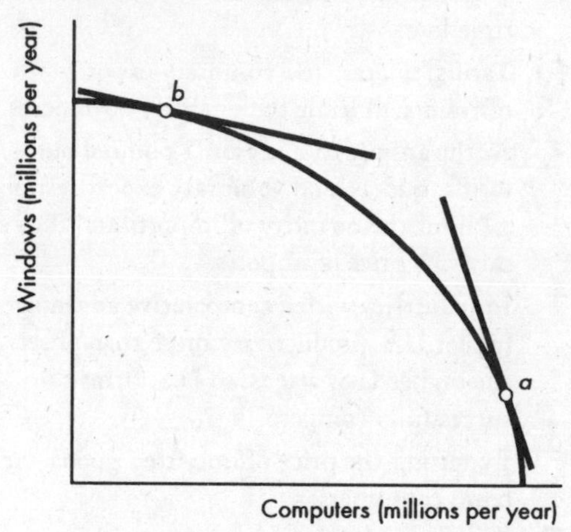

2. a. The opportunity cost in Nip of producing a book is 1 1/2 calculator. To produce 1 more book in Nip requires that a worker be switched from producing calculators to producing books. In 1 hour, 20 books are produced, so 1/20 of an hour is needed to produce 1 book. How many calculators could the worker have produced in this 1/20 of an hour? In one hour, 30 calculators can be produced, so in 1/20 of an hour, the worker could have produced (30)(1/20) = 1 1/2 calculator. Hence the opportunity cost of the book is the 1 1/2 calculators that are not produced. Similarly, the opportunity cost of a book in Tuck is 4 calculators.

   b. The opportunity cost of a calculator in Nip is 2/3 of a book. The opportunity cost of a calculator in Tuck is 1/4 of a book. These answers are calculated similarly to those in part (a).

c. The relative price of a book in Nip is 1 1/2 calculators per book; the relative price of a book in Tuck is 4 calculators per book.

d. In Nip, the relative price of a calculator is 2/3 of a book. In Tuck, the relative price of a calculator is 1/4 of a book.

e. The answers are the same, because the relative price of a good is the same as its opportunity cost.

3. a. Nip has an absolute advantage because its workers are more productive than workers in Tuck. In Nip, 1 worker in 1 hour can produce more calculators than in Tuck and can also produce more books than in Tuck.

b. Nip has a comparative advantage in books and Tuck has a comparative advantage in calculators. Nip has the comparative advantage in books because its opportunity cost of a book — 1 1/2 calculators — is less than the opportunity cost in Tuck — 4 calculators. Tuck has the comparative advantage in calculators for the same reason: The opportunity cost of a calculator is less in Tuck — 1/4 book — than in Nip — 2/3 book.

4. a. Nip has a comparative advantage in books, so Nip exports books; Tuck has a comparative advantage in calculators, so Tuck exports calculators. Note that this answer makes sense: The pre-trade relative price of a book is less in Nip, so producers in Nip will be able to undercut producers in Tuck. Similarly, the pre-trade relative price of a calculator is less in Tuck, so Tuck's producers will be able to undercut Nip's producers.

b. Nip will specialize in books; Tuck will specialize in calculators.

c. Table 22.7 shows the effect of the specialization.

d. In Table 22.7, note that the world production of *both* books and calculators increased. In other words, more books and calculators are available in the world. This outcome demonstrates that both nations can gain from trade. The world gains 100 books and 100 calculators; this gain can be divided so that Nip gains 50 books and 50 calculators and Tuck gains 50 books and 50 calculators.

Table 22.7 Short Answer Problem 4 (c)

Country	**Change in calculators**	**Change in books**
Nip	–300	+200
Tuck	+400	–100
World	+100	+100

5. A tariff on an imported good raises its price to domestic consumers, as the export supply curve shifts upward. As the domestic price of the good rises, the quantity of the good demanded decreases, so the quantity imported decreases. The rise in the domestic price leads to an increase in the quantity of the good supplied domestically.

6. The effect of a quota on the domestic price of the good, the quantity imported, and the quantity of the good produced domestically are exactly the same as the effects of a tariff discussed in the answer to short answer problem 5. The difference is that the rise in the domestic price is not the result of a vertical shift in the export supply curve; it occurs because the quota forces the export supply curve to become vertical at the quota amount.

7. When a country imposes a tariff on its imports, the volume of imports shrink, and the volume of its exports to other countries shrinks by the same amount. Thus a balance of trade is maintained. A tariff limits the amount of goods that other nations can sell to the first country and also lowers the price the other nations receive for their products. Thus, by limiting its imports, foreign nations cannot afford to buy as many exports from the first country, so its exports decrease.

8. a. Figure 22.8 (on the next page) shows the demand and supply schedules.

b. Either from Figure 22.8 or from the demand and supply schedules, the equilibrium price is $45 because at this price the quantity demanded equals the quantity supplied.

c. Forty million watches per year are produced domestically, and 40 million watches per year are purchased by consumers in Norolex.

FIGURE 22.8
Short Answer Problem 8

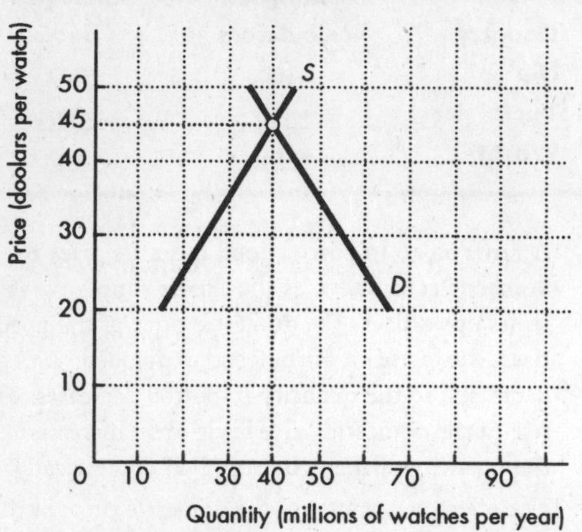

FIGURE 22.9
Short Answer Problem 9

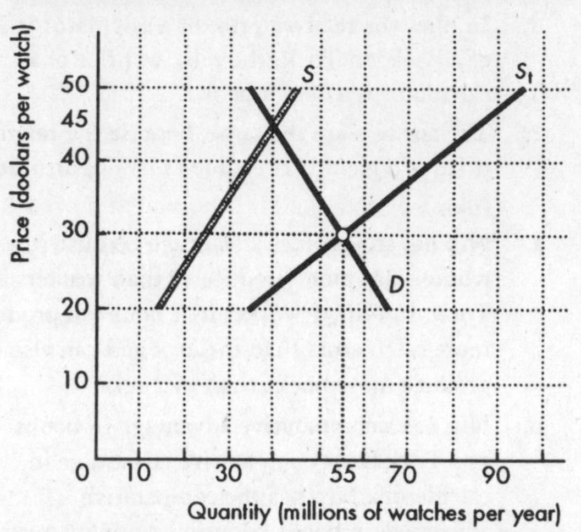

9. a. Table 22.8 shows the total supply schedule. At any price, the total quantity supplied equals the sum of the quantity supplied in Norolex plus the quantity supplied in Switch.
   b. Figure 22.9 shows the total supply curve, S_t, the initial supply curve and the demand curve.
   c. The new equilibrium price of a watch is $30.
   d. At the equilibrium price of $30, consumers in Norolex buy 55 million watches per year. At this price, watch firms in Norolex produce 25 million watches. The difference between the total quantity of watches purchased and the total quantity produced, 30 million watches per year, is imported from Switch.

Table 22.8 Short Answer Problem 9 (a)

Price (dollars per watch)	Quantity supplied in Norolex (millions of watches)	Quantity supplied by Switch (millions of watches)	Total quantity supplied (millions of watches)
$20	15	20	35
25	20	25	45
30	25	30	55
35	30	35	65
40	35	40	75
45	40	45	85
50	45	50	95

10. a. Table 22.9 shows how the tariff affects the supply schedule of imports from Switch. A $15 per watch tariff lowers the receipts of the firms in Switch by $15 per watch. Hence when the price — including the tariff — is $35 a watch, the watch companies receive only $20 per watch. Thus, as the initial supply schedule shows, when the Switch watch companies receive $20 per watch, they supply 20 million watches. The remainder of the supply schedule is calculated similarly.

Table 22.9 Short Answer Problem 10 (a)

Price (dollars per watch)	Pre-tariff quantity supplied by Switch (millions of watches)	Post-tariff quantity supplied by Switch (millions of watches)
$20	20	5
25	25	10
30	30	15
35	35	20
40	40	25
45	45	30
50	50	35

b. The new total supply schedule equals the sum of the Norolex supply schedule plus the new, post-tariff Switch supply schedule. Table 22.10 shows the new total supply schedule.
c. The equilibrium price of a watch is $35.
d. At the price of $35, consumers buy 50 million watches per year. Firms in Norolex produce 30 million watches per year. Imports from Switch are 20 million watches per year.
e. The watch firms and their workers in Norolex have gained. With the tariff, they produce more watches and receive a higher price. Consumers in Norolex and the Switch watch manufacturing firms and their workers have lost. Consumers have lost because they must pay a higher price for a watch ($35 with the tariff compared to $30 without the tariff) and so respond by purchasing fewer watches. Switch firms and workers have lost because the lower price they receive for a watch leads them to produce fewer watches for export (20 million with the tariff, versus 30 million without).

Table 22.10 Short Answer Problem 10 (b)

Price (dollars per watch)	Quantity supplied in Norolex (millions of watches)	Quantity supplied by Switch (millions of watches)	Total quantity supplied (millions of watches)
$20	15	5	20
25	20	10	30
30	25	15	40
35	30	20	50
40	35	25	60
45	40	30	70
50	45	35	80

■ You're the Teacher

1. "Look, you don't have the main idea here. Let's use some numbers because they should help you catch on. Suppose that U.S. wages are 10 times higher than Mexican wages. Now, it's also a fact that U.S. workers' are more productive than Mexican workers. Let's take two industries. In the first, call it industry A, suppose that U.S. workers are 2 times as productive as Mexican workers; in the second, say, industry B, U.S. workers are 20 times as productive. In industry A, U.S. firms won't be able to compete with Mexican firms. Sure, U.S. workers are twice as productive but they are paid ten times as much. Therefore U.S. firms will lose out in this industry. But, in industry B, U.S. firms will drive Mexican firms out of business. Even though U.S. workers are paid 10 times as much as Mexican workers are paid, U.S. workers produce 20 times as much as Mexican workers produce. Hence the per unit cost of the good is less in the U.S., so U.S. firms are going to be able to compete and compete successfully.

   "The United States won't be able to compete successfully with Mexico in producing every type of good or service; but the reason is that the United States does not (and cannot) have a comparative advantage in all goods and services even though it may well have an absolute advantage. But, in the industry with the comparative advantage — industry B in my example — the United States is going to be able to compete and to win the competition."

2. "Well, I'm glad you're catching onto some if the ideas of this chapter, but you're missing another key point. The chapter explains how trade allows a nation to consume more goods and services than it can produce. Obviously, this condition has to make nations engaged in international trade better off.

   "But there's also another a way to tackle this point. I read somewhere that 'trade is not a zero-sum game.' Here's what that means: If you and I voluntarily agree to a trade, like I'll trade my economics notes for your chemistry notes, the trade has to make us both better off. After all, if the trade didn't make me better off, I wouldn't agree to it and if it didn't make you better off, you wouldn't agree to it. This type of trade will enable both of us to raise our grades: me in chemistry and you in economics.

   "Well, it's the same idea with trading between nations. Suppose that we import a VCR from Mexico and the Mexicans use the money we sent them to buy 100 bushels of wheat from Kansas. Essentially, we've traded the 100 bushels of wheat for the VCR. If this trade didn't make us better off, we wouldn't do it. So, too, for the Mexicans involved: If they didn't want the wheat more than the VCR, they won't agree to the transaction. And, as the chapter explained, if we specialize in wheat and Mexico in VCRs, we both will be able to consume more wheat and more VCRs than if we produced VCRs and wheat and Mexico produced VCRs and wheat.

"Or, think about this more generally. For two potential trading partners to be willing to trade, they must have different comparative advantages, that is, different opportunity costs. Then, they will trade and *both* parties will gain. If the countries do not trade, each faces its own opportunity costs. The price at which trade takes place must be somewhere between the opportunity costs of the two nations. The country with the lower opportunity cost of the good in question gains because it receives a price above its opportunity cost. Similarly, the country with the higher opportunity cost gains because it pays a price below its opportunity cost.

"You know, I think this is really cool. What it shows is that just as trade between us makes both of us better off, trade between nations makes both nations better off."

Chapter 23 EMERGING ECONOMIES*

Key Concepts

■ A Snapshot of the World Economy

Nations are divided by the International Monetary Fund into three groups:

- *Industrial Countries* — 23 nations, including the United States, Canada, Japan, Australia, New Zealand, and 18 Western European nations. These nations have the highest average incomes.
- *Developing Countries* — 130 countries throughout the world. These countries have the lowest average incomes.
- *Countries in Transition* — 28 countries that have emerged from the former Soviet Union and Central Europe. Incomes in these nations seem to average about $5,000 per person.

A **Lorenz curve** shows the distribution of income by plotting the cumulative percentage of income against the cumulative percentage of population. The world Lorenz curve shows that the world distribution of income across countries is more unequal than the income distribution within the United States.

For the past decade, world income per person has grown by an average of 2.6 percent a year. Developing nations have, on average, grown more rapidly than developed nations; income per person in the countries in transition have *fallen* an average of 3.4 percent per year.

■ Alternative Economic Systems

All economies face the economic problem of deciding what to produce, how to produce it, when to produce it, where to produce it, and for whom to produce it. Economic systems vary according to property rights and incentives. Property rights determine the ownership, use, and disposal of factors of production and goods and services. Factors of production may be owned by private individuals or the government.

- **Capitalism** — private ownership of capital and land, and incentives based on market prices.
- **Socialism** — state ownership of capital and land, and incentives based on laws and regulations.

Other hybrid economic systems are:

- **Market socialism (decentralized planning)** — state ownership of land and capital with incentives based on a mixture of market prices and regulations.
- **Welfare state capitalism** — private ownership of capital and land, and incentives based on market prices, though the government intervenes to alter prices.

Capitalism uses prices as the key factor in answering the questions that comprise the economic problem. Socialism relies on government planners who produce a central plan that answers those questions.

■ Economic Transition in Russia and Central Europe

Soviet central planning had four key elements:

- an administrative hierarchy;
- an iterative planning process;
- legally binding commands; and
- taut, inflexible plans.

Productivity and consumption per person in the Soviet Union in the mid-1980s was less than 40 percent that of the United States. A period of transition to a market economy began in 1990. This transition had three components:

- Enforcement of the central plan was relaxed.
- Prices were slowly deregulated.
- Limited private ownership of firms was permitted.

* This is chapter 37 in *Economics*.

This transition has had three problems:

- The values and legal system are alien to capitalism.
- Traditional trade flows collapsed so that firms had to search for suppliers and customers.
- A fiscal crisis occurred in which government revenues dried up and were replaced by printing money, which created high inflation.

Transition also has occurred in Central Europe, and the problems have been similar to those in Russia:

- **East Germany** — reunified with West Germany; no fiscal crisis but unemployment has been high.
- **Czech and Slovak Republics** — quickly freed prices and privatized. The economies are now expanding and inflation has been relatively low.
- **Hungary** — had used decentralized planning since the 1960s. A gradual movement to a market economy has fostered economic growth.
- **Poland** — had a fast movement to a market economy, with rapid privatization. The economy has been growing for the last several years and inflation has begun to drop.

China's Emerging Market Economy

China began its command economy in 1949. It was much like that of the Soviet Union, with emphasis on investment in capital-intensive industries.

- The Great Leap Forward of 1958 focused on labor-intensive production, but failed because of political turmoil and poor incentives.
- In 1978, major reforms were introduced. They boosted private incentives in agriculture, and the result has been huge productivity gains and rapid growth.
- Other market-oriented reforms have been made, and China's economic growth rate has been remarkably high: Production per person grew at an annual average rate of 7.5 percent per year from 1978 to 1994.

China's success is the result of four features of its reforms:

- Many new nonstate firms have been formed.
- The gains in productivity at state firms have been large because the managers have been given incentives similar to those faced by managers of privately owned firms.
- China has an efficient taxation system in which firms can keep all profit above a certain level.
- Prices have been deregulated gradually.

Helpful Hints

1. The textbook ends appropriately where it began, emphasizing the universal problems that any economy faces. Foremost among them is the fundamental and universal problem of scarcity, which creates the economic problem and makes choice necessary. No economic system can eliminate scarcity. Each simply confronts the problem in a different way.

   An additional underlying notion that is relevant under any economic system is that individuals will pursue their own best interest as they understand it. This assumption is a postulate about basic human attributes and is independent of the economic environment. However, the specific way that pursuit of self-interest occurs is different under different economic systems because alternative systems provide different incentives and constraints. Socialism does not change the desire to pursue self-interest, as indicated by the fact that managers of socialist enterprises receive bonuses if they achieve certain targets. However, it does blunt people's incentive to innovate and work hard to create more output, as indicated by the fact that socialist economies lag behind capitalist societies in measures of economic growth.

2. The topic of this chapter is of great current practical interest and likely will continue to be for some time into the future. Much of the former socialist world is in a process of economic and political reform. In addition to the ongoing economic reforms in China, great changes are taking place in the former socialist countries of Russia, Poland, Hungary, and Czechoslovakia, among others. The greatest change was the reunification of Germany.

   Many of these countries are taking rather different paths to the goal of a new, more market-oriented economy. You now have a very good foundation in what is occurring in these nations. You may want to keep track of the outcome of these changes, in light of what you have learned in this economics course.

As you continue to observe what occurs in these emerging economies, keep in mind that a market economy requires certain institutions to succeed: a legal system so that people can enter into contracts without fear of arbitrary changes; a viable financial system so that people can borrow and lend; a stable price system so that prices can convey useful information; and property rights so that proper market incentives exist; to name a few. None of the former socialist countries have any of these institutions in place to the degree that they are in the West. Putting these institutions into place will require difficult changes along the road to reform, including large (and seemingly arbitrary) redistributions of income and wealth. These difficulties may create political obstacles to reform — those who stand to lose under reform may obstruct it.

Questions

True/False/Uncertain and Explain

1. The poorest countries in the world are the developing countries.

2. In the mid-1980s, Soviet productivity was higher than U.S. productivity but Soviet productivity was growing much more slowly.

3. Scarcity is a problem for capitalist economies but not for socialist economies.

4. Under capitalism, all capital is owned by the state.

5. The Great Leap Forward initiated in 1958 by Mao Zedong was one of the significant economic successes in modern China.

6. Under capitalism, individual preferences are paramount.

7. One of the problems faced by countries in transition is that their traditional trade flows have collapsed.

8. Soviet central plans were taut, without much leeway for error.

9. Japan and the United States are examples of nations using a capitalist economic system.

10. China's economic growth slowed after it instituted changes that stressed the role of markets.

11. The number of industrial and developing nations is approximately equal.

12. Socialism relies on central planning to solve the economic problem.

13. On average, over the past decade income per person in developing countries has grown more rapidly than income per person in industrial nations.

Multiple Choice Questions

1. The economic reforms of 1978, under Deng Xiaoping,
   a. moved China off the "capitalist road" it had been on under Mao Zedong.
   b. abolished collectivized agriculture.
   c. have resulted in slower economic growth in China.
   d. have made China more dependent on food imports.

2. Under capitalism, information is transmitted
   a. through the planning process.
   b. through price movements.
   c. by capital owners exercising their own influence.
   d. by workers asserting feasibility limits.

3. Under socialism, changes in what is produced are determined by
   a. price movements.
   b. consumers signaling changes in what they want to consume.
   c. firms as they discover which goods and services are most profitable to produce.
   d. the planners' desires as indicated in the central plan.

4. The way in which the "what," "how," "where," "when," and "for whom" questions are answered *always* depends on
   a. relative prices.
   b. the way the economy is organized.
   c. whether there is scarcity.
   d. the preferences of planners

5. Which economic system is characterized by private ownership of capital and incentives based primarily on market prices?
   a. Capitalism.
   b. Socialism.
   c. Market socialism.
   d. Welfare state capitalism.

6. Which economic system is characterized by state ownership of capital and incentives based mainly on market prices?
   a. Capitalism.
   b. Socialism.
   c. Market socialism.
   d. Welfare state capitalism.

7. Which economic system is characterized by state ownership of capital and incentives arising from a central economic plan?
   a. Capitalism.
   b. Socialism.
   c. Market socialism.
   d. Welfare state capitalism.

8. Which economic system is characterized by private ownership of capital and incentives based mainly on market prices though there is considerable state intervention in these prices?
   a. Capitalism.
   b. Socialism.
   c. Market socialism.
   d. Welfare state capitalism.

9. Over the past decade, in which group of nations did average per capita income grow most rapidly?
   a. Industrial countries.
   b. Developing countries.
   c. Countries in transition.
   d. Industrial countries and countries in transition tied.

10. Success of the 1978 Chinese reforms was the result of all of the following <u>EXCEPT</u>
   a. the massive rate of entry of new nonstate firms.
   b. large increases in the productivity and profitability of state firms.
   c. an efficient taxation system.
   d. immediate price deregulation.

11. During the Great Leap Forward in China under Mao Zedong,
   a. agricultural production increased dramatically, but industrial production did not.
   b. the application of new technologies resulted in a significant general increase in production.
   c. China experienced very slow economic growth.
   d. China became a major exporter of grains and cotton.

12. Which of the following nations has predominately a capitalist economic system?
   a. Canada.
   b. Russia.
   c. Sweden.
   d. China.

13. An example of the "what" question of the economic problem is:
   a. Will Leggos be produced?
   b. What will be the income of major league ballplayers?
   c. Steel will be produced in which state?
   d. What is the right answer?

14. The Lorenz curve depicting the distribution of average per capita income among countries lies
   a. on the line of equality.
   b. to the left of the line of equality.
   c. to the right of the line of equality, but not as far out as the Lorenz curve depicting the distribution of income of families within the United States.
   d. to the right of the line of equality and farther out than the Lorenz curve depicting the distribution of income of families within the United States.

15. Central planning in the Soviet Union was characterized by
    a. an administrative hierarchy.
    b. legally binding commands.
    c. inflexible plans.
    d. All of the above.

16. The 1978 Chinese reforms included
    a. a high price of oil.
    b. a trade agreement with the Soviet Union.
    c. more private incentives than before.
    d. a focus on labor-intensive production.

17. Except for East Germany, the transition nations of Central Europe generally have had
    a. fiscal crises.
    b. low unemployment rates.
    c. rapid economic growth but relatively high unemployment rates.
    d. no problems converting their value system to support a market system.

18. The collapse of traditional trade flows is
    a. slowing economic growth in China.
    b. a problem for the Central European nations but not for Russia.
    c. a problem for Russia and the Central European nations in transition.
    d. the result of the fact that money was not important when the Soviet Union was following a central plan.

19. Once producing as efficiently as possibly, which type of economic system can produce at points that lie beyond its *PPF*?
    a. Both socialist and capitalist economies.
    b. Only a socialist economy.
    c. Only a capitalist economy.
    d. Neither socialist nor capitalist economies can produce at points beyond their *PPF*.

20. The transition to a market economy in Russia
    a. started with Joseph Stalin.
    b. has caused output to decline within Russia.
    c. is the result of recent price re-regulation in Russia.
    d. has been hastened by the large number of entrepreneurs in Russia.

21. Recently, Chinese economic growth has been
    a. rapid compared to that of the United States.
    b. about the same as that in the United States.
    c. slower than that in the United States.
    d. not directly comparable to that in the United States.

Short Answer Problems

1. Consider two countries, High and Low, with per capita incomes of $10,000 and $5,000, respectively. The rate of growth of per capita income in High is 1 percent per year.
    a. Suppose that the rate of growth of per capita income in Low is 10 percent per year. What will be the gap in per capita income between High and Low after 1 year? After 4 years?
    b. Suppose that the rate of growth of per capita income in Low is 20 percent per year. What will be the gap in per capita income between High and Low after 4 years? How many years will be needed for Low to surpass High?

2. Again consider the two nations of High and Low. Per capita income in High is $10,000 and in Low is $5,000. Suppose that the growth rate of per capita income is 1 percent per year in High and 4 percent per year in Low.
    a. After 1 year, what is per capita income in High and in Low? After 2 years, what is per capita in these two nations? What is the per capita income gap after 2 years?
    b. After 10 years, what is per capita income in High? In Low?
    c. After 20 years, what is per capita income in the two nations? After 30 years? What conclusion can you draw from these answers?

3. You are an entrepreneur in a developing country and are considering various investments. You have saved a large sum of money and now face two choices: You can smuggle the funds out of your nation and use them in a way that will give you a return of 5 percent. Alternatively, you can use them to build a new factory in your nation that will have a return of 15 percent.
    a. Which is more likely to help your nation grow: Smuggling the funds or building the factory?

b. If you are confident that your nation will enforce property rights so that you will receive the profit from the factory, what are you likely to do: build the factory or smuggle the funds?

c. If you believe that your nation's government is likely to confiscate the factory — that is, your nation does not protect private property rights — what are you likely to do: build the factory or smuggle the funds?

d. What general conclusion can you draw from your answers?

4. Figure 23.1 depicts the market for food in the Russia before it began its transition to a market economy. The price of food was controlled, so it equaled P_c. In Figure 23.1 show the amount of food produced as Q_p and the amount demanded as Q_c. Is there a shortage or a surplus? How was food likely to be allocated?

FIGURE 23.1
The Food Market in Transition

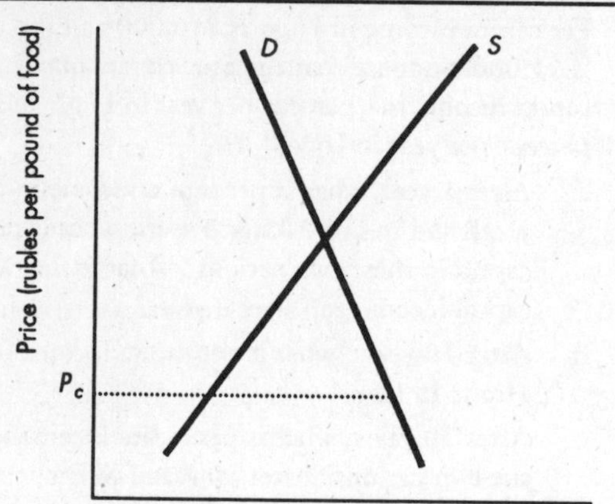

5. Continuing with the situation in problem 4, suppose that, once Russia began its transition to a market economy, the price of food was deregulated so that it was free to reach its equilibrium level.

a. In Figure 23.1 show the equilibrium price as P and the equilibrium quantity as Q.

b. When is more food produced: when the price is controlled or when it is free to reach its equilibrium? When is more food consumed?

c. When the price is deregulated, does it rise or fall? Bearing in mind your answer to part (b), does the price movement reflect a situation in which society, as a whole, is worse off?

6. What are the basic economic questions that any society must decide? Does a capitalist nation or a socialist nation need to answer fewer of these basic questions? Explain your answer.

7. Distinguish between a capitalist economic system and a welfare state capitalist system.

8. You have just bought a small, privatized state firm in a formerly planned economy, which is moving toward a market economy. Briefly explain what decisions you must make as an owner. How will they be complicated by the fact you are operating in this economy as opposed to operating in the United States?

9. Briefly describe the agricultural economic reforms proclaimed by Deng Xiaoping in China in 1978. What has been their effect?

■ You're the Teacher

1. "It's just not fair that some people have such low incomes. I mean, $365 a year in Chad! Come on, this just isn't fair! I think that all industrial nations should give these developing nations as much money as possible." Respond to your friend's comment.

2. "There is a point in this chapter that I just don't understand: Why couldn't socialist nations grow as rapidly as capitalist ones? Didn't the people in those nations care about anything?" This student is close to stumbling on an important assumption made by most economists. The student probably should have understood this point before but clearly did not. Regardless, help the student by explaining what economists assume that people care about and how it related to growth in socialist nations.

Answers

True/False Answers

1. **T** The average income in the developing countries is the lowest of any group.
2. **F** In the mid-1980s, Soviet productivity not only was growing more slowly than that of the United States, but it also was much less than that in the United States.
3. **F** Scarcity is a problem for *all* societies.
4. **F** Under capitalism, the nation's capital stock is owned by private individuals.
5. **F** The Great Leap Forward was a major economic failure.
6. **T** In a capitalist system, individuals' preferences play the major role in determining the answers to the five questions that comprise the economic problem.
7. **T** Because their trade flows have disappeared, firms in these nations must search for new suppliers and new customers.
8. **T** This fact made the plans very hard to fulfill, for a shortfall in one sector was apt to spread to other sectors and cause shortfalls there, too.
9. **T** In both Japan and the United States, most of the capital stock and land are privately owned, and market prices create the incentives to which people respond.
10. **F** China's growth markedly accelerated after it instituted these reforms.
11. **F** Though the precise numbers are somewhat arbitrary, there are many more developing countries than industrial nations.
12. **T** Central planners determine the answers to the economic problem in socialist economic systems.
13. **T** The fact that per capita income grew, on average, more rapidly in developing nations than in industrial nations means that average per capita income in developing nations was catching up to the level in industrial nations.

Multiple Choice Answers

1. **b** Among other market-oriented reforms, the changes made in 1978 abolished collective agriculture in favor of private agriculture, under which individual farmers can rent the land they farm.
2. **b** Changes in prices efficiently convey information so that firms and consumers can respond.
3. **d** Under socialism, planners' decrees about what the nation should produce are all powerful.
4. **b** Different ways of organizing a society will result in different answers to these questions.
5. **a** Capitalist societies allow private individuals to own the capital stock and market prices to provide incentives.
6. **c** In an economy based on market socialism, the state owns the capital stock, and prices provide the incentives for people's actions.
7. **b** Socialism is characterized by state ownership of the capital and incentives arise from the laws and regulations in a central economic plan.
8. **d** Similar to "pure" capitalism, in a system of welfare state capitalism private individuals own the capital stock and respond to market prices, but, unlike "pure" capitalism, government intervenes extensively in markets to affect market prices.
9. **b** On average, income grew most rapidly in developing countries, grew next most rapidly in industrial countries, and fell in the nations in transition.
10. **d** Prices have been deregulated gradually rather than being deregulated immediately.
11. **c** The Great Leap Forward slowed China's economic growth, most likely because it tried to use inappropriate technology and ignored people's incentives.
12. **a** Most of Canada's capital stock is owned by private individuals, and market prices provide the signals to which people respond.
13. **a** The "what" question concerns: "What will be produced?" and the question offered in answer (a) essentially asks whether Leggos will be among the products produced.
14. **d** The farther (to the right) the Lorenz curve is from the line of equality, the more unequal is income distribution. Because world income is distributed less equally than income in the United States, the world Lorenz curve is

farther from the line of equality than the U.S. Lorenz curve.

15. **d** All the answers, along with a reliance on an iterative planning process, characterized Soviet (and all) central plans.

16. **c** In response, the Chinese economic growth rate has soared.

17. **a** East Germany had no fiscal crisis because it reunited with West Germany and was able to rely on the latter's wealth to help finance the government's expenditures.

18. **c** When these nations were centrally planned, trade used to flow throughout the region and the firms did not always know to whom their products were going and from where their supplies were coming.

19. **d** No economic system can produce at a point beyond its *PPF* because the *PPF* shows the limits to what can be produced.

20. **b** Output has fallen severely in Russia.

21. **a** For the past 25 years, output per person has increased by about 7.5 percent annually in China, which is more rapid than in the United States. However, output per person in the United States started at a much higher level than in China, so output per person in China still lags far behind the level in the United States.

Answers to Short Answer Problems

1. a. Because the rate of growth is 1 percent per year in High, per capita income increases from $10,000 to ($10,000)(1.01) or $10,100 after 1 year. In Low, with the rate of growth at 10 percent per year, per capita income increases from $5,000 to ($5,000)(1.10) or $5,500. Thus the per capita income gap between High and Low has fallen from $5,000 to $4,600. In High, per capita income in the next year is 1.01 times per capita income in the current year. Similarly, in Low, per capita income in the next year will be 1.10 times per capita income in the current year. Carrying this procedure out shows that, after 4 years, per capita income will be $10,406 in High and $7,320 in Low. Thus, after 4 years, the per capita income gap will have fallen to $3,086.

   b. If the growth rate in Low is 20 percent, after 4 years per capita income will be $10,368. Per capita income in High will be $10,406 because the growth rate in High is still 1 percent per year. Thus, after 4 years, the per capita income gap between High and Low will have fallen from $5,000 to $37. Per capita income in Low will surpass per capita income in High early in year 5. The conclusion is clear: When a low-income nation is growing much more rapidly than a high-income nation, over-taking occurs quickly.

2. a. As in question 1 (a), after 1 year, per capital income in High is $10,100. Per capita income in Low is ($5,000)(1.04), or $5,200. Then, in year 2, per capita income in High is ($10,100)(1.01), or $10,201. In Low, per capita income is ($5,200)(1.04), or $5,408. In two years the per capita income gap has fallen to $4,793.

   b. In 10 years, per capita income in High is $11,046 and in Low is $7,401. These answers can be obtained in either of two ways. Use High as the example. Then, one method is to use the approach in part (a): Calculate per capita income in the third year by multiplying per capita income in the second year by 1.01. The per capita income in the fourth year then equals the per capita income in the third year multiplied by 1.01. Keep calculating the annual change to get per capita income in the tenth year. Alternatively, note that per capita income in the first year is ($10,000)(1.01). Thus per capita income in the second year equals per capita income in the first year —($10,000)(1.01) multiplied by 1.01, or ($10,000)$(1.01)^2$. Then, per capita in the third year is ($10,000)$(1.01)^3$, and so per capita income in the tenth year is ($10,000)$(1.01)^{10}$.

   c. Per capita income in High after 20 years is $12,202 and in Low is $10,956. After 30 years per capita income in High is $13,478 and in Low is $16,217. The conclusion to be drawn from these results is that, even when the low-income nation is growing just a little more rapidly than the high-income country, per capita income in the initially low-income nation eventually become larger than that in the initially high-income nation. Thus even small differences in growth rates, if maintained long enough, compound to create large changes in income.

3. a. Building the factory will be of greater help in boosting your nation's growth rate.
   b. The return from the factory is significantly larger than the return from smuggling the funds out of the country. In this case you probably will build the factory.
   c. If the government takes over your factory, you will lose your savings. Because you cannot be assured that you will receive the profit from the factory and because you run the risk of losing the funds you invest in it, you probably will smuggle the funds out of the country. Even though they will yield a lower return abroad than you could earn by building the factory, you get the return from the factory only if the government allows you to own it.
   d. The general conclusion from this question is that the lack of private property rights can harm a nation. The nation is better off if you build the factory, and you are more likely to do so when you are confident of receiving the profit from your investment.
4. Figure 23.2 shows the amount produced, Q_p, and demanded, Q_c. There is a shortage of food equal to $Q_c - Q_p$. Because the price is controlled, price movements do not allocate the food. Instead, food was allocated by other means, such as lines and payments made in a black market.
5. a. After the food market was deregulated, the equilibrium price is shown in Figure 23.2 as P and the equilibrium quantity is Q.
   b. Figure 23.2 shows that more food is produced after the price is deregulated. Before, only Q_p was produced; after the deregulation, Q is produced. More food also is consumed after deregulation. Before deregulation, consumers were able to consume only Q_p because that was the amount of food produced. (Even though the quantity of food that consumers demanded was Q_c, only Q_p was produced, and consuming more food than is produced is impossible.) Thus, as a group, consumers are able to consume more food after the deregulation.

FIGURE 23.2
Short Answer Problems 4 and 5

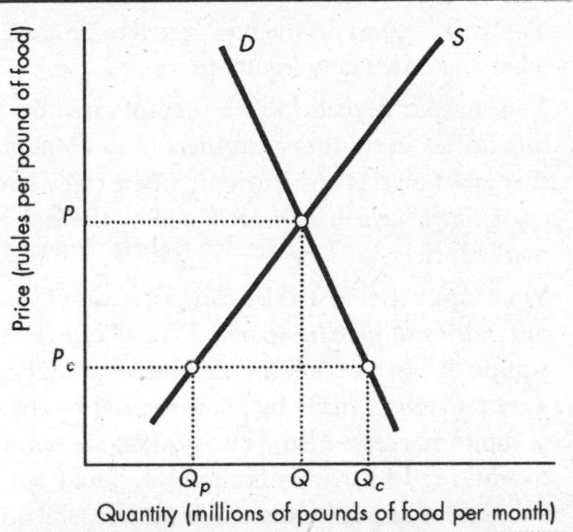

   c. Deregulating the price causes it to rise, from P_c to P. However, this rise in price does *not* signal that society is being harmed. On the contrary, society is better off after the deregulation. Before, when the price of food was controlled, an inefficiently small level of food was produced. After the deregulation, the amount of food produced is the efficient amount. Thus, the deadweight loss from the price control has been eliminated. More intuitively, society is better off precisely because it has more food. With more food being produced, more food can be consumed, and consuming more food makes the nation better off.
6. Every nation must decide what to produce; how to produce it; when to produce it; where to produce it; and for whom to produce it. All nations must somehow answer these questions continuously. Hence both capitalist and socialist nations must answer them. The methods used to answer the questions — as well as the answers themselves — differ among nations.
7. Both capitalism and welfare state capitalism are characterized by private ownership of capital. They differ with regard to the role of the state in the allocation of resources. Capitalism relies on market

allocation of resources, whereas welfare state capitalism is characterized by a significant degree of state intervention in the allocation of resources.

8. You will need to decide how much to produce and what and how many inputs to use.

   Your output decision will be complicated by difficulties in finding customers in an economy that lacks market institutions, where traditional trade flows have disappeared, and by the lack of market prices.

   Your input choice will be complicated by difficulties in getting spare parts and capital equipment in an economy in which such decisions were previously made by planners, and by the lack of input markets. Also, your workers are not used to working in a market economy and may not believe, for example, that their jobs depend on their efforts.

9. In 1978, Deng Xiaoping abolished collective agriculture (state-owned and state-operated farms) and raised prices paid to farmers for many crops. Agricultural land was leased to farmers for the payment of a fixed tax and a commitment to sell part of its output to the state. The main point is that individual farmers were free to decide what to plant and how to produce. Because farmers were able to profit from their productivity, there were new incentives for efficiency. The effects have been striking. The production of agricultural products increased dramatically with the output of some products (those for which the set price was raised the most) increasing by many times their previous levels. China went from being the world's largest importer of agricultural products to being an exporter of these products.

■ You're the Teacher

1. "I hear what you're saying, but keep in mind that 'fairness' is always a normative issue. I know that some of our friends would argue that having to give up some of their income to make people in Chad better off wouldn't be fair.

   "These arguments are fun but I don't think they can ever really be settled. Instead, it's a lot more important to try to determine what institutions help a nation grow more rapidly. After all, if we can figure out what factors help create rapid growth, we can help people in developing countries help themselves. The lessons we can see from our book really make a lot of sense now that we're finishing the course: Setting up property rights so that people aren't afraid to save and make investments; specializing according to comparative advantage; and educating the labor force all seem like good ideas. So, maybe in a few years when we're studying economics in graduate school, we'll be able to look around and see that more developing nations have followed these policies and are now growing more rapidly."

2. "The people in these nations cared about the same things you and I care about. In particular, I really don't think you care too much about what the U.S. growth rate of per capita income has been for the past 5 years; what you really care about is what has been the growth rate of *your* income for the past 5 years. Economists generally assume that people care about themselves and their immediate families. Remember when we talked about the demand curve for different products or the supply curve of labor? We assumed that people were trying to make *themselves* as well off as possible; they were maximizing their utility.

   "Maximizing their utility is what people in socialist nations also were doing. But the incentives those people faced were different from the incentives we face. For instance, when the Soviet Union was centrally planned, losing your job was virtually impossible. Equally difficult was buying much in the way of goods and services. If you wanted to rent an apartment, you had to wait 2 or 3 years, even if you had just gotten married. A telephone required waits of a decade or so, and virtually no one owned a car.

   "These obstacles didn't give people much of an incentive to work hard! If you didn't bother to work, so what? You couldn't get fired. And if you did work hard, so what? You couldn't buy much from a promotion and its accompanying raise! So, not surprisingly, people (looking out for themselves) didn't bother to work too hard and the economies didn't grow very rapidly."

5 GLOBAL ECONOMY

Reading Between the Lines

CHINA'S ENVIRONMENT IS SEVERELY STRESSED AS ITS INDUSTRY SURGES

The slow, hot days of summer are here, and the sun-fed algae is starting to clot the milky surface of Chao Lake. Soon a living scum will carpet a patch the size of New York City. It will quickly blacken and rot — and the 4,000 residents of this lakeside village will face another summer of misery.

Fish will be scarce, and fresh water rife with biological toxins. But that isn't what residents dread the most. "The smell is so terrible you cannot describe it," says Xu Jiajiao, a retired fisherman who still remembers the bountiful lake before it was choked by algae-breeding pollutants.

Rapid development has transformed big tracts of this ancient nation into environmental wasteland. Acid rain nibbles at the great Wall; the Grand Canal in places resembles an open sewer; part of Shanghai is slowly sinking as its water table is depleted; and Benxi, in Manchuria, is so thick with air pollution the city doesn't appear in satellite pictures.

No major economy is growing faster — and nowhere are environmental stresses greater.

When it comes to spending money, most Chinese would rather invest in a new factory than clean up an existing one.

Blame the spirit of paramount leader, Deng Xiaoping's maxim, "To get rich is glorious."

Marcus W. Brauchi, "China's Environment is Severely Stressed As Its Industry Surges," July 25, 1994, P. A1.

■ Analyze It

It is clear from the story that China faces a massive environmental problem. We can analyze some of the trade-offs faced by China by using our economic tools.

1. Draw a *PPF* with the good on the horizontal axis "Quantity of new factories", and the good on the vertical axis "Quantity of cleaned up existing factories." Indicate where China is on this *PPF*. How has China's choice contributed to its economic growth rate?
2. Environmental quality is a normal good; that is, people with higher incomes demand a cleaner environment. Assuming that these demands are actually translated into what occurs, in the *PPF* you already drew, indicate China's production point after its people's incomes have increased. How will this change affect the Chinese growth rate?
3. Is Deng Xiaoping's maxim consistent with providing a clean environment? Be sure to differentiate between the short run and long run.

Mid-Term Examination

1 If the United States has an excess of exports over imports, the United States has a
a. negative trade balance that is financed by U.S. lending to foreigners.
b. negative trade balance that is financed by U.S. borrowing from foreigners.
c. positive trade balance that is financed by U.S. lending to foreigners.
d. positive trade balance that is financed by U.S. borrowing from foreigners.

2 If an efficient country trades with the rest of the world, it produces at a point that lies
a. inside its production possibility frontier.
b. on its production possibility frontier.
c. outside its production possibility frontier.
d. either inside or outside its production possibility frontier.

3 When the full effects are considered, a reduction in tariffs would
a. decrease imports and increase exports.
b. increase imports and decrease exports.
c. increase imports and exports.
d. decrease imports and exports.

4 Which of the following earns revenue for the domestic government?
a. Tariffs.
b. Quotas.
c. Voluntary export restraints.
c. Subsidies.

5 Recent growth in per capital income in the United States is
a. equal to that in China.
b. less than that in China.
c. more than that in China.
d. not comparable to that in China.

6 Preferences of households are the main driving force under
a. socialism.
b. welfare state capitalism.
c. market socialism.
d. capitalism.

7 The term "fiscal crisis" is exemplified by the point that in recent years the
a. Russian government has had a surplus and deflation has been a problem.
b. Russian government has had a surplus and inflation has been a problem.
c. Russian government has had a deficit and inflation has been a problem.
d. None of the above.

8 Following Deng Xiaoping's 1978
a. liberalization of markets, China's agricultural output soared.
b. liberalization of markets, China's agricultural output plunged.
c. collectivization of farms, China's agricultural output soared.
d. collectivization of farms, China's agricultural output plunged.

Answers

Reading Between the Lines

Figure 1 shows the *PPF* between building new factories and cleaning up existing factories. As the story indicated, "most Chinese would rather invest in a new factory than clean up an existing one" so the Chinese economy is operating at point similar to *a*, where many new factories are produced but few existing factories are cleaned up. By producing at this point, the Chinese growth rate has been more rapid than if fewer new factories were produced and more resources were used to clean up existing factories. Investment in new factories contributes to producing more output, so China's total production increases when new factories are produced. Note that the more rapid economic growth does not necessarily mean that the well being of all the Chinese improved. Clearly those people who lived next to Chao Lake would probably have preferred more factories cleaned up and fewer new factories built.

FIGURE 1
China's *PPF*

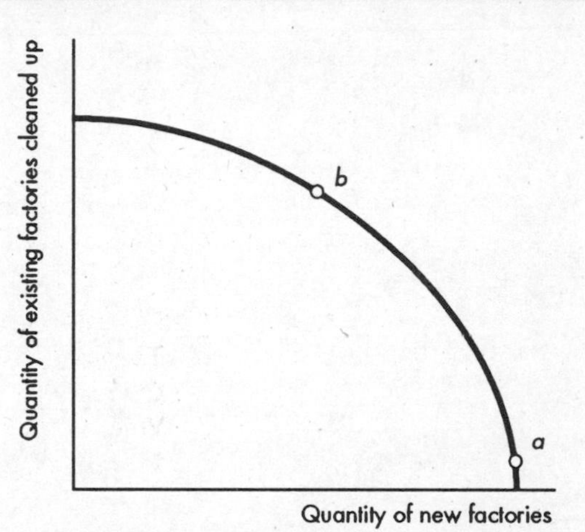

After people's incomes have increased, the demand for a cleaner environment may cause production to move to point such as *b*. We cannot be sure, however, that this will actually occur. China's economy is mixed between reliance upon central planning and markets, so the desires of the planners — as well as the rest of the people — will play a role in determining what is produced. However, if this change in production points occurs, China's economic growth rate will slow, because fewer new factories will be constructed, though the quality of its citizens' lives may rise.

In the short run, Deng Xiaoping's maxim seems to indicate that the more rapid the growth, regardless of its environmental consequences, the better. This belief is probably partially responsible for the severe environmental problems that currently exist in China. In the long run, however, the situation is more subtle. As the Chinese people "grow rich", their demand for a cleaner environment increases. Hence, in the long run, Deng Xiaoping's maxim may lead to a much cleaner environment in China than would otherwise be the case.

Mid-Term Exam

1 c; 2 b; 3 c; 4 a; 5 b; 6 d; 7 c; 8 a.

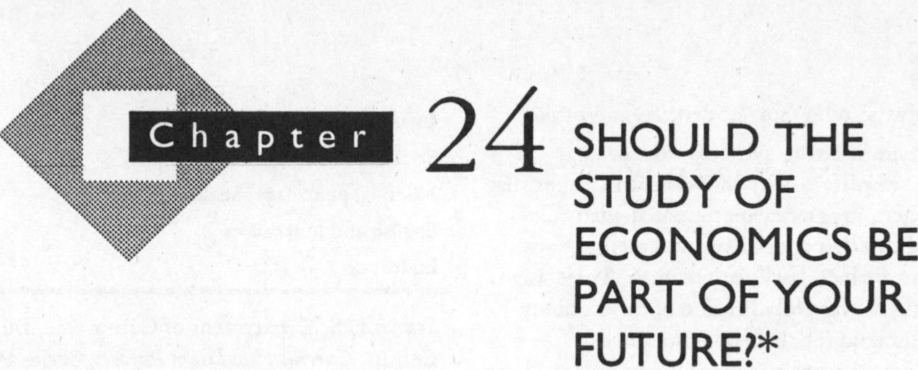

Chapter 24 SHOULD THE STUDY OF ECONOMICS BE PART OF YOUR FUTURE?*

Should You Take More Economic Courses?

Now that you have learned about supply and demand, utility and profit maximization, employment and unemployment, and good old Igor, it is time look to the future.

- Should the study of economics be part of your future?
- Should you take more classes or maybe even major in economics?
- What about graduate school in economics?

As you are well aware, economists generally assume that people try to make rational choices to maximize their own well-being. There is no reason to drop this assumption now. The purpose of this chapter is help you make that rational maximizing choice by providing low-cost information. Let us assess the benefits and see whether they outweigh the costs of studying economics.

Benefits from Studying Economics

Knowledge, Enlightenment, and Liberation

As John Maynard Keynes said, "The ideas of economists ... both when they are right and when they are wrong, are more powerful than is commonly understood. Indeed the world is ruled by little else. Practical men, who believe themselves to be quite exempt from any intellectual influences, are usually the slaves of some defunct economist." Studying economics is a liberating and enlightening experience. You don't want to be the slave of a defunct economist, do you? Liberate yourself. It's better to bring your ideas out in the open, to confront and understand them, rather than to leave them buried.

Knowledge, Understanding, and Satisfaction

Many of the most important problems in the world are economic. Studying economics gives you a practical set of tools to understand and solve them. Every day, on television and in the newspapers, we hear and read about big issues such as economic growth, inflation, unemployment, health care reform, welfare reform, the environment, and the transition away from Communism. Your introduction to economics shows that learning economics will let you watch the news or pick up a newspaper and better understand these issues. As an added bonus, economics helps you understand smaller, more immediate concerns, such as: How much Spam should I buy? Is skipping class today a good idea? Should I put my retirement funds in government bonds or in the stock market? After all, as George Bernard Shaw put it, "Economy is the art of making the most of life." Mick Jagger, who dropped out of the London School of Economics, complains that he "can't get no satisfaction." Maybe he should have studied more economics. The economic way of thinking will help you maximize your satisfaction.

Career Opportunities

All careers are not equal. While the wages in many occupations have not risen much lately, the wages of

---

* This chapter was written by Robert Whaples of Wake Forest University.

"symbolic analysts" who "solve, identify, and broker problems by manipulating symbols" are soaring.[1] These people "simplify reality into abstract images that can be rearranged, juggled, experimented with, communicated to other specialists, and then, eventually, transformed back into reality." Their wages have been rising as the globalization of the economy increases the demand for their insights and as technological developments (especially computers) have enhanced their productivity. Economists are the quintessential symbolic analysts as we manipulate ideas about abstractions such as supply and demand, cost and benefits, and equilibrium.

You can think of your training in economics as an exercise regimen, a workout for your brain.

You will use many of the concepts you have learned in introductory economics during your career, but it is the practice in abstract thinking that will really pay off. In fact, most economics majors do not go on to become economists. They enter fields that use their analytical abilities, including business, management, insurance, finance, real estate, marketing, law, education, policy analysis, consulting, government, planning, and even medicine, journalism, and the arts.

A recent survey of 100 former economics majors at my university included all of these careers. If you want to verify that economics majors graduate to successful and rewarding careers, just ask your professors or watch what happens to economics majors from your school as they graduate.

Statistics from the Bureau of the Census show that across the nation, economics majors earn more than most other majors (see Table 1).

Table 1

Average Monthly Income of People Who Hold a Bachelor's Degree by Field of Study, Spring 1990

Field of Study	Income
Engineering	$3,508
Agriculture and forestry	$3,273
Economics	$2,977
Mathematics and statistics	$2,947
Business and management	$2,780
Other	$2,639
Biology	$2,627
Physical and earth sciences	$2,559
Liberal arts and humanities	$2,239
Psychology	$2,196
Social sciences	$2,118
Nursing, pharmacy, health technologies	$2,056
English and journalism	$2,041
Education	$1,882

Source: U.S. Department of Commerce, Bureau of the Census, *Current Population Reports,* Series P-70, No. 32, "Educational Background and Economic Status: Spring 1990."

Other sources using data on entry-level wages verify these patterns. In 1993 the average annual starting salary of economics and finance majors was $28,584. While this is lower than the salaries for those with degrees in engineering, computer science, chemistry, and math, it is somewhat higher than salaries for those with degrees in business administration. Moreover, the entry-level salary of economics majors beats the entry-level salary of humanities majors by about $4,000, is almost $6,000 higher than the earnings for other social sciences (e.g., psychology, political science, anthropology, sociology), and tops the earnings of school teachers by even more. (*Source: Statistical Abstract of the United States*, 1994, Tables 246 and 289.) These numbers are updated annually, so feel free to look up the latest statistics. In addition, the employment rate of economics majors is higher than that of many other majors, such as those in the humanities and other social sciences. Finally, the supply of new economics majors has been falling lately (down about 10 percent since 1990). Since the demand has remained high, the future promises even brighter prospects for economics majors.

The Costs of Studying Economics

Since the "direct" costs of studying economics (tuition, books, supplies) aren't generally any higher or lower than the direct costs of other courses, indirect costs will be the most important of the opportunity costs to studying economics.

Forgone Knowledge

If you study economics, you can't study something else. This forgone knowledge could be very valuable.

■ Disutility

If you dislike studying economics because you find it boring, tedious, or unenlightening in comparison to other subjects, then the opportunity cost is even higher because your overall level of satisfaction falls. (I know that this is rare, but it does occasionally happen.)

■ Time and Energy

Economics is a fairly demanding major. Although economics courses do not generally take as much time as courses in English and history (in which you have to read a lot of long books) or anatomy and physiology (in which you have to spend hours in the lab and hours memorizing things), they do take a decent amount of time. In addition, some people find the material "tougher" than most subjects because memorizing is not the key. In economics (like physics), analyzing and solving are the keys.

■ Grades

As Table 2 shows, grades in introductory economics courses are generally a hair lower than grades in some other majors, including other social sciences and the humanities.[2] On the other hand, grades in economics are considerably higher than grades in the sciences and math.

Table 2
Average Grades and Grade Distribution by College Major

Department	Mean Grade	% Above B+	% Below B–
Music	3.16	44	21
English	3.12	27	12
Psychology	3.02	28	23
Philosophy	2.99	29	21
Art	2.95	29	24
Political science	2.95	24	23
Economics	2.81	20	31
Chemistry	2.66	17	44
Math	2.53	22	46

Caveat Emptor (Buyer Beware): Interpreting Your Grades Is Not Straight Forward

High grades provide direct satisfaction to most students, but they also act as a signal about the student's ability to learn the subject material. Unfortunately, because the grade distribution is not uniform across departments, students may be confused and misled by their grades. They may think that they are exceptionally good at a subject because of a high grade, when in fact nearly everyone gets a high grade in that subject. The important point here is that you should be informed about your own school's grade distribution. Just because you got a B in economics and an A in history does not necessarily mean that your comparative advantage is in learning history rather than economics. Earning a B or a C in economics could mean that it is the best major for you. It is fun to have a high GPA in college, but maximizing GPA should not be your goal (unless you have a very unusual utility function). Maximizing overall utility is probably your goal, and this might be obtained by trading off a tenth or so of your GPA for a more rewarding major—perhaps economics.

Potential Side Effects from Studying Economics

Studying economics has some potential side effects. I'm not sure whether they are costs or benefits and will let you decide.

■ Changing Ideas about What Is Fair

A recently completed study compared students at the beginning and end of the semester in an introductory economics course.[3] It found that by the end of the semester, significantly more of the students thought that the functioning of the market is "fair." This was especially true for female students. The results were consistent across a range of professors who fell across the ideological spectrum.

For example, the proportion of students who regarded it as unfair to increase the price of flowers on a holiday fell almost in half. The proportion that favored government control over flower prices, rather than market determination, fell by over 60 percent. The study argues that these responses do not reflect changes in deep values, but instead represent the discovery of previous inconsistencies and their modification in the light of new information learned during the semester.

■ Changing Behavior

Many people believe that the study of economics changes students' values and behavior. Some think that it changes them for the worse. Others disagree. In particular, it is argued that economics students become more self-interested and less likely to cooperate, perhaps because they spend so much time studying economic models, which often assume that people are self-interested. For example, one study reports experimental evidence that economics students are more likely than nonmajors to behave self-interestedly in prisoners' dilemma games and ultimatum bargaining games.[4]

This need not mean that studying economics will change you, however. Another study compares beginning freshmen and senior economics students and concludes that economics students "are already different when they begin their study of economics."[5] In other words, students signing up for economics courses are already different; studying economics doesn't change them. However, there are reasons to question both of these conclusions, because it is not clear whether these laboratory experiments using economic games reflect reality. One experiment asked students whether they would return money that had been lost. It found that economics students were more likely than others to say that they would keep the cash.

However, what people say and what they do are sometimes at odds. In a follow-up experiment, this theory was tested by dropping stamped, addressed envelopes containing $10 in cash in different campus classrooms. To return the cash, the students had only to seal the envelopes and mail them. The results were that 56 percent of the envelopes dropped in economics classes were returned, while only 31 percent of the envelopes dropped in history, psychology and business classes were sent in.[6] Perhaps economics students are less selfish than others!

Obviously, no firm conclusions have been reached about whether or how studying economics changes students behavior.

Costs versus Benefits

Suppose that you've weighed the costs and benefits of studying economics and you've decided that the benefits are greater than or equal to the costs. Obviously, then, you should continue to take economics courses. If you can't decide whether the benefits outweigh the costs, then you should probably collect more information — especially if it is good but inexpensive. In either case, read the rest of this chapter.

The Economics Major

The study of economics is like a tree. The introductory microeconomics and macroeconomics courses you begin with are the tree's roots. Most colleges and universities require that you master this material before you go on to any other courses. The way of thinking, the language, and the tools that you acquire in the introductory course are usually reinforced in intermediate microeconomics and macroeconomics courses before they are applied in more specialized courses that you take. The intermediate courses are the tree's trunk. Among the specialized courses that make up the branches of economics are econometrics (statistical economics), financial economics, labor economics, resource economics, international trade, industrial organization, public finance, public choice, economic history, the history of economic thought, mathematical economics, current economic issues, and urban economics. The branches of the tree vary from department to department, but these are common. It will pay to check your college bulletin and discuss these courses with professors and other students.

Graduate School in Economics

■ Preparing for Graduate School in Economics

You can prepare for graduate school in economics by taking several math classes. This would probably include at least two semesters of calculus plus a couple of courses in probability and statistics and linear/matrix algebra. Ask your advisor about the particular courses to take at your college. In addition, the mathematical economics and econometrics courses in the economics department are essential. (*Helpful hint*: Even if you aren't going to graduate school, these mathematical courses can be valuable to you, just as more economics courses can be valuable for nonmajors.)

If your school offers graduate level economics courses, you might want to sit in on a few to get accustomed to the flavor of graduate school.

Most graduate programs require strong grades in economics, a good score on the Graduate Record Examination (GRE), and solid letters of recommendation. It is a good idea to get to know a few professors very well and to go above and beyond what is expected so that they can write glowing letters about you.

■ Financing Graduate School

Unlike some other graduate and professional degree programs, you probably won't need to pile up a massive amount of debt while pursuing a Ph.D. in economics. Most Ph.D. programs hire their economics graduate students as teaching or research assistants. Teaching assistants begin by grading papers and running review sessions and can advance to teaching classes on their own. Research assistants generally do data collection, statistical work, and library research for professors and often jointly write papers with them. Most assistantships will pay for tuition and provide you with enough money to live on.

■ Where Should You Apply?

The best graduate school for you depends on a lot of things, especially your ability level, geographical location, areas of research interests, and, of course, financing. You should talk with your professors about ability level and areas of research. In addition, there are informative articles that give overall departmental rankings and rankings by subfield. See especially John Tschirhart, "Ranking Economics Department in Areas of Expertise," *Journal of Economic Education*, and David Colander, "Research on the Economic Profession," *Journal of Economic Perspectives*, Vol. 3, no. 4, Fall 1989, pp. 137–148. There will probably be more up-to-date rankings by the time you apply. Ask a professor or reference librarian to help you track them down. For smaller specialties (e.g., economic history, urban economics) it is especially important to get up-to-date information on any particular program.

■ What You Will Do in Graduate School

Most graduate programs in economics begin with a year of theory courses in macroeconomics and microeconomics. After a year you will probably take a series of tests to show that you have mastered this core theory. If you pass these tests, in the second and third year of courses you will take more specialized subjects and perhaps take lengthy examinations in a couple of subfields. After this you will be required to write a dissertation — a masterpiece of original research that will contribute new knowledge to one of the fields of economics. These stages are intertwined with work as a teaching and/or research assistant, and the dissertation stage can be quite drawn out. In the social sciences the median time that it takes for a student to complete the Ph.D. degree is about 7.5 years.[7] Be aware that a high percentage (roughly 50 percent) of students do not complete their doctoral degree.

■ What Is Graduate School Like?

Graduate school in economics comes as a surprise to many students. The material and approach are distinctly different from what you will learn as an undergraduate. The textbooks and journal articles you will read in graduate school are often very theoretical and abstract. A good source of information is sitting in on courses or reading the reflections of recent students. See especially *The Making of an Economist* by Arjo Klamer and David Colander (Boulder, Colo.: Westview Press, 1990).

The Committee on Graduate Education in Economics (COGEE) undertook an important review of graduate education in economics and reported its findings in the September 1991 issue of the *Journal of Economic Literature*. COGEE asked faculty members, graduate students, and recent Ph.D.s to rank the most important skills needed to be successful in the study of graduate economics. At the top of the list were analytical skills and mathematics, followed by critical judgment, the ability to apply theory, and computational skills. At the bottom of the list were creativity and the ability to communicate. If you are interested in economic issues but do not have the characteristics required by graduate economics departments, there are other economics-related fields to consider, such as graduate school in public policy. Many economics majors go to business schools to obtain an MBA and are often better prepared than students who have undergraduate degrees in business.

Economics Reading

If you've decided to make the study of economics part of your future, or if you're hungry for more economics, you should immediately begin reading the economic news and books by economists. Life is short. Why waste it watching TV?

The easiest way to get your daily recommended dose of economics is to keep up with current economic events. Here are a few sources to pick up at the newsstand, bookstore, or library over your summer or winter break.

■ The *Wall Street Journal*

Many undergraduates subscribe to the *Wall Street Journal* (WSJ) at low student rates. Join them! Your professor will probably have student subscription forms. Not only is the WSJ a well-written business newspaper, but it also has articles on domestic and international news, politics, the arts, travel, and sports, as well as a lively editorial page (sorry, only one comic strip). Reading the WSJ is one of the best ways to tie the economics you are studying to the real world and to prepare for your career.

■ Magazines and Journals

The Economist, a weekly magazine published in England, is available at a student discount rate of $85/year. Pick up a copy at your school library and you will be hooked by its informative, sharp writing. *Business Week* is also well worth the read.

Also recommended are *Challenge* magazine and *The Public Interest*, two quarterlies that discuss economic policy. Finally, there is the *Journal of Economics Perspectives*, which is published by the American Economic Association and written to be accessible to undergraduate economics students.

■ Books by Economists

I recently asked a group of economics professors from across the country (members of the Teach-Econ computer discussion list) the following question: "A bright, enthusiastic student who has just completed introductory economics comes up to you, the professor, and asks you to recommend an economics book for reading over the summer. What do you suggest?"

Here is what they suggested that you, the bright, enthusiastic student, should read:

■ Top Choices

Milton Friedman, *Capitalism and Freedom.*

Robert Heilbroner, *The Worldly Philosophers: The Lives, Times, and Ideas of the Great Economic Thinkers.*

Steve Landsburg, *The Armchair Economist: Economics and Everyday Life.*

■ Other Good Choices

Alan Blinder, *Hard Heads, Soft Hearts: Tough-Minded Economics for a Just Society.*

Victor Fuchs, *How We Live.*

Paul Krugman, *Peddling Prosperity: Economic Sense and Nonsense in the Age of Diminished Expectations.*

Donald McCloskey, *If You're So Smart: The Narrative of Economic Expertise.*

Russell Roberts, *The Choice: A Parable of Free Trade and Protectionism.*

In addition, Adam Smith's *The Wealth of Nations* is a must read for every student of economics. Written in 1776, it is the most influential work of economics ever. Its insights are still valuable today.

Endnotes

1. This term is used by Robert Reich in *The Work of Nations*. The quote is from p. 178.

2. Richard Sabot and John Wakeman-Linn, "Grade Inflation and Course Choice," *Journal of Economic Perspectives*, Vol. 5, no. 1, Winter 1991, pp. 159–170.

3. Robert Whaples, "Changes in Attitudes about the Fairness of Free Markets among College Economics Students," *Journal of Economic Education*, Vol. 26, no. 4, Fall 1995.

4. Robert H. Frank, Thomas Gilovich, and Dennis T. Regan, "Does Studying Economics Inhibit Cooperation?" *Journal of Economic Perspectives*, Vol. 7, no. 2, Spring 1993, pp. 159–171.

5. John R. Carter and Michael D. Irons, "Are Economists Different, and If So, Why?" *Journal of Economic Perspectives*, Vol. 5, no. 2, Spring 1991, pp. 171–177.

6. "Economics Students Aren't Selfish, They're Just Not Entirely Honest," *Wall Street Journal*, January 18, 1995, B1.

7. See Ronald Ehrenberg, "The Flow of New Doctorates," *Journal of Economic Literature*, Vol. 30, June 1992, pp. 830–875. If breaks in school attendance are included, this climbs to 10.5 years. Of course, some students attend only part time, and most have some kind of employment while completing their degrees.